S0-EGJ-696

A NOBLE COMPANY

A NOBLE COMPANY

Biographical Essays on Notable Particular-Regular Baptists in America

Edited by

TERRY WOLEVER

Volume Three

Particular Baptist Press

Springfield, Missouri

Particular Baptist Press

2766 W. Farm Road 178
Springfield, Missouri 65810

Cataloging data:

Wolever, Terry L., editor 1957 –

1. Baptists – United States – Biographies
2. Baptists – United States – History
3. Regular Baptists – United States

ISBN 1-888514-44-2 Acid-free paper

Printed and bound in the United States of America

Contents

Maps and illustrations:

"Like all pioneers, these preachers were a race of hardy and enterprising men. Vigorous in body and mind, they cherished a not less vigorous zeal for the cause in which they were engaged. . . .At this distance of time, and after so great improvements in the condition of the country, and of society, it is hardly possible to conceive the difficulties which they encountered, and the suffering which they endured. Without public conveyances, or even well-defined roads, they had to track their way, as best they could, through long distances, from settlement to settlement. . . .In all these places they sowed the seed of the Word with a liberal hand; committing it to the waters, confident that it would appear again after many days. And so it did. In these preaching tours of the early fathers, the nucleus of many a church was formed, and Baptist sentiments were widely diffused. . . .We have entered into their labors, and it is good for us to be reminded by whose toils we enjoy our present goodly heritage, and to be stimulated by their example to greater self-denial, and more persevering labors. While therefore these memorials will be specially grateful to those familiar with the scenes and events which they commemorate, they will be interesting and profitable to all."

— *James T. Champlin,*
professor, Waterville College, Maine, in his Introduction to the *Autobiography of Henry Kendall* (1853), iii-v.

Introduction

This third volume in our series covers some of the more pivotal events in the American Baptist experience during the mid to late eighteenth century—the aggressive evangelistic impetus which came about in the midst of the Great Awakening, the beginnings and establishment of educational institutions of higher learning for those of our ministers who desired advanced training, and the founding of the Warren Association, which led to a more concerted and ultimately successful effort to achieve full religious liberty—all set within the context of the tumultuous decades preceding, encompassing, and following the Revolutionary War. Here are the great names of the times—Shubal Stearns, Morgan Edwards, Oliver Hart, Isaac Backus, John Gano, Samuel Jones, Samuel Stillman, Hezekiah Smith and James Manning, but also the significant but "lesser lights," such as Isaac Eaton (1725?-1772), the influential pastor-educator of Hopewell, New Jersey, David Thomas (1732-1812), the noteworthy Philadelphia Association minister who did such an extensive work in Virginia (and who John Mason Peck credited with originating the term 'Regular Baptist'),[1] James Potter (1734-1815), who founded so many of the Baptist churches in Maine, and Andrew Bryan (1737-1812), the former slave preacher who suffered much persecution to establish the first Baptist churches in Savannah, Georgia.

And since the goal of these volumes is not to focus solely on the better-known figures, included in these pages are more of the "unknowns"—ordinary pastors and church members who enjoyed smaller spheres of influence, but whose stories merit retelling.

What will become apparent in all of these essays, is that these men and women, like each of us as part of fallen humanity, had their faults. But what makes them nonetheless a noble company of believers is the conspicuous grace that was yet manifested in their lives and works as they set about to do their Master's business.

Terry Wolever

---

[1] John M. Peck, *"Father Clark," or The Pioneer Preacher. Sketches and Incidents of Rev. John Clark* (New York: Sheldon, Lamport and Blakeman, 1855), 147.

The contributing writers

Peter Beck serves as assistant professor of religion and director of the Honors Program at Charleston Southern University. Since earning his doctorate in historical theology (Southern Baptist Theological Seminary) he has published and presented extensively on Baptist history, Puritan history, and Jonathan Edwards. He and his family live in Charleston, South Carolina, the birthplace of Baptist life in the South. He is the author of *The Voice of Faith: Jonathan Edwards' Theology of Prayer* (2010).

William H. Brackney is Millard R. Cherry Distinguished Professor of Christian Thought and Ethics on the Faculty of Theology at Acadia University in Wolfville, Nova Scotia, Canada. Previously he was Professor of Religion and Chair of the Department of Religion at Baylor University and Dean of Theology at McMaster University with Historical and Theological Faculty Status in the Toronto School of Theology. He also served as Executive Director of the American Baptist Historical Society and Curator of the Samuel B. Colgate Historical Collection. The author of forty books in Baptist Studies, human rights, and the overall Christian Tradition, Dr. Brackney holds degrees from the University of Maryland, Eastern Baptist Theological Seminary and Temple University, where he received his doctorate with distinction.

Jeffrey Brodrick is a school teacher in social studies. He holds advanced degrees in education, technology, and library science. Brodrick is also an adjunct faculty member and D.Min. student at Baptist Bible College, Clark's Summit, Pennsylvania and a past president of the Executive Committee of the Southeastern Pennsylvania Library Association. He is a consulting librarian, and is a credited contributing history researcher for the NBC, CNN and A&E television networks.

John David Broome is a Mississippi native and holds degrees from Pearl River College (A.A.), Mississippi College (B.A.), University of New Orleans (M.A.), and New Orleans Baptist Theological Seminary (B.D., Th.D.). Currently Senior Professor of History and Religion, he joined the faculty of Cumberland College (now University of the Cumberlands) in 1966.

Hywel M. Davies, Graduate of Jesus College, Oxford University in Modern History (1977), received a Ph.D. from Cardiff University in 1985 for his research on Baptists in Wales and North America. He was Visiting Scholar at the Institute of Early American History and Culture in Williamsburg, Virginia in 1980 and Visiting Scholar at the Library Company of Philadelphia in 1987. His published works include the book, *Transatlantic Brethren: Rev. Samuel Jones (1735-1814) and His Friends. Baptists in Wales, Pennsylvania and Beyond* (1995). Davies has also published extensively in scholarly journals in Wales on emigration from Wales to the U.S. in the 1790's, on Goronwy Owen at the College of William and Mary and on Loyalism in Wales in the 1790's. He is the Director of Admissions at Aberystwyth University. He is the treasurer of Bethel Baptist Church, Aberystwyth, and husband of Susan, father to Rhys and Aled and grandfather to Ethan.

Stanley J. Grenz was born on January 7, 1950, in Alpena, Michigan. After graduating from the University of Colorado in 1973, he went on to earn a M.Div. at Denver Seminary (1976) and a Th.D. at the University of Munich. Grenz served as youth director and assistant pastor at Northwest Baptist Church in Denver, 1971-1976. Following his ordination on June 13, 1976, he was pastor at the Rowandale Baptist Church, Winnipeg, Manitoba, 1979-1981, while also teaching courses at the University of Winnipeg and at Winnipeg Theological Seminary (now Providence Theological Seminary). He served as Professor of Systematic Theology and Christian Ethics at the North American Baptist Theological Seminary, Sioux Falls, South Dakota, 1981-1990, and was Pioneer McDonald Professor of Baptist Heritage, Theology and Ethics at Carey Theological College and Regent College, Vancouver, British Columbia. Dr. Grenz had submitted his essay on Isaac Backus to us for this series not long before he passed away at the age of fifty-five on March 12, 2005, at Vancouver.

Walter E. Johnson is a native of Greenville, South Carolina. After attending public schools there from 1960-1972, he obtained his B.A. degree from Furman University in 1977. He then earned his M.Div. (1979) and Ph.D. (1989) from New Orleans Baptist Theological Seminary in Historical and Systematic Theology. Dr. Johnson in addition has completed thirty hours of graduate study in Philosophy at The University of South Carolina, 1981-1982. He has spent his entire ministerial life among the churches of his state, as Minister to Youth at Lee Road Baptist Church in Taylors; interim pastor at Antioch Baptist Church in Woodruff; pastor at Ravenwood Baptist Church, Columbia; pastor at Ebenezer Welcome Baptist Church, Landrum; and as interim pastor successively at Cross Plains Baptist Church, Traveler's Rest; Utica Baptist Church, Seneca; Bethel Baptist Church, Westminster; West Greenville Baptist Church, Greenville; Mt. Airy Baptist Church, Easley; Mt. Pisgah Baptist Church, Easley; Temple Baptist Church, Simpsonville; and Standing Springs Baptist Church, Simpsonville. Dr. Johnson has served as Graduate Assistant in the Department of Philosophy, Columbia, 1980-1982, and is currently Professor of Philosophy and Christian Studies, North Greenville University (since 1992) and Dean of the College of Christian Studies there (since 1997). In addition, he has taught extension courses for the University at Southern Baptist Theological Seminary, Louisville, Kentucky and an academic course in Baptist History and Heritage at the Missionary Learning Center in Richmond, Virginia.

Don Moffitt is a graduate of Baptist Bible College, Clark's Summit, Pennsylvania (Th.B.) and Biblical Theological Seminary, Hatfield, Pennsylvania (M.Div.). After his retirement from Eastman Kodak, he pursued further study at Northeastern Theological Seminary, Rochester, New York, where he received his M.A. in Historical Theology in 2005. Brother Moffitt also founded Backus Book Publishers, Box 17274, Rochester, N.Y. 14617, in 1981, specializing in the reprinting of historical Calvinistic Baptist literature, such as the first separate reprinting of *The First London Baptist Confession of Faith, 1646 edition.*

Thomas J. Nettles is a graduate of Mississippi College (B.A.) and Southwestern Baptist Theological Seminary, Ft. Worth, Texas (M.Div., Ph.D.), and has taught at Southwestern Baptist Theological Seminary, Mid-America Baptist Theological Seminary, Memphis, Tennessee, Trinity Evangelical Divinity School, Deerfield, Illinois and since the fall of 1997, The Southern Baptist Theological Seminary, Louisville, Kentucky. He is the author of several books in Baptist studies, including *Baptists and the Bible, By His Grace and for His Glory,* a three-volume study of Baptist identity entitled *The Baptists* (2005-2007), and the biography, *James Petigru Boyce: A Southern Baptist Statesman* (2009). Since 1976, Nettles has been an instructor in theological education. He is married to Margaret and they have three children and, presently, five grandchildren.

Gerald L. Priest received his B.A., M.Div. and Ph.D. (1988) from Bob Jones University, Greenville, South Carolina. In addition to furthering his education at Wake Forest University and the University of North Carolina at Greensboro, he is also a graduate of the Chaplain Command and General Staff College of the U.S. Army. Dr. Priest has taught at Clearwater Christian College, Clearwater, Florida and Piedmont Baptist College in Winston-Salem, North Carolina. He was the Department Chair and Professor of Historical Theology at Detroit Baptist Theological Seminary, Allen Park, Michigan for many years (retiring in May 2009) and is currently part-time professor at Northland International University (formerly Northland Baptist Bible College), Dunbar, Wisconsin, where he teaches church history and Bible, and in addition, is adjunct professor at International Baptist College, Tempe, Arizona.

Thomas Ray attended Tennessee Temple College in Chattanooga, Tennessee in 1960-1961, before transferring to Garland College in Garland, Texas in 1962-1963, where he graduated with honors, completing his Liberal Arts degree in three years. Having spent some time as a Christian counselor, he taught Pastoral Theology at Pacific Coast Baptist Bible College in California from 1974-1976 and received a Doctor of Sacred Theology degree from Louisiana Baptist University, Shreveport, in May 2004. Dr. Ray was pastor at College Boulevard Baptist Church in Denison, Texas in 1963; Crestview Baptist Church, Irving, Texas, 1964-1968; Central Baptist Temple, Huntington Beach, California, 1968-1976; Alice Avenue Baptist Church, Phoenix, Arizona, 1977-1979; Marsh Lane Baptist Church, Dallas, Texas, 1984-1986; and West Erwin Baptist Church, Tyler, Texas, 1989-1992. His pastorates at the latter two churches were curtailed by his having to resign due to health problems. He now devotes his time to writing and distributing literature through "The Reapers," which he founded in 1970, as well as aiding churches in training persons for evangelistic outreach and small group Bible studies. In addition to regularly contributing a monthly article on Baptist history to the *Baptist Bible Tribune*, Springfield, Missouri, he has also authored the book, *Daniel and Abraham Marshall–Pioneer Baptist Evangelists to the South*, published by Particular Baptist Press in 2006.

George Truett Rogers is a graduate of Hardin-Simmons University (B.A.), Southwestern Baptist Theological Seminary (B.D.), and the University of Colorado (M.A. and Ph.D.). His major doctoral emphasis was in the field of Colonial and Revolutionary American history with his research and publications centered on Baptist work in the Colonial and modern American periods. He has pastored Baptist churches in Colorado and West Virginia, and he has most recently retired from teaching in the Honors College at West Virginia University. He presently lives in Mountain Lake Park, Maryland.

Howard R. Stewart is a native of Philadelphia (born April 21, 1922), where he attended public schools, K through 12. He served in the U.S. Navy during WWII aboard the battleship U.S.S. *Idaho*, participating in eight campaigns, which included thirteen battles in the Pacific Theater of Operations. He was married to Evelyn New on November 25, 1944, who passed away on April 30, 2007. He has two married sons, seven grandchildren and seven great grandchildren. He earned his B.A., Th.B., M.Div., and Th.M. at Eastern Baptist Theological Seminary (Now Eastern University and Palmer Seminary); and a D.Min. at Fuller Theological Seminary. Stewart served pastorates in Pennsylvania, Delaware and California from 1948-1988. He has served as adjunct professor in New Testament at Wesley College, Delaware, and in Baptist History and Polity at the American Baptist Seminary of the West and Fuller Theological Seminary in California. He is the author of *Baptists and Local Autonomy, A Dazzling Enigma—The Story of Morgan Edwards,* and *American Baptists and The Church.* Awaiting publication are "Helpful Rhymes for Senior Times," and "God Had a Plan—An Autobiography." Retired since August 1988, he resides at Atherton Baptist Homes, Alhambra, California.

Earl Waggoner serves Golden Gate Baptist Theological Seminary as both Director of its Southern California Campus and Associate Professor of Theology and Church History. He served three different south Louisiana churches as their pastor from 1992 to 2002. Prior to his June 2012 relocation to Southern California, Waggoner taught ten years for Golden Gate at its Rocky Mountain Campus in Denver, Colorado. He received both M.Div. and Ph.D. (systematic theology) degrees from New Orleans Baptist Theological Seminary. Prior to vocational ministry, Dr. Waggoner served as an active church member and worked in television production. While in Colorado he also did freelance media work and ministered to the baseball community. He and his wife Kris have three adult children.

C. Douglas Weaver received his B.A. at Mississippi College (1978), M.Div. at Southern Baptist Theological Seminary (1981), and PhD. at Southern Baptist Theological Seminary (1985). He was Chair and Professor of Christianity, Division of Religion and Philosophy, Bluefield College, Bluefield, Virginia, 1986-1989, professor at Brewton-Parker College, Mt. Vernon, Georgia, 1989-2003, and has been at Baylor University since 2003, where he was recently promoted to full professor in the Department of Religion. He is a member of the Department's "Historical Studies" area and teaches at the Ph.D., Masters, and undergraduate levels. His current research and teaching focus is on Baptist history and also Pentecostalism. In recent publications, Dr. Weaver offered a survey of Baptist history as a "search for the New Testament church," and offered a new look at the work of the twentieth-century Baptist leader, E. Y. Mullins. In other recent studies, Dr. Weaver has explored the importance of freedom of conscience and the relationship of personal voluntary faith and ecclesiology in Baptist life. He is also part of the Affiliate Faculty at G. W. Truett Baptist Theological Seminary.

Terry Wolever is a graduate of Oklahoma State University, Stillwater (B.Sc., 1982). He is the author of the biography *John Gano, 1727-1804. Pastor-Evangelist of the Philadelphia Association* (2012). His special regional interest is in the early Regular Baptists of the Northeastern United States. He currently serves as editor for Particular Baptist Press, Springfield, Missouri.

Acknowledgments

All of the essays in this volume were composed for this volume, with the exception of the one on David Thomas by C. Douglas Weaver, and the one on Hezekiah Smith by John David Broome, each of which are presented here revised from their original publication in the *Baptist History and Heritage* journal and included with the authors' permission.[2] The essay on Oliver Hart by Thomas J. Nettles, originally written for our series, has also been previously published in his book, *The Baptists*, Volume Two.[3] We are thankful to each writer for their contribution to this work.

We wish to express our appreciation to the staffs of the John Hay Library, Brown University, Providence, Rhode Island; The Historical Society of Pennsylvania, Philadelphia; The American Baptist Historical Society, Atlanta, Georgia; the Franklin Trask Library, Andover Newton Theological School, Newton Centre, Massachusetts; the New Jersey State Archives, Trenton; the Massachusetts Historical Society, Boston; and the Central Baptist Theological Seminary, Plymouth, Minnesota, for the use of portraits and citations from manuscript materials in their collections.

The editor also very much appreciates the time and effort put into this volume by Gary W. Long, who has done much in the way of contacting potential writers for this ongoing series, and by our assistant, Mrs. Patricia Holcomb, who has contributed many hours in both typing and proofing the contents of this book.

T. W.

---

[2] C. Douglas Weaver, "David Thomas and the Regular Baptists in Colonial Virginia," *Baptist History and Heritage* (Nashville, TN: Historical Commission, S.B.C.), 18 (1983), No. 4 (October): 3-19; John D. Broome, "Hezekiah Smith of Haverhill," *Baptist History and Heritage* (Nashville: Historical Commission, S.B.C.), 1 (1965), No. 1 (August): 8-14.

[3] *The Baptists: Key People Involved in Forming a Baptist Identity* (Fearn, Scotland: Christian Focus Publications), 2, *Beginnings in America* (2005): "Oliver Hart (1723-95)," 77-100.

SHUBAL STEARNS
1706 - 1771

by Earl Waggoner

"And so, northward to Virginia, southward into South Carolina and ultimately Georgia, the movement spread. Not only eastward toward the sea, but westward toward the great Mississippi, northwest to Virginia and southward to South Carolina and Georgia, the word went forth from this Zion and great was the company of those who published it, insomuch that her converts were as drops of the morning dew."[1] This quote from Baptist historian William W. Barnes is remarkable for several reasons. The geography mentioned encompasses almost the entire width and breadth of the southeastern United States. The reference is to the wildfire-like spread in the latter eighteenth century of a single religious movement. And most remarkable and interesting is that the movement's founder is an enigma, a virtual unknown.

The man was Shubal Stearns. He is credited with founding the Separate Baptist movement, a force which itself was foundational to the ethos of Baptists in the southern United States. To tell his story requires not just presenting the sparse facts about his life but weaving them together with what is known about the Separates' beginning. So his real story is as much about the group as about the man. The ideas about Stearns which rise to the top are his fervor for evangelism, giftedness to preach, and uncanny ability to identify, equip, and send out others to do the same work.

New Birth, New Light

Shubal Stearns was born on January 28, 1706, in Boston, Massachusetts, to Shubal and Rebecca Larriford Stearns.[2] Raised Presbyterian,[3] Stearns joined the local Congregational church

---

[1] William W. Barnes, "Sandy Creek – The Holy Land of Baptists," *The Chronicle, The Journal of the American Baptist Historical Society*, 19 (1956), No. 2 (April): 71. Barnes' words are almost identical to a quote from Morgan Edwards.

[2] Robert B. Semple, *A History of the Rise and Progress of the Baptists in Virginia* (Richmond: John O'Lynch, 1810), 366.

[3] Morgan Edwards, "Materials Towards a History of the Baptists in North Carolina," in Eve B. Weeks and Mary B. Warren, eds., *Materials Towards*

after he and his family moved to Tolland, Connecticut. Nothing more is known of him prior to a momentous event of 1745. At that point his story becomes grounded in the evangelistic fervor and emotion of the First Great Awakening.

In 1744, itinerant George Whitefield returned to the American colonies to begin his second extensive tour, preaching as he traveled throughout New England. He was a cultural phenomenon in drawing massive crowds with his dramatic, extemporaneous preaching style. Preaching without notes, he believed, rendered him more open to the movement of the Holy Spirit of God.[4] Apparently he was correct, given the revival movement that followed him throughout the colonies, much like it had during his preaching tour of 1739-1740.

Whitefield made an especially dramatic impression on Connecticut. Congregational church leaders and Yale College opposed him, the former drafting a resolution in June 1745, that counseled ministers not to let Whitefield preach in their pulpits and warned citizens not to attend his meetings.[5] But enough people did attend to keep the revival fires burning strong. New Light Congregationalists, so called because they "saw the light" in responding to the spirit of revival, began separating into a new order of Congregationalism. They formed Separate societies (much like early Methodists did while remaining Anglicans), the major precipitating factor of their separation being the desire for a pure, regenerate church membership.[6]

This theological conviction moved many Separates even further, not just in pulling away from the old order, "Old Light" Congregationalists, but also in driving them into the welcoming arms of Baptist churches. It was a natural fit, because not only did both groups—Separate Congregationalists and Baptists—affirm regenerate church membership, but they also loathed government interference in church life and embraced democratic ideals in

---

a History of the Baptists. By Morgan Edwards, A.M. (Danielsville, GA: Heritage Papers, 1984), 2: 93.

[4] *George Whitefield's Journals* (Edinburgh, Scotland: The Banner of Truth Trust, 1978), 205.

[5] William L. Lumpkin, *Baptist Foundations in the South. Tracing through the Separates the Influence of the Great Awakening, 1754-1787* (Nashville, TN: Broadman Press, 1961), 10.

[6] *Ibid.*, 13.

church governance and participation.[7] A final theological hurdle was cleared by these dissatisfied Separates when they denied—based on a faithful reading of Scripture—the validity of infant baptism. Almost half of all ordained Connecticut Separate pastors had become Baptist shortly after 1751.[8] One of those ministry leaders who followed this exact path, from Congregationalist to Separatist to Baptist, was Shubal Stearns.

Stearns was converted at one of the Whitefield meetings in Connecticut, sometime in 1745. Shortly thereafter he became a New Light preacher in Tolland and served the Separatist church there for six years. On May 20, 1751, Stearns became convinced of the unbiblical nature of infant baptism and was immersed by Wait Palmer, pastor of the Baptist church at Stonington, Connecticut. Later that same year, Stearns was ordained to the ministry by Palmer and Joshua Morse, pastor of the New London, Connecticut, Baptist church. Apparently, the Baptist church in Tolland was formed by Stearns and was comprised of former members of the Separate congregation there where he had once ministered.

To Virginia and beyond

After three years of ministry to the Tolland, Connecticut, Baptist congregation, Stearns believed God was calling him to move westward, "to execute a great and extensive work."[9] Thus, in 1754, he and a few followers traveled to Opequon Creek, Virginia (currently Berkeley County, in northeastern West Virginia). He found a Baptist church there already, under the pastoral leadership of John Garrard.

Stearns' willingness to uproot and move some 400 miles is indicative of his passion and zeal for God's work. In relating this story, Robert Semple noted that Stearns had "strong faith in the immediate teachings of the Spirit," and believed "to those who sought him earnestly, God often gave evident tokens of his will. That such indications of the divine pleasure, partaking of the na-

---

[7] *Ibid.*, 15.

[8] The specific numbers are: of thirty-one pastors "in the period 1746-1751, five were Baptists before they were ordained and eight became Baptists soon afterward." A. H. Newman, *A History of the Baptist Churches in the United States* (New York: Charles Scribner's Sons, 1915), 245, quoted in Lumpkin, 18.

[9] Semple, *History of the Baptists in Virginia*, 2.

ture of inspiration, were above, tho' not contrary to reason. . . ."[10] This strong faith in the immediate and very real presence of God, as well as a firm confidence that the Almighty indeed had a will and guided people into it, had grown directly from the seeds of Great Awakening revivalism which had been planted in Stearns' heart. Such faith and confidence in God not only led Stearns and company to Opequon, but would become foundational for the evangelistic theology of the Separate Baptists. Semple further defined the motivations of their collective heart as being grounded in the "two great objects of a Christian's life, the glory of God and the salvation of men."[11]

Though well-received by Garrard, Stearns did not stay still for long. Before departing, however, he joined forces with his brother-in-law Daniel Marshall.

Marshall, his wife Martha (Shubal's sister and Marshall's second wife, who he married in 1747),[12] and their three children had also arrived at Opequon in 1754, after an eighteen-month ministry to the Mohawk tribe in Onnaquaggy, near "the head of the Susquehanna."[13] Missionary living for Marshall and his family had been meager, but his ministry had been successful. However, tribal warfare resulted in the Marshalls' flight and eventual arrival at Opequon. They had labored as Separate Congregationalist ministers and thus had received no denominational financial support.[14] After becoming involved with the Baptist church in Opequon, both Daniel and Martha became Baptists, being baptized by Samuel Heton (or Heaton). Apparently, the Marshalls arrived there before Stearns and his party, for Semple notes that Heton was the immediate predecessor to Garrard.[15]

Continuing toward the west, Stearns, Marshall, and their group stopped next in Hampshire County, Virginia, about thirty

---

[10] *Ibid.*

[11] *Ibid.*

[12] Thomas Ray, *Daniel and Abraham Marshall—Pioneer Baptist Evangelists to the South* (Springfield, MO: Particular Baptist Press, 2006), 5.

[13] Semple, *History of the Baptists in Virginia*, 369.

[14] Ray, *Daniel and Abraham Marshall,* 6.

[15] Semple, *History of the Baptists in Virginia,* 367. Semple notes that the pastoral change occurred around 1755 (*ibid.,* 289).

miles from Winchester. Stearns preached there but became restless, "not meeting with his expected success."[16] Though the directing providence of God may have become hard for Stearns to follow, it became suddenly clear via a letter from some friends in North Carolina. After moving there, they discovered that gospel preaching was greatly desired by the locals, but was simply not to be found. "In some instances they had ridden forty miles to hear one sermon."[17] This must be the divine destination! Stearns, Marshall, their wives and six other couples, plus all their children, packed up and headed further south and west—about 200 miles—to North Carolina.[18] They settled in Guilford (currently Randolph) County near a creek, the name of which they took for their church and settlement, Sandy Creek.

A new day in North Carolina

The North Carolina to which Stearns and company emigrated was a British colony in the midst of strong and vigorous growth.[19] Colonial population hovered around 100,000, with 20,000 to 30,000 inhabitants living in the central and western Piedmont.[20] Only a few villages, and no large towns, dotted this landscape.[21] Stearns' immediate mission field was somewhat "limited by the racial and

---

[16] *Ibid.*, 3; see also 367.

[17] *Ibid.*, 3.

[18] Extant lists of that group provide only the men's names, each one followed by "and wife": Shubal Stearns, Peter Stearns, Ebenezer Stearns, Shubal Stearns, Jr., Daniel Marshall, Joseph Breed, Enos Stimpson, and Jonathan Polk. Interestingly, Morgan Edwards writes that Shubal and his wife, Sarah Johnson (or Johnstone) had no children, so who were Shubal and Shubal, Jr.? Perhaps Shubal the elder is our subject's father, with our man being Shubal, Jr. This is purely conjecture though, based on the mention of Stearns' father's name in Semple, *History of the Baptists in Virginia,* 366, as cited above.

[19] Henry Stroupe, "Shubal Stearns – Sandy Creek's Separate Baptist Leader," *The Chronicle. The Journal of the American Baptist Historical Society*, 19 (1956), No. 2 (April): 60.

[20] *Ibid.*

[21] George W. Paschal, "Shubal Stearns," *Review and Expositor,* 36 (1939), No. 1 (January): 46.

religious character of the [area] settlers."[22] Quakers, Presbyterians, Moravians, and Lutherans were all within about a forty-mile radius of Sandy Creek. While the first three groups were well-served by their respective clergy, the Lutherans were not. They were unreachable by anyone other than a German-speaking minister.[23] Yet, Stearns found a ready audience among the local Anglicans—those who apparently would ride forty miles for a sermon.

Though the Church of England had been the official, established church in North Carolina for over fifty years, its ministers were few and located in the eastern half of the colony. Semple described the Anglicans who surrounded Sandy Creek as "grossly ignorant" of the essential principles of the Christian religion, though they had been raised in a broad but spiritually ineffective Christian context.[24] "Having the form of godliness, they knew nothing of its power."[25] Semple continued, "Having always supposed that religion consisted in nothing more than the practise of its outward duties, they could not comprehend how it should be necessary to feel conviction and conversion: But to be able to ascertain the time and place of one's conversion was, in their estimation, wonderful indeed."[26] For many of them Shubal Stearns would be the one to help them make that wonderful determination.

One other religious group was in the area, too—Baptists. The General Baptists first organized in North Carolina in 1727, under the pastoral leadership of Paul Palmer. By 1750, the Generals had organized sixteen churches throughout the colony.[27] Particular Baptist missionaries, first from South Carolina, then out of the Philadelphia Association, began to reorganize these churches in the early 1750's, so that by 1756, all but one of the General churches had become Particular Baptist.[28] Of special interest was

---

[22] *Ibid.*, 47.

[23] *Ibid.*

[24] Semple, *History of the Baptists in Virginia,* 3.

[25] *Ibid.*, referring to 2 Tim. 3:5.

[26] *Ibid.*, 4.

[27] Paschal, "Shubal Stearns," 43.

[28] *Ibid.*, 43.

a church nearby Sandy Creek, in what was called the Jersey Settlement. Settlers had emigrated there from New Jersey not long before Stearns arrived in North Carolina, taking the name of their home colony, and establishing a church. Its first pastor, John Gano (1727-1804), was credited by Morgan Edwards as being a major influence on the Generals changing to Particulars.[29] Also, Gano was a surprise attender at the second Sandy Creek Association meeting. That event is related below.

Embracing the religious situation which they found upon their arrival in mid-November, Stearns' group built a small meetinghouse and constituted their church on November 22, 1755.[30] Stearns was made pastor, with Marshall and Joseph Breed (neither of whom were ordained) appointed as assistants. Thus was constituted the first Separate Baptist church in North Carolina.

Preacher, pastor, Separate Baptist

Edwards provided an interesting description of Shubal Stearns the preacher: "Mr. Stearns was but a little man, but a man of good natural parts and sound judgment. Of learning he had but a small share, yet was pretty well acquainted with books."[31] This "little man" was a giant in the pulpit, possessing a voice "musical and strong, which he managed in such a manner as. . .to make soft impressions on the heart, and fetch tears from the eyes in a mechanical way."[32] Semple provided a similar description of Stearns' preaching style, attributing its source as having been adopted by Stearns when he was in New England. Apparently the Separates there "had acquired a very warm and pathetic address, accompanied by strong gestures and a singular tone of voice. Being

---

[29] Edwards, "Materials Towards a History of the Baptists in North Carolina," 79.

[30] Edwards notes that the meetinghouse was "little" and "near the present" one he saw in 1771. That latter one was thirty by twenty-six feet in measure. *Ibid.*, 91.

[31] *Ibid.*, 93.

[32] *Ibid.*

often deeply affected themselves while preaching," wrote Semple, "correspondent affections were felt by their pious hearers."[33]

Not surprisingly, the responses of the hearers, "tears, trembling, screams, shouts and acclamations,"[34] as well as "outcries, epilepsies and extacies [sic],"[35] were common expressions among the people who heard Stearns. Indeed, as Semple described, "The people were greatly astonished, having never seen things on this wise before. Many mocked, but the power of God attending them, many also trembled."[36] Edwards described it even more dramatically, declaring "the neighbourhood was alarmed and the Spirit of God listed to blow as a mighty rushing wind."[37] This was Great Awakening Christianity—emotional, affective, Spirit-communicating and inculcating preaching. It had changed Stearns' life, and he was employing it as a tool for God to use in changing others' lives, too. An example of the power of the preached Word comes from this incident involving Elnathan Davis, eventually a pastor at the Haw River church:

> [Davis] had heard that one John Steward was to be baptized, such a day, by Mr. Stearns; now this Steward, being a very big man, and Shubal Stearns of small stature, he concluded there would be some diversion if not drowning; therefore he gathered about 8 or 10 of his companions in wickedness and went to the spot. Shubal Stearns came and began to preach; Elnathan went to hear him while his companions stood at a distance. He was no sooner among the crowd but he perceived some of the people tremble as if

[33] Semple, *History of the Baptists in Virginia*, 4.

[34] *Ibid.*

[35] Edwards, "Materials Towards a History of the Baptists in North Carolina," 92. [Edwards went on to add that these responses to the preaching of the Separate Baptists were "not peculiar to them; the New England Presbyterians had them long before; and in Virginia, it is well known the same effects attend the ministry of some clergymen of the Church of England" —*Ed.*]

[36] Semple, *History of the Baptists in Virginia*, 4.

[37] Morgan Edwards, as quoted in George W. Paschal, *History of North Carolina Baptists* (Raleigh, NC: The General Board, North Carolina Baptist State Convention), 1 (1930): 227.

> in a fit of the ague. He felt and examined them in order to find if it was not a dissimulation; meanwhile one man, leaned on his shoulder, weeping bitterly. Elnathan, perceiving he had wet his white new coat, pushed him off, and ran to his companions who were sitting on a log, at a distance; when he came one said, 'Well, Elnathan, what do you think now of these damned people?' He replied 'There is a trembling and crying spirit among them: but whether it be the spirit of God or the devil I don't know; if it be the devil, the devil go with them; for I will never more venture my self among them.' He stood a while in that resolution; but the enchantment of Shubal Stearns' voice drew him to the crowd once more. He had not been long there before the trembling seized him also; he attempted to withdraw; but his strength failing and his understanding confounded he, with many other[s], sunk to the ground. When he came to himself he found nothing in him but dread and anxiety, bordering on horror. He continued in this situation some days, and then found relief by faith in Christ. Immediately he began to preach conversion work, raw as he was, and scanty as his knowledge must have been.[38]

Thus, the hallmark of Separate Baptist ministry was this type of preaching employed by Stearns. And yet this was not simply the work of a gifted, far from manipulative, communicator. Edwards noted soberly, "I believe a preternatural and invisible hand works in the assemblies of the Separate-baptists bearing down the human mind, as was the case in primitive churches 1 Cor. xiv. 25."[39] Not surprisingly all the Separate Baptist ministers came to imitate the tone and method of their mentor's preaching style, and to great effect.[40]

Stearns' Separates were known for more, however. For the most part, nine rites identified their practice and ecclesial focus. These were, baptism by immersion; the Lord's Supper (initially administered weekly); a "love-feast;" laying on of hands for all new, baptized believers; feet washing; anointing the sick; right

---

[38] Edwards, "Materials Towards a History of the Baptists in North Carolina," 96-97.

[39] *Ibid.*, 93.

[40] *Ibid.*

hand of fellowship; kiss of charity; and devoting children.[41] Also, "ruling elders, elderesses, deaconesses" were recognized as legitimate leaders within the church.[42]

The theological flavor of the early Separates has been said to have been Arminian.[43] However, this idea is based on a single, unsubstantiated statement, written by the Baptist historian David Benedict in 1813. He noted that many of the churches in the early history of the Sandy Creek Association "were formerly thought to lean considerably towards the Arminian system; but they have now become generally, and some of them strenuously Calvinistick [sic]."[44] Beyond that single statement, little substantive proof of deeper theological commitments exists. Paschal maintains that Stearns was not a Calvinist, but his assessment is based more on anti-Calvinist preconceptions and prejudice than solid analysis.[45] Conversely, Stroupe asserts that Stearns successfully combined "evangelistic zeal with modified Calvinistic doctrines."[46] He bases that conclusion on the fact that Stearns was converted under the preaching of George Whitefield, someone known for having such a theological approach. But regardless of Stearns' debt to Whitefield, one can hardly credit the former being a Calvinist simply by association.[47]

---

[41] *Ibid.*, 91. [Edwards noted that some of the Separates did not "regard the nine Christian rites, but only baptism, the Lord's Supper, and imposition of hands" (*ibid.*, 90) —*Ed.*]

[42] *Ibid.*

[43] Paschal, *History of North Carolina Baptists*, 1: 400.

[44] David Benedict, *A General History of the Baptist Denomination in America, and Other Parts of the World* (Boston: Lincoln and Edmands, 1813), 2: 107.

[45] Paschal, *History of North Carolina Baptists,* 1: 401-403. Paschal compares and contrasts two confessional statements reputed to be associated with Stearns. There is no proof that either one was.

[46] Stroupe, "Shubal Stearns," 68.

[47] [While this may be true, some other considerations must be given weight here as well. For example, when Stearns sought out assistance to ordain Daniel Marshall in 1756, the Regular Baptist minister who refused to participate, gave as his stated reasons that "he believed them to be a disorderly set, suffering women to pray in public and permitting every ignorant man to preach that chose; that they encouraged noise and

Given that 1) texts of Stearns' sermons do not exist, 2) observers mention his mode of preaching more than content of theology, and 3) Benedict offers only that one-sentence description, it could be that Stearns was indifferent to either Arminian or Calvinistic allegiance. What we do know for certain is he had a passion for the gospel—being born again, a message delivered with zeal and emotion, activated by the Holy Spirit, and shared with his world. His church was administered according to the rites he found mentioned in Scripture. Deeper, more developed, theological expression of those realities may have been beyond his interest.

Separates and Regulars

As mentioned above, Particular or Regular Baptists were already in the general area of Sandy Creek, at the Jersey Settlement, when Shubal arrived. These Baptists were part of a larger network of Regular Baptists scattered throughout North Carolina. They were Calvinists, articulating their faith with the Philadelphia Confession and belonging to either the Philadelphia or Charleston Associations. Paschal contends that they were not evangelistically inclined, their pastors never traveling to do mission work or establishing new congregations.[48] Though both

---

confusion in their meetings" (Semple, *History of the Baptists in Virginia*, 5), and *not* any difference otherwise doctrinally. This in itself is very telling; plus the fact that Stearns sought out another Regular Baptist, Henry Ledbetter (b.1721) of the Charleston Association, who did assist in the ordination (*ibid.*). In addition, we have the statement of Morgan Edwards, writing in 1772 (less than a year after Stearns' death), that regarding the Regular and Separate Baptists: "The faith and order of both are the same, except some trivial matters not sufficient to support a distinction, but less a disunion; for both avow the *Century-Confession* [i.e. the 1689 or Second London Baptist Confession] and the annexed discipline." (Weeks and Warren, eds., *Materials Towards a History of the Baptists, By Morgan Edwards, A.M.,* 2: 43). Edwards makes no exceptional reference to Stearns on this point —*Ed.*]

[48] Paschal, *History of North Carolina Baptists*, 1: 270. [Paschal later realized this was a mistaken assessment, which he amended 25 years later in Volume Two of his *History* when he wrote, "In reality most preachers of both groups were evangelistic, and with zeal like that of Shubal Stearns were going through all the section west of the Yadkin preaching the gospel of salvation and gathering their converts into churches." *History of North Carolina Baptists*, 2 (1955): 259 —*Ed.*]

groups—the Separates at Sandy Creek and the Regulars—were Baptists, they had enough dissimilarity to remain apart at the time and do their own respective work. Two different experiences illustrate the tenuous nature of their relationship to each other.

One experience involved the ordination of Daniel Marshall. Stearns made it his practice not to ordain a man to the ministry unless he had been called specifically to become a church's pastor. This was the case with Marshall. Though he had preached often, he was not ordained until called by the Abbott's Creek church, located about thirty miles from Sandy Creek. Once the call had been extended (sometime before 1757, according to Paschal),[49] Stearns set about looking for other ordained ministers to participate in Marshall's ordination. A Regular Baptist pastor in South Carolina was petitioned, but he "sternly refused, declaring that he held no fellowship with Stearns' party; that he believed them to be a disorderly set, suffering women to pray in public and permitting every ignorant man to preach that chose; that they encouraged noise and confusion in their meetings."[50] Stearns located another ordained man to assist him with Marshall, but nothing more about the Regular pastor's rebuff is related.

The other experience involved an apparently surprise visit to the Sandy Creek Association by John Gano, then pastor of the Jersey Settlement church. At the second annual associational meeting, in 1759, Gano was "received by Stearns with great affection."[51] However, due to "an unhappy shyness and jealousy between the Regulars and Separates, by the others he was treated with coldness and suspicion; and they even refused to invite him into their Association."[52] Gano, nonetheless, remained as a spectator, refusing to be offended. After leaving the session, Stearns expressed to those assembled how hurt he was at the way they had treated the guest. He "expostulated with them on the matter," persuading them to invite Gano back, this time to preach. They invited Gano to return, and "he cheerfully complied, and his preaching, though not with the New-Light tones and gestures, was

---

[49] *Ibid.*, 292.

[50] Semple, *History of the Baptists in Virginia*, 5.

[51] Benedict, *A General History of the Baptist Denomination,* 2: 50.

[52] *Ibid.*

in demonstration of the Spirit and with power."[53] Gano remained at the meeting, preaching frequently, "much to their astonishment, as well as edification."[54] The gathered association warmed to him and an affectionate relationship was forged. Semple added this comment to his version of the same story: "When Mr. Gano returned to his own country, being asked what he thought of these Baptists, replied, that 'doubtless the power of God was among them; that although rather immethodical, they certainly had the root of the matter at heart.' "[55]

These two incidents highlight key differences between the two Baptist groups. Though the Regulars' theological bent was unquestionably Calvinistic and the Separates' cannot be as definitely determined, the former valued order, lack of emotionalism, and limited participation in worship and preaching. The Separates desired more freedom and emotion in worship and preaching. Nevertheless, when a spirit of maturity and humility prevailed, each group could be won over to the other. Most importantly, the gospel story—"the heart of the matter"—and God's presence in its delivery, were valued by both groups. By 1787, sixteen years after Stearns' death, the Regulars and Separates would be united, with their clarifying names dropped and both groups happy just to be simply Baptists.

For the purpose of our story, the above incidents also reveal important characteristics of Stearns. Namely, he was a man of remarkable humility and charity. Though rebuffed by the South Carolinian Regular pastor, Shubal welcomed Gano with open arms and persuaded his charges to do the same. This response by Stearns toward Gano seems consistent with a description provided by Edwards: "His character was indisputably good, both as a man, a christian and a preacher."[56]

The Regulars may have thought the Separates too disorderly, illiterate, and overly emotional, but the Separates experienced

---

[53] *Ibid.*, 50-51.

[54] *Ibid.*, 51.

[55] Semple, *History of the Rise and Progress of the Baptists in Virginia. Revised and Extended by G. W. Beale* (Richmond: Pitt and Dickinson, 1894), 66.

[56] Edwards, "Materials Towards a History of the Baptists in North Carolina," 93.

amazing growth. The Sandy Creek church grew in short order from the original 16 to 606 members.[57] But Stearns' passion to preach the gospel pushed the Sandy Creek growth out of its own doors. Edwards declared, "The word went forth from this Zion and great was the company of them that published it, in so much that her converts were as the drops of morning dew."[58]

Spread of the gospel happened not just through Stearns' passionate preaching at Sandy Creek, but via his extensive travel throughout central, eastern, and southeastern North Carolina and down into South Carolina, too.[59] In one of the few remaining documents written in his own hand, Stearns reflected on one of those itinerant meetings:

> The Lord carries on his work gloriously in sundry places in this province, and in Virginia, and in South Carolina. There has been no addition of churches since I wrote last year [1764], but many members have been added in many places. Not long since, I attended a meeting on Hoy [Haw] river, about thirty miles from hence. About seven hundred souls attended the meeting, which held six days. We received twenty-four persons by a satisfactory declaration of grace, and eighteen of them were baptized. The power of God was wonderful.[60]

Indeed it was.

Perhaps the most enduring and significant Kingdom contribution made by Stearns was the number of men he sent out as pastors. Through his direct influence, as well as indirectly through all the churches he helped start, some 125 ministers devoted themselves to the gospel, "many of which are ordained and support

---

[57] *Ibid.*, 91.

[58] *Ibid.*, 92. This is the quote mirrored by Barnes in the opening of this essay.

[59] Paschal, *History of North Carolina Baptists*, 1: 304-306.

[60] Letter from Stearns to Connecticut friends, dated October 16, 1765, in Isaac Backus, *Church History of New England, from 1620 to 1804* (Philadelphia: American Baptist Publication and Sunday School Society, 1844), 228.

the sacred character as well as any sett of clergy in America."[61] Edwards documented stories of several of these pastors, some of the narratives smacking of the same drama as Stearns' preaching. For example, Philip Mulkey, eventually pastor of the Deep River church, had the following experience.

> One night (saith his narrative) as I was going home from the house where I had been playing the fiddle to dancers, a hideous spectre (the Devil grinning at him with fiery eyes) presented itself before me just as I opened the door; the effect was, fainting, and continuing as dead for the space of about 10 minutes, as the people about me report the matter; when I recovered, I found an uncommon dread on my spirits, from an apprehension that the shocking figure, I had seen, was the Devil, and that he would have me.[62]

Understandably, this experience contributed mightily to his "transition thence to a state of grace."[63]

Other Stearns-bred ministers included his brother-in-law Daniel Marshall, who preached not only in North Carolina but Virginia, South Carolina, and eventually in Georgia; Samuel Harriss (or Harris), a man of influence prior to his conversion and ultimately a pastor in Virginia; and Elnathan Davis, whose conversion story was related earlier. Also, many of those 125 ministerial "sons" of Stearns helped him start an astounding forty-two churches throughout Virginia, Tennessee, North and South Carolina, and Georgia.

Thus, Sandy Creek was considered by Edwards as the "mother of all the Separate-baptists."[64] Through Stearns' passionate preaching, itinerant work throughout North and South Carolina, and sending out new ministers, the Sandy Creek influence became the Sandy Creek Association.

---

[61] Edwards, "Materials Towards a History of the Baptists in North Carolina," 92.

[62] *Ibid.*, 141.

[63] *Ibid.*

[64] *Ibid.*, 92.

Associational development

By 1758, three churches in North Carolina were identified as Separate Baptist fellowships: Sandy Creek, Deep River, and Abbott's Creek. Shubal Stearns, of course, had been instrumental in starting them all. Amazingly, these three churches had a combined membership of more than 900 by the end of that year.

Stearns understood the value of banding together such a large group of Christians. He possessed organizational skills or, as Semple described, "the talent of arranging the materials when collected."[65] Thus, he determined to create an association out of the three churches and other congregations.[66] Delegates from all these entities would be brought together at Sandy Creek church to create an organization which would "impart stability, regularity and uniformity to the whole."[67] Stearns visited each group, explained his plan, and persuaded them all to join.

Their first meeting was held the second Monday of June, 1758.[68] James Read, who served eventually as a pastor in Virginia, provided this brief description of the meeting.

> We continued together. . .three or four days. Great crowds of people attended, mostly through curiosity: The great power of God was among us: The preaching every day seemed to be attended with God's blessing: We carried on our association, with sweet decorum and fellowship to the end: Then we took leave of one another, with many solemn charges from our Reverend old Father Shubal Stearns, to stand fast unto the end.[69]

---

[65] Semple, *History of the Baptists in Virginia* (1810), 6.

[66] *Ibid.* Semple identified the latter as "some others that exercised the rights of churches tho' not formally organized."

[67] *Ibid.*

[68] Edwards, "Materials Towards a History of the Baptists in North Carolina," 90. Multiple dates have been proposed for this first meeting of the Sandy Creek Association. Semple (*History*, 43) wrote that it was January 1760, while Benedict stated it was January 1758 (*General History*, 2: 49). Given the primacy of Edwards' account, deference is given to his date. Paschal affirms the same, noting other corroborating evidence (*History*, 1: 394 f.).

[69] Semple, *History of the Baptists in Virginia* (1810), 44.

The Sandy Creek Association was off to a good start, gaining the interest of the community and encouraging all the participants. For at least eleven years, the fifty-two-year "old Father" must have been pleased.

In fact, Stearns may have been surprised at how useful the Association proved to be. The meetings certainly provided venues for encouragement to the attending ministers. They gathered for fellowship, but also to hear their brethren preach, sing the songs of Zion, and share stories of God's work throughout the area. According to Semple, "These things so enflamed the hearts of the ministers, that they would leave the association, with a zeal and courage, which no obstacles could impede."[70]

But it had another effect, too. Curious observers gathered at each annual meeting, per Read's narrative, and in so doing "many became enamoured with these extraordinary people, and petitioned the association to send preachers into their neighbourhoods."[71] The requests were granted, preachers answered the calls, and "the associations became the medium of propagating the gospel in new and dark places."[72] The Word was indeed going forth from this Zion, in new and amazing ways.

Stearns was not an absent spiritual landlord, planting the churches and bestowing "solemn charges" upon their ministers just once a year. Though he maintained his ministry at Sandy Creek, he also traveled "a considerable distance in the country around, to assist in organizing and regulating the churches which he and his associates were instrumental in raising up."[73] This continuing itinerant work, now focused on organization as well as evangelism, reflected his broad range of giftedness and pastoral concern. However, the concern may have gone too far.

In 1770, the Association held its annual meeting at the Grassy Creek church, in Virginia. It did not begin well. On the very first day, in the first session of business, a disagreement occurred. Though such would seem a badge of honor for many current-day Baptists, it was not so in the early days of Sandy Creek. That group had resolved to do nothing if not in unanimous agreement.

---

[70] *Ibid.*, 7.

[71] *Ibid.*, 6.

[72] *Ibid.*, 6-7.

[73] Benedict, *A General History of the Baptist Denomination*, 2: 41.

According to Benedict, the process for ironing out disagreements had been determined beforehand and was extensive. "If in any measure proposed, there was a single dissentient, they laboured first by arguments to come to unanimous agreement; when arguments failed, they resorted to frequent prayer, in which all joined. When both these failed, they sometimes appointed the next day for fasting and prayer, and to strive to bring all to be of one mind."[74] These measures were attempted but to no avail. Not until 3 p.m., on the third day of the gathering, did a proposal succeed in gaining unanimity; the log jam was broken. While the exact nature of the initial disagreement is unknown, its resolution is not. That which pleased the entire association finally was a division of the group. The ministers present voted unanimously to divide the Sandy Creek Association into three separate associations, one for each of the colonies represented: Virginia, North Carolina, and South Carolina. When the ministers departed that annual meeting, they would never again meet as one association. Though Stearns' associational dream had died, yet the one association had become three.

What increases the drama of the story is the scope of Stearns' involvement. The year before (September 1769), on the way home from a preaching visit, "he observed in the horizon a white heap like snow; upon his drawing near he perceived the heap to stand suspended in the air 15 or 20 feet above ground."[75] When the heap fell to the ground, it divided into three parts, the largest somehow moving northward and the next largest moving southward. Stearns lost sight of both of these. The third heap stayed where it fell. Stearns' own interpretation of this vision, as related by Edwards, was, "The bright heap is our religious interest; which will divide and spread north and south, but chiefly northward; while a small part remains at Sandy-creek."[76] Stearns was correct; the division of the Association into its three parts occurred the next year. However, Stearns' vision may have been more of a self-fulfilling prophecy than a deeply prophetic announcement.

According to Edwards, the Association's split, carried out in an unsettling manner at that 1770 meeting, was less about growing pains and more about Stearns' misuse of authority. Edwards

---

[74] *Ibid.*, 52.

[75] Edwards, "Materials Towards a History of the Baptists in North Carolina," 94.

[76] *Ibid.*

reveals that the Association "had carried matters so high as to leave hardly any power in particular churches, unfellowshiping ordinations, ministers and churches that acted independent of them."[77] It had become a hierarchical authority, affirming that local churches had complete power over themselves but giving them all the option of transferring such to the Association. Apparently these transfers had been extensive. Benedict offers a further critique: "The good old Mr. Stearns. . .is said to have been the principal promoter of this improper stretch of associational power."[78]

Stearns obviously felt great affection and a high degree of fatherly protection for the Association, as well as so many of its churches, which he had birthed. And yet he crossed a cherished Baptist line by taking away the churches' individual autonomy. The motives may have been protective and noble, but the outcome proved disastrous, and rightfully so. In his analysis of this situation, Glenn Thomas Carson pondered, "What would have been the ultimate ramifications for Baptists in the South if associational power had become the norm?"[79] Thankfully, Sandy Creek Baptists did not let that happen. Though the Association remained the Separate association for North Carolina, it never again was as prominent or influential.

A final blow was dealt to Sandy Creek church and the association just before Stearns died. The Battle of Alamance was fought on May 16, 1771. A precursor to the American Revolution, the fight was between local settlers (whose frustration over British colonial abuse of power had been boiling for three years) and the militia organized and led by Gov. William Tryon. Probably many Regulators were in the Association if not in the actual Sandy Creek church. At the annual meeting in October 1769, those assembled resolved "that if any took up arms against the civil authority he should be excommunicated."[80] While there is no

---

[77] *Ibid.*, 103.

[78] Benedict, *A General History of the Baptist Denomination*, 2: 53.

[79] See his article, "The Sandy Creek Association: A Test of Baptist Polity," *Baptist History and Heritage*, 29 (1994), No. 1 (Jan): 29-32.

[80] Edwards, "Materials Towards a History of the Baptists in North Carolina," 90.

record of any excommunications, there is undisputable record of the outcome of the battle: Tryon and the British won.

Given that victory and that the actual battlefield is less than twenty miles from the Sandy Creek church, many locals left the area after the battle. As Edwards put it, the inhabitants "despaired of seeing better times, and therefore quitted the province."[81] At least 1500 families departed the area, taking the membership of the church down to fourteen.[82] Barely six months after the battle, Shubal Stearns died on November 20, 1771. This date was also two days shy of the sixteenth anniversary of the founding of Sandy Creek church. He was buried in the cemetery of the church.

His legacy

Shubal Stearns was a man of vision. We know very little about the first thirty-nine years of his life. However, from the point of his conversion going forward we see the work of God in using a man for the last twenty-six years of life to do this "great and extensive work."[83] That vision was given by God to Stearns, who was instrumental in carrying it out. Carrying the revival spirit of the Great Awakening to the South, Stearns followed God's guidance and direction, from Connecticut to Virginia to North Carolina. From the banks of a creek which does not show up on many maps, Stearns planted a church which grew in number and influence. He preached passionately and with a unique style—sensing the Spirit, refusing sermon notes, yet zealously calling for repentance and the new birth. As he had been changed, so he was used, by God, to change many others. In the almost sixteen years of his groundbreaking ministry at Sandy Creek, his church grew to 606 members, he birthed forty-two churches, and 125 ministers spread the gospel throughout the southeast. He remains a testimony to following God faithfully.

---

[81] *Ibid.*, 91.

[82] *Ibid.*

[83] Semple, *History of the Baptists in Virginia* (1810), 2.

Further Reading

Clarence C. Goen. *Revivalism and Separatism in New England, 1740-1800. Strict Congregationlists and Separate Baptists in the Great Awakening.* New Haven, CT: Yale University Press, 1962; reprinted Middletown, CT: Wesleyan University Press, 1987.

William L. Lumpkin. *Baptist Foundations in the South. Tracing through the Separates the Influence of the Great Awakening, 1754-1787.* Nashville, TN: Broadman Press, 1961; reprinted Ashville, NC: Revival Literature, 2006.

Josh Powell, "Shubal Stearns and the Separate Baptist Tradition." Thomas K. Ascol, ed. *The Founders Journal.* Cape Coral, FL: Founders Ministries, Issue 44 (Spring 2001), 16-31.

George W. Purefoy. *History of the Sandy Creek Baptist Association, from its Organization in A.D. 1758 to A.D. 1858.* New York: Sheldon and Company, 1859.

Thomas Ray. *Daniel and Abraham Marshall—Pioneer Baptist Evangelists to the South.* Springfield, MO: Particular Baptist Press, 2006.

John Sparks. *The Roots of Appalachian Christianity: The Life and Legacy of Elder Shubal Stearns.* Lexington: University Press of Kentucky, 2001.

Eve B. Weeks and Mary B. Warren, eds. *Materials Towards a History of the Baptists. By Morgan Edwards, A.M.* Danielsville, GA: Heritage Papers, 1984, Volume Two (the Southern Colonies).

Scenes in the life of
Isaac Stelle 1718-1781
NEW YORK
Rocksberry/Schooley's Mtn.
Morristown
New York
Scotch Plains
Piscataqua/Piscataway
Staten Island
Hopewell
Middletown
PENNSYLVANIA
Crosswicks (Upper Freehold)
Pennepek
Philadelphia
NEW JERSEY
Welsh Tract
DELAWARE

ISAAC STELLE
1718 - 1781

by Terry Wolever

In his *Century Sermon* preached at the Philadelphia Baptist Association's annual meeting in October of 1807, Samuel Jones listed eight ministers whom he believed "were in a pretty high degree eminent in their day" in the Association.[1] These were John Davis, of Harford, Maryland; Robert Kelsay, of Cohansey, New Jersey; Peter Peterson VanHorne, of Pennepek, Pennsylvania; Isaac Eaton, of Hopewell, New Jersey; John Walton, of Morristown, New Jersey; Isaac Stelle, Jr., of Piscataway, New Jersey;[2] Benjamin Miller, of Scotch Plains, New Jersey; and John Gano, of New York. Jones added that all these men "were bright and shining lights, especially the last three." The first minister he names among the latter three is the subject of our essay.

His Huguenot ancestry

Like John Gano, Isaac Stelle[3] was descended from the Huguenot refugees that settled in the provinces of New York and East New Jersey in the latter part of the seventeenth century. These Huguenots were sturdy French Reformed Protestants who fled their native country to escape the oppressive persecution of

---

1 Samuel Jones, *A Century Sermon, Delivered in Philadelphia, at the Opening of the Philadelphia Baptist Association, October 6th, 1807* (Philadelphia: Bartram and Reynolds, 1807), reprinted in A. D. Gillette, ed., *Minutes of the Philadelphia Baptist Association, 1707-1807* (Philadelphia: American Baptist Publication Society, 1851), 456.

2 Jones refers to him as Isaac Stelle, *Jr.* so as not to be confused with an uncle of the same name.

3 The correct pronunciation of the surname is monosyllable: *Stelle* as in *tell*. This is verified in the early documents in New Jersey where the name at times appears as Stel, Still, or even Steel. Morgan Edwards in his *Materials Towards a History of the Baptists in [New] Jersey* (Philadelphia: Thomas Dobson, 1792), 26-27, also confirms this by placing the French *accent grave* over the final e in Stellè, to distinguish it as an unstressed second vowel.

the Roman Catholic regime of King Louis XIVth.[4] This monarch began a stringent campaign against the Protestants in the 1660's which culminated with the revocation of the Edict of Nantes on October 18, 1685. For 87 years this Edict, issued on April 13, 1598, had granted some semblance of civil and religious toleration to Protestants in France.[5] The St. Bartholomew's Day Massacre of 1572 was still vividly recalled in the minds of many Huguenots and thousands chose to leave rather than face the certainty of another storm of persecution.[6]

A recent study has shown that out of the total number fleeing France, only 1,500 to 2,000 Huguenots actually emigrated to America. Of these, 804 adults were shown by 1706 to have been settled in the city of New York and its immediate vicinity, which includes New Rochelle, Staten Island and New Jersey.[7]

---

[4] The origins of the name *Huguenot* cannot be stated with certainty. As to pronunciation, hū′ gĕ nŏt is most correct.

[5] On this and many other national policies Louis XIVth, who assumed the title *le Roi Soliel* "The Sun King," didn't display much light and France's loss of the Huguenots was great gain to those countries in which they were dispersed. I've not discovered that there were any immersionists among the Huguenots, but in England and our own country their descendants have furnished us with quite a number of distinguished Baptist ministers—Benjamin and Isaac Stelle, John and Stephen Gano, A. D. Gillette, James P. Boyce and J. C. Philpot to name just a few.

[6] The St. Bartholomew's Day Massacre was a combination of planned assassinations and instigated mob violence directed at the Huguenots by Roman Catholics jealous of their rising influence. Beginning in Paris on August 23, 1572 and extending throughout France, the number killed has been estimated by historians to have been between 5,000 and 30,000 men, women and children. Pope Gregory XIII sent a golden rose of congratulations to French King Charles IX and had a commemorative medal struck for the occasion, with one side bearing his own image and on the reverse an angel with a sword and cross facing the dead Huguenots and the inscription "Ugonottorum strages 1572" ("the slaughter of the Huguenots 1572") overhead. Those who would seek to "balance" the barbarity of this event by recounting crimes committed by Protestants against Catholics would be hard pressed to come even close to the extent of those committed with the official sanction of the Roman Catholic Church.

[7] Jon Butler, *The Huguenots in America. A Refugee People in New World Society* (Cambridge, MA: Harvard University Press, 1983), 47-49. Since the totals are reflective of a period some 10-20 years following the revocation of the Edict of Nantes, Butler rightly assumes that some of

Among those who originally settled on Staten Island was Poncet Stelle, Isaac's grandfather. Poncet Stelle we are told is known in the early records as "Sieur des Loriéres," indicating he was from Loriéres, in southwestern France.[8] Mr. Monnette conjectures that Poncet Stelle "was born probably in or about 1650" at Loriéres and fled France "before 1680,"[9] while another historian more specifically suggests he emigrated "about 1665."[10] From France, Stelle went to Holland and from there to St. Christopher in the Antilles (West Indies),[11] before proceeding on to America. There is an interesting note referring to him in the records during his stay at St. Christopher. He and another Frenchman, then members of the French Protestant Church at St. Christopher, had certificates sent from the church to the "governor and council of Massachusetts" attesting both to their character and religion:

> Certificates from the French Protestant Church at St. Christopher's on the behalfe of Mr. Poncet Stell called the Larier and Frances Ginchard, two French Gentlemen, that they have renounced the Romish Religion in which they were born and bred, and have embraced the true faith and Protestant Religion.[12]

---

these would have been American-born and thus not all original immigrants.

[8] Orra Eugene Monnette, "Poncet Stelle, Sieur des Loriéres, a Huguenot, and some of his New Jersey descendants," *The Grafton Magazine of History and Genealogy* (New York and Boston: The Grafton Press), 2 (1910), No. 3 (February): 141-142; Maud Burr Morris, "Four Generations in America of the Huguenot Family of Stelle," *New York Genealogical and Biographical Record,* 44 (1913): 61, 107. Monnette writes, " 'Stelle' is clearly and undeniably a French patronymic. It is very early found in French records and chronicles and exists in all parts of France today" (142).

[9] Monnette, "Poncet Stelle," 142.

[10] John E. Stillwell, *Historical and Genealogical Miscellany,* Vol. 5: *Early Settlers of New Jersey and Their Descendants* (New York, 1932), 434.

[11] Monnette, "Poncet Stelle," 142. These islands were under French control.

[12] Charles W. Baird, *History of the Huguenot Emigration to America* (New York: Dodd, Mead, & Co., 1885), 1: 206*n.*, citing from the "Orders, War-

This certification that the two men were of the Protestant faith was undoubtedly designed to allay the suspicions of the American authorities that because the men were French, they were also likely Catholic. New England at the time was involved in an ongoing struggle with the French and their Indian allies and King Philip's War (1675-1676) had only recently ended. Animosity between Protestant New England and Catholic New France was at its height. Understandably these Huguenot immigrants, being French, had to assure New Englanders where their sympathies lay.

About the year 1660, a colony of Huguenots settled on the southeastern side of Staten Island (Richmond County,) New York. Here they were ministered to occasionally by the minister of the French Protestant church in the city of New York. Monnette informs us that: "About the same time that several Huguenot families removed from Staten Island and settled in the Hackensack Valley in 1678, others of their co-religionists moved to New York city," among whom was Poncet Stelle.[13]

Poncet Stelle was married in 1682 while residing in New York to Eugenie Legereau, who was also a Huguenot.[14] Their children, nearly all born in the city, were Benjamin, born 1683, Gabriel, 1685, Ambrose, 1687, Madelain, 1689, Isaac, 1690, John, 1693, and possibly Eugenie, "the last," in 1695.[15]

Just prior to or about the year 1693, the Stelle family removed to Monmouth County in East New Jersey. The same year "Pounsett Stelle" was licensed to keep a public inn.[16]

---

rants," etc., Vol. XXXI, page 16, in the Office of the Secretary of State, Albany, N.Y. Baird adds that "as these men had in 1680 been for some time residents here, the date of the certificates may have been earlier by several years."

13 Monnette, "Poncet Stelle," 143.

14 *Ibid*, 144.

15 *Ibid.*, 143, 146. The names are derived from the baptismal records of the French Protestant Reformed Church in New York.

16 *Ibid.*, 144. Monnette writes, "Here the records interchange his name and 'Pontus,' 'Poncet,' 'Pounsette,' and 'Pontius,' by the last of which he is known among his descendants, variously appear."

"Piscataqua"

"When the Stelle family moved to Monmouth County, New Jersey," wrote Monnette, "this was to be the favored home of all but one son, Benjamin Stelle, who entered the Baptist ministry and sometime about 1700 moved to the banks of the Raritan River, in Middlesex County, later to become the pastor of the church there."[17] This became the settlement of Piscataqua, later Piscataway. Monnette directs the reader to James P. Snell's concise account of the origin of this name:

> Piscataqua is an Indian name of one of the tribes in the State of Maine, and also a river called the Piscataqua River, on the boundary line of Maine and New Hampshire. It is recorded that Hugh Dunn, Hopewell Hull, John Martin, Charles Gilman, Robert Dennis, John Smith, John Gilman and Benjamin Hull, who came from Piscataqua, New England, were granted, December 18th, 1666, and May 30th, 1668, the right as Associates and they conferred upon the township the name of the place whence they came, it being known as Piscataqua for some time after the settlement, but now commonly known as Piscataway.[18]

Piscataqua was to become an important center for the Baptists. The church constituted here in the spring of 1689 is the second oldest in the state after that at Middletown (1688) and was one of the five original churches which formed the Philadelphia Association in September 1707. Morgan Edwards, the earliest historian of the Baptists in New Jersey, stated that

> The history of this church from the beginning to the present time, is not easy of acquisition; nor will be altogether certain when acquired: the reason is, their records have been destroyed in the late war.[19]

---

[17] *Ibid.*, 146.

[18] James P. Snell, *History of Hunterdon and Somerset Counties, New Jersey* (Philadelphia: Everts and Peck, 1881), 589.

[19] *Materials Towards a History of the Baptists in [New] Jersey*, 21. Writing in 1789, the "late war" Edwards refers to was of course the American Revolutionary War (1775-1783). He went on to say of his historical researches on the church at Piscataqua that they "have been gleaned,

The first Baptist preachers at the new settlement were Hugh Dunn, John Drake and Edmond Dunham, all "lay brothers," in the words of Edwards.[20] About the year 1689, Thomas Killingsworth (-1709), an English Baptist minister from Norwich who emigrated to the Middle Colonies early on, settled the Piscataqua Baptists into a church and ordained John Drake as their first pastor—an office he held for nearly fifty years, until his death in 1739. "Drake was one of the first settlers," wrote Edwards, "and bore an excellent character."[21]

Benjamin Stelle

There has always been some confusion over just exactly when Benjamin Stelle, the father of our subject and the successor to John Drake as pastor of the church at Piscataqua, was born. Monnette's account, from the baptismal records of the French Church in New York, gives his date of birth as 1683 and this is followed by a number of subsequent historians and genealogists. Howard Stelle Fitz Randolph has clearly demonstrated from the tombstone inscription of Benjamin Stelle that he must have been born no earlier than 1684. Fitz Randolph states that Brown (following Edwards, p. 27) in his history of the church misstated Stelle's age at death from 74 to 76, which was then also copied into Monnette's account.[22] The actual inscription on the stone reads:

---

partly, from public records; partly, from the town book; partly, from the records of the *sabbatarian* church which sprang from this church; and partly from current tradition and the information of ancient persons." The earliest extant records of the church begin with August 29, 1781.

[20] *Ibid.*, 25.

[21] *Ibid.* Drake is believed to have been the nephew of Sir Francis Drake (1545?-1596), and like the famed navigator, hailed from Devonshire, England. James F. Brown, "History of the First Baptist Church, of Piscataway, N.J.," in George Drake, P. A. Runyon and W. H. Stelle, eds., *History of the First Baptist Church of Piscataway. With an account of its Bi-Centennial Celebration, June 20th, 1889* (Stelton, NJ: Bi-Centennial Committee on Publication, 1889), 20.

[22] Howard Stelle Fitz Randolph, "Who was Mercy, the first wife of Rev. Benjamin Stelle?" in Joseph R. Klett, ed., *Genealogies of New Jersey Families. Excerpted and reprinted from the Genealogical Magazine of New Jersey* (Baltimore, MD: Genealogical Publishing Co., 1996), 1: 828*n*. Fitz Randolph's article was originally published in *The Genealogical*

In Memory of
THE REV. BENJAMIN STELLE.
Minister
OF THE BAPTIST SOCIETY
In Piscataway.
Who departed this life Jan. 22, 1759.
Ætat 74.

Your Fathers, where are they? And
the Prophets, do they live
Forever? Zech. 1.5.[23]

But this still would not account for the 1683 infant baptism of Stelle cited by Monnette from the records of the French Church in New York, unless it was taken to be Old Style dating.[24] And there is always the possibility that the age shown on the tombstone inscription is itself incorrect. So it would seem best to leave Benjamin Stelle's date of birth as 1683/1684.

Morgan Edwards wrote of Stelle that he was "said to have been a popular preacher, and a very upright magistrate," while regretting the fact that he could not obtain more information on the preacher.[25] This raises some interesting questions. At what point and through what means did Benjamin Stelle become a Baptist? Was it before he left New York, or after his arrival in

---

Magazine of New Jersey, 2 (1926), No. 1 (July): 93-99. The mistake here is understandable, for Morgan Edwards is usually very reliable. Could it be that the "76" in the published version of Edwards is another printing error?

[23] Brown, "History of the First Baptist Church, of Piscataway, N.J.," 25; with Fitz Randolph, "Who was Mercy, the first wife of Rev. Benjamin Stelle?," 828*n.* This tombstone may be seen in the Piscatawaytown Burial Ground, Edison, New Jersey (see note 30, following). A copy of the will of Benjamin Stelle, 1759, Middlesex County, Number 3327-3328L, Book G, page 31, may be obtained from the New Jersey State Archives, Trenton.

[24] Monnette, "Poncet Stelle," 143, 146.

[25] *Materials Towards a History of the Baptists in [New] Jersey,* 27. "One of [Benjamin Stelle's] sons is yet alive," reported Edwards, "but not a very intelligent man; for which reason (and the loss of the church records) I could not obtain the history of this preacher and 'squire.' "

New Jersey?[26] Likely the transition from a Calvinistic Huguenot to a Calvinistic Baptist would have been a fairly easy one to make after abandoning infant baptism.

In 1708 or 1709, Benjamin Stelle was married to a lady named Mercy. For many years her surname was supposed to have been Drake, but Fitz Randolph made a very good case that Mercy was instead the daughter of Samuel and Mary Hull and the widow of Thomas Piatt when she married Stelle.[27] It was to these parents that Isaac Stelle was born on February 6, 1718, at Piscataqua.[28]

"A peer among his fellows"

Isaac Stelle was the fifth child and third son born to Benjamin and Mercy Stelle. Like so many of our early ministers, we know nothing of his early life and education, or even of his conversion. We do however, know something of his character, family, ministry and influence.

He was married on April 22, 1740, to Christiana Clarkson (1722/3-1778).[29] At the time Stelle was 22 years old, she was 17 or

---

[26] "How many of the settlers [at Piscataqua] were Baptists, or became such after the original settlement, history does not state. More than one writer preceding and succeeding the formation of the Church, alludes to them as forming no inconsiderable part of the population. An Episcopal rector who preached at Amboy in 1711, writing to the Secretary of the 'Society for the Propagation of the Gospel in Foreign Parts,' informs him that 'the Anabaptists swarmed in these parts,' and that they held meetings in the Town House. This Town House stood in the village then, as now, known as 'Piscatawaytown'. . .[and] was built in 1685-1686." Brown, "History of the First Baptist Church, of Piscataway, N.J.," 16-17.

[27] Fitz Randolph, "Who was Mercy, the first wife of Rev. Benjamin Stelle?," 827-833. Fitz Randolph concluded by stating, "That the above evidence does not constitute absolute proof that Benjamin Stelle married Mercy (Hull) Piatt, the widow of Thomas Piatt, is readily admitted, but the circumstantial evidence is unusually strong that such was the case" (833). We agree after reading his article.

[28] *Ibid.*, 828. The other five children are listed as Susannah, born August 3, 1710; Elizabeth, January 30, 1712; Benjamin, September 20 or 21, 1713; John, February 7, 1716; and Rachel, December 11, 1720. Fitz Randolph obtained these names and dates from the "Piscataway Register of Births," as found in the *Proceedings of the New Jersey Historical Society,* Third Series, 3 (1908): 15.

18. The couple would have nine children: Benjamin, born in 1742; Ambrose, in 1743/44; John, in 1746; Abel, in 1748; Joseph, in 1749; Mercy, in 1751; Mary, in 1754; Oliver, on August 1, 1756; and Samuel, 1758.[30] Edwards tells us that these "married into the families of the Crawfords, Dupeaus, Dunhams, Mannings, Stelles, Runyons, Walkers and Taylors; and have raised him [their father Isaac] 37 grandchildren."[31]

The Stelle family came to be in their generations inseparably linked to the prosperity of the Baptist church at Piscataqua. Writing in 1746, Benjamin Stelle related this succinct history of the church to Benjamin Griffith:

> About the year, 1686, Mr. Thomas Killingsworth first planted or settled this church,[32] and preached the gospel to

---

[29] Klett, *Genealogies of New Jersey Families,* 1: 521-522, 2: 490; Fitz Randolph, "Who was Mercy, the first wife of Rev. Benjamin Stelle?," 828.

[30] Oliver B. Leonard, "Outline Sketches of the Pioneer Progenitors of the Piscataway Planters 1666-1716," in George Drake, P. A. Runyon and W. H. Stelle, eds., *History of the First Baptist Church of Piscataway, with an Account of its Bi-Centennial Celebration June 20, 1889* (Stelton, NJ: Published for the Bi-Centennial Celebration Committee by Pakenham and Dowling, New York, 1889), 118. Edwards in his *Materials Towards a History of the Baptists in [New] Jersey,* 27, listed only seven of the children, omitting Ambrose and Mercy. According to the gravestone inscriptions, thankfully preserved 130 years ago in the booklet by Ezra M. Hunt, compiler, *Piscatawaytown Graveyard, Woodbridge Avenue, Edison, New Jersey* (n.p., n.p., 28 Oct. 1880), Ambrose died on February 28, 1760, at the age of 16; Joseph died on March 24, 1837, "in the 88th year of his age"; and Mary died on August 14, 1777, at the age of 26. These Stelle children, together with their parents Isaac and Christiana, and grandparents Benjamin and Mercy (inscribed as "Marcy") are all buried in the Piscatawaytown Burial Ground, which compasses about what is now St. James Episcopal Church, where formerly the Piscataway Baptist Church met. The cemetery may be seen at 2136 Woodbridge Avenue, Edison, Middlesex County, New Jersey, about 1 ½ miles east of Highway 1. The township of Edison is responsible for maintaining the cemetery. The date of birth for Oliver Stelle is from John Littell, *Family Records, or Genealogies of the First Settlers of Passaic Valley and Vicinity* (Feltville, NJ: D. Felt, 1852), 403. Oliver was married to Mary Runyon (1758/9-1813) on January 21, 1778. Littell lists the names of their eleven children. Oliver Stelle died on June 3, 1832.

[31] *Materials Towards a History of the Baptists in [New] Jersey,* 27.

them a considerable time. After his removal, the church had the ordinances of the gospel administered among them until the year 1715; about which time Mr. Drake was ordained, and he continued to preach and to administer the ordinances until about the year 1729; and then, by reason of his great age, he desisted preaching, but continued to administer the ordinances. About that time, Henry Lovall,[33] from New England, came among them, who preached for the space of two years upon trial, and then was ordained, but never administered the ordinances; for, soon after his ordination, he behaved himself in so disorderly a manner that he was excommunicated from the church.

About which time, Mr. Benjamin Stelle was called to preach among them, and was approved and set apart by solemn ordination.

Their number, when first settled, was no more than six persons,[34] and continued very small for the space of twenty years, and then began to increase, and came to be about twenty in number, and is since increased to upwards of one hundred.[35]

---

[32] Morgan Edwards, writing in November 1789, stated that the church was settled or constituted three years later, in the spring of 1689. *Ibid.*, 23. Since the church records were, according to Edwards (p. 31), destroyed during the Revolutionary War, the true date may never be known.

[33] Henry Loveall was the assumed name of Desolate Baker (1694-?), who apparently had been an indentured servant or apprentice on Long Island, ran away from his master, and ended up at the Piscataqua church, where he so deceived the congregation as to receive ordination as their minister in October 1730. About two weeks later it was discovered that he was living in adultery, for which he then was put out of the church. See C. Edwin Barrows and James W. Willmarth, eds., *The Diary of John Comer* (Philadelphia: American Baptist Publication Society, 1892), 113-118; and the author's essay, "Nathaniel Jenkins 1678-1754," in *A Noble Company* (Springfield, MO: Particular Baptist Press), 1 (2006): 340-343.

[34] Edwards, *Materials Towards a History of the Baptists in [New] Jersey*, 23, lists these six persons (all men) as: "Hugh Dunn, who was an exhorter; John Drake, afterwards their pastor; Nicholas Bonham; John Smalley; Edmond Dunham, afterwards minister of the *Seventhday* Baptists; and John Randolph."

[35] Benjamin Griffith, "An Association Book, containing a brief account of the beginning and progress of the churches holding and practicing adult

While Stelle's history gives us no clues as to how or when he became connected with the congregation, it does clearly tell us that he was "called to preach among them, and was approved and set apart by solemn ordination," likely in the years 1730-1731, to assist pastor Drake in the ministry after Loveall's departure.[36] Stelle began attending the annual sessions of the Philadelphia Association as early as 1729,[37] though the early lists of messengers to the meetings do not reflect whether they were licensed, ordained, or any other designation. And since the messengers are not listed in the minutes for 1707-1728, it is entirely possible he may have also been present at previous sessions.

Stelle continued to assist Drake until the latter's death in 1739. As Brown observed, "No stone or mark exists to tell where his body was laid. But his and our Redeemer knows,

'and often from the skies
Looks down and watches all his dust,
Till He shall bid it rise.' "[38]

Stelle ministered from 1739-1751 as sole pastor at Piscataqua after Drake's passing, and, in the words of Brown, "Although years before his death his head became 'frosted o'er with time' we do not learn, either through record or tradition, that the Church grew weary of his ministry and wished him to vacate the field. On the contrary, they clung to him to the last, as one justly entitled to their veneration and love."[39] Brown adds that because Stelle was

---

baptism, and commonly called Baptists, in Pennsylvania and the Jersies," in Gillette, *Minutes of the Philadelphia Baptist Association,* 13.

[36] Brown, "History of the First Baptist Church, of Piscataway, N.J.," 24, was thus mistaken when he wrote that Stelle "was not ordained till after Mr. Drake's death," which occurred in 1739. Concerning Henry Loveall, Edwards tells us that from Piscataqua "he went to Maryland, and raised a church there, which was the first in the state; and afforded materials to form the church whereof rev. John Davis is now pastor. Having behaved ill in Maryland, he went to Virginia and raised another church at Opekon, which was the first in that state, except the Isle of Wight church." *Materials Towards a History of the Baptists in [New] Jersey,* 26.

[37] Griffith, "An Association Book," 30.

[38] "History of the First Baptist Church, of Piscataway, N.J.," 23.

held "in high esteem by his fellow citizens, offices of honor and trust had been thrust upon him. He was a Justice of the Peace, a chosen Freeholder for ten consecutive years, a Collector of Taxes from 1727-1731, and Overseer of Roads after as well as before his ordination."[40]

Isaac Stelle was called upon to assist his aging father in the ministry in 1751. Exactly when he was ordained that year cannot be determined.[41] "What his educational advantages had been, we know not," wrote Brown, "but he appears to have been a man of more than ordinary vigor and sprightliness of mind; a peer among his fellows, and from the first able to hold a conspicuous position among his brethren in the ministry, and a large place in their hearts."[42] The truth of this is borne out in the variety of duties he performed at the appointment of the Philadelphia Association: as one of the four men selected in 1756 to oversee the work of Isaac Eaton's new Latin Grammar School "for the promotion of learning amongst us," at Hopewell, New Jersey; preaching the annual associational sermon in 1759, 1766 and 1774; serving as alternate preacher for the same in 1752, 1758 and 1765; as clerk in 1763; as writer of the Association's "Pastoral Address" or Circular Letter in 1763, 1767 and 1770; as their messenger to other associations in

---

39 *Ibid.*, 25. Except for Benjamin Stelle's note in his history of the church that by 1746 the membership of the Piscataqua church (which was in part widely dispersed) had "increased to upwards of one hundred" persons, no other statistics are known to exist from the time of his ministry there, 1730/1-1759.

40 "History of the First Baptist Church, of Piscataway, N.J.," 24.

41 The Statement by Edwards in his *Materials Towards a History of the Baptists in [New] Jersey,* 27, that Isaac Stelle "became minister of Piscataqua in 1752, as an assistant to his father," would appear to be incorrect in point of time for this reason: at the annual meeting of the Philadelphia Association in September 1751, Isaac Stelle, who was present at the session, was appointed as an alternate to preach the associational sermon the following year in 1752. It would be highly unlikely that an unordained minister in the Association would be so appointed, therefore his ordination must have occurred before September of 1751. James F. Brown, a later pastor of the church and the church's bicentennial historian, seems to have also taken notice of this, for he states without equivocation, that Stelle "was ordained as assistant to his father in 1751 . . ." "History of the First Baptist Church, of Piscataway, N.J.," 26.

42 "History of the First Baptist Church, of Piscataway, N.J.," 26.

1766, 1767 and 1774; and as moderator of the annual meetings in 1776 and 1780.[43] Under the ministry of the Stelles, the church at Piscataqua became one of the more significant churches in the Association. The congregation also brought forth two other important daughter churches within the bounds of the Association—Scotch Plains, in 1747 and Morristown, in 1752.[44] These two congregations in turn produced the other ministers named by Samuel Jones at the beginning of our essay, along with Isaac Stelle, as "bright and shining lights" in the Association's history—Benjamin Miller and John Gano.

"swarms detached from the old hive"

The members of the Piscataqua church at mid-century for various reasons were scattered over a large area. Some of them began to see the need of forming their own local congregations. The first of these daughter churches came to be organized at Scotch Plains, in Essex County. Morgan Edwards, in another of his humorous analogies, gives this account of the friendly separation:

> For the origin of Scotchplains (as a church) we have no further back to look than Sep. 8, 1747; for theretofore all Baptists in this part of the country were members of *Piscataqua* church: but, growing numerous, and distance considerable, the mother church detached from the old hive, a swarm, and formed them into a distinct society, the day and year above-mentioned: the names were *William Darby, Recompence Stanbury, John Lambert, John Stanbury, John Dennis, Henry Crossley, John Sutton, Isaac Manning, Mary Bradwell, Mary Green, Mary Dennis, Tibia Sutton, Catherine Manning, Sarah Decamp, and Sarah Peers*: the same year they joined the association.[45]

---

[43] Gillette, *Minutes of the Philadelphia Baptist Association,* 67-68, 74, 76, 78, 89-90, 92, 95-97, 102, 105-106, 113, 131, 140, 143, 155.

[44] Edwards, *Materials Towards a History of the Baptists in [New] Jersey,* 69, 72-73; Griffith, "An Association Book," 22.

[45] *Materials Towards a History of the Baptists in [New] Jersey,* 69. Abel Morgan and James Mott of the church at Middletown assisted in this constitution. Griffith, "An Association Book," 22.

The "swarm" may in part have had reference to the numerous, unnamed children associated with these households.

Benjamin Miller was ordained as pastor of the new church on February 13, 1748, and continued in that capacity until his death in 1781. Miller had been converted under a sermon by the famous Presbyterian minister Gilbert Tennent, but later adopted Baptist sentiments.[46] Edwards, after noting that Miller had been raised up at Scotch Plains, stated that he "was an exception to the proverb which saith, 'that a prophet is not without honour save in his own house [Matt. 13:57],' " and "all that hath been said of a good, laborious, and successful minister, will apply to him."[47] Stelle and Miller became close friends, so much so that Edwards, who knew them both, remarked that Miller's "usual companion in travels" was Isaac Stelle; "lovely and pleasant were they in life," he added, "and in death they were not much divided, the one having survived the other but 35 days."[48]

In the fall of 1752 and the spring of 1753, Stelle was a key participant in the formation of two more churches, this time in Morris County, as seen in these narratives by Benjamin Griffith:

---

[46] *Ibid.*, 70-71. Interestingly, it was through the counsel of the Tennents and Benjamin Miller, that another young Presbyterian named John Gano came to adopt Baptist views.

[47] *Ibid.*

[48] *Ibid.*, 71. Stelle died on October 9, 1781 and Miller on November 14, 1781. In reflecting on the deaths of these two men, in a letter to the London Baptist minister Benjamin Wallin in May 1783, James Manning wrote, "Rev. Messrs. Miller and Stelle, of the Scotch Plains and Piscataway churches, two eminent Baptist ministers, died nearly two years ago. Their people have not yet found Elishas to take their places." Reuben A. Guild, *Life, Times, and Correspondence of James Manning, and the Early History of Brown University* (Boston: Gould and Lincoln, 1864), 295. Manning was obviously referring to Miller and Stelle as the Elijahs of their day, whose mantles had not yet been taken up. Samuel Jones in his *Century Sermon* likewise wrote of these men, "May the God of Elijah grant that a double portion of their spirit may rest on all, that stand as watchmen on Zion's Walls." Gillette, *Minutes of the Philadelphia Baptist Association*, 456. At the ordination of Manning on April 19, 1763, John Gano (Manning's brother-in-law) preached the sermon, Isaac Eaton gave the charge, and "his beloved friend," Isaac Stelle, offered the prayer. Guild, *Life, Times, and Correspondence of James Manning,* 35-36.

THE CHURCH AT MORRISTOWN,

IN MORRIS COUNTY, NEW JERSEY.

Several of the members of the church of Piscataqua, living in Morris county, remote from that church, requested a dismission, to the end they might be constituted a distinct church by themselves; and accordingly they appointed to meet on the 11th day of August, 1752; and having Mr. Benjamin Miller, Mr. Isaac Stelle and Mr. Isaac Eaton for their assistance, and after having improved the fore part of this day in fasting and prayer, they were regularly incorporated in the usual manner, and the right hand of fellowship given to them as a sister church of Jesus Christ, and as such recommended to God by solemn prayer, and on the 4th day of October following, were admitted into the Association.

* * * * *

THE CHURCH AT ROCKSBERRY,

IN MORRIS COUNTY, N.J.

A number of persons, baptized on profession of faith, residing at Rocksberry aforesaid, being desirous to put them in church order, for their better convenience, benefit, and edification; and being dismissed by the church they were related to, they appointed the 12th day of May, 1753; and having procured the Rev. brethren, Isaac Stelle, and Malachia Bonham, for their assistance, they were constituted after the same manner as other churches, the said ministers giving them a hand of fellowship as a sister church; and, at the Association in October following, were, upon their request, received into the number of our associating churches: their number then being fourteen persons.[49]

---

[49] Griffith, "An Association Book," 22-23. The Rocksberry church was synonymous with Schooley's Mountain, by which it was also known. John Gano was settled as the first pastor at Morristown, while Henry Crosley was the first pastor at Rocksberry. For additional brief overviews of the two churches, see Edward Howell, "Historical Sketch of the Baptist church at Morristown," in *Minutes of the Thirty-Ninth Anniversary of the*

The church at Morristown has an interesting background. Around the year 1717, a man named David Goble arrived there with his family from Charleston, South Carolina. They being Baptists, wrote Edwards, soon "invited Baptist ministers to preach at their house," in particular Isaac Stelle, and that by his repeated labors and the labors of some others, "several were turned from darkness to light, and went to Piscatauqua for baptism." Stelle and the others continued their visits, which duly necessitated the building of a meetinghouse by the Gobles at their own expense in order to accommodate the growing number of hearers.[50] At the time of the church's constitution in August of 1752, 16 persons named by Edwards, including the Gobles, were dismissed by the church at Piscataqua to join their new local body.[51]

In April 1766, the Baptist church at Middletown dismissed 47 of its own members living at Crosswicks (later Upper Freehold) in Monmouth County, in order that they might form themselves into a separate body of believers. Following receipt of their letters of dismissal, the Crosswicks congregation agreed to send for the assistance of Isaac Stelle, Benjamin Miller and Peter Peterson VanHorne, "who came according to appointment on the 10th day of May 1766."[52] The official record to the day's meeting goes on to read:

North New Jersey Baptist Association (Deckertown: Sayer and Noble, 1872), 17-24; and "Historical Sketch of the Schooley's Mountain Church," *Minutes of the Fortieth Anniversary of the North New Jersey Baptist Association* (Deckertown: Sayer and Noble, 1873), 24-28.

[50] *Materials Towards a History of the Baptists in [New] Jersey,* 72-73. Edwards does not tell us when Stelle began his evangelistic labors at Morristown, nor does he inform us as to when the Gobles built their meetinghouse. It is possible that Stelle began his ministry there while licensed but not yet ordained, that is, prior to 1751, or in the 1740's.

[51] *Ibid.*, 73. Edwards gives the date of the constitution of the Morristown church as *July* 11, 1752, while Griffith states it was *August* 11, 1752. The August date is given again by Gillette in the chart of the member churches on page 93 of his *Minutes of the Philadelphia Baptist Association.*

[52] Helen Polhemus, ed., *The Church Book of the Upper Freehold Baptist Church. A Copy of the Original Church Records begun in 1766* (Imlaystown, NJ: The Upper Freehold Baptist Church, 1972), [4].

Mr. Stelle was principally active in the Constitution. When all were met together, Mr. Stelle made a short address, respecting the occation and importance of our Meeting, & solemnly prayed for the divine Blessing to attend the Proceeding, he was succeeded by the Prayers of the other ministring Brethern. Prayer being ended, he re[a]d the Dismission from Middletown. Then called the Names of the Consituents, to which each present, answered; after which he Produced a Church Cove[na]nt, which being re[a]d, was unanimously subscribed. A Copy of which is here inserted viz: We whose names are hereunto anexed, being Members of the Church of Christ at Middletown & Crosswicks in the County of Monmouth in the Eastern Division of the Province of new Jersey which Church owns & Professes the Articles of Faith & Practice and Plan of Church Disciplin[e] as expressed & contained in a confession of Faith, which was adopted by the Baptist association met at Philadelphia Septem. 25. 1742. with the addition of two articles, viz. the Imposition of hands & singing of Psalms in Publick worship, together, with a short Treatise of Church Disciplin[e].[53] Not from any Dislike to the faith or Practice of the Church, we belong unto,[54] but from an apprehension that it will be for edification & benefit, to be constituted a Church in gospel order at Crosswicks; and having obtained the suffrage of the s[ai]d Church, & Dismission from them for this Purpose, we having set apart the 13th Day of May anno Domini 1766, & having Called to our assistance our Rev.[d] Brethren Isaac Stelle & Peter Peterson Vanhorn, and having spent part of s[ai]d day in fasting & Prayer: We do freely & voluntarily enter into the same Covenent Relation together, and agreement with one another distinct & separate from that Church, as we were in & under, with them, whilst Members together with them, that is to say in words Following, viz. We who live in & about Crosswicks, in the County & Province affors[ai][d] who decide to walk together in the fear of God, do thro' the assistance of his holy Spirit Profess our deep & serious humiliation for all our Transgressions. We do solemnly in the Presence of God, and of each other, under a sence of our own unworthiness, give up ourselves to the

---

[53] Written by Benjamin Griffith (1688-1768) and published with the first edition of the Philadelphia Baptist Confession in 1743.

[54] At Middletown.

> Lord, to each other in a Church-State according to the apostalick Constitution, that he may be our God, & we may be his People thro' the everlasting Covenant of his free grace, in which we hope to be accepted with him, thro' his blessed Son Jesus Christ, whom we take to be our high Priest, to Justify & Sanctofy us, and our Prophet to teach us, and to [be] subject to him, as our Law giver & the King of Saints, and to Conform to all his holy laws & ordinances, for our groath, Establishment and Consolation, that we may be as an holy Spouse unto him and serve him in our generation, and wait for his Second appearance as our glorious Bridegroom: being fully satisfied in the way of Church Communion, and of the Truth of grace, in some good measure, upon one another's Spirits, we do Solemnly Joyn ourselves together in an holy union & fellowship, humbly submitting to the Discipline of the gospel and all holy Duties required of a People in such a spiritual Relation.[55]

This was immediately followed by eight stated promises to which all the members joining in covenant relation to the church must agree, which in turn was followed by a listing of the names of the 34 men and women who united at that time.[56] After subscribing their names they were "Pronounced a regular Church of Jesus Christ." Following the singing of "the 7th hymn of Dr. Watts's first book," Benjamin Miller "ascended the Pulpet, and Delivered a Solemn Discourse from these words, 'as ye have therefore received the Lord Jesus, so walk ye in him.' Col. 2.6."[57] The members then chose their own officers and "unanimously agreed" that their "esteemed Brother David Jones should continue in the exercise of his ministerial gifts."[58]

---

[55] Polhemus, *The Church Book of the Upper Freehold Baptist Church,* [4-5].

[56] *Ibid.*, [5-6]. Edwards, *Materials Towards a History of the Baptists in [New] Jersey,* 105-106, lists the same 34 persons with the exception that he has *Mary* Vaughn where it is *Mercy* Vaughn in the original church record, along with some variation in surname spellings.

[57] Polhemus, *The Church Book of the Upper Freehold Baptist Church*, [6].

[58] *Ibid.* This was David Jones (1736-1820), who had moved to Middletown in 1761 to study for the ministry under pastor Abel Morgan (1713-1785). See the essay on Jones by G. Truett Rogers on pages 401-425, following.

Abel Morgan of Middletown continued to supply the new church at Crosswicks at "Communion Seasons" until October 1766, when the members sent a letter to the Philadelphia Association requesting assistance in the ordination of Jones as their pastor. Stelle and Miller promised to answer the request and accordingly arrived at Crosswicks on November 12, 1766.

> Mr. Stelle preached the ordination sermon, which was very suitable, & met with great approbation. The words of his Text were, 'and the things that thou hast heard of me, among many witnesses, the same commit thou to faithful men, who shall be able to teach others also.' 2 Tim. 2.2. After sermon was ended Mr. Stelle descended from the pulpit, and proposed several questions to Mr. Jones, respecting his Call to the work of the Ministry and of his faith in the Lord Jesus Christ, and of his Purposes to continue in the work of the Ministry; After which both Mr. Stelle and Mr. Mil[l]er prayed, & Proceeded solemnly by laying their hands on Mr. Jones, at which Time Mr. Mil[l]er fervently prayed for the gifts of the Holy Spirit. Prayer being finished, they both gave him the right hand of fellowship as a sign of their acknowledgement of him as an ordained Brother in the ministry of the gospel of Christ. . .[59]

Two other Baptists from Piscataqua, Benjamin Reuben and Joseph Randolph, together with a Baptist from Coventry, England named John Haywood, settled in the neighborhood of Manahawkin, also in Monmouth County, about the year 1760. These three men and six others (including four from the Scotch Plains meeting) were formed into a Baptist church by Benjamin Miller in 1770.[60]

Possessing "a disposition uncommonly amiable"

The dismissals from Piscataqua and the general unsettledness of the country at the time of the French and Indian War, accounts for the greatly decreased membership of the church from the

---

[59] *Ibid.*, [6-7].

[60] Edwards, *Materials Towards a History of the Baptists in [New] Jersey,* 113-114. This church appears in the Associational Minutes only through 1776 and apparently, like others, disbanded during the Revolutionary War.

"upwards of one hundred" reported by Benjamin Stelle in 1746,[61] to the 41 members listed in the first statistics given on the church in the Associational minutes for 1762. The statistics do reveal however, as seen in the chart below, a slow but steady growth in the membership during Isaac Stelle's ministry:

Year	baptized	deceased	excluded	members
1762	1	1	0	41
1763	2	0	0	43
1764	17	1	1	58
1765	4	2	0	60
1766	3	0	0	63
1767	0	0	0	63
1768	4	2	0	64
1769	7	2	0	69
1770	8	2	0	73
1771	1	1	0	72
1772	1	0	0	73
1773	2	2	2	72
1774	0	0	0	72
1775	3	0	0	75
1776	2	2	0	75

In these 15 years for which we have figures,[62] it will be noticed that there were only two years in which no baptisms were reported by the church. It will also be seen that there was a considerable accession made to the membership by baptism in 1764. This and

---

[61] Griffith, "An Association Book," 13.

[62] Gillette, *Minutes of the Philadelphia Baptist Association,* 88, 91, 94, 96, 100, 103, 106, 111, 117, 122, 127, 133, 146, 153, 157. One member was received by letter in 1773 (p. 133). Some of the figures given between 1768 and 1773 as transcribed by Gillette don't quite add up. Due to the Revolutionary War, which began on April 19, 1775, there are no statistics given for the church between 1777 (when Philadelphia was occupied by the British army and no meeting was held that year) and 1781, when Isaac Stelle died. A note in the minutes for 1781 reads: "As no letters came to hand from Piscataqua, Welsh Tract, Montgomery, Scotch Plains, and several other churches belonging to this Association, we are unable to give any just account of their present numbers." In 1784, the year after hostilities officially ceased, the church reported 40 members. *Ibid.,* 179, 203. The war had clearly impacted the churches of the Association.

exceptional figures given for other churches that year prompted the Association to remark in its Pastoral Letter: "The letters from the several churches brought us the pleasing news, that the Lord is carrying on his work with power in sundry places; that peace and concord abound in our congregations, blessed be his holy name."[63]

The Piscataqua church by 1775, with 75 members and an unknown number of other "hearers" attending on Isaac Stelle's ministry, would have made it a fairly large Baptist congregation by eighteenth-century standards.[64]

Reuben Guild wrote in the nineteenth century that Stelle seemed to him to have been possessed of "a temperament exceedingly active, and a disposition uncommonly amiable."[65] What led Guild to arrive at such an estimation? Stelle's "exceedingly active" temperament may be readily seen in the variety of duties he was entrusted with by the Association. And to say that Stelle was possessed of an "uncommonly amiable" disposition may as easily be deduced from the remarks made concerning him by his contemporaries. To be *amiable,* by dictionary definition, means that one characteristically displays agreeable personal qualities, such as genuine kindheartedness and friendliness.[66] Morgan Edwards, who knew Stelle personally, said this of him:

> I need not publish the goodness of the man, and the excellency of his preaching; for many are now alive who know both, and who regard him as their spiritual father. He was remarkable for his travels among the *American* churches in company with his other self, rev. Benj. Miller.[67]

---

[63] *Ibid.*, 92.

[64] A successful gospel ministry however, can never be measured solely in terms of *numerical* growth, but in terms of *spiritual* growth. Are the members of our churches growing in the grace and knowledge of the Lord Jesus Christ? That is the real question, no matter how large the membership.

[65] *Life, Times, and Correspondence of James Manning,* 36*n*.

[66] Should this not be a desirable character trait of *every* Christian, in light of the admonitions to such given in God's Word?

[67] *Materials Towards a History of the Baptists in [New] Jersey*, 27. By "his other self" Edwards meant that Miller was very much like Stelle.

In recalling Stelle's ministry, these were the chief attributes of the man—his goodness and the excellence of his preaching, that came to Edwards' mind. This combination would certainly have made Stelle "uncommonly amiable" as a minister. And when contentions arose in and between churches of the Association—as at Cohansey in 1767 and between First and Second New York in 1772, he was selected to accompany other ministers to help settle those disputes.[68] Among his peers he became known affectionately as "our beloved Brother Stelle."[69]

His pastoral addresses

Though we have no extant sermons by Isaac Stelle by which we might hope to convey some sense of the "excellency of his preaching" remarked upon by Edwards, yet we do have three examples of the annual "Pastoral Address" which were written by Stelle at the appointment of the Philadelphia Association for the years 1763, 1768 and 1770.

In the first of these, Stelle made special mention of the recent ingathering of believers. "We find there is an addition to our churches of eighty-one members this year more than last," he wrote, "which is great cause of thankfulness to God, and encouragement to us all. May fervent zeal for the cause and interest of our dear Redeemer ever animate our souls."[70] Stelle then closed his letter with these positive words of admonition:

> And now, brethren, receive a word of exhortation in love. Strive to abound in vital piety; see that you walk worthy of the vocation wherewith you are called. Be careful to maintain a steady course of cheerful obedience to God all the days of your life. Neglect not prayer, neither family nor closet [i.e. private]. Strengthen the hands of your ministers,

---

[68] Gillette, *Minutes of the Philadelphia Baptist Association,* 102, 123, 129. In October 1773, Stelle was also appointed with six other ministers to meet at Oyster Bay, Long Island, on November 10th, "to give them the help they requested, and also to provide [pulpit] supplies for them this year." *Ibid.*, 129.

[69] *Ibid.,* 140. This appellation was given Stelle in the minutes for 1774. A former usage of the term "amiable" carried with it the idea of being lovely or loveable.

[70] *Ibid.*, 90. As seen earlier, Stelle's Piscataqua church experienced an influx of new members the following year.

> and encourage their visits to vacant places. Delight yourselves in the word, worship and ordinances of God. Make the sacred oracles the rule of all your actions. Learn, by Christ's sermon on the mount, to forgive your enemies; strive to live peaceably with all men.
>
> May you ever be able to walk together in the unity of the Spirit and bond of peace, provoking one another to love and good works: and that being by promise united to an inheritance among them that are sanctified, you may at last hear the voice of the heavenly bridegroom say unto you, Come up hither; which, may God of his infinite mercy grant for Jesus sake. Amen.[71]

Stelle's exhortation abounds with the language of Scripture. And most assuredly he had taken to heart his own counsel of being careful "to maintain a steady course of cheerful obedience to God."

In his 1768 letter, Stelle again expressed the encouragement felt by the Association as a whole "with the accounts sent us from different churches, particularly the good news of the increase of Christ's kingdom on earth, for which we praise God, and pray for you that your faith fail not."[72] He went on to charge the Association's membership to "Do all things whatsoever may tend to promote brotherly love and charity," while reminding them "that unity is the best security the church of Christ can have against attacks from every enemy; that if divided, you fall a more easy prey to your adversaries; that you cannot injure one another without injuring yourselves also; that by attending too much to distinctions and speculations, you rob your own souls of the real comfort of religion."[73]

Stelle's third address of 1770 related the news of considerable additions having recently been made to the Warren and Virginia Associations, which he used as an example both to call forth praise and exhort to prayer his own Association by writing,

> We rejoice that the Lord Jesus doth still walk in the midst of his golden candlesticks. O, may he continue and increase his glorious work, so that the number of converts to him may be as the drops of morning dew! And while we hear good news

---

[71] *Ibid.*

[72] *Ibid.*, 105.

[73] *Ibid.*, 105-106.

> from distant places, may it excite in us earnestness productive of fervent prayer to God for a revival of his work amongst us, which, of late, is rather decaying.[74]

After noting the death of John Walton, pastor of the Morristown church, Stelle called upon believers to reflect upon the uncertainty of their earthly lives. "Now dear brethren," he continued, "as we are about parting from each other, we would write to you as though we were writing our last; and this should induce you to attend [i.e. give heed to what is said] as though you were never to hear from us again. . .strive to walk together in unity of the Spirit and bonds of peace. Neglect not the use of the Bible, nor public worship, nor private prayer. Set the best examples before, and give good and wholesome advice to all under your care. Watch over all your thoughts, words, and ways, remembering that the glory of God and your present comfort much depend thereon. . .and let the world see by every part of your conduct that there is a divine reality in your religion. May the Lord open your ears to our words, and abundantly bless our advice to your hearts."[75]

The Stelles enter their rest amidst war

Just six months prior to the beginning of the American Revolution, Isaac Stelle was requested to preach the opening sermon at the proposed bi-annual meeting held at Philadelphia in October 1774. In 1773, it had been suggested and approved that the Association meet twice a year, as seen in this entry in the minutes:

> Agreed, that by reason of the distances of several of our sister churches to the eastward, the Association should meet twice in the year; once at New York, on the Wednesday after the fourth Lord's day in May, at 3 o'clock, for the conveniency of said eastern churches; and at Philadelphia, on Wednesday after the second Lord's day in October. The sermon to be preached, at New York, by Rev. Samuel Jones, or, in case of failure, by Rev. Abel Morgan; that at

---

[74] *Ibid.*, 115. The Virginia Association later became known as the Ketocton Association.

[75] *Ibid.* The annual "Pastoral Address" came to be more commonly known as "Circular Letters."

> Philadelphia by Rev. Isaac Stelle, or, in case of failure, by Rev. William Rogers.[76]

For the meeting Stelle chose as his text Jeremiah 23:28, "The prophet that hath a dream, let him tell a dream; and he that hath my word, let him speak my word faithfully. What is the chaff to the wheat? saith the Lord." Stelle's good friend Benjamin Miller was then chosen as moderator of the meetings.[77] In addition, Stelle was asked to be part of a committee to form an official reply, to be inserted in the minutes, respecting some concerns raised by the Welsh Tract church about a book written by Morgan Edwards.[78] The statement as composed by Abel Morgan, Isaac Backus, Isaac Stelle and Samuel Jones read:

> Whereas, a book was published, entitled, 'The Customs of the Primitive Churches,' which the author proposed should be altered, amended, and corrected, by his ministering brethren, and then re-printed for the use of the churches, which was never done; and whereas, we have reason to think, that it is understood by many abroad to have been adopted by use in its present form, as our custom and mode of church discipline and practice; it is therefore thought meet, that we should thus publicly testify to the contrary, as it is not, nor ever has been adopted by us, or by any of the churches belonging to the Association.[79]

The Association that year also took up for consideration such diverse topics as the catechizing of youth, ecclesiastical oppression

---

[76] *Ibid.*, 131. Each of these two meetings is presented separately in their entirety in the official minutes for 1774.

[77] *Ibid.*, 140.

[78] *The Customs of Primitive Churches; or a set of propositions relative to the name, matterials, constitution, power, officers, ordinances, rites, business, worship, discipline, government, &c. of a church; to which are added their proofs from Scripture; and historical narratives of the manner in which most of them have been reduced to practice.* Philadelphia: Printed by Andrew Stewart, 1768. Because of Edwards' standing in the Association as pastor of the Philadelphia church, his book on church polity was taken by some as expressive of the official views of the Association.

[79] *Ibid.*, 141.

in New England, support of Rhode Island College and the doctrine of the Trinity.

Regarding the question as to whether the Association should meet twice a year, in May and October, and in two different cities, and discovering that the experiment that year was "not answering so well as expected," it was agreed to go back to meeting once annually.[80]

Stelle and William Worth, pastor of the Pittsgrove church, were appointed that year to visit the Ketocton Association in Virginia as messengers. This was Stelle's second visit to that association.[81]

The Association bestowed its final honors on Isaac Stelle when they chose him as moderator of their sessions in 1776 and again in 1780.[82] These were tumultuous times of war in the land and the last references made to the respected minister in the official minutes. This period in Stelle's life was a mixture of spiritual refreshing, personal bereavement, and ministry amid war's devastation. Hezekiah Smith (1737-1805), pastor, chaplain, and itinerant evangelist from Haverhill, Massachusetts, spoke of attending a "great meeting at Piscataqua" on June 2, 1776, where he heard Abel Morgan "preach in the forenoon," and where he himself preached that afternoon.[83] Christiana Stelle, Isaac's wife of 38 years, passed away on the morning of September 27, 1778.[84]

---

[80] *Ibid.*, 143.

[81] *Ibid.* Stelle, in the company of John Davis and John Blackwell, had eight years before been assigned as messengers to visit the new Virginia (Ketocton) Association, which had just been organized on August 19, 1766, and to hand deliver a letter from the Philadelphia Association written by Morgan Edwards. *Ibid.*, 97.

[82] *Ibid.,* 155, 169, 172.

[83] John David Broome, *The Life, Ministry, and Journals of Hezekiah Smith, Pastor of the First Baptist church of Haverhill, Massachusetts 1765 to 1805 and Chaplain in the American Revolution 1775-1780* (Springfield, MO: Particular Baptist Press, 2004), 438. Smith had preached at Stelle's meetinghouse on at least one other occasion that we know of, on Thursday afternoon, October 8, 1772. *Ibid.*, 385.

[84] Thomas B. Wilson, ed., *Notices from New Jersey Newspapers 1781-1790* (Lambertville, NJ: Hunterdon House, 1988), 1:17. The notice given in the *New Jersey Gazette,* as transcribed by Wilson, reads as follows: "7 Oct. 1778: On the 27th ult[imate] in the morning, Mrs. Christian[a] Stelle, wife of the Rev. Isaac Stelle, at Piscataway, in her 55th year. Her remains

The mother of all his children, she was sure to be missed in many homes. On July 13, 1779, while en route to Philadelphia, he called on James Manning and others at Cranbury (later Hightstown), New Jersey, informing them that accounts had been received of the burning of New Haven by the British and that they were "destroying all in their way in that quarter."[85] Stelle not long after was married to Katherine (or Catherine) Green, by a license dated January 5, 1780.[86]

On March 1, 1781, Isaac Stelle drew up a will to make provision for his family. He began by writing that he was "sick and weak in body but in some Good measure of mind and memory (thanks be to God for the same)." He must have felt that his appointed time of departure was near at hand, leaving detailed instructions for the care of his spouse:

> my will & pleasure is that my Beloved wife Catherine Stelle should have all she Brought to me with her[87] Either in Creatures household goods or whatsoever; to dispose of at her pleasure. And also a full Right & priviledg[e] in the two Rooms at the East End of my Dwelling House together with some priviledg in my milk room & orchard with firewood for her use. And also the priviledg of one Horse & Two Cows to be keep [kept] on my place to be provided for both summer & winter by my four sons namely John, Joseph, Olliver & Samuel Stelle. And also the sum of twenty four pounds in money which shall be made Equally Good to her as Silver or Gold: that is to say to be paid by my four sons above named Yearly & Every Year Each an Equal part all which priviledg & payments shall stand & remain Good to her so long as she

---

were interred the next day in the publick burying ground in that town." See also Klett, *Genealogies of New Jersey Families,* 1: 521-522; 2: 490.

[85] Guild, *Life, Times, and Correspondence of James Manning,* 277.

[86] Klett, *Genealogies of New Jersey Families,* 1: 522; Fitz Randolph, "Who Was Mercy, the First Wife of Rev. Benjamin Stelle?," 828. Like his father Benjamin, Isaac was married twice.

[87] Upon their being married.

> shall Remain my widdow and no longer.[88] Which priviledges & money I give to her in Lue [lieu] or instead of her thirds.[89]

Stelle likewise made remarkable provision for Mary Manning:

> I give to my Daughter Mary Manning the sum of four hundred & fifty pounds to be paid her as shall be hereafter mentioned....I Give & bequeath to my Daughter Mary Manning the sum or value of four hundred & fifty pounds to Come out of my Estate that is to say & it is my will & pleasure that she shall have the priviledg of taking in part of s[ai]d four hundred & fifty pounds as many articles shall be vallued by two Indifer[e]nt persons agreed upon by the parties conserned.[90]

The sons were also granted various items from the estate.

We can find no better tribute to conclude this essay on Isaac Stelle with than these words written by the tenth pastor of the church, James F. Brown:

> Mr. Stelle did not attain to the venerable ages of his predecessors, being scarcely sixty-three years old when the Lord called him to rest from his labors. But his works followed with him, to be, with him, held in everlasting remembrance.[91] His pastorate covered twenty-two years, his entire ministry twenty-nine years, and, excepting his occasional missionary tours and one or two visits to Rhode Island, were confined exclusively to this Church. In Piscataway he was born and born again, licensed and ordained. In Piscataway he lived, labored and died. His remains were placed by the side of his father's. The inscription on the stone reads:

---

[88] In other words, in the event she remarried, the sons were no longer obligated to make these annual payments to their stepmother.

[89] Will of Isaac Stelle, 1781. Middlesex County. Number 5999-6000L, Book 24, page 44. New Jersey State Archives, Trenton.

[90] *Ibid.* Since his daughter Mary had died in 1777, this may actually be a daughter-in-law, or widow of one of his sons.

[91] Rev. 14:13; Psalm 112:6.

In Memory of ye
REV. MR. ISAAC STELLE,
Baptist Minister of ye Gospel of Christ,
At Piscataway,
Who departed this life
Oct. ye 9th, 1781, in ye 63d year of his Age.

A loving Husband, a tender Parent and a
Friend to all that love ye
Lord Jesus.

No more ye Gospel Trumpet sounds
By him who had much given,
One in this Lower World imployed
But now imployed in Heaven.

Mr. Stelle left seven sons and two daughters. His son Benjamin, graduated at Princeton in 1766, and soon after establish a Latin School at Providence, which was largely patronized. It was a daughter of this gentleman who became the second wife of the Hon. Nicholas Brown, the distinguished benefactor of Brown University.[92] Mr. Stelle was also Clerk of the Baptist Church in Providence for many years.

The descendants of the Rev. Benjamin and Rev. Isaac Stelle are spread over all the country. They are in our chief cities and in country places, occupying the marts of business, or engaged in husbandry and manufactures, or pursuing various professional callings. Their influence in this Church from the beginning, and in the Baptist Israel at large, is not to be estimated in time. May all that bear the name, as they multiply through future generations, be in no wise unworthy of their honored ancestors.[93]

---

92 This was Mary Bowen Stelle, the granddaughter of Isaac Stelle. She was married to Nicholas Brown on July 22, 1801. See Reuben A. Guild, *Chaplain Smith and the Baptists; or Life, Journals, Letters, and Addresses of the Rev. Hezekiah Smith, D.D., of Haverhill, Massachusetts 1737-1805* (Philadelphia: A.B.P.S., 1885), 334, 358.

93 "History of the First Baptist Church, of Piscataway, N.J.," 28-29. As we stated in Volume One of *A Noble Company,* "ye" was a common abbre-

Brown took note of the fact that only ten days after Stelle passed away, General Cornwallis surrendered the British army at Yorktown, Virginia.[94]

It was during the ministry of Brown, who was pastor from 1868 to 1878, that significant changes were made to the community in and around Piscataway. In 1870, the Township of Raritan, composed of sections formerly belonging to Piscataway and Woodbridge Townships, was incorporated. And the Stelle family, which owned considerable holdings of land, had just divided their large tracts into smaller plots. The village about the Baptist church, known as "Baptist Roads," was renamed Stelton (a contraction of "Stelle-town") in their honor.[95] This alteration indirectly led to the church being renamed in their honor as well:

> In Piscatawaytown, where there was a larger settlement than that in Stelton, the ladies had long felt the need of a building to accommodate the Sunday School. Classes had been taught there since 1820 and, for many years, it had been necessary to meet in homes. In 1875, church members freely subscribed $2,500 and 'a neat chapel of ample dimensions' was erected to meet the spiritual needs of the community. In addition to the Sunday school, services were held there three Sunday afternoons a month, with Dr. Brown officiating.
>
> With the building of the Piscatawaytown Chapel, in order to avoid confusion, the mother church became known as the Stelton Baptist church. However, the corporate name remained the First Baptist Church of Piscataway until 1964.[96]

---

viation for "the," as "yt" was for "that," and therefore is not intended to be read as "ye" but "the" on these gravestones. It is not of the same usage of course as the personal pronoun "ye."

[94] *Ibid.* As noted earlier, the Stelle family gravesites may be visited at the Piscatawaytown Burial Ground in Edison, New Jersey, at the former site of the Piscataqua Baptist Church.

[95] Mrs. Charles W. Jorgensen, Jr., *History of the Stelton Baptist Church (Formerly The First Baptist Church of Piscataway). 275th Anniversary Week, May 10th to May 17th, 1964* (Stelton, NJ: The Stelton Baptist Church, 1964), 33; William Nelson, ed., *The New Jersey Coast in Three Centuries* (New York: The Lewis Publishing Co., 1902), 3: 396.

[96] Jorgensen, *History of the Stelton Baptist Church,* 33.

& one Cow out of my Stock before
ghter Mary Manning the Same
ate that is to Say & it is my will
four hundred & fifty pounds As Mary
ticles Shall be Valued by two
Bequeath all the Rest of my
lly Divided amongst them all
bles they paying Each one of
ny part of the above Sd foure
er or gold the one half of Said
half in two years after my Decd
by John Stelle Joseph Stelle Oliver
hn I hereby Give them full power
ions herein Contained in this my
& former wills made by me owning
tament In witness whereof I
and Date first above written
to be his Last will & Testament

Isaac Stelle

Signature of Isaac Stelle on his will, reproduced here actual size. To the right of his name was applied a wax seal, which has since been covered with a piece of paper. Courtesy New Jersey State Archives, Trenton.

Further Reading

James F. Brown, "History of the First Baptist Church, of Piscataway, N.J.," in George Drake, P. A. Runyon and W. H. Stelle, compilers. *History of the First Baptist Church of Piscataway, with an Account of its Bi-Centennial Celebration June 20, 1889, and sketches of Pioneer Progenitors of Piscataway Planters.* Stelton, NJ: Published for the Bi-Centennial Celebration Committee by Pakenham and Dowling, New York, 1889, 11-76.

Morgan Edwards. *Materials Towards a History of the Baptists in [New] Jersey.* Philadelphia: Thomas Dobson, 1792; facsimile reprint Enid, OK: Regular Baptist Publishing, Inc., 1998.

Abram D. Gillette, ed. *Minutes of the Philadelphia Baptist Association, 1707-1807.* Philadelphia: American Baptist Publication Society, 1851; reprinted Tricentennial Edition with new comprehensive indexes, maps and illustrations, Springfield, MO: Particular Baptist Press, 2002.

Mrs. Charles W. Jorgensen, Jr. *History of the Stelton Baptist Church (Formerly the First Baptist Church of Piscataway). 275th Anniversary Week, May 10th to May 17th, 1964.* Stelton, NJ: The Stelton Baptist Church, 1964.

Oliver B. Leonard, "Outline Sketches of the Pioneer Progenitors of the Piscataway Planters 1666-1716," in George Drake, P. A. Runyon and W. H. Stelle, comp. *History of the First Baptist Church of Piscataway* (see the Brown citation above), 1889, 110-118.

Maud Burr Morris. *The Stelle Family of New Jersey: A Compilation.* Moss, 1903.

JAMES BOWND ? - ?
EPHRAIM BOWND 1719? - 1765

by Terry Wolever

Sometimes a painful necessity will bring about a separation of the members of one church to begin a new work in the same community. James Bownd was the leading founder of the Second Baptist Church in Boston in 1743, while his son Ephraim Bownd became its first pastor. The two were zealous upholders of the doctrines of grace among the Baptists of Boston at a time when the standard of truth there seemed to be faltering. In this essay we will revisit their story.

Events leading to the pastorate of Jeremiah Condy

The First Baptist Church of Boston was begun at Charlestown, Massachusetts when a group of Calvinistic Baptists, some of whom had recently departed their Congregational churches and others who had arrived from Particular Baptist churches in England, came together to unite in worship around their commonly-held principles in June 1665.[1] In its first 73 years, the church enjoyed a succession of six pastors—Thomas Goold 1665-1675, John Russell, Jr. 1679-1680, co-pastors Isaac Hull 1682-1689, 1694-1699 and John Emblem 1684-1699, Ellis Callender 1708-1726 and his co-pastor Elisha Callender 1718-1726, who succeeded Ellis as pastor 1726-1738. These men had all ministered to the congregation within the context of the doctrines of grace.[2]

---

[1] For more on the founders of this church see the author's previous essays in *A Noble Company* on Thomas Goold, John Russell, Sr., John Russell, Jr. and William Turner. For a full history of the church see Nathan E. Wood, *The History of the First Baptist Church of Boston, 1665-1899*. Philadelphia: American Baptist Publication Society, 1899.

[2] William McLoughlin's statements that the First Baptist Church "had been Calvinistic at its founding by Thomas Goold in 1665, but as it grew respectable and ordained elders who had been educated at Harvard, it gradually adopted the Arminian views of Harvard," that Elisha Callender (1692-1738) "leaned toward the Arminian liberalizations of Calvinism that he encountered at Harvard" and that his nephew John Callender (1706-1748) "appears to have adopted the Arminianism of Harvard," in his notes to *The Diary of Isaac Backus* (Providence: Brown University Press, 1979), 1: 578, 2: 839-840 and suggested elsewhere in his writings,

With the arrival of Jeremiah Condy soon came a change in doctrinal sentiments, which was not at all agreeable to a significant portion of the church.

Jeremiah Condy, Jr. was born in Boston on February 9, 1708. After graduating from Harvard College in 1726, he taught school at Boston in 1729. From 1730-1738 he lived in England. It was there he was contacted by the First Baptist Church about the possibility of ministering to them. Condy arrived from London on August 20, 1738. The church immediately sent word congratulating him on a safe voyage and desiring him to preach to them on one part of the Lord's day. Two months afterwards at a meeting of the church on October 12th, it was unanimously voted to extend to Condy an invitation to accept the pastoral charge of the church. Deliberating two months more, he accepted their call on December 24th.[3] Following the precedent set by the previous pastor, Elisha Callender, the church invited Congregational ministers to participate in the ordination and settlement of Condy. The ordination service took place on February 14, 1739, with John Callender, pastor of the First Baptist Church, Newport, Rhode Island, preaching the sermon on the occasion.[4] These proceedings did not sit well with some of the neighboring Baptist churches. Isaac Backus informs us that the Baptist church at Swansea had taken such exception to the church's decision to invite Congregational ministers to the ordination council as to send them the

---

are interpretations not in accord with what we've also read about the Callenders. The resulting strong reaction to Condy's Arminian sentiments by some of the members of the congregation would in itself be sufficient witness that the doctrine was being newly presented among them.

[3] Frederick L. Weis, *The Colonial Clergy and the Colonial Churches of New England* (Lancaster, MA: The Society of the Descendants of the Colonial Clergy, 1936), 61; Wood, *The History of the First Baptist Church of Boston*, 233.

[4] The sermon by Callender was published as *A Sermon Preach'd at the Ordination of Mr. Jeremiah Condy to the pastoral care of the Baptist Church in Boston, Feb. 14th. 1738, 9*. Printed by S. Kneeland and T. Green, in Queen-street, 1739. When Elisha Callender was ordained pastor of the church on May 21, 1718, the service was conducted by three Congregationalists, whereas with Condy's ordination, while Congregationalist ministers again participated, Baptist minister John Callender led the service. See the essays on Elisha Callender and John Callender in *A Noble Company*, Volume 2.

following letter beforehand in an effort to get them to reconsider the matter:

Swanzey, February 8, 1738-9.[5]

We, the subscribers, of the Baptist Church of Christ in Swanzey, under the pastoral care of Elder Samuel Maxwell: to the Baptist Church of Christ in Boston, sendeth greeting, wishing grace, peace and mercy, in our Lord Jesus Christ, may be multiplied.

Beloved Brethren: We rejoice to hear that the loss of your minister is so likely to be made up in the settlement of another whom we hear you have chosen to supply the place of your deceased pastor. But we shall be sorry to hear that you make use of, or improve, other ministers of other persuasions in the ordination of him whom you have chosen for that work; for we believe it to be not agreeable to your own principles; for we suppose you do not look upon them as persons regularly baptized, and, for that reason, not qualified to ordain your minister; for we do not find by the rules of the gospel of our Lord Jesus Christ that any were received into the Christian church before baptism, much less to ordain others to the work of the ministry. Therefore we pray you to take it into your serious consideration, before you proceed; for if you proceed in that way, it will be a matter of grief to us, and we believe to the whole church, and particularly to our brothers and sisters in Providence. Therefore, brethren, we leave these things to the blessing of Almighty God, praying that he would give you grace and wisdom in all things to do his will. So, not having opportunity to call the church together, we thought it our duty to send these lines, in love and good will towards you. So we take leave to subscribe ourselves, your beloved brethren in the bonds of the gospel,

Jonathan Kingsley, &c.

Beloved Brethren, we desire that this letter may be communicated to the church before they proceed to the ordination of their pastor.[6]

---

[5] Under the Old Style calendar, the new year began on March 25th, hence the double dating common during this period. February was the 12th month of the year 1738, Old Style and the 2nd month of 1739, New Style.

"How much of this protest was due to doctrinal strictness, and how much to the fact that the Newport Church was invited and the Swansea and Providence churches were not, it is now impossible to tell," wrote Wood.[7]

The growing dissatisfaction with Condy

Protests from without a church can be more easily dealt with than those coming from within. The First Baptist Church was now beginning to experience such internal dissent. "Mr. Condy was a gentleman of superior powers and learning, and of a very respectable character," wrote Isaac Backus, "but the sentiments he had imbibed about the doctrines of sovereign grace, impeded his public usefulness in the ministry."[8] It would appear that Condy did not express those beliefs until well after he became pastor, so we cannot be sure at what point in time he actually came to embrace Arminianism—whether before or after becoming pastor. He did however, become confident enough in his views to begin making them known in no uncertain terms by the early 1740's.[9]

This was the time of the Great Awakening. George Whitefield was making his first evangelistic tour of New England. He arrived at Newport on Lord's day evening, September 14, 1740 and proceeded to preach throughout the region, including Boston. At

---

[6] Isaac Backus, *A History of New England, with Particular Reference to the Denomination of Christians Called Baptists*. Second Edition, with Notes by David Weston (Newton, MA: The Backus Historical Society, 1871), 2: 33*n*.

[7] Wood, *The History of the First Baptist Church of Boston*, 235-236.

[8] Backus, *A History of New England*, 2: 276-277. Wood informs us that Condy married Sarah Drowne, daughter of Deacon Shem Drowne of the First Baptist Church. *The History of the First Baptist Church of Boston*, 236.

[9] C. C. Goen in his *Revivalism and Separatism in New England, 1740-1800. Strict Congregationalists and Separate Baptists in the Great Awakening* (Middletown, CT: Wesleyan University Press, 1987), 238, writes that the "first note of discord" against Condy's ministry came on February 1, 1742, when member Elizabeth Pitson wrote a letter of complaint. Her complaint, while not specified in the records, was such as led her to be "much impressed by the text, 'Come out from among them and be ye Separate' "(2 Cor. 6:17).

the conclusion of the day's preaching, Whitefield entered into his journal for October 12th these observations of the city:

> Blessed be God for what things he has done in Boston! I hope a glorious work is now begun, and that the Lord will stir up some faithful laborers to carry it on. Boston is a large, populous place, very wealthy. Has the form kept up, but has lost much of the power of religion. I have not heard of any remarkable stir for these many years. Ministers and people are obliged to confess, that the love of many is waxed cold. Both, for the generality, seem to be too much conformed to the world. There is much of the pride of life to be seen in their assemblies. Jewels, patches, and gay apparel are commonly worn by the female sex; and even the common people, I observed dressed up in the pride of life. There are nine meeting-houses of the Congregational persuasion, one Baptist, one French, and one belonging to the Scotch-Irish. One thing Boston is very remarkable for—the external observance of the Sabbath. Men in civil offices have a regard for religion. The governor encourages them, and the ministers and magistrates are more united than in any other place where I have been. Both were exceedingly civil to me during my stay. I never saw so little scoffing, never had so little opposition. But one might easily see much would hereafter arise, when I came to be more particular in my application to particular persons; for I fear many rest in a head-knowledge, are close pharisees, and have only a name to live. It must needs be so when the power of godliness is dwindled away, and where the form only of religion is become fashionable among people. Boston people are dear to my soul. They were greatly affected by the word, followed me night and day, and were very liberal to my dear orphans.[10] I promised, God willing, to visit them again, and intend to fulfil my promise when it shall please God to bring me again from my native country. In the meanwhile, dear Boston, adieu. The Lord be with thy ministers and people, and grant that the remnant which is

---

[10] Whitefield routinely took up collections during his preaching engagements for the several orphan houses he supported both in Britain and America.

still left according to the election of grace, may take root downwards, and bear fruit upwards, and fill the land.[11]

It is indeed sad to relate that the 'one Baptist' meetinghouse in Boston was unsupportive of Whitefield. Pastor Condy, described as "a man of totally different temperament" than his predecessor, Elisha Callender,[12] was seemingly indifferent to the religious excitement surrounding him. Baron Stow writes,

> Mr. Condy seems not to have participated, either personally or relatively, in any of the good effects of the revival whose gracious fruits were multiplied around him. But a few of the more spiritual members of his Church became 'partakers of the benefit,' and experienced such a deepening of the work of grace in their own hearts, as made them discontented under his ministry. They regarded his preaching as grievously defective in the exhibition of Christian doctrine, and took occasion repeatedly to express to him their decided dissatisfaction. But, as he was sustained by a large majority of his Church, and doubtless considered them as meddlesome enthusiasts, infected with the 'New Light mania,' their remonstrances, however sincere and modest, were utterly unavailing.[13]

It was James Bownd who seems to have first had leadership of these dissenters within the congregation. Such dissent is always a grave matter and should never be entertained without much prayer and personal self-examination. For the church is the Lord's and not ours, which makes it imperative that things are handled in a most careful and responsible manner.

---

[11] Joseph Belcher, *George Whitefield: A Biography, with Special Reference to His Labors in America* (New York: American Tract Society, 1857), 173-174.

[12] Goen, *Revivalism and Separatism in New England*, 237.

[13] Baron Stow, *A Discourse, delivered at the One Hundredth Anniversary of the Organization of The Baldwin Place Baptist Church, July 27, 1843* (Boston: Gould, Kendall and Lincoln, 1843), 10-11. Baron Stow (1801-1869) was pastor of the Second Baptist Church (later renamed the Baldwin Place Baptist Church in honor of its well-known pastor, Thomas Baldwin) from 1832-1848 and wrote this centennial history of the church during that time of ministry.

Very little is known of James Bownd except that he was originally from England.[14] His son Ephraim Bownd (or Bound),[15] born about the year 1719, had apparently experienced the saving grace of God during the late revival season, but was reluctant to have Condy baptize him until the pastor made it clear where he stood on some cardinal truths. This must have been a difficult situation for both parties, for it was Condy who had performed the wedding ceremony in Boston between Ephraim and his wife Eunice Marston on December 6, 1739.[16]

The dissenters decided to formally address their concerns to both Condy and the other members of their church. The substance of their complaints were set forth in this letter, dated Boston, September 29, 1742:

> To the Rev. Mr. Condy, Minister, and to the Brethren of the Baptist Church, Boston—
>
> We, the subscribers hereunto, having withdrawn for some time from the public worship and communion with the said Church, do hereby lay before you the reasons why we absent ourselves.
>
> 1. We have for a considerable time been dissatisfied with Mr. Condy's doctrine, being, for our parts, of the opinion, from the many discourses which we have heard him deliver from the pulpit, and from conversation with him at several times, that he is what we call an Arminian, in that, as we apprehend, he holds to General Redemption, is a Free-Willer, holds a falling from grace, and denies original sin. We mean by his denying original sin, that he softens, moderates and explains away the guilt, malignity, corruption and depravity of human nature, exactly in like manner as the high Arminian clergy ever do.

---

[14] Backus, *A History of New England*, 2: 421-422.

[15] As Stow observed in his history, "There is some uncertainty about the orthography of his name. Dr. Baldwin uniformly wrote it Bound. His own signature is sometimes in one form, and sometimes the other. Mr. Proctor, the clerk, always wrote it Bownd." *Discourse, delivered at the One Hundredth Anniversary of the Organization of The Baldwin Place Baptist Church*, 15*n*.

[16] Edward W. McGlenen, comp., *A Report of the Record Commissioners of the City of Boston, containing the Boston Marriages from 1700 to 1751* (Boston: Municipal Printing Office, 1898), 209.

2. We conceive we have just grounds to think that he denies the doctrines of election and predestination. If Mr. Condy does not deny these two last-mentioned doctrines, we freely confess that we do not now, nor ever did, nor could understand the scope, drift or design of his sermons, nor of his conversations, when we have heard him discourse on these points of our faith last mentioned. And what further confirms us in our apprehension, that he denies or does not hold election, is this—He publicly owned at a church-meeting that he never had preached it and believed he never should; at the same time alleging this as a reason for his conduct, that if he should preach up election, he should thereby offend the greater part of his church. This excuse we look upon as no sufficient reason for his declining to instruct his people in this important doctrine, but rather ought to have animated him, if he believed the truth of the doctrine himself, to set his church right in an article of such importance, and the more so, if it was as he suggested that the greater part of his church would be disgusted thereat. We hope we need not take up your time nor our own, in proving to Mr. Condy, or to you, that it is the indispensible duty of a faithful minister of Christ, to declare to his Church the whole counsel of God, be who will, or how many soever, offended thereat; so that we are ready to conclude, as we but now hinted, that Mr. Condy does not believe the said doctrine of election himself.

3. We are enough dissatisfied with his way of thinking on that great, that most solemn doctrine of regeneration; he positively denying that we are passive therein; and whenever we have heard him discourse on the new birth, which we don't remember to be often, we say, to our apprehension, his sermons or discourses thereon were so defective, so ill-grounded, so intermixed with Arminianism, or man's free-agency and co-operation therein, and at all times so widely different from what our Lord taught and intended thereby, that we cannot avoid questioning, in our own minds, whether he has ever experienced the saving operation of that most important doctrine in his own soul.

4. We were sufficiently affrighted at a declaration of Mr. Condy, in one of his sermons, wherein he affirmed that Christians cannot know or distinguish the operation of the Spirit of God upon their souls, from the operation of their own minds. This assertion we look upon to be of the most

dangerous tendency, a striking at the root and main evidence of the Christian's consolation and hope, a rending of foundations, a miserable affront to a great number of texts in God's word. And, were there any truth in this presumptuous assertion of Mr. Condy's, would it not make St. Paul himself a downright visionary and enthusiast, for affirming to the Christians of his time that the Spirit itself beareth witness with our spirits that we are the children of God?[17] In a word, we look upon this assertion which we complain of, to be a direct inlet or introduction to Deism and Infidelity, though by no means do we think that Mr. Condy introduced it among us with that view.

What is abovementioned, which, for method's sake, you observe to be reduced under respective heads, is, upon the whole, the substance of what administered occasion for our uneasiness and withdrawal from Mr. Condy's ministry.

Your ease and contentedness under Mr. Condy's preaching, your acquiescence in and attachment to his doctrines, must necessarily oblige us to conclude that, either yourselves are of the same way of thinking with him, or that for your parts you never observed that he preached in such a delinquent manner as we have now suggested, or else that the above exceptions on which we ground our uneasiness and separation, are of so trivial a nature, and so inconsiderable, as not to merit your attention or our separation.

We proceed, purposing to be as brief as is consistent with the weight of the affair, and our being rightly understood. What we have further to observe, we shall sum up as followeth, and which we desire you would be pleased to attend to.

If you are, as some of you have often declared, desirous of our return to our places in the Church, we do then humbly and in Christian meekness, and in all simplicity of soul, request of Mr. Condy, and you, the brethren of the Church, for Christ's sake, for the sake of the Baptist Church, and for our sakes, to draw up a Declaration of your Faith as to these following articles:—

1. Eternal Election;
2. Original Sin;
3. Grace in Conversion;

---

[17] Rom. 8:16.

4. Justification by Faith;
5. The Saints' Perseverance.

These we take to be main, essential points. These are the good old Protestant doctrines, taught and recorded in the articles of the Church of England, which our first reformers from Popery contended so earnestly for against their implacable, bloody adversaries, the Papists, and the popishly-affected English Clergy of their times. As to other articles of less consequence, if we are not all exactly like-minded, we shall waive such inferior points, and not make a separation for matters of small moment. The Baptist Church, where you at present worship, was founded on this principle—FREE GRACE—or, to vary the phrase, your godly ancestors, the first founders of the said Church, were strict Calvinists, as to the points aforementioned, nor would they, by any means, as we can prove, suffer a Free-Willer or Arminian, if they knew a person so to be, to join with the Church.

It is high time, we think, and we hope you will so think, also, to know what are the principles of the present Baptist Church in Boston, especially as it is feared and rumored that this Church is, in part, gone off from the faith once delivered to the saints—the faith by which your pious predecessors overcame the world, and which in them, it is abundantly manifest, worked by love. This, by the grace of God, they held fast in one spirit, and with one mind, being in nothing terrified by their adversaries.[18] In this faith your dear godly fathers lived, we know, exemplary, and died triumphantly.

We would not be understood to think or mean, by what has been said, that truly because the Baptist Church was once Calvinistical, or that because your godly ancestors were of these and such opinions, therefore you are obliged to be so too, without searching, proving and thinking for yourselves. By no means. We utterly disclaim such unworthy sentiments. On the contrary, we would have all men use the like liberty as we do, namely, to judge for ourselves. But then, please to observe, if you are indeed, upon further conviction, gone off from those principles aforementioned, or if you really never held those points of faith before hinted at, or

[18] Phil. 1:27-28.

hold other opinions reverse to them, we say that you ought, we think, in such a case, in point of duty, if it is desired of you, generously, openly and above-board, to declare your principles, that so, those who may hereafter have an inclination to join with your church, or others who may perhaps have mistaken your sentiments, and so have withdrawn from you—that such persons, we say, may know your terms of Church communion, and thereby, if they approve them, be induced to cleave unto you. We are now willing to return to our former places with you, if we can find that your principles and practices correspond or are the same with those on which (by the grace of God) our Church was first founded. But if your articles of faith are in fact opposite, or contrary to those on which this Church was at first established, you cannot, we think, justly blame or upbraid us for separating from you (no, the schism will be somewhere else) and uniting with others who are like-minded with ourselves, as to the articles aforementioned.

Now the Lord give you understanding in all things, and may your hearts be directed into the love of God, and be ready always to give an account of the hope that is in you, with meekness and fear.[19] The grace of our Lord Jesus Christ be with you all.

James Bownd,
John Dabney,
Thomas Boucher,
John Proctor.

Appended to this letter as recorded, is the following additional paragraph, with the sign manual of two other persons:—

We, the under-written signers, by the grace of God, are fully convinced of our duty to submit ourselves to the sacred ordinance of believers' baptism, and have been desirous to join in full communion with the Baptist Church in Boston. But apprehending from the many sermons which we have heard Mr. Condy preach, that his principles are corrupt, and contrary to the great doctrines of grace laid down in the Gospel, we dare not in conscience apply to him for baptism,

---

[19] 1 Peter 3:15.

nor dare we attempt to join with his church, until we know what principles they are of.

Ephraim Bownd,
Thomas Lewis.[20]

Commenting on what he refers to as the letter's "rather extreme charges," C. C. Goen thought that they "stretch the truth somewhat. The church was reputed to be Calvinistic," he argued, "but its Confession of Faith, adopted in 1665 and never altered, is completely silent on the distinguishing points of Calvinism."[21] As discussed in our first volume, such interpretations stem from a misunderstanding of the Confession's purpose at the time it was written.[22] But to remove any doubt as to where these Boston Baptists stood doctrinally, one need only reference their statement made just 15 years later in 1680, that "we own in every particular" the "Confession of Faith lately put forth by our Brethren in Old England," that is, the Second London Baptist Confession of 1677.[23]

Wood's assessment that Condy "was reputed to be an Arminian in his views, but it would appear that he was only lukewarm in regard to high Calvinistic views,"[24] seems to miss the mark, given the specific nature of the above charges made concerning his teaching, coupled with the fact he never publicly denied any of them. The dissenting faction questioned Condy's contention that if he were to preach on the doctrine of election, "he should thereby offend the greater part of his church." Yet it cannot be denied that

---

[20] Stow, *Discourse, delivered at the One Hundredth Anniversary of the Organization of The Baldwin Place Baptist Church,* 56-61. Since this letter is integral to an understanding of the separation, I have quoted it in full.

[21] Goen, *Revivalism and Separatism in New England,* 238*n*.

[22] See the author's essay on "Thomas Goold 1607-1675," in *A Noble Company* (Springfield, MO: Particular Baptist Press), 1 (2006): 90*n*.

[23] John Russell, Jr., *A Brief Narrative of Some Considerable Passages Concerning the First Gathering, and further Progress of a Church of Christ, in Gospel-Order, in Boston, in New-England, Commonly, (though falsly) called by the Name of Anabaptists* (London: Printed by J. D., 1680), as transcribed by Terry Wolever, ed., *A Noble Company* (Springfield, MO: Particular Baptist Press), 2 (2011): 472.

[24] Wood, *The History of the First Baptist Church of Boston*, 236.

there were now a significant number of members who had either come to agree with Condy's views, or had no real issue with them. In the words of Whatley, "Every one wishes to have truth on his side, but it is not every one that sincerely wishes to be on the side of truth." The church voted unanimously that the letter should not be publicly read "and that no action be taken." According to Wood, Condy "pocketed the letter and the church made strenuous efforts to win these brethren back to its fellowship. Messengers were sent to them," he added, "but all in vain." They were all finally "Suspended from Communion" in 1743.[25]

The new church is organized

"Having withdrawn from their brethren for reasons such as have been specified, it is natural to suppose, that they would not fail to give special prominence, in their articles of organization, to those cardinal doctrines for the sake of which they were making large sacrifices, and assuming peculiar responsibilities," wrote Stow.[26] The basis of the new meeting was set forth in this letter:

> Boston in New England, July 27, 1743.
> *Wednesday*, 9 *o'clock*, *A.M.*
>
> We, the subscribers hereunto (being by the grace of God Believers baptized on confession of our faith in the Lord Jesus Christ, and members of the First Baptist Church in Boston, New England), having for several weighty and important reasons (which are set forth in a letter dated Sept. 29, 1742, directed and sent to Mr. Jeremiah Condy, by him to be read and communicated to those who adhere to him and his notions of religion),[27] withdrawn ourselves from the said Condy and his associates, because we are fully persuaded in our own minds that the said Condy either never held, or if he ever did hold the great doctrines of Grace

---

[25] *Ibid.*, 241. One must wonder, if the Lord's truth was desired to be had, why the church would have declined to read or discuss the dissenters' letter, reasonable as it was.

[26] Stow, *Discourse, delivered at the One Hundredth Anniversary of the Organization of The Baldwin Place Baptist Church,* 14.

[27] See above.

laid down in the Gospel, he is gone off or departed from the same, together with those persons who still adhere to him, as is more particularly set forth by us in the aforementioned letter, which said letter Mr. Condy and his brethren have contemned and thrown aside, and have all along denied and still persist in a refusal to give us Christian satisfaction as to those important objections and other very material points laid down in the said letter—

We, therefore, through grace, being still inclined and enabled to hold fast those great, though now much exploded doctrines of Election, Justification by faith alone, particular redemption, final Perseverance, and Original Sin, or the total depravity and absolute enmity of all mankind (by their fall in Adam) to God and the Gospel of his Son, until irresistible Grace doth change the hearts of those who are the Elect of God, on which great and essential principles the Baptist Church in Boston was first founded, and on which last mentioned principles, as they are fully set forth and enumerated in that Confession heretofore put forth by the Baptized Churches in England, entitled 'A Confession of Faith put forth by the Elders and Messengers of many Congregations of Christians baptized upon confession of their faith in London and the country,'[28] we, the said subscribers hereunto, do now solemnly and in the presence of the great God our Creator, Redeemer and Sanctifier, covenant, engage, profess and declare ourselves to be established, purposing by the Lord's Grace enabling us, to continue in the same unto our lives' end. We do therefore, we humbly hope, in the fear and love of God, and we trust with a single eye to the interest of Christ, and for the further increase, welfare and flourishing estate of our said Baptist Church, proceed in the manner and form following, having first set our names hereunto—that is to say—

James Bownd,
John Proctor,
Ephraim Bosworth.

Wednesday, P.M.

John Dabney and Thomas Boucher, who were baptized in England upon confession of their faith, and who were

[28] The Second London Baptist Confession of Faith of 1677, more popularly known by the date of its later reprinting in 1689.

sometime since in communion with Mr. Condy and those who yet adhere to him, but being fully convinced that it was their bounden duty to withdraw from them for the reasons aforegiven, have this day, as well as at sundry times heretofore manifested their desire to us the aforenamed subscribers to be admitted as members in full communion with us whom they look upon and acknowledge to be the First Baptist Church in Boston,[29] professing themselves to be like-minded with us as to all the doctrines contained in the Confession of Faith aforementioned, and we being satisfied as to the truth of their declaration of their being like-minded with us as to principles, and being well acquainted with their Christian-like conversation and behaviour, do unanimously consent and agree to receive, admit and accept of them as united brethren and fellow-members of the First Baptist Church in Boston.

Witness our subscription hereunto the said 27th of July, 1743.

James Bownd,
John Dabney,
Thomas Boucher,
John Proctor,
Ephraim Bosworth.[30]

That same day Ephraim Bownd presented himself to be numbered with these five men. It is reasonable to assume that the wives of those who were married among them were also a part of this constituent membership, but as was sometimes the case at the time, only the male heads of families were so named. In order to be qualified for membership, Bownd had earlier visited Brimfield, where he received baptism at the hands of Ebenezer Moulton, pastor of the church and one "whose principles he

---

[29] Stow notes here: "This assumption was for a long time tenaciously maintained, and it was not until one generation had passed away, that the Church would consent to be called the Second Baptist Church." *Discourse, delivered at the One Hundredth Anniversary of the Organization of The Baldwin Place Baptist Church,* 64*n.* However, to avoid any confusion I will refer hereafter to the church as Second Baptist.

[30] *Ibid.*, 62-64.

preferred to those of Mr. Condy."[31] In the succeeding months Bownd was the Boston church's "principal leader in religious services." This entry in the records of the Second Church tells of his joining the little band:

> Our loving friend, Ephraim Bownd, whom we all look upon and esteem to be a believer in Christ, and who was heretofore baptized on a confession of his faith by Elder Moulton, Pastor of the baptized Church of Christ in Brimfield, having testified his desire to join with us and to be admitted as a brother and fellow-member with us, the First [i.e. Second] Baptist Church in Boston, declaring himself to be fully of our opinion as to the doctrinal points exhibited in the aforementioned Declaration of Faith put forth by the baptized Churches as aforesaid, and we being fully satisfied as to his faith, and thoroughly acquainted with his life and conversation, do unanimously and with hearts flowing with joy and thanksgiving, admit and receive him as a dear brother in Christ, and a fellow-member with us of the said First Baptist Church in Boston, signified by our setting our hands hereunto.
>
> James Bownd,
> John Dabney,
> Thomas Boucher,
> John Proctor,
> Ephraim Bownd,
> Ephraim Bosworth.[32]

These six, together with Thomas Lewis, formed the constituting male members of the church. "The records of that solemn transaction," writes Stow, "most clearly indicate that these seven believers had a proper sense of the responsibility they were

[31] Stow, *Discourse, delivered at the One Hundredth Anniversary of the Organization of The Baldwin Place Baptist Church,* 15. Ironically, Condy had earlier participated in the ordination of Moulton as pastor of the church at Brimfield, Massachusetts on November 4, 1741. See Wood, *The History of the First Baptist Church of Boston*, 240.

[32] Stow, *Discourse, delivered at the One Hundredth Anniversary of the Organization of The Baldwin Place Baptist Church,* 65. Stow exclaimed, "Faithful disciples of Jesus! They laid their foundation deep and broad in the great doctrines of the New Testament, and to this fact may be attributed, under God, the stability of the superstructure." *Ibid.*, 14.

assuming, and of their entire dependence upon the Divine blessing for the success of their enterprise."[33]

Ephraim Bownd's ordination as pastor

The question remaining to be answered at the meeting was who would pastor the new church? The members met again that Wednesday evening, July 27, 1743, at the home of James Bownd to make a determination. Some months before that time the church had set a day of fasting and prayer "to implore counsel and direction from our ascended Saviour how we should proceed in our low and forlorn estate, beside many weekly meetings of prayer for the same purpose."[34] John Proctor was asked to record the proceedings of this important meeting, which thankfully have been preserved for us:

> After prayer [was] made and a suitable conference had with each other, it was unanimously agreed that the following declaration, mind and intention of us the aforenamed brethren of the First [i.e. Second] Baptist Church in Boston, should be minuted down and recorded as followeth:—
>
> That whereas by the declension of the aforenamed Mr. Jeremiah Condy from many of the fundamental principles held and maintained by our godly fathers and predecessors, the first founders of the Baptist Church in Boston, and by us also, the aforenamed subscribers, held and maintained, we have for that reason been obliged in point of conscience to withdraw from any worship and communion with the said Condy and his associates who still abide with him and, as we have abundant reason to think, are like-minded with him, and stand culpable of the like delinquency and declension from many great and fundamental truths laid down in the gospel:—
>
> And whereas it is now near a twelve month [i.e. a year] that we have been waiting to observe whether the said Mr. Condy and his adherents would accede to or comply with the proposals we laid before them in the letter so often before referred to, and which we were so ardently desirous from our very souls that they would listen and respond to, but all

---

[33] *Ibid.*, 13.

[34] *Ibid.*, 68.

in vain and to no purpose, to our great grief and anguish of soul:—

And, further, being well informed that there are many pious and well disposed persons, sound in the faith and order of the Gospel, who are desirous to submit themselves to the sacred ordinance of believers' baptism, and to join themselves in full communion with us, and we also ourselves longing to have the Lord's Supper to us administered according to our Lord's command, and the stated times appointed for the celebration thereof by our Church: —

We do therefore, unanimously, and with one heart and mind further proceed and say, that, from the observations which we have made on the conduct, gifts, and graces which shine and abound in our beloved brother Ephraim Bownd, and from many fervent prayers, sermons and other spiritual discourses which have many times been uttered and delivered by him in our hearing, to our great consolation and joy, we now do look upon it to be our bounden duty not to slight or disregard so great a gift as the Lord in his mercy has been pleased to raise up for us in our low estate, but thankfully adoring the rich goodness of God to usward, to prize, countenance and encourage the same by calling our said brother Ephraim Bownd to the Eldership and ministerial office among and over us, and we do hereby invite, request and call our said much respected and beloved brother Ephraim Bownd to the Eldership and pastoral charge over us the said First [Second] Baptist Church in Boston, requesting of him his speedy answer and acquiescence to this our Call, especially considering that several persons for many months past have been waiting to submit to the ordinance of Baptism, and are still waiting and longing for that ordinance and for the Supper, but are kept off and put back for want of an administrator; and it is desired that our brother Boucher immediately inform our said brother Ephraim Bownd with this vote and request of the Church. And O, that it would please the Lord Jehovah, our Strength and our Salvation, to look upon us and bless us with all the increase of God.[35]

---

[35] *Ibid.*, 66-67.

Boucher went directly to Bownd with the request of the church and returned that evening to report that he had delivered the message. "Some time after," the record continues, "brother Bownd came in, and after prayer publicly made by him for direction, and some retirement to think upon the Church's call, accepted of the same." Upon voting to set apart the first Wednesday in September 1743, by prayer and fasting "for the ordination or laying on of hands on our said beloved brother Ephraim Bownd to the pastoral charge" of the church, they adjourned the meeting at about 9 p.m.

Arrangements were made for ordination service and the ministers chosen to participate, all Baptists, were contacted to request their assistance. It is at this point that the historical narratives become intriguing, to say the least. Isaac Backus informs us that like Condy, most of the other Baptist ministers in New England were in his words "prejudiced against the late revival of religion," which caused the new congregation to find "it difficult to obtain help in the ordination of their minister." He then tells us this led the church to contact Valentine Wightman (1681-1747), pastor of the First Baptist Church in Groton, Connecticut, who Backus writes, "was clear in that work, but he was advanced in years, and could not well travel so far as Boston; therefore this church sent some of their members to meet him" at an agreed place of rendezvous "somewhere in his neighborhood," which they settled on being at Warwick, Rhode Island.[36] What makes this extraordinary is that Wightman, according to his own statements, did not hold to the doctrine of particular redemption! —which is to say, he was a General Baptist.[37] Yet what becomes evident from the manuscript evidence is that the other participating members of the church (John Proctor and Thomas Boucher) as well as at least some of the other invited ministers, appear to have been unaware of Wightman's views in this regard. This is also borne out by the fact that the official minutes of the Second Baptist Church tell us that the ministers called upon to assist in the ordination of Bownd—Wightman, Daniel Whipple, pastor of a Baptist church "in the upper part of Groton" (who very likely accompanied Wightman on the trip), the before-mentioned Ebenezer Moulton, of

[36] Backus, *A History of New England*, 2: 422.

[37] MS "Elder Bound's ordination 1743." A record of the proceedings of Ephraim Bownd's ordination service, as related by David Sprague to Isaac Backus. Isaac Backus Papers, Andover Newton Theological School, Newton Centre, Massachusetts.

Brimfield (who was unable to attend) and Thomas Green, pastor of the Baptist church in Leicester, Massachusetts were selected, because, "We apprehend them to be sound, clear, and zealously affected to the doctrine of free and sovereign grace, and absolutely averse to the Pelagian and Arminian tenets."[38]

This occasioned quite a lively debate when they all came together at Major Jos[eph?] Stafford's place in Warwick, where the service was to be held. Adding greatly to the subsequent turn of events was the fact that Wightman had invited still another minister, David Sprague (1707-1777), pastor of the Baptist Church at North Kingston, Rhode Island, to take part, but had sent him "no acc[oun]t of E[phraim] B[ownd's] principles" beforehand. In a conference with Wightman at the meeting, Sprague (who related an account of the meeting to Isaac Backus) said he immediately sought to defer the ordination. Moreover, Wightman informed Proctor and company that the other elders were "against his [Wightman] having any hand" in the service, he "being declared to be a person y^{t} [that] did not hold particular Redemption—he himself replied He did not hold particular Redemption, but always believed persons were Condemned for y^{r} [their] own sins."[39] But Bownd had already had hands laid on him by Wightman that morning in order to satisfy this requirement by the Six-Principle ministers in attendance prior to his ordination. On learning this, Sprague "Expostulated w[it]h Ep[hraim] B[ownd] as coming und[e]r hands y^{n} [then] only to be ordain[e]^{d}—because V[alentine] W[ightman] w[oul]d not [perform the service] without [it]." Wightman's reply on behalf of Bownd was brushed aside by Sprague, who "Insisted this would not save his Credit." Bownd was said to have "went out at this talk."[40] Sprague then

> bore testimony ag[ains]t y^{e} [the] whole—especially ag[ains]t V. W[ightman]—having any hand—unless He will now declare he is not in Comm[unio]^{n} w[it]h our Ch[urc]h[e]s at Newport &c. V. M. w[oul]d not declare such a Seperation

---

[38] Stow, *Discourse, delivered at the One Hundredth Anniversary of the Organization of The Baldwin Place Baptist Church*, 16.

[39] MS "Elder Bound's ordination 1743," [1-2].

[40] *Ibid.*, 3. Wightman had previously written to Proctor informing him he would not assist in the service unless Bownd agreed to have hands laid on him beforehand.

> especially with E[lder] S[prague]—we y^{re}fore [therefore] agre[e]d not.[41]

At this point Pastor Whipple rose and said he believed Bownd to be "well qualified" and "a work of God," and thought it not "fit to keep of[f] his hands for all ye world." Sprague "here repeated he could not bid y^{m} [them] Godspeed & they w[oul]d bring a stain &c.—& left them."[42]

What transpired next is to this writer the most puzzling exchange of the whole meeting. For Sprague adds that a Capt. John Wait had told him "after the ordination" and "before many," that he told Wightman he could not perform the service for Bownd,

> if he held such Doctrines as they viz: as particular Redemption—or if he ordain^{d} a man y^{t} [that] Did—
>
> V. W[ightman] replied that Eph[raim] B[ownd] had signified to him or satisfied him he Did not hold it—w[he]^{re}upon Eph. B. was Called & He declared He did not hold Particular Redemption but declared his opinion. Mr Butcher[43] replied if that was his opinion it was not his, i.e., Butchers & he left ye Room in Disgust—Mr Sprague asked V. W[ightman] w[hethe]^{r} this was True & he declared it was True & here also to other people—Dr. Wait says his Brother told him ye same.
>
> V. W[ightman] has since openly Expressed his Griefe & sorrow for the affair—& w[oul]d have been Excused—but they pleaded his promise by [it overcame?] his Resolut[io]^{n} to let y^{m} [them] alone—& ready to say never will [he] be again Concerned in Such an affair—[44]

What are we to make of this? Was Valentine Wightman's grief and sorrow "since," over the general conduct of the meeting in which he had a part? Or was it possibly also over the fact he had

---

[41] *Ibid.*, [3].

[42] *Ibid.*

[43] Thomas Boucher, of the Second Baptist Church, Boston, who as seen earlier, accompanied Bownd to the meeting.

[44] MS "Elder Bound's ordination 1743," [4].

related something to Capt. Wait (or Wait to others alleging Wightman had told him) about Ephraim Bownd that in the end was not true (or that he learned afterwards had been misunderstood)? We may never know. It does however, seem incredible that Bownd would have told someone he didn't believe in particular redemption, when this was one of the core doctrines of the new church which his father James had helped found and of which Ephraim was to become the first pastor of, seeing the latter had confessed to be "like-minded with" them as to all the doctrines contained in their Confession of Faith (which included particular redemption); together with the fact that the church itself, "being satisfied as to the truth of [his] being like-minded" with them, had allowed him to affix his name to their statement of belief less than two months earlier on July 27th (see above).

Despite all of the contention which perhaps no one anticipated on the occasion and "after a perfectly satisfactory examination," writes Stow, Bownd was ordained that Wednesday, September 7, 1743, in Warwick. Thomas Green opened the service. Valentine Wightman then preached the sermon and prayed over Bownd at the imposition of hands by himself, Green and Whipple. Green afterwards delivered the charge.[45] Bownd might be criticized for allowing Wightman to participate after the latter made his views known, yet with all having made the trip for that purpose and with Bownd having invited the elderly minister to assist in his ordination (which he graciously consented to do), their decision would seem to have been the most charitable course to follow. And it seems apparent that Ephraim Bownd corrected any misunderstanding of his doctrinal views either before or after his arrival back at Boston, for there is no evidence of any subsequent controversy over what had transpired at the service.

"By the best information which I have been able to obtain," said Thomas Baldwin, "it appears that Mr. Bound, though a plain, unlettered man, was an able minister of the New Testament. Like Apollos, he was mighty in the scriptures, and the want of human learning was abundantly made up by that gracious unction with which God was pleased to favour him."[46] Another writer observed

---

[45] Stow, *Discourse, delivered at the One Hundredth Anniversary of the Organization of The Baldwin Place Baptist Church*, 16; MS "Elder Bound's ordination 1743," [4].

[46] Thomas Baldwin, *A Discourse, delivered Jan. 1, 1811, at the opening of the New Meeting-House belonging to the Second Baptist Church and*

concerning the new work in Boston, "It appears that a number of others were prepared to join them, whenever they should embody a church on evangelical principles. Hence, these brethren had no sooner agreed to rear the standard of the cross, than a number more, to the amount of thirty, came forward and united with them."[47]

Bownd was also reputed to have been "a very evangelical and interesting preacher."[48] And so he must have been, for the new work greatly prospered, with members being added from "nearly all of the towns within a radius of twenty miles, and even from places still more remote. Such was its prosperity," remarked Stow, "that in five years the number of members had increased to one hundred and twenty, and for ten years no act of discipline was found necessary."[49] Among those uniting with this body early on was Phillip Freeman, who was afterwards appointed a deacon. Freeman, we are told,

> had been baptized in London, and was a staunch friend and supporter of the great principles which he found embraced in our Declaration of Faith, and in the 'Embodying Covenant,' to which the members had given their signatures. He sent over an account of the origin and doctrines of the Church to the Rev. Dr. [John] Gill, pastor of the Baptist Church in Carter Lane, London, and author of a voluminous Exposition of the Bible, which so much pleased that illustrious divine, that he expressed his approval by a generous donation of a complete communion service, seven suits of 'baptismal garments,' and a valuable collection of books. Accompanying these articles, were several acceptable

---

Society in Boston (Boston: Lincoln and Edmands, 1811), 25. God has often schooled such plain, unlettered ministers in the most profound truth.

[47] Anon., "History of Revivals of Religion in Boston." *The American Baptist Magazine* (Boston: Putnam and Damrell), 13 (1833), No. 2 (February): 53. The writer does not tell us if all of these initially came from First Baptist, but it can be safely assumed that most all of them did.

[48] Thomas F. Caldicott, *A Concise History of the Baldwin Place Baptist Church, together with the Articles of Faith and Practice* (Boston: William H. Hutchinson, 1854), 23.

[49] Stow, *Discourse, delivered at the One Hundredth Anniversary of the Organization of The Baldwin Place Baptist Church,* 18.

> donations from other individuals, who sympathized with the infant Church in its efforts to honor the truth and the institutions of Christ.[50]

From October 3, 1742 until June 3, 1745, the new congregation met at the home of James Bownd on Sheaf Street, at the corner intersecting Snowhill Street, near Copp's Hill. On the latter date they removed to John Proctor's schoolhouse, where they continued to meet until Lord's day, March 15, 1746, "when the first sermon was preached in their new meeting-house, which stood on the spot now occupied by the church."[51] The meetinghouse, erected on land donated by Deacon Bosworth, was described as a 45′ by 33′ wooden building, "finished in a plain, but decent style." It contained 32 pews total, with 26 pews on the lower floor and six in the east gallery, in front of the women's gallery. One of the upper pews was appropriated for "the singers." The seats in the west gallery were free and were most often occupied by seafaring men, "as they were, from time to time, in port." At the head of the broad main aisle near the pulpit "was prepared a font or cistern, in which the candidates were immersed: it continued in use for more than forty years."[52]

---

[50] *Ibid.*, 18-19. Backus relates in greater detail the items Gill sent over as having been, "for the communion table, one large cup, four smaller ones, two dishes and two plates, also one large, rich damask table cloth; also seven complete sets of baptismal garments, namely, one for the minister, and three for men and three for women; also books to the amount of about fifty dollars. At the same time they received a further gift of forty-eight volumes of the late Rev. Mr. Hill's Sermons; (an Independent minister in London, successor to Dr. Ridgely.) Mr. Hill's sermons were sent by his father, the editor, to be given away at the discretion of the church." *A History of New England*, 2: 422.

[51] Caleb H. Snow, *A History of Boston, the Metropolis of Massachusetts, from its Origin to the Present Period* (Boston: Abel Bowen, 1828), 230. John Proctor, one of the three founding members, was a native of Boston and a public schoolteacher.

[52] *Ibid.*, 230-231; Caldicott, *A Concise History of the Baldwin Place Baptist Church*, 23; Stow, *Discourse, delivered at the One Hundredth Anniversary of the Organization of The Baldwin Place Baptist Church,* 17; Stow tells us that "though the water of the Charles River, under the classical name of 'Mill-Pond,' flowed within twenty feet of the rear of the building, yet they saw reasons for administering the ordinance, as we do now, in the presence of a quiet congregation." *Ibid.*, 17-18.

The church's participation in the cause of religious liberty

In the following decade of the 1750's, members of the Second Church actively participated in meetings convened to address the concerns of the country churches regarding the oppressive actions of the Congregational Standing Order and aimed at securing religious liberty in the colony. The first of these took place at Medfield, Massachusetts on March 15, 1753. John Proctor and Phillip Freeman represented the Second Baptist Church at the meeting, with Proctor being unanimously chosen as moderator. Proctor was also chosen as agent to England to carry their memorial and petition before the king and council. At the second meeting held at Bellingham, Massachusetts on May 23, 1753, Pastor Bownd attended with Proctor. Proctor was chosen moderator and Bownd clerk. And at the third meeting at Boston on February 6, 1754, though Freeman alone attended from the church, he was chosen clerk of the proceedings.[53]

A major figure who would emerge in the struggle for religious liberty in New England was Isaac Backus (1724-1806). On Wednesday, June 23, 1756, Bownd was in Middleboro, where he had been asked to participate in the ordination council for Backus, who had only recently come to embrace Baptist principles, along with the majority of his congregation. In his diary entry for the day, Backus gives an account of the service, telling how he went to the meetinghouse early to pour out his soul to God in prayer before the elders began arriving. The ordination council consisted of Ephraim Bownd and Joseph Collins from the Second Baptist Church, Boston and Richard Round, Squire Bullock and Joshua Briggs from the Second Baptist Church in Rehoboth. Round was chosen moderator of the meeting and Bownd as clerk. After declaring themselves satisfied with the principles of both Backus and the church, they went out before "a great Congregation of people," where Bownd preached from the text of Daniel 12: 3, "And they that be wise shall shine as the brightness of the firmament; and they that turn many to righteousness as the stars forever and ever." Backus recalled that Bownd showed, "first, what was implied in man's being turned to righteousness. Secondly, how ministers are made use of, in turning persons to righteousness. Thirdly, the great encouragement that is given to such as are

[53] McLoughlin, *The Diary of Isaac Backus*, 3: 1558-1561, where the full account of these proceedings may be seen. The remonstrance to Governor William Shirley and the general Court may be read on pages 1565-1576.

faithful and successful in this work—They shall shine as the brightness of the firmament and as the stars forever and ever." Backus added that Bownd "handled these points with great clearness, tho' not with extraordinary power: yet while he spake the nature and weightiness of a ministers Work opened with fresh clearness to my soul, which lead me to view the necessity and importance of allways cleaving near to God in order to discharge these great duties aright."[54] Little could Bownd have realized at the time what an influential figure Backus would become in American Baptist history.

It is not surprising that Backus, himself a Calvinist, would choose to be in close association with Boston's Second Baptist Church. Backus preached to Bownd's congregation on at least five different occasions between 1759 and 1765.[55] Concerning the first time, on Thursday, January 11, 1759, Backus wrote,

> in the evening I preacht at Mr. Bownd's meeting-house which was the first time I ever preacht there and truly 'twas a sweet and Solemn time: truth flowed free and I believe was freely received by many Souls. O bless the Lord my Soul! Afterwards I supt with Mr. Bownd and lodged at Deacon Collins's.[56]

Bownd's closing years

In 1763, Bownd suffered a paralytic stroke. Though debilitated, he continued to preach occasionally at the meetinghouse until his death. He was assisted in the ministry from October 1763 until November 1764, by Samuel Stillman. On a visit to Boston in December of 1763, Backus took note of the fact "that people flock after Mr. Stillman very much."[57] The church had hoped that

---

[54] McLoughlin, *The Diary of Isaac Backus*, 1: 419-420.

[55] These were 1) Thursday evening, January 11, 1759, 2) Lord's day, September 30, 1764, 3) Friday afternoon, October 5, 1764, 4) twice on Lord's day, November 18, 1764, and 5) twice again on Lord's day, March 24, 1765. McLoughlin, *The Diary of Isaac Backus*, 1: 419-420, 578-579, 583; 2: 595.

[56] McLoughlin, *The Diary of Isaac Backus*, 1: 503.

[57] *Ibid.*, 1: 542.

Stillman would succeed Bownd as pastor, but Stillman chose instead to succeed Condy and accept the pastoral charge at the First Baptist Church in November 1764, which not only alienated Stillman from the membership at Second, who were grieved by his action, but widened the breach for a time between the two Boston churches. However, as Stow reminds us, there is "no evidence that Mr. Stillman was, in this matter, guilty of any thing dishonorable. He preferred, as would any man, the situation of sole Pastor to that of colleague. He saw in the First Church an open field for extensive usefulness, while there was no certainty, that, in case of the decease of Mr. Bownd, he should be his successor. He had faithfully fulfilled his contract, by laboring one year, and he perceived no good reason for declining the proffered situation."[58]

The last years of Bownd's ministry were fraught with some difficulties relating to his congregation. In a letter addressed to Isaac Backus in September 1764, Bownd wrote,

> Rev[d] Sir,
>
> Mr. Proctor was y[ou][r] way last week who would have acquainted you of the troubles that my self & the Church at present labor under. The bearer hereof the Rev[d] Mr. Hyndes will be able to acquaint you of our unhappy circumstances. The intent of my present writing is to pray your help & assistance a Sabbath or more. Excuse any thing further now & pray for me & the Church under our weakness & affliction. I conclude, having reference to Mr. Hyndes that he will state our affairs to you, and am Dear Sir y[ou][rs] y[ou][r] Brother in the Gospel,
>
> Boston Sep[r] 10th 1764. Ephraim Bownd[59]

We are not aware today what all these troubles involved, but in spite of them the church grew to the extent that at the time of

---

[58] Stow, *Discourse, delivered at the One Hundredth Anniversary of the Organization of The Baldwin Place Baptist Church,* 22-23.

[59] MS letter from Ephraim Bownd to Isaac Backus, Andover Newton Theological School, Newton Centre, Massachusetts. The "Rev. Hynds" likely refers to Ebenezer Hinds (1719-1812), pastor of the Second Baptist Church at Middleboro, Massachusetts, 1758-1793.

Ephraim Bownd's death, the congregation was said to have been twice the size of the First Baptist Church.[60]

As Bownd's health continued to decline, the congregation set apart Friday, October 5, 1764, "as a day of fasting and prayer for his recovery, if it may be the will of God, or otherwise that he would appear for their help as he sees best."[61] Isaac Backus preached to Bownd's congregation one last time on Lord's day March 24, 1765, during the latter's final illness. In his journal entry for that day Backus wrote:

> Preacht twice to Mr. Bound's people; tho' 'twas so stormy that but few met and the Storm brought in the tide so as to do a great deal of damage in town. Mr. Bound is yet in a weak condition, and they have no stated supply yet they have been wonderfully provided for.[62]

Ephraim Bownd passed away three months later on Tuesday, June 18, 1765. Backus, on hearing of the death of his friend, said the news "much affected" his mind. He wrote that Bownd died "much lamented, though with great comfort in his own soul."[63]

It might be asked, what became of the First Baptist Church? While under Condy's Arminian leadership the church had seriously declined. Condy resigned as pastor of the church in August 1764 and lived in retirement in the city until his death in 1768.[64] His successor Samuel Stillman not only restored the congregation back to its original Particular/Regular doctrinal foundation, but the church under his capable hands regained its former strength and grew both in size and influence. Yes, it was under the leadership of a Calvinist (and a high Calvinist at that) that the First Baptist Church was restored back to spiritual and numerical prosperity. Both the First and Second Baptist Churches of Boston greatly prospered under their evangelical Calvinistic

---

[60] Goen, *Revivalism and Separatism in New England*, 239.

[61] McLoughlin, *The Diary of Isaac Backus*, 1: 579.

[62] *Ibid.*, 2: 595.

[63] *Ibid.*, 2: 599; Backus, *A History of New England*, 2: 422. Backus did not learn of Bownd's death until Saturday the 29th, while he was ministering at Bellingham. I have not been able to discover when his father James Bownd passed away.

[64] Wood, *The History of the First Baptist Church of Boston*, 243.

pastors, Samuel Stillman and Ephraim Bownd. We emphasize this point due to the fact that Christian people are often told that Calvinistic theology will ruin a church and its evangelism and that only by proclaiming John 3:16 apart from John 6:44 can a congregation be expected to thrive. Here, and in other cases we could cite, one may see indisputably that the exact opposite was true.

Further Reading

Thomas Baldwin. *A Discourse, delivered Jan. 1, 1811, at the opening of the New Meeting-House belonging to the Second Baptist Church and Society in Boston.* Boston: Lincoln and Edmands, 1811.

Thomas F. Caldicott. *A Concise History of the Baldwin Place Baptist Church, together with the Articles of Faith and Practice. Also an Alphabetical and Chronological Calendar of the Present Members*. Boston: William H. Hutchinson, 1854.

Baron Stow. *A Discourse, delivered at the One Hundredth Anniversary of the Organization of The Baldwin Place Baptist Church, July 27, 1843*. Boston: Gould, Kendall and Lincoln, 1843.

Nathan E. Wood. *The History of the First Baptist Church of Boston, 1665-1899.* Philadelphia: American Baptist Publication Society, 1899.

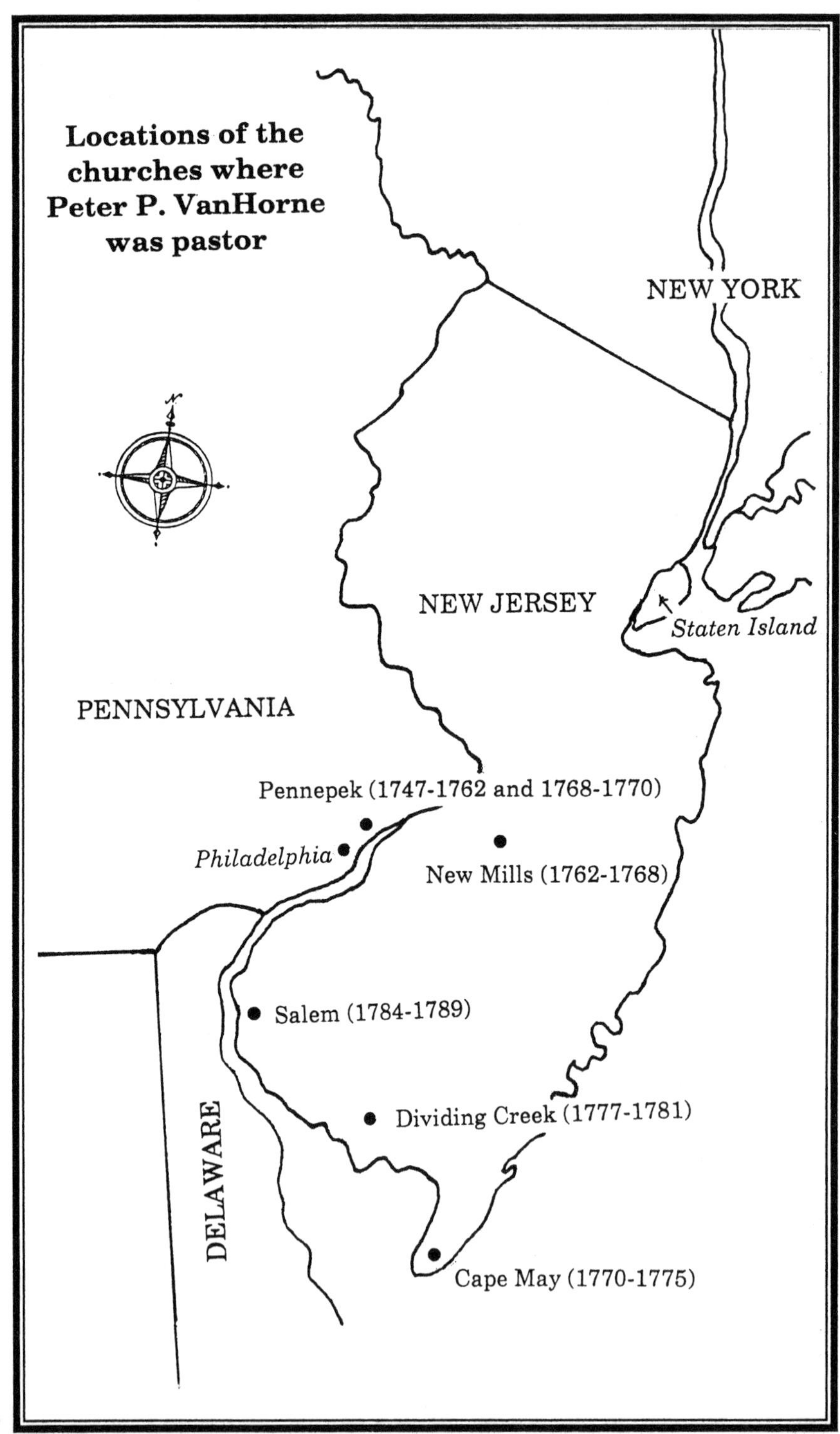
Locations of the churches where Peter P. VanHorne was pastor
NEW YORK
NEW JERSEY
Staten Island
PENNSYLVANIA
Pennepek (1747-1762 and 1768-1770)
Philadelphia
New Mills (1762-1768)
Salem (1784-1789)
DELAWARE
Dividing Creek (1777-1781)
Cape May (1770-1775)

PETER PETERSON VANHORNE 1719 - 1789

by Gerald L. Priest

George W. Paschal writes that, from its beginning in 1707, the Philadelphia Baptist Association (PBA) was blessed with ministerial leaders who were "men of culture and education, who guided them wisely, instructed their members in Christian doctrine, helped them avoid errors, and secured harmony and union" among various Baptist churches. One way they did this was sending "out missionaries to other colonies to secure acceptance of their principles.... In this they were...assuming a leadership to which their advantages had entitled them, and for which they...[felt] responsible."[1] This description is exemplified in the life and ministry of Peter Peterson VanHorne (or often, Vanhorn), distinguished Particular Baptist pastor and able promoter for the doctrines of grace.

His Dutch ancestry and early associations

Shortly after Pennsylvania colony was chartered in 1681, several Dutch families from New Jersey and Long Island began settling in Bucks County (est. 1682) to take up farming.[2] Among these the name Vanhorn became prominent.[3] One of the early residents of Middletown Township (est. 1692) was that of a Lutheran minister, Dr. Peter Vanhorn, and his wife Elizabeth.[4]

---

[1] *History of North Carolina Baptists* (Raleigh: General Board, North Carolina Baptist State Convention), 1 (1930): 44-45.

[2] Penn's liberal policies encouraged the settlement of many ethno-religious groups, which proved eminently providential for Baptists, who prospered in the colony.

[3] The 1790 census identified twenty-nine separate Vanhorn households in Bucks County. [The surname is spelled variously in the records as Vanhorn, Van Horn and VanHorne. For consistency with our series, in reference to Peter Peterson and his son William, we will use the spelling VanHorne —*Ed.*]

[4] William W. H. Davis, *History of Bucks County Pennsylvania from the Discovery of the Delaware to the Present Time*. Second Ed., rev. and enl. (New York: Lewis Publishing, 1905), 143. Two assumptions are made in this description—that Peter Vanhorn was a Lutheran minister and that

Here their son, Peter Peterson, was born August 24, 1719.[5] Possibly through the influence of the Pennepek Baptists, young Peter accepted Baptist principles and was immersed on September 6, 1741.[6] He married Margaret Marshall in 1745, and two years later was ordained and installed as pastor of the Pennepek church.[7] Peter's son William (1747–1807), the oldest of eight children, was pastor of the Scotch Plains (NJ) Church for twenty-

---

he was a doctor. The first assumption is based on the testimony in several sources that his son Peter Peterson was bred and educated a Lutheran, and that the latter's father is listed in Vanhorn genealogies as a minister. Therefore, the senior Vanhorn was probably a Lutheran minister who was given the honorary title "Dr." However, clear cut evidence is lacking for both assumptions. According to research by Vanhorn/VanHorne family genealogists, Peter Peterson's grandfather, Barent Christiansen Vanhorn, was born in Hoorn, North Holland in 1651, came to East New Jersey around 1667, and married Geertje Claussen in 1679. He became a wealthy land owner, eventually purchasing 1,000 acres in Bucks County, Pennsylvania. He had been christened in the Dutch Reformed Church. Obviously, Peter Peterson came to believe that membership via pedo-baptism, whether it be in the Dutch Reformed Church of his grandfather or the Lutheran Church of his father, was unscriptural.

[5] Peter Peterson was the sixth of eleven children (five brothers and five sisters). Davis, *History of Bucks County*, 94. Vanhorn family researchers tell us he also had three half-brothers and one half-sister from his father's previous marriage. Their various internet sites may be consulted by the reader under "Vanhorn Family."

[6] Horatio Gates Jones, *Historical Sketch of the Lower Dublin (or Pennepek) Baptist Church* (Morrisania, NY, n.p., 1869), 23. The immersion could have taken place at Southampton Township, where a group from Pennepek held a monthly service. In 1731, a meetinghouse was erected there.

[7] William Nelson, *New Jersey Biographical and Genealogical Notes from the Volumes of the New Jersey Archives with Additions and Supplements* in *Collections of the New Jersey Historical Society* (Newark: New Jersey Historical Society), 9 (1916): 206. Morgan Edwards names the children of Peter P. and Margaret VanHorne as being William, Gabriel, Peter, Aaron, Thomas, Elizabeth, Marshal and Charles. Eve B. Weeks and Mary B. Warren, eds., *Materials Towards a History of the Baptists. By Morgan Edwards, A.M.* (Danielsville, GA: Heritage Papers, 1984), 1: 9. Such close proximity to Middletown would have made church attendance very convenient for VanHorne.

two years,[8] and is frequently mentioned in the PBA minutes along with his father.[9]

Throughout his ministry Peter Peterson VanHorne was an active participant in the PBA as local pastor and itinerant evangelist. We will briefly examine the remarkable ministry of this faithful servant of Christ in three areas: his pastorates, his contribution to the PBA as reflected in its records, and the vital role he played in the transformation of the General Baptists of the South into Particular Baptists.

VanHorne was the pastor of several Baptist churches within the Philadelphia Association. Most of the congregations under his care grew numerically, but were not without their problems. Interestingly, the circumstances of his relocations are quite varied and invite review.

Pennepek (established 1688)

To be called as pastor of the flagship church of Pennsylvania Baptists would be a highly esteemed honor. VanHorne enjoyed this privilege for 15 years, from 1747 to 1762.[10] Evidently this young Dutchman's ministerial gifts grew to such maturity in a relatively short time that he secured the attention of Pennepek's leadership upon the departure of Jenkin Jones in 1746 to assume the pastorate of the Philadelphia Baptist Church, which up to that

---

[8] J. H. Parks and James D. Cleaver, *History of the Scotch Plains Baptist Church from Its Organization on the Fifth of August 1747 to Its One Hundredth and Fiftieth Anniversary on the Fifth of August 1897* (Scotch Plains, NJ: Scotch Plains Baptist Church, 1897), 15-19.

[9] William VanHorne was given a financial grant for his education by the PBA in 1770. He took advantage of this offer by attending the academy established at Pennepek Church by Samuel Jones, Peter VanHorne's successor. In 1791, William was assigned the PBA's circular letter, an eloquent and passionate address on the subject of perseverance. Among several duties assigned to him by the PBA was that of librarian in 1780. A. D. Gillette, ed., *Minutes of the Philadelphia Baptist Association, 1707-1807* (Philadelphia: American Baptist Publication Society, 1851), 114, 170, 272-277.

[10] It is during his pastorate at Pennepek that VanHorne represents the PBA in his ventures south, resulting in the reconstituting of General Baptist into Particular Baptist churches. Of this more will be written below.

time, had been a ministry of Pennepek. VanHorne was ordained on June 18, 1747 (possibly at Southampton) and then installed as Pennepek's eighth pastor.[11] Pennepek's historian, Horatio Jones, states only that VanHorne labored "with acceptance" until his resignation on February 7, 1762.[12] Shortly after his installation in 1747, a question arose whether to permit "a gifted brother to preach the gospel, who refuses to communicate with them, unless they will comply with his own terms?"[13] Such highhandedness, recognized by the Association's negative response, would indicate that the "gifted brother" was someone other than VanHorne, if Jones's epithet of "acceptance" has any merit. The fact that VanHorne was welcomed by the Pennepek congregation to fill the pulpit again for roughly two more years (1768–1770) during Samuel Jones's pastorate, would surely render him acceptable.[14]

Seeing a need for planting another Baptist church, VanHorne began meeting with a small group of believers at New Mills, New Jersey in 1762. A year and a half later he, along with four other members of Pennepek, requested dismissal in order to be con-

---

[11] Interestingly, VanHorne is listed as a messenger at the PBA meeting for 1746, a year before his ordination. This suggests that he was already active in ministry. No doubt, the lengthy but favorable response to a query by the Philadelphia church regarding acceptability of preaching without ordination must have resonated with him. Gillette, *Minutes of the Philadelphia Baptist Association*, 50-52.

[12] Horatio G. Jones, *Historical Sketch of the Lower Dublin (or Pennepek) Baptist Church*, 23-24.

[13] Gillette, *Minutes of the Philadelphia Baptist Association*, 56.

[14] The fact that Samuel Jones is listed as the pastor of Pennepek for these years would indicate that VanHorne was simply performing the duty of a pulpit supply during Jones's absence. An indication of VanHorne's concern for an orderly church is reflected in another query put forth at the PBA's 1749 meeting. The issue had the potential of dividing the church: should members who obstinately support excommunicated persons be publicly censured? The answer was affirmative. Gillette, *Minutes of the Philadelphia Baptist Association*, 59-60. Lower Dublin must have endeared itself to VanHorne if, as the record shows, he owned a hundred-acre farm with livestock and a servant in nearby Bibury Township—a comfortable glebe for a Baptist pastor. William H. Egle, ed., *Provincial Papers: Proprietary, Supply, and State Tax Lists of the City and County of Philadelphia for the Years 1769, 1774, and 1779* (Philadelphia: William Stanley Ray, 1897), n.p.

stituted a church there, which was granted.[15]

New Mills (established 1764)

In 1750, a Baptist layman invited friends to worship with him in his home at New Mills (Pemberton) in Burlington County, New Jersey.[16] Soon the little band of believers were able to purchase property for a house of worship. Beginning in 1752, the PBA provided ministers for pulpit supply.[17] Among these was Peter Peterson VanHorne, who organized the church in 1764. All indications point to a prosperous ministry. As founding pastor, VanHorne saw the advantage of the church's membership in the PBA and wasted no time in petitioning for it during the October 1764 meeting, even though the membership totaled only nine persons.[18] Within a few months the church had more than doubled in size with the addition of ten new members. By the next year, the number had increased to thirty, and in 1766, to thirty-eight.

---

[15] MS Minutes of the Pennepek (Lower Dublin) Baptist Church 1687-1894. American Baptist Historical Society, Microfilm R-7D, 106. See also the Appendix on page 540, following. It is significant that VanHorne, along with other persons, sought *permission* for dismissal. In keeping with PBA polity, pastors were considered to be *first* members of their church. This underscores the seriousness with which early Particular Baptists considered congregational membership, and illustrates their high regard for *orderly* churches.

[16] To anyone familiar with the history of PBA church polity, it should be clear that local ministries were frequently but occasionally organized with devout Baptist laymen concerned about worship. Normally churches were not recognized as being officially established until an ordained pastor was installed, and approval by other churches of like faith obtained. Pastorless churches were considered "destitute," and in need of pulpit supply, for which the PBA assumed responsibility. The goal, of course, was "settling" a permanent resident pastor. This factor explains why colonial Particular Baptists were so earnest in pursuing educational opportunities for gifted men. Lay ministries needed trained leadership!

[17] James W. Willmarth, "Historical Sketch of the Pemberton Baptist Church," in *The Sixty-Second Anniversary of the West Jersey Baptist Association, Held with the Dividing Creek Baptist Church, from Tuesday, Sept. 9, to Thursday, Sept. 11, 1873* (Wilmington, DE: James and Webb, 1873), 32-33.

[18] Gillette, *Minutes of the Philadelphia Baptist Association*, 91.

When VanHorne left in 1768, the church had forty-nine members.[19] In nearly every case, the additions were by baptism, which would indicate conversions. It is evident that VanHorne was zealous in preaching the gospel, thereby realizing the abundant fruit of an evangelistic ministry. Having successfully organized the New Mills group into an independent Baptist church, he resigned his pastorate on April 2, 1768 to return to Pennepek, where he filled the pulpit for two years.

Cape May (established 1712)

The Baptist church at Cape May in the village of Cape May Court (Middle Township), was the first church of any denomination to be established in the county of Cape May, New Jersey. As early as 1675, a Baptist ministry was organized in the county under English laymen George Taylor and Philip Hill. Following the deaths of these faithful men, others came to minister, including Thomas Griffith of Welsh Tract, Delaware. On his recommendation, another Welshman, Nathaniel Jenkins, agreed to be their minister. He then led them, with the assistance of a ministerial delegation from the Cohansey Baptist Church, to be officially constituted a Baptist assembly on June 24, 1712.[20] The delegation's article of approval significantly underscores the church's responsibility to maintain a godly witness:

> Inasmuch as you have covenanted together to walk in church fellowship according to Gospel institution; we do in the presence of God declare you to be a church of Jesus Christ; and shall desire the God of all grace to bless you in that state and relation; that you may be established in all truth, grounded and rooted in right belief and gospel sanctity; that you may become a pillar and ground of truth, and behave yourselves as real citizens of Gospel Zion and of the Household of Faith.[21]

---

[19] Willmarth, "Historical Sketch of the Pemberton Baptist Church," 33.

[20] Allen J. Hires, "Historical Sketch of First Cape May Baptist Church," in *The Fifty-Eighth Anniversary of the West New Jersey Baptist Association, Held with the Burlington Baptist Church, From Tuesday, Sept. 14th, to Thursday, Sept. 16th, 1869* (Wilmington, DE: H. and E. F. James, 1869), 27-28.

[21] *Ibid.*, 28.

Unfortunately, the church had not been living up to the expectation of its covenant when VanHorne arrived as its fifth pastor on April 7, 1770. The church had been without pastoral leadership for four years, and "it appears from the records that [the congregation had come]...through much tribulation.... consequently, she remained weak and small."[22] The church minutes record several instances of disciplinary action against drunkenness, card playing, and lewd behavior. In spite of such obstacles, during his first year VanHorne baptized four persons, the first converts the church had seen in as many years. The number of members had remained virtually unchanged at around sixty for over a decade. The minutes also reveal the displeasure of VanHorne with the congregation in not being provided his promised salary.[23] An amicable arrangement was made, but when the year 1775 brought with it the death of his wife on March 8th and membership fell to fifty-seven, the pastor decided it was time to leave that July for another field.

Dividing Creek (established 1761)

It is not clear how VanHorne was occupied during the four-year interim between pastorates (1775–1779). It is conceivable that he returned to his farm in Pennsylvania. We do know that his connection with Dividing Creek began in 1777, with the death of its founding pastor, Samuel Heaton. Thereafter VanHorne began filling the pulpit every two weeks until he was asked to assume the pastorate two years later.[24] He must have been encouraged by the prospect of renewing his pastoral ministry at a church with a successful past and a much more promising future than he may have perceived was to be had at Cape May.

Dividing Creek Baptist Church in Cumberland County, New Jersey was formed by a group of settlers from Cohansey. In 1760,

---

[22] *Ibid.*, 29.

[23] *Baptist Church of the Middle Precinct of Cape May Minute Book 1766-1792*, New Jersey Historical Society, MG 1236.

[24] Ellis L. Stager, "Historical Sketch of the Dividing Creek Baptist Church," in *The Sixtieth Anniversary of the West New Jersey Baptist Association, Held with the Mount Holly Baptist Church, from Tuesday, September 12th, to Thursday, September 14th, 1870* (Wilmington, DE: James and Webb, 1871), 29.

Heaton arrived with his family from Cape May, and upon his advice, the group obtained letters of dismissal from their home churches in order to constitute a new work on May 30, 1761.[25] Heaton was immediately chosen pastor, a position he held for sixteen years. During his ministry, upwards of fifty were baptized into fellowship with the church as compared to sixteen during the same time period at Cape May.[26] A historical sketch of the church commends VanHorne for the continuation of this evangelistic emphasis: "Taking into account the sparse population of this section of the country at that early day, it is the part of Christian candor to recognize...[his] four years of pastorate as a grand success, for within that period forty-seven were added to the church, forty-three by baptism."[27]

Salem (established 1755)

A company of English settlers founded the town of Salem on the east bank of the Delaware River in 1675. They so named it with the expectation of blessing and prosperity for the new community. After Elias Keach came to the area preaching and baptizing new converts in 1688, the resulting group of Baptists in the vicinity regarded themselves as simply an extension of the Pennepek church. When the Cohansey church was constituted in 1690, most of the Salem Baptists united with it until 1755. At that time the Salem group constituted its own church after receiving the gracious approval of Cohansey:

> Dear Beloved Brethren and Sisters, We have taken your request into serious consideration and do think there is abundant reason in what you desire. We do consent therefore that you may proceed as you have proposed, and

---

[25] See the "Memorial" to this effect in Gillette, *Minutes of the Philadelphia Baptist Association*, 81-82.

[26] Stager, "Historical Sketch of the Dividing Creek Baptist Church," 26-28.

[27] *Ibid.*, 29. We see no mention of Peter VanHorne in the Associational Minutes after 1774 until he reappears in the list of ministers for 1781, as pastor of Dividing Creek (Gillette, *Minutes of the Philadelphia Baptist Association*, 179). The table records thirty-seven baptisms for that year—an amazing statistic when one considers a sparse population for that area, coupled with the adversities of the Revolutionary War!

> form yourselves into a distinct Gospel Church; which, whenever accomplished, we shall dismiss you from membership with us. We pray that it may be for God's glory, the interest of Christ's Kingdom, and the comfort of your souls. Amen.[28]

That same year the church applied for and was accepted into membership with the PBA.[29]

When VanHorne arrived in 1784 as the fifth pastor of the church, he was afforded the pleasure of occupying a parsonage which had been newly erected for the previous pastor, Abel Griffith. This was to be VanHorne's last pastorate. He died on September 10, 1789, after serving Salem Baptist for five years. One tribute given him was not especially flattering: "His pastorate with this church does not appear to have witnessed any special progress in the interests of the church. At the close of his pastorate, which was in the 34th year of the history of the church, the total membership was only 31, which was 15 less than it was six years previous."[30] Offsetting this negative aspect is the honor he received from his PBA brethren two years before his passing:

---

[28] John R. Murphy, "Historical Sketch of First Baptist Church, Salem, N.J.," in *The Fifty-Ninth Anniversary of the West New Jersey Baptist Association, Held with the Woodstown Baptist Church, from Tuesday, Sept. 13th, to Thursday, Sept. 15th, 1870* (Wilmington, DE: H. and E. F. James, 1870), 26.

[29] See Gillette, *Minutes of the Philadelphia Baptist Association*, 72. It was at this same meeting that the PBA appointed two brethren (Benjamin Miller and Peter Peterson VanHorne) to visit North Carolina.

[30] Murphy, "Historical Sketch of the First Baptist Church, Salem, N.J.," 30. We are left to wonder about the unfortunate decline in membership from a high of fifty-four in 1786, to a precipitous drop of thirty-six the next year and then to thirty-one in 1789, the year of VanHorne's death. A remarkable turn around occurred the very next year (1790) with a report of twenty-eight baptisms, boosting the membership to fifty-nine! All of these statistics are available in the *Minutes of the Philadelphia Baptist Association* for the appropriate years. The fact that VanHorne's successor, Isaac Skillman, was required to sign an agreement with the church that he would maintain pastoral responsibilities and not "leave nor absent himself from the necessary services of said congregation without permission," suggests a reaction to frequent (unapproved?) absences by VanHorne. Thomas S. Griffiths, *A History of Baptists in New Jersey* (Hightstown, NJ: Barr Press, 1904), 47.

composing the circular letter, an examination of which follows.

Associational contributor

The minutes of the Philadelphia Baptist Association reflect a genuine comradery and spirit of deference coupled with a deep-rooted commitment to Baptist principles and sound theology. One can note how, time and again, corporate resolutions and constituent responses were the product of careful scriptural reflection. Peter Peterson VanHorne was both a contributor and a benefactor of that process. We should also note that the spirit of unity prevailed at their assemblies. It is a tribute to their charitable spirit to see how these predominantly British and Welsh pastors welcomed among them a young Dutchman and former Lutheran(!), mentored, and developed him into a seasoned minister.

We first meet VanHorne in the pages of the PBA minutes at the annual session of 1746, subscribing to the pastoral salutation sent to member churches, in which we read these weighty words: "Be diligent in reading the holy Scriptures, which are our only rule of faith and obedience, without which we can have no saving knowledge of God, or of Jesus Christ our Redeemer and hope."[31] How thoroughly Protestant, how inherently Baptist is this statement(!) which provided the foundation upon which that grand Association stood and from which it operated. There is no reason for us to believe that VanHorne ever departed from it, but every reason to suggest that he conscientiously upheld it. He rapidly earned the confidence of his seniors. In 1749, he was asked to preach the Association's introductory sermon at the following year's meeting, and again in 1766, for the meeting in 1767.[32] This was no trivial task, since what was said helped reinforce the doctrinal standard for Particular Baptists throughout the colonies. In 1756, he was asked to be part of an oversight committee responsible "to raise a sum of money towards the encouragement of a Latin Grammar School for the promotion of learning amongst us, under the care of Brother Isaac Eaton."[33] This effort resulted in

---

[31] Gillette, *Minutes of the Philadelphia Baptist Association*, 50.

[32] *Ibid.*, 63, 99-100. [His text for the September 1750 meeting is unknown, but at the meeting of October 13, 1767, VanHorne preached a message on final perseverance from Hebrews 10:14 —*Ed.*]

[33] *Ibid.*, 74.

the first official Baptist school in America, the Hopewell Academy.

The year 1761 was especially significant for VanHorne. He was given two important tasks by the Association: 1) writing its circular letter to the member churches, and 2) sending a request to the Particular Baptists in London for support of the Hopewell Academy. In the first task, VanHorne represented a spirit of unanimity and zeal in admonishing the churches to read and study the Scriptures, be found often at the throne of grace in prayer, be constant in the worship of God, instruct youth with wholesome literature, and to "make use of Christ in all his offices, titles, and relations." In the second, he addressed his British counterparts courteously but forthrightly. He drew on their mutual affirmation of the Second London Confession of 1689, confided the destitute condition of Baptist churches in America and the desperate need of funding the Academy to supply their want. His appeal was mainly for books: "We have also, of late, endeavored to form a library at Philadelphia, for the use of our brethren in the ministry, who are not able to purchase books. This design also wants the assistance of our brethren in England."[34] The letter was short, concise, and cordial.

Another burden the PBA leadership accepted for themselves was visiting other Baptist associations which it had nurtured. This meant several days of wearisome travel to annual meetings in distant places and absence from pastoral duties. But they believed the opportunity to provide encouragement and counsel was worth the effort. In 1775, VanHorne was to share the responsibility with Morgan Edwards of visiting the southern associations.[35]

The last achievement for VanHorne on behalf of the PBA was the privilege of writing the 1787 circular letter. He is now in his sixty-eighth year; having been the senior pastor of five churches, he writes from extensive experience and insight. Typically, the circular letter was intended to be a brief doctrinal exposition of a specific article of faith found in the PBA's confession. The reason for this was made abundantly clear at its 1774 meeting in New York: "Let diligent care be used to caution the churches against innovation in doctrine and practice, and to watch against errors and avoid them wherever they rise, and by whomsoever they may be propagated."[36]

---

[34] *Ibid.*, 84-85.

[35] *Ibid.*, 149.

[36] *Ibid.*, 136.

VanHorne chose to treat the doctrine of sanctification. In the preface to his remarks he first congratulates the Federal Congress for its deliberations in the formation of a constitution, which "offered to establish an efficient government, which, we hope, may, under God, secure our invaluable rights, both civil and religious."[37] VanHorne was well aware that such a government was indefinite until approved by the states. Therefore, in the midst of uncertainty, a sure and positive message on sanctification was entirely appropriate. His three points were: 1) an explanation of sanctification, 2) reasons why it is necessary, and 3) the happy effects of it. He defines sanctification as a setting apart of a person or thing to the peculiar service of God. He then relates the doctrine to regeneration while admitting a distinction as indicated in 1 Corinthians 6:11, "But ye are washed, but ye are sanctified." He writes,

> In regeneration we receive a new nature of principle, and sanctification is the growing of that new nature to the stature of a man in Christ Jesus. The washing of regeneration is never repeated, but the renewing of the Holy Ghost is carried on through the whole life of a Christian, till he ascends to be with Jesus, Phil. 1.6. It is the Holy Ghost which begins it, and it is his work to finish it.[38]

It is clear from his remarks that both regeneration and sanctification have been preordained by the sovereign Godhead: "The council of God has ordained this way to make us meet for...[the] state of glory [or glorification]." The actual work of sanctification is by the Spirit; 2 Thessalonians 2:13—"chosen unto salvation, through sanctification of the Spirit."

The necessity of sanctification is due to the fall of man, which has incapacitated us for communion with God. "Without holiness, no man shall see the Lord." Second, it is necessary to glorify God. Third, it fulfills the design of Christ to accomplish redemption in His elect. The effects of sanctification include detestation of sin. "No man can loathe himself till he is born of God," he wrote,

---

[37] *Ibid.*, 230. The Particular Baptists were almost unanimously patriotic in support of opposition to the British in the War of Independence. Peter VanHorne's son, William, served as a chaplain for the American troops, a service that several other Baptist leaders performed as well.

[38] *Ibid.*, 231.

because the new man only sees the deformity of sin. After he is turned he truly repents after a godly sort, and is humbled in dust and ashes before God; firmly believing that nothing can deliver him from guilt, but the precious blood of the dear Redeemer."[39] A second effect is deliverance from the deeds of the law as the basis of divine acceptance. Finally, as a warning against failure to hold justification and sanctification inseparably, he admonishes, "Beware of all who applaud the imputed righteousness of Christ, and, at the same time, either deny the work of the Holy Spirit in sanctification, or speak lightly or reproachfully of it." Likewise, "he...who would either verbally or doctrinally exclude the imputed righteousness of Christ, and at the same, make great professions of holiness and zeal for religion, ought to be considered as an inveterate enemy to the blessed Redeemer and his truth."[40]

VanHorne's orthodoxy, expressed in this sermon, helps us understand why he was asked to answer a desperate need for the amendment of doctrine in certain southern churches which were proven to be out of order.

Doctrinal messenger

Around 1754, PBA leaders learned that some Baptist churches in North Carolina which had been established upon Arminian or free-will doctrines, had been admitting members on the basis of immersion without requiring any evidence of true conversion. Many of these were General Baptist churches, formed in the early 1700's by elders Paul Palmer and Joseph Parker and evangelist William Sojourner. Some had immigrated from southern Virginia, specifically Isle of Wight County. John Tyler mentions that, as early as 1700, a group of General Baptists had settled in this area and gradually migrated into eastern North Carolina, starting churches, such as Meherrin (Hertford County), Sandy Run (Bertie County) and Fishing Creek (Wilkesboro). It was also from Isle of Wight that Sojourner brought a small group to form the Kehukee Church in 1742.[41] Benedict describes these churches as "the most

---

[39] *Ibid.*, 232.

[40] *Ibid.*, 233.

[41] John E. Tyler, "Sandy Run Baptist Church, Roxobel, Bertie County, North Carolina: a history in recognition of its bicentennial 1750-1950" (Thesis prepared for the church, 1950; MS #CRMS 059, Z. Smith Reynolds Library, Wake Forest University, Winston-Salem, NC), 3. Accessed online

negligent and the least spiritual community of Baptists, which has arisen on the American continent" and in dire need of "renovation."[42] In 1751, Particular Baptist pastor Robert Williams, from Welsh Neck (SC), attempted to reclaim some of them. Shortly after Oliver Hart arrived to assume the pastorate of First Baptist Church, Charleston (SC) in 1749, he organized the Charleston Baptist Association (1751). When Fishing Creek was admitted to this association in 1758, it confessed that previously a lack of discipline and proper understanding of Christian doctrine existed there. The majority of its membership had been "destitute of real religion."[43] John Gano had also become aware of the condition of these churches during his itinerant visits into Virginia and the Carolinas. Visiting Fishing Creek in 1754, he found the church in need of solid preaching, which "much engaged" him, and resulted in several "hopeful conversions."[44]

The next year (1755), after Gano presented their state at the annual meeting, the PBA decided to send two messengers to assist in reorganizing the General Baptist churches and correcting their errors. These were Benjamin Miller from Scotch Plains Baptist Church and Peter Peterson VanHorne from Pennepek.[45] As a result of their efforts, a number of churches were reorganized

---

March 22, 2012.

[42] David Benedict, *A General History of the Baptist Denomination in America, and Other Parts of the World* (Boston: Lincoln and Edmands, 1813), 2: 98.

[43] Wood Furman, *A History of the Charleston Association of Baptist Churches in the State of South Carolina* (Charleston, SC: J. Hoff, 1811), 13.

[44] Stephen Gano, ed., *Biographical Memoirs of the Late Rev. John Gano* (New York: Southwick and Hardcastle, 1806), 65. Gano saw revival take place in several of the churches he visited in the South. For a full discussion of his ministry see Terry Wolever, *The Life of John Gano, 1727-1804. Pastor-Evangelist of the Philadelphia Association.* Springfield, MO: Particular Baptist Press, 2012. Upon his arrival at Fishing Creek, Gano was initially refused an interview by the ministers, but they were soon convinced of their errors. See Edwards, *Materials Towards a History of the Baptists*, 2: 79.

[45] Gillette, *Minutes of the Philadelphia Baptist Association*, 72. According to Paschal, VanHorne was one of the PBA's "ablest and most trusted ministers." *History of North Carolina Baptists*, 1: 209.

along Regular Baptist lines.[46] The first church they visited was Fishing Creek (est. 1745), which they reconstituted into a Particular Baptist church on December 6th.[47] They next visited Kehukee. Its pastor, Thomas Pope, had already converted to Calvinist doctrine. Now, through the influence of Miller and VanHorne, the church was also convinced to become Particular Baptist on December 11th. According to Paschal, the typical procedure required an examination by the visiting pastors to see if applicants had actually been converted prior to baptism. He states that the examinations imposed "rigid Calvinist rules," implying that the process was legalistic, when, in fact, it was an orderly spiritual process which would help guarantee the purity of Christ's church, something which heretofore had not been realized.[48] Semple writes that by the effectual preaching of Miller and VanHorne "many precious souls were raised from the sleep of death.... Their...preaching [was]...not with enticing words of man's wisdom, but in demonstration of the Spirit and power. Many of the members of the churches were convinced of the incorrectness of the Arminian doctrine and relinquished it."[49] Benedict adds, "By the labors of Mr. Gano, and also of Messrs. Miller and VanHorne, a great work was effected among this people, which consisted not merely in the important business of reforming their creed and purifying their churches, but also in reviving the power of godliness amongst [them]."[50]

By the spring of 1761, eleven North Carolina General Baptist churches had been reorganized into Particular Baptist churches—

---

[46] James L. Clark, *To Set Them in Order: Some Influences of the Philadelphia Baptist Association Upon Baptists of America to 1814* (Springfield, MO: Particular Baptist Press, 2001), 93.

[47] Wood Furman, *A History of the Charleston Association of Baptist Churches* (Charleston, SC: J. Hoff, 1811), 62. "These two ministers had previously worked together the year before, when they had constituted a church of fourteen persons at Winter Run, Maryland, on November 1, 1754." Wolever, *The Life of John Gano*, 74.

[48] *History of North Carolina Baptists*, 1: 214.

[49] Robert B. Semple, *A History of the Rise and Progress of the Baptists in Virginia*, rev. and enl. G. W. Beale (Richmond, VA: Pitt and Dickinson, 1894), 447.

[50] *General History of the Baptist Denomination*, 2: 99-100.

four of these (Fishing Creek, Kehukee, Bear Creek, and Swift Creek) through the ministry of Miller and VanHorne.[51] Perhaps the finest honor paid these faithful messengers from the PBA comes from Kehukee historians Burkitt and Read who record that, when these men came into North Carolina to visit the churches and preach the gospel, they were at first feared but then "cordially received."

> Their preaching and conversation seemed to be with power, the hearts of the people seemed to be open, and a very great blessing seemed to attend their labors. Through their instrumentality, many people were awakened; many of the members of these churches were convinced of their error, and were instructed in the doctrines of the Gospel; and some churches were organized anew, and established upon the principles of the doctrine of *grace*. These churches, thus newly constituted, adopted the Baptist confession of faith, published in London in 1689, containing thirty-two articles, and upon which the *Philadelphia* and *Charleston* Associations are founded.... Thus, by means of those ministers who visited the churches, several were reformed, and the work of reformation progressed, until the greater part of what few churches were gathered in North Carolina, both ministers and members, came into the *Regular Baptist* order.[52]

Yet undoubtedly these men would agree that the highest tribute belongs to

> Almighty God, [who] by his grace, has been pleased to call us...out of darkness into his marvelous light, and all of us have been regularly baptized upon a profession of our faith in Christ Jesus, and have given up ourselves to the Lord, and to one another, in a Gospel church way, to be governed and guided by a proper discipline agreeable to the word of

---

[51] For a complete list of the churches see Paschal, *History of North Carolina Baptists*, 1: 211, or as cited in Wolever, *The Life of John Gano,* 77. Ten years after their arrival Kehukee led the way in organizing most of the converted churches into an association (1769).

[52] Lemuel Burkitt and Jesse Read, *A Concise History of the Kehukee Baptist Association: from Its Original Rise to the Present Time* (Philadelphia: Lippincott, Grambo and Co., 1850; facsimile reprint, New York: Arno Press, 1980), 28-29.

> God: We do, therefore, in the name of our Lord Jesus, and by his assistance, covenant and agree to keep up the discipline of the church we are members of, in the most brotherly affection towards each other.[53]

The varied experiences of VanHorne's pastoral ministry and the mixed responses to it are indicative of the nature of Baptist ecclesiology in the American Colonies during the 1700's, which could be expressed in one word—*unrest*. Even though the middle colonial region experienced unusual religious freedom due to Quaker proprietorships, this did not relieve Baptists from problems which often attend liberty. While the leadership of the PBA seemed to work harmoniously, this was not always the case with their constituent churches, as evidenced by the several queries submitted and the various conflicts discussed among congregations, sometimes requiring church discipline and even expulsion. Add to these the problems fomented by the Revolution, which created havoc for many a congregation, and the doctrinally dysfunctional churches in the South, which required courageous confrontation. Pastors like VanHorne, whose gifts were in demand for correspondence, negotiation, and extended absences for pulpit supply to destitute churches,[54] inevitably created hardships for themselves and their constituents, stretching both to their limits. What is extraordinary is how VanHorne and his companions bore such challenges with incredible wisdom, humility, and especially perseverance. It is interesting that a sermon VanHorne was asked to deliver before the PBA, although not recorded, was on this very topic.[55] What happened in the South was a remarkable instance of perseverance in the gracious truths of the gospel and the reward was the fruit they bore in doctrinally sound churches. Such change is striking evidence of the power of God's gracious gospel to change lives for His glory.

---

[53] *Ibid.*, 30.

[54] *Minutes of the Philadelphia Baptist Association* for 1757 included the admonition to member churches "to spare their ministers as much as possible to supply 'vacant places' making 'pressing calls...for ministerial helps' " (p.75). VanHorne frequently accommodated this request: to Manahawkin in 1771, Upper Freehold in 1766, Pennepek, 1768-1770, and no doubt others as well.

[55] Gillette, *Minutes of the Philadelphia Baptist Association*, 100.

Further Reading

Susan Armour. *300: 1712-2012. First Baptist Church of Cape May.* Cape May, NJ: First Baptist Church, 2012.

William W. H. Davis. *History of Bucks County, Pennsylvania. From the Discovery of the Delaware to the Present Time.* Second Edition, Revised and Enlarged. New York and Chicago: The Lewis Publishing Company, 1905: "The Van Horn Family," contributed by R. Winder Johnson, 92-97.

Abram D. Gillette, ed. *Minutes of the Philadelphia Baptist Association, 1707-1807.* Philadelphia: American Baptist Publication Society, 1851; reprinted Tricentennial Edition with new comprehensive indexes, maps and illustrations, Springfield, MO: Particular Baptist Press, 2002.

Eve B. Weeks and Mary B. Warren, eds. *Materials Towards a History of the Baptists. By Morgan Edwards, A.M.* Danielsville, GA: Heritage Papers, 1984, Two Volumes.

JOHN DAVIS
1721 - 1809

by Don Moffitt

The planting of Baptist churches in colonial Maryland was an effort that initially did not seem to meet with much success. As JoAnne Rogge, in an unpublished thesis, has noted:

> In 1742 the first Baptist church in Maryland was constituted at Chestnut Ridge, northwest of Baltimore Town, that church now being called Sater's in honor of the founder, Henry Sater. A second Maryland Baptist church was begun at Winter's Run in Baltimore County (1754) but later when Harford County was created, it became the Harford Church. A third church was established at Frederick, also the Seneca Church, and these four were the only Baptist churches in Maryland prior to the Revolutionary War.[1]

Of the four churches mentioned, two are of interest when considering the life and ministry of John Davis. The first of these is the church founded at Chestnut Ridge by Henry Sater (1690-1754)[2] and the second is the church at Winter's Run founded by John Davis. Davis was to pastor this church for fifty-three years,

---

[1] JoAnn Rogge, "The Harford Baptist Church" (Baltimore: typescript, dated March 10, 1971), 1. According to John Asplund, *The Universal Register of the Baptist Denomination in America, For the Years 1790, 1791, 1792, 1793, and Part of 1794* (Boston: John W. Folsom, 1794), 23, the two churches at Frederick's Town and Seneca Creek (both Particular Baptist) were constituted the same year, 1772.

[2] In 1709 at the age of nineteen, Sater, an Englishman, had emigrated to America. Arriving on the coast of Virginia, he settled in the northern part of Maryland. He made his living as a tobacco farmer on property acquired through a small land grant. Eventually his holdings grew to over a thousand acres. It was on this land that he, as a committed Baptist, was to provide land and a meetinghouse for the Baptists. Sater opened the meetinghouse for any Baptist minister who happened to be traveling through, affording them an opportunity to preach. Sater's commitment to the Baptist cause came to fruition in 1742, when he organized Maryland's first (General Baptist) church on July 10th, with fifty-seven persons signing their "solemn league and covenant."

resulting in a long and fruitful ministry. Under his leadership the church joined the Philadelphia Association (October 7, 1755),[3] established a number of daughter churches and was instrumental in organizing what came to be known as the Baltimore Baptist Association. The significance of this pastor and his church cannot be underestimated.

His early life and marriage

John Davis was born on September 10, 1721 at Pennepek, Pennsylvania,[4] the son of Daniel and Mary (née Mann) Davis. Within three years the family had come to reside in Montgomery, Pennsylvania. Here Daniel Davis was received into the membership of the Baptist church on June 21, 1724.[5] The log meetinghouse, built in 1720, was the center of a large and thriving Welsh community. A larger, stone meetinghouse was constructed in 1731.[6] Fifteen years later, John Davis was baptized (most likely by Pastor Benjamin Griffith) on March 9, 1746, and also received into this growing church. By 1742, he had married Jane VanVost (1726-1822).[7] She is named as the "wife of John Davis" at the time of her own baptism at the Montgomery church on May 12th of that

---

[3] A. D. Gillette, ed., *Minutes of the Philadelphia Baptist Association 1707-1807* (Philadelphia: American Baptist Publication Society, 1851), 71-72, 93.

[4] Morgan Edwards, "Materials Towards a History of the Baptists in Maryland" (1772), in Eve B. Weeks and Mary B. Warren, eds., *Materials Towards a History of the Baptists. By Morgan Edwards, A.M.* (Danielsville, GA: Heritage Papers, 1984), 2: 27.

[5] Edward Mathews, *History of Montgomery Baptist Church in Montgomery Township, Montgomery County, Pennsylvania* (Ambler, PA: A. K. Thomas, 1895), 10. When Mary Davis was received into the church is not recorded, only that she, "Mary, widow of Daniel Davis," died in November 1774. *Ibid.*, 15.

[6] *Ibid.*, 7, 23.

[7] *Ibid.,* 11; Edwards, "Materials Towards a History of the Baptists in Maryland," 27. Her dates are found in "Harford (Old Brick) Baptist Church, Harford County," Henry C. Peden, Jr., ed., *A Collection of Maryland Church Records* (Westminster, MD: Willow Bend Books, 2000), 277.

year.[8] The couple would have one daughter, named Hannah (1742-1778).[9]

Establishing the Baptist church at Winter's Run

The Baptist church founded by Henry Sater at Chestnut Ridge, Maryland in 1742, had some among its members who, according to Morgan Edwards,

> being inclined to the sentiments of the Particular-baptists, invited their ministers to preach among them about the year 1747; they continued their visits, and found the following persons sound in the faith viz., Wm. Grafton, John Sumner, Thomas West, John Sheperd, John Dean, Abraham Jarrot, Wm. Brown, Wm. Grafton Jur., Mary West, Temperance Robinson, Eleanor Jarret, Mary Talbot, Christiana Baker, Mary-ann Stafford. These 14 persons were Nov. 1, 1754, constituted into a church by means of Rev. Messrs. Benj. Griffiths and Peter P. Vanhorn. . . .No remarkable event hath happened since, except they, in 18 years, increased from 14 to 138, and have acquired the reputation of good and pious people. . .[10]

---

[8] Mathews, *History of Montgomery Baptist Church*, 11.

[9] Edwards, "Materials Towards a History of the Baptists in Maryland," 27-28; David Fridley, "Aldersons of Harford Co., MD," in *Alderson Roots and Branches*, 5 (1994), No. 4 (June): 37-39, which is accessible online. Several sources give the year of Hannah Davis's birth as 1742, which would mean John and Mary Davis were married no later than that date. [In his article, pages 37-38, Fridley makes the common mistake of confusing the Particular-Regular Baptists of this period with the later Primitive Baptist movement of the 1820's-1830's, due to their shared beliefs in election and particular redemption —*Ed.*]

[10] Edwards, "Materials Towards a History of the Baptists in Maryland," 27. [This account by Edwards of there already being some "inclined to the sentiments of the Particular-baptists" in the Chestnut Ridge congregation as early as 1747, who "invited" Particular Baptist ministers to preach among them, makes his earlier statement that "In 1752, the Particular-baptist ministers visited the northern parts [of Maryland] *and proselyted 14* souls [emphasis mine] which, in 1754, were constituted into a church near Winter-run" (*ibid.*, 25), surely an initial mistaken inference —*Ed.*]

This was the beginning of the Particular Baptist Church at Winter's Run, Maryland, the first of that order in the colony.[11] It was originally known as the Winter's Run church due to the location of its meeting near the forks of a brook called Winter's Run. The church itself went through a number of name changes over the years. Subsequently known as the Harford Church, it was also known for a time as the Old School Baptist Church.[12] But the name that it finally came to be known by is the Old Brick Baptist Church. The church was referred to by this name because it was constructed using bricks that were originally shipped from England.[13]

The new church made a call to John Davis to come to Maryland and be their first pastor, and he was subsequently ordained to the gospel ministry at his home church in Montgomery in April 1756.[14]

---

[11] Edwards wrote, "These are so called from their holding the doctrine of Particular Redemption etc. Their faith and order are exactly the same with those of their Brethren in Pennsylvania with whom they stand connected in Association." *Ibid.*, 27.

[12] [Maryland Baptist historian John F. Weishampel tells us that "At one time, Harford was the largest and most flourishing Baptist Church in Maryland. From 1799 to 1803, there was a gracious revival there, increasing the membership to 226." But within two decades of Davis's death, the congregation, "became affected with anti-missionary views and lost its power for usefulness." *History of Baptist Churches in Maryland Connected with the Maryland Baptist Union Association* (Baltimore: J. F. Weishampel, Jr., 1885), 28. It was the leadership that made the difference here as in other churches during the anti-mission controversy and not the church's Calvinistic doctrinal basis. For as Weishampel here stated, the Harford Church under Davis, *as a Particular Baptist congregation*, had been "the largest and most flourishing Baptist Church in Maryland" — *Ed.*]

[13] *The Harford Baptist Church*, 1. See also Fridley, "Aldersons of Harford Co., MD," 37. The connection to John Davis lies in the fact that the Rev. John Alderson, Sr., of Bucks County, PA, moved to the Shenandoah Valley about 1755. His son, Thomas (born 1744), was to marry Hannah Davis, the only daughter of John and Jane Davis, on December 15, 1767.

[14] Edwards, "Materials Towards a History of the Baptists in Maryland," 27; Gillette, *Minutes of the Philadelphia Baptist Association*, 78. [It is quite possible that Davis had accompanied his pastor Benjamin Griffith into Maryland when the latter went there to assist in the constitution of the Winter (or Winter's) Run church in 1754, if not before or since, which may be how the church became acquainted with him —*Ed.*]

That same year he and his family removed to Maryland, where, says Edwards, he "took on him the care of the church."[15] As J. F. Weishampel writes,

> This excellent man was then thirty-five years old and remained pastor for *fifty-three* years, leaving behind him a record of good work. Through his zeal, Harford church became the progenitor of the Maryland Baptist Associations. In 1781, the "General Baptist Church" at Chestnut Ridge had become *extinct*, and in its place in the same building, another church had been organized by Bro. Davis and his brethren.
>
> They also organized missions at Patapsco and Westminster, with a total membership of 138. Subsequently, these faithful workers established Churches at Taneytown and Gunpowder, and in 1785, eleven members of Harford Church took letters and organized the *"Church of Baltimore,"*. . .They built a meeting house on the corner of Front and Fayette streets, on the present site of the shot tower.[16]

Not much appears to be known of John Davis regarding his life outside of the ministry. What we do know is that at his coming to settle in Maryland, he did not meet with a friendly reception. "When he first arrived," wrote Edwards, "he was very roughly treated by the neighbours, the magistrates and the court, publickly affronting him and using indirect arts to drive him out of the province; but now [1772,] the men who were his bitterest enemies are his good friends; and treat him with honour and respect."[17]

That Davis may have pursued successfully other endeavors seems to be indicated by an incident that transpired later in his life. The marriage of Thomas Alderson to his daughter, Hannah, produced five children. Two of these children, Abel and Naomi, apparently lived with their grandparents while growing up. Abel was to marry in 1804 and was granted a parcel of land from his grandfather Davis.

---

[15] *Ibid.*

[16] Weishampel, *History of Baptist Churches in Maryland*, 10.

[17] Edwards, "Materials Towards a History of the Baptists in Maryland," 28. [Edwards may have received this information directly from either Davis or his wife —*Ed.*]

> The tract, containing 165 acres, was known as "Davis's Cheerful Innocence" and was transferred to Abel for the consideration of "his natural love and affection he bears and has for the said Abel Alderson his grandson…"[18]

Abel and Naomi were to inherit the Davis estate upon his death. While it may not seem like much, tax and census records indicate that around 1800, Davis held one tract of land consisting of 165 acres and one building with a combined value of $455.63. Along with this, he held three slaves.[19]

Of greater abiding interest are his labors in the ministry. Two years following his ordination and becoming pastor of the Winter's Run church, Davis attended the annual associational meeting of Philadelphia on October 3, 1758, where it was

> Ordered, that a testimonial be given and signed by the Rev. Jenkin Jones, minister of the Baptist meeting, or congregation, in Philadelphia, to Rev. John Davis, late of Bucks county, in Pennsylvania, but now of Baltimore county, in the province of Maryland, certifying his regular ordination, according to the rites, ceremonies, and approved forms and usages of the Baptist church, and also his purity of life, manners, and conversation; and recommending him to the favor of all Christian people, where he now does, or may hereafter happen to dwell.
>
> In pursuance of the above order, the following testimonial and certificate was given and signed by the Rev. Mr. Jones to the Rev. John Davis:
>
> 'To all Christian people to whom these presents shall come:
>
> I, Jenkin Jones, minister of the Baptist meeting or congregation of the city of Philadelphia, do send and certify, that the bearer hereof, Mr. John Davis, late of Buck's county, in the province of Pennsylvania, but now residing and dwelling in Baltimore county, in the province of Maryland, in the month of April, in the year of our Lord, one thousand seven hundred and fifty-six, was regularly admitted, ordained, and received holy order to preach the

---

[18] Fridley, "Aldersons of Harford Co., MD," 39.

[19] Henry C. Peden, Jr., *Inhabitants of Harford County Maryland* (Westminster, MD: Willow Bend Books, 1999), 85.

> gospel of our Lord and Saviour Jesus Christ, to all people, according to the rites and ceremonies, and approved forms and usages of the Baptist church; and that at all times, before and since his ordination aforesaid, for any thing heard, known, or believed to the contrary, he lived a holy and unblemished life, as well in his conversation as in his actions. And I do humbly recommend him to the notice, esteem, and regard of all Christians, where he now does, or hereafter may, reside, or with whom he may have conversation or dealing.
>
> In testimony whereof, and by order of the general meeting or Association aforesaid, I have hereunto set my hand, at the city of Philadelphia, the sixth day of October, in the year of our Lord, One thousand seven hundred and fifty-eight.
>
> Jenkin Jones.'[20]

This step may have been taken as a means of providing Davis with some official sanction as a preacher in light of the opposition he was then facing at Winter's Run.

Preaching the gospel seems to have been the desire that gripped his heart. His labors to that end were well known. Fifty years after his death, George F. Adams in Sprague's *Annals of the American Pulpit*, would observe:

> He traveled much, preaching Christ wherever he went. The woods, the school-room, the barn, the cabin, the parlour, equally with the meeting-house, were all to him places of worship and of labour for Christ's sake.[21]

From 1799 to 1803, Davis had an associate in the ministry, Absalom Butler. The blessing of God resulted in a period of continuous revival during which the number of members "was considerably more than doubled."[22] His preaching ministry was

---

[20] Gillette, *Minutes of the Philadelphia Baptist Association*, 77-78.

[21] Biographical account of John Davis in a letter by George F. Adams, dated Baltimore, March 24, 1859, in William B. Sprague, ed., *Annals of the American Pulpit* (New York, Robert Carter and Brothers, 1865), 6 (Baptist): 70

[22] *Ibid.*

enhanced by the establishing of preaching stations "at various points where he preached at stated intervals, until the missions were able to support themselves."[23]

The Baltimore Baptist Association (1793)

The difficulty in ministering during colonial times is well illustrated by the pastorate of John Davis. His church at Winter's Run was initially small. It was also scattered and only able to observe the Lord's Table on a rotation basis once every two months.[24] Mutual support in ministry and from other Baptist churches was often necessary for the survival of these churches. This may account in part for why the church joined the Philadelphia Baptist Association.[25]

Though the geographically larger associations, the Philadelphia in the North and the Charleston in the South, were important in the support of many of the smaller churches, it was the more local associations that ministered directly to them. One such association was the Baltimore Association, founded in 1793 by Davis and the churches he planted.[26]

---

[23] Joseph T. Watts, *The Rise and Progress of Maryland Baptists* (Baltimore?: Maryland Baptist Union, [1953]), 13.

[24] Edwards, "Materials Towards a History of the Baptists," 27. "This church consists of 4 branches," wrote Edwards, "one near Winter-run where is a neat brick meeting house, 41 feet by 30, erected in 1762 on a lot of 4 acres purchased of James Amos; another branch is near Chestnut-Ridge where they have the use of the house belonging to the General-baptists; another at Patapsco where is a house built in 1770 on land given by Dutton Lane; the fourth near Winchester where a meeting is held in a school house....The families are about 200 whereof 138 persons are baptized and in the communion which is here administered at each place in rotation, once in two months."

[25] Weishampel, *History of Baptist Churches in Maryland*, 10.

[26] *Ibid.*, 11. Weishampel writes: "The names of the churches and delegates originating this body were as follows: —Harford, Alex. Lemon, John Prichard, Abs. Butler, J. Davis; representing 106 members. Frederick Town, Thos. Beatty, Joseph Coleman, Elijah Beatty, Absalom Bainbridge; 36 members. Hammond's Branch, Brice Gassoway, James Warfield, Chas. Rogers; 29 members. Taneytown, Thos. Jones, Benj. Cornel, David Walter; 27 members. Seneca, Lawrence Alnutt, Howard Griffith, Nich. Dorsey; 52 members. Huntington [i.e. Huntingdon County], Pa., Samuel Lane, 16 members.—Total, 226 members." Weishampel also informs us

Associational involvement with the churches covered a number of areas. One of these was pulpit supply and the Harford Church benefited directly through the supply of their pulpit for several years after the death of John Davis.[27] Davis himself was active in the association serving as moderator on two occasions (1794 and 1799), preaching and authoring circular letters to the churches on behalf of the association. In 1793, he preached the convening message to the gathered delegates from 2 Corinthians 8:23. It was appropriately titled, "The Messengers of the Churches, the Glory of Christ."[28]

Another of the efforts of the association in behalf of the churches was the sending of the "circular letter." These were letters written, usually in answer from an inquiry from a church, to clarify a doctrinal issue or deal with a specific problem that had arisen within the churches. The 1795 letter, written by John Davis, dealt with the nature of faith. Specifically, Davis discussed the relationship between a strong and a weak faith. His opening remarks reveal his heart for the churches.[29] The letter itself is

---

that the new Association was "styled at first, the Baptist Association of the Western Shore of Maryland, to distinguish it from the Salisbury (Eastern Shore) Association, but in 1794, upon the adoption of a Constitution, it assumed the title of 'Baltimore Baptist Association' " (*ibid.*, 10).

[27] Watts, *Rise and Progress of Maryland Baptists*, 14.

[28] Joseph H. Jones, *History of the Baltimore Baptist Association* (Baltimore, T. A. Rhodes, 1872), 3. That preaching was central to the associational meetings is noted by Jones. Regarding the 1798 meeting he points out: "At this meeting there were two sermons on Friday, three on Saturday, and three on Lord's Day. It will thus be seen that most of the time was taken up with religious exercises, generally a stand being erected in a grove near the meeting house, where the gospel would be proclaimed to hundreds, and sometimes to thousands; for persons for fifty and some from a hundred miles off, would attend those meetings, and for weeks previous would be preparing so as to have no obstacle in the way to prevent them enjoying this highly esteemed privilege" (*ibid.*, 5).

[29] *Minutes of the Baltimore Baptist Association, Held at Baltimore-Town, August 8, 9, 10. 1795* (Baltimore: Samuel Sower, 1795), 9-12. The preface to his letter reads: "Having had a comfortable interview with each other, and a pleasing intelligence from the churches, that they are firmly attached unto the truth they profess, trusting that they endeavour to adorn the doctrines of the Gospel by a holy living—may the Lord cause the churches to grow in grace and that the beauty of vital holiness and brotherly love, may abundantly appear among the Brethren—may not the

divided into three sections. The first section deals with both weak and strong faith. To show how they are alike, Davis makes five points. First, both are rooted in the free grace and electing love of God—"as many as were ordained to eternal life believed." Second, the cause of the weak and strong faith is the same. It is the Spirit of God, see Colossians 2:12. Third, they do not differ in their essence. Both agree in the nature of man. Fourth, they do not differ as to their object, both look to the promises as made in Christ as the foundation of their hope. Finally, they do not differ as to their goal. Both desire the glory of God and the salvation of the soul.

Davis then reminds the churches that there are some differences between a weak faith and a strong faith. Strong faith is never grounded in ignorance or total darkness, while a weak faith may not have a clear knowledge or understanding of the work of Christ. Second, the differences may sometimes be ascribed to the age of faith. A mature faith may be strong and sturdy, while a younger faith may be like a new sprout, small and easily broken. Another way they differ depends on where they grow. Strong faith may grow in fertile, well watered soil, while weak faith may struggle to exist in soil that is barren and dry. The strength of faith may also be determined by the number and nature of trials that one experiences.

In contrast to a strong faith, Davis shows that a soul of weak faith may not be sure that Christ is its Savior. He goes on to note that a weak faith may not see that Christ is its friend, but it does see that sin is its enemy. Thirdly, a weak faith will find that unbelief and hardness of heart are burdensome and troublesome. Weak faith does not rest in the confidence of its profession, rather, it is always looking to the means of grace to be persuaded of its reality. Weak faith concludes that trust must be put in Christ even though, if like Esther, one must say, "if I perish, I perish." It can only be assumed that when churches are exposed to this level of teaching on a subject like faith that their understanding of the

---

day of small things discourage you, but rejoice that there is small beginnings; it was not always so as even now; remember he that sowed the mustard seed, he did it in his own time, and in his own time, he can cause it to grow up to a large tree—be encouraged then, to wait patiently in the use of God's appointed means, you know not how soon he may raise up many sons and daughters unto Abraham, and add many unto his little churches, such as shall be saved" (*ibid.*, 5-8).

matter will be biblically based, rooted in a firm understanding of scripture.

The following year Davis again had the honor of preaching the introductory sermon at the meeting of the Association at Taneytown, on September 24th at 1 p.m., choosing as his text Job 34:2-4, "Hear my words, O ye wise men, and give ear unto me, ye that have knowledge: For the ear trieth words, as the mouth tasteth meat: Let us choose to us judgment; let us know among ourselves what is good."[30]

One anecdote survives regarding "Father Davis" in his latter years. It appears that in his old age "he fell into the habit of reading his Bible as he was riding to his appointments." Joseph H. Jones, "informed by one who knew him well," says that when Davis would sometimes be late in getting to the meeting,

> he would very pleasantly say: 'well brethren, old John Davis is as sure as a gun, but not quite so quick.' Frequently this detention would arise from his becoming so engaged in his meditations on the way, that the horse upon which he rode would stop in a fence corner, nipping grass, while he, with Bible in hand, would sit upon his saddle, until some passer by would say to him: 'Father Davis, it is near meeting time!' The reply would be, 'Is it? dear me.' It is said this was no unfrequent occurrence.[31]

His legacy to Maryland's Baptists

In 1803, a few years before Davis died, the association noted how God was blessing. There can be no question that the gospel was spreading. To twenty-first-century Americans who are used to the concept of autonomy and individualism, even in ministry, such co-operative efforts might be expected to impede the progress of the gospel. Yet the 1803 associational meeting could report:

---

[30] *Minutes of the Baltimore Baptist Association, Held at Taney-Town, Maryland, Sept. 24, 25 & 26, 1796* (Fredericktown, MD: Matthias Bartgis, 1796), 1. As noted earlier, Davis was chosen moderator of the annual meeting three years later in 1799. See *Minutes of the Baltimore Baptist Association, Held at The Baptist Meeting-House, near Reister's-Town, in Baltimore County, On the 24th, 25th, 26th and 27th Days of May, 1799* (n.p., n.d.), 2.

[31] Jones, *History of the Baltimore Baptist Association*, 31.

> From the letters that we have laid before us, we gather the pleasing intelligence that the cause of Christ within our bounds is generally flourishing, some of almost every age and description have been made willing in the day of Divine power [Psalm 110:3], to lay down their arms of rebellion and bow to the scepter of King Immanuel.[32]

The assessment of the association was a fitting summary of the work in Maryland.

Davis's converts were not only to plant churches, some of them would exercise their influence through their ministry in unexpected ways. One example is found in the ministry of William Parkinson (1774-1848). Parkinson was converted and baptized under Davis. He was ordained at the age of twenty-two in April, 1788. Because of his ability to preach, he was chosen in 1801 to be the Chaplain of the United States Congress. As chaplain he would hold two Sunday services, one in the morning at the capitol and one in the evening at the treasury building. His ministry was so well received that he would observe, "I have the pleasure of stating that the president has missed but one of my meetings at the capitol."[33]

The ministry of Davis was to end with his death in 1809. It was a ministry that consisted of preaching, evangelizing and pastoring. Upon learning of his passing, the Baltimore Association would enter in its minutes: "Brother John Davis, upwards of fifty years

---

[32] *Ibid.*, 7. The association noted further: "During the last year a goodly number have been baptized on profession of their faith in Christ, and added to the churches we represent, and from present appearances we are encouraged to believe that the kingdom of Satan is tottering, that the prejudices of education and the shackles of human tradition are becoming weak, and that the time set to favor Zion is drawing near. While heaven is smiling on us, be persuaded, dear brethren, as much as in you lies, to walk worthy of your holy vocation, strive to keep the unity of the spirit in the bond of peace. Remember infidels are observing our weakness, and hypocrites are spying out our liberties, in short, we are in an enemies land, and should always be on our watch-tower. Let us then as the followers of the Lamb, labor to let our light so shine before men, that they may see our good works and glorify our Father who is in heaven. Let us labor to lay aside every weight and the sin that most easily besets us, and run with patience the race that is set before us, looking unto Jesus the author and finisher of our faith."

[33] Watts, *Rise and Progress of Maryland Baptists*, 15.

pastor of the church in Harford, departed this life in February last, aged 87 years. *Precious in the sight of the Lord is the death of his Saints.*"[34]

Further Reading

Morgan Edwards, "Materials Towards a History of the Baptists in Maryland," in Eve B. Weeks and Mary B. Warren, eds. *Materials Towards a History of the Baptists. By Morgan Edwards, A.M.* Danielsville, GA: Heritage Books, 1984. Volume Two of two.

Abram D. Gillette, ed. *Minutes of the Philadelphia Baptist Association, 1707-1807.* Philadelphia: American Baptist Publication Society, 1851; reprinted Tricentennial Edition with new comprehensive indexes, maps and illustrations, Springfield, MO: Particular Baptist Press, 2002.

Joseph H. Jones. *History of the Baltimore Baptist Association.* Baltimore: T. A. Rhodes, 1872.

John F. Weishampel, Jr., ed. *History of Baptist Churches in Maryland Connected with the Maryland Baptist Union Association.* Baltimore: J. F. Weishampel, Jr., 1885.

---

[34] Jones, *History of the Baltimore Baptist Association*, 9. The author is indebted to Pastor Doug Richey of Excelsior Springs, Missouri, for graciously sharing his collected materials on John Davis, which greatly aided in the writing of this essay.

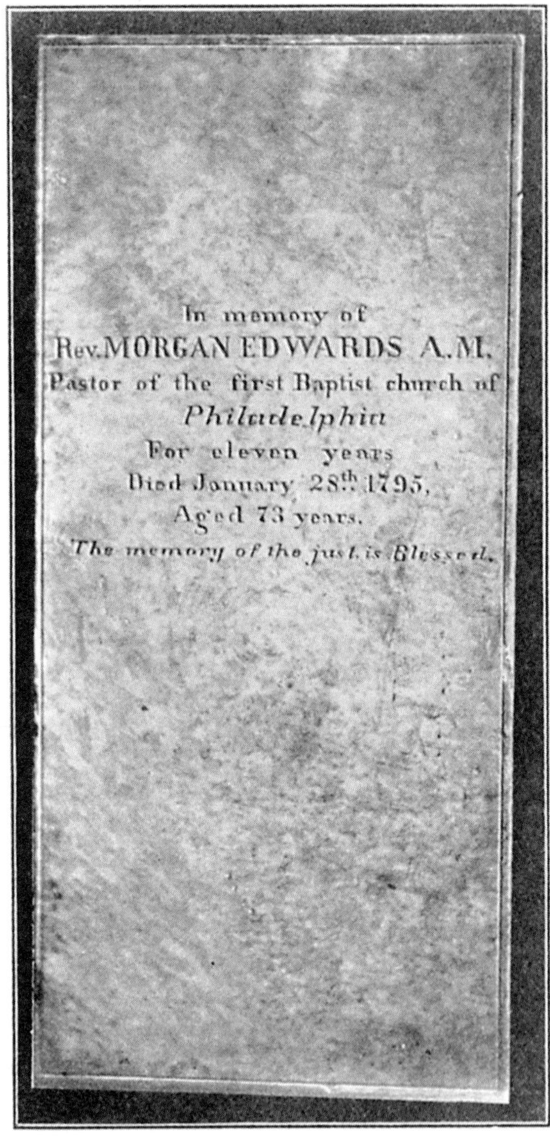

Original gravemarker of Morgan Edwards, now kept with those of other early former pastors, inside the First Baptist Church building, Philadelphia. Photograph by Thornton M. Lynch.

MORGAN EDWARDS
1722 - 1795

by Howard R. Stewart

"Morgan Edwards is the single most important leader in the history of Baptists in America." So spoke the late Dr. William McLoughlin of Brown University on January 24, 1992.[1] When asked why he considered Edwards to be so important with such persons as Isaac Backus, John Leland and others having greater visibility in Baptist history, he said, "They influenced us in only one or two areas, whereas Morgan Edwards directly influenced American Baptist church life in more areas than anyone else."

Who was Morgan Edwards?

Morgan Edwards was a Welsh Baptist minister, who after serving churches in England and Ireland between 1743 and 1761, came to America to be pastor of the Baptist Church in Philadelphia.

He has been described by Baptist historian William Cathcart in 1876 as "a man of great ability and general worth, but eccentric."[2] He also charged Edwards with being the only Tory among Baptist ministers during the struggle for American independence.[3] Later research has shown that he was not the only Baptist minister who was a Tory.[4]

The description of Edwards as "eccentric" has some merit, for he was often a puzzle to his peers and to latter-day Baptists as well. For example, over a fifteen year period he was troubled by a premonition that he would die on March 9, 1770, and the fact that

---

1 Personal interview with Dr. William McLoughlin at Brown University on Friday, January 24, 1992. Tape recording of the interview in the possession of the author.

2 William Cathcart, *The Baptists and the American Revolution* (Philadelphia: S.A. George & Co., 1876), 70-71.

3 *Ibid.* 70.

4 Howard R. Stewart, *A Dazzling Enigma: The Story of Morgan Edwards* (Lanham, MD.: University Press of America, 1995), 306.

he gave credence to the premonition created problems for him with some of his fellow-Baptists.

In addition, Edwards was not adverse to imbibing alcoholic beverages and for some years remained an outspoken critic of the movement toward independence for reasons of religious liberty. Despite his love for gathering historical data, he left little information about his own family. Finally, at one point he was accused of being a Universalist because of his personal support of a fellow minister, though he disagreed with his theology.

Historian Cathcart's terse treatment of Edwards in his earlier book was changed to a very flattering affirmation in the article written by a contributor in his *Baptist Encyclopedia*, first published in 1881, where it is said of him:

> Morgan Edwards was a man of refined manners and shone to particular advantage in good society. He was a master of scholarly attainments. His attachment to Baptist principles was intense and no man since the days of the Apostles ever showed greater love, or made more costly sacrifices for them than he did. He was full of generosity, he would give anything to a friend or to a cause dear to him. Edwards was a man of uncommon genius in his day, and none since his time have surpassed him.[5]

Morgan Edwards influenced Baptists as a preacher, evangelist, historian, educator, ecclesiastic, author, denominational leader and lecturer.

"A man full of Welsh fire"

It should not seem strange that Morgan Edwards has been portrayed as a "man so full of Welsh fire that he could not hold his tongue."[6] He was born in Wales of Welsh parents on May 9, 1722, near the town of Pontypool, Monmouthshire.

He was named after his father and his only sibling was his brother James, born in 1731. The senior Morgan was a man of the soil, but he surrounded his sons with books and provided well for

---

[5] William Cathcart, *The Baptist Encyclopedia* (Philadelphia: Louis H. Everts, 1881), 362.

[6] Thomas Armitage, *A History of the Baptists* (New York: Bryan, Taylor and Co., 1887), 723.

their schooling. Pontypool's major industry was the Hanbury Iron Works, with the Hanburys being prominent members of St. Cadoc's Anglican Church. The Edwards family also belonged to that church, and it was there baby Morgan received the rite of infant baptism.

His primary education included two components, an encouraging learning environment at home and attendance at the Evans' Grammar School, which majored in providing a thorough classical education. Here Morgan Edwards learned religious principles, Latin, Greek, classical literature, geography and other subjects. He completed his studies at the Evans' school at sixteen years of age, and went on from there to the Trosnant Academy. In that same year an even more important event occurred with the conversion of Morgan Edwards to Jesus Christ and his entrance into a Baptist church.

His conversion experience in Wales

"You cannot imagine the joy I felt." Thus did Morgan Edwards describe his experience of conversion in a 1764 sermon to his congregation at Philadelphia.[7] His conversion, however, must be seen against the backdrop of the religious climate in Wales at that time.

The religious atmosphere in Wales included both moribund churches and fervent revival. In the early part of the eighteenth-century, many churches were spiritually neglected and dying because so many clergy had to be bi-vocational or serve multiple parishes. By 1713, great numbers of people began to flock to a number of Anglican preachers who had experienced true conversion. As a result, many lay conversions took place under the umbrella of the Anglican church. By 1738, this continuing revival had touched St. Cadoc's church in Pontypool, exposing Morgan Edwards to the gospel. The two major factors which played important roles in Edwards' conversion and his transition from

---

[7] Morgan Edwards, "Behold What Manner of Love," 1764, n.p. MS at the time part of the Crozer Collection, Colgate Rochester Divinity School, Rochester, New York. [The Edwards collection was purchased late in 2012 by the Special Archives and Collections department of the James P. Boyce Library, Southern Baptist Theological Seminary, Louisville, Kentucky, from Central Baptist Theological Seminary in Plymouth, Minnesota, which had the collection about five years —*Ed.*]

Anglican to Baptist were Pastor Miles Harry (1700-1776) and the Penygarn Baptist church.

Edwards passed through a period of intense inner struggle before he yielded to faith in Christ. He described his preconversion lifestyle in these words:

> I was formerly as wild and as worthless as any other; and should have been so yet had not the unmerited love of God laid hold of me, and raised me to the state I am in now.
>
> * * * * *
>
> My conduct from my youth up to the time of my conversion had been base and shameful. The thoughts of it make me drop the head, and the eyes together. O that what I did had not been done! That I had not been till I had been good—I possess the sins of youth—I cannot forget them.[8]

About this time Miles Harry, who has since been thought to be "probably the outstanding Welsh Baptist minister of his time,"[9] entered his life. At precisely what point he came in to Edwards' spiritual struggle can only be guessed, but he was a key person both in his conversion and his early Christian experience.

Long after his conversion experience, which occurred in 1738,[10] Edwards related the experience to the congregation at Cork, Ireland, on July 20, 1756:

> I can remember my convictions and conversion: I know how God in kindness broke in upon me when I like the Israelites at Mount Sinai feared and trembled; when the pains of hell got hold of me he then said to me fear not for I am thy God, be not dismayed for I am with thee: he then said to me thy

---

[8] *Ibid.*

[9] A. C. Underwood, *A History of the English Baptists* (London: The Carey Kingsgate Press, 1947), 164. It is reported that Harry baptized "hundreds of believers" in the course of his itinerant ministry. Selwyn Gummer, "Trosnant Academy," *The Baptist Quarterly* (London: Baptist Union Publication Dept.), 9 (1926): 44. In addition he helped constitute churches, set up the earliest printing press in that part of Wales and played a major role in establishing Trosnant Academy.

[10] Morgan Edwards, *Materials Towards a History of the Baptists in Pennsylvania* (Philadelphia: Joseph Crukshank and Isaac Collins, 1770), 48. Though he only writes, "[I] Embraced the principles of the Baptists in 1738," this was more than a mental assent to a set of theological tenets.

> sins are forgiven be of good cheer; he then seals his love to me and in the interim my heart filled with love to him, all my soul was kindness and affection, and tho' a little before I was in such bondage that [if] all the world were to tell me that God would not forgive me I would not believe; but then again if the world were to tell me that I should die eternally I could not credit them.[11]

Next came Edwards' baptism and membership in the Penygarn Baptist Church, where he joined several other young men in a pool of preachers who were spreading the Gospel in the area around Pontypool. Following his conversion he became part of the student body at the Trosnant Academy.

"A Baptist minister possessed of superior learning"

Morgan Edwards has been viewed as one of the better educated American Baptist ministers of the eighteenth century. Reuben Guild described him as a "Baptist minister possessed of superior learning,"[12] and Stephen A. Swaine called him a "master of scholarly attainments."[13] Two schools provided the training grounds for his education for ministry, the Trosnant Academy in Wales and the Bristol Academy in England.

The Trosnant Academy was started by John Griffiths, a Baptist layman, who was aided by Miles Harry. It began (by 1734) in a rented house in Trosnant and while it was primarily for the training of ministers, it offered a program of general education. Morgan Edwards spent four years at Trosnant and came under the influence not only of John Griffiths, but headmaster John Matthews as well.

John Griffiths would play a significant role in bringing Morgan Edwards to America in 1761, while John Matthews would be instrumental in sending forty young men into the Baptist ministry during his death-shortened, five-year tenure at Trosnant. Edwards

---

[11] Morgan Edwards, MS sermon, "And Manoah Said," No. 416, n.p.

[12] Reuben A. Guild, *Early History of Brown University, Including the Life, Times and Correspondence of President Manning, 1756-1791* (Providence: Snow and Farnham, 1896), 12.

[13] Stephen A. Swaine, *Faithful Men or Memorials of Bristol Baptist College and Its Distinguished Alumni* (London: Alexander Shepherd, 1884), 68.

was so well trained in the classics at Evans' Grammar School that he was able to excel at Trosnant. There he also came to the attention of the leading Baptist ministers of England when each year Miles Harry included his name among Welsh students recommended for aid from the Particular Baptist Fund of London.

In 1742, Morgan Edwards moved to the Bristol Academy for another year of study. Bristol is the oldest Baptist college in the world, having been launched in 1679. Edwards was not the only young Welshman to cross the River Severn from Wales to attend the school. From 1734 to the end of the eighteenth century, at least ninety students made the journey.[14] Five of these are singled out as persons of distinguished ability: Thomas Llewelyn (1741), Morgan Edwards (1742), Benjamin Francis (1753), William Richards (1775), and Morgan John Rhys (1782).[15] Again, a minister and a church were to play an influential role in Edwards' life while at Bristol. The headmaster, Bernard Foskett (1685-1758), brought his love of learning, expansive reading and an evangelical Calvinism to bear upon Morgan Edwards. The church was the Broadmead Baptist Church of Bristol, a major force for evangelical Calvinism in that part of England.

Morgan Edwards was thus himself an evangelical Calvinist when he left Bristol Academy in 1743, to become pastor of the Baptist church in Boston, Lincolnshire.

The extant sermons and other writings all show Morgan Edwards to be one of the number of Baptist preachers who were Calvinistic preachers with warm evangelistic hearts. The area around Bristol was greatly influenced by the revivals of Wesley and Whitefield. That influence was felt in the Broadmead Baptist church, which was a member of the evangelistically oriented Western Baptist Association. Indeed, that church called Bernard Foskett in 1720 from the Little Wild Street Baptist church in London, pastored by Joseph Stennett (1692-1758). Morgan Edwards was often invited to preach in that church.

When he came to the end of his term at Bristol Academy, Morgan Edwards drew up a series of five academicals or formal papers covering several major doctrinal themes of Calvinism.[16]

---

[14] Norman S. Moon, *Education for Ministry—Bristol Baptist College, 1679-1979* (Bristol: Bristol Baptist College, 1979), 17.

[15] *Ibid.*, 18.

[16] Morgan Edwards, (MS Academicals), 1743, McKesson Collection, John Hay Library, Brown University, Providence, R.I.

The Particular Baptist Church in Boston, Lincolnshire

Morgan Edwards was a single, twenty-one-year-old young man when he arrived as pastor of the newly organized Particular Baptist church in Boston, Lincolnshire in 1743. When he came to Boston, the General Baptists in that part of England were in a state of theological upheaval. Socinianism had made deep inroads into the Baptist churches in the County, but the church in Boston was still a strong General Baptist church, with John Goode as its pastor.

Particular Baptists began to meet in Boston about 1727 and by 1742 had erected a meetinghouse. It was a small congregation and Morgan Edwards had to supplement his salary with teaching opportunities and itinerant evangelism. The church was called the Ebenezer Baptist Church and by 1770 had spun-off another church called the Salem Baptist Church. It is safe to assume that some of its initial growth resulted from the theological discontent among the General Baptists as people sought the more certain doctrinal teaching provided by Edwards. After seven years at Boston, Edwards went to Cork, Ireland, to become associate pastor of the Baptist church in 1750.

The Baptist Church at Cork, Ireland

Edwards was still unmarried when he went to Cork in 1750, but when he left in 1759, he was both married and without another pastorate. His ministry at Cork was as an assistant to Ebenezer Gibbons, who served that church from 1729 to 1764.

The years in Cork were a mixed blessing for Edwards. While there he married Mary Nun (or Nunn), the daughter of Joshua and Ruth Nun, prominent members of the congregation. Mary conceived children several times at Cork, but all the children died in childbirth. Edwards was ordained at Cork on June 1, 1757, but was rejected as the one to assume the mantle of the ailing Gibbons.[17] In 1759, he was asked to leave to make way for someone else. It was also in Cork where he and his wife both experienced premonitions of their deaths. For Mary it came true as she related it, but not so for Morgan.

---

[17] Edwards, *Materials Towards a History of the Baptists in Pennsylvania*, 48. Interestingly enough, Edwards served in the ministry for fourteen years before he was ordained. Dissenters in the eighteenth century did not rush their candidates for the ministry into ordination.

One of the benefits Edwards received from his ministry at Cork was the continued development of his preaching ability. A number of his sermons from Cork are still extant and compare well with those of his best years at Philadelphia.[18] Some in the church thought he delivered his sermons in a "heavy manner" and that his preaching would not bring people into the church. The church book indicates that the majority in the congregation liked Edwards, but that did not prevent his forced termination.

In June of 1759, Morgan and Mary Edwards left Cork to represent the Cork church at the annual meeting of the Irish Baptist Association in Dublin. It would be his last service to the church. Following the meeting he went to London to await the next development in his ministry. It would be seven months before his next pastorate evolved with the Particular Baptist Church in Rye, Sussex.

The Particular Baptist Church at Rye, Sussex

Morgan Edwards' pastorate at Rye lasted only one year (1760-1761), but it permanently impacted the church, and set the stage for his greatest years at Philadelphia. The church at Rye was a young church, but the people who had formed the church were a feisty, squabbling lot. The result was a shrinking of the membership, so that only thirteen people were present when Edwards presided at a communion service on March 23, 1760. When he left in February of the following year, he was so loved by the people that they offered financial inducements beyond their means for him to stay. In tribute to him they put his farewell sermon in print.[19]

The year at Rye was one of revival, spiritually and numerically. Before he came, the church was involved in doctrinal disputes with other churches, held in disrepute in the community, torn by internal spats, unable to support a pastor and almost comatose. When Edwards left they were at peace with their sister churches, reconciled to each other, respected in the community, able to pay a full salary and growing. The church worship services were filled

---

[18] Formerly in the Crozer Collection at the Colgate Rochester Divinity School, Rochester, N.Y. and now at Southern Baptist Theological Seminary, Louisville, Kentucky.

[19] *A Farewell Discourse, delivered at the Baptist Meeting in Rye on Feb. 8, 1761.* Dublin, 1761.

and many freewill offerings were gladly taken. Many new people had united with the church.

The townspeople, at first hostile to Edwards, soon came to respect and support him. The town leaders invited him to their homes and special events, offered sound advice and gave extra help during an illness. They even offered to contribute more money to offer him a higher salary which was already the best he had received. With all these positive things happening, why did Edwards choose to accept the call to leave his native land and travel thousands of miles by sea to a land still in a primitive state?

Two men provide the answer to that question, John Griffiths and John Gill. John Griffiths (1731-1811), who started the Trosnant Academy, came to Philadelphia in 1759, two years before Morgan Edwards. This ardent Baptist layman knew Morgan Edwards, but he also knew John Gill (1697-1771), board chairman of the Particular Baptist Fund in London. The board of that fund not only helped to support ministers and churches, but also acted as a clearing house for recommending names to pastorless churches. John Gill also knew Morgan Edwards from years of association through the Particular Baptist Fund.

John Griffiths wrote a letter to John Gill, requesting the name of a person who could come to Philadelphia to be pastor of a church which was then in a dying state. Gill sent them the name of Morgan Edwards, even though the qualifications listed in the letter were extremely high for that time. Gill named Edwards as one who "came the nearest of anyone who could be obtained."[20]

The Baptist Church at Philadelphia

When Morgan and Mary Edwards arrived in Philadelphia on May 23, 1761, they came to the most progressive city of the American colonies. Its forty thousand inhabitants had paved streets in straight lines, a public square in each quadrant of the city, a marketing area near the waterfront, religious liberty, a bustling economy, fire companies, street lighting, trash collection, a hospital, a theater, a college and a thriving community of artists. It was an "exciting and exuberant town;" a city second in size only to London in the British Empire.

---

[20] John Rippon, ed., *The Baptist Annual Register, for 1794, 1795, 1796-1797* (London: Dilly, Button, and Thomas, et al., 1797), 310. Memorial Sermon, William Rogers, February 22, 1795.

This Baptist congregation, begun in 1698, had been served by Pastor Jenkin Jones since 1746. He had been in failing health for some years and the church had suffered serious decline under supply preaching. After Jones's death in July 1760, the church began its search for a new pastor, but because they had drawn up such high qualifications there were few men interested in the pastorate. It was then that John Griffiths was authorized to write John Gill for assistance.

During the Philadelphia years, Morgan and Mary Edwards had two sons, William or Billy as he was known, and Joshua, named after his maternal grandfather.

Billy was born in 1762, attended the grammar school associated with the College of Philadelphia for two years and following the death of his mother in August of 1769, transferred to the academy connected with Rhode Island College at Providence. Like his father, he majored in classical literature and following grammar school attended Rhode Island College, from which he graduated in 1776. At some point subsequent to his graduation, Billy persuaded his father to send him to Wales or Ireland where he could stay with his paternal or maternal grandparents.

Billy Edwards kept a loyalty to the British crown and the growing movement toward independence in America was becoming too much for him. He eventually joined the British army, rose to the rank of colonel, but never fought in the American Revolution. At some point he disappeared without a trace and was never heard from again. Later trips by his father and brother failed to find what became of him.

Joshua was born in 1765 and began attending the academy at the College of Philadelphia at the age of six. By the time he was eleven, he was working in an apothecary shop and in 1782, enlisted in the United States Navy as a surgeon's mate. His navy tenure was long enough to earn a pension and following the death of his father in 1795, he journeyed to England in a futile effort to find some trace of his brother. Upon his return to Philadelphia he married and went into the apothecary business.

Joshua named his one son after his father, who also joined the navy at age fourteen. After his naval service, the younger Morgan (1807?-1893) became an evangelist, in some cases using his grandfather's sermons, and was credited with over ten thousand conversions in the Midwest. In addition to Morgan, Joshua fathered five daughters. He was able to maintain good health until his death in 1854 at age eighty-nine.

Morgan Edwards served the First Baptist Church in Philadelphia for ten action-filled years. He immediately began to make improvements in the worship services, created a more orderly discipline, recruited new ministers, became involved in the community and associational life and attracted many new people through his preaching.

Because of his Welsh love of singing, Edwards led the congregation to purchase their own Psalters for congregational singing and hired a chorister to lead them. He also instituted changes in the observance of the ordinances and the collection of pew rentals. The most startling change came when the congregation voted to raze their meetinghouse and replace it with a new and larger one seating several hundred people.

Edwards brought a new dimension of order and compassion to the process of church discipline. In addition, a long-standing restriction on women's participation in the life of the church was set aside during Edwards' tenure.[21] He gave the church a higher visibility in the city by his teaching at the College of Philadelphia and becoming friends with such civic leaders such as Benjamin Franklin.

Morgan Edwards was one of the truly great preachers in his time. He meticulously prepared every sermon, wrote out a full manuscript, but never read his sermons. His delivery was slow and deliberate and he wore a gown in the pulpit. Edwards held the attention of his hearers by what he said and the way he said it. Undoubtedly his most famous sermon was the so-called death sermon, which came about from the circumstances of his wife's death.

Mary Edwards died on August 16, 1769, during her eighth pregnancy. She, Edwards once stated, was "very near and dear to me."[22] She had previously told her husband in Cork that she had a premonition she would die in her eighth pregnancy—and she did. The experience reinforced Morgan's own premonition that he

---

[21] [As Stewart explains in his fuller biography of Edwards, just before the death of Jenkin Jones, a business meeting was held under the leadership of Deacon Samuel Davis which rescinded the right of women to vote in church affairs. On appeal, Edwards restored their voting rights, which they previously held for many years. See *A Dazzling Enigma*, 167-168 — *Ed.*]

[22] Morgan Edwards, *A New Year's Gift* (Newport, RI: Solomon Southwick, 1770), 8.

would die on March 1, 1770. In confidence he shared that experience with Ebenezer Gibbons, but Gibbons told others about it and it soon became common knowledge. Thus, as the year 1770 approached, the level of interest in his death was increasing. The circumstances of his wife's death only intensified the interest and the gossip.

To offset the ghoulish cloud developing around him, Edwards decided to clarify the matter in a sermon on January 1, 1770, he called "A New Year's Gift." It was a sermon in which he urged people to receive God's gift of grace in Christ immediately because no one knew the day of their death. He included a reference to his own premonition as he spoke of others having a similar experience. Some later writers and historians have unfairly accused Edwards of preaching his own funeral sermon, but a reading of the sermon belies that assertion.

A little over a year and a half after that sermon, Edwards submitted his resignation as pastor on July 8, 1771, in order to accept a position as an evangelist for the Philadelphia Baptist Association that fall.[23] He had been moderator of the association and its long-time clerk. His keeping the minutes of the church and as clerk of the association brought a level of accuracy not known before. At his suggestion, a fund to support a traveling evangelist was established by the Association in 1766. While serving as an evangelist himself for the Association in 1771-1772, he collected a wealth of historical data which he later used in writing a new type of history of the Baptists.[24]

Undoubtedly one of Morgan Edwards greatest achievements was leading the Philadelphia Association to found Rhode Island College (1764) and spending two years in the British Isles raising money for its support. The college later became Brown University. He produced our first manual on Baptist polity[25] and proposed a

---

[23] First Baptist Church, Philadelphia, Churchbook No. 2, July 8, 1771 entry, n.p.

[24] A. D. Gillette, ed., *Minutes of the Philadelphia Baptist Association, 1707-1807* (Philadelphia: American Baptist Publication Society, 1851), 97, 119, 124. Edwards' name is prominent throughout the associational minutes during this period. Of his proposed twelve volumes of "Materials Towards a History of the Baptists" (one for each province), only two, the one on Pennsylvania (1770) and the one on New Jersey (1792), were published during his lifetime.

[25] *The Customs of Primitive Churches; or A Set of Propositions Relative to the Name, Materials, Constitution, Power, Officers, Ordinances, Rites,*

plan for a national body which many years later influenced the organization of the General Missionary (or Triennial) Convention in 1814. Without question, Morgan Edwards was the dominant personality among the Baptists of America in the eighteenth century. Yet, for many years his loyalty to the crown has stained his reputation.

It is no secret that Morgan Edwards was still loyal to the British as the American colonies rushed toward their independence from the mother country. He did, however, publicly renounce that loyalty on August 7, 1775, a full eleven months before the signing of the Declaration of Independence. The chief reason he retained his loyalty was his desire to have the power of the crown to protect the freedom of Baptists to practice their faith. But Edwards has had two other issues which have dogged his steps down the road of Baptist history: alcohol and Universalism.

Morgan Edwards learned to use alcohol freely as a youth before his conversion. Following his conversion he ceased to be a heavy drinker, but continued the moderate use of wine on social occasions and periodic visits to the pubs. During a period following the death of his third wife,[26] the disappearance of his oldest son and the stress of health problems, he had one occasion when he over-imbibed in a pub. This was witnessed by a man who reported it to the Baptist church in Philadelphia. Edwards suffered a period of suspension of his membership for several years over that incident before being restored. He completely renounced all drinking following that experience.[27]

When Elhanan Winchester (1757-1797) was compelled to resign the pastorate of the Baptist church in Philadelphia in 1781, because he was preaching universalist doctrine, Edwards signed

---

Business, Worship, Discipline, Government, &c. of a Church. Philadelphia: Andrew Stewart, 1768.

[26] Twenty-one months after the death of his first wife Mary, Edwards was married to his second wife Elizabeth Singleton, on May 3, 1771. When she died the following year, he married the widow of Washington Nathaniel Evans of the Welsh Tract in Delaware in 1774. There is no record of her first name.

[27] Edwards reported to Samuel Jones (1735-1814), pastor of the Pennepek Baptist Church that he had made a firm commitment as of October 31, 1785, to abstain from further drinking, even in moderation. MS letter from Morgan Edwards to Samuel Jones, dated November 7, 1785. Jones Collection, John Hay Library, Brown University, D 2470.

the petition for his removal only as a protest against that doctrine, but not as support for Winchester's removal. This was later interpreted as agreement with Winchester's universalism. The truth is that Edwards was unequivocal in his denial of universalism and his signature on that petition made his disagreement clear. He did, however, know the pain of being forced to resign and that was why he reluctantly signed the petition.[28]

"A time to die"

The death of Morgan Edwards occurred on January 28, 1795, in his seventy-third year of life. He was interred with his first wife and deceased children under the aisle of the First Baptist Church in Philadelphia. A memorial service in his honor was held at the church on February 22, 1795. In 1860, his remains were trans-

---

[28] [In his funeral sermon preached on the occasion of Edwards' death, William Rogers stated,

> *A good report* our departed brother also had: the numerous letters brought with him across the Atlantic from the Rev. Dr. John Gill, and others, *reported* handsome things of him; and so did, in return, the letters that went from America to the then Parent Country. *Evil reports* also fell to his share; but most of these were false reports, and therefore he gave credit to them as a species of persecution: and even the title of a *Deceiver* did not escape him. Often has he been told that he was an Arminian, though he professed to be a Calvinist; that he was an Universalist in disguise, &c. yet, he was *true* to his principles. These may be seen in our confession of faith, agreeing with that republished by the Baptist churches assembled at London, in the year 1689. He seldom meddled with the five polemical points; but when he did, he always avoided abusive language. The charge of universalism brought against him was not altogether groundless; for though he was not an universalist himself, he professed a great regard for many who were, and he would sometimes take their part against violent opposers, in order to inculcate moderation.—Obituary for Morgan Edwards, in Rippon, *The Baptist Annual Register, for 1794, 1795, 1796-1797,* 309.

I have read in the manuscript sermons of Edwards where he did on occasion depart from certain aspects of what would be considered Calvinistic orthodoxy, but I agree with Stewart that he did not cross the line into Universalism—though he may be rightly criticized for his attachment to some of its advocates —*Ed.*]

ferred to Mount Moriah Cemetery on the southwestern edge of the city, after the church relocated to another site.

Morgan Edwards was undoubtedly *the* outstanding leader among American Baptists of the eighteenth-century. Indeed he may well have been our most outstanding leader to this day. Let history's judgment of his place among us be based on his contributions to our growth and development and not on his idiosyncrasies. He was at times an enigma, but a dazzling one to be sure.

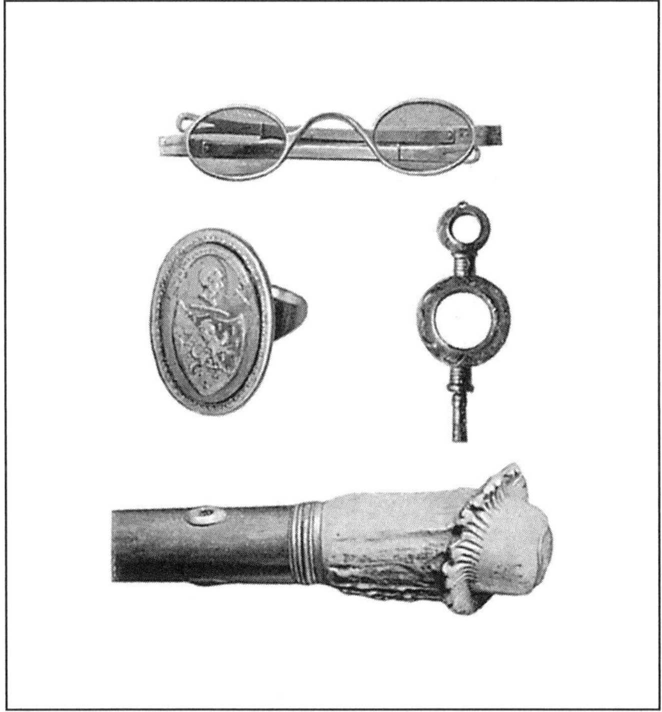

A collection of items which belonged to Morgan Edwards: green spectacles, seal ring, watch-key, and cane.

Further Reading

Howard R. Stewart. *A Dazzling Enigma. The Story of Morgan Edwards.* Lanham, MD: University Press of America, Inc., 1995.

Thomas R. McKibbens, Jr. and Kenneth L. Smith. *The Life and Works of Morgan Edwards.* New York: Arno Press. 1980.

Morgan Edwards, *The Customs of Primitive Churches; or A Set of Propositions Relative to the Name, Materials, Constitution, Power, Officers, Ordinances, Rites, Business, Worship, Discipline, Government, &c. of a Church.* Philadelphia: Printed by Andrew Stewart, 1768.

Eve B. Weeks and Mary B. Warren, eds. *Materials Towards a History of the Baptists. By Morgan Edwards, A.M.* Danielsville, GA: Heritage Papers, 1984. Two volumes.

Abram D. Gillette, ed. *Minutes of the Philadelphia Baptist Association, 1707-1807.* Philadelphia: American Baptist Publication Society, 1851; reprinted Tricentennial Edition with new comprehensive indexes, maps and illustrations, Springfield, MO: Particular Baptist Press, 2002.

William W. Keen. *The Bi-Centennial Celebration of the Founding of the First Baptist Church in the City of Philadelphia, 1698-1898.* Philadelphia: American Baptist Publication Society, 1899.

MATURIN BALLOU
1722 - 1804

by Terry Wolever

Unlike many of the other essays in this volume, this study was not born out of a sense of Maturin Ballou's greatness among his contemporaries, for he was not counted as such, at least as far as we know this side of glory. But rather his life's experience is related out of the need to portray the example of a godly pastor who went about his Master's business in a faithful but unheralded way in a small field. Here one will find an account of the trials of a subsistence living, coupled with a sad but not uncommon occurrence among such faithful ministers—the apostasy of their own children. Perhaps others who have found themselves in just such a situation will be benefited in some way by this minister's story.

Ancestry and early ministry in Rhode Island

Maturin (mă tū′ rĭn) Ballou was born at Smithfield, Providence County, Rhode Island on Tuesday October 30, 1722,[1] the fifth child and eldest son of eleven children born to Peter and Rebecca (née Esten) Ballou. Peter Ballou (1689-1754), by occupation a farmer and cooper, was said to have been "a very conscientious and morally exemplary man."[2] Peter's father, John Ballou, was recognized by the General Assembly in 1684 for his services during the Indian War. Maturin's great-grandfather of the same name, Mathurin (the original *h* being silent) Bellau (b. 1632) with his wife Hannah (née Pike) came to settle in Providence, Rhode Island as early as 1646 and was quite possibly a French Huguenot.[3]

---

[1] Thomas Whittemore, *Life of Rev. Hosea Ballou; with Accounts of His Writings* (Boston: James M. Usher, 1854), 18. Much of what we know about Maturin Ballou must necessarily be drawn from the biographies written on his famous son, the Universalist Hosea Ballou (1771-1852).

[2] Hosea S. Ballou, *Hosea Ballou, 2d, D.D., First President of Tufts College: His Origin, Life, and Letters* (Boston: E. P. Guild and Co., 1896), 14.

[3] *Ibid.*, 11, 13; Adin Ballou, ed., *An Elaborate History of the Ballous in America* (1888), vi; hereafter cited as *History of the Ballous in America*. Hosea S. Ballou dismissed the claim made by Adin Ballou that Mathurin

Very little is known of Maturin's childhood. But in adulthood he was described as having become "a large man" in stature, "with a peculiar native grace in his air."[4] He also excelled as a horseman. It was said that all of his sons were good horsemen, "but Rev. Maturin was accounted a better horseman still."[5]

Maturin Ballou was married while in his early twenties to Lydia Harris (1725-1773), daughter of the Quaker Richard Harris, at Smithfield in 1744. Together they would have eleven children, with the first nine being born in Rhode Island: 1) Mary, born October 30, 1745, at Smithfield; 2) Benjamin, born November 8, 1747, at Smithfield; 3) Amey, born June 6, 1750, at Smithfield, who died at age six in 1756; 4) Lydia, born October 21, 1752, at Smithfield; 5) Maturin, Jr., born July 8, 1755, at Pawtucket, who died at age 35; 6) David, born September 15, 1758, at Pawtucket; 7) Nathan, born September 9, 1760, at Scituate; 8) Sarah, born May 4, 1763, at Scituate; 9) Phoebe, born May 24, 1765, at Scituate, who died as a young woman at the age of 20; 10) Stephen, born September 1768, at Richmond, New Hampshire; and 11) Hosea, born April 30, 1771, also at Richmond.[6]

Maturin Ballou appears to have been the first preacher in the family. He received no formal theological training that we are aware of, but that was not uncommon among pastors of rural churches in that day. He was "strictly Calvinistic in his opinions," wrote one author, and "a very affectionate parent," who "fervently desired the conversion of his children."[7] His first three pastorates were all within his native state of Rhode Island, being first settled

---

Bellau was of Norman-English ancestry from the time of William the Conqueror.

[4] Hosea S. Ballou, *Hosea Ballou, 2d*, 15.

[5] *Ibid.*

[6] Whittemore, *Life of Rev. Hosea Ballou*, 18, 23-27; Maturin M. Ballou, *Biography of Rev. Hosea Ballou. By his youngest son* (Boston: Abel Tompkins, 1852), 17-18; Oscar F. Safford, *Hosea Ballou: A Marvellous Life-Story* (Boston: Universalist Publishing House, 1889), 17*n*. Maturin Murray Ballou (1820-1895), named after both his grandfather and the Universalist John Murray (1741-1815), was the founding editor of *The Boston Globe* newspaper. To avoid confusion, hereafter when naming Maturin M. Ballou in this essay, I'll refer to him as M. M. Ballou.

[7] Whittemore, *Life of Rev. Hosea Ballou*, 41.

briefly as pastor of the Baptist church at Smithfield, from 1752-1753, then for five years as pastor at Pawtucket, 1754-1759, and lastly at Scituate, 1759-1768.[8]

In the fall of 1767, Ballou made a journey to the site of the new community of Richmond, New Hampshire, where he purchased 80 acres of uncleared land that October for £15.[9] Here he removed with his wife Lydia and eight of their children from Scituate, probably in the spring of 1768. The oldest son, Benjamin, now 21, chose to remain at Scituate.

The new field at Richmond, New Hampshire

The town of Richmond was first chartered in 1735, though under a different name. When New Hampshire became a separate colony, the town was incorporated under its present name in 1752, but it was not until the year 1762, in the words of one historian, that "the tide of emigration commenced in force" to the area.[10]

Oscar Safford has well summarized the likely motivations behind Ballou's decision to remove to this new community:

> We may wonder, indeed, that Rev. Maturin Ballou, in middle life, with a large family already dependent upon him, should voluntarily become a resident of this almost unbroken wilderness. He was, we conjecture, influenced mainly by two motives. It was natural for him, in the first place, to desire to secure for his children a better worldly prospect than he had himself inherited. This he might hope

---

[8] Frederick L. Weis, *The Colonial Clergy and the Colonial Churches of New England* (Lancaster, MA: The Society of the Descendants of the Colonial Clergy, 1936), 26-27 (with some changes); Safford, *Hosea Ballou*, 16. "Shortly after the birth of [David Ballou], the family removed to Scituate, R.I., and settled in that part of the town now known as Foster." Whittemore, *Life of Rev. Hosea Ballou*, 18.

[9] Adin Ballou, *History of the Ballous in America*, 67.

[10] William Bassett, *History of the Town of Richmond, Cheshire County, New Hampshire, from its First Settlement, to 1882* (Boston: C. W. Calkins and Company, 1884), 10. The town's former name was Sylvester-Canada, in honor of Capt. Joseph Sylvester of Scituate, Massachusetts, who died in the 1690 assault on Quebec. Richmond was renamed by Governor Benning Wentworth after Charles Lennox (1735-1806), 3rd Duke of Richmond, who strongly advocated colonial independence.

> to do by becoming a landholder in a pioneer settlement. The other motive we find in the attraction of the family tie. Among the first settlers were Anthony and Uriah Harris, brothers of his wife, also two of her sisters and their families, all Baptists. . . .With such neighbors to offer welcome, it was reasonable for him to hope a forest-home would not be altogether lonely. When Mr. Ballou and his wife Lydia visited their kindred in the wilds they were, we easily conjecture, earnestly invited to cast their lot with the invaders of the wilderness. Still another motive may have had strong influence—perhaps even the strongest—with the Baptist preacher; namely, his desire to establish in the new country a Baptist church. He had been a Baptist preacher fifteen years. He was now forty-five; when he was thirty, with a large family looking to him for sustenance, and without special education, he had entered on his chosen vocation. He had preached the Baptist doctrine successively at Smithfield, Pawtucket, and Scituate, in Rhode Island. It is superfluous to say he had not found his path of life free from anxieties. We assume that in the prospect opening before him at Richmond to found the second Baptist church in New Hampshire, he saw promise of a continuance of the same life-struggle. For the sake of his children he was with this prospect content.[11]

Ample testimony has been given respecting Ballou's Christian deportment. One of his grandsons remembered him as being "remarkable for his unostentatious manner, his forgiving spirit and meekness, and the strict consistency of a life devoted, as he truly believed, to the service and glory of his Divine Master."[12] Another grandson said he had "the reputation of great gentleness, goodness, and piety; was respected and much esteemed; but was not eminent as a public speaker."[13] Not *eminent*, perhaps, but was nevertheless, "a devout and eloquent preacher of the Scriptures."[14]

---

[11] Safford, *Hosea Ballou*, 15-16.

[12] M. M. Ballou, *Biography of Rev. Hosea Ballou*, 16.

[13] Hosea S. Ballou, *Hosea Ballou, 2d*, 15.

[14] M. M. Ballou, *Biography of Rev. Hosea Ballou*, 28.

Two years after Ballou's arrival at Richmond, the Baptist church was formally constituted. He was ordained as pastor on September 27, 1770.[15] Divine services were initially held at his home and "sometimes at Deacon Simeon Thayer's, and at Elder Artemas Aldrich's," until the first meetinghouse was built in 1780.[16] The land for the building was conveyed to the church by Hezekiah Man. This meetinghouse was well constructed and sturdy. It was described by the town's historian in 1884 in this manner:

> The building is thirty by forty feet, of solid oak timber of huge dimensions, and would last another century if protected from the weather. The interior arrangement was patterned after the style of the period, with high pulpit, in front of which was the deacon's seat. It has square box pews, and galleries on three sides, with no fireplace or other provision for warming. The town altered and repaired the house in 1884, at an expense of $150. The box pews were removed and benches substituted instead, was plastered overhead, a chimney built, and stove put in.[17]

In addition to clearing and farming their land, Maturin Ballou derived the family's income from teaching school and making spinning wheels.[18] It was his conscientious belief "that he ought

---

[15] John Asplund, *The Annual Register of the Baptist Denomination in North America; to the First of November, 1790* (n.p., preface dated Southampton County, VA, 1791), 10; Isaac Backus, *A History of New England, with Particular Reference to the Denomination of Christians Called Baptists.* Second Edition, with Notes by David Weston (Newton, MA: Backus Historical Society, 1871), 2: 539.

[16] Bassett, *History of the Town of Richmond*, 223. Deacon Thayer would later embrace Universalism. See Safford, *Hosea Ballou*, 44.

[17] Bassett, *History of the Town of Richmond*, 185-186. An illustration of this meetinghouse appears on page 185. Bassett explains that the town had an interest in maintaining the meetinghouse because since August 1782, town meetings were also held there.

[18] Adin Ballou, *History of the Ballous in America*, 66. Hosea Ballou informs us that his father Maturin Ballou had "taught a large school and had good compensation" at Foster, Rhode Island. M. M. Ballou, *Biography of Rev. Hosea Ballou*, 58.

Maturin Ballou's homestead at Richmond, New Hampshire.

not to receive any remuneration whatever, either pecuniary or otherwise," for his ministerial services. Consequently, "as he devoted himself with the utmost zeal and the most untiring assiduity to his calling, and was possessed of little or no personal estate, his family were all obliged to labor very hard, merely to obtain a simple subsistence."[19] Though the Apostle Paul himself had chosen this same course,[20] still under divine inspiration he had also given the prescribed standard whereby "the Lord ordained that they which preach the gospel should live of the gospel" (1 Cor. 9:14), which follows what Jesus had previously told His disciples, "the laborer is worthy of his hire" (or wages), Luke 10:7. Thus Maturin Ballou may have placed himself and his family under an unnecessary hardship. After all, as far as we know, the Apostle Paul had no wife or family to care for.

Then again, it could just be, in Ballou's case, that due to the circumstances of the time and place in which he labored, the members of his church may have been in dire straits themselves, which compelled him from the kindness of his heart not to seek their support. This would seem to be suggested by the following statements by a grandson of Maturin Ballou, who though a Universalist and not sympathetic to his grandfather's views, preserved this tribute to the Baptist minister's self-denial:

> The character of [Maturin Ballou] reminds us of one of those stern old Cameronians of Scotland,[21] so well described by one of the first writers of the age. With but little sympathy for his creed, we must nevertheless respect his sincerity; nor can we wonder at all, with his education in the faith which he preached, and hampered by the illiberal spirit of the period, which seemed to mildew every generous prompting of the human heart, that he clung to it with inflexible tenacity. But we must contemplate with unqualified admiration the heroic self-denial, the martyr-like firmness, with which this servant of the Lord pursued what he believed to be the path of his duty, amidst circumstances of such extraordinary deprivation. Truly, he abandoned all to serve

---

[19] M. M. Ballou, *Biography of Rev. Hosea Ballou*, 24.

[20] 1 Cor. 4:11-12; 9:3-18.

[21] As the followers of the Scottish Covenanter Richard Cameron (? -1680), who were Reformed Presbyterians, came to be known.

> his Master. His severest trial must have been to witness the privations of his family. A man can endure in his own person what it costs him agony to witness inflicted on those nearer and dearer to him than life itself.
>
> * * * * *
>
> This is probably by no means an isolated case of trial. It is but a type of the condition of many of the early settlers in a new country,—in short, a picture of American pioneer life. It is from such beginnings, and under such circumstances, that the most useful and energetic of our countrymen have sprung. It is not to the lap of luxury that we are to look for the source of manly character and virtues.[22]

In any event, the hardships of the family were very real. For example, when writing of Hosea Ballou, their youngest son, one biographer noted that

> from his earliest childhood, Mr. Ballou was accustomed to toil and labor, and this too under the hardships of a scanty supply of food and clothing. So destitute even of the most ordinary articles of raiment, or the means of procuring it, was his father's family, in the times of his boyhood, that many a long week has he passed without an under garment of any kind upon his person, and without shoes or stockings for his feet, even during the inclemencies of winter, when his employment would frequently call him abroad for a large portion of the day![23]

Even so, the home had love, and with that love a most valuable possession—the Word of God, as Hosea's biographer goes on to tell us:

> Some further idea of the limited means of his father's family, and the extraordinary disadvantages under which his early progress was made, may be gathered from the fact, that the only books the house contained, or in fact that the family had access to at all, were a Bible, an old dictionary,

---

[22] M. M. Ballou, *Biography of Rev. Hosea Ballou,* 25-26. There is some indication that Ballou had previously followed this practice during his pastorates in Rhode Island as well.

[23] *Ibid.*, 24-25.

> and a well-thumbed pamphlet of the scriptural story of the tower of Babel. A newspaper in the days of which we write, in the town of Richmond, would have been considered a most rare curiosity. . . .It has been remarked of the sacred volume, that as the face of nature is bedecked with colors and adornments to render it agreeable to the senses, so its pages are filled with that luxury of poetry and language and incident which commends it to every imagination. . . .Need we count that house poor in literary possessions which contains a Bible?[24]

Along with their everyday struggles on their farms, the Ballous and other Baptists had to endure the religious persecution from their immediate neighbors. On September 10-12, 1771, Maturin Ballou attended the annual meeting of the Warren Baptist Association, held at Sutton, Massachusetts, where his church was received into the membership.[25] In its letter to the Association that year, the Richmond church explained the nature of this opposition while at the same time making an appeal for counsel:

> We request some special advice on several occasions: for we are young in such cases, for we meet with great opposition in our province, and the main point of their objection is, they say our settlement is not according to law, so that they threaten to pay no regard to our certificates given to our brethren living in other towns. Another particular is, it is so ordered in our charter by the king's grant, that one whole share of land shall be given to the Church of England, one whole share to the incorporated society to propagate the gospel in foreign parts, and one whole share to the first settled minister of the gospel in said town. These are the express words in the charter of our town. Our elder being the first, we think it belongs to him, but being opposed by the inhabitants of the town of other denominations, we ask your advice, what we had best do. Further, there are a number of brethren in the town of Rindge, in our province, who are embodied in church state, with government and

---

[24] *Ibid.*, 30-31.

[25] *Minutes of the Warren Association, Held at Sutton, In the Province of Massachusetts-Bay, September, MDCCLXXI* (Boston: Printed by John Broyles, in Marlborough Street, 1771), title page.

> articles of faith agreeable to ours, and are under our care to assist them in administering the ordinances of the gospel. These brethren have suffered much by the inhabitants of their town, who have taken away their cattle and sold them at the post for their minister's rates, and they are threatened still to be used in like manner; they require us to make request for them, what they had best do. [26]

At this time and for many years afterwards, dissenters from the Congregational Standing Order in New England were required to pay an assessed rate to support the local parish's appointed Congregational minister and the upkeep of his meetinghouse, even though they might never attend services there. When the Baptists, Quakers and others refused to pay these rates from their already meager annual incomes, the Congregationalists, in conjunction with the local authorities, would confiscate their livestock or other property to sell and thereby collect the money. The Association responded to the Richmond church's letter by requesting that James Manning, president of Rhode Island College, write to Hezekiah Smith of Haverhill (who was the agent appointed by the Association to seek redress from government officials in such cases), to see if a remedy might be had to their situation. The letter read as follows:

> Newport, May 1, 1771.
>
> Dear Sir:
>
> I perceive, by an application made to a neighboring Baptist church, that the people in Richmond, in Hampshire Government (I mean the Baptist church there), are in great distress on account of the taxes for the clergy; and so are the Baptists in sundry other towns thereabouts. The charter gave a farm to the first settled minister in that town; and Mr. Ballow, the Baptist minister, was the first, though a Friend [or Quaker] speaker was there before him. Now the Friends have united with the Presbyterians,[27] and voted the farm for the use of the town. Upon the whole they seem troubled much, and some are likely to be totally ruined by

---

[26] Backus, *A History of New England*, 2: 539.

[27] It was not uncommon for writers of the period to use the term Presbyterians for Congregationalists, as Manning does here, when he is actually referring to the Congregationalists at Richmond.

the Presbyterians. Now if you can lend any aid or assistance, you will do them a singular favor; and I have been urged to write to you, that, if possible, you might make interest with the Governor, or some of the great men, to redress these grievances. I received a letter from Mr. Edwards, dated March, which informs me that he has a law of New Hampshire which obliges the Baptists to pay their ministers,—that is, Presbyterian ministers,—and he is greatly afraid they will fall into the snare. Pray do your utmost to prevent the Baptists from taking the benefit of that law; for the Presbyterians will triumph in that case. Mr. Rogers, the bearer, will give you information of my affairs, and other matters in these parts; so that nothing remains but to desire you with Mrs. Smith to pay us a visit soon, to whom with yourself I give my sincere love, and remain, sir,

Your very loving friend,

James Manning.[28]

Ballou's name regularly appears in the subsequent minutes of the Warren Association, but he seems to have been unable due to his circumstances to attend the annual sessions very often. Between 1772 and 1790 (when he is last listed as pastor at Richmond), he was only present at four meetings.[29]

Great sorrow befell the Ballou home in 1773, when Lydia Ballou passed away. "My mother died when I was about two years old, and, of course, I do not remember her," wrote Hosea, their youngest child, "but from all I can learn of my mother, I am satisfied that she was of a most tender and kind disposition. But the treasure was gone before I could realize its value."[30] Maturin Ballou's grandson, M. M. Ballou, youngest son of Hosea Ballou, says that after her death,

---

[28] Reuben A. Guild, *Life, Times, and Correspondence of James Manning, and the Early History of Brown University* (Boston: Gould and Lincoln, 1864), 186-187. What specifically came of this effort I have not discovered.

[29] The years in which he was present besides 1771 were 1774, 1777, 1780 and 1787. For a record of the proceedings see Terry Wolever, ed. *Minutes of the Warren Baptist Association. Volume One: The First Sixty Years 1767-1827*. Springfield, MO: Particular Baptist Press, to be printed, D.V., 2013.

[30] M. M. Ballou, *Biography of Rev. Hosea Ballou*, 22.

> The care and guidance of the family then fell upon the father, whose means for providing for his children's necessities were of the most simple and limited character. This parent, a pious and devout preacher of the Calvinistic Baptist denomination, endeavored, to the best of his ability, to bring up his large family to fear and serve a God who was merciful to those whom from all eternity he had elected to be heirs of eternal life, but who was full of holy wrath towards the greater portion of mankind;—a faith which the honest parent little thought, at the time, his youngest son...would so successfully battle against in the spiritual warfare of after years.[31]

In the year following the death of his first wife, Maturin Ballou was married to Lydia Bliss on September 15, 1774. There were no children from this second marriage.

In 1775, the church at Richmond became divided over the controversy concerning ministerial taxes and glebe lands, with the result that a second Baptist church was formed, with Artemas Aldrich as pastor.[32] Their meetings at first were likely held at Aldrich's house. About four years later, the town of Richmond experienced a great revival in which about forty persons were added to the membership of the two churches.[33] Though the First Church received but a small percentage of these, it still reported a total of 83 members to the Warren Association that September.[34]

Ballou was able from time to time to itinerate to some of the nearby towns and settlements. He occasionally preached to the

---

[31] *Ibid.*, 22-23.

[32] Bassett, *History of the Town of Richmond*, 223, 227; Asplund, *The Annual Register of the Baptist Denomination in North America*, 10. The First Baptist Church is shown in 1790 with 65 members, the Second with 45. Bassett has the date of the Second church's constitution as being in 1776, Asplund as 1775.

[33] *Ibid.*, 227.

[34] *Minutes of the Warren Association, in their Meeting at Royalstone, [Massachusetts,] September 12th and 13th, 1780* (Boston: n.p., 1780), 2. According to the Associational minutes, First Baptist had 79 members in 1778, so it would appear that the great majority of the new converts in 1780 were added to the membership of Second Baptist. The Second church was never connected with the Warren Association.

believers at Dublin, New Hampshire, until a Baptist church was organized there on December 7, 1785.[35] And on November 12, 1787, Ballou assisted in organizing the Baptist church at Putney, Vermont. This latter event proved to be more significant, in that he was one of the nine constituting members and was chosen the church's first minister. Over the next few years he would alternate his time between here and First Richmond.[36]

David and Hosea Ballou's descent into error

We now come to a series of events that must touch the heart of any true Christian and even more so the heart of a loving parent who would naturally desire that their children would come to know and worship the Lord in spirit and in truth (John 4:24). The leaven of Universalist teaching that was to eventually lead four of Maturin's sons astray (three during his lifetime and one after his decease), began with his son David Ballou (1758-1840).

In the winter of 1788-1789, the community of Richmond experienced the beginnings of another spiritual awakening. Many souls were converted and the saints much encouraged. In addition to this genuine work of God, however, serious error had also entered the town through the influence of Caleb Rich (1750-1821). Rich came to Richmond after being excluded by the Baptist church at nearby Warwick, Massachusetts, for his ecstatic visions. Among other things, he claimed to have had visions of personal visits by a "spirit guide" and on another occasion by an angel. After embracing Universalism, Rich then founded his "New Religious Society" at Warwick in 1773, believed to be the first Universalist church organized in America.[37] One writer has suggested that he "gave the first impulse to Universalism in the northern section of

---

[35] Charles Mason, et al., *The History of Dublin, N.H., containing the Address by Charles Mason, and the Proceedings at the Centennial Celebration, June 17, 1852; with a Register of Families* (Boston: John Wilson and Son, 1855), 190. Maturin and his son Maturin, Jr. attended the church's constitution representing Richmond's First Baptist Church.

[36] Henry Crocker, *History of the Baptists in Vermont* (Bellows Falls, VT: The P. H. Gobie Press, 1913), 209.

[37] John Murray's church in Gloucester, Massachusetts, is often credited with being the first such organization, but only because Rich's congregation had no legal status.

Massachusetts and the southwestern section of New Hampshire."[38]

In 1781, Rich was ordained as minister not only at Warwick but to two other such organizations established in Richmond and Jaffrey, New Hampshire. "By the Baptists in general, the elder was regarded as an apostate, and the sentiments which he cherished were denounced as the rankest heresy," wrote Whittemore.[39] Yet there were some gullible hearers. Safford informs us:

> Among the persons in Richmond who gave credence to the message of Rev. Caleb Rich were Mr. James Ballou, and his sons James, Jr., and Silas. There was a distant relationship between this family and that of Rev. Maturin Ballou, ranging somewhere in the second or third degree of cousinship. These Ballous became champions of the heresy preached by Rev. Caleb Rich.[40]

Universalism teaches that every person who has ever lived will ultimately be redeemed by God. As with all such pseudo-Christian movements, Universalists embrace a host of other serious errors as well, including a denial of the Trinity and with it the deity of Christ, His vicarious atonement, imputed righteousness and the depravity of mankind, among others. Samuel Bigelow (1738-1807), pastor of the Baptist church at New Salem, Massachusetts, rightly concluded that universal salvation was "completely calculated to suit the carnal mind." By the summer of 1789, David Ballou, at the age of 30, had been won over to their arguments.[41] He would play an important role in the course of the next few years in establishing his younger brother Hosea in Universalism.

Hosea Ballou had already been engaging the above-named cousins and some other townsmen on the subject, at first defending the orthodox position of his father, while at the same time wrestling with his own doubts. Hosea's skepticism regarding the faith he was taught in the home and church at Richmond began when he was a boy. He surely had some honest questions

---

[38] Whittemore, *Life of Rev. Hosea Ballou*, 46.

[39] *Ibid.*

[40] Safford, *Hosea Ballou*, 32.

[41] *Ibid.*, 38.

and no one would doubt his sincerity, but still they proceeded from a heart of unbelief, a heart unrenewed by the grace of God. Hosea recalled,

> I was remarkably inquisitive, even when a mere boy, about doctrines. I was fond of reasoning on doctrinal points, studied and talked much upon the subject of free will and necessity. I well remember to have surprised my honored father with such a question as the following: 'Suppose I had the skill and power out of an inanimate substance to make an animate, and should make one, at the same time knowing that this creature of mine would suffer everlasting misery,—would my act of creating this creature be an act of goodness?' The question troubled my father, and I let it pass without an answer.[42]

The question troubled his father, we presume, not because it presented an insurmountable difficulty, but because his son was questioning the goodness of God, in creating those sinners whom he knew would never be saved.[43] This may be reasonably deduced from the second quotation, following. Hosea had been taught aright, but could not reconcile himself to his own depravity nor to the depravity of all men—nor indeed to the distinguishing grace of God. He wrote,

> We were all taught, and in our youth all believed, that we were born into the world wholly depraved, and under the curse of a law which doomed every son and daughter of Adam to eternal woe. But at the same time God had made provision for a select number of the human family, whereby they would be saved by the operations of the divine Spirit, which would result in what was called conversion, sometime during the life of those elected. Those who were not elected would remain without any effectual calling, die, and be forever miserable.[44]

---

[42] M. M. Ballou, *Biography of Rev. Hosea Ballou*, 36.

[43] The Apostle Paul deals with this very objection in Romans chapter 9.

[44] *Ibid.*, 23. Hosea Ballou went on to remark that "When I was a youth it was the sentiment of all Christian people, as far as I knew, that not more than one in a thousand of the human family would be saved from endless condemnation." I have never met with such a sentiment or statement in

Hosea Ballou's skepticism of the teaching under which he was raised understandably caused his father no little anxiety for his son's spiritual state, as M. M. Ballou tells us:

> These frequent questions had the effect of causing the father much uneasiness of mind, and he used often to express great solicitude and fear for the present and future welfare of his son. Many were his endeavors to convince Hosea of the dangerous character of the sentiments that seemed to be springing up spontaneously in his heart, but the unprofitable nature of these efforts soon became apparent, from the fact that the simple, natural arguments of the son confounded the father. Boy as he was, he would not take the assertions of faith for argument, but insisted upon reason, and understanding at all times the 'root of the matter.'[45]

This last sentence is very telling. Hosea Ballou, according to his son, M. M. Ballou, *would not take the assertions of faith for argument, but insisted upon reason, and understanding at all times the "root of the matter."* This has ever been the way of the skeptics we have known. If all of their questions fail to be answered to their own satisfaction on a spiritual matter, they will not receive it as truth! This calls again to mind the words of Samuel Stennett (1728-1795), who wrote,

> What men do not care to believe they will take pains to persuade themselves it is not true. They will employ all their ingenuity to find out objections, and having cast them with great eagerness into the opposite scale to positive unexamined evidence, will at length pronounce confidently against the truth, and in favour of error. Such is the manner of the world, and thus do men impose upon themselves in a

---

all the literature I have read by Christians from this period. Universalists will often make these spurious claims and draw such stark contrasts in their writings in order to arrest the reader's attention when confronting Calvinistic theology, which to them is their greatest foe. Here we "which believe and know the truth" (1 Tim. 4:3), must bear in mind the prophetic warning of the Apostle Peter that "there shall be false teachers among you, who privily shall bring in damnable heresies....And many shall follow their pernicious ways; by reason of whom the way of truth shall be evil spoken of" (2 Peter 2:1-2). Universalism is just such a heresy.

[45] M. M. Ballou, *Biography of Rev. Hosea Ballou*, 36-37.

> thousand questions, civil and religious, which thwart their inclinations.[46]

In Hosea Ballou's case, this was due to the fact that in reality he was still unconverted—he had not that faith which is "the substance of things hoped for, the evidence of things not seen" (Heb. 11:1). And we know that "the natural man receiveth not the things of the Spirit of God: for they are foolishness unto him: neither can he know them, because they are spiritually discerned" (1 Cor. 2:14). Though his son's questions may indeed have 'confounded' him at the time, Maturin Ballou nonetheless had a God-given faith that he himself was yet in the way of true righteousness. This gave him a spirit of humble forbearance as he lovingly sought to recover his sons from error. He chose not to cut-off his sons and disown them, but to seek the Lord for His mercy and their recovery. "To the honor of this truly pious and devout parent, it should be remembered," remarked M. M. Ballou, "that these controversies never elicited an unchristian spirit, or the least anger towards the child. This was a natural and beautiful characteristic of his father's disposition."[47]

Hosea Ballou's profession of faith and subsequent exclusion from the Richmond church

Hosea Ballou at the age of 17 made what can only be termed a spurious profession of faith in January 1789, during the revival in Richmond. This is conceded even by his own biographers, one of whom wrote this about the subject:

> there being what was termed a reformation in the town of Richmond, [Hosea] Ballou was induced, believing it to be his duty, to become a professor of religion, and accordingly at that time he joined the Baptist church, of which his father was pastor, in the month of January, 1789. It is very evident that he was partly induced to this circumstance by the bearing of external circumstances and the immediate associations about him, such as observing the conduct of others of his own age, who at that time made a formal and

---

[46] Samuel Stennett, *Discourses on the Parable of the Sower* (London: A. Rivington and J. Marshall, 1787), 259-260.

[47] M. M. Ballou, *Biography of Rev. Hosea Ballou*, 37.

> public profession of faith, and also by what he knew very well to be his father's earnest desire. It seems, therefore, that these matters, rather than any earnest mental conviction of faith, were instrumental in leading him to join the church as he did,—inasmuch as none of those objections which he had often made to his father's belief, had yet been cleared up to his mind.[48]

Hosea Ballou's brother Stephen, as well as their father, sought to turn his mind from speculations into the right path. Hosea Ballou in his own words tells of one such effort:

> In the spring following my union with the Baptist Church, I went with my brother Stephen, next older than myself, who had joined the church a short time after me, to Hartford, in New York, then called Westfield, where we spent the summer. In this town there was a Baptist congregation, enjoying the pastoral labors of Elder Brown, on whose ministry we attended.[49] My brother was apprehensive that my mind was inclined to Universalism, and told me that he had a desire that I should converse with Elder Brown on the subject, by which means he hoped I should become fully convinced that the doctrine was false, and be more settled in the belief of which I had made profession. There was, at my brother's request, a conference appointed for Elder Brown to convince me that I ought to give no heed to the doctrine which labored in my mind. Accordingly we met. The Elder requested me to turn to some passage of Scripture which appeared to me favorable to Universalism, promising to do his endeavors to show me the error of applying it in favor of such a doctrine. I opened to the fifth chapter of Romans. I directed him to the eighteenth verse,[50] and told him I was

---

[48] *Ibid.*, 38. Hosea Ballou's own words were: "At this time I became more specially attentive to the subject of religion, and thought it my duty to become a professor, and to join the church, which I did, in the sincerity of my heart, in the month of January, 1789." Whittemore, *Life of Rev. Hosea Ballou*, 49.

[49] The church at Westfield, New York, had been formed not long before, in 1788. Amasa Brown was the pastor. Asplund, *The Annual Register of the Baptist Denomination in North America*, 18.

[50] Romans 5:18 reads: "Therefore as by the offense of one judgment came upon all men to condemnation; even so by the righteousness of one the

> unable to understand the passage if it agreed with the doctrine of the eternal reprobation of any of the human family [i.e. that any would be eternally lost]. He immediately began, in his way, to speak very loudly, and nothing to the subject. When he would stop, I had only to inform him that what he had offered had no relation to the text I had produced; and, by showing him that the same *all men* who were under condemnation in the first member of the text were under justification in the last, evidently confused his mind, and immediately turned it sour. He was no longer able to converse with a right spirit, and prudence dictated a discontinuance. My brother grew more uneasy, and told me he was sorry I had conversed with Elder Brown; 'for,' said he, 'as he could by no means answer you, and as he manifested anger, you will think you had the best of the argument, and will feel encouraged to indulge favorable thoughts of Universalism.'[51]

Stephen was right—for this was the result. Even its advocates have said that at this period "Universalism was but little known,"[52] and it is no wonder that numbers of our ministers at the time expressed some bewilderment in confronting it. In addition, the Universalists themselves at this early stage were not agreed as to what their own doctrinal views were. Still, it could not be said that Pastor Brown handled the situation well at all. A young man came to him with honest questions and with a non-combative disposition. If Brown could not speak directly to the subject at that time, he should have been willing to humbly acknowledge the fact

---

free gift came upon all men unto justification of life." This verse is a cardinal text to Universalists. But when set within the entire context of Romans chapter 5, the teaching of Paul becomes plain: as all in Adam are under condemnation, so all those in Christ are justified by His righteousness unto eternal life. This justification comes through the free gift of faith, 5:1, 15-18. See also Ephesians 2:8-9; Philippians 1:29.

[51] Safford, *Hosea Ballou*, 34-36; I see no reason to question Hosea Ballou's truthfulness in relating these events. An earlier version (not differing in the essential details of the meeting itself) may be seen in M. M. Ballou, *Biography of Rev. Hosea Ballou*, 44-45. "This circumstance [his meeting with Brown] tended rather to strengthen my mind in favor of universal and impartial grace," he later wrote (*ibid.*, 45).

[52] Whittemore, *Life of Rev. Hosea Ballou*, 44.

and say so. The Ballou brothers were going to be there all summer. He could have suggested a date soon after when they could meet again once he had prayerfully studied the issue, while at the same time seeking wisdom and counsel from the Lord. Instead, as I fear has all too often been the case, Brown took umbrage at the young man's question because he had no immediate answer to it, then flew into a loud and angry retort nowhere to the purpose. Pastors and teachers should learn from this poor example. If you don't have the answer, say so, and then request another meeting after you've had time to prayerfully study the subject. Don't address the matter superficially and by all means keep your word and meet at the appointed time. Be friendly and sincere and imagine yourself in the place of the inquiring soul.

Stephen Ballou, being but a new believer himself, was no doubt embarrassed by Brown's angry reaction to his brother's questions, but his well-meaning endeavor to correct his brother was not in vain. Though the outcome was not what he had hoped for, Stephen nevertheless had acted in the right out of a heart of loving concern.

Hosea Ballou recognized the danger to his soul should he now be mistaken, having denied the beliefs he had been taught and had once openly professed himself, but as his biographer reasoned,

> why should his Heavenly Father have implanted in his heart an earnest desire for the salvation of all mankind, unless that desire was susceptible of gratification, as is every appetite, mental or physical, with which we are endowed by nature? Such thoughts caused him much and incessant anxiety of mind, because the very fact of his entertaining them, if the doctrine he had professed was true, endangered his eternal salvation; while, on the other hand, if this creed was not that taught by God's revealed word, then he was needlessly suffering, to a degree that greatly depressed him.[53]

On arriving back, he found that his brother David during his absence had fully embraced Universalism. By the fall of 1789, Hosea Ballou's mind had also become "quite settled in the belief that God will finally have mercy on all men."[54]

---

[53] M. M. Ballou, *Biography of Rev. Hosea Ballou*, 40.

[54] Whittemore, *Life of Rev. Hosea Ballou*, 63.

Hosea chose to work in Richmond on his brother David's farm. Here David greatly aided him in study. Firmly established in his convictions, Hosea Ballou "at length declared himself a believer in the final salvation of the whole human family."[55] The reaction was only what could have been expected:

> Great was the surprise, disappointment, and chagrin of his father and friends generally. Being looked up to by the young men of his own age as a sort of leader in their secular plans and games, the influence of his example was greatly feared as operating upon the younger portion of the church; and as his joining it had been the occasion of much rejoicing at the time, so his declaration of unbelief in its faith was the cause of a proportionate degree of sorrow.[56]

Hosea Ballou gave this account of his subsequent meeting with the Baptist church:

> I now sometimes spoke my sentiments at meetings at my brother's house. The church of which I was a member thought it a duty to call me to answer for the course I had taken, and I was called upon to meet the accusation of believing in the salvation of all men. I attended, but did not feel it my duty to deny the charge, or to renounce my belief. I was therefore excommunicated from the church, my letter of excommunication carefully stating that no fault was found in me, my belief in the salvation of all men excepted. I shall ever remember the tears which I shed on this solemn occasion.[57]

---

[55] M. M. Ballou, *Biography of Rev. Hosea Ballou*, 39-40. As with all such errorists, Hosea Ballou ultimately relied more on his own subjective rationalizations than the revealed Word of God.

[56] *Ibid.*, 40-41.

[57] *Ibid.*, 41. I have not been able to determine the precise time of Ballou's exclusion from the Baptist church at Richmond. It likely occurred sometime in 1790, but could also have occurred as late as the summer of 1791. I am puzzled by the fact that so significant an event is not specifically dated in the biographies of Hosea Ballou I've seen. He had not at this point had time to formulate his other heretical beliefs, hence the church's only excluding him on the one charge.

The church was right to exclude Ballou, thereby giving notice to both him and to those in the congregation who might have been under his influence that he had greatly erred from the faith. And what of his father Maturin Ballou? Safford observed,

> The grief of the father over his youngest son's change of belief was probably lessened by the shock not coming singly. His youngest son could not seem to him so much deserving of blame as the mature son David, who was by nature peculiarly calm and meditative. Why this philosopher among his children should peril his soul with such a heresy remained to the father an unexplained mystery.[58]

One of Hosea Ballou's biographers related the following story which, though intended to be a humorous anecdote, nonetheless clearly demonstrates how Hosea Ballou had come to identify his own views as being those of the Bible:

> It was about this period that [Hosea] Ballou, ever in search of improvement, possessed himself of some book of a liberal religious character as to the sentiments it inculcated, when his father, chancing to see him reading it, told him decidedly that he would not have Universalist books in his house. Promptly acquiescing, as he always did, in his father's directions, a few days subsequent, the parent, on returning home, found Hosea reading a book beside the wood-pile, out of doors. 'What book are you reading there?' he asked. 'A *Universalist* book,' replied the son respectfully. An expression of dissatisfaction escaped the father, as he turned away and entered the house. Watching until his son had placed the book in the wood-pile, and left the spot, the parent resolved to possess himself of it, and perhaps even destroy it. But, lo! when he opened it, he found it was the Bible.[59]

"The kind-hearted father did not accept his son's new faith," wrote Safford, "but his love for his youngest child, to whom he had been both father and mother, remained during his life fond and

---

[58] Safford, *Hosea Ballou*, 38.

[59] M. M. Ballou, *Biography of Rev. Hosea Ballou*, 41-42.

tender."[60] Hosea Ballou went on to become a leading theologian, author and preacher of Universalism. As an example of just how far he had departed from the faith, one need only read this excerpt from his own writings:

> the doctrine of the Trinity, holding that Christ is equal to God, or, in other words, is God, being the second person in the holy Trinity. All these notions, as it appeared to me, were essential errors, constituting a mass of confusion. I soon renounced all these views, and preached only God, and one mediator between God and man, the man Christ Jesus....I went to my work in earnest, laboring, with all my skill and with all my limited talents, to convince my brethren in the ministry, and all who heard me preach, that the doctrines of the Trinity, of depravity, of eternal penalty, etc., were neither the doctrines of the Scriptures nor of reason.[61]

Hosea Ballou succeeded in converting his oldest brother Benjamin Ballou (1747-1834), who before had been an occasional preacher among the Baptists, to Universalism. One other brother, Nathan Ballou (1760-1838), who provided the care for his father in his last days and afterwards in 1804 went to reside in Monroe Massachusetts, where his brother David had previously removed, became a Universalist as well. These were obviously not true believers to begin with, or they would never have fallen away. Maturin Ballou's other children who remained true to the faith after such a falling away, must have been a cause for rejoicing!

Maturin Ballou did attend some of his son Hosea's meetings in the area. These were most likely in the form of weekday lectures or sermons, which were commonplace at the time. It has been reported by Hosea Ballou's biographers that on one such occasion

---

[60] Safford, *Hosea Ballou*, 39.

[61] M. M. Ballou, *Biography of Rev. Hosea Ballou*, 70. However agreeable Hosea Ballou may have been in his person, and by all accounts he was, nevertheless as a theologian or expositor of the Bible it can only be said that he displayed an extraordinary penchant for circumventing the plain declarations of God's Word in order to be able to arrive at the conclusions he did. One could not by any means believe as he did and be a Christian. He was said to have been quite eloquent in his sermons however, and eloquence combined with error has never failed to win converts among the unregenerate.

as Maturin listened, "tears were seen to run down his furrowed cheeks, and he would express his admiration of his son's sagacity and logical powers."[62] The admiration was not said to have extended to his son's doctrinal sentiments, but only to his mental acuteness and "logical powers." This in itself says a lot. Maturin Ballou is never reported to have said that his son was honoring Christ or preaching the gospel, for he was certainly doing neither. And one must wonder—might those tears, which Whittemore would have us believe were being shed in admiration, have actually been shed in sorrow for the error he was hearing from his son? This would be a more consistent viewpoint, given what we already know to be true.

His grandson Hosea Ballou, 2nd (1796-1861), claimed to have had "a strong impression that it used to be said that [Maturin Ballou] became a Universalist before he died."[63] But this was nothing more than wishful thinking, for even fellow-Universalist M. M. Ballou himself had emphasized the point over forty years earlier that Maturin Ballou stayed true to the orthodox faith, when he wrote:

> He remained a highly respected and influential member of the Baptist church until the time of his death, at the age of eighty-two years. When his son differed from him so materially in faith, though it sorely grieved the parent's heart, it never for a moment influenced him in his affection for his child. His conduct towards him was uniformly kind and solicitous, as was also the son's regard for his father of the most loving and respectful character.[64]

---

[62] Whittemore, *Life of Rev. Hosea Ballou*, 22. Whittemore makes the questionable assertion that Maturin Ballou "heard his son Hosea preach frequently, sometimes in the old Baptist pulpit at Richmond (for Hosea, though a Universalist, was admitted there), and in some other places." It would be highly unlikely, given the fact that Hosea Ballou was excluded from the Baptist church at Richmond for Universalism, that he would afterwards be admitted to preach there. At a later date, perhaps noting this inconsistency, Safford more cautiously writes of the same event, that it took place "in the Richmond church, *or in a church near Richmond*" (emphasis mine). Safford, *Hosea Ballou*, 69.

[63] Hosea S. Ballou, *Hosea Ballou, 2d*, 15.

[64] M. M. Ballou, *Biography of Rev. Hosea Ballou*, 16-17. That Maturin Ballou remained steadfast to the Baptist faith is also the view of Safford, *Hosea Ballou*, 68-69. Whittemore, on the other hand, indulged his own

Maturin Ballou's last years of ministry

Maturin Ballou continued as pastor of the First Baptist Church at Richmond until 1790, while at the same time pastor at Putney, Vermont. The First and Second Baptist churches in Richmond, having been refreshed by the revival just experienced and with an influx of about a hundred new members, had come to the decision to lay aside their longstanding differences and reunite as one congregation. Part of the compromise reached by the two churches was that the pastors of each—Maturin Ballou at First Baptist and Artemus Aldrich at Second Baptist—would be given orderly dismissals and a new pastor chosen for the united congregation. Ballou was accordingly dismissed on March 18, 1790. This providentially worked out for good, since the Baptists at Putney were able to construct their first meetinghouse that same year. Ballou's dismissal at Richmond meant he could now devote himself exclusively to the building up of this church. And with two of his sons renouncing their former faith that year it was probably thought best that he begin anew in another field. Isaac Kenney (1751-1801) became pastor of the reunited church at Richmond in 1792 (or possibly in late 1791).[65]

Ballou continued on as pastor at Putney, Vermont until about 1793. During his time there, the church was blessed with a revival season under his preaching which led to some 40 converts being baptized.[66] He returned again to Richmond in 1793, where for a

---

paradox concerning Maturin Ballou when he wrote, "Towards the close of his life his sentiments were thought to be much modified; but he made no profession of a change of opinion, and died in the communion of a Baptist church." *Life of Rev. Hosea Ballou*, 22. We would ask, by whom were his sentiments "thought to be much modified"? If they were indeed modified, why are we not told in what sense were they 'thought' to be 'much modified'? Then again, if he "made no profession of a change of opinion," why would he have been thought to have 'much modified' his sentiments in the first place?

[65] These events are reconstructed here utilizing a wide variety of sources. Kenney was not a stranger to the town, for he was listed as an assistant to Pastor Aldrich at the Second Baptist Church in 1790. See Asplund, *The Annual Register of the Baptist Denomination in North America*, 10.

[66] Crocker, *History of the Baptists in Vermont*, 209.

time he assisted pastor Isaac Kenney.[67] At its request the Richmond church was dismissed from the Warren Association on September 10, 1794, to unite with the Leyden Baptist Association.[68] After Kenney resigned the care of the church two years later in 1795, Ballou chose to remain. Whittemore gave this concise review of his final days:

> He continued to reside in Richmond, preaching in the neighboring towns, maintaining his connection with the Baptist denomination, and evincing a deep interest in its welfare and in the conversion of sinners, until, at the age of fourscore, he felt himself admonished to abstain from his public labors; and after a serene quiet of two years, he yielded up his spirit to the God who gave it. . ."[69]

Maturin Ballou passed away quietly among the people he had served so long on November 3, 1804, at the age of 82.[70]

Tragically, there have been many other souls seduced by the delusion of Universalism and its attendant errors. Among whom we could name a daughter of the famous missionaries to Burma, Adoniram Judson and his second wife Sarah Hall Boardman Judson. Abigail Ann Judson (1835-1902), likewise had been taught well the true way of salvation by her parents, pastors and friends, but she never experienced genuine conversion and eventually by the late 1870's had apostatized from the way of truth altogether into both Universalism and Spiritualism. Mercifully, neither of her parents lived to see it.[71]

---

[67] John Asplund, *The Universal Register of the Baptist Denomination in North America, for the Years 1790, 1791, 1792, 1793, and part of 1794* (Boston: John W. Folsom, 1794), 13, where Ballou is shown as being in the category of "the itinerants, or helps" at the Richmond church with Isaac Kenney.

[68] *Minutes of the Warren Association, held at the Congregational Meeting-House in Templeton, September 9 and 10, M,DCC,XCIV* (Boston: Manning and Loring, 1794), 6; Backus, *A History of New England*, 2: 539.

[69] Whittemore, *Life of Rev. Hosea Ballou*, 21.

[70] *Ibid.*

[71] Sadly Abby Ann Judson wrote, "I once believed in the limited, partial, wrathful, and unreasonable god of the old orthodoxy. I thought my nature

Some very important reminders may be drawn from this essay:

1) Grace is not inherited. Neither is it a universal birthright. Each soul stands alone before God and is accountable to Him. "For it is written, As I live, saith the Lord, every knee shall bow to me, and every tongue shall confess to God. So then, every one of us shall give account of himself to God" (Romans 14:11-12).

2) While there is life, there is hope. God may yet be gracious in turning a soul from the way of destruction. Pray that the Lord might be pleased to make the gospel effectual in that person's life. Salvation is truly of the Lord (Jonah 2:9b; Psalm 110:3).

3) Those truly saved, like Maturin Ballou, will persevere in the faith to the end, being "kept by the power of God through faith unto salvation" (1 Peter 1:5).

Maturin Ballou's story is one for the commonplace minister, faithful to the charge the Lord has given him. Without the countless multitude of such laborers for Christ down through the ages, both the elect of God and even the world itself would have missed untold blessings.

---

was corrupt, that there was no good thing in me, that my corrupt nature was inherent in me, and that I had intensified it by millions of wrong thoughts, words and deeds, and that my only hope was in having Jesus bear my sins, and save me by his blood. . . .Those who had not gone through [this] one little gate, of which billions of the human race had never even heard, were to be in hell. . .What a horrible state of affairs! What an awful universe! And what an unreasonable God!. . .Friends, progression is a better thing than redemption or salvation; development is better than fall; and continued and ever advancing life is better than resurrection." *Why She became a Spiritualist: Twelve Lectures delivered before the Minneapolis Association of Spiritualists, by Abby Ann Judson. Daughter of Adoniram Judson, Missionary to the Burmese Empire, November 30, 1890-March 15, 1891* (Minneapolis: Alfred Roper, 1891), 68, 79, 243. Judson died at the age of 67 from extensive burns she received in a fire at her home in Worcester, Massachusetts in December 1902.

Further Reading

William Bassett. *History of the Town of Richmond, Cheshire County, New Hampshire, from its First Settlement, to 1882.* Boston: C. W. Calkins and Company, 1884.

Terry Wolever, ed. *An Anthology of Early Baptists in New Hampshire.* Springfield, MO: Particular Baptist Press, 2001.

Terry Wolever, ed. *Minutes of the Warren Baptist Association. Volume One: The First Sixty Years 1767-1827.* Springfield, MO: Particular Baptist Press, to be published, D.V., 2013.

OLIVER HART
1723 - 1795

by Thomas J. Nettles

Oliver Hart was born July 5, 1723, in Warminster, Bucks County, Pennsylvania. His parents, John and Eleanor Hart, taught him Christian truth from his earliest years. Hart often heard preaching from the Tennents and George Whitefield during the most fruitful period of the First Great Awakening. George Whitefield's earnest doctrinal exhortations brought profound conviction to the young Hart. He was converted in 1741 and baptized on April 3rd by Jenkin Jones, when not quite 18 years old. This fruit of the First Great Awakening remained. Hart's Christian world view, his zeal for the church and the truth had long term impact for the influence of Christianity, particularly Baptist life, on America.

His call to the ministry

The Baptist Church at Southampton, Pennsylvania, licensed Hart to preach on December 20, 1746. In his diary, he describes this event: "I was called by the church to the exercise of my gift, December ye 20th, 1746, being 23 yrs. and 5 months old."[1] His marriage to Sarah Brees came on February 25, 1748, with Peter Peterson VanHorne, a minister in the Philadelphia Association, performing the ceremony. Their first child, Seth, was born on November 18th of that year.

On October 18, 1749, almost three years after his licensing, he was ordained to the gospel ministry. In 1749, he is listed as one of the ministers of the Philadelphia Association.[2] In that year

---

[1] A Copy of Original Diary of Rev. Oliver Hart of Charlestown, Pastor of the Baptist Church of Charlestown from a mimeographed copy made in 1949 by Loulie Latimer Owens. She wrote, "This mimeographed edition has been prepared for preservation in a number of libraries and Baptist historical collections." At times it appears that the typist did not understand the word that Hart intended to use or was not familiar with the contemporary formation of some of the letters. Page numbers will be from this mimeographed copy and referred to as Diary.

[2] A. D. Gillette, ed., *Minutes of the Philadelphia Baptist Association, 1707-1807* (Philadelphia: American Baptist Publication Society, 1851), 59.

Benjamin Griffith (1688-1768) presented "An essay on the power and duty of an Association of churches," which Oliver Hart and the other ministers signed. He later, or sooner, made use of this in his Charleston ministry. An urgent call to the Philadelphia Association to send ministers to the South found immediate response from Hart. "I embarked at Philadelphia on board the ship St. Andrew, James Abercrombie Commander, for Charles Town, South Carolina, on ye 13th day of November 1749 and arrived at Charles Town the 2nd day of December following, out 19 days."[3] His wife, then pregnant with their second child, stayed behind until June, two months after the birth of the girl, Eleanor. She arrived on July 26, 1750, after a twenty-eight-day journey, as the wife of the pastor of the First Baptist Church, for Hart had been called to the pastoral charge in February and would continue there for thirty years.

Shaping the man

According to Wood Furman in his history of the Charleston Association, the arrival of Hart constituted a joyful aspect of the special providence of God:

> The settlement of Mr. Hart in Charleston, is an important event in the annals of these churches. His unexpected arrival while the church was destitute of a supply, and immediately after the death of the excellent man [Isaac Chandler or Chanler[4]] who had occasionally officiated for them, was believed to have been directed by a special providence in their favour. He undertook the pastoral office with much seriousness, and soon entered on an extensive field of usefulness. His ardent piety and active philanthropy, his discriminating mind and persuasive address, soon raised him high in the esteem of the public, and gave him a distinguished claim to the affections of his brethren.[5]

---

[3] Diary, 2.

[4] [See the essay on Isaac Chanler (1701-1749) in Volume Two of *A Noble Company*, 301-320 —*Ed.*]

[5] Wood Furman, *A History of the Charleston Association of Baptist Churches in the State of South Carolina* (Charleston: From the Press of J. Hoff, 1811), 7-8.

Basil Manly, Sr. (1798-1868), pastor of First Baptist of Charleston from 1826-1837, described the time before Hart arrived as "a dark day." With the death, "his melancholy removal," of their fortnightly preacher, Isaac Chanler, "all had now sunk with him into the cold embrace of death." Manly represented the church as having been brought into the "greatest straits, that they may better appreciate and improve the blessings" to come. With the coming of Oliver Hart, "the Lord had provided an instrument by which he designed greatly to promote the cause of truth and piety in the province."[6]

Hart's remarkable ministry and personal pilgrimage at Charleston unfolded the decrees of God for his life, revealing an experience of both the severity and the mercy of God. The title he gave his diary reads, "A memorandum containing some of the most remarkable concurrencies on providence relative to or noticed by an unworthy traveler towards the New Jerusalem, who desires ever to esteem himself a stranger and sojourner in this dreary wilderness."

Many times the journey indeed was dreary and the road parched. Six of the eight children he and his first wife Sarah had failed to survive him. His first child, Seth, died October 22, 1750, "aged one year, eleven months, and four days." Hannah, the third child, died September 2, 1753, aged 9 months. The births of Oliver, John and Joseph followed in 1754, 1758, and 1760. Joseph died in 1761, at approximately 12 months of age. Mary Baker, the seventh child, was born in September 1762.

His daughter Eleanor married Thomas Screven, descendant of the first pastor of the church, William Screven, on March 6, 1770. The Screven's daughter, Sarah, was born December 4, 1770. A most trying series of deaths occurred within two years of the birth of this first grandchild. In June, 1772, the grandchild, Sarah, died, aged eighteen months. On October 19th, three days old, Hart's eighth child, named Sarah after the grandchild, died. The next day, October 20th, Hart's wife, also named Sarah, died. Hart recorded in his diary:

> My dear wife, Sarah Hart, departed this life about 3 o'clock on Tuesday morning October ye 20th, 1772, aged 42 years,

[6] Basil Manly, Sr., *Mercy and Judgment: A Discourse containing Some Fragments of the History of the Baptist Church in Charleston, S. C.* (Delivered by request of the Corporation of Said Church, September 23rd and 30th, A. D. 1832: Press of Knowles, Vose, and Co., 1837), 30-31.

> 10 months and 13 days. When married (which was Feb. 25, 1747/48) she was 18 years, 2 months and 18 days old. We lived together 24 years, 7 months and 25 days when death separated us.[7]

This providence of grief soon gave way to a providence of bliss. After six months, Hart began a courtship with a widow, Mrs. Anne Grimball. This led to marriage one year later. Hart had baptized Mrs. Grimball in May of 1770 and she was widowed in June of that year. She was said to have "behaved worthy of her profession" as a Christian. As a widow, she "demeaned herself with so much prudence, circumspection and integrity as to gain the esteem and applause of all her acquaintances." As an unmarried woman, as a wife, and as a widow she "sustained an unsullied character" and became "a pattern and ornament to her sex." As Hart tried to write about her, he disclaimed any ability fully to show forth the loveliness of her character. In spite of this literary shortcoming he nevertheless testified, "I speak not at random or by guess, having had sufficient tryal of her virtues, it being now twelve months since I had the pleasure to call her my own, and I esteem that as one of my happiest days that put such a prize into my bosom." So certain was he of this that he could seal it with his blood. A lady's handwriting added in the margin, "I blush to read this. O, the goodness of him that wrote this."[8]

His married daughter, Eleanor, whom he called Nellie, became very ill in November, 1774; though "her life hung in dreadful suspense for a long time," she was delivered from death. Hart prayed that she would "never forget this great deliverance from death."[9]

That same month a dear friend, ill for some time, did not experience that same deliverance. Francis Pelot and Hart became fast friends shortly after Hart's arrival in Charleston in 1750. The friendship expanded into a pastoral relationship most endearing to Hart when he helped ordain Pelot to the gospel ministry on January 11, 1752 [according to the dating of his diary]. Through the urgings of Hart, Pelot had acquiesced to the desires of many that he be set apart to the ministry. Hart preached his ordination

---

[7] Hart, Diary, 6.

[8] *Ibid.*, 7.

[9] *Ibid.*

sermon from Matthew 10:6, "Behold, I send you forth as sheep in the midst of wolves. Be ye therefore wise as serpents and harmless as doves." Hart gave the highest encomiums to the ministry of Pelot in describing his preaching. "He did not content himself with delivering a little dry morality," Hart would observe with empathetic approval, "but unfolded and applied the great and glorious doctrine of the Gospel." Pelot knew how "rightly to divide the word of truth" in giving both the saint and the sinner "their proper portion." On issues of assurance, he could "search out the hypocrite" and remove any false evidences from his hands.[10]

Through the years he enjoyed many happy, encouraging, and edifying times of ministry and social fellowship with him. Basil Manly observed that Pelot was "a man of classical education, and of kindred feelings and spirit with" Hart, assuredly a "ready and able co-adjutor."[11] To Hart he was a "sincere open, constant and hearty friend, could keep a secret, and in short, few men were ever better qualified for friendship than he." Hart had performed the second wedding ceremony for Pelot on October 6, 1761, and Pelot returned the favor to Hart on the latter's second marriage in April of 1774. Pelot's first wife of almost twenty years had died on August 29, 1760. Hart observed that "In this second marriage [to the widow of William Screven] Mr. Pelot was again blest with a pious prudent and suitable companion by whom he had four children." On October 16, 1774, Hart preached for Pelot and, in the words of his diary, "Monday I took my last farewell of my dear friend Pelot and returned home, little thinking then that I should see my friend no more." In November of that year, Pelot died. Hart grieved deeply, not only over the loss of a soul-mate in the ministry, but for the larger Baptist cause in the South. Pelot was his "dear friend and brother" and his death left a huge gap in the future of all that Hart held dear.[12] As he wrote,

> A greater loss the Baptist interest could not have sustained by the death of any one man in the Province. His family, his church and the neighborhood will feel a sensible and irreparable loss, and as to my own part, I have lost the best friend and compelor [sic, but surely this is supposed to be

---

10 *Ibid.*, 8.

11 Manly, *Mercy and Judgment*, 33.

12 Hart, Diary, 7-9.

> "counselor"] I ever was blest with in the world; the most intimate friendship had subsisted betwixt us for about four and twenty years. In all which time I ever found him a faithful friend and gratified to give advice in the most critical cases.[13]

Some ministerial contacts caused as much distress as others did joy. A good relationship turned sour causes pain. Nicholas Bedgegood came to America from England in 1751 when he was twenty years old. He worked for some years for the orphanage George Whitefield sponsored in Georgia. By 1757 he had come to Charleston, had reached Baptist convictions, and was baptized by Hart. Along with Samuel Stillman, Bedgegood was ordained to the gospel ministry on February 26, 1759. Hart and Pelot presided, with Pelot preaching the sermon. Soon Bedgegood played the role of Hart's assistant.

The difference between the two men in formal education struck some of the wealthier members of the congregation as constituting an awkward incongruity. Bedgegood was "a classical scholar, and an accomplished speaker." Hart, on the other hand, had "no more than a plain English education."[14] Although his talents clearly qualified him for the pastoral office and his application to study more than compensated for the absence of earlier opportunity, these dissatisfied members sought to supplant Hart and place Bedgegood in as pastor.

Before proceeding to the end of this story, one must know that however striking and impressive Bedgegood might have been, he could not have been so superior to Hart in talent and piety as to justify the attempted usurpation. Manly says Hart's "preaching attracted considerable attention" and his character "universal respect." A man with a less spiritual mind "would have found enough food for self gratulation in the general approbation with which he was received by all ranks."[15] Richard Furman described his mentor, Oliver Hart, in these words:

> In his person he was somewhat tall, well proportioned, and of a graceful appearance; of an active, vigorous constitution,

---

[13] *Ibid.*, 7.

[14] Furman, *History of the Charleston Association*, 75-76.

[15] Manly, *Mercy and Judgment*, 35.

> before it had been impaired by close application to his studies, and by his abundant labours; his countenance was open and manly, his voice clear, harmonious and commanding; the powers of his mind were strong and capacious, and enriched by a fund of useful knowledge; his taste was elegant and refined. Though he had not enjoyed the advantages of a collegiate education, nor indeed much assistance from any personal instruction, such was his application, that by private study, he obtained a considerable acquaintance with classical learning, and explored the fields of science; so that in the year 1769, the college of Rhode Island, in honor to his literary merit, conferred on him the degree of master in the liberal arts.[16]

Furman also serves as witness to a time when "the power of divine grace was eminently displayed in this church."[17] Manly calls it a "great work of grace" in which "very many, especially of the young, were brought to a knowledge of the truth."[18] Hart gives a brief but energetic notice in his diary, "Revival of Religion. The remarkable revival in our church began in August 1754."[19] Samuel Stillman was among those converted at this time. Both Furman and Manly point to Hart's intense desire for usefulness as shown in a section of his "Diary." This entry immediately preceded the spiritual awakening of that year:

> Monday, August the 5th, 1754. I do this morning feel myself oppressed under a sense of my barrenness: Alas! What do I for God? I am indeed employed in his vineyard, but I fear to little purpose. I feel a want of the life and power of religion in my own heart: This causes such a langour in all my duties to God: this makes me so poor an improver of time. Alas! I am frequently on my bed when I ought to be on my

---

16 Richard Furman, *Rewards of Grace conferred on Christ's Faithful People: A Sermon, Occasioned by the Decease of the Rev. Oliver Hart, A.M. Pastor of the Baptist Church at Hopewell, in the State of New Jersey* (Charleston: Printed by J. M'Iver, 1796), 23.

17 *Ibid.*, 25.

18 Manly, *Mercy and Judgment*, 35.

19 Hart, Diary, 3.

> knees—to my shame. Sometimes the sun appears in the horizon, and begins his daily course, before I have paid my tribute of praise to God: and perhaps, while I am indulging myself in inactive slumbers. Oh! Wretched stupidity! Oh! That, for time to come, I may be more active for God! I would this morning resolve, before thee, O! God, and in thy name and strength, to devote myself more unreservedly to thy service than I hitherto have done: I would resolve to be a better improver of my time than I have heretofore been: to rise earlier in the morning, to be sooner with thee in secret devotion, and Oh, that I may be more devout therein! I would be more engaged in my studies. Grant, O, Lord! That I may improve more by them! And when I go abroad, enable me better to improve my visits; that I may always leave a savour of divine things behind me. When I go to thy house to speak for thee, may I always go full fraught with things divine, and be enabled faithfully and feelingly to dispense the word of life. I would begin and end every day with thee: Teach me to study thy glory in all I do: And wilt thou be with me also in the night watches; teach me to meditate of thee on my bed; may my sleep be sanctified to me, that I may thereby be fitted to thy service, nor ever desire more than answers this important end. Thus teach me to number my days, that I may apply my heart unto wisdom.[20]

A man of such ability, devotion, zeal and piety could not be expected to acquiesce to the pretensions of superficial pride on the part of some of the members and perhaps of Bedgegood himself. Hart opposed the plan as a matter of conscience. His detractors, nevertheless, judged his opposition as an expression of envy and jealousy toward the polished Bedgegood. When their plan failed, those members withdrew from the church and Bedgegood removed to Pedee. His name appears as pastor of Welsh Neck church following Evan Pugh. He served as clerk of the Association from 1758-1764 and preached the Associational message in 1761 and 1765. Soon Bedgegood married; his misfortune in that consisted of the discovery that he already had a wife in England. He sought to

---

[20] Both Furman (*Rewards of Grace,* 25) and Manly (*Mercy and Judgment,* 34) quote this in full. It does not appear in the Owens copy. Perhaps both had access to a manuscript that included it or, more likely, Manly copied the extract from Furman's memorial sermon. The scripture verse Hart references in the last sentence is from Psalm 90:12.

defend himself by alleging that he heard that his wife in England, who would not come with him to America, was dead. In 1771, the Associational minutes say, "Mr. Nicholas Bedgegood, summoned by letter to appear before the Association to answer a charge of the sin of polygamy."[21] He failed to appear, however, when summoned before the Association, which promptly disowned him as a minister of the Gospel.

Chastising the culture

God's holy interaction with his creation shapes not only the character of man, but warns nations and cultures of judgment. As Hart observed many remarkable events, he began to feel that a pattern of just severity characterized the chain of warnings and subsequent relentings.

Hart records a "great and terrible" hurricane that struck "Carolina" on September 14, 1752, in which "my house was washed down and all I had almost totally destroyed." Also, he was witness to the birth of a grotesquely unformed child, a newborn that lived 48 hours that he described in detail. He called it a "most deplorable object of a child," and after describing its ears and nose as bare holes and its eyes as "lumps of coagulated blood" remarked that they were "ghastly to behold." A great and destructive tornado hit Charleston on Monday, May 4, 1761. Hart describes its movement, size, and ferocity. He remarked also how it was met en route by another gust that made it more agitated but altered its direction. "The strong gust from the northward which checked the progress of the pillar of destruction in its way from Wappoo Creek seems to have been sent by Providence for the preservation of Charles Town which had it kept its then direction must have been driven before it like chaff." Remarkable also was the gift of "Divine favour" that protected lives. In all the destruction, only four people lost their lives.[22]

On January 15, 1778, a great fire broke out on the north end of town carried by a high wind. Efforts to control it were vain as "flakes of fire were carried through the air" and the fire "seemed to laugh at their feeble efforts to extinguish its flames." Not until the

---

[21] This quote is taken from a hand-written collation by Basil Manly of actions taken by the Association. It appears at the end of a bound volume of the Minutes of the Charleston Association from 1775.

[22] Hart, Diary, 3-4.

wind abated could the fire be brought under control and finally was extinguished by 10:00 in the evening. One-fourth of the town, including most of the business district, was reduced to ash. "May I never see such another day," Hart wrote.[23] In the Associational letter that year, Hart drew attention to this providential warning:

> We esteem it a signal favor from the Lord, that but few of our brethren were considerable sufferers by the late dreadful conflagration in this town, and that their Meeting-house, although in imminent danger (having taken fire three times) was preserved. O, that while the judgments of God are abroad in the land, the inhabitants thereof would learn righteousness!

Subsequent events, however, convinced Hart that Charleston did not read the signs right on the fire. "The judgments of God are now opened over the land," Hart opined, "and the inhabitants ought to learn righteousness."[24] He was convinced that the state of war and all its attendant horrors together with the "late dreadful conflagration in this town" manifested the voice of God as "so many loud calls to repentance, reformation of life, and prayer that the wrath of God may be turned away from us." The fire was scarcely extinguished, however, and up popped "balls assemblies, and dances in every quarter; and even in some of those houses which miraculously escaped the flames." Hart predicted that "greater judgments will yet light upon us unless we repent."[25]

The situation called for brave action. Hart preached against the activity that he felt revealed the shallowness and worldliness of Charleston's elite; he would aim at a "popular darling vice; one that hath been much caressed, and that too by the more polite part of the world."[26] In order to shake Charleston to sobriety in con-

---

[23] *Ibid.*, 10.

[24] Oliver Hart, *Dancing Exploded: A sermon showing the unlawfulness, sinfulness and bad consequences of balls, assemblies, and dances in general,* in L. A. Osborne *The Patriot Preachers of the American Revolution* (New York: L. A. Osborn, 1860), 233.

[25] *Ibid.*, 234.

[26] *Ibid.*, 235. Hart knew his stance would be controversial, unpopular, and ridiculed. "He, however, who ventures to attack vice in a public manner, ought to be possessed of some degree of fortitude and resolution; for sin is

templation of the chastising hand of God he preached on March 22, 1778, "Dancing Exploded: A sermon showing the unlawfulness, sinfulness and bad consequences of balls, assemblies, and dances in general."

Other providential warnings followed in quick succession. Another storm in August, 1778, would have destroyed all crops and ships in the harbor and put the entire town under water had its direction not changed about 3:00 P. M. "Thus God favors sinful Charleston." A fire on December 8, probably set "by the hands of some vile Tory," broke out at Queen Street and consumed several houses. A gun exploded on Edisto Island killing a soldier. Hart responded, "Thus uncertain is life. O may I always hold my self in readiness for death." A possible plot for destruction and riot in the town was discovered in the evening so that "Thro' mercy no harm came of it." A threatened attack by the enemy British in May, 1779, ended in a retreat of the British army, "Thus sinful Charles town was delivered at this time." Hart then set forth the particulars by which "the providence of God in the defeat of Gen. Provost's design on Charles Town" could be discerned.[27]

Such warnings followed by deliverance did not continue, however, and Hart's warning that "greater judgments will yet light upon us unless we repent" came to pass. The alarm that a British fleet had appeared off Stono Bar shocked Charlestonians on February 11, 1780. Hart was taken with a fever that day and advised by his doctors to leave town in light of the impending attack, "which would render it an unfit stand for me in my weak state."[28]

Sickness was only one, and perhaps the least, reason that Hart was advised to go. William Rogers mentions the weightier reason in his funeral sermon concerning Hart: "In the month of February, 1780, owing to his warm attachment to the American Revolution, it was thought adviseable that he should leave Charleston, as the British troops were preparing to lay siege to it."[29] Before following

---

a monster of more than a thousand heads; should he slay some, there will be others yet remaining, and he may expect to be attacked."

27 Hart, Diary, 11-12.

28 *Ibid.*, 13.

29 William Rogers, *A Sermon Occasioned by the Death of the Rev. Oliver Hart....Preached at Hopewell, New Jersey, April 24, 1796* (Philadelphia: Printed by Lang and Ustick, 1796), 20.

Hart out of Charleston, we must pause to see why not only his health, but his safety, would be enhanced by flight.

Hart, as indicated by his suspicion of the plot of a "vile Tory," carried himself with dignity and purpose as a child of freedom, independence, and self-determination for America. On July 4, 1776, Hart records "the thirteen united colonies of North America were declared free and independent states by the continental congress." In March of the following year "South Carolina broke off the British yoke and established a new form of Government upon a free and generous plan, our rulers being chosen from among ourselves. May we never again be enslaved."[30] Furman characterized Hart as "ardent in his love of liberty, and rationally jealous for the rights of his country." As early as July 31, 1775, after hearing of Lexington and Concord, Hart had been selected by the council of safety along with William Henry Drayton and the Presbyterian minister William Tennent for special duty. Rogers denotes their task "to reconcile, if possible, a number of the inhabitants who were disaffected towards a revolutionary government."[31] Furman described Hart's involvement as his taking "an early and decided part in those measures which led our patriots to successful opposition against the encroachments of arbitrary power."[32]

Hart displays with clarity and vigor his own feelings about the cause of the Revolution in a sermon preached in 1789 entitled, *America's Remembrancer, with Respect to Her Blessedness and Duty*. After speaking of God's providence in the discovery and settlement of America, Hart acknowledges an initial satisfaction with the treatment England gave the colonies and her tolerable response to any statement of grievances. In short, "We conceived our charter-rights were tolerably copious, and were perfectly easy and pleased with our situation."[33]

Things changed. Hart increases in the energy of his story when recalling the events of only fifteen years previous to the sermon.

---

30 Hart, Diary, 12-13.

31 Rogers, *Sermon Occasioned by the Death of the Rev. Oliver Hart,* 23.

32 Furman, *Rewards of Grace,* 26.

33 Oliver Hart, *America's Remembrancer, With Respect to Her Blessedness and Duty. A Sermon, Delivered in Hopewell, N.J., on Thanksgiving Day, November 26, 1789* (Philadelphia: Printed by T. Dobson, 1791), 8.

Great Britain was "the aggressor" against a former child now grown to maturity. He tells the story with passion:

> Indeed it was time to emancipate ourselves;. . .and when compelled thereto, we submitted with tears in our eyes. Britain beheld with a jealous eye, our growing opulence, and formed a resolution to nip our rising glory in the bud. The parliament framed oppressive acts, for this purpose. They not only embarrassed our trade and commerce, but taxed us without our consent; and proceeded so far as to declare that of right they might bind us in all cases whatsoever. Our situation at that period was truly alarming. A state of the most abject slavery, like some evil Demon, stared us in the face. What could we, the devoted sons of America, now do? Tamely to put on the shackles fabricated for us, we apprehended, would argue a meanness of soul, unworthy the offspring of Freemen—a baseness, derogatory to the dignity of human nature. . . .We therefore petitioned—we remonstrated—but obtained no relief. We then associated, and formed articles and resolutions of economy and non-importation; hoping these measures would open the eyes of our oppressors. But our peaceable associations were confused into factious riotous mobs; and only productive of severer menaces from Britain. . . .Congress was formed. . .in the common cause of their country [and] united as one man . . .the provinces. . .again humbly petition the throne, and remonstrate with parliament. But the haughty monarch was deaf to our supplications, and the Almighty parliament spurned our remonstrances. Instead of a redress of grievances, more roaring bulls were sent over against us; accompanied with thundering cannon to affright us into submission. . . .It was now high time for America to arise, stand on her own feet, and make preparation for defence. By a vote of Congress, we were therefore declared, Free and independent States. And after a solemn appeal to the great God, with respect to the justness of our cause and sincerity of our intentions, we had recourse to arms. . . .This critical juncture brought America's virtue to the test, and evinced that it was full proof. . . .We are now free from our former shackles, and enjoy peace, with all its concomitant blessings. We are acknowledged, even by that King who, by malpractices, forfeited all just claim to our allegiance, A free, sovereign, and independent Nation. And unless our

> sins prevent, we shall certainly be the most favoured of all nations under heaven; yes we are so already.[34]

Like his younger contemporary, Richard Furman, Hart would have been a prime target for reprisals had he been captured by the British. The virtual certainty of their assault on Charleston, therefore, made his escape necessary. From Charleston, he went to the home of Nellie and her husband, Thomas Screven. For two months he stayed there, petitioning God "with prayers and tears that poor Charles Town might be spared." The "hideous roar of cannon by day and night" made the end seem inevitable, but he never gave up until he heard of the surrender, which happened on May 12, 1780. In the meantime, Hart had moved further from Charleston, having to take leave of his family, after he learned that the enemy were within a few miles of him. Concerning this he wrote, "I then packed up a few clothes in haste, and about 12 o'clock took leave of my dear wife and the family (the most affecting parting I ever experienced) and mounting my horse, set off but whither I was going or when I should return I knew not, but endeavored to leave my connections and place myself in the hands of the great and wise Disposer of all events."[35]

Later, in George Town, he learned that 1500 British soldiers were marching to the place. At this point of the flight he knew he could not return to his family and remarked, "I was distressed at the thought of leaving my dear Mrs. Hart and family in the hands of the enemy, but it was out of my power to help them. Committing into the hands of a merciful God, therefore, I proceeded on my journey."[36] He continued his flight, being accompanied along the way by a variety of persons, including his dear friend and fellow Baptist minister, Edmund Botsford (1745-1819), pastor at George Town, for 700 miles of the trip.

He preached in several places and in August baptized a convert in the North River, with a Presbyterian congregation looking on. He preached to them, seeking to prove "that believers are the only proper subjects of baptism and that dipping in water is essential to the mode of administration." He remarked that few of them had

---

[34] *Ibid.*, 8-12

[35] Hart, Diary, 13.

[36] *Ibid.*, 14.

ever heard or seen the like; "however, they behaved well."[37] He and Botsford visited in the home of John Leland, only 26 years old at the time, who eventually became the most popular Baptist preacher in Virginia and a pioneer in religious liberty. He had just recovered from a severe bout of sickness.

Hart went on to Baltimore and finally on October 10th, arrived in Philadelphia, where a momentous providence greeted him. "I had my first interview with Rev. Mr. (since Dr.) William Rodgers [sic] who with his lady, kindly invited me to make their house my home."[38] On successive days he visited with his sister, his brother Joseph, and saw his home where more than 57 years before he had been born. He attended the meeting of the Philadelphia Association on October 17th, the place where he initially heard the call to the South. Samuel Jones (1735-1814), pastor at Pennepek, which was founded by Elias Keach (1665-1699) and was the first church of the Association, preached the Associational Sermon. The text must have been very encouraging to Hart in light of the troubles in his cherished Charleston. Jones preached on Matthew 16:18, "And I say also unto thee, That thou art Peter, and upon this rock I will build my church; and the gates of hell shall not prevail against it."

His later ministry at Hopewell, New Jersey

On October 30, 1780, the Hopewell church invited Hart to come as interim until May. In December, he settled into the parsonage and procured his niece, Nelly Thomas, to keep his house. After another ten months, making an eighteen-month separation, his family was able to join him. The years at Hopewell saw a gradual decline in the community and a corresponding decline in church membership. The Association kept records of all additions and deletions from its member churches. During the years 1781-1795, the total membership declined from 213 to 150. During that time 41 were added to the church by baptism and 15 by presentation of a letter from another church. Sixty-two, however, were dismissed by letter and 42 died. Another 14 were excommunicated and 7 were restored.

The church in Charleston called Hart to return after the war. At Hart's advice and continual insistence, they eventually were

---

[37] *Ibid.*

[38] *Ibid.*, 15.

enabled to procure the services of Richard Furman. He served as pastor from 1787-1825.

A review of his publications

Hart's work in the "church militant" was the crowning passion of his life. Of six printed sermons, two concern the order and purpose of the church: *A Humble Attempt to Repair the Christian Temple,* preached in 1785, and *A Gospel Church Portrayed and her Orderly Service Pointed Out,* in 1791. In both cases, Hart preached the opening sermon at the meeting of the Philadelphia Association and responded to requests that the sermon be preserved in print. Within these two sermons he gives an artistic presentation of the structure and constitution of the church. Both sermons take the Old Testament temple as a type of the Christian church. Zerubbabel's rebuilding of the temple, in the first case, and Hezekiah's re-establishment of orderly worship in the temple, in the second, form the respective historical and scriptural allusions foundational to Hart's analogy.

The earlier sermon concentrated on engaging in the worship of God in the right manner. The church must have the right officers leading, which are bishops (pastors) and deacons. Hart lists seven duties of the pastor and four separate items of serving for the deacons. Bishops must preach, administer ordinances, rule the church, visit the sick, comfort the saints, reprove vice, and refute error and heresy. Deacons must serve four tables: the Lord's table, the minister's table, the table of the poor, and the church's table.

The same picture emerges in 1791, as Hart reiterates that the church has two officers, "Ministers and deacons," both of whom should be "inducted into office in a regular orderly way." Foremost among the mandated activities of these officers is the preaching of the gospel. The purpose of this "is to save sinners, of Adam's race, from eternal misery, in a way consistent with the claims of a violated law, and the honour of the divine perfections and government."[39]

Intimately interested in the concerns of truth, Hart never lost an opportunity to place urgent injunction on the preacher. Preparation stood high in Hart's view of the qualifications for that

---

39 Oliver Hart, *A Gospel Church Portrayed, and Her Orderly Service Pointed Out—A Sermon, Delivered in the City of Philadelphia at the Opening of the Baptist Association, October 4, 1791* (Trenton, NJ: Isaac Collins, 1791), 23.

calling. In Charleston, he took young ministers under his own instruction. He urged the Association to seek ways of establishing formal instruction for those called to ministry. He led in establishing "The Religious Society" in 1755 and in 1757 queried the Association: "Whether there could not be some method concluded upon, to furnish with suitable degrees of learning, those among us who appear to have promising gifts for the ministry?" As a result, the Association began the Education Fund. Hart served as a trustee and as its first treasurer.[40]

Hart exhorted his fellow ministers, that is, his "venerable fathers and dear brethren in the ministry," to "labor for every qualification." They should not despise "the aid of human literature" but should see "learning as an excellent handmaid to grace." Without such aid "it will be difficult, if not impossible, to expound some passages of Scripture." None of this aid, however, replaced the gift and graces of the Spirit by which a man is rendered apt to teach.[41]

Nor will any amount of zealous preparation excuse doctrinal deviation. Constructing the temple God's way means that only approved materials are placed in the structure. In preaching the gospel the minister will explain what Paul calls "the form of sound words." For Hart that included sublime and important doctrines. Preachers should preach the "pure gospel," without blending law and gospel, grace and works but salvation "through Christ, in a way of free rich and sovereign grace."[42] Only through these biblical teachings, presented in a way warranted by God, will right construction take place.

> The being of God—A trinity of persons in the Godhead—The fall of Adam and the imputation of his sin to his posterity—the corruption of human nature, and impotence of men to that which is spiritually, or morally good—The everlasting love of God to his people—The eternal election of a definite number of the human race to grace and glory—the covenant of grace—Particular redemption—Justification by the imputed righteousness of Christ—Pardon and reconciliation

---

[40] Basil Manly, *Mercy and Judgment*, 38-39.

[41] Oliver Hart, *A Humble Attempt to Repair the Christian Temple* (Philadelphia: Printed by Robert Aitken, 1785), 46.

[42] Hart, *A Gospel Church Portrayed*, 23.

AN HUMBLE ATTEMPT TO REPAIR THE CHRISTIAN TEMPLE.

A

SERMON,

SHEWING

The business of officers and private members in the church of *Christ*, and how their work should be performed; with some motives to excite professors ardently to engage in it.

Preached in the CITY of

PHILADELPHIA,

October 21st, 1783,

AT THE OPENING OF THE

ASSOCIATION,

And published at their REQUEST.

By OLIVER HART, A. M.

And are built upon the foundation of the Apostles and Prophets, Jesus Christ himself being the chief corner stone.

In whom all the building fitly framed together, groweth unto an holy Temple in the Lord. Eph. ii. 20, 21.

PHILADELPHIA:

Printed by ROBERT AITKEN, at Pope's Head, in Market Street.

M. DCC. LXXXV.

Facsimile of the original title page to Oliver Hart's *A Humble Attempt to Repair the Christian Temple* (1785). Collection of Terry Wolever.

> by his blood—Regeneration and sanctification by the influences and operation of the Holy Spirit—The final perseverance of the saints in grace—The resurrection of the dead, and eternal judgment. This is the epitome of the faith which was once delivered to the saints, which ministers are to preach, and for which they should earnestly contend. The tenor of this compendium evidently proves, that salvation is not of works, but of grace. And these doctrines are to be preached faithfully, without fear of offending man, clearly and distinctly, without terms and conditions, to be performed by us; and without offers and tenders of grace. Otherwise we blend law and gospel, grace and works, Christ and Moses; and thereby involve the christian doctrine in the greatest inconsistencies and absurdities. It were to be wished that ministers would be consistent with themselves as also with the gospel; and not one while preach that salvation is of grace; and then, introduce such terms, offers and conditions, as would lead us to believe that it is not of faith, but as it were by the works of the law.[43]

His list shows his strong Calvinism and his concern, along with many of his brethren in the Philadelphia Association, that the declaration of the gospel not be reduced to the concept of an "offer" of the gospel.[44] His chasteness in language testifies to his firm and fervent commitment to the sovereign unilateral prerogatives of God and the utter dependence of the sinner on God in every step of the work of salvation. He warns that preachers should guard against inserting "terms and conditions, to be performed by us." Just as carefully must the minister avoid "offers and tenders of grace."[45]

---

[43] Hart, *A Humble Attempt to Repair the Christian Temple,* 14-16.

[44] This reflects the controversy that originated in England over the use of the word "offer" when referring to the proclaimer's presentation of the gospel call to repentance. John Gill's *Body of Divinity* and Commentaries held a place of great esteem among the Baptists both in Philadelphia and Charleston. He gave clear enunciation to his conviction that grace is not "offered" to anyone, not even the elect. Instead grace, operative from the sovereignty of God and as a manifestation of his everlasting love, *bestows* all the blessings of salvation.

[45] Hart, *A Humble Attempt to Repair the Christian Temple*, 14-16.

This disciplined zeal, however, did not interrupt Hart's practice of seeking to persuade sinners to believe the gospel. Hart had a keen missionary and evangelistic zeal, demonstrated in his ministry and preaching and in his concerns for the destitute areas of South Carolina. As stated earlier, he believed that "the grand design of this institution [preaching] is to save sinners, of Adam's race from eternal misery." He considered it the "most important service that ever demanded the attention of man" and that the task is enough to make a man "of any sensibility tremble" since he stands between "the living God and dead sinners."[46] In his closing remarks on the funeral sermon for William Tennent, Hart gave fervent urging to the "sinners" that they "strive to enter in at the strait gate." He exhorted them to "Labour for the renovation of your souls; and rest not without an interest in Christ." Should they find that, their "happiness is secured, but without it, in vain will you expect to enter into heaven."

Considering all that is at stake and the grand benefits of service to God, Hart said, "I hope to be pardoned, though I should here exhaust the little skill I have in the art of persuasion." He then addresses the "impious sinner" who asks, in the words of Job's speech about the wicked, "What is the Almighty, that we should serve him? And what profit should we have, if we pray unto him?" Is there any benefit in being religious and joining those who seek to build the Christian temple? Most assuredly, Hart insisted, arguing with his unconverted inquisitor in Paul's words, "Godliness is profitable unto all things, having promise of the life that now is, and of that which is to come." To be sure that the transcendent importance of the issue didn't slide away, Hart gave one last stroke to the issue in laconic brevity, "More cannot be desired."[47]

Even a man of his engaging manliness and warmth and freedom and ease of striking and apt expression had no power to change the sinner's heart. "Does success depend on the overtures of the minister?" he asks. "Were he possessed of the wisdom of Solomon, the firmness of Elijah and the zeal of Phineas,"—a striking array of human talent—and add to that "the engagedness of Paul and the eloquence of Apollos, he would be unequal to the

---

[46] Hart, *A Gospel Church Portrayed*, 23.

[47] Hart, *A Humble Attempt to Repair the Christian Temple*, 43-44.

task." This is because "a divine energy, only, can render his labours successful."[48]

The labors of the ministry for true doctrine might call for martyrdom. God's truth weighs more than life itself and must be preserved above one's own life. When infidelity arises and wolves seek the destruction of God's flock, Gospel ministers must be fit to "make head against such invaders of truth." Shall they sit down, or fold their hands, or tamely stand by while the foundations of religion are sapped and the bride of Christ is poisoned? Shall ministers be so unfaithful as to make "no attempt to prevent the infection?" No, they must labor to build up the church of Christ by "preaching, praying, disputing and writing for the defence of the gospel. Yes! And if called to it—rather seal the truth with their blood."[49]

In the work of "repairing" the temple, ministers must be governed by Scripture, motivated by love to God, work to the glory of God, maintain courage and fortitude, labor heartily, and continue with persevering constancy. They are not to be among those who "have slunk away like cowards." The regulative principle operates in this task if it is to be done "in the right manner." Every part of the work must conform to that "divine and unerring rule—the holy scriptures." Workmen should never "deviate an hair's breadth" from the "sure and tried rule which hath never failed."[50] This point governed his own description in the 1791 sermon as he determined to draw "descriptive characters from the unerring rule of sacred truth."[51]

Motivations for such a work abound. Not only has God Himself called His workers to it (and "who can withstand the injunctions and solicitations of the infinitely wise, powerful and gracious God?"), but in itself the work is good, honorable and pleasant. Beyond that the work carries with it great profit ("all faithful labourers in it are graciously and amply rewarded") and enjoys the presence of the great Jehovah Himself. This reality is the *ne plus ultra*, no other motivation of like attraction can be offered. "Should this consideration fail of exciting professors of all ranks and orders

---

[48] Hart, *A Gospel Church Portrayed*, 23.

[49] *Ibid.*

[50] Hart, *A Humble Attempt to Repair the Christian Temple*, 35.

[51] Hart, *A Gospel Church Portrayed*, 8.

to engage with ardor in building the christian temple," Hart muses, "we have no other motive to offer—our pinions fail—we can soar no higher."[52]

For the correct ordering of this service, so exuberantly described in the previous section, Hart sets forth those parts of church government and practice that Scripture mandates. After an enforcement of the Scriptural offices, pastors and deacons and their central purpose in the church, Hart unfolds the corporate duties of the church in its public setting. Social and public prayer, singing the praises of God (a moral duty), and administering the ordinances of the Lord's Supper and baptism also constitute aspects of public worship. Church discipline, scrupulously carried out in accordance with Scripture method for offenses outlined by the Scripture, with the patience and compassion demonstrated by the Almighty in His patience and long-suffering, is an essential element of maintaining purity and beauty in the church. Sunday in Hart's traditional Baptist/Puritan understanding, is the Christian Sabbath. He gives a full four pages of discussion to this issue in the sermon, enforcing his belief with strong reasoning that the resurrection, a day on which Christ entered into his rest, made the "first day of the week [become] the Christian Sabbath."

None of these requirements, however, has any effectual profit performed in a merely perfunctory manner. The blessing of the Spirit alone gives vitality. "The form of godliness, without the power, is like a body without a soul—a dead carcass." Hart insisted on this point with all the conviction of his fervent heart. "Upon the whole," he preached, "I apprehend the spirituality of worship consists in communion with God, through Christ, by the operations of the Holy Ghost." Aware that some might be afraid of the doctrine of divine influence and discard it as "enthusiastical," Hart embraced the necessary work of the Spirit as "the quintessence of religion, without which there can be no spiritual—no acceptable worship at all." He then urged this reality on his hearers, "O, may we experience more of these divine influences! That we may be more spiritual in all the parts of religious worship."[53]

Another important aspect in Hart's view of the church is what he called the "communion of churches" or associational life. Both sermons treat the subject. Hart himself participated actively in

---

[52] Hart, *A Humble Attempt to Repair the Christian Temple*, 41-44.

[53] Hart, *A Gospel Church Portrayed*, 37-38.

both the Philadelphia and Charleston Associations. Richard Furman acknowledged the importance of Hart as the initiator of associational organization in the South. Furman says, "He was the prime mover in that plan for the association of churches, by which so many of our churches are very happily united at the present day."[54] His son, Wood Furman, recalls the founding of the Charleston Association:

> Mr. Hart had seen, in the Philadelphia Association, the happy consequences of union and stated intercourse among Churches maintaining the same faith and order. To accomplish similar purposes, an union of the four Churches before mentioned was contemplated and agreed on. Accordingly on the 21st of Oct. 1751 Delegates from Ashley River and Welch Neck met those of Charleston in the said City. The Messengers from Euhaw were prevented from attending. It was agreed that an annual meeting should thenceforward be holden on Saturday preceding the 2d Sabbath of Nov. to consist of the Ministers and messengers of the several Churches: that the two first days should be employed in public worship, and a Sermon introductory to business preached on the Monday following at 10 o'clock.[55]

In 1767, the Charleston Association adopted the Second London Confession as its doctrinal statement and appointed Hart and Pelot, according to Manly "an able and ready co-adjutor,"[56] to "draw up a system of Discipline agreeable to Scripture to be used by the Churches."[57] They used the essay produced by Benjamin Griffith which had been adopted by the Philadelphia Association in 1749. Oliver Hart's name first appears in the Philadelphia minutes in that year. Though Hart and his co-worker "borrowed many hints" from that document, they found some things in it "exceptionable" and wanted to produce something more explicit. They acknowledge very forthrightly, and might one say proudly, their indebtedness to the "late learned, pious and judicious Dr.

---

[54] Richard Furman, *Rewards of Grace*, 26.

[55] Wood Furman, *History of the Charleston Association*, 8-9.

[56] Manly, *Mercy and Judgment*, 33.

[57] Wood Furman, *History of the Charleston Association*, 12.

Gill, for what is taken from his Exposition and Body of Divinity."[58] After some revisions with the help of Morgan Edwards and David Williams, Hart saw the document through the press in 1773.

In Hart's opinion, the natural relation between churches brought them together in acts of brotherly love, fellowship, council, sharing a supply of ministerial gifts with those that are destitute, giving material aid to indigent churches, and coming together to help settle disputes. That these natural and necessary interactions in brotherly love may "ripen to maturity," the churches should "associate, and become an ecclesiastical body; to meet, by their delegates, periodically, for the transaction of business."[59] In the sermon he lists seven advantages of an association of churches and in the Summary of Church Discipline he lists twelve.[60] In the 1785 sermon, Hart emphasizes a point concerning the association that appeared clearly in the Discipline when he reminded them, "You assume no higher title than that of an Advisory Council." He went on, in accordance with the statement of Discipline, "You, therefore, impose not your sentiments on the churches, under pain of excommunication."[61] The Association maintained the right, however, to "judge for itself what churches shall be admitted into confederacy with it, and to withdraw from all acts of communion and fellowship" with churches that hold erroneous principles or doctrine.[62]

---

58 Preface to *A summary of Church Discipline* (Charleston: Printed by David Bruce, 1774), as found in *Some Southern Documents of the People Called Baptists,* ed. Rondel Rumburg (Birmingham: Society for Biblical and Southern Studies, 1995), 172-173.

59 Hart, *A Gospel Church Portrayed*, 31-32.

60 The sermon seven include: 1) a general knowledge of the state of the churches is obtained; 2) they promote brotherly love; 3) it establishes the doctrines of grace; 4) a standard against error, heresy, and innovation in doctrine and worship; 5) cases too difficult for a particular church may be solved; 6) destitute churches may receive supplies; 7) a fund for education and other purposes may be raised. The twelve roughly correspond to the seven with the addition of hearing an aggrieved church member, hearing an aggrieved party in a church that has no recourse but the association, settling contentions between sister churches, and properly testing candidates for the ministry.

61 Hart, *A Humble Attempt to Repair the Christian Temple*, 50.

62 Hart, *A summary of Church Discipline*, 207. On the former point, the Summary of Church Discipline stated, "The Baptist Association therefore

A preacher with piety and truth

Hart's zeal for a well-ordered church was a function of his zeal for Christ and His truth. He gave unrelenting effort ever to be a herald of the truth of sovereign grace, while walking personally under the discipline of Scripture and its clear exhortations for purity, humility, earnestness, and holiness. In his funeral oration for Hart, Richard Furman characterized Hart as a "Calvinist, and a consistent, liberal Baptist." He continued,

> The doctrines of free, efficacious grace, were precious to him; Christ Jesus, and him crucified, in the perfection of his righteousness, the merit of his death, the prevalence of his intercession, and efficacy of his grace, was the foundation of his hope, the source of his joy, and the delightful theme of his preaching.[63]

Furman, a keen observer of preachers and preaching, described Hart's sermons as "peculiarly serious, containing a happy assemblage of doctrinal and practical truths." Doctrinal preaching, as a matter of fact especially suited him, for he was prepared "by an intimate acquaintance with the sacred scriptures, and an extensive reading of the most valuable, both ancient and modern, authors."[64] William Rogers observed these same things in Hart's ministry, describing him as "sound in the faith and an uniform advocate, both in public and in private, for the doctrines of free and sovereign grace."[65]

On at least three occasions Hart preached ordination sermons built on 1 Timothy 4:16. Edmund Botsford, Joseph Cook, and Samuel Stillman all heard Hart admonish them to take heed to themselves and to doctrine. They would constantly remember

---

arrogates no higher title than that of an Advisory Council, consistent with which epithet, it ought ever to act, when it acts at all, without intruding on the rights of independent congregational churches or usurping authority over them, Matt. 23:10-12."

[63] Furman, *Rewards of Grace,* 24.

[64] *Ibid.*

[65] Rogers, *Sermon Occasioned by the Death of the Rev. Oliver Hart,* 22.

their own interest in Christ and the work of grace in their souls. He reminded them:

> You cannot be qualified to deal with wounded spirits, unless you have been sensible of your own wounds. It is not possible you should, in a suitable Manner, direct Sinners to Christ, without an actual Closure with him yourselves.[66]

In speaking to the candidates for ministry about their doctrine, Hart said, "In general you will insist upon the two following Topics, namely our apostacy from God, and our Redemption by Jesus Christ, which will very naturally lead you to take notice of the Transactions of God in eternity, with reference to your salvation." They were to bear in mind that the persons for whom God's salvation has been given "are a certain, select number, out of the Race of Mankind, who are redeemed by his blood, justified by his righteousness, called by the inscrutable operations of his Spirit, sanctified by his grace, and finally glorified." These doctrinal concerns permeated Hart's outlook. In his brief associational letter of 1775, Hart encouraged its churches to "Guard against Error, Heresy, and every Species of corrupt Doctrine; labour that you may be sound in the Doctrines of Grace, and that you may feel their vital Influence on your Hearts. Contend earnestly for the Faith once delivered to the Saints."[67]

Hart's return to New Jersey in 1780 brought his immediate participation again in the Philadelphia Association. Through cordial communication between Baptist associations, the Philadelphia Association had maintained knowledge of Hart and his work at Charleston. They knew of his aptness and reputation as a preacher. In 1780, therefore, at the Associational meeting the minutes recorded, "Rev. Oliver Hart of Charleston, South Carolina" was present, and, along with three others, was admitted "to the full privilege of members." He was "unanimously requested to preach" on the evening of Wednesday, October 18. In 1782, he was chosen moderator. He also presented the associational letter. The

---

[66] The details of this sermon are reported in Robert A. Baker, *Adventure in Faith: The First Three Hundred Years of First Baptist Church, Charleston, South Carolina* (Nashville: Broadman Press, 1982), 139-142.

[67] Oliver Hart, Circular Letter, *Minutes of the [Charleston] Baptist Association, held in Charlestown, February 6th, 7th and 8th, 1775* (Charleston: n.p. [1775]), 4.

association had begun the practice in 1774, that "the contents of the general letter to the churches consist of an improvement of some article of our Confession of Faith, following the order therein observed." In accordance with that practice, his letter treated the eighth chapter of the Confession, Christ as mediator.[68]

In this letter, Hart demonstrates the justness of William Rogers' estimate of his preaching in saying, "The sum and substance of all his discourses were founded on the great atonement, yet he studied variety, for he never lost sight of the Bible-system in any of its parts."[69] The full range of theological considerations surrounded the exposition of his theme. First, essential trinitarianism undergirds the entire scheme as he looks into "the transactions of the Deity from eternity" and discusses the eternal covenant of redemption. In eternal counsel the Triune Jehovah instituted the voluntary submission of the Son as the means to save a chosen people. "Jehovah, the Father, in his manifold wisdom, having predestinated a select number of the fallen race to the adoption of children, by Jesus Christ, according to the eternal purpose which he purposed in Christ Jesus our Lord, now proposed the business or work of saving the elect, to Jehovah the Son." The fall and the consequent inability of man to "repair the injuries done by sin or to restore himself to the divine favor" made necessary the provision of an able, suitable, and qualified mediator. Christ's deity, "of the same nature and essence of Jehovah the Father" makes Him able. The mystery of the human nature taken "in union with and subsist[ing] in the person of the Son of God" makes Him suitable.

As mediator He sustained several characters or offices which qualify Him for His work. He is covenant head to the elect; He is surety of His people, in which office He took His people's whole debt to the law upon Himself "in consequence of which, the elect...were set free;" He is an advocate "for all the chosen people of God" whose advocacy proved "efficacious to the pardoning, justifying, and glorifying an elect world." The Son is a prophet, in which office He teaches "powerfully and efficaciously by His Word and Spirit;" He is priest, in which capacity He "was offered up a

---

[68] For the full text of the sermon see Gillette, *Minutes of the Philadelphia Baptist Association,* 181-191.

[69] Rogers, *Sermon Occasioned by the Death of the Rev. Oliver Hart,* 22.

sacrifice to satisfy divine justice[70] for the sins of an elect world;" He is king, as which He gives the saints "the most glorious charter of privileges contained in the covenant of grace."

A large spectrum of other doctrines dart in and out of the presentation. Particularly prominent is the doctrine of justification. Hart delineates the components of justification four times in this letter and makes several other allusions to it in passing. The tandem of forgiveness and imputed righteousness built on Christ's death and perfect obedience drive these discussions, for as he writes,

> 2. Christ is the surety of his people. As such, he drew nigh to God, in covenant, and engaged to do and suffer all that the law and justice of God required, to make satisfaction for their sins. He put himself in their law place, took the whole debt of his people upon himself, and became responsible for it. They owed a debt of obedience to the law, and a debt of punishment for the violation of it; this double debt he assumed payment of, and did pay: . . .
>
> The law must be kept, or man could not be saved. It is holy, just, and good, righteous in all its demands. Perfect obedience it positively requires; a single deviation therefrom exposes to the curse, Gal. iii. 10. Had Christ failed only in one point, his mediation would have been of no avail. But his obedience was complete. Divine justice could not charge it with the least flaw. . . .
>
> Again, Christ, as mediator, not only kept the law inviolable, but he died the cursed death of the cross, to atone for the sins of his people. . . .And when his soul was made an offering for sin, and divine wrath was poured out upon him to the uttermost, he cried out, 'My God! My God! Why hast thou forsaken me?' Matt. xxvii. 46. Thus Jesus, the Mediator, suffered for us men, and for our salvation. . . .
>
> Second. With regard to the law of God. The mediatorship of Christ hath restored to the law all its rights and honors; for he hath magnified the law and made it honorable, by yielding a perfect obedience to it, and dying to make satisfaction for the breach of it. . . .

---

[70] One of the remarkable features of this sermon is the number of times Hart quotes verbatim from the Baptist Catechism as a foundation for his theological exposition. He does this at least on seven occasions.

> Justification is also through the mediatorship of Christ, 'in the Lord shall all the seed of Israel be justified, and shall glory.' Isa. xlv. 35. The righteousness of Christ, as mediator, is the sole matter and cause of a sinner's justification before God, Rom. v. 17, 18. This righteousness Christ wrought out by his active and passive obedience to the law; and by it, 'all that believe are justified from all things, from which they could not be justified by the law of Moses,' Acts xiii. 39.[71]

A death of dignity and deference

Upon his death in 1795, the Associational minutes recorded, "It hath pleased God, in the year past, to remove from the church militant to the church triumphant, that burning and shining light, the Rev. Oliver Hart, A. M., of Hopewell, New Jersey."[72]

Hart depended on this work of Christ for the eternal health of his own soul and would admonish his heirs in the faith to do the same. Hart even unto death saw himself as utterly destitute of any merit of his own but fully accepted before the throne of God by virtue of the righteousness of the Beloved Son. He died as he lived; even in death, the providence of God amazed his soul with its wisdom and mercy and the righteousness of Christ constituted his only hope. William Rogers, for whom Hart named his last child, a son who was eleven when his father died,[73] preached Hart's funeral sermon. He reminded Hart's bereaved children to "Let his quiet exit, and full belief in the promises cause them to arrest every improper complaint, and as professors of our holy religion, may they be still, knowing that God hath done it." Such deference to God's will helps "improve this most afflicting stroke of an unerring providence" to their spiritual good and the honor of Him who wounds and heals, who kills and makes alive. Rogers, in a footnote to the printed version of the sermon, provided a chronicle of the "quiet exit" of Hart:

---

[71] Oliver Hart, Circular Letter on Christ as Mediator, in Gillette, *Minutes of the Philadelphia Baptist Association*, 186, 188, 190.

[72] Gillette, *Minutes of the Philadelphia Baptist Association*, 323.

[73] William Rogers Hart was born December 13, 1784. Rogers, *Sermon Occasioned by the death of the Rev. Oliver Hart*, 29*n*.

> For many months previous to his death he repeatedly said that he viewed himself as *a dying man.*—A few days after he was taken with his last illness, and while he was able to walk about the room, he called for his Will, gave it to a friend, and desired him to get his remains conveyed to Southampton [Pennsylvania], the *family burying place.*—It was with such difficulty at this time that he drew his breath, and the agony he was in was so great, that he said, *he should not think it strange if he should go into convulsions. —The struggle for breath broke a vessel, and he spat a quantity of blood*—yet not a *single murmur, or undue complaint!*—He would frequently lift up his hands and say, *poor mortal man!*—A friend once replied, *this mortal shall put on immortality*—he answered, *yes! yes!*—He would often say, *I want, I want!* —being asked what he wanted?—*I want the will of the Lord to be done!* The Rev. Mr. Van Horne called to see him; he asked him if he felt comfortable, he replied, GOD *is an all sufficient* SAVIOUR!
>
> A person who at one time was sitting by, and observing his great bodily distress, said *how happy for Mr. Hart that he has but one work to do!* Dying was meant—He immediately replied CHRIST *is the end of the law for* RIGHTEOUSNESS *to every one that* BELIEVETH!
>
> Dec. 29. He called for all around him *to help him praise* GOD *for what he had done for his soul*—being told he would soon join the glorious company of saints and angels, he replied, *enough, enough!*
>
> Dec. 30. His cough and spitting of blood increased, and every breath was accompanied with a groan!
>
> When he died, he just put his head a little back, closed his eyes as if he were going into a sleep, and EXPIRED!!![74]

Thus ends our story of Hart. If his twofold hope can be learned, it is all that can be desired of such a writing. We must trust the unerring providence of God and lean wholly on the blood and righteousness of Christ.

---

[74] Rogers, *Sermon Occasioned by the Death of the Rev. Oliver Hart,* 28-29.

Further Reading

Robert A. Baker, Paul J. Craven and R. Marshall Blalock. *History of the First Baptist Church of Charleston, South Carolina, 1682-2007.* 325th Anniversary Edition. Springfield, MO: Particular Baptist Press, 2007. This edition contains the complete texts of each of the funeral sermons for Oliver Hart, by Richard Furman and William Rogers, referred to in this essay, as well as the "Sketch of the Life and Character of Mrs. Ann Hart," originally published in 1814.

Wood Furman. *A History of the Charleston Association of Baptist Churches in the State of South Carolina.* Charleston, SC: J. Hoff, 1811.

Abram D. Gillette, ed. *Minutes of the Philadelphia Baptist Association, 1707-1807.* Philadelphia: American Baptist Publication Society, 1851; reprinted Tricentennial Edition with new comprehensive indexes, maps and illustrations, Springfield, MO: Particular Baptist Press, 2002.

Oliver Hart, Diary. As transcribed by Loulie L. Owens, 1949. 18 pages.

Leah Townsend. *South Carolina Baptists, 1670-1805.* Florence, SC: The Florence Printing Company, 1935. Currently available in a facsimile reprint from Higginson Book Company, Salem, Massachusetts.

Isaac Backus

ISAAC BACKUS
1724 - 1806

by Stanley J. Grenz

Much of the credit for placing the Baptist cause in New England on firm footing ought to go to the eighteenth century pastor and activist, Isaac Backus. In fact, so significant was his role that Backus has appropriately been hailed as "the father of American Baptists."[1]

Early influences

Isaac Backus, who was born on a Connecticut farm January 9, 1724, lived during tumultuous times. During his youth, the ecclesiastical face of New England was in the process of being reshaped. This process was precipitated by the arrival in the colonies of the British evangelist, George Whitefield.

Whitefield's itinerant preaching inaugurated the Great Awakening, a revival of such significance that it has been called the American "national conversion." But the revival also produced a deep cleavage within the established Congregational churches of New England between the Old Lights, the church leaders who were put off by the excesses of the revivalists, and the New Lights, those who had been touched by revival or who supported it. At first, the New Lights sought to be catalysts for renewal and reform with the established churches. Conflict inevitably arose, however. The revivalists' efforts were met with antagonism and opposition, especially among the clergy. The New Lights in turn began questioning the spiritual integrity of an ecclesiastical system that opposed itinerant preaching and failed to emphasize what had become a hallmark of the revival, the necessity of personal conversion. As a result, many New Lights began holding worship services apart from the established churches, earning for themselves the name Separates.

At the time of his birth, Backus's parents, Samuel and Elizabeth (née Tracy) Backus, were nominal Congregationalists. When the fervent preaching of the itinerants swept the area, Isaac's recently-widowed (1740) and severely-depressed mother

[1] Mary H. Mitchell, *The Great Awakening and Other Revivals* (New Haven, CT: Yale University Press, 1934), 27.

experienced a renewal of faith and became an enthusiastic supporter of the revival, opening her home for meetings of prayer and exhortation. For his part, Isaac was deeply impressed with what he saw happening in the neighboring community of Norwich, Connecticut, and he desired the conversion so many others were experiencing. Not knowing how one received such an experience, he sought the counsel of his minister, Benjamin Lord. Lord, however, adhered to the rationalist theology of the day which held that if the sinner leads an upright life, God will in due time grant salvation. Consequently, the pastor advised his young inquirer, "Be not discouraged, but see if God does not appear for your help."[2] Backus found this advice unacceptable and continued his search for salvation. When he finally concluded that his personal striving was totally useless, Backus's quest was rewarded. On August 24, 1741, while alone in a field he experienced conversion,[3] and soon after he received the "inner witness" assuring him that he was indeed a true saint predestined for salvation.

Five years later (September, 1746), Backus was the recipient of a second divine encounter, "an internal call to preach the gospel." In the meantime, the Backus family had become part of the Separate congregation that had formed in Norwich. Immediately after receiving his call, Isaac "tested his gift" by preaching the Sunday sermon at the New Light church. He spent the next year on the itinerant circuit. Then at the age of twenty-four and without any formal theological education, Backus was called to the pastorate of a similar group in Titicut parish, Massachusetts.

The pastor-statesman

Backus's years as a Separate were filled with strife. Because theirs was an illegal congregation, his church members faced conflicts with the Massachusetts government over religious taxation. This incident triggered his involvement in what would occupy him most of his life, the struggle for separation of church and state.

---

[2] Isaac Backus, "Isaac Backus' Life: An Account of the Life of Isaac Backus," unpublished manuscript, 11. Also found in Isaac Backus, "Isaac Backus, his writing containing Some Particular account of my Conversion," unpublished manuscript, 5.

[3] Backus describes this event in his "Account of the Life of Isaac Backus," 16-18; and his "Account of my Conversion," 5-6.

Backus had barely joined the cause when his participation was interrupted (in the summer of 1749) by a grave theological controversy that was already threatening to split the entire Separate movement—the explosive issue of believer's baptism. A two-year personal struggle followed. Backus knew that to abandon pedobaptism was to secede from the Separates just when success appeared on the horizon. Yet he also realized that not only was the New England form of covenant theology not taught by the Bible, it was used to justify the ecclesiastical evils of the day, including the parish system, religious taxes, and the aristocratic structure of the church.[4] Convinced by such considerations, Backus was baptized by immersion on August 22, 1751. For five subsequent years he struggled to maintain a congregation that would practice both infant baptism and believer's baptism, only to discover that the theological controversy was too divisive. The final resolution came in 1756. Backus dissolved the congregation and formed an immersionist church in the adjacent town of Middleboro.

The story of the Middleboro congregation was repeated in many other Separate churches. As these congregations accepted baptistic principles, they naturally sought the same exemption from religious taxes older dissenting bodies enjoyed. The Massachusetts government, however, saw the matter otherwise. These Separate Baptists had separated from the established Congregational fold, their members could not be dismissed from supporting the established churches financially. To prevent any loophole by which the new dissidents might obtain exempt status, the Massachusetts legislature in 1753 added a new requirement, stipulating that the certificates issued by individual dissenting congregations must be validated by three other "Anabaptist" churches in the region.

The attempt to tighten up the requirements, however, backfired. It alarmed the older Baptist congregations, who in response drafted a remonstrance to the Massachusetts general court and raised funds to send a representative to England with their grievances. Further, the act did not plug the hole in the dyke, for by failing to define "Anabaptist," it simply allowed the Separate Baptist congregations to validate certificates for each other. Most importantly, however, the law accelerated the movement of open-communion churches to closed-communion status; and it caused the closed-communion churches to realize their fundamental ties first to each other and then with the old

[4] William G. McLoughlin, *Isaac Backus and the American Pietistic Tradition* (Boston: Little, Brown and Co., 1967), 62.

Baptists, whom they had themselves previously ostracized. Ironically, then, the Massachusetts law was the first step in the rejuvenation of the New England Baptists.

The key figure in this rejuvenation process was Isaac Backus. Backus saw almost immediately the importance of close ties among all churches holding Baptist beliefs. Therefore, between 1756 and 1767, he traveled nearly 15,000 miles within the region,[5] visiting old Baptist churches, open-communion congregations, and new groups who sought his help in the task of organizing as churches. The process was augmented as well by the Philadelphia Baptist Association, with whose help the New England Baptists in 1764 founded Rhode Island College (now Brown University) and, in 1767, the Warren Baptist Association.

Although originally established for the purpose of aiding local churches, the Warren Association soon became the political arm of the New England Baptists in a renewed struggle against the establishment, a struggle triggered by the difficulties faced by many of the newer churches in their efforts to obtain exemption from religious taxation. In 1769, the association appointed a grievance committee to collect the complaints of churches and, under Backus's leadership, to present a petition to the Massachusetts legislature. Drawing from the slogans of the independence-minded colonists, the petition condemned the certificate system as "taxation without representation" and claimed that liberty of conscience was a natural right.

Despite the pleas of the Baptists, however, the certificate system and the injustices in its administration continued, injustices which led to a turning point in Backus's own thinking. He concluded that God had appointed two kinds of government, the civil and the ecclesiastical, which ought never to be "confounded together," and that the union of the two governments in the New England colonies must be broken if America were to become a truly Christian land.[6] In September, 1772, the grievance committee was reactivated under Backus's own leadership. On the basis of his two-governments theory as well as its corollary, the right of the Christian to disobey when the governments had indeed been "confounded together," the committee suggested to the association meeting in September, 1773, a new tactic: Baptists

---

[5] Robert G. Torbet, *A History of the Baptists* (Philadelphia: Judson Press, 1950), 235.

[6] See McLoughlin, *Isaac Backus and the American Pietistic Tradition*, 123-127.

should refuse *en masse* to turn in exemption certificates. In typical Baptist fashion the association voted to leave this decision with each church, but to aid financially those who suffered as a result of their non-compliance with the certificate law.

The Baptists viewed the first meeting of the Continental Congress in Philadelphia (September 5, 1774) as their opportunity to appeal to a body higher than the Massachusetts legislature without appearing disloyal. Backus was among those sent by their constituents to join with a group being formed by the Baptists and Quakers of Philadelphia. At the suggestion of the Quakers, the envoys gained a meeting (October 14, 1774) with the Massachusetts congressional delegation together with several sympathetic delegates from other colonies. The Baptists presented a statement, which included Backus's two-government theory and the Baptist arguments on behalf of their concept of liberty of worship.[7] The meeting, however, turned out to be a mistake. Not only did the Baptists fail to accomplish their goal of focusing national attention on their plight, their common cause with Tory Quakers and neutral, if not Tory, Philadelphia Baptists added to the suspicion in New England that they too were unpatriotic. Having failed in Philadelphia, the Baptists were forced again to appeal to the Massachusetts assembly, doing so in July, 1775, shortly after the Revolutionary War had begun.

The next opportunity to bring about change in Massachusetts came in 1779, when a convention was called for the purpose of writing a new state constitution. Backus lobbied intensively for the inclusion of a bill of rights, but the new constitution did not totally separate church and state and leave the "rational soul" free to find "true religion," as Backus had desired. Despite voting irregularities, the legislature declared the constitution law in 1780. In the wave of renewed persecution against the Baptists who refused once again to pay the religious tax, the legislature ignored completely all petitions and protests. As a result, the struggle shifted to the courts.

The Baptists won an important victory in 1782, only to see the decision reversed two years later. The second court decision made the situation worse, for it stated that only incorporated religious societies were entitled to legal recognition. Against the advice of Backus, many churches began complying with the law. They incorporated, paid the tax, and then sued to have their taxes go to support their own Baptist minister.

---

[7] *Ibid.*, 131.

The Baptist efforts to eliminate religious taxation had not been successful. Yet, a climate of broad acceptance and toleration had been attained by 1785, and New England Baptists began to turn their attention away from the political struggle to the task of evangelism. Even Backus found himself forced to devote much of his effort to other needs, for new sects and non-Calvinist theologies were making inroads among the Baptists. He sought to counter these trends through sermons and tracts which attacked the heresies and defended the outlook he had experientially found to be true. Then, Middleboro honored their Baptist minister by electing him as a delegate to the Massachusetts convention which debated the newly-proposed United States Constitution, a trust to which Backus gave much attention before finally voting against the consensus of his constituents and in favor of ratification.

At the Warren Association meeting on September 6, 1788, Backus called for a renewal of the struggle against the establishment. Although out of deference to the aging warrior, the association appointed a committee to write a petition and offer it to the legislature at its own discretion. The delegates then presented Backus with a new challenge—a journey to the South to aid in a revival currently taking place there. This he did, returning enthusiastic in 1790, but unable to produce a similar renewal in his home state.

Backus's health began to fail in 1798, and his wife of nearly fifty-one years, Susannah, died on November 24, 1800.[8] The year 1806 was Backus's last. He suffered a stroke in March, preached his last sermon on April 3rd, suffered a second stroke on April 23rd, but lingered until November 24th, on which day the eighty-two-year-old Baptist statesman died. Although he did not live to see the disestablishment of the Congregational churches in Massachusetts, his lifetime goal nevertheless became a reality on November 11, 1833.

A review of Backus's beliefs

From 1754 until his death, Backus penned thirty-seven tracts and pamphlets, a three-volume ecclesiastical history of New

---

[8] [Isaac was married to Susannah Mason (b. January 24, 1725) on November 29, 1749 at Rehoboth, Massachusetts. They had nine children—six daughters and three sons —*Ed.*]

England, written at the request of the Warren Association,[9] a subsequent abridgement,[10] and numerous petitions and newspaper articles, plus unpublished sermon manuscripts, a lengthy diary and other personal accounts,[11] parts of several autobiographical works, and an assortment of short pieces on various topics. By means of these writings he sought to direct the Baptist cause through troubled waters. He spoke out about the Calvinism/Arminianism conflict and covenant theology; about the nature of the church, its officers and the ordinance of baptism; and about the relationship between the ecclesiastical and civil spheres. These publications reveal a man motivated by what he saw as God's truth and keenly aware of the mood of his times.

Theological foundations. Backus did not view himself as an innovative theological thinker. He accepted the Calvinist theology of Jonathan Edwards (1703-1758), mediated to him by the Awakening, with which he then blended (with some disagreements) the philosophy of John Locke (1632-1704), so important to the colonists. His primary task was that of calling New England back to what he believed to be right theology, convinced that doctrinal and ecclesiastical purity would in turn lead to a properly ordered society. Three theological themes loom as central to his thinking and as foundational to his understanding of this properly ordered society.

First, Backus built from the typical Calvinist emphasis on the sovereignty of God. For him God is the absolutely sovereign governor of the universe to whom all earthly governments must appeal for legitimization:

> That there is one supreme BEING whose kingdom ruleth over all is the first and capital article of truth which no nation upon earth were ever able to erase entirely out of their minds. For no government could ever be established among themselves without appeals to HIM for the truth of what was

---

[9] *A History of New England, With Particular Reference to the Denomination of Christians Called Baptists*. Boston, three volumes: 1 (1777), 2 (1784) and 3 (1796).

[10] *An Abridgement of the Church History of New England, from 1602 to 1804*. Boston: Printed for the Author, by Ensign Lincoln, 1804.

[11] See William G. McLoughlin, ed. *The Diary of Isaac Backus*. Providence, RI: Brown University Press, 1979. Three volumes.

asserted, and to avenge injustices and the violation of contracts and engagements.[12]

The second doctrine crucial to Backus was anthropology. Influenced by Edwards and Locke, he saw the intellect as the controlling faculty in the human person, dominating even the will.[13] Hence, Backus maintained that humans as created by God were to be governed by "reason and a well informed judgment," which would be influenced by the externally applied "motive" of the divine command to love God. Rather than the ability to act without any motive (which is impossible), freedom, in turn, entails acting consistent with reason, albeit reason informed by God's revelation.[14] This led Backus to an optimistic view of truth, understood as an objective force that "certainly would do well enough if she were left to shift for herself."[15]

Sin, in contrast, is the product of human yielding to another external motive, "the conceit that man could advance either his honor or happiness by disobedience instead of obedience," injected by "the father of lies." This evil imagination "usurped" the place of a properly informed reason, a usurpation which continues in the history of every person and brings with it the rebellion that characterizes each human. The result is depravity, the situation in which reason no longer rules over the actions of the individual.[16]

Given this deplorable condition, Backus added in true Calvinist fashion, only divine influence can restore reason to its rightful place.[17] Such divine influence is mediated by the Scriptures, "our

---

[12] Isaac Backus, *Truth is Great and Will Prevail* (Boston, 1781), in William McLoughlin, ed., *Isaac Backus on Church, State, and Calvinism: Pamphlets, 1754-1789* (Cambridge, MA: Harvard University, 1968), 402.

[13] Isaac Backus, *The Sovereign Decree of God* (Boston, 1773), in McLoughlin, *Isaac Backus on Church, State, and Calvinism*, 297.

[14] Isaac Backus, *The Doctrine of Sovereign Grace Opened and Vindicated* (Providence: John Carter, 1771), 60-62.

[15] Isaac Backus, *A Seasonable Plea for Liberty of Conscience* (Boston, 1770), 12.

[16] Isaac Backus, *An Appeal to the Public for Religious Liberty*, in *Isaac Backus on Church, State, and Calvinism*, 311.

[17] Backus, *The Doctrine of Sovereign Grace*, 62.

only perfect rule,"[18] which are designed to act against the "evil imaginations" and to combat ignorance, thereby bringing freedom.[19] Divine assistance via both "light and truth" results in entrance into faith—the acceptance of the real truth about God and oneself. Christ is "the author and finisher" of this faith, the Word is the means of its coming to a man,[20] and thus it is a grace produced in man by an external cause:

> it is admitting the testimony of another, and not any work of ours; our character has no concern in the affair, as to whether we are poor or rich, worthy or unworthy, for it depends entirely upon the evidence that we have of the creditability of the speaker: And though we often strive against, or try to avoid the light, because our deeds are evil, yet when our souls are brought to receive divine truth it is no more of our work than it is to see and enjoy the light when the sun shines, Psal. lxxxiv, 11, John iii, 14-20. The light directs our way, and we are influenced by the objects which we view, to avoid what appears odious or dangerous, and to pursue what we think is agreeable with all our might. So by faith the soul flies to Christ to supply all its wants, and cleaves to him in the way of holiness. . . .[21]

This faith results in obedience to God:

> There are three things in faith which powerfully excite to obedience, and guard against all the snares of sin: The believing soul views the precept to be true and excellent, therefore to be obeyed; the promise to be sure and sufficient,

---

[18] Isaac Backus, *All True Ministers of the Gospel are Called unto that Work by the Special Influences of the Holy Spirit* (Boston: Printed by Fowle, 1754), 16.

[19] See, for example, Isaac Backus, *The Doctrine of Particular Election and Final Perseverance* (Boston, 1789), in McLoughlin, *Isaac Backus on Church, State, and Calvinism*, 451.

[20] Isaac Backus, *True Faith Will Produce Good Works* (Boston: Printed by D. Kneeland, for Philip Freeman, 1767), 31. See also *An Abridgement of the Church History of New England,* 239: "faith cometh by hearing the Word of God. Romans x. 17."

[21] Backus, *The Doctrine of Sovereign Grace Opened,* 25.

> therefore he shall be supported; and faith presents eternal things as near and real, therefore to be regarded without delay. And if we carefully observe, we shall find that in these are the main springs of obedience, and that the contrary is the root of all mischief.[22]

In short, faith is the assent to the real truth about God and man, which comes about by means of an overwhelming external motive and which results in a willing submission to the reasonable precepts of God.[23]

In Backus's mind the entrance into the state of faith, or the acceptance of God's truth, occurs at a specific point in time, that is, before this moment in time the individual does not possess faith whereas after that moment he does. At this point in time, something occurs in the individual, namely regeneration or the new birth, the necessity of which is one article in the doctrine of Christ, for "no man can see his kingdom nor have right to any power therein without regeneration, John i, 12, 13 and iii, 3."[24] But men cannot be regenerated unless they are first brought to a realization of their need, a realization which likewise is externally produced. The agent which produces an awareness of one's need is the law as found in God's word, so that "nothing but the divine law . . .brought home with convincing power, can make them (i.e. men

---

[22] Backus, *True Faith Will Produce Good Works,* 35.

[23] [This is not to suggest that Backus believed salvation consists only in mental assent to the truth, for as he also writes, "Saving faith is a receiving with all the heart the witness and testimony that God has given of eternal life in his Son, and he who believeth not hath made him a liar, 1st John v. 9-12, the evidence of which truth shines so clear as to leave all without excuse, who do not believe with all their hearts; while every soul that is made willing by divine power to receive his testimony [Psalm 110:3], and set to his seal that God is true [John 3:33], knows that the *faith is not of himself,* it is the gift of God." *The Doctrine of Sovereign Grace,* 14. Backus further notes that it is perfectly consistent of God to "plainly set life and death before all men by the ministry of his work, and call them all to turn and live; although he does not intend to exert his almighty power to save any others but those that he has given to his Son, John vi. 37 and xvii. 2." *Ibid.*, 66-67 —*Ed.*]

[24] Isaac Backus, *An Appeal to the People of the Massachusetts State Against Arbitrary Power* (Boston: Benjamin Edes and Sons, 1780), 391.

in general) truly sensible of the soul-slavery that they are in,"[25] the entire process being in final analysis, effected by "the power of the Holy Ghost, Matt. iii, 11 and John iii, 5, 8."[26] This process comes about in the following manner:

> When He (i.e. the Spirit of God) sets home the law upon a sinner's conscience, he is made to know that he is a guilty soul before God, as certainly as if his name was expressed in God's sacred book: for it lays open his particular sins, and charges them home upon his conscience with power; and thus the Word of God becomes a 'discerner of the thoughts and intents of the heart,' Heb. iv, 12. So when a soul has a discovery of Christ he sees Him not only to be a Savior in general, but also that He is just such a Savior as he needs.[27]

This then results in a recovery of man's original state of spiritual life:

> As natural life is lost when the union between soul and body is dissolved; so our spiritual life was lost by revolting from God, and is recovered only by reconciliation and union with him. By the divine Spirit the soul is cut off from nature's stock, and grafted into Christ, the true vine, whereby they have such a vital union with him as to receive strength and nourishment from him, to bring forth fruit. . . .[28]

Thus Backus's theology of conversion is a theology of the Word and the Spirit: the gospel proclamation, which is basically the demands of God as expressed in his law plus the work of Christ to save those who are disobedient to the law, is so impressed by the Holy Spirit upon a man's reason that his conscience cries up his guilt and his mind sees the reasonableness of the whole message

---

[25] Isaac Backus, *An Appeal to the Public for Religious Liberty, Against the Oppression of the Present Day* (Boston: John Boyle, 1773), 311.

[26] Backus, *An Abridgement of the Church History of New England*, 239.

[27] Backus, *All True Ministers of the Gospel*, 76. But see his *Sermon on Acts 17* for the additional element of repentance.

[28] Isaac Backus, *Gospel Comfort under Heavy Tidings* (Providence, RI: John Carter, 1769), 6.

so as to embrace the truth. In conversion reason is once again allowed to carry out its God-given task: "It (i.e. conversion) is not a creation of new faculties, but the giving new ideas and dispositions, which were our indispensable duty before, but our evil hearts were contrary thereto."[29]

Such an outlook upon conversion obviously demands that other men play a role in the process. Their job is that of proclaiming the gospel message, of holding forth clearly the truth of God. Herein is the importance of the use of means (which has been mentioned earlier). But since the final power producing regeneration is the Holy Spirit, the means which men legitimately use are limited to these just mentioned. Any use of force in this affair is strictly forbidden. Further, this outlook upon conversion as a Spirit-produced event by means of the proclaimed Word, denies the validity of all systems which place regenerative significance upon any acts which a man might do for himself (e.g., Wesley),[30] or that one might do for another (such as in sacramentalism).[31]

It is easily seen that in Backus's thought such a conversion experience will always result in certain changes. On the one hand, the true convert will now believe differently than before:

> Those who are looked upon to be converted, though many circumstances of their change are very various; yet all agree in the purity and strictness of the divine law, and that their hearts as well as lives have been filled with sin, and from thence give in to the justice of God in their condemnation: And hold their justification to be entirely by Christ's righteousness, received by faith. . . .[32]

On the other hand, if the evil imaginations which had blocked acceptance of man's duty to obey God have now been overcome by the Spirit's power (at least to the extent that the individual now

---

[29] Backus, *A History of New England*, 2 (1784): 264.

[30] See Isaac Backus, *The Doctrine of Particular Election and Final Perseverance, Explained and Vindicated* (Boston: Samuel Hall, 1789), 453, 461.

[31] Backus, *An Abridgement of the Church History of New England*, 239.

[32] Isaac Backus *Spiritual Ignorance Causeth Men to Counter-act Their Doctrinal Knowledge. A Discourse from Acts xiii. 27* (Providence: William Goddard, 1763), 20.

freely accepts his duty), then at least the desire to follow God's commands should be present in the life of the believer even though he may often fail to carry them out. After writing the above, Backus adds, "Yet a view of that is so far from making them careless in their behavior, that they discover an earnest desire to know and conform to all of Christ's commands and ordinances; they show much love to God's people, earnest concern for the salvation of souls, and the like."[33]

Since conversion always results in a changed life, it is possible to determine one's own spiritual status, as well as the status of others. For this reason, Backus on several occasions admonishes his readers to look to their own condition[34] and even sets down certain formulas to follow in this enterprise. One "use" which he concludes from the existence of two families of men, the children of the bondwoman and those of the free, is this:

> Then, surely 'tis of infinite importance for each soul to know which mother they belong to. And the Scriptures have given many plain marks whereby we may come to know how our case is. For brevity's sake I shall instance but one, which is that If thou art a child of the freewoman, it is become thy *liberty* to walk in holiness.[35]

Then Backus explains that one difference between the greatest hypocrite and the least Christian lies in the motives from which they pay regard to God's commands—the hypocrite is motivated by fear of hell whereas the Christian is motivated by his knowledge of God's love for him and a delight in, and a love for, God's law. Elsewhere, Backus elaborates further upon this same idea, suggesting the following as a basis for self-appraisal:

> Have you been made to know the dreadfulness of being without Christ, without God in the world? And have you been driven out of every other refuge, so as to take sanctuary in Christ alone? One peculiar excellency of the knowledge of him is, that it transforms the soul into his

---

33 *Ibid.*, 20-21.

34 E.g., *All True Ministers of the Gospel*, 117.

35 Isaac Backus, *A Short Description of the Difference Between the Bondwoman and the Free* (Boston: Green and Russell, 1756), 160-161.

likeness. . . .The views they (i.e. saints) have of him now, through a glass darkly, cause a self-loathing for their former actings against him, and a longing after conformity to him in heart and life. . . .[36]

But to prevent any true believers from falsely misunderstanding the spiritual struggle which they may be experiencing, he says,

Methinks I hear some such say, 'Alas, I fear that I am a child of the bondwoman, for I often drag on heavily in duty, and I feel my heart so dull and backward to spiritual exercizes that I can't think there is any grace in it.' But this short question may easily decide the case, viz., Is it the divine commands which are burdensome to thee or thy vile heart that often hinders thee from doing the things that thou wouldest? God's service is a weariness to hypocrites, Amos vii, 5; Mal. i, 13. But saints delight in his law after the inward man though they find a law in their members warring against it, Rom. vi, 21, 22, 23. Carefully observe this distinction and you may come to know what your condition is.[37]

Similarly, upon the basis of Jesus' statement that we shall know them by their fruits,[38] Backus claims that believers can know the condition of others:

Indeed fruits comprehend all that men 'bring forth out of their hearts,' in their principles, experience, conversation, and conduct; and hereby we are to 'know them,' and to act towards them according to the clearest light we can gain.[39]

---

[36] Backus, *Gospel Comfort Under Heavy Tidings*, 12.

[37] Backus, *A Short Description of the Difference Between the Bond-woman and the Free*, 162.

[38] E.g., *A Letter to the Reverend Mr. Benjamin Lord, of Norwich* (Providence, 1764), 30, citing Matt. vii. 6, 15, 16, and Luke vi. 44-45.

[39] Backus, *True Faith Will Produce Good Works,* 75. Also *Spiritual Ignorance*, 19-20 and *A History of New England*, 2: 90.

In all of this Backus emphasized the individual. It is the individual in whom reason was originally designed to rule, in whom reason's role has been usurped by evil imaginations, and therefore in whom God's solution is to be operative. Likewise, it is the individual whom the Holy Spirit teaches the truths of God's Word. For this reason "religion is ever a matter between God and individuals,"[40] "a voluntary obedience unto God,"[41] a relationship mediated only by the Word as it is illuminated to the believer by the Holy Spirit.

Backus's third foundational doctrine was ecclesiology. Like others of his day, he accepted without variation of thought the differentiation between the invisible church of all the elect and the visible church, the earthly institution. But in contrast to the Congregationalists, he demanded a radical application of the pure church ideal, leading to the conclusion that the visible church is a voluntary society of believers,[42] united by a voluntary covenant:

> All who have this work (i.e. the new covenant, which is 'the writing of the law of love in the believer's heart, which yields a free consent to it') wrought within them ought to confess the same with their mouths, and to receive each other as Christ received them, to the glory of God. Says the apostle, they first gave their own selves to the Lord, and unto us by the will of God. Rom. x, 10; xv, 7; II Cor. viii, 5. This is the exact nature of a church covenant; which shows that no person can be brought into it without his own consent, that the covenant cannot bind any person or community to act any thing contrary to the revealed will of God, nor ever exempt any from their obligation to act agreeably thereto with their hearts.[43]

---

[40] Isaac Backus, *A Door Opened for Religious Liberty* (Boston, 1783), in McLoughlin, *Isaac Backus on Church, State, and Calvinism*, 432.

[41] Isaac Backus, *Government and Liberty Described* (Boston, 1778), in McLoughlin, *Isaac Backus on Church, State, and Calvinism*, 351.

[42] Backus, *A Door Opened*, 432.

[43] Isaac Backus, *A History of New England, with Particular Reference to the Denomination of Christians Called Baptists.* Second Edition, with Notes by David Weston (Newton, MA: Backus Historical Society, 1871), 2: 304.

This understanding of God, the human person, and the nature of the church led to Backus's appraisal of the New England situation and his radical proposal for society, namely, the separation of church and state.

Church and state. Three premises stood at the heart of Backus's understanding of church and state. First, Backus held that government is intrinsic to human existence. As creatures of God, humans are placed within the framework of government, in that they fall under the providence of the God who governs creation. In contrast, then, to the teaching of many of his contemporaries including John Locke, Backus emphasized with Roger Williams that government and liberty are not incompatible. Rather, because humanity was created under divine providence,

> it is so far from being necessary for any man to give up any part of his real liberty in order to submit to government that all nations have found it necessary to submit to some government in order to enjoy any liberty and security at all.[44]

In this way, human government became for Backus the agent of God, divinely instituted and necessitated because of human rebellion against the divine rulership.[45]

Second, Backus held that God had instituted two different governments, the civil and the ecclesiastical, each with differing tasks and spheres of responsibility: "Men have three things to be concerned for, namely, soul, body, and estate. The two latter belong to the magistrate's jurisdiction, the other does not."[46] In order to fulfill its task of governing the "bodies and estates" of humans, the civil government has two basic duties. It is "to punish such as work ill to their neighbor," and to carry out this duty, and this one alone, the magistrate "bears the sword."[47] Likewise, "all

---

[44] Isaac Backus, *An Appeal to the Public for Religious Liberty* (Boston, 1773), in McLoughlin, *Isaac Backus on Church, State, and Calvinism*, 312.

[45] Backus, *History of New England* (1871 ed.), 2: 321.

[46] Isaac Backus, *Policy as Well as Honesty Forbids the Use of Secular Force in Religious Affairs* (Boston: 1779), in McLoughlin, *Isaac Backus on Church, State, and Calvinism*, 381.

[47] Backus, *History of New England* (1871 ed.), 2: 265.

who are in authority" are to "protect and encourage such a quiet and peaceable life in all Godliness and honesty."[48]

Although admitting certain structural similarities between the two governments, Backus adamantly argued that the two are separated by a major difference. Unlike the situation in the church, "dominion" in the civil sphere is not "founded in grace." In saying this, Backus was opposing the widely held viewpoint of his day that "religion endows the subjects of it with a right to act as lawgivers and judges over others."[49] Rather, he envisioned the civil government as defending its citizens against the hostilities of others and promoting upright living by means of respectable magistrates who are elected by the entire population regardless of religious persuasion.

The distinction between the civil and ecclesiastical governments suggested to Backus that there must be a twofold separation of the two. Of course, the church must not interfere in the civil sphere. This is demanded by the Lord's exclusion of the sword from his kingdom,[50] he asserted, as well as by the nature of religion itself. Hence, Backus wrote, "as the Baptists hold all religion to be personal, between God and individuals, and that all church power is in each particular church, it is impossible for them ever to form any great body, that can be dangerous to any civil government."[51]

Worse in Backus's eyes than the threat of ecclesiastical interference in the civil sphere is the reverse problem, the use of secular force in religious matters. According to Backus, the civil government must not legislate in the ecclesiastical sphere, because Jesus declared that his kingdom "does not receive its support from earthly power, but from TRUTH."[52] In one of his most famous statements on this topic, Backus declared,

---

[48] Backus, *An Address to the Inhabitants of New England* (Boston, 1787), in McLoughlin, *Isaac Backus on Church, State, and Calvinism*, 446.

[49] Backus, *History of New England* (1871 ed.), 1: 373.

[50] Backus, *Policy as Well as Honesty*, 375.

[51] Backus, *History of New England*, preface to volume 3, 2 (1784): viii.

[52] Isaac Backus, *A Letter to a Gentleman*, (n.a., 1771), 5.

> The business of laws is not to provide for the truth of opinions, but for the safety and security of the commonwealth, and of every man's goods and person; and so it ought to be; for truth certainly would do well enough if she were once left to shift for herself. She seldom has received, and I fear never will receive, much assistance from the power of great men; to whom she is but rarely known, and more rarely welcome. She is not taught by laws, nor has she any need of force to procure her entrance into the minds of men. Errors indeed prevail by the assistance of foreign and borrowed succours.[53]

In spite of his call for what in his day appeared to be a radical separation between church and state, Backus did not see the two spheres as being competitive. Nor did he dispute the long held view that religion is important to society.[54] The point of fundamental disagreement with his opponents lay with their suggestion that the importance of religion to society granted to the civil government the right to secure legislatively the benefits of religion.[55] Backus questioned whether that worthy goal could even be attained by such means. Instead, he advocated a different approach to securing the piety necessary to society. Civil government must limit its role to that of creating a climate in which truth is free to act. Piety in turn would be guaranteed to society by the sovereign God through the convincing power of truth by means of the missionary enterprise of the church, as individuals are converted and consequently become good citizens.[56]

Backus, then, envisioned a "sweet harmony" between church and state.[57] Christ is to be sovereign in his church. Through his people, Christ draws the individual members of society to acknowledge the truth of Christianity. This in turn benefits the

---

[53] *Ibid.*, 5-6. Here, Backus is quoting from John Locke, *A Letter Concerning Toleration* (London, 1689, et var.).

[54] Backus, *Policy as Well as Honesty*, 371.

[55] *Ibid*, 374-375.

[56] Isaac Backus, *The Kingdom of God Described by His Word* (Boston, 1792), 14; Backus, *History of New England* (1871 ed.), 2: 378.

[57] Isaac Backus, *A Fish Caught in His Own Net* (Boston, 1768), in McLoughlin, *Isaac Backus on Church, State, and Calvinism*, 190-191.

state, because "real Christians are the best subjects of civil government in the world."[58]

Third, while denying the civil sphere a role in matters of the church, Backus did advocate governmental activity in the realm of morality. Following Locke and the Enlightenment, Backus believed that certain truths of morality and religion were present to all humans regardless of confessional persuasion, being mediated to them by reason. These truths or duties taught by natural religion, including justice, peace, sobriety, and even petition and thanksgiving to God,[59] fall under the jurisdiction of civil government. Legislation in these areas does not entail a denial of religious liberty, for such laws merely force citizens to act according to reason, which is freedom in the true sense. Truths that are available only by special revelation, in contrast, lie outside the civil sphere.[60]

In short, according to Backus, government is a legitimate institution derived from God. The civil and religious spheres are distinct entities, separated in function and in fact. Morality falls under the domain of both, being divided into each sphere according to the distinction between natural truth of reason and supernatural truth of revelation.

The Baptists in God's program. In addition to defending evangelical Calvinism and advocating the separation of church and state, Backus offered a far-reaching perspective on the nature of the Baptist cause. He was convinced that the positions he and the Baptists were formulating were not only logical and biblical, but were the natural outgrowth of the entire Puritan heritage of both Old and New England. Hence, rather than being a sectarian group as the Puritan establishment suggested, his adopted denomination stood at the forefront of the entire Reformation. In short, Backus was able to bring a formerly outcast, sectarian group on the fringe of the Puritan commonwealth into the center of the American religious community.

Backus accomplished this goal through an ingenious reinterpretation of the apocalyptic imagery of the book of Revelation,

---

[58] Backus, *An Abridgment of the Church History of New England*, 245.

[59] Backus, *History of New England*, 1: 361.

[60] For a fuller discussion see Stanley J. Grenz, "Isaac Backus and Religious Liberty," *Foundations. A Baptist Journal of History and Theology* (American Baptist Historical Society), 22 (1979), No. 4 (Oct.-Dec.): 352-360.

especially the figures of the two beasts. Since Luther, Protestant apologists had linked the first beast with ancient Rome, but had asserted that the second, Antichrist figure was the bishop of Rome. Consequently, in his apologetic for the Protestant cause Jonathan Edwards had claimed that Puritan New England was the scene of the climax of the battle between Christ and Antichrist.

Backus altered this interpretation. He claimed that the pope was the *first* beast. The second beast did not arise until the Protestants, following the church against which they were protesting, joined church and state together and used the power of the state against their dissenting sisters and brothers. In this manner Antichrist, wounded in the Reformation, had raised its ugly head first in England and subsequently in the colonies. The very Massachusetts fathers who had built a Christian commonwealth to combat the papal Antichrist, Backus argued, were responsible for giving place to the real Antichrist—the church-state union—within the city upon a hill. Consequently, Backus argued, the apocalyptic conflict was still raging in New England. By clinging to the concept of a national church and its corollary, infant baptism, the New England establishment was refusing to allow Christ to be sole ruler and supporter of his church. Backus likewise asserted that the mingling of church and state was responsible for thwarting the reformation process and preventing a return to the primitive purity of Christ's church. When true separation of church and state would be inaugurated, truth would be set free to do its work of convincing all God's people of all the principles of Reformation theology and polity. This would constitute the church's victory over Antichrist and the dawning of the era of truth and righteousness marked by Christ's complete rule in His church.[61]

By means of his subtle alteration of the reigning interpretation of the apocalyptic drama, Backus placed the small, despised, dissenting sect on the pinnacle of the Puritan rendition of church history. Whereas the Massachusetts fathers had thought that the Reformation culminated with them, giving their experiment the significance of constituting a city on a hill for the rest of the world, Backus argued that subsequent history disproved this claim. He asserted that the despised Baptists—and not New England's Congregationalists—were the vanguard of the entire reformation process and the most reformed of the reformation churches.—

[61] Isaac Backus, *The Testimony of the Two Witnesses* (Providence: Printed by Bennett Wheeler, 1786), 31.

Further, Backus envisioned a not-too-distant day when *all* Christians would see the light God had allowed the Baptists alone to see already. On that day, all Christians would acknowledge the principles of believer's baptism and the sole lordship of Christ over his church apart from the meddling of human legislators.

Summarizing his contributions

Not only was Backus a crucial leader of his day, he also made a lasting contribution to the Baptist cause in America. Backus's legacy lies in the type of Calvinistic theology he embraced, the church-state theory he developed, and the understanding of the role of the Baptist movement in the on-going reformation he envisioned.

First, Backus contributed to the developing theology of the Baptist movement. More particularly, he became the bearer of the theological orientation that came to characterize the denomination as a whole at this crucial stage in its history. Under Backus's leadership the evangelical Calvinism he inherited from Jonathan Edwards and the Separates replaced the Arminianism that had come to predominate in the older Baptist churches. In so doing, however, Backus actually became a transitional theological figure. Although he saw himself as a stanch Calvinist, he actually helped pave the way for the revivalism of the nineteenth century. He held unwaveringly to the Calvinist distinctive of the sovereignty of God in election. Yet, Backus's understanding of this principle was shaped by the Great Awakening and the Enlightenment. Edwards and Locke shifted Backus's attention to the human person—especially the human faculty of reason—as the location where God's eternal decrees find their outworking. It was a short step from his emphasis on individual reason to the revivalist emphasis on individual will, generally expressed in terms of "decisions for Christ."

Backus was surely correct in finding the basis of evangelism in the sovereignty of God and the importance of human obedience, rather than in God as the source of human happiness, so prevalent in revivalism. Similarly, Backus's emphasis on covenant (conversion as a covenant with God and the church as a covenant community) offers a needed corrective for much Baptist thinking that builds largely on the individualism of the Baptist heritage while ignoring the communal dimension of faith, which for earlier Baptists formed the context for an emphasis on the individual.

Backus's second contribution was in the area of church and state. His efforts in this area led one observer to offer this accolade: "no individual in America since Roger Williams stands out so preeminently as the champion of religious liberty."[62] This dimension of Backus's work has spilled over denominational boundaries, having had lasting importance for the United States as a whole. The program he outlined was adopted to a large extent by the new republic and has remained the dominant position into the present. By means of an emphasis on the freedom of truth, Backus sought a balance between a transcendent grounding of government and individual religious liberty. He likewise championed liberty of the individual conscience, while acknowledging the importance of religion to the well-being of society. Although the theory is not without difficulties, over two hundred years of subsequent American history have confirmed the basic correctness of Backus's position. Personal religious conviction does contribute to the well-being of society. And such conviction ultimately cannot be forced or legislated, but must arise from the hearts of its citizens.

Finally, Backus offered a powerful vision of the role of the Baptists in reformation history. Here, however, his lasting influence is less pronounced. The churches in America did in time come to embrace disestablishment, as Backus had hoped. But this victory brought neither the universal acceptance of believer's baptism nor the one truly reformed church. After his death even many of Backus's own spiritual children lost his vision. Rather than continuing his struggle for the reformation of the one church, they settled for the enjoyment of the place in the American religious community his efforts in part won for them. As respected members of the community of churches, the Baptists by and large embraced the denominationalism that gained widespread adherence in the nineteenth century, by means of which the various competing groups could affirm each other as comprising together the one body of Christ despite their lack of theological and organizational unity.

The reformation which Backus envisioned, the goal which he inherited from those whom he saw as his predecessors and which marked him as a Puritan, has never been completed. On the contrary, reformation remains the task of the church in every age. Backus's declaration that the Baptists have an important role to

---

[62] William Henry Allison, "Isaac Backus," in Allen Johnson, ed., *Dictionary of American Biography* (New York: Charles Scribner's Sons, 1928), 1: 471.

play in that reformation stands as an important challenge to his heirs in every generation.

Standing in the legacy of the "radical reformation," Baptists have historically called other Protestants to apply consistently the principles of the protest against traditionalism, sacramentarianism, sacerdotalism, and authoritarianism. To this end, throughout their history Baptists have asserted that all creeds and ecclesiological systems must be measured according to the Scriptures, and they have emphasized the importance of such crucial principles as the personal nature of the Christian faith and religious liberty. This witness has not been unsuccessful. However, the gains of the past are never sufficient. Therefore, if today's Baptists are to maintain the legacy of their forebears, they must reaffirm the goal and vision of Isaac Backus, and on the basis of that overarching vision contribute to the fulfillment of the mission of the one Body of Christ.

Further Reading

Stanley J. Grenz. *Isaac Backus—Puritan and Baptist.* Macon, GA: Mercer University Press, 1983.

Alvah Hovey. *A Memoir of the Life and Times of the Rev. Isaac Backus, A.M.* Boston: Gould and Lincoln, 1858; facsimile reprint Harrisonburg, VA: Gano Books, 1991.

William G. McLoughlin, ed. *The Diary of Isaac Backus.* Providence, RI: Brown University Press, 1979. Three volumes.

William G. McLoughlin. *Isaac Backus and the American Pietistic Tradition.* Boston: Little, Brown and Company, 1967.

William G. McLoughlin. *Isaac Backus on Church, State, and Calvinism. Pamphlets, 1754-1789.* Cambridge, MA: The Belknap Press of Harvard University Press, 1968.

An old print of the Baptist meetinghouse at Hopewell, New Jersey.

ISAAC EATON
1725? - 1772

by Walter E. Johnson

The eighteenth century was a period of significant growth for Baptists in America, both numerically and organizationally. In 1700, there were only 24 Baptist churches in America with 839 members. By 1790, they numbered 979 churches, with 67,490 members. These churches were organized into at least 42 associations, and were planning to organize on a national basis. The Baptists had adopted a confession of faith in 1742, formed a Baptist college in 1764 (Rhode Island College, later called Brown University), struggled for and achieved religious liberty, and hammered out a theology of evangelical Calvinism.[1] Capable leadership was a main factor in this substantial growth. One such leader was Isaac Eaton.

Family background and early ministry

Eaton was born in Montgomery, Pennsylvania, in late 1725 or early 1726. His father, Joseph Eaton (1679-1749), had emigrated from Wales as a lad about the year 1686. At the time of Isaac's birth, Joseph was pastor of the Baptist church at Montgomery, a member of the Philadelphia Baptist Association. In 1743, a split occurred in the membership of the Montgomery church over whether to relocate the church meetinghouse and over a Christological issue. Joseph Eaton sided with the group that petitioned the Montgomery church for dismissal in order to start a new church (New Britain) and affiliate with the Philadelphia Association. Joseph Eaton served as pastor of this body until his death on April 1, 1749. The New Britain church formally incorporated in 1754 and was accepted into the Association in 1755.[2]

[1] H. Leon McBeth, *The Baptist Heritage: Four Centuries of Baptist Witness* (Nashville: Broadman Press, 1987), 200.

[2] Morgan Edwards suggested that the doctrinal issue was "too inconsiderable to produce the effects it did," since both sides agreed on the full deity of Christ and His equality with the Father. See his *Materials Towards a History of the Baptists in Pennsylvania* (Philadelphia: Joseph Crukshank and Isaac Collins, 1770; reprint, Enid, OK: Regular Baptist Publishing, 1998), 50-51. However, the issue was regarding the eternal generation and Sonship of Jesus Christ, which Joseph Eaton evidently

Joseph Eaton advocated the "Maydoc myth," the belief that America was discovered and settled in the twelfth century by the Welsh prince Maydoc. This belief further motivated the Welsh Baptists in the Delaware Valley to evangelize the area, having "an urgency to save their lost brethren's souls."[3]

Joseph Eaton had eight children by his first wife, Gwen Morgan; Isaac was one of the three children born to Joseph's second wife, Uria Humphreys.[4] Isaac was saved at an early age and joined the Southampton Church soon after that congregation was organized.[5] According to church records, in December of 1746, Eaton and Oliver Hart (1723-1795) "were called to be on trial for the work of the ministry, to exercise at the meetings of preparation or in private meetings that might for that purpose be appointed."[6] This approval for ministry was followed by ordination on November 29, 1748, when Eaton was twenty-four years of age and being called to pastor the church at Hopewell, New Jersey.[7] At some point he was married to Rebecca Stout (–1794), by whom Edwards tells us, "he had many children: some died single; but

---

denied. Fortunately, at the 1743 meeting of the Philadelphia Association, in a written statement, Eaton acknowledged his error. See A. D. Gillette, ed., *Minutes of the Philadelphia Baptist Association, 1707-1807* (Philadelphia: American Baptist Publication Society, 1851), 47-48.

[3] Hywel M. Davies, *Transatlantic Brethren: Rev. Samuel Jones (1735-1814) and His Friends: Baptists in Wales, Pennsylvania, and Beyond* (Bethlehem, PA: Lehigh University Press, 1995), 169.

[4] Edwards, *Materials Towards a History of the Baptists in Pennsylvania*, 51-52. [They were married on March 17, 1724 —*Ed.*]

[5] Edwards indicated that the church at Southampton did not fully organize until 1746; thus Eaton would have been about 21 years old. Gillette informs us that the precise date of the church's constitution was April 8, 1746 and that it joined the Association on September 24th of that year. *Minutes of the Philadelphia Baptist Association*, 93.

[6] Robert A. Baker and Paul J. Craven, Jr., *Adventure in Faith: The First 300 Years of First Baptist Church, Charleston, South Carolina* (Nashville: Broadman Press, 1982), 126. Edwards states that Eaton had come to Hopewell in April 1748. *Materials Towards a History of the Baptists in [New] Jersey*, 48.

[7] William Cathcart, ed., *The Baptist Encyclopedia* (Philadelphia: Louis H. Everts, 1881), 357.

Joseph, David, and Pamela [or Pamelia] married into the families of the Turners, Potts, and Humphreys, and have raised him 8 grand children."[8] Eaton would remain at Hopewell until his death twenty-six years later in 1772.

The Hopewell Church had been organized in 1715, an offshoot of the Middletown Church. Jonathan Stout moved from Middletown to become the first settler in Hopewell. The church was organized in Stout's home, where it met for thirty-two years until building its first meetinghouse in 1747. After Eaton's death, Oliver Hart served as pastor from 1780 or 1781 until his own death in 1795.[9] Hart came to Hopewell from the pastorate of the First Baptist Church of Charleston, South Carolina, where his political activities as a patriot forced him to flee the British.[10]

From all indication, Eaton's ministry at Hopewell was very productive. In the words of one historian, "rich blessings descended upon his pastorate."[11] Morgan Edwards tells us there were several remarkable seasons of revival. We read for example, in 1764, that one hundred and twenty-three converts were added to the church. And in 1775-1776, one hundred and five more were united with it.[12] In his Philadelphia Association centennial sermon in 1807, Dr. Samuel Jones listed Eaton as one of the leading ministers in the Association's first century.[13] Unfortunately, by the

---

[8] Morgan Edwards, *Materials Towards a History of the Baptists in [New] Jersey* (Philadelphia: Thomas Dobson, 1792; facsimile reprint, Enid, OK: Regular Baptist Publishing, Inc., 1998), 50. [Thomas S. Griffiths in his *History of Baptists in New Jersey* (Hightstown, NJ: Barr Press Publishing Co., 1904), 69, speculates that Isaac Eaton's wife Rebecca "may have influenced his coming to the church" —*Ed.]*

[9] Griffiths, *A History of Baptists in New Jersey,* 67.

[10] Baker and Craven, *Adventure in Faith*, 173-174.

[11] Cathcart, *The Baptist Encyclopedia,* 357.

[12] *Materials Towards a History of the Baptists in [New] Jersey,* 46.

[13] Samuel Jones, *A Century Sermon. Delivered in Philadelphia, at the Opening of the Philadelphia Baptist Association, October 6th, 1807* (Philadelphia: Bartram and Reynolds, 1807), as republished in Gillette, *Minutes of the Philadelphia Baptist Association*, 456.

early years of the nineteenth century the church would lose its evangelical fervor and effectiveness.[14]

While effective as a pastor, it is through his involvement in cooperation with the Philadelphia Association that Eaton is most remembered. In 1752, Eaton was instrumental, along with Isaac Stelle and Benjamin Miller, in organizing the Morristown church. Its first pastor, John Gano (1727-1804), and Gano's first convert, Hezekiah Smith (1737-1805), became prominent Baptists in early America.[15] Even more significant however, was Eaton's involvement with the earliest attempts at more formally organized higher education for Baptists in America.

Hopewell Academy

Opportunities for ministerial training for Baptists were all but nonexistent in Eaton's day. As a rule, Baptists had not placed a high priority upon education for their ministers, stressing personal piety and Holy Spirit empowerment instead. This, along with the scarcity of Baptists and a lingering suspicion of an educated ministry, inhibited progress toward developing needed educational institutions. That is not to say that all Baptists looked with disdain upon an educated ministry; many Baptists realized the importance of trained ministry.[16] Yet, options were extremely limited. McBeth delineated these options:

> Baptist ministers who desired education had three choices. They could return to England, which a few did before the

---

[14] Conflicting reasons are suggested for this decline. Writing in 1898, Henry Vedder indicated that Hopewell's numerical and spiritual decline resulted from its adoption of anti-mission sentiments and its association with "Old School" or "Primitive Baptists." See Henry C. Vedder, *A History of the Baptists in the Middle States* (Philadelphia: American Baptist Publication Society, 1898), 47. In 1904, Thomas S. Griffiths suggested a different cause: "the church has deserted the Gospel of grace." *A History of Baptists in New Jersey*, 69.

[15] Walter R. Greenwood, "Historical Sketch of the First Baptist Church, 1752-1927," in *One Hundred Seventy-fifth Anniversary of the Morristown Baptist Church, September 15-18, 1927* (Morristown, NJ: First Baptist Church, 1927), 10.

[16] McBeth, *The Baptist Heritage*, 235; and Robert G. Torbet, *A History of the Baptists.* Third edition (Valley Forge, PA: Judson Press, 1973), 305.

> Revolution made that less feasible; they could read on their own; or they could attend Harvard or Yale....However, Baptists faced harassment and second-class treatment at these schools. Further, many were proselyted to the state religion before graduation, giving rise to the saying that you could send a Baptist to Harvard but could not get one out.[17]

McBeth later mentioned a fourth option for ministerial students: to "read theology" with a seasoned minister, living in the minister's home, and participating in his ministerial duties.[18]

In 1756, the Philadelphia Baptist Association addressed the lack of educational opportunities for Baptists in America. At its annual meeting on October 5th, the Association voted "to raise a sum of money toward the encouragement of a Latin Grammar School, for the promotion of learning among us, under the care of the Rev. Isaac Eaton, and the inspection of our brethren, Abel Morgan, Isaac Stelle, Abel Griffith, and Peter P. Van Horne."[19] The school, though primarily devoted to the training of young men for the ministry, trained for other professions also.[20] Thus, to Isaac Eaton belongs the honor of being "the first man among the *American* Baptists, who set up a school for the education of youths for the ministry."[21]

The Association fully supported the Hopewell school during its continuation, raising nearly £400 for its support.[22] The school

---

[17] McBeth, *The Baptist Heritage,* 235. Harvard and Yale were controlled exclusively by the Congregationalists at this time; the College of New Jersey at Princeton was Presbyterian; and William and Mary of Virginia and the University of Pennsylvania were under Episcopal control.

[18] McBeth, *The Baptist Heritage,* 236-237.

[19] Reuben A. Guild, *Early History of Brown University, Including the Life, Times, and Correspondence of President Manning* (Providence, RI: Snow and Farnham, 1897), 8-9.

[20] Morgan Edwards wrote in his quaint way, "All that received the first rudiments of learning at Hopewell School did not prefer the church," indicating that some men were trained for other professions. *Materials Towards a History of the Baptists in [New] Jersey*, 49.

[21] Edwards, *Materials Towards a History of the Baptists in [New] Jersey,* 49-50.

[22] *Ibid.*, 49*n*.

operated effectively for eleven years (1756-1767), during which time it "succeeded beyond the fondest expectations of her most loyal friends and promoters."[23] Much credit for this success is attributed to Eaton's unique qualifications. In addition to his also having studied medicine,[24] Guild noted that "for this work his natural endowments of mind, his rare personality, his varied attainments in knowledge, and his genuine piety, happily qualified him."[25] Thomas S. Griffiths was more specific concerning Eaton's abilities in relation to his greatest life's work:

> Mr. Eaton was one of the world's great men; not alone in his natural endowments and culture, but as much in the appreciation of the claims of the future upon him and of his relations to that future. His forecast in founding a school of universal qualities, and also, his choice of location, the heart of the country, the center if its wealth, and of its social forces, amid the men of the only Baptist Association in the country and in a colony of the largest liberties, having guarantees in its settlers, 'Friends' [or Quakers] and Baptists, unlike other colonies.[26]

Eaton had remarkable academic credentials as well. He received three Master of Arts degrees, one each from the College of New Jersey in 1756, the College of Philadelphia in 1761, and Rhode Island College in 1770, after the closing of Hopewell Academy.[27]

Eaton died on July 4, 1772, at the age of 47. He was buried in the Hopewell Church, the head of his grave being near the base of the pulpit. The congregation marked this spot with a marble memorial inscribed in part as follows:

---

[23] James L. Clark, *To Set Them in Order; Some Influences of the Philadelphia Baptist Association Upon Baptists of America to 1814* (Springfield, MO: Particular Baptist Press, 2001), 33.

[24] Edwards, *Materials Towards a History of the Baptists in [New] Jersey*, 50.

[25] Guild, *Early History of Brown University*, 9.

[26] Griffiths, *A History of Baptists in New Jersey,* 69.

[27] William B. Sprague, ed., *Annals of the American Pulpit* (New York: Robert Carter and Bros., 1865), 6 (Baptist): 89.

In him, with grace and eminence, did shine;
The man, the Christian, scholar, and divine.[28]

At Eaton's funeral, Associational leader Samuel Jones paid tribute to the Hopewell pastor and educator, surely one of early America's greatest, but often neglected, Baptists. At the end of the service, Jones said,

> It might be expected I should say something concerning him; and verily much might be said with the greatest truth. The natural endowments of his mind; the improvement of these by the accomplishments of literature; his early, genuine, and unaffected piety; his abilities as a divine and a preacher; his extensive knowledge of men and books; his catholicism, prudence, and able counsels, together with a view of him in the different relations, both public and private, that he sustained through life with so much honour to himself and happiness to all who had connection with him, would afford ample scope, had I but abilities, time, and inclination, to flourish in a funeral oration. But it is needless, for the bare mentioning them is enough to revive the idea of him in the minds of all who knew him.[29]

Eaton's theology

In spite of Eaton's extensive education and teaching ministry, he was not a prolific writer. In fact, only one work from his pen is extant: the ordination sermon he preached for John Gano in May of 1754 entitled, *The Qualifications, Characters and Duties, of a good Minister of Jesus Christ, considered,* published in 1755.[30] Although not strictly a theological work, several noteworthy doctrinal and practical emphases surface which reveal the heart of this early American Calvinistic Baptist.

---

[28] Edwards, *Materials Towards a History of the Baptists in [New] Jersey*, 48. [This marker may be seen on page 233 —*Ed.*]

[29] Cathcart, *The Baptist Encyclopedia,* 357.

[30] This sermon is reprinted in its entirety in Terry Wolever, *The Life of John Gano, 1727-1804. Pastor-Evangelist of the Philadelphia Association* (Springfield, MO: Particular Baptist Press, 2012), Appendix B, 363-382.

Eaton held the Bible in high esteem, equating its words with the very words of God. For Eaton, the Bible is both necessary and sufficient for the Christian life. Its guidance is necessary in that Christ, he wrote, "hath given us His Word to judge by, and act from."[31] Furthermore, the Bible is necessary in that it is nourishment for the soul as food is for the body, and by it one increases "mightily in the knowledge of Divine truth."[32] Eaton did not follow the modern practice of setting one portion of Scripture against another, as if some portions were more accurate than others. Rather he urged ministers to "declare the whole counsel of God" and warned them not to "keep back any part of the portion which belongs to the children of God."[33]

Eaton also understood the Bible to be sufficient for all that the Christian needs to know for salvation from sin and service to God. Eaton compared the minister, as the Apostle Paul did in 2 Corinthians 5, to an ambassador:

> As an ambassador in a foreign court represents the person of his prince, and is to negotiate in the most weighty affairs relating to the honour of his sovereign, though not to propose any new terms, neither is he to deviate from those made by his master, but always to stand firmly attached to the interests and honour of his rightful lord. So the ambassadors of Christ are sent forth by Him to carry on the Treaty of Peace with mankind, in the Name, and by the authority of, Christ; and exactly according to the platform laid before them, and upon no consideration to propose any new or other method of obtaining the Divine regard . . .[34]

The Scriptures are necessary for both doctrine and practice. The Scriptures are sufficient in that the truths of the faith are fully revealed in them.[35]

---

[31] *Ibid.*, 365.

[32] *Ibid.*, 367.

[33] *Ibid.*, 370.

[34] *Ibid.*, 374.

[35] *Ibid.*, 370.

Eaton's high view of Scripture was matched by his equally exalted view of the church and its ministry. The church as comprised of "the excellent ones of the earth," is so closely related to Christ that to serve it is to serve Jesus.[36] The call to minister within the church is "the highest station that ever mortal man can be placed in this world."[37] Whereas the local church is to be governed by the congregation,[38] the minister is given authority to rule in the church. While the minister is not to lord it over God's people, still he must fulfill his roles described in Scripture as leader, ruler, shepherd, and elder.[39]

Winthrop Hudson has noted that the rugged individualism of American society has had an adverse effect on Baptists, leading them to over-emphasize the individual aspect of the Christian life to the neglect of its social nature. By contrast, Eaton struck the biblical balance between the church as a corporate body and the importance of the individual before God. Whereas Eaton understood the call to the ministry as *personal*—between the individual and God—involving an internal call by the Holy Spirit,[40] he did not interpret the call to ministry as *private*—as *merely* between the individual and God. It is the responsibility of the congregation to aid the individual in discerning the call to ministry. "The authority of a Gospel church over her members, the right she hath to all the gifts of every individual, discovers something in this affair."[41]

This esteemed view of the church is nowhere more evident than in Eaton's understanding of the qualifications of its ministers. He again found the biblical balance—this time between the heart and the head. Eaton stated that the minister must have an experimental knowledge of the work of grace in the heart. "And

---

[36] *Ibid.*, 366.

[37] *Ibid.*, 382.

[38] *Ibid.*, 372-373. The reference was to the church's right to call its own pastor. Eaton approvingly referred to "the opinion of a set of learned men in New England" in this regard, an apparent reference to New England Congregationalism.

[39] *Ibid.*, 377.

[40] *Ibid.*, 372.

[41] *Ibid.*, 372-373.

how any person may be called a good minister of Christ, whilst a stranger to, and an alien from, God, and never felt the powerful efficacy of Divine grace in renewing his soul," he writes, "is beyond my comprehension."[42]

The minister also is to be a man of prayer, praying for himself and interceding for both the saints and sinners. The minister is to be a model of Christian living. Being in such a high-profile position, the minister has the opportunity to convince others that there is more to religion that a mere name, and that true godliness influences one's lifestyle. "No one knows what influence the courteous, meek, religious and affable conversation of such has upon others," he wrote.[43]

Along with experimental religion, the call to ministry equally involves the natural powers of faculties of the mind. Eaton asked, "How shall persons addict themselves to the work of the ministry, whose powers of mind, at their highest pitch, are but shallow and contracted?"[44] Possessing a gifted mind, the minister must exercise it in the study of various disciplines. He must have, says Eaton,

> some acquaintance with the original languages, wherein the Scriptures were penned, so as to know the import of words, and their radices; especially of the New Testament, which all must allow to be greatly beneficial; together with some knowledge of the sciences, especially logic, rhetoric, natural and moral philosophy, &c.[45]

Above all, the minister must have knowledge of Divine truth. In particular, Eaton noted the importance of systematic theology for the work of ministry. Recognizing the underlying unity of Scripture, he contended that the minister must be competent in

---

[42] *Ibid.*, 368.

[43] *Ibid.*, 379.

[44] *Ibid.*, 370.

[45] *Ibid.*, 371. Eaton acknowledged that God has often used unlearned men in service of the church but warned that such instances are the exception and should not be used to invalidate learning.

dealing with the great doctrines of the Gospel, "their nature, distinction, and mutual dependence."[46]

The minister also should be cognizant of the various arguments used by worldly wisemen to oppose the truths of the Gospel. Without such knowledge the minister will be unable to silence those who challenge the truth of God's Word. Eaton warned against an ignorant ministry as well as an irreligious and negligent ministry.[47]

Having recognized the significance of the ministry, Eaton urged the church to pray for its ministers, to encourage them, and to hold them in high esteem. He exhorted them to support them financially to the extent that they could avoid, if possible, what today is called bi-vocational ministry. He writes:

> For my part, I do not see how a man can act up to the duties of his calling in this respect, and to be by far the greater part of his time employed in secular affairs. Nor how such congregations will answer it before God (in another day) who are able, and yet force their minister to labour for his own and family's reasonable support.[48]

Eaton also challenged churches to be careful as to not send unqualified men into the ministry.[49]

Eaton's Calvinistic theology is nowhere more clear than in his understanding of sin and salvation. Following the influential Philadelphia Confession of Faith, Eaton believed in original sin and human depravity stemming from Adam's Fall. He spoke of man's depravity and pollution of sin as part of man's inherent nature. Man is an enemy to God, in revolt against God, and not subject to the law of God. As a result, man is by nature under the wrath of God. In Eaton's characteristically biblical fashion, he averred that man is impotent to bring about the changes neces-

---

[46] *Ibid.*, 367.

[47] *Ibid.*

[48] *Ibid.*, 376.

[49] *Ibid.*, 380.

sary for reconciliation with God.[50] Man's only hope is in "the powerful efficacy of Divine grace in renewing his soul."[51]

This efficacious grace of God is grounded in the person and work of Jesus Christ, who is "the Way, the Truth, and the Life," the only medium of our access to, and acceptance with, the Father.[52] This reconciliation is procured both "through the perfection of the satisfaction made by Christ, and the prevalency of His intercession."[53]

Avoiding the pitfall of hyper-Calvinism, Eaton recognized the church's responsibility to carry God's message of redemption to those in sin. It is the particular responsibility of the minister sincerely to strive for the good of immortal souls. This involves informing the unbeliever of his condition before God and of the hope that is in Christ. The gospel message must make a clear distinction between the law and the gospel, showing the role of each in God's economy of salvation.[54] Obviously, Eaton was more concerned with the sinner's salvation than he was in producing in them a false self-esteem. Eaton's exhortation to evangelism exudes passion:

> Let us have the weight of the work before us lay heavy on our minds. Does not the deplorable case of our fellow men call for tears of sorrow, and the strongest endeavours to reclaim them? How many of our friends, and those under our charge, are going quickly to destruction, dishonouring our God, rejecting our precious Redeemer? Let us up and be doing. Let us exert ourselves instrumentally to pluck them as brands out of the burning; and doctrinally arrest them in their wild career, denouncing the awful penalties of Jehovah's violated law, as the artillery of heaven, charged with divine wrath against them whilst persisting in their vile practices. Let us engage their warmest thoughts to seek after peace through the peace-speaking blood of the New

---

[50] *Ibid.*, 370.

[51] *Ibid.*

[52] *Ibid.*, 376, following John 14:6.

[53] *Ibid.*, 370.

[54] *Ibid.*, 375-376.

> Covenant. Let us unfold the transcendent beauties of a dying Redeemer, telling them that mercy yearns in the Father's bowels.[55]

It would be difficult to find a better example of speaking the truth in love.

In light of Eaton's belief that salvation is of the Lord, three additional matters are noteworthy. First, Eaton specifically advocated the use of all prescribed methods to reach the lost. He clearly understood that salvation is of the Lord, but equally understood that God uses the efforts of His people to bring the lost to the Savior.[56] Second, since salvation is of the Lord and not of man, God will count His people as faithful, even when they are not successful at winning the lost.[57] Third, while God's people are to long for the conversion of souls, it is God who saves, and the honor and glory of God is the ultimate goal.[58]

The Christian's concern for others is not confined to their spiritual welfare, but is to extend to their physical well-being as well. The child of God is "to bestow acts of charity to the needy," following the example of Jesus, who was kind and compassionate to the poor and the infirm.[59]

His long-term influence

Although his name is seldom mentioned with the high-profile leaders of Baptist life in America, nevertheless, Isaac Eaton's contribution is significant. All who have been trained at Baptist institutions in America, or who have benefitted from those who were, are indebted to Eaton. His impact was both immediate and long-range.

Eaton's immediate impact was on the men whom he touched through his ministry as a pastor and teacher, men who served Baptists as competent leaders at an important time in our history.

---

[55] *Ibid.*, 380-381.

[56] *Ibid.*, 382.

[57] *Ibid.*

[58] *Ibid.*, 370.

[59] *Ibid.*, 378.

Hopewell Academy existed particularly for the training of ministers, but its students included many who, as noted earlier, went into other vocations. Edwards listed twenty-five prominent men who attended Hopewell, training for professions other than the ministry. These included men foremost in politics, law, business, medicine, and the military. One student, David Hoel (Howell), became a member of Congress.[60]

The list of ministers who studied at Hopewell in its short, eleven-year history reads like a 'who's who' of Baptists of the period:

> Among them may be mentioned his first pupil, James Manning; Hezekiah Smith, "the great man of Haverhill," and the distinguished Chaplain of the revolution; Samuel Stillman, the eloquent preacher of Boston; Samuel Jones, who was informally invited to succeed Manning in the Presidency of Rhode Island College; John Gano, Manning's brother-in-law, the fearless Chaplain, and "a pastor and a prince among the Baptists hosts of Israel"; Oliver Hart, the beloved pastor and patriot of Charleston, South Carolina; Charles Thompson, the Valedictorian of the first graduating class under Manning; William Williams, also of this class, the founder of an academy in Wrentham; Isaac Skillman, of Boston, a member of the famous "Committee on Grievances"; John Davis, of Boston, the first agent of the churches of the Warren Association; David Jones, the eminent pastor, patriot and chaplain; and John Sutton who accompanied Manning on his first visit to Rhode Island in behalf of the College.[61]

The existence of Baptist institutions of higher learning in America testifies to Eaton's long-range contribution. As the instructor of the initial Baptist venture in America for training its young men for the ministry, much was riding on the success of

---

[60] Edwards, *Materials Towards a History of the Baptist in [New] Jersey*. 49. John Hart also was influenced greatly by Eaton's pastoral ministry. Residing near Hopewell Church, Hart was one of the most eminent figures of the Revolutionary period. He was a member of the Continental Congress and a signer of the Declaration of Independence. [See the essay by Sam Tullock on John Hart in *A Noble Company*, 2: 441-456 —*Ed.*]

[61] Guild, *Early History of Brown University,* 9-10.

Hopewell Academy. The eventual success of the academy under Eaton's leadership greatly encouraged Baptists to press on in further educational enterprises and similar institutions began to appear. For example, Dr. Samuel Jones, a Hopewell graduate and pastor of the Pennepek or Lower Dublin Baptist Church near Philadelphia, administered a boarding school from 1765-1795, where classical and theological subjects were taught. Many effective Baptist leaders, ministers and other professionals were trained there.[62] Other academies included one by Dr. John Stanford in New York and another at Bordentown, New Jersey, operated by Dr. Burgiss Allison in 1778.[63]

Although anti-education sentiments persisted among some Baptists in the Philadelphia Association, the Association persevered in its efforts to organize a Baptist college. Eaton's success at Hopewell was, to a large measure, responsible for the success of the effort, an effort which culminated in the founding of Rhode Island College in 1764. According to Guild, "The success of the Hopewell Academy inspired the friends of learning in the denomination with renewed confidence, and incited them to establish a college." A contemporary of Eaton wrote,

> Many of the churches. . .being supplied with able pastors from Mr. Eaton's academy, and being thus convinced, from experience, of the great usefulness of human literature to more thoroughly furnish the man of God for the most important work of the Gospel ministry, the hands of the Philadelphia Association were strengthened, and their hearts were encouraged to extend their designs of promoting literature in the Society (denomination) by erecting. . .a college or university, which should be principally under the direction and government of the Baptists.[64]

---

[62] Torbet, *History of the Baptists,* 308 and Clark, *To Set Them in Order,* 37.

[63] Henry C. Vedder, *A Short History of the Baptists* (Philadelphia: The American Baptist Publication Society, 1907), 352; and Clark, *To Set Them in Order,* 38.

[64] Quoted in Guild, *Early History of Brown University,* 10. Guild noted that this quote was attributed to Morgan Edwards, but may have come from Judge Howell.

James Manning (1738-1791), pastor of the Baptist church at Warren, Rhode Island, was installed as the first president of Rhode Island College. Manning was one of Eaton's first students at Hopewell and was brought to a saving knowledge of Christ through his mentor at Hopewell.[65] Eaton had the honor of giving the charge at Manning's ordination service.[66] Vedder observed that "if the Hopewell Academy had done nothing more than give the world James Manning, it would be entitled to the gratitude of Baptists for all times."[67]

With "hands strengthened and hearts encouraged" by the success of Hopewell and, subsequently, the establishment of Rhode Island College, Baptists moved to establish other educational institutions. Among the most notable are Columbian College, established in the District of Columbia (1821) and Newton Theological Institution, the first Baptist graduate school in the United States, established in Newton Centre, Massachusetts (1826). Such progress for Baptist higher learning in America is a reminder of the importance of Isaac Eaton, who, unfortunately, is today as obscure as he is significant.

---

[65] Vedder, *A Short History of the Baptists*, 352.

[66] Guild, *Early History of Brown University,* 36-37.

[67] Vedder, *A Short History of the Baptists*, 352.

Further Reading

Morgan Edwards. *Materials Towards a History of the Baptists in [New] Jersey*. Philadelphia: Thomas Dobson, 1792; facsimile reprint, Enid, OK: Regular Baptist Publishing, Inc., 1998.

Abram D. Gillette, ed. *Minutes of the Philadelphia Baptist Association, 1707-1807*. Philadelphia: American Baptist Publication Society, 1851; reprinted Tricentennial Edition with new comprehensive indexes, maps and illustrations, Springfield, MO: Particular Baptist Press, 2002.

Photograph of the gravemarker for Isaac Eaton at the historic Baptist meetinghouse at Hopewell, New Jersey.

Portrait of John Gano, first published in the October 1850 issue of *The New York Chronicle*, a Baptist periodical. It is not known whether this steel engraving was based on an original painting of Gano made from life. If so, the painting is now missing. From the author's collection.

JOHN GANO
1727 - 1804

by Terry Wolever

A contemporary minister, Morgan John Rhees, Sr. (1760-1803), confided in his diary after visiting the aged John Gano in Kentucky in the spring of 1795, that he believed him to be "one of the greatest travelling preachers in America."[1] There were indeed few Baptist ministers at the time who had journeyed to the extent Gano did in preaching the gospel of God's grace, for he is known to have preached in each of the original thirteen colonies[2] (in most of them a number of times), as well as in what was considered the "far west" of his day, Ohio and Kentucky. He also assisted in constituting at least eleven churches[3] and participated in the ordination services of pastors and deacons throughout the country, including the first non-Catholic ordination in the Old Northwest Territory.[4] And what a preacher he must have been!—on one particularly notable occasion in September 1771, he is said to have

---

[1] MS Diary of Morgan John Rhees, entry for April 21, 1795. John Hay Library, Brown University.

[2] I have not come across any evidence that Gano went as far north as Maine, but in any event, Maine was in his lifetime (and until 1820) a part of Massachusetts.

[3] These would be the Baptist church at the Jersey Settlement, NC (1758); the Gold Street or First Baptist Church, New York (June 19, 1762), of which he became pastor; Warren, RI (Nov. 15, 1764); Coram, L. I. (Nov. 1, 1765); Beauty Spot, SC (June 15, 1768); Lyon's Farms, NJ (Apr. 16, 1769); Second Baptist Church, New York (June 5, 1770); Kingstreet, CT (Nov. 3, 1773); Stamford, CT (Nov. 6, 1773); First Baptist Church, Staten Is. (Dec. 30, 1785); and Nobletown, later West Hillsdale, NY (May 8, 1787), where his son Stephen became pastor. We know that Gano also intended to constitute the branch of his church at Peekskill, NY, as early as March 1772, and again in late 1773, but he doesn't appear to have succeeded in this. The record shows they were not formally constituted until 1788.

[4] Gano assisted pastor John Smith in ordaining Daniel Clark as assistant pastor of the Baptist church at Columbia in what is now the state of Ohio on September 21, 1792. A. H. Dunlevy, *History of the Miami Baptist Association; From its Organization in 1797, to a Division in that Body on Missions, etc. in the Year 1836* (Cincinnati: Geo. S. Blanchard, 1869), 21.

preached to about a thousand persons assembled at the large Second Baptist meetinghouse in Newport, Rhode Island—the same number reportedly drawn there earlier by the famous George Whitefield.[5] The comparison between the two men was not lost on Isaac Backus, who once observed after Gano itinerated in New England that "his preaching seems to be as much admired as Mr. Whitefield's."[6] In the brief context of this essay we'll look at some of the more striking features of this man's life and ministry.

Ancestry and early life

John Gano was born on July 22, 1727, at Hopewell, New Jersey, the third son and fifth child of Daniel and Sarah (née Britton) Gano. Daniel had only recently removed the family from Staten Island to Hopewell. John's paternal great-grandfather François (or Francis) Gayneau,[7] of the Huguenot or French Protestant faith, had fled the Island of Guernsey after the tyrannical monarch Louis IV of France in 1685 revoked the Edict of Nantes (1598), which for almost a century had given the Huguenots a large measure of religious and civil liberty in the Catholic-dominated nation. François had been warned (by a neighbor) of his intended execution. "He thereupon," recalled John Gano in his *Biographical Memoirs*, "chartered a vessel, removed his family on board, and, in the morning, was out of sight of the harbour. . .On his arrival in America, he settled in New-Rochelle,

---

[5] Franklin B. Dexter, *The Literary Diary of Ezra Stiles, D.D., L.L.D., President of Yale College* (New York: Charles Scribner's Sons, 1901), 1: 159. At this period Morgan Edwards could write that Gardner Thurston's Second Baptist "meeting-house and congregation are the largest among the Baptists in all New England." "Materials Towards a History of the Baptists in Rhode Island." *Collections of the Rhode Island Historical Society* (Providence: Hammond, Angell and Co.), 6 (1867): 42.

[6] William G. McLoughlin, ed., *The Diary of Isaac Backus* (Providence: Brown University Press, 1979), 1: 583. George Whitefield (1714-1770) is generally considered the greatest evangelist of the eighteenth century.

[7] The French spellings of the surname, Gayneau and Gaineau, would suggest that the correct pronunciation of the surname is Gā'nō, which is the way it is pronounced by some of the direct descendants I've met here, though I also know of others in different branches of the family who pronounce it Gŭ'nō.

in the state of New-York, and lived to the age of one hundred and three."[8]

In the spring of 1734, when John was but six years old, he was "seized with a severe sickness," from which he did not recover until the fall. He was to learn afterwards that the linen had been procured with which to bury him, as he was not expected to live, since in his own words, he had lain "a great part of the time perfectly senseless."[9]

Following his recovery, he was sent by his parents to "a common country school." This comprised only a part however, of what Gano termed his "strict religious education." He tells us his mother was "a pious Baptist," while father on the other hand was "a steady Presbyterian," who saw to it that he was "well acquainted" with the Westminster Confession of Faith and Catechism.[10]

Early in life Gano experienced "some severe convictions of sins" and was well aware that he must at some point die and face the judgment. He also knew that he "must be renewed by grace, or perish as a sinner." But these sobering considerations were of short duration and soon passed from his mind. By the time he was in his teen years, he had overcome his earlier frailness and had become a vigorous young man. This healthful vitality however, had its own drawbacks. "As I advanced in years," he wrote, "I progressed in youthful vanity and sin. I became exceedingly anxious to excel my companions in work and amusements, and especially in their country frolics and dances." He was frequently admonished by his parents for overwork, but still more frequently, he adds, "for my attachment to vanity."[11]

His shameful pursuits and conduct brought considerable grief to his Christian parents. An encounter with his mother one day particularly arrested his attention, as he relates in his narrative:

---

[8] Stephen Gano and Daniel Gano, eds., *Biographical Memoirs of the Late Rev. John Gano, of Frankfort, Kentucky. Formerly of the City of New York* (New York: Southwick and Hardcastle, 1806), 10. Hereafter cited as *Biographical Memoirs of John Gano.*

[9] *Ibid.*, 11.

[10] *Ibid.*, 12.

[11] *Ibid.*, 12-13.

> I cannot charge myself with irreverence to my parents; but when my pious mother would expostulate with me, I seized the opportunity to vindicate myself. One morning when I came into her presence, having been out late the night before, she fixed her eyes upon me, said not a word, and the pious parental tear stole down her cheek, which struck me with more conviction than I ever remembered to have felt before, which I could not eradicate by any reply. . .[12]

His conversion and call to the gospel ministry

The Heaven-sent spiritual movement known as The Great Awakening was sweeping through the Middle Colonies in the early 1740's. George Whitefield and his ministerial associates and supporters, attended with the Divine blessing, were rejoicing in the fruit being born of their gospel labors all along the eastern seaboard. "Scarcely a community wholly escaped the influence of the revival," wrote A. H. Newman.[13]

It was at this time that Gano experienced another spiritual crisis in his life. When he was about the age of fifteen (or sometime in 1743), his older brother Stephen, then twenty years of age, died. "He was," writes Gano, "before, and in the first part of his illness, deeply concerned for the salvation of his soul, of which, before his death, he professed a strong hope, and what he said under his conviction, greatly engaged my resolution to seek an acquaintance, if possible, with Christ." In retrospect, Gano believed that probably the greater part of this mental and spiritual exercise on his part "flowed from natural affections, as time gradually wore it away."[14]

Two or three years following the death of Stephen Gano, all of the family except for John and his father Daniel were "brought exceedingly low" by dysentery. A brother and two sisters eventually succumbed to the illness and died.[15] As one of the sisters died in her twentieth year, this was all the more alarming to John

---

[12] *Ibid.*, 13-14.

[13] A. H. Newman, *A History of the Baptist Churches in the United States* (New York: The Christian Literature Company, 1894), 242.

[14] *Biographical Memoirs of John Gano*, 14.

[15] *Ibid.*, 14-15.

Gano. For it seems that his father had early on resigned himself to a prophecy which he had taken to heart, "with apparent cheerfulness," that he would have many children, but that three of them would die in their twentieth year. Incredibly, John Gano recalls that he "often heard" his father mention this prediction! Since it now appeared on the verge of fulfillment, with his brother Stephen and now a sister dying at the age of twenty, John wondered if he was destined to become the third child to die at that age. "As I was next in point of years," he wrote, "this thought continually haunted me, and made me sensible that I was not prepared for such an awful change. Whenever I could dispel those gloomy thoughts, I was more at ease, and more vile and vain than ever, which continued and even increased."[16]

Gano informs us that his "next younger brother, soon after this, died in the twentieth year of his age."[17] Though the prophecy had come to pass and Daniel Gano, being fully assured of it, had cheerfully resigned himself in any event to the good will of God in the matter, still it might initially strike one as inappropriate that he should have made this known to the anxiety of his wife and children. But what if his motivation in doing so was to impress upon his family, as all Christian parents should, the uncertainty of life and the need to be prepared to die?

That December 25th, 1745, would prove to be the beginning of an earnest spiritual quest for the now eighteen-year-old John Gano. While it was his determination "to spend a jovial evening" in celebration of the holiday with what he called his "frolicing companions," the Lord had other plans. Abiding within Gano was just enough spiritual concern that upon being made aware there was a sermon to be preached near his home that same day, he concluded to attend both. The message he heard brought about a life-changing series of events, which he recounted in these words:

> After sermon, my mind turned on the inconsistency of my conduct, in spending the day, where God was served, and the night, in the service of the devil. This led me to consider more closely than ever, that if a day was regarded as the birth of Christ, a holy Saviour, through whom alone we could look for salvation,—how improper it was to spend it in open rebellion! This brought me to a resolution,—that I would spend my time in a more consistent manner, than I

---

[16] *Ibid.*, 15.

[17] *Ibid.*, 15*n*.

> had done—and, blessed be God, before the year terminated, I was brought under serious impressions, which arose from a conversation with a person, whom I supposed really pious and sincere. . . .It became my ardent wish, that if there was a possibility of pardon for my sins and transgressions, I might not rest either night or day until I obtained it. . . .But I soon found by experience, what I had learned from my Bible, that a change of heart was necessary; and that the power of God's grace only could accomplish it; which, I was afraid, would never be granted. I was, however, determined to seek it to the latest hour of my existence. I cannot express the anguish, with which my mind was frequently oppressed, with the idea of being eternally banished from God, in endless despair, to everlasting destruction. I saw I deserved it, and at times concluded it was unavoidable.[18]

Gano tells us that from that time, the nature of his convictions were altered and his "grief was greater." He then shares how it was that God brought him to rejoice in His salvation:

> I knew that I must be changed, and that it was to be effected by God, and that he would affect it was my fervent wish. But how he could be just and save me I knew not: that he could be just and condemn me, appeared plain. In this state, I remained for some time. And it was some satisfaction to my mind, that God would secure his own glory, and the honour of his Son. In this temper of mind, the way of salvation, through the life, death, and mediation, of the glorious Saviour, appeared plain. I contemplated on the amazing wisdom and goodness of God, and condescension of Christ. My soul was enraptured, amazed, and confounded, that with all my ingratitude, I could still be saved. My mind was enlightened, and my guilt and fear of punishment was removed.
>
> Yet, notwithstanding the alteration I felt, I am not sensible that I thought of its being a real conviction; I was afraid my convictions would not be lasting; I prayed for a continuance of them. I was constrained at times to rejoice in God and his salvation; and in this state continued some time, until a sermon from these words, with light and power fasted [i.e. fastened] on my mind: '*Jesus, thou Son of David,*

[18] *Biographical Memoirs of John Gano*, 16-19.

> *have mercy on me'* [Mark 10:47]. I trust they were so applied, that I could not put them from me. They opened the way of salvation, the suitableness, fulness, and willingness of God; and I was enabled to appropriate them to myself, and rejoice in Christ. This was the time, from which I dated my conversion, and I think I walked in the light of God's countenance, and had many blessed promises, which strengthened and confirmed my hope in, and humbled me before God.[19]

Gano was no sooner converted than he began seeking opportunities for gospel witness. There were a number of young people in his neighborhood "who were under serious concern for their souls." During the distress of his own spiritual awakening he had warned them of their exposure to the wrath of God. "I could now point out to them, Christ," he wrote, "and the method of salvation through him. As my soul felt what I said, it seemed as if God made them sensible of it."[20] They began to meet in the evenings for prayer and conversation. Gano later considered this a useful part of his early Christian life and his inclination was to become a preacher, though for the time he thought it his duty "to wait and pursue literary acquirements."

He had not as yet made an open profession of faith nor joined any church. His initial desire was to join his father's denomination, the Presbyterians. In preparing to do so, he experienced an unexpected change in sentiments, as he explains:

> For some reasons, I wished to join that of the Presbyterian; and as a communion season was approaching, I expected some examination. I took the Westminster confession of faith, and the Bible, with a view honestly to profess them. The doctrines appeared thoroughly grounded, and perfectly consonant with the Bible, until I came to the doctrine of baptism. The proofs there adduced, fell far short of my expectations, and appeared foreign to the point.—I then took the Bible, especially the New Testament, and searched it for months together; and enquired for, and obtained all the disputes, especially in favour of infant baptism, that I

---

[19] *Ibid.*, 19-20.

[20] *Ibid.*, 21.

> could hear of; I, however, could find nothing that seemed to me to amount to a divine warrant.[21]

Gano then decided to go to the local presbytery to converse with others and hopefully receive more instruction on the subject. There he met with "a Mr. Tennant," who was quite possibly William Tennent, Jr. (1705-1777), pastor of the Presbyterian church at Freehold, New Jersey. He recalled that on arriving to discuss the matter with Tennent,

> A favorable opportunity presented, and from my attachment to the man, and a deference to his opinion, and the confidence he appeared to have of the justice of infant baptism, I was induced to embrace his sentiments. But on my road home, it turned in my mind, that this was not the way I had obtained the hope of salvation, or consonant with my former resolutions, to make the word of God my only rule of faith and practice. Let Mr. Tennant be ever so good a man, his belief, is not a divine warrant for me to act upon. Before I got home, I was determined to try farther to see for myself.[22]

Soon after this, Benjamin Miller (1715?-1781), Baptist minister at Scotch Plains, New Jersey, asked Gano why he did not "profess Christ openly, and join some church." Gano replied that he was unsettled on the matter of baptism. Miller told Gano that God's Word and Spirit would direct him, and if he attended to these impartially, they would remove his doubts; "and if they did not make [him] a Baptist, he did not wish to do it."[23] This conversation led Gano to inquire if he had indeed acted impartially in looking at the question. "I was soon convinced I had not," he writes, "but had only searched for something to confirm me in the doctrine of infant baptism, which I had received from my education. I really think, that if any person was ever induced to take the word of God in hand, with a fervent desire to be free from all prepossessions, to

---

[21] *Ibid.*, 21-22.

[22] *Ibid.*, 22.

[23] *Ibid.*, 22-23.

see the truth as it really was, and to let the Bible be their guide, I was."[24]

Taking the Bible as his guide, Gano searched out what it had to say on the issue. He began to see the fallacy of carrying over rites from the Old Testament into the New and mixing them together, as his pedobaptist friends had done with their infant sprinkling. "I then endeavoured," he recalled,

> to learn my duty from the New Testament, as being a New Testament ordinance, and found that it was from Heaven,[25] had its authority from God, and became binding by a positive command. The characters of those, who were to be baptized were, *disciples*, *penitent believers*, and such as had received the Holy Ghost. I could not find by any of the apostles' practice, that any others were encouraged or permitted, unless they intruded as Simon Magus did. And the apostles declared him to have no part or lot in that matter.[26] The end and design was to fulfil righteousness—to answer a good conscience.[27] All things considered, I could see no ground for infant baptism in the New Testament. I next turned my attention to the mode, which appeared so plain in the example of Christ, in the places where he administered, and the reasons why he administered in those places, insomuch, that I was soon established in the belief, that *immersion* was the only mode, which could be gathered from the New Testament; and with this mode my conscience pressed me to comply. I then addressed my father on the subject. I told him 'his constant religious care over me entitled him to all the gratitude I was capable of rendering, yet I must beg his indulgence. I believed he was conscientious in having me baptized in my infancy, as he supposed, and I had tried to suppose, it right. But, on the whole, I was convinced it was my duty to be baptised by immersion; and that it relied on the profession of my own

---

[24] *Ibid.*, 23-25.

[25] Mark 11:30.

[26] Acts 8:9-24.

[27] Matt. 3:15; Rom. 6:16-18; 1 Peter 3:21.

> faith, if the church would receive me.'[28] He replied, 'that what he did, he thought right, and in the discharge of his own conscience. If I was conscientious, (and he was thankful to God, that he had reason to believe I was, from his observance of my searching the scriptures and the time I had taken therein, and the books I had read,) I had his full and free consent; and it was my duty to make profession.—That whenever I went to offer myself, he would go with me, and give the church his consent, and answer any inquiries, respecting my life, if they chose to make any; and that he would go and see me baptized.[29]

Gano was baptized (probably in the summer of 1747) and joined the Baptist church at Hopewell. He was among fifty-five others who had been added to the church that year as fruits of a season of revival.[30] In addition John Hart (1713?-1779), who would later be one of the signers of the Declaration of Independence, donated a three-quarter-acre tract of land that year to the Baptists on which to build a meetinghouse.[31] Yet the church was still lacking a most vital asset—its own pastor.

The church had been without a settled pastor ever since its constitution thirty-three years before in 1715, relying all the while on supplies to fill the pulpit. Gano tells us that after joining the church, he was "treated more like an old, than a younger member," in that he was soon invested with some important responsibilities, including being appointed a messenger to the Philadelphia Association and, along with Elder Jonathan Stout, engaged "to obtain

---

[28] Gano here emphasizes being baptized on the profession of his *own* faith due to the fact that when he was sprinkled in infancy, being an unconscious baby, his sponsors acted 'in faith' in his stead before God. He had now come to realize that the cart had been put before the horse—he had been 'baptized' before he himself believed.

[29] *Biographical Memoirs of John Gano*, 25-27. Gano tells us that his father eventually came to profess a belief in believer's immersion before he died.

[30] Morgan Edwards, *Materials Towards a History of the Baptists in [New] Jersey* (Philadelphia: Thomas Dobson, 1792; facsimile reprint Enid, OK: Regular Baptist Publishing, Inc., 1998), 46.

[31] *Ibid.* The first forty-one years (1706-1747), or until the meetinghouse was built, services had been held "chiefly at the dwellings of the Stouts," who were a family prominent among the founding members. *Ibid.*, 52.

stated supplies to keep up the communion seasons," from Benjamin Miller's new congregation at Scotch Plains. Gano counted Miller as "one of the most useful ministers in that day"[32] and the two would become close friends in the ministry.

On being apprised of a possible candidate for pastor, Stout and Gano were commissioned by their church to make a personal visit to the Southampton Baptist Church, located southwest of Hopewell across the border in Pennsylvania, in order "to obtain a worthy young minister" named Isaac Eaton (1725-1772), who had recently been licensed. Their meeting resulted in a tentative agreement by Eaton to assume the pastorate at Hopewell, which was undoubtedly an occasion of rejoicing to both parties.

Eaton arrived at Hopewell in April of 1748. He was settled as pastor on the 17th of that month and formally ordained on November 29th.[33] In Gano's estimation, Eaton proved "not only a great acquisition and a useful minister to Hopewell church, but to the churches all around," for God's power seemed to attend the new pastor's preaching of the Word and a considerable number were consequently added to the church. "I was also blessed with a judicious and useful minister and friend," said Gano, "who was able to instruct me in the classics, and who was desirous to do it."[34] On settling in at Hopewell, Eaton began working with Gano in his preparatory studies for the ministry. But again doubts over his own worthiness began to consume Gano's thoughts.

By the year 1749, Gano had entered into his greatest spiritual struggle since becoming a Christian. "I was so terrified," he wrote, "with the importance of the ministerial work, and conceiving that neither providence, nature, or grace, had qualified me for that arduous office, that I determined to relinquish the idea, and return home. . . .I meant, however, to live a steady and uniform Christian life. I was much in prayer, and enjoyed a nearness to God in his word."[35] But his calling would not abate. In his earnest

---

[32] *Biographical Memoirs of John Gano*, 28.

[33] Edwards, *Materials Towards a History of the Baptists in [New] Jersey*, 48; Thomas S. Griffiths, *A History of Baptists in New Jersey* (Hightstown, NJ: Barr Press Publishing Co., 1904), 67-68 (where through a typographical error the numbers in the date appear as 1874 instead of 1748).

[34] *Biographical Memoirs of John Gano*, 28-29.

[35] *Ibid.*, 30.

endeavors to seek the Lord's will, Gano finally came to the conclusion that if Providence so ordered that his church at Hopewell should call him, and he could be freed from his worldly concerns, he would devote himself to the gospel ministry. With Eaton's encouragement, Gano resumed his education with an eye towards the ministry.[36]

It wasn't long before Gano began more formal training under a Presbyterian minister from Connecticut. Then the time arrived when he believed he was ready to pursue study at the local College of New Jersey (later Princeton), which was then located at Newark. About the year 1751-1752, he began frequently attending the examinations there. The president of the school, Aaron Burr, Sr. (1716-1757), took a liking to Gano and encouraged the young man by telling him he might enter the college whenever he chose, provided he was found to be fit to do so upon taking the required examination. But as Gano lamented, "unfortunately I was taken sick, before I had made but very little progress in the classics. My sickness was probably owing to my too close application to study, and the want of exercise. The doctors and my friends, advised me to take a journey, and relax my mind from study."[37]

Gano heeded the advice and in the company of three ministers—Isaac Sutton, John Thomas and Benjamin Miller, took a journey to Virginia in 1752, in response to a request from the two churches there at Opequon and Ketocton. It would be the first of a series of visits to the South that Gano would make in succeeding years. While on this trip, though he was reluctant to do so, Gano was urged to preach and exhort by both Thomas and the people they ministered to. It was discovered that not only was he a gifted preacher, but the people readily attended to his ministry of the Word.

On returning to New Jersey (in either late October or early November, 1752), Gano intended to travel directly to Newark and resume his studies at the college. But on passing through Hopewell, he was informed by pastor Isaac Eaton, that there were some who believed he had acted in a disorderly manner by preaching in Virginia without being either licensed or ordained. Perhaps fearing the report would injure Gano's reputation, Eaton advised him to remain in town until after the following Lord's day, "that he might call a church meeting for the purpose of settling the matter." At the appointed meeting Gano, convinced he had acted

---

[36] *Ibid.*, 35-37.

[37] *Ibid.*, 39.

in good conscience before God, did not believe that repentance on his part was needed and therefore he endeavored to acquit himself as best he could of any wrongdoing. The inquiry resulted not in Gano being disciplined, but instead a time was appointed for him to preach before the church.[38]

It was on November 19, 1752, that John Gano was "called to exercise his gifts in a public way," before his home church at Hopewell. The following year he was again requested to preach to the church, but this time with a view to being licensed. In the words of the churchbook entry, Gano "exercised according to the satisfaction of the church," on January 20, 1753 and that spring, on April 14, 1753, at the age of twenty-five, was licensed by the Hopewell church to preach "wheresoever providence should give him a call." [39] Gano intended to return and complete his education, "but was prevented by frequent interruptions."[40]

Now with the approval and encouragement of his brethren, Gano began to engage in some local preaching and assisting neighboring ministers. In so doing he gained invaluable experience that would serve him well in the future.

His first pastorate and marriage

In the summer of 1752, a Baptist church had been constituted at Morristown, roughly 35 miles northeast of Hopewell. Isaac Stelle and Benjamin Miller supplied the new church its first two years, or until May of 1754, when Gano began ministering there.[41] The church at Opequon, Virginia, had obviously been impressed

---

[38] *Ibid.*, 51-52.

[39] Hopewell Baptist Church Book, Hopewell, New Jersey. [n.p.]

[40] *Biographical Memoirs of John Gano*, 52. Gano was prevented by circumstances from ever completing the course of study at the College of New Jersey (Princeton). He therefore did not graduate from the school, as claimed in some accounts.

[41] The Morristown Baptist Church Book reads: "1754, May. Mr. John Gano came to us and continued to preach for us till October following when he went on a journey to Carolina." As we shall see later, Gano was not officially settled as pastor of the church at Morristown until October of 1755, though as Morgan Edwards correctly states, "He took the oversight of the church in 1754." *Materials Towards a History of the Baptists in [New] Jersey*, 74.

with Gano's abilities on his former visit there and wished to have him come among them again as well. Gano made known his desire to be ordained to Pastor Eaton, who no doubt was delighted by the news, and agreed to conduct the service. Thus on May 29, 1754, he was ordained at the Hopewell Baptist church, with the participating ministers "Imploring Divine blessings in his behalf." He now conducted his ministry at the Morristown church on a more regular basis, with a determination to visit the church at Opequon in the fall. Sometime this year, Gano also "formed a matrimonial engagement" with Miss Sarah Stites, the daughter of John Stites, Sr., mayor of Elizabethtown, New Jersey, and his wife Margaret. Gano intended to marry her after he returned from his trip to the South.[42]

On October 8, 1754, Gano attended the associational meetings at Philadelphia, where the members decided to receive into fellowship the two churches at Ketocton and Opequon.[43] After the meetings, Gano began his journey southward into Virginia, intending to mediate a dispute which had arisen between the church at Opequon and their minister, which he says was "amicably adjusted." He then visited the church at Ketocton, where he administered the Lord's Supper.[44]

Gano afterwards proceeded on into North Carolina, "to comply with a pressing request" from one Samuel Newman, "which he left with some acquaintance of his" at Opequon.[45] This request led Gano to determine he would visit the Jersey Settlement in the Yadkin River area of northwestern North Carolina. Sometime in late 1754 or in early 1755, a large portion of the congregation of Gano's mentor, Benjamin Miller, at Scotch Plains, New Jersey, along with others, had migrated there. The place was soon appropriately known as "the Jersey Settlement." Knowing they were good friends, and with Gano being at Morristown and Miller

---

[42] *Ibid.*, 55, 79-80. In addition to being mayor of Elizabethtown, John Stites, Sr. was a ruling elder in the Baptist church at Scotch Plains. Reuben A. Guild, *Life, Times, and Correspondence of James Manning, and the Early History of Brown University* (Boston: Gould and Lincoln, 1864), 33.

[43] A. D. Gillette, ed., *Minutes of the Philadelphia Baptist Association, 1707-1807* (Philadelphia: American Baptist Publication Society, 1851), 71.

[44] *Biographical Memoirs of John Gano,* 55-56.

[45] *Ibid.*, 57-58.

pastor of the congregation less than twelve miles to the southeast at Scotch Plains, Gano was sure to have been already well informed about this new settlement in North Carolina. Following stops at the Fishing Creek and Tar River churches, Gano arrived at the Jersey Settlement, "where," he says, "I spent some time, and preached often, with some appearance of success."[46]

When it came time for him to leave the Jersey Settlement, Gano planned to ride still further southward to Charleston. By the time he got there, the rigors of his overland travel had taken quite a toll on his clothing. He expresses his embarrassment on arriving at Ashley River, but also tells of unanticipated blessings in this excerpt from his narrative:

> My coat, which had grown thread-bare almost, by my long journey, made me look rather outlandish; and I saw it created a great deal of suspicion in Mr. Stephens,[47] who closely examined me, but finally treated me very brotherly, and made me very welcome. The next day he insisted on my preaching for him. His congregation, of white people, was small; but the blacks were very numerous. To this latter class, he had paid much attention, and was very useful to them. After service was over, he told me, I made a very good negro preacher. When I came out of the house, the negroes stood in two rows, and as I passed, they pronounced many blessings on me, for taking so much care of their souls. This humbled me before God, and I then thought, I would, for the future, take more pains with souls, and especially with negroes; and I now wish I had more strictly adhered to my determination.[48]

Oliver Hart, pastor of the First Baptist Church of Charleston, had also extended an invitation to Gano to preach. It was sometime in early 1755 (likely March), that John Gano preached at the First Baptist meetinghouse at Charleston. Among his hearers was the celebrated George Whitefield. Gano's unfeigned humility may be seen in his remarks on this occasion:

---

[46] *Ibid.*, 65.

[47] John Stephens, pastor of the Baptist church at Ashley River.

[48] *Biographical Memoirs of John Gano,* 55-56.

> Mr. Hart, spread word among the people, that I was to preach. I went with my tattered garb on; and when I rose to speak, the sight of so numerous and brilliant an audience, (among whom were twelve ministers, and one of whom was Mr. Whitefield,) for a moment, brought the fear of man on me; but, blessed be the Lord, I was soon relieved from this embarrassment: the thought passed my mind, I had none to fear, and obey, but the Lord.[49]

Gano conferred with Hart and others while in Charleston regarding the situation at the Jersey Settlement, which led to an interest by Hart and the Charleston Association in the work there.

After a visit to Savannah, Gano returned to Charleston, again preaching there and at Ashley River. He then began making his way back homeward, now riding northeastward, "by the way of [the] Black River," intending to go to Mars Bluff, on the west side of the Pee Dee River. He preached at a Mr. Screven's place and was ready to cross the Black River. Despite the arduous journey, Gano obviously retained his ready wit, for as he writes,

> In my way to Mars-bluff, on the Pedee, I lodged at the ferry-man's house. He observed, that he believed I was a minister, and wished me to tell him of the best and shortest way to heaven. I told him that Christ was the best way; and that he must become experimentally acquainted with him, and believe him, which was the hope of glory. That after he had obtained this, the shortest way, that I knew, would be to place himself in the front of some army, in an engagement.[50]

Preaching at other stops along the way, Gano arrived back home at Morristown in June of 1755, after about a nine month absence.[51] He then traveled over to Connecticut Farms, New Jersey, to see Sarah Stites, to whom he was engaged previous to

---

[49] *Ibid.*, 67.

[50] *Ibid.*, 69.

[51] The Morristown Baptist Church Book reads: "1755, June. Mr. J. Gano returned from Carolina and again went on to preach for us." As cited in Norman Fox, *Preachers and Patriots, The Rev. John Gano, The Rev. Hezekiah Smith. D. D.* (Morristown, New Jersey, 1904), 9.

his journey. They soon married, though we do not know the place or precise date this occurred. It would most likely have been in the fall of 1755. With the assistance of his new father-in-law, Gano purchased a small farm near Morristown, which he said was "in the neighbourhood of the then infant Baptist church, where I had formerly preached."[52] "We soon took possession of our farm," he wrote, adding, "[t]he church at Morristown gradually grew, and the congregation gradually increased."[53]

In October of 1755, Gano, "at the earnest request of the church," became officially settled as pastor. Gano and the congregation agreed to "the sum of forty pounds a year" as his salary.[54]

The same month, Gano traveled to Philadelphia where he attended the meetings of the Philadelphia Association on October 7, 1755. There he presented before his brethren the state of the churches in North Carolina. At the request of the Fishing Creek church, Gano represented their case to the Association, that "they had been a numerous society but without discipline or a proper acquaintance with Christian doctrines, and the majority destitute of real religion."[55] The Association, recognizing the desperate plight of this church, and some others visited by Gano, "Appointed, that one ministering brother from the Jerseys, and one from Pennsylvania, visit North Carolina: the several churches to contribute to bear their expense."[56] Those appointed for this visit to North Carolina were Benjamin Miller of the Scotch Plains, New Jersey church, and thirty-six year-old Peter Peterson VanHorne,

---

[52] *Biographical Memoirs of John Gano*, 79. Interestingly, Sarah Stites had not yet made a public profession of faith when they were married. For a discussion of this subject, see my fuller biography, *The Life of John Gano, 1727-1804. Pastor-Evangelist of the Philadelphia Association* (Springfield, MO: Particular Baptist Press, 2012), 71-73.

[53] *Biographical Memoirs of John Gano*, 80-81.

[54] Morristown Baptist Church Book, as cited in Fox, *Preachers and Patriots, The Rev. John Gano, The Rev. Hezekiah Smith, D. D.*, 9.

[55] Wood Furman, *A History of the Charleston Association of Baptist Churches in the State of South Carolina* (Charleston: J. Hoff, 1811), 62.

[56] Gillette, *Minutes of the Philadelphia Baptist Association*, 72. New Jersey was formerly divided into the two provinces of East New Jersey and West New Jersey until 1702, when they were reunited, but were still commonly referred to long afterwards as "the Jerseys."

pastor at the Pennepek church in Pennsylvania. The Association requested that VanHorne set out on the trip on Tuesday, October 28, 1755,[57] reflecting the urgency with which they viewed the situation. This was only two weeks after the association met.

Miller and VanHorne first visited the church at Fishing Creek in Granville County, North Carolina, whose case Gano had set before the Association. This church had been a General Baptist meeting for ten years, since their founding in 1745 as a branch of the Kehukee church in Edgecombe (now Halifax) County. Thirteen persons had come to believe the Doctrines of Grace, both through the faithful preaching of James Smart, who had embraced Particular Baptist views four years earlier, and the visit and ministry of John Gano there. These thirteen persons, who "upon examination" were "judged to be experimental Christians," were gratefully reconstituted as a Particular Baptist church on December 6, 1755, with the able assistance of Miller and VanHorne.[58] Additions were soon made to this number "by baptism and from among their former members by a new examination," so that by the time the church was admitted to the Charleston Association in 1756, it consisted of fifty members.[59]

Miller and VanHorne then rode over to the Kehukee meeting, reorganizing that church in like manner on December 11, 1755.[60] As George Paschal wrote, "[t]heir example was soon followed by most of the other General Baptist churches of North Carolina."[61]

David Benedict, referring to this transformation of the Baptist churches in North Carolina, wrote that "the introduction of

---

57 *Ibid.*, 73. Miller is not shown as being present at the October 7, 1755 meeting of the Association, but VanHorne is.

58 Furman, *History of the Charleston Association*, 62, and Morgan Edwards, "Materials Towards a History of the Baptists in the Province of North Carolina," in Eve B. Weeks and Mary B. Warren, eds., *Materials Towards a History of the Baptists. By Morgan Edwards. A.M.* (Danielsville, GA: Heritage Papers, 1984), 2: 84. Furman gives the number of constituting members as fourteen, but Edwards names thirteen.

59 Furman, *History of the Charleston Association*, 55 and 62.

60 Edwards, "Materials Towards a History of the Baptists in the Province of North Carolina," 2: 82.

61 George W. Paschal, *History of North Carolina Baptists* (Raleigh, NC: North Carolina Baptist State Convention), 1 (1930): 210.

Calvinistic sentiments among them. . .had the happy effect of purifying the churches." In addition he concluded that "Mr. Gano appears to have shaken the old foundation, and begun the preparation of the materials which Messrs. Miller and Vanhorn organized into regular churches."[62] In other words, Gano's tour of 1754-1755 provided the real catalyst for the resulting changes in doctrine and church order among the Baptists in North Carolina.

For this transformation of the General Baptist churches in North Carolina into Particular/Regular Baptist churches, Gano, VanHorne and Miller have been sharply criticized by some later historians—yet not without a good deal of misrepresentation.[63]

His ministry at the Jersey Settlement

As stated earlier, through the visit of Gano, the Charleston Association came to have an interest in the work at the Jersey Settlement. At their annual session on November 13, 1755, the Association sought to secure an itinerant missionary willing to minister in these neighboring provinces. Oliver Hart made "repeated solicitations" to Gano "to undertake the service," citing the latter's previous visit to the Carolinas and his acquaintance with the people there.[64] Hart's persistence soon prevailed and as Gano wrote later, "I was induced to engage in a second journey."[65]

---

[62] David Benedict, *A General History of the Baptist Denomination in America, and Other Parts of the World* (Boston: Lincoln and Edmands, 1813), 2: 98-99.

[63] For more on this see *The Life of John Gano, 1727-1804* (2012), 77-92.

[64] *Biographical Memoirs of John Gano*, 81 and Furman, *History of the Charleston Association*, 10.

[65] *Biographical Memoirs of John Gano*, 81. These appointments by the Philadelphia Association in October 1755, and the Charleston Association in November 1755, culminating in John Gano's visit to the Jersey Settlement in Western North Carolina have been viewed by historian Robert Baker as marking "the beginning of the first associational mission program in American Baptist history." See Robert A. Baker, "The Contributions of South Carolina Baptists to the Rise and Development of the Southern Baptist Convention." Lynn May, Jr., ed., *Baptist History and Heritage* (Nashville: Historical Commission, S.B.C.), 17 (1982), No. 3 (July): 4. Thus it was that the two Calvinistic Baptist associations in America in the mid-eighteenth century came to jointly initiate home mission work among the denomination in America.

On August 18, 1756, the Morristown church "met for business," and "after prayer to God for direction," agreed to allow Gano to visit the Carolinas, "they hoping that on his return he would be satisfied to stay with them." Accordingly, he left for the journey on August 29, 1756.[66] He writes:

> I therefore set out, and, when I arrived at the Yadkin [i.e. Jersey Settlement], in North-Carolina, I was strongly solicited to move among them. They sent two messengers to my church, to give me up. I requested them to let the matter rest, till my return from South-Carolina, to which they consented. Upon my arrival in South-Carolina, I was happy in the appearances of religion in many places.[67]

Gano returned to the "Yadkin," or Jersey Settlement, shortly after. Wood Furman gave this assessment of his labors there:

> He devoted himself to the work: it afforded ample scope for his distinguished piety, eloquence and fortitude; and his ministrations were crowned with remarkable success. Many embraced and professed the Gospel. The following year [1757] he received from the [Charleston] Association a letter of thanks for his faithfulness and industry in the mission.[68]

Taking some representatives of the Jersey Settlement's congregation along with him, Gano headed for home in April of 1757, about eight months from the time he had left Morristown.[69] Convinced that the Jersey Settlement was in much greater need of his aid than his congregation at Morristown, he had brought along some help to make his case. The church replied to Gano, "we deem you the best judge, and are willing to leave the matter with God, and your own conscience. If you think it your duty to leave us, we cannot insist upon your stay;" to which Gano responded, "that as they had left the matter to me, it appeared to be my duty to go to

---

66 Morristown Baptist Church Book, as cited in Fox, *Preachers and Patriots: the Rev. John Gano, the Rev. Hezekiah Smith*, 11.

67 *Biographical Memoirs of John Gano*, 81.

68 Furman, *History of the Charleston Association*, 11.

69 *Biographical Memoirs of John Gano*, 81.

that people, who were entirely destitute, and that it was not for want [or lack] of attachment to them."[70]

With great reluctance, the Morristown church, in true Christian benevolence, on June 24, 1757, agreed to give up their beloved pastor.[71] Gano writes, "I made preparations for removal, disposed of my property, and wrote to the church in North-Carolina. I at length took leave of the church and my friends, and started [September 25, 1757] on a long, expensive, and tedious journey...[72]

Gano and his family arrived at the Jersey Settlement "through the goodness of God," as he wrote later, "in about five weeks, after traveling about eight hundred miles."[73] Here Gano purchased land beside Swearing Creek and immediately began building a house. His neighbors cut the logs and assisted their new minister in the construction work. By late winter or early spring, the Gano family was able to move in.[74] And now that he was there, "the people met, and determined on building a meeting house." The meetinghouse "was completed in a few months," Gano recalled. Necessity soon brought Christians from other backgrounds to worship together with the Baptists, for, as Gano wrote, "there was no other place of worship near, and there was a great collection of inhabitants of different denominations, [so] they all attended."[75]

Gano also took an interest in what was going on among the Separate Baptists at nearby Sandy Creek and possibly at the request of others, decided to attend their associational meeting in 1759. "He was sent it seems," writes Robert B. Semple, "to inquire into the state of these *New Light Baptists*. He was received by [Shubal] Stearns with great affection. But the young and illiterate

---

[70] *Ibid.*, 82.

[71] Morristown Baptist Church Book, 12.

[72] *Biographical Memoirs of John Gano*, 83; Edward Howell, "Historical Sketch of the Baptist Church at Morristown." *Minutes of the Twenty-first Anniversary of the East New Jersey Baptist Association, held with the First Baptist Church, Elizabeth, June 4th and 5th, 1872* (Newark, NJ: Jennings and Hardham, 1872), 26-27.

[73] *Biographical Memoirs of John Gano*, 83.

[74] Garland A. Hendricks, *Saints and Sinners at Jersey Settlement. The Story of Jersey Baptist Church* (Charlotte, NC: Delmar Co., 1988), 13.

[75] *Biographical Memoirs of John Gano*, 83.

preachers were afraid of him, and kept at a distance." But in learning after a few days of hearing that Gano's preaching "was in the Spirit of the Gospel," their "hearts were opened, so that before he left them they were greatly attached to him." On returning home and being asked what he thought of these Baptists, Gano replied, that *"doubtless the power of God was among them; that although they were rather immethodical, they certainly had the root of the matter at heart."*[76] Gano did not see so much of a *doctrinal* problem with the Separates, as with their *methodology*. In this respect, he reflected the general sentiment of the Regular Baptists towards the Separates.

That same year of 1759, the Jersey Baptist church was admitted into the Charleston Association.[77] Not long afterwards, Gano was compelled to remove with his family from the Jersey Settlement. "The reason of my leaving this place," he tells us, "was the war with the Cherokee Indians."[78] Gano had received a captain's commission from Governor Dobbs, but with there being no immediate call for his services, and with his wife and two young sons exposed to danger due to the escalating war with the Cherokees, he resigned his commission and late in the year 1760, removed with his family back to New Jersey. "Under the protection of a kind Providence," wrote Gano, they arrived safely at the residence of his father-in-law John Stites at Elizabethtown.[79] His decision to leave the Jersey Settlement was made with great reluctance, yet with the confident belief that he would return again.

Interim ministry at Philadelphia and New York, 1760-1761

On July 6, 1760 Jenkin Jones, the venerable pastor of the First Baptist church in Philadelphia, passed away. At the suggestion of the Particular Baptist Fund Board in London, the widowed church that September extended an invitation to Morgan Edwards (1722-1795), then pastor of a church at Rye, Sussex, which was accepted.

---

[76] *A History of the Rise and Progress of the Baptists in Virginia* (Richmond, VA: John O'Lynch, 1810), 65-66.

[77] Furman, *History of the Charleston Association*, 55.

[78] *Biographical Memoirs of John Gano*, 85.

[79] *Ibid.*, 85.

During the eight-month interval between Jones's death and Edwards' arrival, the church at Philadelphia had "made application" to John Gano and to Benjamin Miller to visit them in the meantime and minister. "It was represented," Gano later wrote, "that they had been so particular in the requisite qualifications for a minister, that it had given offence to the preachers; so that they were entirely destitute." Miller, who was still pastor of the church at Scotch Plains, New Jersey, was making quarterly visits to the branch of his church meeting in New York, which was also in need of a settled pastor. Gano wrote that Miller "had been a successful minister in New York, and had baptized sundry persons there." Gano, deciding he could supply both congregations, "visited New York and Philadelphia, alternately," spending two Sundays at a time in each place.[80] Thus Gano and Miller were now laboring together again in another field, this time in New York.

The church at New York sent word to Gano in the spring of 1761, requesting him to remove there, knowing his engagement at Philadelphia would be ending soon. Gano answered that he would consent to go to New York for one year, provided he could take three months of that time to visit North Carolina. To this they agreed, and what began as a nine-month commitment turned into a twenty-six year association for John Gano and the First Baptist Church of New York.

His third and longest pastorate, in the city of New York

In the eighteenth century, the city of New York bordered within the confines of Manhattan Island, geographically twelve and a half miles at its longest and two and a half miles at its widest. Though there had been a previous attempt to establish a church in the city twenty years earlier by the General Baptists, the first Regular Baptist church in the city began in the home of Jeremiah Dodge in 1745. This meeting soon became a branch of the church at Scotch Plains, New Jersey, some 22 miles to the southwest of Manhattan, and therefore under the pastoral care of Benjamin Miller. Miller administered the ordinance of the Lord's Supper to them once quarterly, while the believers in New York themselves went forward with establishing the work.

On February 10, 1759, the trustees of the church purchased some land that fronted on the west side of Gold Street. The lot lay

---

[80] *Ibid.*, 86.

just south of Fulton Street and between it and John Street. To this was added property to the north. On this property, a section then known as "Golden Hill," the congregation erected a small frame meetinghouse, which was opened for services on March 14, 1760.[81] Gano, who as related, had made the commitment to come to the city that spring, may have been there in time to conduct these opening services, but we are not sure. He does tell us that when he did arrive there, he observed that members of the church "had finished a meeting-house, and had began a parsonage-house; and they seemed disposed to do any thing, to render me happy."[82]

A year after his coming, Gano led the New York membership in the spring of 1762 to apply to the Scotch Plains church by letter for dismissal in order to constitute their own church. On Saturday, June 12, 1762, with the aid of Benjamin Miller, the twenty-seven former members of the Scotch Plains church were formally constituted as the Baptist Church in the City of New York.

With the church now formally organized, thirty-five-year-old John Gano entered into his pastoral ministry in New York with characteristic earnestness. As to his method of conducting meetings, Gano briefly stated, "My usual services, on Lord's days, were, preaching three times; and I gave a lecture weekly." The members of the church, he writes, "were speedily increased; and a hopeful work began. At every church-meeting there was a number who offered themselves."[83]

On March 23, 1763, James Manning was married to Miss Margaret Stites, younger sister to John Gano's wife Sarah, making the two men brothers-in-law.[84] Manning would become a leading figure among the Baptists in New England and the Mannings and the Ganos would maintain a close-knit and mutually rewarding family tie throughout their lives. The following year, when Rhode Island College (now Brown University) was founded under Man-

---

[81] Morgan Edwards, "Materials Towards a History of the Baptists in New York," as cited in Benedict, *A General History of the Baptist Denomination*, 1: 538; W. Carlin and E.R.B., *Souvenir of the First Baptist Church of the City of New York* (New York: The First Baptist Church, 1904), [4].

[82] *Biographical Memoirs of John Gano*, 87.

[83] *Ibid.*, 87.

[84] Reuben A. Guild, *Early History of Brown University, Including the Life, Times, and Correspondence of James Manning, 1756-1791* (Providence, RI: Snow and Farnham, 1897), 34, 36.

ning's leadership with the support of the Philadelphia Association, Gano was one of the original incorporators listed in the school's charter of March 2, 1764.[85] Manning was also the leading spirit behind the founding of the Warren Baptist Association on September 8, 1767, while Gano was chosen that day as the Association's first moderator.

Meanwhile, the Gold Street church continued to grow and prosper under Gano's ministry. Within a year the meetinghouse had become too small for the congregation and in 1763 was enlarged "to meet their increasing needs."[86] William Parkinson noted that even the enlarged house "was generally well filled and often too small. Nor were the people hearers of the word only," he added, "for it was the pleasure of God so to attend his own truth, as delivered by his servant, that many were turned to the Lord and added to the church."[87]

On Saturday, March 17, 1764, in New York, during one of his visits to the city, Hezekiah Smith, after hearing her profession of faith and examining her testimony, baptized Gano's wife Sarah along with one other person, likely in the East River. "It is supposed that 3 or 4 thousand People attended at the Water," Smith noted in his journal. He stayed with the Ganos until the following Saturday, the 24th. "Surely God is Wonderfully at work in New York," he wrote, "Christians are refreshed, Sinners awak[e]ned crying out what must they do to be Saved."[88]

With these blessings came the difficulties which seemingly beset every good work. Gano names three persons who were

---

[85] Walter C. Bronson, *The History of Brown University, 1764-1914* (Providence, RI: Brown University, 1914), 501, 503. Gano's name is not found in the index for this work, though he is shown on these two pages.

[86] *Souvenir of the First Baptist Church of the City of New York*, [5].

[87] William Parkinson, *Jubilee: A Sermon, Containing a History of the Origin of the First Baptist Church in the City of New York, and its Progress* (New York: Printed for William Parkinson, 1813), 16. Gano said that the church "at this time, had increased to two hundred in number," which probably included the 'hearers' as well as members. *Biographical Memoirs of John Gano*, 88.

[88] John D. Broome, *The Life, Ministry, and Journals of Hezekiah Smith. Pastor of the First Baptist Church of Haverhill, Massachusetts 1765 to 1805 and Chaplain in the American Revolution 1775 to 1780* (Springfield, MO: Particular Baptist Press, 2004), 242.

especially troublesome during his ministry in New York, as well as the fact that a division in the church happened at about the same time over hymn-singing methodology, resulting in the formation of the Second Baptist Church in the city in June of 1770.

In October 1773, Gano was appointed by the Philadelphia Association as their "evangelist or messenger of the churches" for the ensuing year,[89] an assignment which would eventually take him through New England, each of the Southern Colonies, upstate New York and Vermont. Beginning his journey on November 2, 1773, he would not arrive back to New York until May 6, 1774.

On May 25-26, 1774, Gano's church at New York hosted an experimental spring session of the Philadelphia Association. The regular fall session would also be held that October. This bi-annual meeting was an attempt to make it convenient for the messengers from the churches more northeastward to attend. Though he had not yet completed his preaching tour of the colonies, on the 26th,

> A motion [was] made, that Brother John Gano should give an account of his travels to the southward: he accordingly did, by which it appears he has been indefatigable in his labors, and that a minister, travelling annually, according to the plan proposed, may answer very valuable purposes.[90]

On June 1st, 1774, Gano ventured forth on the last stage of his preaching tour of the colonies, this time riding northward along the Hudson River, then over to Vermont, and from there down into Massachusetts, Connecticut, Rhode Island and back home.[91]

On September 7, 1774, he attended the commencement service at Rhode Island College. There he met with Isaac Backus and other Baptist leaders interested in securing full religious liberty in New England. That October 14th, Manning, Backus, Gano and other concerned persons met with representatives of the Continental Congress at Carpenter's Hall in Philadelphia, where Manning presented their memorial on religious liberty. Though

---

[89] MS John Gano's diary and expense account for his preaching tour of 1773-1774 in New England, the South and New York. John Hay Library, Brown University, [1].

[90] Gillette, *Minutes of the Philadelphia Baptist Association*, 135.

[91] John Gano's diary and expense account, [21-25].

their plea was rebuffed, the action was not in vain and proved a means of enlightening the public at large of their views.

The Revolutionary War and its aftermath

When war finally ensued with Great Britain on April 19, 1775, many of the nearly 22,000 residents of New York, well aware of the strategic value of their city to both sides, had already begun to evacuate the city, moving into the surrounding countryside and neighboring colonies. The membership of the First Baptist Church began to disband and flee as well, though Gano himself chose to stay. "The war now coming on, obliged the church to separate, and many removed from the city, in almost every direction, through the union," he recalled. While awaiting the expected assault, Gano relocated his family from New York to safety. "I was invited," he wrote, "by Mr. Peter Brown, of Horseneck, in the edge of Connecticut, to remove my family to his house, as he understood I was determined to remain in the city, till the enemy entered it."[92]

On January 1, 1776, Gano agreed to become chaplain of the 19th Continental Regiment.[93] Before leaving the city, Gano administered the ordinance of baptism for the last time on April 28, 1776.[94] The British Navy arrived off Staten Island on June 29th, where they disembarked troops three days later. On August 22nd, the British began landing an additional 15,000 troops on Long Island, near Gravesend.[95] Gano now realized he had waited too late and lamented that after the British Navy had taken possession of both the North and East Rivers, "this left me with no possible opportunity of getting my household furniture."[96]

Gano finally left the city on September 14th. "I was obliged," he wrote, "to retire, precipitately, to our camp." The following day, September 15, 1776, "after a little skirmishing," he tells us, "the

---

[92] *Biographical Memoirs of John Gano*, 92-93.

[93] Francis B. Heitman, *Historical Register of Officers of the Continental Army During the War of the Revolution, April, 1775, to December, 1783* (Washington, D.C.: W. H. Lowdermilk and Co., 1893), 186.

[94] *Souvenir of the First Baptist Church of the City of New York,* [5].

[95] Oscar T. Barck, *New York City During the War for Independence* (New York: Columbia University Press, 1931), 46-47.

[96] *Biographical Memoirs of John Gano*, 93.

British took possession of the city, and our army was driven to Hærlem heights."[97]

On October 12th, in a move aimed at cutting off the American army from the mainland, the British made their way up the East River to attack the Continentals from the rear. Alerted to the danger, the Americans retreated to White Plains, where, Gano says, "General Washington had the greater part of his army, excepting those that were employed in Pennsylvania." Here on October 28-November 1, 1776, another engagement took place. Amid the confusion of the battle, Gano soon found himself in harm's way, as he describes to us in this account:

> On the heights of White-plains, we had a warm, though partial battle; for not a third of our army, or probably of theirs, was brought into action. My station, in time of action, I knew to be among the surgeons; but in this battle, I, somehow, got in the front of the regiment; yet I durst not quit my place, for fear of damping the spirits of the soldiers, or of bringing on me an imputation of cowardice. Rather than do either, I chose to risk my fate.[98]

It was mainly due to this exploit that Gano came to be known as "the fighting chaplain," though there is no evidence that Gano himself ever carried or fired a weapon, or that he engaged in any personal combat at all during the war. In fact, when writing on this same incident later, his son Stephen informs us that his father was unarmed during the engagement.[99]

Now living as refugees, Gano's family moved about from one location to another. James Manning expressed his concerns at not knowing the whereabouts of Gano and his family in a letter dated November 13, 1776, to a friend in England: "My dear Brother Gano has suffered greatly by the war, and where he now is with

---

[97] *Ibid.*, 93.

[98] *Ibid.* This calls to mind the conversation Gano had over twenty years earlier with the ferryman in South Carolina who asked him the best and shortest way to heaven (see page 250). Little did Gano know that here at White Plains he would find himself in just such a situation—in the front of an army during an engagement!

[99] Stephen Gano, Sarah Gano Ludlow, et al., "Sketch of Dr. Stephen Gano." Orrin B. Judd, ed., *The New York Chronicle* (New York: Holman and Gray), 1 (1849), No. 6 (June): 196.

his distressed, numerous family, I cannot learn, as I have never had a line from him since he was obliged to quit New York."[100]

On November 21, 1776, Gano received appointment as chaplain of the 5th New York Regiment, an office he would retain for the next six months.[101] On May 27, 1777, he resigned as chaplain of the 5th New York Regiment, but was requested to stay on, which he agreed to do out of a sense of duty, though he found life in the army to be disagreeable to him personally.

Following a harrowing near escape from the British and Hessian assault on Fort Montgomery in the Hudson highlands (where he was stationed in 1777), and his participation in the famous Sullivan Expedition of 1779, Gano spent the remainder of the war apart from any major engagements. When word of peace came, he was called upon to dismiss the troops in prayer at their New Windsor Cantonment in New York on April 19, 1783.[102]

After an extended absence due to the war, John Gano attended the meetings of the Philadelphia Association on October 21-23, 1783. Since his church was still dispersed, the delegates took the unusual step of voting to receive him individually as a member before then choosing him as Moderator of the meetings!

On November 2, 1783, Congress ordered that the Continental Army be disbanded. Gano was formally discharged the next day.[103] The last British forces left New York on November 25, 1783, and Washington and his army then re-entered the city. Gano himself did not return to the city until near the end of December. As he sadly recalled, "we poor ruined Yorkers returned to our disfigured houses. My house needed some repairs, and wanted some new furniture; for the enemy plundered a great many articles."[104]

The meetinghouse itself had been badly damaged, having been used by the British as a prison, an infirmary and later a stable for

---

[100] Guild, *Early History of Brown University*, 295.

[101] Heitman, *Historical Register of Officers of the Continental Army During the War of the Revolution*, 186.

[102] *Memoirs of Major-General William Heath. Written by Himself* (Boston: Thomas and Andrews, 1798; repr. New York: William Abbatt, 1901), 341.

[103] Francis J. Sypher, Jr., *New York State Society of the Cincinnati. Biographies of Original Members and Other Continental Officers* (Fishkill, NY: New York State Society of the Cincinnati, 2004), 167.

[104] *Biographical Memoirs of John Gano*, 116.

cavalry horses. On his return to the city Gano, in the striking words of Thomas Armitage, "found emptiness, desolation and ashes."[105] Nevertheless, Gano and his small band, said Jonathan Greenleaf, "all set to work like men to repair their desolation."[106] "We collected of our church," wrote Gano, "about thirty seven members, out of upwards of two hundred. Some were dead, and others scattered into almost every part of the union. Some had turned farmers; but the most of these returned to the city."[107]

"The Lord looked graciously upon us," said Gano, "we soon had a large congregation, numbers were sensibly convicted, and many were brought to bow the knee to king Jesus."[108] William Parkinson added that the church was "in a short time, raised to a more flourishing condition, than she had ever enjoyed before: most of the members who had been scattered abroad, were, in the course of Providence, brought back to the city and to the church; and the circumstance of so long a separation, and a review of the toils, dangers and the privations sustained during the war, made the blessings of peace and of Christian society, peculiarly valuable and pleasant."[109]

The call to Kentucky and final years of ministry

The year 1787 would prove to be one of great significance in the life of John Gano. On August 24th, his eldest son Daniel Gano removed from Trenton, New Jersey to Kentucky, where he became one of the first settlers of Frankfort.[110] This event may have been the first to turn John Gano's thoughts towards Kentucky. But it was in the fall of 1787 that he would be directly challenged to become involved in the work of the gospel there. This seems to

---

[105] *A History of the Baptists* (New York: Bryan, Taylor, & Co., 1887), 755.

[106] Jonathan Greenleaf, *A History of the Churches, of all Denominations, in the City of New York* (New York: E. French, 1846), 227.

[107] *Biographical Memoirs of John Gano*, 116-117.

[108] *Ibid.*, 117. Gano first administered baptism again in the city on September 4, 1784. Parkinson, *Jubilee: A Sermon*, 18.

[109] Parkinson, *Jubilee: A Sermon,* 19.

[110] *The Biographical Encyclopedia of Kentucky* (Cincinnati, OH: J. M. Armstrong and Company, 1878), 129.

have first come about when the Philadelphia Association met that year in New York on October 2-5. As he explains in his *Biographical Memoirs*,

> The reason of my removal to Kentucky, I shall here state. One Mr. William Wood, came from that country, and gave a very exalted character of the state of it. He made several encouraging proposals to me to go there, said there was a prospect of usefulness in the ministry, the necessity of an old experienced minister to take care of a young church there, and flattering temporal prospects for the support of my family. For these reasons I concluded to remove. Besides, I was considerably in debt, and saw no way of being released, but by selling my house and lot. This I concluded would clear me, and enable me to purchase waggons and horses to carry me to Kentucky.[111]

Gano soon called for a meeting at the church to state his intentions. The church members "were much grieved at the prospect of parting with him."[112] As Gano was now nearly 61 years old, his plans were viewed as an unrealistic fancy by some members of his congregation, but he remained undaunted. That he was willing to begin anew in a different field of endeavor well illustrates his flexibility—and too, his pioneer spirit.

On Saturday, April 5th, 1788, Gano administered baptism at the church for the last time to three persons.[113] A few weeks later on Tuesday, April 22nd, Gano, his wife Sarah, their son John Stites Gano and six others requested letters of dismissal from the First Baptist Church. Though John Gano's dismissal was granted on April 22nd, he actually didn't take his leave as pastor of the church at New York until Lord's day, May 4, 1788, after having served 25 years, 10 months and 15 days there.

The Ganos followed on a considerable wave of immigration which swept into Kentucky in the first decade following the Revolutionary War. They were part of one such emigrant group

---

[111] *Biographical Memoirs of John Gano*, 11.

[112] "The First Baptist Church, Book of Records." First Baptist Church, New York, 87.

[113] *Ibid.*, 94. These three "the next day came under imposition of hands and were received to full communion in the Church."

planning to rendezvous at their new home in Kentucky, consisting of a number of families and individuals from at least three Baptist churches—the First Baptist Church of New York, William VanHorne's Baptist church at Scotch Plains, New Jersey, and Oliver Hart's Baptist church at Hopewell, New Jersey.

On Monday, May 5, 1788, the Ganos and company began their long journey westward. They traveled into New Jersey to meet first with the party from the Scotch Plains church. The following Wednesday, May 7th, they continued on with the trip, making their way across southern Pennsylvania in their two-horse "Jersey wagons," to Fort Pitt, where they then took portage to the Ohio River. John Gano gave these sober recollections of the experience:

> I encountered more difficulties than I had calculated for. In going down the Ohio river, one of my boats unfortunately overset, and turned every thing into the river. They who were in her, narrowly escaped, by cutting the ropes which tied the horses, so that neither man nor beast were lost. But I lost some very valuable property, which I never could replace. I also lost all the provender for my horses, which at that time was a very serious misfortune. However, as there were others in company from New Jersey, and of my acquaintance, I was amply supplied with that necessary article. We landed at Limestone, on the 17th of June, A.D. 1787;[114] and soon after set out for Washington, in Kentucky, where I safely arrived. I here preached to my companions and the inhabitants, from these words; *'So we got all safe to land'* [Acts 27:44].[115]

John and Sarah Gano soon entered into the fellowship of the Town Fork Baptist church, which was located near Lexington. It wasn't long before he became actively involved in other aspects of Baptist life in his new surroundings—itinerant preaching, attending associational meetings and serving on committees. Gano had brought to Kentucky the same gifts and evangelistic spirit which had made him such a notable figure back East. Testimony was borne to his abilities at the time by Presbyterian minister David

---

[114] The year was actually 1788. This error in the date made by either Gano or the printer of his *Biographical Memoirs* has understandably been repeated by many historians.

[115] *Biographical Memoirs of John Gano*, 119-120.

Rice (1733-1816), who was himself newly-arrived from Virginia. Rice initially despaired of finding true gospel preaching in this new field, but experienced a marked change in his outlook after hearing John Gano preach near his home, as his biographer shares in this excerpt from his *Memoirs*:

> Not finding much of the power of religion in his own denomination, [Rice] began to look to other denominations to see if things were any better there. . . .About this time an old disciple, Mr. Gano, of the Baptist church, came from the state of New York. Mr. Rice had been formerly acquainted with his character, and was rejoiced at his arrival. He at length preached within about four miles of his house. 'I heard him,' says he, 'with great avidity and satisfaction. He appeared to me to preach the gospel in its native simplicity, with honest intention to promote the glory of God and the good of men. He preached in the neighbourhood a second and a third time, and still in the same spirit. To me he appeared as one of the ancient Puritans risen from the dead.'[116]

Soon after, perhaps less than a year after their arrival in Kentucky, Sarah Gano was seriously injured in a fall from her horse while on a visit to Frankfort, which her husband says, "made her a cripple the remainder of her life." Adding to her debility was the fact that not long after settling in to their new home at Frankfort, she was "seized with the pleurisy," a painful inflammation of the membranes of the lungs.[117] After a protracted illness, she passed away at their home near Frankfort on April 23, 1792. John Gano attributed her death to her pleurisy, which he said, "terminated her existence, after languishing a short time." While he expressed that it was "happy for her, I trust, she soon removed to that building of God, a *'house not made with hands, Eternal in the heavens,'* " he admitted that as for himself, "alas! I was too unprepared for such a shock. In all her lameness," he recalled, "I had her cheering company and conversation, and was enlivened by a hope of her recovery. But when this fatal stroke

---

[116] Robert H. Bishop, ed., *An Outline of the History of the Church in the State of Kentucky, during a Period of Forty Years, Containing The Memoirs of Rev. David Rice,* etc. (Lexington : T. T. Skillman, 1824), 70-71.

[117] *Ibid.*, 121.

was given, I was bereft of all consolation, and had not the word and power of God sustained me through it, I must have sunk beneath the stroke."[118] His wife of 37 years and the mother to all of his children was now gone. Their friend Lewis Craig preached her funeral sermon and William Hickman gave the eulogy. Her body was laid to rest in the cemetery near the Baptist meetinghouse at Forks of Elkhorn Creek.

On June 1, 1792, only five weeks after the passing of Sarah Gano, Kentucky became the fifteenth state in the Union. Three days later on Monday, June 4th, John Gano was chosen chaplain of both houses of the Kentucky Legislature at their first sitting at Lexington.[119] This honor would be bestowed again six years later in 1798.[120] And he was not to remain a widower for long. Following the Elkhorn Association's meeting on Saturday, September 1, 1792, at which he was chosen moderator,[121] God's unerring providence found him being called back to North Carolina that fall in order to attend to some urgent business concerning the land he had sold in Rowan County, and as he relates, "Here I found and obtained another companion. She was the widow of Captain Thomas Bryant, and daughter of Colonel Jonathan Hunt. She was a communicant in a Baptist church in that neighbourhood."[122] The two entered into a marriage bond on April 15, 1793 in Rowan

---

[118] *Biographical Memoirs of John Gano*, 121-122.

[119] Zachariah F. Smith, *The History of Kentucky from its Earliest Discovery and Settlement, to the Present Date* (Louisville: Courier Journal Job Print Co., 1886), 312; John T. Christian, *A History of the Baptists of the United States. From the First Settlement of the Country to the Year 1845* (Nashville, TN: Broadman Press, 1926), 2: 293.

[120] "Journal of the House of Representatives," in *Acts Passed at the First Session of the Seventh General Assembly for the Commonwealth of Kentucky* (Lexington, KY: James H. Stewart, 1798), 10.

[121] "Minutes of the Elkhorn Baptist Association, Kentucky, 1785-1805," in William W. Sweet, *Religion on the American Frontier. The Baptists, 1783-1830* (New York: Henry Holt and Co., 1931), 450-451. Gano would serve as Moderator of the Elkhorn Association five times: in 1788, 1789, 1791, 1792, and 1793 (at the South Elkhorn special session). *Ibid.*, 428, 431, 441-442, 447-448, and 457, respectively; and of the Salem Baptist Association once, on October 3, 1789.

[122] *Biographical Memoirs of John Gano*, 122-123.

County and either on or soon after that date were married.[123] David Benedict commented that in her, Gano "found an amiable help-meet for his declining years."[124]

Gano himself suffered a series of physical calamities which came upon him in the fall of the year 1798, when he too fell from a horse, fracturing his shoulder blade. This in turn led to a paralytic stroke which he says, "affected the whole of one side of me, one ear, an eye and half my face, and rendered me almost speechless. This remained for about ten months, when I partially recovered. I have now, abundant cause to sing of the mercies and goodness of the Lord, that during all this illness, my reason was as good as ever it was."[125] William Hickman, a close friend of John Gano, sent a letter to one of Gano's children, in which he said that upon hearing Gano "had a paralytic shock," immediately went to see him. On arriving, Hickman asked Gano how he did? He answered that he was *half* dead. Admitting his own estimate of Gano's condition was not optimistic, Hickman wrote:

> I did not then believe he would ever come out of his house, again, alive. He seemed willing to resign all to God, and to bear what he was pleased to lay on him; wishing the prayers of God's people, and that the travelling preachers would call, converse and preach. At such times, which frequently occurred, he would sit in his chair and exhort to duty, and to flee from vice. His longing, to get out amongst his brethren, so raised his spirits, that in about a year, he ventured, in a carriage, to the Town Fork, Bryants, and other places. When we apprehended his fatigues were too great, while preaching, some friend would support him, when he would preach with renewed ardour.[126]

Just prior to his injuries, Gano had attended the meeting of the Elkhorn Association on Saturday, August 11, 1798, at noon, held

---

[123] Marriage Bond of John Gano and Sarah Bryan[t], dated April 15, 1793. State of North Carolina, Department of Cultural Resources, Raleigh.

[124] Benedict, *A General History of the Baptist Denomination in America*, 2: 315-316.

[125] *Biographical Memoirs of John Gano*, 127-128.

[126] *Ibid.*, 133-134.

at the nearby Forks of Elkhorn church, where he delivered the introductory sermon from the text of 2 Peter 1:15, "Moreover I will endeavor that ye may be able after my decease to have these things always in remembrance." By utilizing his well-known propensity to choose texts to suit a particular occasion, Gano manifested that he had become persuaded months before his stroke that his time was short.[127] On December 29th, believing his earthly life to be near an end, he made out his last will and testament.

What has come to be known as the Great Revival in the West began in 1797 and reached its culmination in Kentucky at the turn of the century. Though the minutes of the Elkhorn Association in August of 1800 revealed that since their last session a respectable number of 82 persons had been baptized and 96 received into the churches by letter, by the time of their next meeting in 1801 a total of 3,011 baptisms would be reported by the churches of the Association![128] The Town Fork church itself experienced an increase in membership from 46 reported in 1800 to 118 in 1801.[129] "This blessed harvest of souls, appeared to increase his joys," wrote Hickman of Gano, while observing that he was also "desirous of being, as in years past, in the vineyard, although his half dead side forbid it." Even so, Gano would occasionally ride his horse to the meetinghouse, said Hickman, "where he would exhort, preach, pray and give counsel, sound and good, while he was supported by two persons to steady him. At other times he would go to the water side at the administration of the ordinance of baptism, and advocate that mode."[130]

Writing perhaps from information received from his father-in-law Stephen Gano, David Benedict further tells us of John Gano, that in regards to the paralytic shock received years before,

> he never fully recovered; but his speech was restored, and he had the use of his limbs so far, that he was able to be

---

[127] "Minutes of the Elkhorn Baptist Association, Kentucky, 1785-1805," in Sweet, *Religion on the American Frontier. The Baptists, 1783-1830*, 477, 479-480.

[128] *Ibid.*, 484-486 (for year 1800) and 486-488 (for year 1801).

[129] *Ibid.*, 485, 487.

[130] *Biographical Memoirs of John Gano*, 134.

> carried out to meetings, and preached frequently, especially in the time of the great revival, in an astonishing manner. While the Arian affair, mentioned in the history of the Elkhorn Association,[131] was agitating the minds of many of the Kentucky brethren, this able advocate for gospel truth was carried to Lexington, assisted into the pulpit, where he preached a masterly discourse in defence of the proper Deity of the Saviour, which was thought to have had a considerable influence in checking the prevalence of that erroneous system, which many were previously inclined to embrace.[132]

More often, however, Gano was found to be confined to his bed, as William Hickman related in this account of his friend:

> My visits to this father in Zion, being frequent, he one day, wished to have the worship of God attended in his house. I spoke from these words: *'Lord help me'* [Matt. 15:25]. I discovered him to be much in tears, and he appeared much affected. When dismissed, while lying on the bed, he seized my hand, and in an extacy exclaimed, 'The Lord has helped me!' His cup appeared full and running over; and he often expressed a wish to depart, and be with Christ, which was far better; [133] but patience he seemed to crave, and I believe God granted his request; for he had every mark of a soul waiting on God.[134]

Hickman visited Gano again the last week of his life, beginning on Sunday, August 6, 1804, just four days before he passed away. He left a moving account of his last days with Gano in this final recollection:

> I went to see him, and he appeared much altered, which induced me to think he was near *home*. He appeared smiling, and in no great misery; nor would he ever own that

---

[131] See this history in Benedict, *A General History of the Baptist Denomination*, 2: 229-235.

[132] *Ibid.*, 2: 316.

[133] Alluding to Psalm 23:5 and Phil. 1:23.

[134] *Biographical Memoirs of John Gano*, 134-135.

> he was. His appetite failed him, and in the course of that week he wore away much; yet his senses and reason continued. Myself and his family, set up the whole night, and I asked him a number of questions, being desirous of knowing the exercise of his mind. He appeared permanently fixed on *Jesus, as the rock of ages*. I asked him, what I should request of God in his behalf? His answer was, that he might enjoy his right mind, and be resigned to God's will. His anxious eyes were upon his weeping children. The night before he expired, I went to see him, went to the bed side and took hold of his hand, and asked if he knew me? he motioned in the affirmative. I asked him if he was in much pain? he spoke so as to be heard, and said *no*. I then asked him if he wanted to be with Jesus? he said *yes!* This was the last word, which could be understood, at least, as far as my recollection serves me. I went to prayer with the family and friends, after which, he was taken with a fit, which continued with but little alteration till morning; when business called me away. I bid him farewell in my mind, no more expecting to see him in life. I went to visit another sick person in the course of the day, and called again in the evening, when I found him still breathing. It had been my wish, for years, to close his eyes in death, should I survive him; but another call happening that evening, I left him in the hands of a faithful and able friend, and about ten o'clock of that night, being [Thursday] the 10th, day of August 1804, he got dismission from the church militant to the church triumphant; being in the 78th year of his age.[135]

It must have been a day of sadness intermingled with joy as the bearers of his casket conveyed his body to the gravesite. Gano was buried next to his first wife Sarah in the cemetery near the Baptist meetinghouse at Forks of Elkhorn Creek. The grave marker was made in the same simple fashion as hers. His marker read:

SACRED
to the
MEMORY
of
THE REV. JOHN GANO
Who departed this life the 10th day of August,

[135] *Ibid.*, 135-137.

A. D., 1804, in the 78th year of his age.
The Grace of our Lord Jesus Christ
Be with You All. Amen.[136]

In 1806, Stephen Gano, in a loving tribute to his late father, shared these simply-worded remembrances of him:

> it is but a testimony of respect in me, just to say, that as a husband, he was faithful and loving;—as a father, kind and indulgent;—as a friend, sincerity ever shone in his heart;—and as a Christian, he was emphatically the follower of Jesus Christ, in all his imitable examples.[137]

Further Reading

Stephen Gano and Daniel Gano, eds. *Biographical Memoirs of the Late Rev. John Gano, of Frankfort, Kentucky. Formerly of the City of New York*. New York: Southwick and Hardcastle, 1806.

Terry Wolever. *The Life of John Gano, 1727-1804. Pastor-Evangelist of the Philadelphia Association*. Springfield, MO: Particular Baptist Press, 2012.

Lee Sayers Johnson, "An Examination of the Life of John Gano in the Development of Baptist life in North America 1750-1804." Ph.D. dissertation, Southwestern Baptist Theological Seminary, Fort Worth, Texas, 1986.

---

[136] From the author's line by line transcription of the stone. Gano and his first wife's remains were later removed by the D.A.R. in 1916 to the Frankfort Cemetery. New blue granite markers were placed at their gravesite and that of William Hickman (who is buried beside them there) by the Baptist History Preservation Society in 2001. I have not discovered when Gano's second wife passed away or where her gravesite is.

[137] Preface to *Biographical Memoirs of John Gano*, vii.

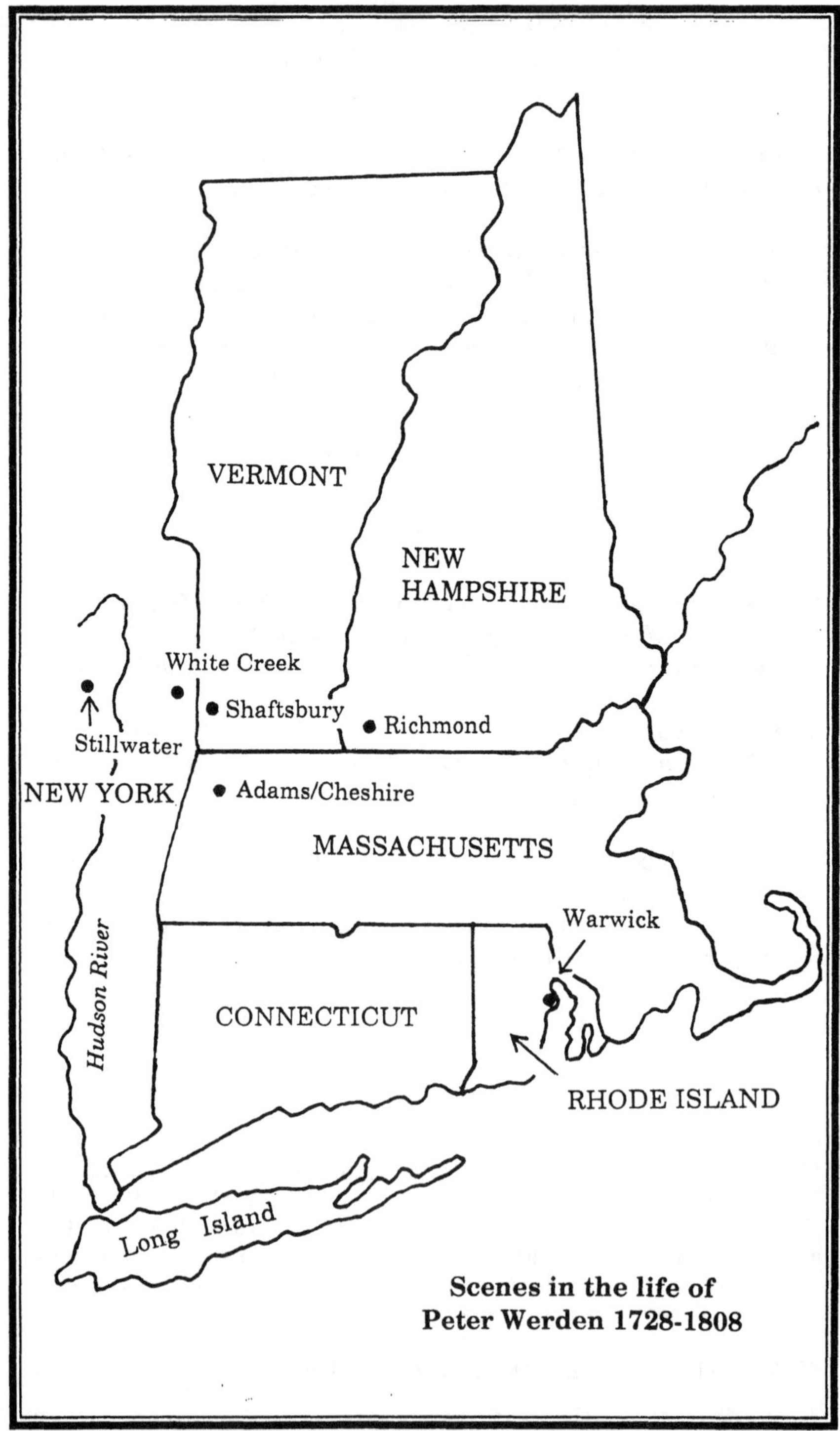

Scenes in the life of Peter Werden 1728-1808

PETER WERDEN
1728 - 1808

by Terry Wolever

It was said at the time of his death in 1808 at the age of 79 that Peter Werden was "the Patriarch of the Baptist churches in New England."[1] In addition he was eulogized as "the founder, father, and guardian angel" of the Shaftsbury Baptist Association.[2] Another has described him as "a fervent and useful preacher," who was "remarkable for integrity, discretion and self-control."[3] This says quite a lot about his stature among his contemporaries, and in the context of this brief essay we will seek to become re-acquainted with this esteemed gospel minister and leader.

A providential opening at the gallows

Peter Werden was born on June 6, 1728. His sole biographer John Leland (1754-1841), was either unaware of or chose not to preserve any details of his friend and fellow minister's early life.[4]

---

[1] Henry Curtis, *Conflicts and the Triumphs of the Christian Soldier; a Sermon on the occasion of the Death of Jesse B. Worden, with Sketches of his Life, Labors, and Character* (Lewisburg, PA: 1855), as cited in William B. Sprague, *Annals of the American Pulpit* (New York: Robert Carter and Bros., 1865), 6 (Baptist): 688.

[2] Notice on the occasion of his death in the *Minutes of the Shaftsbury Baptist Association, 1808*, as cited in Stephen Wright, *History of the Shaftsbury Baptist Association, from 1781-1853* (Troy, NY: A. G. Johnson, 1853), 116.

[3] Sprague, *Annals of the American Pulpit*, 6: 688*n*.

[4] John Leland, "A Biographical Sketch of the Life and Character of the Rev. Peter Werden," in Thomas Baldwin, ed., *The Massachusetts Baptist Missionary Magazine* (Boston: Manning and Loring), 2 (March 1808-December 1810), Number 11 (September 1810): 348. This sketch, which Leland drew from the sermon he delivered at Werden's funeral, was reprinted in David Benedict, *A General History of the Baptist Denomination in America, and Other Parts of the World* (Boston: Lincoln and Edmands, 1813), 2: 401-404; in Miss L. F. Greene, ed., *The Writings of the Late Elder John Leland* (New York: G. W. Wood, 1845), 319-321; abridged in Charles G. Sommers, William R. Williams and Levi L. Hill, eds., *The Baptist Library: A Republication of Standard Baptist Works*

Leland thankfully did share however, the following account of Werden's spiritual awakening:

> In his first religious exercises, he was led to dig deep into his own heart, where he found such opposition and rebellion, that when he obtained pardon, he attributed it to sovereign grace alone; which sentiment, so interwoven in his soul, he ever proclaimed aloud to a dying world. Nothing appeared to be more disgustful to his mind, than to hear *works* and *grace* mixed together, as the foundation of a sinner's hope. To hold forth the Lamb of God as a piece of a Saviour; or to consider the self-exertions of a natural man, to be the *way* unto Christ, the true and *only way*, were extremely displeasing to that soul of his, which delighted so much in proclaiming eternal love, redeeming blood, and matchless grace.[5]

Werden was married to Mary (or Mercy) Moon (1723-1805), daughter of Ebenezer Moon, Jr. and his wife Elizabeth, on August 18, 1749 at Richmond, Rhode Island.[6] He was ordained to the gospel ministry at Warwick, Rhode Island on May 21, 1751,[7] just shy of his 23rd birthday. When he first began preaching, his Calvinistic sentiments were not always welcomed, as Leland recalled, for "he was too much of a New-Light, and too strongly

---

(Prattsville, NY: Robert H. Hill, 1841), 1: 237-238; and retitled as "Elder Peter Werden, of First Cheshire, Massachusetts," in Wright, *History of the Shaftsbury Baptist Association*, cited above, 349-351. Werden's surname appears at times as "Worden," though Leland spelled it "Werden." The "o" spelling has been followed by some descendants.

[5] Leland, "Biographical Sketch of the Rev. Peter Werden," 349. Werden's tombstone states that he was "Converted by the mighty power of God to the Lord Jesus Christ May 9th 1748."

[6] The marriage record shows her name as Mary, while the constituent member list of the Baptist church at Adams, Massachusetts shows her name as Mercy, so it is difficult to know which is correct.

[7] Isaac Backus, *A History of New England, with Particular Reference to the Denomination of Christians Called Baptists*. Second Edition with Notes by David Weston (Newton, MA: Backus Historical Society, 1871), 2: 471. A point of confusion exists in that Backus noted earlier in his *History* that Werden was ordained on May 17th. *Ibid.*, 79*n*. He also mentioned that at the time he wrote, the Baptist church "in the west part of Warwick," where Werden had been ordained, had dissolved. *Ibid.*, 288.

attached to the doctrine of salvation by sovereign grace, to be generally received among the old Baptist churches in Rhode-Island, which had been formed partly upon the Arminian plan." But a singular event was to providentially open the way for him. A criminal by the name of Carter was to be executed at Tower Hill. As was usual in that day, the event drew a large crowd of curious spectators from all across the colony. Leland tells what happened next:

> While the criminal stood under the gallows, young Werden felt such a concern for the soul of this unhappy criminal, that he urged his way through the crowd; and being assisted by the Sheriff, he gained access to Carter, and addressed him as follows: 'Sir, is your soul prepared for that awful eternity, into which you will launch in a few minutes?' The criminal replied, 'I don't know that it is, but I wish you would pray for me.' In this prayer, Mr. Werden was so wonderfully assisted in spreading the poor man's case before the throne of God, that the whole assembly were awfully solemnized, and most of them wet their cheeks with their tears. This opened a great door for his ministrations, both on the Maine [or mainland] and on the island.[8]

Werden itinerated at Warwick, Coventry, "and many other places, with good success," for about 18 years, before removing with his wife and their four children[9] from Warwick, Rhode Island to the New Providence Purchase in Berkshire County, Massachusetts. There the Werdens would experience great spiritual blessing in a series of God-sent awakenings to their congregation.

The settlement and church at New Providence

In 1762, Massachusetts sold some of its township lots in the western portion of the province to prospective settlers. Most of these lay in Berkshire County. Col. Joab Stafford became chiefly instrumental in leading the emigration from Rhode Island to the lands in Berkshire. As historian James Barker explained,

---

[8] *Ibid.*, 348-349.

[9] These children, all born at Coventry, R.I., were: Abigail, born on September 19, 1750; Esther, born April 19, 1753; Lucinda, born May 21, 1755; and Judah, born May 16, 1756. There likely were other children who may not have survived childhood, which was common at the time.

> These earlier settlers came more largely than the settlers of any other considerable portion of Berkshire from the Colony of Rhode Island and Providence Plantations. They were descendants, some of them of the very men who were the first to follow Roger Williams to Rhode Island, and generally they were men who had inherited and imbibed the spirit of her free institutions, and were educated in the religious beliefs prevalent in that colony rather than in the orthodoxy of the Massachusetts Colony.
>
> * * * * *
>
> The story of the men who made the New Providence Purchase, and in 1767 removed their families and goods from Rhode Island to the splendid eminence which they christened New Providence Hill in affectionate remembrance of the hill in Providence, and there assayed to found a new community, is worthy to be told.[10]

Providence Hill was later renamed Stafford's Hill in honor of Col. Joab Stafford. In looking over the scene in the late nineteenth century, Barker gave this description through the eyes of a skillful town historian of what he saw:

> On our right rise the grassy slopes of Stafford's Hill, a few apple trees on the summit being all that from this point is visible to indicate that it has been the site of a village. On the left rises Mount Amos, wooded on its northern slope, but clear and smooth on its southern, where, among the maple trees, the early settlers used to keep the sugar boiling while the wolves howled around the fires in the night. Far below, at the north, is the Adams valley and, perhaps, a mile in advance of you, if your eyes are keen, you can see rows of white stones by the roadside, another resting place of these first settlers of New Providence. It occupies a little plateau with but a gentle slope toward the west, the road sweeping

---

[10] Judge James Barker, "Early Settlement of Cheshire," the Introductory Chapter in Ellen M. Raynor and Emma L. Petitclerc, *History of the Town of Cheshire, Berkshire County, Massachusetts* (Holyoke, MA and New York City, 1885), 10. For the interested reader, Barker goes on to describe in detail who these settlers were and the locations of the lots they purchased.

> around it down the hill with a dark, solemn spruce tree standing in the background.
>
> It was here that these Rhode Islanders of the Baptist denomination planted their first church and set up the public worship of God. No trace remains upon the spot of the ancient building, nor any mark by which to fix its location, but tradition says that it was next to the road and that its site is now occupied by graves.
>
> The building, however is now standing on the northern slope of the hill to which it was removed, and where, as a two-story red farm house, it still does duty in the cause for which it was framed and raised. It has changed its uniform, but still does service in sustaining the preaching of the word in the New Providence Purchase.[11]

Among this new colony of Baptist emigrants were some of Werden's former hearers in Coventry, Rhode Island, who desired to organize a church and sent for Werden to come among them as their minister. Werden removed to the area in 1769.[12] On August 28th of that year he helped organize this congregation of believers there into "the Baptist Church in Adams" (later known as the First Baptist Church of Cheshire).[13] The 13 constituent members, eight men and five women, were listed as being "Rev. Peter Werden, Eunice Bennet, Joab Stafford, John Lee, Betsy Read, Samuel Low, John Bucklin, Deliverance Nichols, Joseph Bennet,

---

[11] *Ibid.*, 18.

[12] Leland mistakenly dates Werden's arrival at Adams as being in 1770. "Biographical Sketch of the Rev. Peter Werden," 349.

[13] Josiah G. Holland, *History of Western Massachusetts. The Counties of Hampden, Hampshire, Franklin, and Berkshire* (Springfield, MA: Samuel Bowles and Co., 1855), 476; John W. Barber, *Historical Collections, relating to the History and Antiquities of Every Town in Massachusetts* (Worcester: Dorr, Howland and Co., 1839), 67. The village at Adams was originally named East Hoosuck. "The town of Cheshire was incorporated on the 14th of March, 1793. The title of the Act indicated that its territory was made up of parts of the towns of Lanesborough, Windsor, Adams and of the District of New Ashford not having been incorporated as a town until May 1, 1836." Barker, "Early Settlement of Cheshire," 9.

Mercy Werden, Martha Lee, John Day, [and] Alma Low." Werden officially became pastor of the new church in January 1770.[14]

Barker has characterized Werden as "a remarkable man; somewhat unlettered, perhaps, but full of grace and zeal, and actuated by love of God and man. . . .The discipline of his church was strict, and it cannot be doubted that its work was of the utmost importance to the well being of the community."[15] Indeed, Barker wrote that he believed the new church, "more than anything else, must have educated the men and women of Cheshire and moulded the life of the town."[16]

The proprietors at New Providence were not obligated to devote a part of their purchase towards the support of the new church. Even so, as Barker informs us, "Nicholas Cook and Joseph Bennet learning that a church had been thus founded at New Providence, gave by deed on the 17th of January 1770, 50 acres of their best land on the northern slope of the hill to Joab Stafford, in trust as a ministerial lot or glebe land for the support of a preacher." On this land Peter Werden lived and from it he obtained his subsistence.[17]

Isaac Backus tells us that an uncommon death in early 1772, together with the sermon delivered at the funeral, were the means by which the Lord brought about the initial revival at Cheshire. He went on to say that in the fall of that year, "the work came on more powerfully, and prevailed through the winter."[18] Pastor Werden and the deacons at Cheshire gave a written account of this wonderful season of revival, "the most material part" of which was preserved by Backus as follows:

> The children of God began to be more manifestly quickened, and more earnestly engaged than they before had been.

---

[14] Ellen M. Raynor and Emma L. Petitclerc, *History of the Town of Cheshire, Berkshire County, Massachusetts* (Holyoke, MA and New York City, 1885), 22.

[15] Barker, "Early Settlement of Cheshire," 19.

[16] *Ibid.*, 18.

[17] *Ibid.*, 19. Barker states that it was during the ministry of one of Werden's successors, Elder Samuel Bloss, that the meetinghouse itself was relocated to this glebe land. See also Holland, *History of Western Massachusetts*, 476.

[18] Backus, *A History of New England*, 2: 471.

Love and unity daily increased, and concern of mind began to be powerful on the minds of the unregenerate; and not long after, some began to give hopeful evidences that they had passed from death unto life. The first of our young converts that made a public declaration of what God had done for them, were received into the church and baptized on November 15, 1773. Soon after this, distress of soul, and awakenings on the consciences of sinners, became more general, so that it was manifest by their uncommon attention and solemnity in public meetings, and their earnest inquiries and lamentable complaints in their private conversation, that the Spirit of God was operating on many of them; and in the course of the ensuing winter and spring, we had reason to hope that near forty were savingly brought home to God, by a living union to Jesus Christ. Our number of members has increased to about eighty. And although upon the most close inquiry, there appears to be great variety of circumstances in the subjects of the late work, yet in several things there appeared a general agreement. A clear conviction of sin, of the universal depravity of human nature, the reasonable requirements of God's holy law, his just declaration of vengeance against sin, and the total shutting up of all the sources of their natural hope, which is ever seeking some legal qualification to prepare for God's mercy; and then a discovery of the all sufficient righteousness of the Son of God, as Mediator between God and man, a sensible union to God, love to holiness, hatred of sin, union to the children of God, and pity and benevolence to all mankind; in these and in other things of like nature, there appeared a very general agreement. The means of awakening people among us have been various, as, the preaching of the word, prayer, exhortation, religious conversation, occurrences of divine providence, and the like; but the public relations of experiences of those who have been wrought upon, have been as frequent a means as any. The most of the subjects of this work were in the vigor of youth, from fifteen to twenty-five years: though we have reason to think that some who were advanced in age, and some little children, have been made the happy partakers of the salvation of God. This church does not receive any as members, but such as give satisfying evidences that they are born of God, neither have they table-communion with any but those who profess and practice believers' baptism. They make no bar of communion, whether persons come under hands or not.[19] They hold to a general right in the brethren to improve their gifts, and yet believe that the church ought to exercise government therein, so that the church may be edified by the gifts of the brotherhood. We believe the entire depravity of human nature, and that the justification of a sinner before God is alone in the righteousness of Christ. This was publicly read and acknowledged by the church as a true relation.

Peter Worden, Elder,
Jonathan Richardson,
Stephen Carpenter,
Samuel Low, } Deacons.

January 15, 1774.[20]

Three more visitations of revival would follow over the next two decades. The first, described by Backus as “another powerful work,” would increase the church’s membership to 133 persons by 1782. “A great blessing was again granted in 1788,” he went on to write, “which caused the addition of eighty members to this church in a year. A like favor was given again in 1791, so that the next year they had a hundred and ninety-four members.”[21] Though

---

[19] In other words, Werden’s congregation practiced closed communion, but did not make the imposition or laying on of hands upon all baptized believers (as opposed to only ministers, deacons and possibly licentiates) a prerequisite to taking the Lord’s Supper.

[20] Backus, *A History of New England*, 2: 471-472.

[21] *Ibid.*, 472. These figures may not appear so substantial by today’s standards, but in the eighteenth century this was quite a large congregation for a small rural community in Western Massachusetts. As Stephen Wright has noted: “In regard to the revivals of Eld. Werden’s ministry, it may be proper to remark, that the early period of his ministry in Cheshire, before the population had become densely settled, and while many things hindered the rapid growth of churches generally, besides his advance age, it was not to be expected under such circumstances, that large additions would reward the labors of a minister in a single town. He was over 40 years of age when he removed thither, and when we first find the statistics of his church in 1786, he was nearly 60 years of age; and yet the returns of that year give his church a membership of 117.” *History of the Shaftsbury Baptist Association*, 350*n*.

there were eventually some necessary exclusions, nonetheless the new membership in the main proved to be genuinely born again.

In later reflecting on Werden's ministry, John Leland, who came with his family to settle in Cheshire in February, 1792 and assist in ministry at the Second Baptist church in town at the time of the last revival season, had this to say about his fellow-laborer:

> From the sternness of his eyes and the blush of his face, a stranger would have been led to conclude that he was sovereign and self-willed in his natural habit of mind; but on acquaintance, the physiognomist would have been agreeably disappointed.[22] He has so much self-government, that he has been heard to say, that, except when he had the smallpox, he never found it hard to keep from speaking at any time, if his reason told him it was best to forbear; and no man possessed finer feelings, or treated the characters of others with more delicacy than he did. He had an exalted idea of the inalienable rights of conscience; justly appreciated the civil rights of man, and was assiduous to keep his brethren from the chains of ecclesiastical power.
>
> His preaching was both sentimental and devotional, and his life so corresponded with the precepts he taught, that none of his hearers could justly reply, 'Physician, heal thyself.'[23]

Founding of the Shaftsbury Baptist Association

Perhaps Peter Werden's greatest contribution to aiding the rise and progress of Regular Baptist principles in the Northeast was the leading role he took in founding and establishing the Shaftsbury Baptist Association. Werden, along with William Wait, Joseph Cornell and Lemuel Powers, were said to have been "the principle ministers" who participated at the organizational meeting of the Association in 1780.[24] The five constituting churches were the West (or First) Shaftsbury, Vermont, pastor

---

[22] A physiognomist is one who seeks to determine from a person's face or countenance an index to their character.

[23] Leland, "Biographical Sketch of the Rev. Peter Werden," 350.

[24] Benedict, *A General History of the Baptist Denomination*, 1: 335.

Ebenezer Willoughby; East (or Second) Shaftsbury, Vermont;[25] Adams (later First Cheshire), Massachusetts, pastor Peter Werden; Stillwater, New York, pastor Lemuel Powers; and White Creek, New York, pastor William Wait. Cornell was pastor of the Baptist church in Manchester, Vermont, which did not join this association, but later joined the Vermont Baptist Association, formed in 1787.

The Shaftsbury Association soon grew to become a strong and influential body. In the first six years, or by 1786, the Association had grown from five to fifteen member churches and Werden's church in Adams had the honor of hosting the associational meeting that summer on Wednesday, June 14th.[26]

Stephen Wright, historian of the Association, wished to point out its Calvinistic theological basis at this period, citing the following entry from the Minutes of the year 1788, which he wrote, "may be useful in exhibiting the specific doctrinal views of the ministers and churches of that age":

> *Whereas*, the intention of this association, in the first and third queries in the minutes of the last session, was not fully understood by our brethren at a distance: therefore *voted*, that it is expedient to communicate our ideas in the following manner:
>
> 1. Whether all men, or any part of them, are actually discharged from the condemnation of the law, by the atonement of Christ, without the special application of that atonement by the Holy Spirit?

---

[25] In 1813, Benedict reported that the East, or Second Shaftsbury church "has no pastor, and never had; but they have a worthy exhorter among them, by the name of Downer, who is now 80 years old." *A General History of the Baptist Denomination*, 1: 336. Wright confirms this by stating that the church had "no settled pastor among them. A licentiate named Cyprian Downer was helpful by his labors, in keeping them from entire dissolution; as also were the labors of another Brother usually denominated Deacon Gideon Slye." *History of the Shaftsbury Baptist Association*, 289. John Asplund mistakenly lists Cyprian Downer at the West (First) Shaftsbury and Willoughby at the East (Second) Shaftsbury. *The Universal Register of the Baptist Denomination in North America, 1790-1794* (Boston: John W. Folsom, 1794), 17.

[26] See *Minutes of the Shaftsbury Baptist Association, at their Annual Convention, held at Elder Warden's Meeting-House, in Adams, 1786.* Albany, NY: Charles R. Webster, 1786.

Answer: in the negative.

2. Whether the benefits of the great atonement, as they respect the eternal salvation of man, are applied to any except the elect?

Answered in the negative. And so the body adjourned.[27]

By 1790, the Adams church reported having 177 members.[28] At the annual associational meeting held at Stockbridge, Massachusetts on June 1-2, 1791, Werden, Stephen Gano (then pastor at Hillsdale, New York) and Justus Hull (pastor at Little Hoosick, New York) were asked to prepare a Circular Letter "on the subject of the power of an association." The three were requested to prepare the letter during that year's sessions after Ebenezer Willoughby, who had been assigned the task the year before, reportedly "accidently mislaid" his own letter on the subject.[29] The Werden-Gano-Hull Circular Letter is a remarkable achievement in its concise and yet at the same time comprehensive treatment of the subject, especially considering the time constraint under which the three labored to get it written. Said Wright, "It is a document worthy of the age, and deserving present study among our churches, for the sound views of church order it exhibits. Which of the committee produced it, we are unable to say."[30]

"All men are born free"

Nearest the site of the Adams church was the property of Samuel Low, who was one of the wealthiest and most prominent men in the community. He was also among those who had helped found both the settlement and the church at New Providence. Barker tells us that in 1763, Low "was entrusted with the duty of organizing a lottery to raise and grade the streets of Providence, Rhode Island." An interesting controversy arose between Low, a member of the Adams church, and Pastor Werden. In New Providence, Low owned at least four slaves we know of—William

---

[27] Wright, *History of the Shaftsbury Baptist Association*, 22.

[28] John Asplund, *The Annual Register of the Baptist Denomination in North America; To the First of November, 1790* (Preface dated Southampton County, VA, July 14, 1791), 5.

[29] Wright, *History of the Shaftsbury Baptist Association*, 29.

[30] *Ibid*. This Circular Letter may be read in Wright, 30-35.

Dimon, Molly Dimon and their two children, one of whom was named Antony. "About 1790," writes Barker, Low removed to Palatine, New York, "having freed old William and Molly," but taking Antony and his sister with him. Afterwards, Low applied to the church at Adams for an orderly dismissal, but was refused unless he would free the two children.

The matter issued in a lengthy correspondence between Low and Werden. One of the letters from Pastor Werden, which reveals something of his mind on the subject of slavery, read in part:

> Dear Brother—
>
> We received your letter and the brethren hath heard it re[a]d. That part that concerneth Antony and it doth not serve our minds. Our minds is that your duty was to have set him at liberty at the age of twenty-one which was about a year ago. And as to the bills of cost that you speak of you and he must settle that yourselves. We look upon it that we have nothing to do in that matter. We wish you, very dear brother, to attend to the proposition that you mentioned—all men are born free. Therefore our request and desire is that you liberate him emmediately to ease our sister and ourselves of our pain, as we think it will dishonor our profession if it is not dun.
>
> Adams, March 2d, 1792.[31]

Low had obviously been a member in good standing while he held all four members of the family in bondage. Even so, Werden and other members may have all the while objected to the practice of slavery, bearing with Low until he made the decision to divide the family by keeping the son and daughter as slaves and taking them with him. The church, as stated, believed it would dishonor their profession as Christian people to allow this to happen without expressing their displeasure with Low's actions. Though the outcome of the controversy is uncertain, Low surely would have conceded to his pastor's request and freed the two.

"A distinguished nursery for Baptists"

The nine years of the Shaftsbury Association, from 1792 to 1800, were characterized by Wright as embracing

[31] Barker, "Early Settlement of Cheshire," 19-20.

> a period of enlargement and prosperity among most of the churches,—in which great showers of Divine Grace descended upon all the hills of Zion. The extension of our peculiar sentiments as a denomination,—in the multiplication of converts,—the formation of new and strong churches in important places,—and the increase of ministers of the Word of Life,—able and successful men, distinguishes this period of the existence of the association more than any other.
>
> From 26 churches, 19 ministers, and 1,754 members in 1791,—the association was enlarged in these nine years, to 46 churches, having 33 ministers, and more than 4,100 members. This has been an interesting chapter to the writer, and no doubt it will be equally satisfactory to the Christian reader, awakening his gratitude to God, for the wonders of his redeeming grace, among the churches, in those days of our Fathers.[32]

During this same period, Werden enjoyed the confidence of his fellow ministers. Wright stated that at the Association's meeting of June 4-5, 1794, held at Pownal, Vermont, "the venerable Peter Werden of 1st Cheshire, the father or founder of this Association, now 66 years of age, was chosen Moderator."[33]

As noted earlier, on March 14, 1793, the town of Cheshire was incorporated from parts of Adams, Lanesborough and other surrounding communities. The church, now known as First Baptist Church, Cheshire, had become the focal point of Werden's life and labors, in a ministry that would span almost 37 years. Leland wrote of Werden that

> Sound judgment, correct principles, humble demeanor, with solemn sociability, marked all his public improvements, and mingled with all his conversation in smaller circles, or with individuals.
>
> In him, young preachers found a father and friend; distressed churches, a healer of breaches; and tempted souls a sympathizing guide. From his first coming to this place, until he was 70 years old, he was a father to the Baptist

---

[32] Wright, *History of the Shaftsbury Baptist Association*, 37.

[33] *Ibid.*, 41.

churches in Berkshire and its environs, and in some sense an apostle to them all.

His many painful labours for the salvation of sinners, the peace of the churches, and purity of the ministers, will never be fully appreciated, until the time when he shall stand before his Judge, and hear the words of his mouth, 'well done good and faithful servant.'[34]

Leland also spoke of the "number of revivals" that had taken place in the town and congregation where Werden resided and preached, and how "a number of ministers have been raised up in the church of which he was pastor."[35] David Benedict would later expand on Leland's observations by favorably noting that the town of Cheshire "has been a distinguished nursery of Baptists for many years." "Great numbers have been baptized in it," he went on to say, "who have removed to other places; but there yet [1813] remain two churches, which, together, contain upwards of two hundred and fifty members."[36]

In 1795, Werden was present at the preliminary meeting called to arrange the organization of the Otsego Baptist Association in New York. This new association was held in special regard recalled Wright, due to the fact that some of its members were "the sons and daughters of the Shaftsbury Association, who had emigrated into the then wilderness of Central New York."[37]

Letters to a Friend (1796)

As could be expected, Baptists weren't the only religious group to move into Berkshire County when land was made available. A large body of The Society of Friends (or Quakers) from Smithfield, Rhode Island and Dartmouth, Massachusetts had come there at the same time. Not at all reconciled to each other by a great

---

[34] Leland, "Biographical Sketch of the Rev. Peter Werden," 349.

[35] *Ibid.*, 350.

[36] Benedict, *A General History of the Baptist Denomination*, 1: 438. The Second (Six-Principle) Baptist Church of Cheshire was founded by Nathan Mason on September 21, 1771. *Ibid.*, 439; Barber, *Historical Collections*, 67.

[37] Wright, *History of the Shaftsbury Baptist Association*, 50-51.

disparity in their beliefs, the Baptists and Quakers found common cause in dissent from the Standing Order—but that was about the limit of their commonality. The two sides often engaged one another in lively, yet in the main civil, debate, either through appointed public meetings or more often, through the printed page. The Baptists rightly viewed the Quakers as a heretical sect, though the former were able by principle to tolerate the latter residing among them, unlike the Congregationalists.

In the year he died, Quaker Job Scott (1751-1793) published an influential work, *The Baptism of Christ a Gospel Ordinance: Being altogether Inward and Spiritual*.[38] Four posthumous editions soon followed, two in 1794 and two more in 1796. As the title suggests, Scott was upholding the Quaker view that there are no "outward" ordinances, such as water baptism and the Lord's Supper, but that these take place inwardly and are purely of a spiritual nature. This of course runs directly counter to the New Testament revelation and typifies the lack of solid biblical exegesis common to Quaker writings.

In 1796, Peter Werden replied to Job Scott in what would be his only published work, a 64-page pamphlet entitled, *Letters to a Friend*.[39] The pamphlet is a credit not only to Werden's capable defense of the orthodox position, but also to his friendly manner of approach to the controversy. Werden makes it clear in the Introductory Letter of his reply that he had been personally acquainted with Scott in the past, but apparently was unaware he had died just three years before. This unawareness would not have been an unusual circumstance for the time and given the fact that Scott's pamphlets continued to be printed could have suggested to Werden that he was yet living. In any event, though his ten "Letters" were addressed to Scott, it was to Scott's arguments, even more specifically those of the Quakers in general, that Werden was actually directing his remarks.

---

[38] Job Scott. *The Baptism of Christ a Gospel Ordinance: Being altogether Inward and Spiritual: Not, like John's, into Water; but, according to the real Nature of the Gospel, into the very Name, Life and Power, of the Father, and of the Son, and of the Holy Ghost.* Providence, R.I.: Printed by J. Carter, 1793.

[39] Peter Werden. *Letters to a Friend: Containing Remarks on a Pamphlet Written by Job Scott, Entitled, The Baptism of Christ a Gospel Ordinance, Being altogether Inward, Spiritual, &c.* Lansingburgh, NY: William W. Wands, for the Author, 1796. Starr's *Baptist Bibliography* shows the work at only 48 pages, but it is actually 64 pages in length.

Wright thought that while Werden's "spirit is good" in the pamphlet and gives evidence of his "intellectual power, as well as [his] religious principles," it seemed to him "he presses the argument pretty close home upon the writer he is reviewing."[40] Possibly so, but Werden was contending for vital truths, and such a direct dealing can hardly be avoided altogether in such an endeavor. He was undoubtedly the right man for this needful task.

Early on in his *Letters*, in digressing for the moment from his argument on the text of John 3:30, where John the Baptist exclaims, "He must increase, but I must decrease," Werden paused to appropriate the passage to reflect on his own life and ministry:

> *He must increase*, that is, the same work goes rapidly on in his hands. *But, I must decrease*, as much as to say, I have almost done my work of preaching and baptising in person, but then I rejoice that the same work is in better hands; he that hath the bride is the bridegroom. Had John seen that the gospel which he preached and the ordinance that he administered in the name of God, would have ceased, then adieu to his joy; Herod would have had no occasion to cut off his head: I presume, it would have broken his heart, and he would have died in despair. In contemplating this subject, it naturally brings the following experience to mind: I have been young—have had considerable attendance and success in preaching the gospel and baptising—I now decrease—my work is almost done: but when I consider, and see with mine eyes, that God has sent a goodly number into the work, and given them both skill and success; so that there is a very great increase to what there was forty years ago: I rejoice; but, ah! I decrease.[41]

It gave Werden no small measure of consolation to know that the Lord was raising up others to enter into the field he had spent his own life laboring in.

"Fresh tokens of his Redeemer's favor"

The growing popularity of John Leland, now settled as pastor of the Third Baptist Church in Cheshire, combined with Werden's

---

[40] Wright, *History of the Shaftsbury Baptist Association*, 351*n*.

[41] Werden, *Letters to a Friend*, 10.

failing health, began affecting the attendance at First Church, to the extent that, according to Wright, "his membership became very much reduced before his death."[42] Yet there was no bitterness between the two pastors, and Leland had only good things to say about Werden. The simple truth was the old saint was no longer the man he once was and was nearing the end of his course. As Leland observed,

> For about 10 years his physical and mental powers have been on the decline; and how many times have we heard him rejoice, that others increased, though he decreased: but his superannuation was not so great, as to prevent the whole of his usefulness; and his hoary head was a crown of glory unto him.[43]

The Lord graciously continued to reward Werden's faithfulness by adding members to his congregation even as others departed, even as he became more infirm with age. In the years 1800 and 1801, Wright informs us that

> while other branches of Zion around were being favored with the dews of Divine grace, his people were not left entirely desolate, nor his soul uncheered by fresh tokens of his Redeemer's favor upon his ministry. In two years the pleasing addition of some 22 [persons] were reported to his church, while he was attaining the age of 73 in life, and the 50th year of his public ministry. And still in 1804, we find him adding 12 more in a year to his flock, and three or four in the subsequent years of his lengthened pastorate of 38 years among that one people, until he fell with his armor on, nobly contending for truth, and encouraging the hearts of his brethren, in the 80th year of his age, and to the last Sabbath of his eventful life. Is not this 'bearing fruit even in old age' (Psalm 92:14)?[44]

It may have been that like John Gill, the famed English Baptist, his faithful supporters in the church could not bear to

---

[42] Wright, *History of the Shaftsbury Baptist Association*, 350*n*.

[43] Leland, "Biographical Sketch of the Rev. Peter Werden," 350.

[44] Wright, *History of the Shaftsbury Baptist Association*, 350-351*n*.

part with him for another pastor. And so on a winter's day, February 21st, 1808, Peter Werden truly 'fell with his armor on.' John Leland, in delivering the sermon at his funeral, told those gathered together,

> A number of times he has been heard to pray, that he might not outlive his usefulness, which has been remarkably answered in his case, for the Sunday before he died, he preached to the people—he preached his last.
>
> The disease which closed his mortal life, denied his friends the solemn pleasure of catching the balm of life from his lips, in his last moments. He had finished his work before, and nothing remained for him to do, but to die. Socrates, the patient philosopher, said to have never been angry in his life, when dying was vexed. The cause was this: his pupils asked him what he would have them do with his *body* after he was dead. To whom he sternly replied, 'have I been so long with you and taught you no better? After I am dead, what you see will not be *Socrates.—Socrates* will then be among the Gods.'—the improvement which I now make on the words of this philosopher is this: what we see here lying before our eyes, is not *Werden*, this is but the shell; his soul is now among the angels and saints in light, before the throne of glory. I will not say that his soul is under the altar with others, crying, 'how long, O Lord, holy and true, dost thou not judge and avenge our blood on them that dwell on the earth,' because he did not offer his life upon the altar of martyrdom; but I have an unshaken belief that his soul has left all its tribulation, being washed and made white in the blood of the Lamb, and is now basking in the sun-beams of immortal noon.[45]

The Shaftsbury Association paid tribute to Werden with this notice of grateful remembrance in their official Minutes for 1808:

> DIED, February 21st, 1808, Elder PETER WERDEN, of Cheshire, in the 80th year of his age. For dignity of nature, soundness of judgment, meekness of temper, and unwearied labors in the ministry, but *few* have equalled him in this age. He was the founder, father, and guardian angel of this

[45] Leland, "Biographical Sketch of the Rev. Peter Werden," 350.

Association, until his age prevented. He followed the work of the ministry about 60 years; and then,

> 'Like old *Elijah*, in a fiery car,
> He rode to Heaven, to be a shining star;
> May some *Elisha* catch his sacred robe,
> And smiting Jordan cry, *Where is Elijah's God?*'[46]

Further Reading

John Leland, "A Biographical Sketch of the Life and Character of the Rev. Peter Werden," in Thomas Baldwin, ed. *The Massachusetts Baptist Missionary Magazine*. Boston: Manning and Loring. Volume 2 (March 1808-December 1810), Number 11 (September 1810), 348-350. Reprinted in Miss L. F. Greene, ed., *The Writings of the Late Elder John Leland* (New York: G. W. Wood, 1845), 319-321.

Peter Werden. *Letters to a Friend, Containing Remarks on a Pamphlet by Job Scott, Entitled The Baptism of Christ a Gospel Ordinance, being altogether Spiritual, Inward, &c.* Lansingburgh, NY: William W. Wands, for the Author, 1796.

James Barker, "Early Settlement of Cheshire." The Introductory Chapter in Ellen M. Raynor and Emma L. Petitclerc. *History of the Town of Cheshire, Berkshire County, Massachusetts.* Holyoke, MA and New York City, 1885, 9-21.

David Benedict. *A General History of the Baptist Denomination in America, and Other Parts of the World.* Boston: Lincoln and Edmands, 1813. Volume 1, 438-439; Volume 2, 401-404.

Stephen Wright. *History of the Shaftsbury Baptist Association, from 1781-1853.* Troy, NY: A. G. Johnson, 1853.

[46] Wright, *History of the Shaftsbury Baptist Association*, 116.

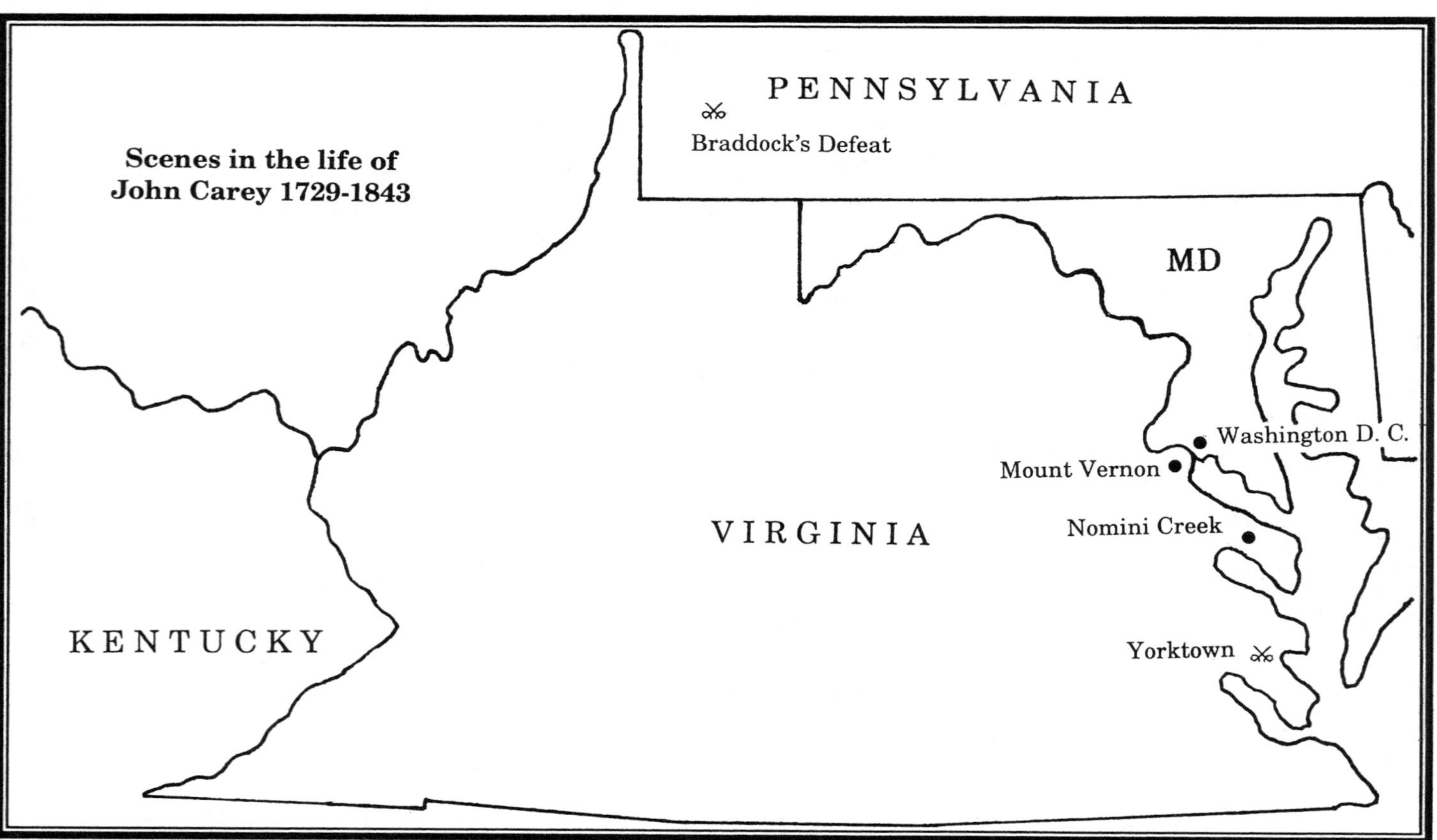
Scenes in the life of
John Carey 1729-1843
PENNSYLVANIA
Braddock's Defeat
MD
Washington D. C.
Mount Vernon
Nomini Creek
Yorktown
VIRGINIA
KENTUCKY

JOHN CAREY
1729 - 1843

by Terry Wolever

The Providence of God will sometimes uniquely unite in friendship the lowliest of persons with the greatest of public figures. Such was the case with the subject of this essay. Though outwardly poor and despised by the generality of his fellow men, John Carey was nonetheless esteemed by the Lord and those fellow believers who knew him well. Thankfully some aspects of his long and interesting life, through a brief account, were preserved by Obadiah B. Brown (1779-1852), pastor of the historic First Baptist Church of Washington City (Washington, D.C.) and one who knew and respected this "old disciple" as a longtime member of his congregation.[1]

A freeborn servant of African descent

John Carey differed from most other persons of color for his time in that though he was of African-American heritage, his mother had been emancipated before his birth and therefore he was born a free man in Westmoreland County, Virginia in August of 1729. Being freeborn did not remove the societal prejudice confronting him; nonetheless, and significantly, he was never to become one of the many thousands of slaves in the colony.[2] Instead he was able through perseverance to make his own way in life as best he could by hiring himself out as a servant.

---

[1] Obadiah B. Brown, "John Carey—Aged 114 Years," in Rufus Babcock and John O. Choules, eds., *The Baptist Memorial and Monthly Chronicle* (New York: John R. Bigelow), 2 (1843), No. 9 (September): 265-267. Spencer Cone, who noticed the biographical sketch of Carey on the occasion of his death in the pages of *The Religious Herald* (Richmond), submitted it with an introductory recommendation to the editors of *The Baptist Memorial*, in which he stated it "deserves a more permanent home than a weekly paper can give." The article was reprinted five years later in an edited format under "John Carey" in Thomas W. Haynes, *Haynes' Baptist Cyclopedia* (Charleston, SC: Samuel Hart, et al., 1848), 135-138.

[2] It has been estimated that in 1730, there were about 30,000 slaves in Virginia. The number grew to well over 140,000 by 1760. See Thomas L. Purvis, *Colonial America to 1763* (New York: Facts on File, 1999), 128.

His early association with George Washington

It was while in Westmoreland County that Carey began a lifelong acquaintance and friendship with none other than George Washington. Washington, born in the same county on February 22, 1732,[3] was about two and a half years younger than Carey and having known the latter from his youth, was said to have been "much pleased" with him. Brown recalled that Carey, though not yet a Christian, was an outwardly moral man, whose "energy, fidelity," and "decision of character," were "traits which Washington knew how to appreciate as well in an humble African, as in one of his own complexion."[4]

Washington inherited the Mount Vernon estate upon the death of his brother Lawrence in 1752. When he embarked on a military career two years later, he employed John Carey as a personal servant. We know that in addition to Carey, Washington had a mulatto slave for a servant both during and after the Revolution named William "Billy" Lee (1750-1828). Before his death, Washington made special provision for Lee in his will, "granting him his immediate freedom, an annuity of thirty dollars during his natural life, or support, if he preferred (being incapable of walking or any active employment) to remain with the family." Wrote Washington, "This I give him as a testimony of my sense of his attachment to me, and for his faithful services during the Revolutionary War."[5] While Washington's attitude was initially consistent with that of most other Virginia landowners, it has been well documented that he grew increasingly averse over the years to the institution of slavery. By 1770, he owned 87 Negroes, but two years later made the decision to stop buying slaves altogether. In the Fairfax County Resolutions of 1774, which Washington co-authored, it was stated, "during our present difficulties and distresses, no slaves ought to be imported, . . .and we take this

---

[3] Washington's date of birth was February 11 under the reckoning of the Old Style calendar, which was changed to the New Style two decades later, which moved the previous dates ahead by 11 days.

[4] Brown, "John Carey," 265.

[5] William C. Nell, *The Colored Patriots of the American Revolution* (Boston, MA: Robert F. Wallcut, 1855), 218. Lee appears in a well-known portrait of the Washington family painted by Edward Savage at Mount Vernon after the war.

opportunity of declaring our earnest wishes to see an entire stop forever put to such wicked, cruel, and unnatural trade."[6] The following decade his position on slavery became even more pronounced. In a letter to General Lafayette in April 1783, he wrote:

> The scheme, my dear Marq[ui]s which you propose as a precedent, to encourage the emancipation of the black people of this Country from that state of Bondage in w[hi]ch they are held, is a striking evidence of the benevolence of your Heart. I shall be happy to join you in so laudable a work; but will defer going into a detail of the business, 'till I have the pleasure of seeing you.[7]

And in a letter to Robert Morris in April 1786, Washington declared, it was not his wish "to hold the unhappy people, who are the subject of this letter, in slavery. I can only say that there is not a man living who wishes more sincerely than I do, to see a plan adopted for the abolition of it."[8] He had come to conclude the practice "introduces more evils than it can cure" and would not gradually cease of its own accord, but would have to be abolished through "Legislative authority."[9]

Service in the French and Indian War

According to Carey, Washington employed him as his personal servant "in his earliest military campaigns." Would this have included the venture made into the disputed Ohio Territory in the spring of 1754? This event brought on the war and led to Washington's only military surrender at the improvised Fort Necessity in Western Pennsylvania on July 4, 1754. Perhaps Carey was there, but all we are specifically told about is his being

---

[6] Peter Force, ed., *American Archives*. Fourth Series (Washington, DC: Matthew St. Clair and Peter Force), 1 (1837): 597.

[7] Letter to Marquis De Lafayette, dated Headquarters, Newburgh, New York, April 5, 1783, in John C. Fitzpatrick, ed., *The Writings of George Washington, from the Original Manuscript Sources, 1745-1799* (Washington, DC: United States Government Printing Office), 26 (1938): 300.

[8] Letter to Robert Morris, dated Mount Vernon, Virginia, April 12, 1786, Fitzpatrick, *The Writings of George Washington*, 28 (1938): 408.

[9] *Ibid.*; and Letter to Lafayette, dated Mount Vernon, May 10, 1786, *ibid.*, 424.

with then Lt. Col. Washington on General Braddock's ill-fated expedition in the summer of 1755. At the time Carey would have been 25 years of age.

Gen. Edward Braddock (1695-1755) had been appointed Commander in chief of the British forces in North America in 1754. Arriving in Virginia in February 1755, he immediately set about making preparations to drive the French from their forts on the Ohio River. The first target would be Fort Duquesne. In March, the large force of British regulars and American militia made its way out of Virginia and into the wilderness of Pennsylvania. It is interesting to speculate that Carey may also have made the acquaintance of the not yet famous Daniel Boone (1734-1820), who had joined the expedition as a teamster and blacksmith.

En route, Washington became so ill on June 14th he had to travel in one of the wagons. He would remain ill for the duration of the campaign, though his presence would still prove a decisive factor in the outcome of the battle.

Less than 10 miles from Fort Duquesne, on the afternoon of July 9, 1755, the British and Americans were ambushed by the French and Indians near the Monongahela River. Panic ensued and disaster quickly befell Braddock's command. In a letter addressed to his brother, John Augustine Washington, dated Fort Cumberland, July 18, 1755, Washington wrote, "I now exist and appear in the land of the living by the miraculous care of Providence, that protected me beyond all human expectation; I had 4 Bullets [pass] through my Coat, and two Horses shot [from] under me, and yet escaped unhurt."[10] His actions that day helped save the British and Americans from an even greater catastrophe. Nevertheless, the casualties were heavy and there was nothing to do but retreat. Braddock, who had been mortally wounded, died four days later on July 13th.

Though Carey told Brown he was with Col. Washington "on the battlefield of Monongahela, on the 9th of July, 1755," Brown did not relate in his article the extent of his involvement or just where he was at in the actual engagement. Consequently, these details are now lost to us. In any case, Carey shared in the tragedy of the

---

[10] Fitzpatrick, *The Writings of George Washington*, 1 (1931): 152. For a stirring account of the engagement and the events immediately leading up to it, see Douglas S. Freeman, *George Washington, a Biography* (New York: Charles Scribner's Sons), 2, *Young Washington* (1948): chapters 1-5.

experience and undaunted, continued with Washington until the close of his military services in the war in December of 1758.[11]

Washington presents Carey with one of his coats

Nearly two decades later Carey found himself reunited once more with Washington in a military capacity during the American Revolutionary War of 1775-1783. Apparently in the intervening years they had maintained their friendship and when Washington was elected Commander in chief of the Continental Army on June 15, 1775, Carey again accompanied him into the field. Washington was now 43 years of age, Carey was 46. Both were in the prime of life. Carey served the American cause in different capacities throughout the war, which means that along with enjoying the successes, he endured the tremendous hardships. As Brown informs us:

> Sometimes he served in the ranks of the army, and sometimes he was the personal attendant of his revered general. He loved Gen. Washington as a child loves his father; and till within a short time of his death, he would talk of scenes and battles of both the wars, with a memory as perfect as of events just past; and in such minute accordance with the records of history, as to show he had been a close observer of the deeds of the great Washington.[12]

At the close of the war, when it came time for Carey to take leave of his commander, General Washington presented him with one of his military coats, "the same which he had worn in the siege of Yorktown, when he consummated his military glory, as a token of his approbation and esteem of the fidelity of this devoted

---

[11] Brown, "John Carey," 266. Under a new and experienced British commander, John Forbes (1710-1759), Washington returned to Fort Duquesne in a successful campaign which took the French stronghold on November 25, 1758—the French having abandoned it in the face of superior forces. The settlement there was renamed Pittsburg and the fortification Fort Pitt, both in honor of William Pitt (1708-1778), the new Prime Minister who formulated the plan for its capture. Washington resigned his commission and returned to Mount Vernon in December.

[12] Brown, "John Carey," 266.

servant and patriot." After Carey's passing, Pastor Brown had this to say about its significance to him:

> This coat, John often wore to church, till within the last fifteen years. He set a value upon it above all price, as a memento of his beloved General; and though reduced to extreme poverty, no offers of money could induce him to part with it. John was full six feet high, about the size of the general he had served, and the coat suited him quite well. He has died in its possession, and the coat is quite a curiosity. It is of a coarse texture, a fair sample of the times in which it covered the greatest national chieftain that ever lived, in the person of the commander of the armies of a new republican empire, struggling for existence. It is of blue cloth with buff facings and large flat gilt buttons; in the same fashion of that in the National Institute, which he wore when he resigned his commission.[13]

What a wealth of firsthand information on George Washington would have been available from Carey!—and yet it appears that historians of the time were either unaware of this association, or if they were aware, failed to avail themselves of what he could have shared with them.

"A hopeful subject of divine grace"

Following the war, Carey returned to Westmoreland County, Virginia, where he continued to reside for many years. It was here amid familiar and peaceful surroundings that he became "a hopeful subject of divine grace" and was baptized as a believer by Henry Toler (1761-1824). This would have occurred during the time Toler was pastor of the Nomini Creek Baptist Church in Westmoreland County. This church, founded by Lewis Lundsford and Toler, was formally constituted on April 29, 1786, and became a member of the Dover Baptist Association.[14] Toler was pastor there from the church's constitution to about 1816.

---

[13] *Ibid.* Washington was 6′ 2″ tall. It would be of interest to know what became of this coat and if it is still in existence in a private or public collection somewhere. It obviously would have great historical value.

[14] Robert B. Semple, *A History of the Rise and Progress of the Baptists in Virginia* (Richmond, VA: Printed by John O'Lynch for the Author, 1810), 130-133. David Benedict points out that by 1809 the Dover Association

At some point John Carey made the decision to remove to the new capital at Washington, D.C. Perhaps he wanted to reside in the city named in honor of the general and first president with whom he had served for so many years. We know that about the time of the close of the War of 1812, Carey became connected with the First Baptist Church of Washington City. Charles P. Polk, one of the original constituting members of the church, related the details of its founding to the Baptist historian David Benedict, who then preserved them in his narrative as follows:

> When the General Government was removed from Philadelphia to this newly established metropolis, a few Baptist members, some of whom were in its employment, belonging to different churches, removed hither, about the same time. These persons had frequent conversations on the advantages which might result to them, from church fellowship; and having made previous arrangements for the purpose, were, on the 7th of March, 1802, in the Hall of the Treasury Department, constituted into a church by the assistance of Messrs. Jeremiah More, Lewis Richards, William Parkinson, and Adam Freeman. Their number was only six, viz. Charles P. Polk, from Baltimore, John Burchan, from New York, Charles Rogers, from Maryland, Cephas Fox, from Virginia, and Joseph Barrows and wife, from Philadelphia.
>
> A few days after the church was constituted, the brethren began to solicit the aid of the citizens, towards erecting for them a place of worship: in their attempts they were greatly assisted by Rev. William Parkinson, who was then officiating as Chaplain to Congress; and so successful were their exertions, that they soon obtained sufficient means to purchase a lot in the west end of the city, 75 feet by 37, and to build a handsome house, 42 feet by 32, in which the first sermon was preached by Mr. Parkinson, on the 14th day of November, 1802.

---

was "the largest body of Baptist communicants in America, and probably in any part of the world; although it contains but 37 churches, and but 24 ordained ministers, who are pastors of churches." That year the Association "contained 9628 members, many, and perhaps some thousands of whom, were Africans." The largest church in this body was Toler's at Nomini, consisting of 875 members. *A General History of the Baptist Denomination in America and Other Parts of the World* (Boston: Lincoln and Edmands, 1813), 2: 87-88.

> Previous to this event, the church had received the addition of five members, and continued gradually to increase for a number of succeeding years. It was supplied with preaching pretty frequently by the neighbouring ministers, both in Virginia and Maryland, but had no pastor until 1807, when Rev. Obadiah B. Brown, a native of Newark, New Jersey, and who was then preaching in that town, by the call of the church, removed amongst them, and assumed the pastoral office, which he still continues to fill with reputation and success. Mr. Brown also generally officiates as Chaplain to one branch of the National Legislature, during its sessions.[15]

Spencer H. Cone (1785-1855), pastor of the First Baptist Church of New York from 1841 until his death, had previously been a member of the First Baptist Church of Washington. He recalled that Carey "was received as a member of the 1st Baptist church, Washington City, within a few months of the time when I united with it."[16] He then went on to say of Carey, "having been myself engaged from 1812 to 1814, in defending our Common Country against an invading foe, I could not but feel a special regard for the man who had waited upon the person of Washington, throughout the Revolutionary struggle."[17]

---

[15] David Benedict, *A General History of the Baptist Denomination in America, and Other Parts of the World* (Boston: Lincoln and Edmands, 1813), 2: 19-20. Brown remained as pastor of the church until 1850, when "growing physical infirmities prevented his officiating longer." William Cathcart, ed., *The Baptist Encyclopedia* (Philadelphia: Louis H. Everts, 1881), 148.

[16] Edward W. Cone and Spencer W. Cone, *Some Account of the Life of Spencer Houghton Cone. A Baptist Preacher in America* (New York: Livermore and Rudd, 1856), 136-138, do not specifically tell us when Cone united with the church. Brown however, stated that Carey had been a member "for the last 28 years of his life," which would place his joining the church within the first six months of 1815. Brown, "John Carey," 266.

[17] Brown, "John Carey," 265. Cone had served as a company commander during the War of 1812. There are no references to our John Carey in any of the published papers, letters or diaries of George Washington that I could find. Since Washington is known to have destroyed a significant amount of his correspondence before he died, this would not be in itself a sufficient reason to dispute Carey's account. Not only was Carey himself considered a man of exceptional integrity, but both Obadiah Brown and

John Carey was "an exemplary member of the First Baptist Church," wrote Pastor Obadiah Brown, who further stated,

> His piety has never been doubted by those who knew him. He was always clear in the doctrine of salvation by the grace of God, in the Lord Jesus Christ; and as he advanced in years, that Saviour who first taught him to hope in his mercy, became more and more precious to his soul. If martial scenes which engrossed a full portion of his earlier manhood, often recurred to the memory of his declining years with enlivening interest, the manifestation of his Saviour's love, and the prospect which it opened to him of brighter scenes than mortal vision could endure, would often kindle his soul into rapture. He retained his faculties remarkably well for his age, though the infirmities of such a weight of years necessarily weakened the powers of his mind. But in every infirmity, Jesus Christ and his promises were first in his mind; and to the last period of his mortal life, he manifested an unshaken confidence in God his Saviour, which bore him triumphantly through the vale of death.[18]

From the time of his childhood and on into middle life, Carey had braved many dangers through which he was no doubt spared by the Lord. But what must have been one of the most difficult trials of his life was when he failed to receive his well-earned pension for his years of service during the American Revolution. The death of Washington on December 14, 1799, the burning of the War Office on November 8, 1800, (where the military roll on which he was listed as serving in the Revolutionary War was believed to have been destroyed) and the lack of other required evidence, caused his name to be omitted from the pension list. "Since the decline of life deprived him of the strength to labor," wrote Brown, "he has subsisted partly on the bounties of the benevolent, but in a great measure upon the regular allowance made him by the church to which he belonged."[19] Efforts were

---

Spencer Cone seem to have had complete confidence in the faithfulness of his testimony.

[18] Brown, "John Carey," 266.

[19] *Ibid.*

made on his behalf both by Pastor Brown and other Christian friends to right the situation. As late as 1842-1843, Representative George W. Briggs of Massachusetts, having become acquainted with Carey's character and condition, sought through a joint resolution of Congress to grant him a pension for the remainder of his life. On Wednesday, January 18, 1843, he introduced his request to the House, which

> On motion of Mr. Briggs,
>
> *Resolved*, That the Committee on Revolutionary Pensions be instructed to inquire into the expediency of giving a pension to John Cary, (a free colored man,) a native of the county of Westmoreland, and State of Virginia, now a resident of this District, who says he was a body servant of General Washington at the time of Braddock's defeat, in 1755, and was present at that battle; and, also, that he was a servant of General Washington's at the surrender of Cornwallis, in 1781, and who is believed to be one hundred and twelve years old.[20]

When Pastor Brown informed Carey about what Congressman Briggs was trying to do, Carey "responded with a prayer, that the Lord would reward Mr. Briggs for his kindness to a poor unworthy servant of God," adding, "I need but little, and but for a very little time." The measure passed in the House of Representatives but failed in the Senate. On March 1, 1843, "Mr. Briggs moved to discharge the Committee of the Whole from the further consideration of the bill for the relief of John Carey, a colored servant of General Washington," but not before stating his conviction that "there was no doubt that he had served General Washington, both at Braddock's defeat, and during the revolutionary war."[21] Despite the disappointing news, Brown tells us that the Lord raised up friends to assist Carey, "and he did not suffer while he lived."[22]

---

[20] *Journal of the House of Representatives of the United States, at the Third Session of the Twenty-Seventh Congress Begun and Held at the City of Washington, in the Territory of Columbia, December 5, 1842* (Washington, DC: Gales and Seaton, 1843), 218.

[21] *Congressional Globe*. 27th Congress (Washington, DC: Blair and Rives), 12 (1843), No. 16 (Friday, February 10, 1843): 241; and No. 22 (Wednesday, March 1, 1843): 340.

[22] Brown, "John Carey," 267.

"While on earth he lived obscurely great"

Carey's earthly tabernacle finally dissolved and he passed away to the land of eternal day at 9:00 p.m. on Friday, June 2, 1843, "in the 114th year of his age."[23] He was survived by his wife, then about the age of eighty. Brown recalled Carey's final days with these words:

> [His wife] gave him all the assistance he needed in his infirmity. The last Sabbath of his life, he walked out and attended the public worship of God. On Monday morning, he told his wife he should leave her this week, for his Lord had called him, and he should cheerfully obey the summons. Monday night, he was taken with a chill, which proved the secession of vitality.—He continued however, till Friday night, when he fell asleep.[24]

The day following his death, Brown penned this eulogy as a final tribute to Carey:

> While on earth he lived obscurely great; for he glorified God in his body and spirit.[25] In the depth of poverty he enjoyed the blessing of royalty; for God his Saviour resided with him, and lived in his heart. In the confidence of faith, he realized that he was born a prince of the kingdom of glory. God was his father; Christ his brother; angels were his ministers; and heaven was his destination. In the assurance of this hope, he lived above the world, waiting for the happy moment which should change his faith to vision, and consummate his hope in glory.[26]

---

[23] *Ibid.*, 265. Such longevity, while uncommon, was not an altogether rare occurrence among African-Americans of this period. Another black veteran of the Braddock campaign, Samuel Jenkins, reportedly died at the age of 115, according to the Lancaster, Ohio *Gazette*, in February 1849. Nell, *The Colored Patriots of the American Revolution*, 214.

[24] *Ibid.*, 267.

[25] 1 Cor. 6:20.

[26] Brown, "John Carey," 267.

Spencer Cone, who as seen earlier had expressed a feeling of "special regard" for this man "who had waited upon the person of Washington throughout the Revolutionary struggle," added, "I rejoice to know, that John enjoyed the infinitely higher honor of waiting upon the Great Captain of our Salvation, to the day of his death; who according to his promise brought off the old soldier at last, *more than conqueror*."[27]

Further Reading

Obadiah B. Brown, "John Carey—Aged 114 Years," in Rufus Babcock and John O. Choules, editors. *The Baptist Memorial and Monthly Chronicle*. New York: John R. Bigelow, Volume 2 (1843), Number 9 (September), 265-267.

Douglas S. Freeman. *George Washington, a Biography*. New York: Charles Scribner's Sons. Volume Two: *Young Washington*, 1948.

William C. Nell. *The Colored Patriots of the American Revolution, with Sketches of Several Distinguished Colored Persons: To Which is Added a Brief Survey of the Condition and Prospects of Colored Americans*. Boston: Robert F. Walcutt, 1855.

Robert B. Semple. *A History of the Rise and Progress of the Baptists in Virginia*. Richmond, VA: Printed by John O'Lynch for the Author, 1810.

Dorothy C. Winchcole. *The First Baptists in Washington, D.C., 1802-1952*. Washington, D.C.: First Baptist Church, 1952.

[27] *Ibid.*, 265. The scripture referred to is Romans 8:37.

DAVID THOMAS
1732 - 1812

by C. Douglas Weaver

Histories of Virginia Baptists in the colonial South have concentrated primarily on the contributions of the Separate Baptists. Any recognition of the Regular Baptists, however, always mentions the leadership of David Thomas. This essay will examine the contributions of David Thomas to colonial Baptist life. After a brief look at the religious climate of colonial Virginia, a brief biography of Thomas and his leadership in Regular Baptist beginnings will be offered. Based on the presupposition that Thomas was representative of Regular Baptists, this group's relationship to Separate Baptists will be examined. The attitude of the Regulars toward non-Baptist groups and the colonial government will follow. The activity of Thomas as a Kentucky Baptist will conclude the study.

Religious climate of Colonial Virginia

In the colonial period, the Church of England was the legally established state church in Virginia. Religious commitment, however, was in a depressed condition. Many Anglican ministers were leading immoral lives, and their preaching was characterized by cold, stilted sermons on morality that included little evangelistic doctrine. Indeed, the consensus of many church historians is that the established church was a failure as a spiritual factor in the colonial era.[1] Amidst this context, revivalistic awakening came to Virginia.

Wesley Gewehr identified the period 1740-1790 as the era of the Great Awakening in Virginia.[2] The Presbyterians were the first to bring the awakening to Virginia. In 1743, Samuel Morris, a Presbyterian from Hanover County, acquired a collection of

---

[1] Devereux Jarratt, *The Life of the Reverend Devereux Jarratt* (Baltimore: Warner and Hanna, 1806), 98-99. William Meade, a prominent Anglican bishop, asserted that the spiritual problem among the Anglicans was due to the fact that there was no bishop in America. See William Meade, *Old Churches, Ministers and Families of Virginia* (Philadelphia: J. B. Lippincott and Co., 1872), 1: 15.

[2] Wesley M. Gewehr. *The Great Awakening in Virginia, 1740-1790.* Durham, NC: Duke University Press, 1930.

George Whitefield's sermons. Morris shared the sermons with neighbors at his home, and the crowds became so large that a meetinghouse was built to accommodate the listeners. Soon, other communities invited Morris to read sermons. Spiritual awakening resulted, and other Presbyterian ministers began to arrive from New Jersey and Pennsylvania. The movement flourished, reaching a climax with the ministry of Samuel Davies. The Presbyterian revival declined in 1759, however, when Davies left Virginia.[3]

The Presbyterian awakening had only limited effect. The high educational standards of the ministry and the intellectual requirement of elaborate creeds were not conducive to reaching the common people. Consequently, the movement only influenced a small area in east-central Virginia. The movement, however, was an important forerunner to the Baptist phase of the awakening. The concept of revival was established in the colony which paved the way for a more aggressive evangelism by the Baptists.[4]

The rapid growth of the Baptists was the second phase of awakening in Virginia. The Baptist movement was more popular with the common people. W. T. Thom argued that "The people needed a distinctive symbol and a comparatively formless faith; they found the one in adult baptism by immersion and the other in the wide compass of Bible teaching wherein the devout and emotional soul finds what it seeks."[5] Gewehr added that "as was the case in other churches, the Great Awakening caused a division among the Baptists into conservative and revivalist wings."[6] He identified the Regular Baptists as the conservative faction and the

---

[3] Davies emphasized that the Presbyterian movement was not designed to overthrow the Anglican Church. He once told an Anglican bishop from London that there would not have been a dissenter in Virginia if the Anglican clergy had preached the evangelical doctrines they subscribed to in their thirty-nine articles of faith. See William Foote, *Sketches of Virginia: Historical and Biographical* (Richmond: John Knox Press, 1850), 194-195.

[4] William L. Lumpkin, *Baptist Foundations in the South. Tracing through the Separates the Influence of the Great Awakening, 1754-1787* (Nashville: Broadman Press, 1961), 108.

[5] William T. Thom, *The Struggle for Religious Freedom in Virginia: The Baptists* (Baltimore: John Hopkins University Press, 1900), 32.

[6] Gewehr, *The Great Awakening in Virginia*, 107.

Separates as the continuators of the awakening because they were the heirs of the Whitefield revival.[7]

Historians agree that the Separate Baptists were the primary contributors to the Baptist phase of awakening. The role of the Regular Baptists, however, should not be denigrated. When the Presbyterian awakening declined in 1759, only a few Baptists were left in the colony. Though the Separates would eventually outnumber the Regulars, during the 1760's, the primary growth among Baptists was with the Regulars. By 1770, they had 624 members in ten churches that were scattered in seven counties, primarily in northern Virginia.[8] Indeed, the Regulars helped prevent the torch of awakening from fading out when the Presbyterian movement declined. Their most influential leader, David Thomas, is the subject of this study.[9]

Brief biographical sketch of David Thomas

David Thomas was born August 16, 1732, at London Tract, Pennsylvania. He was educated under the eminent Baptist leader, Isaac Eaton, at Hopewell Academy, New Jersey. James B. Taylor noted that Thomas's educational achievements "were such that Rhode Island College [now Brown University] gave him the Master of Arts" degree in 1755.[10] Thomas left Pennsylvania in 1760 for Berkeley County in northern Virginia as a "self-appointed missionary."[11] He preached there for about eighteen months.

In 1762, Thomas moved to Fauquier County, establishing and becoming the minister of Broad Run Church, which became the center of his evangelistic activities.[12] For the next several years,

---

[7] *Ibid.*, 107-109.

[8] *Ibid.*

[9] Gewehr identified a third phase of the awakening with the Methodists. This occurred after the Baptist success, in the latter half of the 1770's.

[10] James B. Taylor, *Virginia Baptist Ministers*, Series 1 (Philadelphia: J. B. Lippincott and Co., 1859), 43.

[11] *Ibid.*

[12] [It would appear that it was here that Thomas was married to the widow, Catherine Shrieve (née Martin). The couple had four children by 1772: Sarah, John, Elizabeth and Mary. Eve B. Weeks and Mary B.

Thomas was the preeminent Regular Baptist in Virginia. Thomas returned to Berkeley County in 1788 and became the minister of Mill Creek Church after the death of the church's pastor and Thomas's close friend, John Garrard. Thomas remained at Mill Creek until 1796 when he moved to Kentucky. The move was occasioned by trouble at the church. Semple noted that the church initially rejoiced in Thomas's ministry, but eventually "some of the members becoming wise in their own conceit took it into their fancy that Thomas preached false doctrine."[13] The church's records only partially elucidated the controversy. They stated that Thomas was charged with permitting the church to be disorderly, drawing a group of members around him into a body contrary to the stated discipline of the church. The records never indicated that Thomas was asked to resign. Thomas, however, evidently became discouraged by the controversy and left Virginia for Kentucky.[14]

While on the Kentucky frontier, Thomas, now sixty-four years old, continued serving churches possibly until 1808. Semple closed his account of Thomas's activity by stating that the aged minister was almost blind and living in Jessamine County in 1810. Thomas died in 1812.[15]

Regular Baptist beginnings and the leadership of David Thomas

Earliest Regular Baptists in Virginia.—In 1743, Edward Hayes and Thomas Yates, members of a General Baptist Church at Chestnut Ridge, Maryland, led a group to settle in Berkeley County, Virginia. Their pastor, Henry Loveall, followed them and the Mill Creek Church was organized. The church remained

---

Warren, eds., *Materials Towards a History of the Baptists. By Morgan Edwards, A.M.* (Danielsville, GA: Heritage Papers, 1984), 2: 36 —*Ed.*]

[13] Robert B. Semple, *A History of the Rise and Progress of the Baptists in Virginia*, rev. by G. W. Beale (Philadelphia: American Baptist Publication Society, 1894), 418.

[14] Minutes, Mill Creek Church, June, 1796. Mill Creek is also called Opequon/Opekon on several occasions. Berkeley County is now in West Virginia.

[15] Semple, *History of Baptists in Virginia*, 380*n*. See also Leo T. Crismon, "Virginia Baptist Ministers Who Migrated to Kentucky Before 1800," *The Virginia Baptist Register* (Richmond: Virginia Baptist Historical Society), 16 (1977): 769.

General Baptist until Loveall was excluded for licentiousness. In 1751, the church, being without a minister and in general disorder, requested assistance from the Philadelphia Association. In 1752, the association sent four representatives to Mill Creek. Consequently, the church was reorganized upon the Calvinistic principles of the Philadelphia Association. This was the first Regular Baptist church in Virginia.[16] During the next ten years, until 1762, only two other churches, Ketocton (also 1751) and Smith's Creek (1756), were organized.[17]

Possible involvement of Thomas in earliest beginnings.—Historians have claimed that David Thomas made several ministerial excursions into Virginia before arriving in Berkeley County in 1760. Perhaps that occurred, but attempts to document specific involvement have revealed historical inaccuracies. The most widespread error derived from the failure to distinguish the identities of John Thomas and David Thomas. Several historians asserted that David Thomas was a member of the Philadelphia entourage to Mill Creek in 1751. Moreover, Benedict suggested that David Thomas became the first pastor of Ketocton Church the same year.[18]

The confusion was evidently due to John Gano's autobiographical account of the events of 1751. Gano, one of the Philadelphia representatives, described one of his colleagues simply as "Mr. Thomas." The evidence, however, indicates that the man in question was John Thomas. First, John, not David, Thomas was active in the Philadelphia Association during the 1750's.[19] Second, Gano did say that he and Mr. Thomas visited a

---

[16] Semple, *History of Baptists in Virginia*, 419.

[17] *Ibid.*, 377; Gillette, *Minutes of the Philadelphia Baptist Association*, 93.

[18] David Benedict, *A General History of the Baptist Denomination in America, and Other Parts of the World* (Boston: Lincoln and Edmands, 1813), 2: 26, 29. See also William Cathcart, ed., *The Baptist Encyclopedia* (Philadelphia: Louis H. Everts, 1881), 147; Reuben E. Alley, *A History of Baptists in Virginia* (Richmond: Virginia Baptist General Board, 1974), 53. Garnett Ryland did make the correct distinction between John and David Thomas. He did not, however, explicate the evidence. See Garnett Ryland, *The Baptists of Virginia, 1699-1926* (Richmond: Virginia Baptist Board of Missions and Education, 1955), 10.

[19] A. D. Gillette, ed., *Minutes of the Philadelphia Baptist Association, 1707-1807* (Philadelphia: American Baptist Publication Society, 1851), 71-72.

church, currently without a minister, that Mr. Thomas had recently constituted.[20] This was probably the Ketocton Church, as the minutes of the Philadelphia Association recorded that John Thomas was the minister there in 1752.[21] Finally, Gano reported that his colleague, Mr. Thomas, was an ordained minister.[22] David Thomas, however, was not ordained until 1760.[23]

Contribution of Thomas to the spread of the Regulars.—The account of David Thomas as a leader among the Regular Baptists must begin when he came to Berkeley County on a "ministerial visit"[24] in 1760. While preaching in the area of Mill Creek Church, Thomas was introduced to Peter Cornwell, who lived on Broad Run in Fauquier County. Cornwell, only recently converted, desired that the Baptist message be taken to Fauquier County. Upon meeting Thomas, Cornwell invited him to preach at Broad Run. The preaching was so well received that Thomas agreed to settle in Fauquier County.[25] In 1762, Broad Run Church was constituted by Thomas and John Marks, the pastor of Ketocton Church. Thomas was received by letter from the Baptist church in Vincent, Pennsylvania, and after submitting a certificate of his ordination from the Philadelphia Association, he was called as minister of Broad Run.[26] Semple providentially described the events that led to the formation of the church:

> It could be said, that if they had made Paul high-priest, instead of sending him to Damascus, he would not have spread the Gospel among the Gentiles. So also, if Mr.

---

[20] Stephen Gano and Daniel Gano, eds., *Biographical Memoirs of the Late Rev. John Gano of Frankfort, Kentucky. Formerly of the City of New York* (New York: Southwick and Hardcastle, 1806), 40.

[21] Gillette, *Minutes of the Philadelphia Baptist Association*, 93.

[22] Gano, *Biographical Memoirs*, 45.

[23] Gillette, *Minutes of the Philadelphia Baptist Association*, 86. See also Morgan Edwards, "Materials Towards a History of the Baptists in Virginia" (MS, 1772), 25.

[24] Semple, *History of Baptists in Virginia*, 378.

[25] William Fristoe, *A Concise History of the Ketocton Baptist Association* (Staunton, VA: Printed by William Gilman Lyford, 1808), 6.

[26] Minutes, Broad Run Church.

> Thomas had not happened to meet with these men [Cornwell and a friend]. . .he might never had gone to Broad Run, and from thence over a great part of Virginia by which thousands were turned from darkness to light. These things in the eye of mere reason look like contingencies; but by the eye of faith they are all plainly viewed as the contrivance of Infinite Wisdom. . . .[27]

In 1766, Broad Run joined the churches of Mill Creek, Ketocton, and Smith's Creek in the formation of the Ketocton Association, the first Baptist association in the colony. Thomas was one of the association's organizers.[28] Broad Run Church, under the leadership of Thomas, became the most important church to the growth of the association. The church became a center of evangelism, functioning as a mother church whose members produced many new churches. Due to the evangelistic efforts of Thomas, eight new churches were added to the association during its first decade.

Thomas served as the minister of several of these new churches, in addition to his position at Broad Run. The other churches had ministers who all recognized Thomas as their "spiritual father."[29] These young preachers, especially William Fristoe, Richard Major, Daniel Fristoe, Jeremiah Moore, and Nathaniel Saunders, were some of the fruits of Thomas's ministry who continued the Regular Baptist contribution to the awakening.[30]

---

[27] Semple, *History of Baptists in Virginia*, 379.

[28] Fristoe, *Concise History of the Ketocton Baptist Association*, 7-11. Fristoe noted that the churches separated from the Philadelphia Association for reason of travel convenience.

[29] Edwards, "Materials Towards a History of Baptists in Virginia," 31. See Appendices A and B for churches served and influenced by Thomas.

[30] *Ibid.*, 31-33; Semple, *History of Baptists in Virginia*, 385, 395, 399. [John L. Dagg related an interesting anecdote concerning William Fristoe and David Thomas, which was as follows:

"William and Daniel Fristoe were baptized by Thomas at Chappawamsic, eight miles from Dumfries, and became eminent and laborious ministers for Christ.

* * * * *

Relationship of Thomas and the Regular Baptists to the Separate Baptists

Regular Baptist growth continued throughout the colonial era. The Separate Baptists, on the other hand, increased at a phenomenal rate, especially after 1770, and soon became the majority Baptist group. The two groups remained divided, however, until 1787.[31]

Comparison of Beliefs and Attitudes of Regulars and Separates.—The differences that kept the two groups divided were never great. Semple suggested that the breach was never wide but that jealousy played a major role.[32] There were differences, however, in degree. These can be seen in an analysis of Thomas's portrayal of Regular beliefs and attitudes, briefly compared to the Separate tradition.

Confessionalism.—The Regular Baptists were heirs of the beliefs of the Philadelphia Association, adopting the Philadelphia

---

The Philadelphia Baptists maintained the system of faith usually styled Calvinistic, which is set forth in their confession of faith. This doctrine was at first taught by Mr. Thomas, but after a time he was thought to waver in his exposition of it. In one of his public discourses, he said, 'Who is John Calvin? A persecuting bigot. Who was James Arminius? A meek and humble disciple of Christ.' In this strain he contrasted the characters of the two men, giving preference to the latter; and was understood to give preference to the system of doctrines which he taught. The young disciples were grieved that their father in the Gospel had departed from the truth, as they had first learned it from him; and they held a private, sorrowful meeting, to determine what ought to be done in this case. At this meeting it was decided to be their duty to labor, as children with a beloved parent, to bring back their spiritual guide to the good old path from which he was wandering. William Fristoe was selected to perform this very delicate and responsible service. Tremblingly, yet firmly, he approached the venerated man, reminded him of the truth which they had once learned from his lips, and reasoned with him out of the Scriptures. His mission appears to have been successful, for confidence in the orthodoxy of their spiritual leader was afterwards restored." Edward W. Cone and Spencer W. Cone, *Some Account of the Life of Spencer Houghton Cone* (New York: Livermore and Rudd, 1856), 179-180 —*Ed.*]

[31] Glynn R. Ford, "The Baptist District Association in Virginia, 1766-1950; A Study in Baptist Ecclesiology" (unpublished Th.D. dissertation, Southern Baptist Theological Seminary, 1961), 232.

[32] Semple, *History of Baptists in Virginia*, 383.

Confession of Faith of 1742.[33] In fact, Thomas published *The Virginian Baptist* (1774), which contained his own edited version of the confession, as an apology for the Baptist cause in Virginia.[34] Concerning the confession, Thomas declared, "it contains a just view of all our religious principles without any variation; or the least difference in any respect."[35]

In desiring union, the Regulars thought that the Separates should be willing to adopt a confession of faith. In contrast, a number of the Separates were averse to accepting confessions. These Baptists feared that confessions would lead to formality and deadness and would divert them from their sole authority, the Bible.[36]

Doctrine.—Regular Baptist doctrine was Calvinistic. Concerning the creation and the fall of man, Thomas argued that Adam had been created righteous, having been given sufficient power to resist all temptations. Adam, however, freely chose to break the divine law. Thomas concluded, "He [Adam] fell: And we in him. So that his sin is now justly imputed to everyone descending from him in the ordinary way of generation. And human nature is also, fearfully corrupted and depraved, as the deserved punishment of his detestable apostasy from God. This is what we call original sin."[37] Because man is a transgressor from the womb, regeneration is necessary, according to Thomas. The new birth cannot be wrought by man himself; rather, it is the product of irresistible grace.[38]

In his description of the Regulars' Calvinistic doctrine, Thomas also delineated the beliefs in particular atonement, predestination,

---

[33] The Philadelphia Confession of 1742 was a later edition of the English Particular Baptist Second London Confession of 1689, with some additions.

[34] Thomas also published *The Novelty of Novelties Examined* (1782).

[35] David Thomas, *The Virginian Baptist; or A View of Defense of the Christian Religion as it is Professed by the Baptists of Virginia* (Baltimore: Enoch Story, 1774), 3. Ryland, *The Baptists of Virginia*, 24, noted that Thomas condensed the thirty-four chapters of the Philadelphia Confession into 17 articles, revising, omitting, and adding with much freedom.

[36] Fristoe, *Concise History of the Ketocton Baptist Association*, 21-22.

[37] Thomas, *The Virginian Baptist*, 9.

[38] *Ibid.*, 12.

faith as a supernatural gift from God, justification as imputed righteousness, and perseverance. Concerning eternal security, Thomas surmised that Christians "are kept by the power of God unto Salvation so that although sin still remains in them, and they too often contract new guilt on their consciences; yet they are secured from final apostasy and can never fall quite away to perdition."[39]

Regarding doctrine, the Separates unlike the Regulars, did not emphasize systematic theology. Lumpkin commented that the Separates "had neither aptitude nor inclination to be heavily theological. The subtleties of speculative thought held no attraction for them."[40]

The Regulars' major criticism was that some of the Separates held Arminian theology. The Separates were definitely more aggressive in style, being more enthusiastic in their proclamation. The Separates, however, would have perceived themselves as Calvinistic.

Preaching.—Baptist ministers of the colonial period engaged in much itinerant preaching. David Thomas utilized this method effectively in spreading the Baptist message across northern Virginia. In 1763, the year after he settled at Broad Run in Fauquier County, he extended his preaching and became the first Baptist preacher in Orange and Culpeper Counties.[41] Benedict

---

[39] *Ibid.*, 15.

[40] Lumpkin, *Baptist Foundations in the South*, 62. [Lumpkin's characterization must be gauged by the fact that each of the early leaders of the Separate Baptists—Daniel Marshall, Abraham Marshall and Shubal Stearns, both composed and assisted in composing Calvinistic confessions of faith for their churches and associations. See Thomas Ray, *Daniel and Abraham Marshall—Pioneer Baptist Evangelists to the South* (Springfield, MO: Particular Baptist Press, 2006), Appendixes F, G and H; and Robert I. Devin, *A History of Grassy Creek Baptist Church* (Raleigh, NC: Edwards, Broughton and Co., 1880), 43-45. One must wonder also, if Abraham Marshall, for example, "had neither aptitude nor inclination to be heavily theological," as Lumpkin suggested above, why would he write that, at least on one occasion, he "perused" (that is, by definition, "read through, as with thoroughness or care") John Gill's *Body of Divinity*? See *Memoirs of the Late Abraham Marshall* (1824) as reprinted in Ray, *Daniel and Abraham Marshall*, 100. In addition, Marshall listed Gill among those he thought "the brightest geniuses on earth." *Ibid.*, 176 —*Ed.*]

[41] Fristoe, *Concise History of the Ketocton Baptist Association*, 62. The minutes of Smith's Creek Church bear witness to Thomas's itinerant

remarked that the fame of Thomas's preaching brought listeners from sixty miles away.[42]

One of the Regulars' main discomforts concerning the Separates was their style of preaching and the effects it produced. Indeed, the Separate John Leland described the Regulars as "solemn and rational," whereas the Separates were "the most zealous" and "very noisy."[43] Both Thomas and the Separates believed that preaching should be evangelical, stressing the necessity of new birth. Thomas asserted that preaching was the vehicle whereby the sinner must be convinced of his hell-bound wrathful nature. The opportunity for "full, free, and everlasting salvation,"[44] however, obviated the need for the sinner to fall into a state of despair which produced excessive physical manifestations at conversion. Thomas criticized the Separates for these "horrid vociferations and obstreperous commotions."[45] He asserted that this excessive enthusiasm never resulted from his preaching, nor was it approved by Regular Baptist churches "as any part of religion."[46] He concluded that he could "find no account of it in the word of God."[47]

Education and Poverty.—Robert Torbet has noted that in the popular colonial mind, the Separates occupied a clearly defined social status in which their critics viewed them as ignorant and poor enthusiasts. In contrast, Regulars were the better educated town people.[48]

---

activity. They indicate that Thomas participated in a communion (1763) and performed a baptism (1790). See John Wayland, *Virginia Valley Records* (Strasburg, VA: Shenandoah Publishing House, Inc., 1930), 53, 62.

[42] Benedict, *A General History of the Baptist Denomination*, 31.

[43] L. F. Greene, ed., *The Writings of the Late Elder John Leland* (New York: G. W. Wood, 1845), 105.

[44] Thomas, *The Virginian Baptist*, 59.

[45] *Ibid.*, 63.

[46] *Ibid.*

[47] *Ibid.*

[48] Robert G. Torbet, *A History of the Baptists* (Valley Forge: Judson Press, 1978), 223.

Though historians have classified the Separates as belonging to a lower socioeconomic class than the Regulars, the latter were willing to identify themselves as Baptists of the "poorer sort."[49] Thomas was proud that many of his constituents were poor and uneducated. He concluded,

> Are we poor? GOD has chosen the poor of the world. Are we a simple unlearned people? GOD has chosen the foolish things of the world to confound the wise. . . .The truth is, poverty, the want of erudition and the malice of an ungodly world, are just so many more likely characters of GOD's election than the contrary.[50]

On the other hand, David Thomas has been proclaimed as the most learned and scholarly of colonial Virginia Baptists.[51] In contrast to the Separates, he saw the value of an educated ministry. Education was a serviceable handmaid for the Christian. Education was not to be idolized, however. When used alone, it was insufficient to show the way to salvation.[52]

For Thomas, an educated ministry, rather than one which relied on immediate inspiration, was desired. This conviction was a stumbling block in his attitude toward the Separates. His first confrontation with the Separates vividly illustrated his reservations toward their lack of education.

In 1763, Thomas was invited by Allen Wiley to preach in Culpeper. Opposition from residents was so fierce that Thomas traveled to Orange where he was able to preach without interference. Wiley wished for Thomas to preach frequently in

---

[49] Fristoe, *Concise History of the Ketocton Baptist Association*, 64.

[50] Thomas, *The Virginian Baptist*, 55.

[51] George W. Beale, "Baptist Beginnings in Virginia," in Charles F. James, *Documentary History of the Struggle for Religious Liberty in Virginia* (Lynchburg, VA: J. P. Bell Co., 1900), 211. In *The Virginian Baptist,* Thomas utilized the writings of the early Church Fathers (in Latin) and referred to numerous English divines. William Wirt said that Thomas "took no part in the management of domestic affairs, but left all worldly business to his wife; and devoted himself exclusively to his books and his pulpit." See Lewis P. Little, *Imprisoned Preachers and Religious Liberty in Virginia* (Lynchburg, VA: J. P. Bell Co., 1938), 40.

[52] Thomas, *The Virginian Baptist*, 56.

Culpeper; however, the itinerant was constantly requested to preach in areas where there was less opposition. Since Wiley could not acquire the services of Thomas as often as he desired, he traveled to Halifax County in southern Virginia to request some Separate Baptists to come to Culpeper. Samuel Harriss came to Culpeper, but was similarly opposed as Thomas had been previously. Before Harriss left Culpeper, however, he encouraged some young converts to exercise their gifts and to begin holding services. These men, among them Lewis and Elijah Craig, had previously been awakened by the efforts of Thomas. Following Harriss's admonition, services were held and several new converts were made. The young exhorters, however, requested Thomas to come and "preach for them and teach them more perfectly."[53] Upon his arrival, Thomas voiced disapproval of the preaching of such untrained and uneducated men. Semple commented, "This was like throwing water on their flaming zeal. They took umbrage and resolved to send for Harriss."[54]

Efforts at Reconciliation.—The first confrontation of Regulars and Separates after the Culpeper incident occurred in 1767 in Orange County. Some Separate preachers, including Samuel Harriss and James Read, were exhorting to large crowds. Present in the gathering were Thomas and another Regular minister, John Garrard. John Leland reported that the two groups met "like the two seas in St. Paul's shipwreck. . .assembled in conference but did not so happily unite, as candor desired."[55] Semple suggested that the crowd primarily identified with the Separates and opposed union. As a result, both groups held meetings the following day and administered baptism. The breach was widened.[56]

The two Baptist groups, however, in the main continued to desire union. In 1769, the Regulars of the Ketocton Association sent messengers to the Separates of the Sandy Creek Association (North Carolina). The Regulars asked, "If we are all Christians, all Baptists, all New Lights, why are we divided?"[57] The Separates, however, rejected this plea for union because they had insufficient

---

[53] Edwards, "Materials Towards a History of Baptists in Virginia," 77.

[54] Semple, *History of Baptists in Virginia*, 36.

[55] Leland, *The Writings of the Late Elder John Leland*, 105.

[56] Semple, *History of Baptists in Virginia*, 10.

[57] Edwards, "Materials Towards a History of Baptists in Virginia," 113.

knowledge concerning the beliefs and practices of the Regulars. Another merger was attempted in 1773 when Regulars of the Kehukee Association approached the Separates. Union was again unsuccessful. The Separates criticized the Regulars for having an unregenerate church membership and for not insisting on simplicity of dress but allowing "superfluity of apparel."[58]

Achievement of Union.—The attitudes of Regulars and Separates concerning confessions, doctrine, the style and effects of preaching, and education were representative of real and significant differences between the two groups. They never functioned as permanent roadblocks, however. As the two groups grew through revival and as contact between them increased, the differences diminished. The Regulars, though already evangelistic, became more so and identified further with the masses of common people. Fristoe commented that union was possible when the factions realized that "they were of the same sentiment."[59]

Gradually, the Separates modified their stance toward confessions. They were willing to accept the Regulars' confession with the stipulation that it was not a binding statement of faith. Drawn together by revivalism, the issue of religious liberty during the Revolution was the climactic push towards union. In 1787, the two groups united and renamed themselves the United Baptist Churches of Christ in Virginia.[60]

One can conclude that union with the Separates was an enduring goal of the Regulars. The environment created by attitudes such as the one epitomized by Thomas facilitated this quest. Rebuffed by the crowd at Culpeper in 1767, Thomas still communicated with Separates. For example, when James Ireland was imprisoned for preaching, Thomas sent a letter to Ireland admonishing him to keep the faith. Ireland's biographer spoke of the letter as from one who was "signally blessed to him [Ire-

---

[58] Lemuel Burkitt and Jesse Read, *A Concise History of the Kehukee Baptist Association* (Halifax: A. Hodge, 1803), 42-43. Separates required a convert to recite his experience publicly before baptism. Interestingly, Thomas in *The Virginian Baptist* agreed. He also denounced "superfluity in apparel" (p. 20).

[59] Fristoe, *Concise History of the Ketocton Baptist Association*, 21.

[60] Ford, "The Baptist District Association in Virginia, 1766-1950; A Study in Baptist Ecclesiology," 233.

land].”[61] A safe conjecture is that Thomas and his Broad Run Church were involved in the Ketocton attempt to effect union in 1769. Moreover, when Thomas wrote *The Virginian Baptist* in 1774, he never referred to a breach among Baptists. His purpose was to present the Baptist faith. He still criticized some Separate Baptist practices, but he was willing to report them as Baptist. Thomas was willing to follow the maxim ‘unity amidst diversity’ because he valued union. Indeed, Thomas was denouncing superfluity in dress and advocating a regenerate church membership, the two items emphasized by the Separates in their rejection of the Kehukee plea for union.

Relationship of Thomas and Regular Baptists in non-Baptist groups

David Thomas and the Regular Baptists were not ecumenical in the modern sense that they were willing to hold communion with non-Baptist groups. Indeed, Thomas practiced closed communion, observing the ordinance strictly with other Baptists. He never claimed, however, that Baptists were the only Christians.[62] Thomas admitted that the visible church, the whole body of professing believers living on earth, belonged to diverse denominations that differed greatly in form and ceremonies.[63] He justified closed communion, however, on the basis of church order. Just as the master of a house has the indispensable right to deny entrance to persons who refuse to submit to discipline and government, the church must deny communion until persons “are reconciled to our order.”[64]

Presbyterians.—The only evidence concerning any specific activity of Thomas with another denomination was his interaction with the Presbyterian minister Amos Thompson of Loudoun County. Morgan Edwards, the Baptist historian, and Archibald Alexander, the Presbyterian minister, related two separate inci-

---

[61] James Ireland, *The Life of the Rev. James Ireland* (Winchester, VA: Printed for the publishers by J. Foster, 1819), 179. Ireland was in the Culpeper jail from November 1769, to April 1770.

[62] Thomas, *The Virginian Baptist*, 44-45.

[63] *Ibid.*, 24.

[64] *Ibid.*, 44.

dents of diametrically opposed sentiments. Edwards described how Thompson, "having done him [Thomas] much mischief before,"[65] challenged the Baptist leader to a public dispute. Thomas accepted the challenge and won the debate. There were two proofs of Thomas's victory, according to Edwards. First, Thompson was excessively angry on the stage, "freezing and scolding and waxing scurrilous."[66] Second, an elder, the clerk, and eight other members of Thompson's parish left Thompson and joined the Regular Baptists. Edwards added that Thompson was a source of harassment for three years.[67]

Alexander's story, however, painted a picture of friendly cooperation between Edwards' two antagonists. The Presbyterian story contended that Thomas requested Thompson to preach at a Baptist gathering. Thomas had been threatened with violence by some profane and lawless men. He wanted the presence of Thompson, a man of gigantic frame and brawny arms, to quell any possible violence. Thompson came and dispersed the trouble-makers, reminding their leader that "he could hurl him [the leader] to the earth in a moment."[68] Alexander concluded, "Father Thomas received no further molestation."[69]

Taking into account the apologetic embellishments of both historians, one can surmise that Thomas, as a Baptist, naturally bore the occasional scorn of other religious groups. The rejection of infant baptism for believer's baptism by immersion would assure criticism.[70] Thomas possessed an ecumenical spirit. His attitude toward the Anglican Church, at least up to 1774, vividly illustrated that attitude.

Anglicans.—In denying an accusation that Baptists were heretics split off from the Church of England, Thomas quickly asserted that the established church was a Christian church,

---

[65] Edwards, "Materials Towards a History of Baptists in Virginia," 25.

[66] *Ibid.*

[67] *Ibid.*

[68] James W. Alexander, *The Life of Archibald Alexander, D. D.* (New York: Charles Scribner, 1854), 230.

[69] *Ibid.*

[70] Thomas, *The Virginian Baptist*, 50. He included an extensive defense for immersion in response to critics.

possessing many sound articles of faith. Thomas was a dissenter because many elements of Anglican church order, such as infant baptism, did not agree with Scripture.[71] Thomas defended his right to exhort evangelical doctrine to adherents of the established church, yet this was not done in a presumptuous manner. Thomas concluded that "as to the established church, we humbly thank her for all her favours. And if any of our sect have spoken disrespectfully of her as such, I freely allow it was imprudence in them to do so."[72]

Thomas's attitude starkly contrasted that of the Separates towards the established church. Torbet noted that the Separates "did not hesitate to criticize the Episcopal clergy as being unspiritual, worldly in their practices; and more concerned with their salaries than with the service which they might render to God."[73] The disparity of the attitudes of the two Baptist groups toward the Anglicans was due to various factors. The Anglicans were more favorable to the educational and economic standards of the Regulars. Another major factor, however, was the Regulars' more cooperative attitude toward the government.

Relationship of Thomas and the Regular Baptists to the Government

Civil Harassment.—The persecution of Separate Baptists by the colonial civil authorities has been well chronicled. The Separates generally would not comply with the Act of Toleration which required dissenters to obtain licenses to preach. They believed that their authority to preach came from God alone. Moreover, the licenses restricted a dissenter to preaching in one meetinghouse. Separates would not be restricted in their itinerancy.[74] During the course of opposition, at least thirty-four Separates were imprisoned at the hands of local legal authorities. These civil officials often suppressed the Separates at the

---

[71] *Ibid.*, 41.

[72] *Ibid.*, 43.

[73] Torbet, *A History of the Baptists*, 239.

[74] Lumpkin, *Baptist Foundations in the South*, 110; Gewehr, *The Great Awakening in Virginia*, 126-27. Fristoe, *Concise History of the Ketocton Baptist Association*, 71, discusses the difficulty in obtaining a license.

encouragement of Anglican ministers who despised the Baptist enthusiasts.[75]

In comparison with the Separates, the Regulars generally escaped severe civil harassment—only one imprisonment occurring. In the early years of preaching, however, Thomas was assaulted on several occasions. Edwards surmised, "if we may judge of a man's prevalency against the devil by the rage of the devil's children, Thomas has prevailed as a prince."[76] Harassment of Regulars, however, was not as intense because they obtained licenses according to the Act of Toleration. Civil officials often were unaware or overlooked that Regular itinerancy did not confine itself to the required one meetinghouse. Gewehr suggested that three factors contributed to the better treatment of the Regulars by the civil officials and the Anglican ministers: the Regulars' willingness to obtain licenses, the less demonstrative nature of the Regulars in comparison with the Separates, and the respect garnered from the fact of Thomas's education.[77]

One could suggest that Thomas's openness toward the Anglicans was facilitated by their tolerant attitude toward his status as a dissenter. The explanation should not be ruled out. On the other hand, it is not necessary to denigrate Thomas's motives. The Regulars considered the Anglican Church as Christian. They also emphasized that they were law abiding citizens of the colony.[78]

Religious Liberty.—Virginia Baptists exerted a powerful influence in the fight for the disestablishment of the Anglican Church and the realization of religious liberty. Of the two Baptist groups, the main contributors were the Separate Baptists. The influence of leaders such as John Leland and Samuel Harriss and the indefatigable effort of the Separate Baptists' General Committee in lobbying the Virginian legislators is a well-deserved chapter in

---

[75] One Anglican minister compared the Separates to gnats: "though they can neither give pleasure nor do any good, they do not want either the disposition or the ability (of) those little insignificant animals to tease, to sting, and to torment." The Anglicans disliked the wild enthusiasm of the Separates and were alarmed at their phenomenal growth. See Thomas E. Buckley, *Church and State in Revolutionary Virginia, 1776-1787* (Charlottesville: University Press of Virginia, 1977), 14.

[76] Edwards, "Materials Towards a History of Baptists in Virginia," 26.

[77] Gewehr, *The Great Awakening in Virginia*, 115.

[78] Thomas, *The Virginian Baptist*, 33.

the history of the Separate Baptist tradition. The Regular Baptists, however, were not silent in the fight. The attitude of David Thomas is instructive regarding their role.

The precursor to the fight for religious liberty was a concern for fair treatment according to the stipulations of the Act of Toleration. The first petition of the colonial legislature came from the Regular Baptists in 1770. They requested military exemption for their licensed preachers and called for the negation of the restriction which prohibited a minister from preaching but in one meetinghouse.[79] A petition from the Ketocton Association in 1774 reiterated the plea for unrestricted preaching.[80]

In August, 1775, Separate Baptists made the first organized step among Virginian dissenters for religious freedom and the separation of church and state. The revolution was impending and the satisfaction with "toleration" had disappeared in favor of the fight for political and religious liberty.[81] The pilgrimage of David Thomas dramatically revealed the Regular Baptist shift from emphasis on toleration to freedom.

At the time of the publication of *The Virginian Baptist* (1774), Thomas exhibited a tolerant attitude toward the Anglicans and a conciliatory spirit toward the English government. Thomas contended that Baptists were not concerned with the government of the colony at their meetings except in the form of prayer for the welfare of the inhabitants. Thomas was content with English rule, noting that Baptists were loyal and "heartily acknowledged as our rightful king," King George III of England.[82] Thomas continued that Baptists completely respected the laws of the colony and desired no further liberty than to worship God "without molestation."[83] Even taking into account apologetic distortion, Thomas exhibited satisfaction with the current state of English-dominated

---

[79] The petition is signed by "Protestant dissenters of Baptist persuasion." The legislature rejected the plea for military exemption and did not vote on the question of meetinghouses. See Thom, *The Struggle for Religious Freedom in Virginia*, 28-29.

[80] James, *Documentary History of the Struggle for Religious Liberty in Virginia*, 38.

[81] Ryland, *The Baptists of Virginia*, 95.

[82] Thomas, *The Virginian Baptist*, 33.

[83] *Ibid.*

affairs. The seeds for the espousal of total religious liberty, however, were present in *The Virginian Baptist*. Concerning soul liberty, Thomas declared, "The *Almighty* alone has reserved the government of conscience to himself, nor is it subject to any inferior jurisdiction. It ought not to be, nay it cannot be savaged by human authority."[84]

As the spirit of revolution gripped Virginia, Thomas became a leader for the patriotic cause.[85] On May 19, 1776, during the first meeting of the Virginia Convention, which was convened to deal with the ramifications of independence, Thomas's church at Occoquon presented a petition. The petition requested complete religious liberty and the discontinuance of financial support for the Anglican clergy.[86] This petition was the forerunner of a great influx of petitions to the Convention by dissenters.[87]

When the Virginia Convention adjourned in July, 1776, a Bill of Rights had been passed. Through the work of James Madison, the concept of toleration had been abrogated in favor of religious freedom. The legislature, however, had deliberately differentiated between free exercise of religion and the disestablishment of the church, approving the former and rejecting the latter. Dissenters viewed the two concepts as necessarily linked, especially the termination of all taxation for religious purposes.[88] Thomas contributed to the dissenting cry for justice with a poem against religious taxation:

> Tax all things, water, air, and light,
> If need there is, yea tax the night
> But let our brave heroic minds
> Move freely, like celestial winds.
> Make vice and folly feel your rod,
> But leave our consciences to God.[89]

---

[84] *Ibid.*, 17.

[85] A contributor to Cathcart's *Baptist Encyclopedia*, 1148, noted that Thomas Jefferson and Patrick Henry held Thomas in high regard.

[86] Ryland, *The Baptists of Virginia*, 98.

[87] Thom, *The Struggle for Religious Freedom in Virginia*, 32.

[88] Buckley, *Church and State in Revolutionary Virginia, 1776-1787*, 18.

[89] *Ibid.*, 22.

When the Virginia legislature convened in the fall of 1776, all persons were freed from the requirement to support any church. Though the work of leaders like James Madison and Thomas Jefferson was central, the dissenting voice of men like Thomas was an influential factor.[90]

Of course, the battle for religious liberty had really just begun in 1776. The Separate Baptists were especially active through their lobbying agency, the General Committee (1784-1787). No further evidence exists concerning the specific activity of Thomas in the struggle for liberty. The Ketocton Association, however, participated in the efforts of the General Committee. Indeed, the victory of liberty was climaxed by the union of the two Baptist bodies.[91]

Thomas as a Kentucky Baptist

The Great Revival struck the frontier of Kentucky in 1801-1802. Baptists prospered. The following table reveals the dramatic gains.[92]

Year	Associations	Churches	Members
1800	7	106	5,119
1803	10	219	15,495

The climax of the revival was the union of Regular and Separate Baptists in Kentucky. David Thomas was once again in the midst of an awakening. Now an aged minister, he felt the need to reassert his evangelistic heritage by answering the critics of the revival. Consequently, he published *The OBSERVER Trying the Great Reformation in This State* (1802).

Evaluation of Great Revival.—At the outset of *The OBSERVER*, Thomas contended for the divine origin of the revival. The devil could not have designed the revival. It would be contra-

---

90 The emphasis on the contributions of Thomas is only an attempt to highlight the Regular Baptist role in the fight for liberty. See Buckley, *Church and State in Revolutionary Virginia, 1776-1787,* for an excellent analysis of the contributions of the Presbyterians and the critical work of political leaders like Jefferson.

91 Alley, *A History of Baptists in Virginia*, 60.

92 J. H. Spencer, *A History of Kentucky Baptists* (1886; facsimile reprint, Lafayette, TN: Church History Research and Archives, 1986), 1: 541.

dictory for the devil to persuade people to desist their vices for "a stated course of severe virtue, and serious devotion."[93]

Thomas applauded the utility of revival. Many were truly converted. Even those only outwardly reformed, charged Thomas, were attending services which might unmask their "secret unbelief."[94] Indeed, the revival might be foreshadowing greater things to come.

The author's primary objective, however, was to answer the charge that the excessive physical manifestations that accompanied the revival disqualified it as a delusion. Thomas asserted that the presence of physical manifestations did not indicate pro or con concerning the existence of a revival. He noted, however, that "it may be hard to find an account of any extraordinary reformation of religion, either in Europe or America, at least of late years, without the concomitance of such appearances."[95] Thomas surmised that it was no surprise for a criminal to be seized with agonizing fits when he was confronted with the judgment of a human court. Analogous to the human scenario, Thomas continued, "And pray, what is this, to the horrendous doom of eternal damnation pronounced by the infinite Jehovah?. . .is it a wonder that many of them [sinners] should cry out with horror?"[96]

Thomas, however, never approved of the revivalistic excesses. They almost always ceased, according to the author, when the believer gained a competent measure of knowledge. Real religion was to be found in the heart, consisting of a "sedate, silent, tranquil contemplation of infinite perfection."[97] The kingdom would come, not with pomp and parade, but like the chaste virgins of old, veiled rather than exposed to full view.[98]

Throughout his ministry, Thomas preached the evangelistic message of new birth. Yet his attitude toward revival exhibited a

---

[93] David Thomas, *The OBSERVER Trying the Great Reformation in This State* (Lexington, KY: Printed by John Bradford, 1802), 10.

[94] *Ibid.*, 33.

[95] *Ibid.*, 21.

[96] *Ibid.*, 23.

[97] *Ibid.*, 39.

[98] *Ibid.*

maturity of thought. In *The Virginian Baptist*, Thomas decried the physical manifestations of the Separates. As an elder statesman in *The OBSERVER*, he remained consistent in his negative critique of enthusiasm. Yet, Thomas had learned to better accept the excesses. Though not a part of the central thrust of mature religion, they might accompany the novice in his sense of religious despair.

Activity as an aged minister.—Most of the ministry of Thomas in Kentucky was conducted in the Elkhorn Association of Regular Baptists. Only a little evidence exists regarding any specific ministerial activity. Thomas did help to form the Bracken Association, an offshoot of Elkhorn.[99] Probably due to his age and increasing blindness, Thomas was seldom a messenger to the Elkhorn Association,[100] whereas he continuously represented Broad Run at the meetings of the Ketocton Association.[101] While at East Hickman Church, 1801-1805, Thomas was recognized as one of three ministers "on equal footing."[102] The other two ministers, however, were heavily involved in associational activities and moderated church business sessions much more frequently than Thomas.[103]

Though the church records offer a limited picture,[104] the feeling they convey is that the aged Thomas was akin, in modern terms, to a revered pastor emeritus. Though age and health restricted his activity, Thomas was a respected minister whose opinion was still powerful. He published his view of the Great Revival in *The OB-*

---

[99] Crismon, "Virginia Baptist Ministers Who Migrated to Kentucky Before 1800," 769.

[100] Minutes of the Elkhorn Baptist Association (KY), 1785.

[101] Minutes of the Ketocton Baptist Association (VA), 1766.

[102] Minutes, East Hickman (KY) Baptist Church, November, 1802, 66.

[103] Thomas did prepare East Hickman Church letters for the associational meetings for June 13, 1801; July 3, 1802; July 2, 1803.

[104] Colonial business meeting records were terse. For example, Broad Run Church began to record fuller records on April 28, 1785, at the request of Thomas. For a discussion of frontier business meeting records, see T. Scott Miyakawa, *Protestants And Pioneers* (Chicago: University of Chicago Press, 1964), 38.

SERVER at the request of others.[105] As an aged minister, he still continued to be a source of inspiration. S. H. Ford ebulliently described Thomas just before his death:

> Intelligence still beams out, though the windows of the soul are closed. The scholar, the thinker, the man of energy and of power, are seen still in their partial eclipse. . .retired from the battlefield, his fight finished; whose life had been one of dauntless, aggressive, uncompromising valor. . .and had been blessed, oh! as few men living had been.[106]

Conclusion

Walter B. Shurden identified four dominant traditions among Baptists of the South. One of these was the Charleston tradition, epitomized by Richard Furman and the Charleston Association of South Carolina. Shurden stated that this tradition was characterized by "order." Theological order was maintained by the Charleston Association's adoption of the Philadelphia confession of Faith. The confession was rooted doctrinally in the Calvinism of the English Particular Baptists. Ecclesiological order was maintained by balancing the demand for local church autonomy with cooperation in associational life. Concerning liturgical order, Shurden suggested that the Charleston tradition "represented a style in public worship that was ordered and stately, though pulsating with evangelical warmth."[107] Finally, Charleston emphasized ministerial order which saw the value of an educated ministry.

The description of the Charleston tradition by Shurden can also be applied to the Regular Baptist tradition of colonial Virginia. Regular Baptists in Virginia were another manifestation of the tradition of order. Theologically, they also adopted the Calvinistic Philadelphia confession. Ecclesiologically, the Ketocton Association had its roots in the Philadelphia Association. The emphasis on

---

[105] Thomas, *The OBSERVER Trying the Great Reformation in This State*, iii.

[106] S. H. Ford in Taylor, *Virginia Baptist Ministers*, 47.

[107] Shurden, "The Southern Baptist Synthesis: Is It Cracking?" *Baptist History and Heritage* (Nashville: Historical Commission, S.B.C.), 16 (1981), No. 2 (April): 4.

associational cooperation was vividly seen in the life of the Ketocton Association and the leadership of Thomas and his Broad Run Church. As noted earlier, many of the Regular ministers regarded Thomas as their spiritual father. In addition, Thomas often itinerated with John Garrard, the minister of Mill Creek Church. The Regular Baptists of Virginia also exhibited liturgical order, especially in comparison with the Separates. Thomas's preaching was "pulsating with evangelical warmth."[108] Order was desired, however, as the Regulars criticized the wild enthusiasm and excessive physical manifestations which characterized the Separates. Finally, ministerial order was vividly illustrated by the importance that Thomas attached to an educated ministry.

David Thomas was the leader, the historian's representative figure, of the tradition of order in Virginia, the Regular Baptist tradition. This study, by viewing the tradition through the eyes of Thomas, does not infer that diversity was not present in Regular Baptist life. The conviction that Thomas embodied the Regular tradition, however, is clearly justifiable. His contributions to the spread of the Regular tradition throughout northern Virginia were unsurpassed among the Regulars. As church planter, itinerant minister, or spiritual father, his influence was pervasive. Thomas's Broad Run Church was the heartbeat of the Ketocton Association. Moreover, Thomas was the spokesman for the Regular cause with his publication, *The Virginian Baptist*, the first printed presentation of Baptist faith and order in Virginia.

By examining the life of David Thomas, this writer has sought to give credit to the contributions of the Regular Baptists to Baptist foundations in colonial Virginia. Too often these Baptists have been slighted at the expense of the Separate Baptists. Indeed, the Separates became the dominant thrust behind the growth of Baptists after 1770. They justly deserve the appellation of the major contributor to the Baptist phase of the Great Awakening. The Regulars, however, sustained the awakening begun by the Presbyterians.

Perhaps the Regulars were not the real continuators of the revival, as Gewehr asserted, if revival meant the extension of the spirit of George Whitefield. Their liturgical order was not as conducive as the enthusiasm of the Separates to Whitefield-styled revival. The Regulars, however, solidly established the Baptist foundation in Virginia. During the 1760's, they experienced growth under the evangelical message of Thomas and his protégés.

---

[108] *Ibid.*

Any history of colonial Baptists in Virginia needs to acknowledge the contributions of both the Regular and Separate Baptists. They represent the two dominant traditions in colonial Baptist life. Their diversity enriches the understanding of Baptist heritage. Their ability to achieve unity amidst diversity was an important achievement.

Further Reading

Morgan Edwards, "Materials Towards a History of the Baptists in Virginia." Eve B. Weeks and Mary B. Warren, eds. *Materials Towards a History of the Baptists. By Morgan Edwards, A.M.* Danielsville, GA: Heritage Papers, 1984. Volume Two, 33-77.

William Fristoe. *A Concise History of the Ketocton Baptist Association*. Staunton, VA: William G. Lyford, 1808.

William Lumpkin. *Baptist Foundations in the South. Tracing through the Separates the Influence of the Great Awakening, 1754-1787*. Nashville, TN: Broadman Press, 1961. Reprinted Asheville, NC: Revival Literature, 2006.

Garnett Ryland. *The Baptists of Virginia, 1699-1926*. Richmond: Virginia Baptist Board of Missions and Education, 1955.

Robert B. Semple. *A History of the Rise and Progress of the Baptists in Virginia*. Richmond: John O'Lynch, 1810. Revised Edition by George W. Beale. Philadelphia: American Baptist Publication Society, 1894.

JAMES POTTER
1734 - 1815

by Jeff Brodrick

Within a few months after Jonathan Edwards at Northampton, Massachusetts experienced what he called the "shower of God's blessing," and what would soon become known generally as The Great Awakening, a Presbyterian gentleman and his wife were welcoming a son into their home in the Pejepscot[1] area of the District of Maine in the Commonwealth of Massachusetts. This son would, in the providence of God, experience spiritual awakenings and revivals later as an itinerant Baptist evangelist. He would also plant a number of solidly Calvinistic Baptist churches in the boundaries of his native-born territory during a period of thirty-four years of ministry.

His early life and spiritual impressions

James Potter was born on February 22, 1734, in Brunswick, Cumberland County, Maine.[2] He is a confirmed sixth generation American and also the sixth of eight children born to William and Catherine Potter, despite the conflicting claims found in many genealogies of the Potters as contained in early published Maine histories.[3]

---

[1] The Pejepscot Committee was formed in 1714. Pejepscot is now much of Brunswick, Topsham and Harpswell, Maine.

[2] Brunswick is located near the coast of Maine approximately 25 miles northeast of Portland. It is also the birthplace of Harriet Beecher Stowe, Henry Wadsworth Longfellow and Joshua Chamberlain (Civil War era general and 32nd governor of Maine). Potter's birthplace is indicated by the first line of his narrative.

[3] I found while searching various Potter family records that there are many inaccuracies. It took a great deal of time and two trips to Bowdoin, Maine, to confirm the above data by untangling the confusing accounts. For example, there were at least three contemporaries named James Potter in official district records. A concise genealogical lineage of Elder Potter, as best I was able to determine it, is as follows: Robert Potter (1628-1690) and Isabella Anthony were the American immigrant ancestors of James Potter. They made their home in Ipswich, Massachusetts, lived there their entire lives and were Puritans. Among the children of Robert and Isabella was Anthony, born in 1652 at Ipswich.

In his diminutive autobiography, James Potter informs the reader that when he was about two years old he and his parents moved to Topsham (now in the county of Lincoln) to reside. "My parents were strict Presbyterians," he wrote, "and carefully instructed me in the first principles of religion: they set before me life and death, good and evil; warned me against swearing, lying, Sabbath-breaking, and evil practices; they encouraged me in the pursuit of morality, to say the catechism and a form of prayer."[4]

At the age of eight years old, James became very concerned about the matter of prayer. He began to think that he had never prayed before, but simply repeated the best form "without the exercise of the heart" and that this kind of prayer was mockery. Eventually, through the saving knowledge of the Lord Jesus Christ, he would discern how to pray as he later confesses, "according to the light I had."[5]

James was thirteen in 1747, when the great evangelist George Whitefield was spreading the Gospel message throughout New England. James had heard many individuals in his own town railing against this messenger of the Gospel. "There was a great outcry amongst the people against Mr. Whitefield, and the people who followed him; that he went about breaking up churches,

---

Anthony married Elizabeth Stone after his first wife died. Elizabeth and Anthony had several children and one of their sons, Samuel (1656-1714), married Joanna Wood. To Samuel and Joanna was born David Potter in 1685. He eventually married Mary Merriam. The first son born to this union was William Potter (1715-1747). William would marry Catherine Mustard. William and Catherine are the parents of James Potter, the subject of this essay. The *Bath Daily Times*, Tuesday Evening, March 11, 1924, in the "Historical Data Regarding Early Folk in Topsham" section, states that James Potter "was called 'elder,' also called 'miller' to distinguish him from his uncle James, and because he was concerned at the mills at the falls." Another secondary source, Jesse W. P. Purdy, *The Whitmore Genealogy: a record of the descendants of Francis Whitmore of Cambridge, Massachusetts (1625-1685)* (Reading, PA: Pengelly and Bros., 1907), says that he was called 'Elder Potter' because he was one of the first Baptist ministers in Maine.

[4] *Narration of the Experience, Travels and Labours of Elder James Potter, Minister of the Gospel, and Pastor of the Baptized Church in Bowdoin, Commonwealth of Massachusetts, Published by Request of Many of the Friends of Zion* (Boston: Lincoln and Edmands, 1813), 1. Hereafter cited as Potter, *Narration*.

[5] *Ibid.*, 6.

deluding the people," he would later recall.[6] James, very likely instilled with great moralistic foundations as a teen, further added, "Those who raged against Mr. Whitefield appeared to be wicked, spiteful and self-righteous...I believed Mr. Whitefield to be a man of God, and that the moving under his preaching was a genuine work, although I never was among or heard any of it."[7]

On the 26th day of August, 1747, James and his family suffered a heavy loss. While most of the records of this event simply state that his father was "killed by Indians," the Massachusetts archives present a fuller depiction. This account reads:

> Four days subsequent the Indians fired upon a canoe, containing four persons, as it was coming up through the Narrows of Cow Island. The boat contained Mr. and Mrs. Moffit, *William Potter* and William Thorn, a soldier in Topsham under Captain Burns. [Mr.] Moffit and Potter were killed.[8]

Subsequently, William Potter's widow married Edward Cunningham.

"If God did not help me there was no help"

James Potter tells us his next serious encounter with spiritual concerns came two years later, as he shares in this excerpt:

> When about fifteen years old, I was very much exercised in my mind concerning delusion, which set me to pray and search the scriptures that I might know the meaning of it; and it appeared to me that deluded persons were left to despise the plan of redemption, invent a plan of their own, and then pervert scripture to support it; and if God left them to their own inventions to believe a lie, they would grow bold and labour to make proselytes, and speak wickedly against

---

[6] *Ibid.*

[7] *Ibid.*

[8] George A. Wheeler, *History of Brunswick, Topsham, and Harpswell, Maine: including the ancient territory called Pejepscot* (Boston: Alfred McDue and Son, 1872), 61, who footnotes Williamson, Smith and McKeen, *Massachusetts Records*, 73: 163-164. Emphasis mine.

> the truth...I endeavored to pray that I might not be left to pervert the scriptures.[9]

As his narrative attests, for the next few years he would indeed himself pervert the scriptures. At age twenty he admits that he "began to be very worldly," with his "heart much set upon the riches and pleasures of the world."[10]

Nevertheless, from time to time he would realize what he says was the "awakening of my conscience, which constrained me to refrain from outward sins, praying and reading the scriptures. . .I thought I was willing to receive Jesus Christ as offered in the gospel. . .then election came up in my mind, 'that it is not of him that runneth or willeth, but of God who sheweth mercy' [Rom. 9: 16]. The enmity that then arose in my mind against God and his purposes cannot be expressed; yet I believed that he had a plan which was immutable."[11]

Still not fully persuaded, Potter continued to perform, "all the good that a fallen man can do. . .thus I went on sinning and reforming until I lulled my conscience to sleep; and then to the world and its vanities after this manner, till I was about forty-six years old."[12] Within this period (certainly by the time he was twenty-four or five), James had married Mary Spear (or Speer) of Brunswick[13] and the Lord would bless the couple with nine children while they lived in Topsham, Maine.[14]

---

[9] Potter, *Narration*, 6.

[10] *Ibid.*

[11] *Ibid.*, 7.

[12] *Ibid.*

[13] "Mr. James Potter, Jun., of Topsham and Mrs. Mary Speer of Brunswick, Dec. 5, 1759." "Intentions of Marriage in Maine," in *Putnam's Monthly Historical Magazine* (Salem, MA: The Salem Publishing and Printing Company), 6 (new series, 4; 1896): 22.

[14] The children were: 1) Martha, born in 1760, who married first Josiah Simpson; then Simon Conner; 2) John, born in 1766, who married Abigail Farnham; he died December 10, 1855, at the age of 89 years and 4 months and was buried in the South Bowdoin Cemetery; 3) Edward, born in 1768; 4) Robert, born in 1769 (local records say that he was a twin of John, which, if true, would mean he was also born in 1766), who married Hannah Reed; he died July 25, 1819, in Washington County, Illinois; 5)

James Potter with his family moved from Topsham to Bowdoin (pr. Bōw-dĭn), Lincoln County, Maine[15] on January 16, 1781.[16]

When the Potter family of eleven souls arrived in a what he saw as a spiritually barren Bowdoin, James Potter stated, "there were five persons in this place who appeared to be pious people; these kept up a society meeting, and met together on the Lord's day, singing, reading, praying and conversing together. . .at the conclusion of the meeting one Lord's day one of the leading members asked me to pray, I answered him I could not."[17] Ten days later, Potter was traveling with this leading member and says that "after about three miles, I asked him why he asked me, an unbeliever to pray? He answered that he did not know but it was my duty. I asked him if a number of Christians were earnestly engaged to get a petition well indited [or composed] to send to the throne of grace, whether they would employ a child of the devil for that purpose? He answered no."[18]

William, born in 1770, who was unmarried and reportedly died at sea; 6) Matthew, born in 1772, who married Martha Spear; he died of "Bilious Colic" at the age of 27 years; 7) Katherine, born in 1774, who married Capt. Thomas Dunham; 8) Elizabeth, born in 1775; 9) Mary, born in 1776, who married Samuel Whitmore; she died December 2, 1828. Local records, and Purdy, *The Whitmore Genealogy* (1907), 62.

[15] According to the United States Federal Population Censuses, the town was in Lincoln County until 1860. Then it changed to Segadahoc County.

[16] By this time, the War for Independence from England had fully commenced. Many of James's relatives served in the Revolutionary War. One such relative, a cousin named James, born in Topsham, enlisted as a private soldier in December, 1775, for the term of one year in Captain York's company, Col. Phinney's regiment of the Massachusetts line. There are a few records, including D.A.R. lineages, which incorrectly place Elder Potter in the War (see D.A.R. Book 1904, XLIX: 385-386 and Book LXV: 107-108). Some of the aforementioned records conclude that Private James Potter is the same as the subject of this essay. This is unlikely since this particular soldier in these lineages requested a soldier's pension (which I was able to obtain a facsimile copy of), which clearly indicates otherwise. The date of the pension application is 1818 and he is shown as being age 63. This would make his date of birth to be about 1754/5. Elder Potter was not only born in 1734, but he died in 1815!

[17] Potter, *Narration*, 7.

[18] *Ibid.*

On Friday, September 28th of the same year (1781), Potter unpretentiously recalled,

> I was confused in my mind, and went about my work having no inclination to converse with any person. I seemed inwardly fractious, having no more than usual convictions of the state I was in. The Saturday night following a vast eternity opened to my view, time shrunk into nothing, and I saw myself a dreadful sinner. My mind flew from one object to another, if peradventure I might find some means to alleviate my distress. Every object I sought fled from me but my own wicked heart; my sleep left me, and I wondered at the patience of God with me.[19]

Finding a quiet place at the break of dawn, he attempted to pray, but again he says, "it appeared to me like mocking God. I thought of all the means I had tried in the past, but they appeared less than vanity."[20] When the day broke it was Sunday. James remembered a sermon book from the church that he had borrowed some time before. He later wrote,

> I went into the house, it being the Lord's Day, September 30th, but was very careful not to let my wife know my troubled state of mind. I told my wife that she and as many of the family might go to meeting as could, and they accordingly went.[21]

After the family departed he examined the book, finding one sermon in particular that arrested his attention. "The sermon treated on effectual calling. I had a desire to know the meaning of such a call, and began to read the introduction. As I read I tried to recollect what the subject matter of it was, but could not." Potter sat for several minutes, closed the book and resolved that he could not find favor with God. "If God did not help me there was no help, and I believed it. Then I prayed to God that he would enlighten my understanding by his Spirit, that I might understand what I

---

[19] *Ibid.*, 8.

[20] *Ibid.*

[21] *Ibid.*, 9.

read."[22] As he read about *the* particular call to mankind, he began to see that

> The law of God was set before me, and my conduct from my youth up was clearly displayed to my mind, justice cried, 'the soul that sinneth, it shall die [Ezek. 18:4, 20].' When I read the part on effectual calling, the gospel brought to my view the plan of salvation through our Lord and Saviour Jesus Christ. It appeared glorious and beautiful beyond description; I began now to dread sin more than hell.[23]

As Potter recounts, it would not be until the first of October while lying in bed that he recognized that the

> Lord was pleased to grant me special influences of his Holy Spirit like a mighty rushing wind. . .In a moment my sin, guilt and trouble were gone, and I was filled with peace with God. I now believed that I was born of God. . .now I saw that this change in me sprang from God's eternal electing love. . . I lay in bed and praised God, but did not speak above my breath, so that my wife was not awakened.[24]

He reports that this was about 2 a.m., when he was saved by the grace of God. After rising from their slumber, he told his wife and family, the neighbors, and anyone who would hear, that "the Lord has made me a new creature. . .'behold all things are become new' [2 Cor. 5:17]. . .It seemed to me the heavenly host were rejoicing that such a prodigal was brought home to God." Fearlessly, James Potter went to meeting, prayed every time he could, and told the saved and the unsaved what a reformation the Lord had worked in his life. All the while, he exclaimed, "Glory be to God I had the Spirit of Christ with me wherever I went."[25]

After this miracle of the new birth, Potter began to wonder what the Lord would do with him concerning what he called a

---

[22] *Ibid.*

[23] *Ibid.*

[24] *Ibid.*, 13.

[25] *Ibid.*, 13-14.

profession of religion.[26] The call to ministry and the truth of the Scriptures began to weigh heavy upon him. A month later, he visited the Congregational church in Harpswell, Maine, twenty-five miles south of his Bowdoin home. "I paid attention to the sermon," he wrote,

> but was so confused in mind that I had no satisfaction. Before [the minister] broke bread, he requested me to come forward; I went into the broad aisle, expecting to be questioned concerning my faith, but was not. The minister read the covenant, to which I assented, and then took my seat. I partook with them, but felt neither union nor fellowship.[27]

He decided to no longer take communion with them, and asked the minister to meet with him and hear his concerns. The minister consented and came to the Potter residence with a number of persons from this congregation. James Potter told his curious guests,

> I could not see any warrant in scripture, or their platform, to baptize unbelievers' children. They said it was a custom got into the churches, and they knew not how it could be got out. I then asked them by what rule they received unregenerate persons into the church. They said they could not search men's hearts. I told them that some of the members of that church confessed to me that they had no idea that they were Christians. They answered, these things were too high for us to meddle with. . .I told the Christians wherever I conversed that I never would go forward in any Christian duty until I had 'thus saith the Lord.'[28]

In a short time after, Potter, while considering the poverty of pedobaptism,[29] the potential importance of being baptized by immersion, and those Baptists who were known for this doctrine,

---

[26] *Ibid.*, 14.

[27] *Ibid.*

[28] *Ibid.*, 15.

[29] Potter had been "christened" at Brunswick.

remembered, "There were no travelling ministers in this way, and all I heard about the Baptists was that they were a deluded people. I thought they held some things right, as baptism by immersion. . .but had no further trial on my mind concerning [my own] baptism."[30] However, after reading the eighth chapter of Acts and praying for God's enlightenment, he "began the chapter again, and read to these words, 'if thou believest, thou mayest.' In a moment my eyes and understanding were opened to behold things in a different light. I saw myself unbaptized, and all others, who were not baptized by immersion upon a profession of faith."[31] He sought out other Christians in the society, who believed this as well. "But," he writes,

> I was disappointed; they cried out, 'it is the Baptist delusion.' I told them I never saw a Baptist in my life, nor read any of their books.[32] They were much concerned about me, and labored with me in love. They furnished me with books of the opposite sentiment. I read them, and told them they contradicted the scriptures. They attempted to prove that Enon was a small place of water, and Jordan was not more than ankle deep.[33] They continued to reason with me, until I was confirmed in believers' baptism.[34]

He shares that a reformation commenced in the town concerning *believer's* baptism. Even his oldest daughter, Martha, was baptized by immersion a month later. He began to go and speak regularly "house to house" and called to mind that "The old Christians manifested a fellowship with me as one called to preach." However, within himself he also felt "a doubting and

---

[30] Potter, *Narration*, 15.

[31] *Ibid.*

[32] There were established Baptist works in the surrounding areas by this time, but perhaps if William Screven's church would have remained in Maine, it would have been even more likely for him to have seen a Baptist.

[33] John Gill's, *Infant-baptism a part and pillar of Popery* (London, 1766, et var.), even today presents the definitive refutation of this idea.

[34] Potter, *Narration*, 16.

mistrust" as to whether he was called to preach, but he continued to pray to God for direction.[35]

In March of 1782, Nathaniel Lord came to Bowdoin.[36] Potter reminisced that Nathaniel Lord was "the first Baptist we had seen or heard,"[37] and after the first meeting, tells us:

> [I] spoke to him and informed him that I heard he was a Baptist. He said he was. I desired him not to tell me one word of what he held to, because they say I am a Baptist, and I will relate to you what I believe. I did so, concerning the faith and order of the primitive church of Christ, as I received it from the scriptures. He said if I believed what I had told him, I was a Baptist, for I had told him everything that Baptists believe and hold.[38]

Armed with this new confirmation, James Potter proceeded to travel into neighboring towns. "To many it was a strange thing to see such a worldling leave his business and become a preacher," he wrote.[39] Some of the clergy were not too happy about his new-found occupation. "[One] minister informed me there was no need of my preaching there. I told him I had not found a darker place, or one that needed preaching more than that in all my travels."[40] This boldness would always characterize his future sermons and fervency in planting Baptist churches.

A Baptist evangelist is equipped

James Potter believed that God had, "overruled for good my joining the Congregational church, as it was the means of giving

---

[35] *Ibid.*, 17.

[36] Nathaniel Lord (1754-1832) came from Massachusetts.

[37] Potter, *Narration*, 18.

[38] *Ibid.*, 18.

[39] *Ibid.*, 17; he was an independent farmer, but also ran a mill.

[40] *Ibid.*, 17.

me freer access among them."[41] He could preach and freely expound Baptist beliefs. He tells us that he

> travelled about four years [1782-1786] without license or recommendation from church or people. . .sometimes I was questioned by the clergy by what authority I did these things? I answered by the same authority that the woman of Samaria and blind Bartimeus did.[42]

From the early spring of 1782 until his death thirty-three years later, James Potter tirelessly spread the good news of the Gospel while traversing the interior of his native-born territory. George A. and Henry W. Wheeler remark in their *History of Brunswick, Topsham and Harpswell Maine* (1878) that, "An Ecclesiastical History of the Baptist Church in the state of Maine subsequent to the American Revolution would read like a biography of Elder James Potter."[43] Indeed, in 1782, when he began a tour which encompassed the next sixteen years, in having reconciled all of his accounts afterward, Potter realized that he had spent "$300 for clothing, horses and horse furniture [i.e. tack]."[44]

The records of several local church histories, Bowdoinham Baptist Associational minutes, Maine histories, as well as his own narrative, provide a rich accounting of his years as an itinerant Baptist evangelist. Maine Baptist historian Henry Burrage fittingly stated, "Potter, full of evangelistic zeal, was not slow to take advantage of the opportunities thus afforded for preaching the glad tidings."[45]

---

[41] *Ibid.,* 18. Joshua Millet, *A History of the Baptists in Maine* (Portland: Charles Day and Company, 1845), 454, claimed Potter was a member of the Congregational Church at Harpswell.

[42] Potter, *Narration,* 18.

[43] Part II, Chapter 12: "Ecclesiastical History of Brunswick," 352.

[44] Potter, *Narration*, 28. This amount, over sixteen years, would be $129,000 by today's standard, using the consumer price index and Samuel H. Williamson's, "Seven Ways to Complete the Relative Value of a U.S. Dollar Amount, 1774 to Present," *Measuring Worth* (2011).

[45] Henry S. Burrage, *History of the Baptists in Maine* (Portland, ME: Marks Printing House, 1904), Chapter 7, "Beginnings of the Bowdoinham Association," 86.

James Potter's scheduled and spontaneous meetings were something like the narrative in Scripture of the Acts of the Apostles and unarguably a personal self-actualization of the commission of Christ to go first to Jerusalem, then to Samaria, and from there to the uttermost parts of the earth. Starting in his hometown, Potter states, "A reformation began in Bowdoin, March 1782, and went on gradually through the spring and summer." In the remaining spring of 1782, he began to travel into neighboring towns, "some," he writes, "by invitation, to others by impression laid upon me, which never failed. I found in every place that I visited, numbers to attend, but best of all was that a divine power attended to awaken, convince and convert sinners."[46]

Potter, after evangelizing Bowdoin, then came "under travail of mind for perishing sinners"[47] at Bowdoinham. On visiting them he recollected,

> I enjoyed the sensible presence of my Lord, felt love towards all men, and concluded no person could hate me. They had heard of the reformation at Bowdoin, and of my traveling from town to town. A meeting was appointed, and the people flocked to hear; while I was speaking to their ears, I believe the Lord was speaking to their hearts. I tarried one week, preaching every day from house to house, the people acknowledging the power of God was among them.[48]

He also recorded that one night while at Bowdoinham, he "Lodged with someone who held the Arminian sentiment and who was seized in the night with such fear and trembling, as to shake the bed where he lay which alarmed all of the house. I conversed with him, but to no purpose."[49]

Continuing onward in his travels, Potter

> set forward [to Smithfield Plantation,][50] on a Saturday, my mind being exercised with apprehensions whether I should

---

[46] Potter, *Narration*, 19.

[47] *Ibid.*

[48] *Ibid.,* 20.

[49] *Ibid.*

[50] Incorporated as the Town of Litchfield in 1795.

> have the Divine presence with me. I had a great sense of my own weakness and ignorance, praying all the way as I went, that if the Lord had not sent me, he would confound me before the people. Before I entered the place, it pleased God to shed abroad his love in my heart, which banished all doubts, and increased my strength. I entered the first house, and began discoursing with the family concerning their soul affairs, then to the next, and soon discovered signs of conviction. . .They requested me to appoint a meeting among them, which I did the following Lord's day.[51]

Many hearts received the word and souls were saved. Furthermore, he added, "I tarried there six days with them, preaching and conversing house to house. . .and I went home confirmed that the Lord had sent me there to preach the gospel."[52] People came from Pownalborough[53] to these meetings as well. As Potter exclaimed, there was "Great reformation here. . .as many as forty gave satisfactory evidence of change."[54]

After all of these gatherings and while at Brunswick, Potter's place of birth, he preached twice on the Lord's Day at two locations. After the first meeting, he writes, "I went to the southeast part of the town, where they received me kindly, and the neighbors invited together to attend meeting; afterwards I visited different parts of the town, having the pleasure to see a reformation begun there."[55]

At this time, Potter likewise visited Topsham, "but saw no fruit there attending my labors."[56] Later he visited Burnt-Meadow (afterwards Lisbon), with "the people generally attending and

---

[51] Potter, *Narration*, 20.

[52] *Ibid.*

[53] The town of Pownalborough incorporated on February 13, 1760. The name of Pownalborough was changed to Wiscasset June 10, 1802. *The Bangor Historical Magazine*, 7 (Bangor, ME: J. W. Porter, 1892): 17.

[54] Potter, *Narration*, 20.

[55] *Ibid.*

[56] This is where he was married and raised his family; a prophet without honor in his own country?

behaving discreetly."[57] While recalling this visit he remarked, "Sometimes in preaching I have had such a sense of the state of sinners, together with a clear view of the plan of redemption, being much engaged in prayer and preaching, I then concluded much good would be done." He quickly added that, "Since then I have been taught the most engag[ing] and powerful frames are utterly insufficient to effect any impressions that are lasting and profitable without a divine blessing."[58] Potter expressed this full assurance that salvation was by grace alone when he eventually noted: "The Lord visited them in his own time and brought a number out of darkness; [now] a 50 member church."[59]

Next, he spent eight days on Sebascadigen (also written as Sebascadise) Island near Harpswell, Maine, where, he observed, "Both saints and sinners bid me welcome."[60]

It was in the fall that Isaac Case came to Maine.[61] "When I saw him he was twenty-one years old," recalled Potter, "I rejoiced that the Lord had sent him amongst us to preach the Gospel where the harvest was so great and the laborers so few. . .I heard him preach with engagedness and becoming zeal for the cause of truth and glorified God on his behalf."[62] Henceforth, somewhat like Paul and Silas, James Potter and Isaac Case began to travel together, conduct many meetings and plant churches.

In the early part of 1783,[63]

---

[57] Potter, *Narration*, 20.

[58] *Ibid.*, 21.

[59] *Ibid.*, 22. A fifty-member church as of 1813, the date of Potter's *Narration*.

[60] Potter, *Narration*, 21.

[61] Isaac Case was born at Rehoboth, Bristol County, Massachusetts on February 25, 1761. In 1783, he was ordained as a Baptist evangelist and made his way to Maine. After a long and fruitful ministry, he died in Readfield, Maine on November 3, 1853. [See the essay on Isaac Case in Volume 4 of *A Noble Company* —*Ed.*]

[62] Potter, *Narration*, 21.

[63] Potter wrote, "in the Winter."

> Elder Case and myself went to *Thomaston* and preached, when a great reformation began. This reformation spread into neighboring towns. . .when I have heard converts attributing their first awakenings to me as an instrument, I have been led to examine myself lest my heart should be puffed up with pride, and Satan get an advantage over me, and under these views, have concluded that if they saw me as I appeared to myself, they would be far from bestowing any commendation upon me.[64]

As the year progressed, so did Elder Potter. Coming to New Gloucester again,[65] he later commented,

> There had been some previous awakenings amongst them in the Freewill order. I preached there, and the people were attentive to hear the word; they reasoned with me in a calm and moderate way upon the doctrines of the gospel. They alleged that it was hard that after all their doing and exertions there was no promise of mercy. I answered that God required faith and repentance. After our controversy on the doctrines of the gospel several of them renounced the Freewill sentiments and embraced the doctrines of free grace.[66]

At Monmouth he writes, "I discovered no fruit in this place to satisfaction,"[67] while in Bath, he "enjoyed sensible tokens of the divine presence." Moreover, he added,

> in that town there were some experienced Christians who adorned their profession; they were the means of strengthening of my hands and encouragement to my heart; of stopping the mouths of gainsayers, and blessed be God he gave me to drink of the water of life. Christians were

---

[64] Potter, *Narration*, 21

[65] Burrage, *History of the Baptists in Maine*, 98.

[66] Potter, *Narration*, 23.

[67] *Ibid.*, 22.

> revived and several persons gave comfortable evidence of a change.[68]

Some of these went to the Harpswell church. Potter continued:

> In the same year [1783] I was impressed with a great desire to visit *Lewiston*. As I went, I believed that I should see some effect of my labor. When I arrived I met a person in the field and told him I was come to visit the people in that town, and to speak to them in the name of the Lord. He looked upon me as though I had come from a different world.[69]

Potter says when he left to go to the neighbor to tell them, "what the Lord had done for my soul, and my desire in coming to visit them, the first person with whom I conversed being disturbed, followed me, as he came to the door his mind was touched. We conversed some. . .and appointed a meeting the next day, which was Tuesday." The meetings continued through the week. "On the Lord's day," wrote Potter, "we had a meeting in the centre of the town, when the people flocked from all parts and Jesus the Master of assemblies came among us."[70]

Also in 1783, Potter preached at Little River Plantation, where "but little fruit appeared." He also preached at Greene (where later a church was formed; 70 members), Littleborough (now Leeds; Thomas Francis would found a church there), New Sandwich (now Wayne; where Potter founded a church), Wales (where a church was formed; 40 members), and Woolwich, where "Reverend Benjamin Randall had organized a Freewill Baptist Church as early as 1781."[71] From 1783-1785, Potter visited Litchfield, Readfield, Winthrop, Washington, Mount Vernon, Hallowell, Augusta, Dresden, Georgetown, New Castle, New-Milford, Edgecomb, Ballstown, Davistown, Harlem, Fairfax, and Nobleborough. At each place he shared the gospel of Christ and planted churches. On one occasion during his travels, he says,

---

[68] *Ibid.,* 23.

[69] *Ibid.,* 24.

[70] *Ibid.* He founded a church here—60 members.

[71] Burrage, *History of the Baptists in Maine*, 138.

> I met an old acquaintance, who rejoiced to see me, and expressed a hope of happiness. I asked him what he depended upon to keep him in a state of grace? He said he depended partly on Christ, and partly on his own obedience. I told him if what he told me was true, he had no dependence, for Christ had no partners in saving sinners.[72]

By 1784, many churches were forming from the nucleus of believers in each town where Potter had ministered. A church was planted in Harpswell, which Potter then joined.[73] At Bowdoinham a church was formed, with Job Macomber from Middleboro, Massachusetts ordained as pastor. This ordination was presided over by Isaac Case and Simon Locke of Coxhall.

In 1785, a church was organized at East Brunswick. That year Potter was ordained on the fifth day of October at the Harpswell church, "with liberty to travel," or itinerate.[74] Isaac Case preached the ordination sermon. Shortly thereafter, Potter accepted the pastorate at Harpswell, although he continued to make Bowdoin his home.[75] It must be noted that Potter wrote that he was, "frequently [away] from home eight or nine weeks at a time," but rejoiced, "When my work was done I returned home satisfied."[76]

It was in August of 1786, that Potter began to be spiritually disheartened and candidly he confesses in part,

> I appeared to myself in the Lord's vineyard like the barren fig tree, when the Lord in mercy shewed me my back-slidings, wonderings and nonconformity in duty, so that I did loathe myself, and hunger and thirst after righteousness. I prayed to the Lord that he would be pleased to purge me from all filthiness of flesh and spirit that I might perfect

---

[72] Potter, *Narration*, 30.

[73] Burrage, *History of the Baptists in Maine*, in a footnote on page 87, discusses whether Potter was baptized at this time or not. The Bowdoinham Association minutes quoted by Burrage, inform us that the Harpswell church was organized on January 20, 1785, at New Meadows, now East Brunswick (*ibid.*, 87).

[74] Potter, *Narration*, 25.

[75] Burrage, *History of the Baptists in Maine*, 87.

[76] Potter, *Narration*, 25.

> holiness in the fear of the Lord [2 Cor. 7:1]. I related my trials to the church, and requested them to pray for me, and did believe that the Lord would once more set me at liberty from all sinful entanglements.[77]

The first Baptist association in Maine is formed

It was on May 24, 1787, that delegates from the Baptist churches at Bowdoinham, Harpswell and Thomaston,

> met in the dwelling house of Job Macomber in Bowdoinham, and organized the Bowdoinham Association. . .with a total of 138 members. . . .Elder James Potter preached a suitable discourse from Luke 5:34, 35, 'Can ye make the children of the bridechamber fast, etc.' . . .The design of the organization was stated in these words, 'In associating together we disclaim all pretensions to the least control on the independence of particular churches. Our main design is to establish a medium of communication relative to the general state of religion—recommend such measures, give such advice and render such assistance as shall be thought most conducive to the advancement and the power and enlargement of the Redeemer's Kingdom in the world.'[78]

The following "Summary of Doctrines" was adopted by this first Baptist association in Maine:

> 1st. We believe that the Scriptures of the Old and New Testaments contain the mind and will of God, delivered to us by holy men of old, inspired thereunto by the Holy Ghost; and that they are the perfect and only rule of faith and practice.
>
> 2d. That there is only one living and true God, eternally existing and mysteriously manifested to us in three distinct persons,—the Father, the Word (or Son) and the Holy Ghost, who are of the same essence, power and glory.
>
> 3d. That God created man at first in his own moral image, in which man continued not, but sinned, lost his holiness, contracted guilt, became wholly indisposed to good, inclined to evil and justly exposed to temporal and eternal

---

[77] *Ibid.,* 29.

[78] Burrage, *History of the Baptists in Maine*, 87-88.

misery, and that such is now the character and condition of all Adam's posterity by nature.

4th. That the recovery of fallen, sinful man to holiness and eternal life is wholly of divine, unmerited grace through the mediation and expiatory sacrifice of our Lord and Saviour, Jesus Christ, which grace is displayed in election, vocation, remission, justification and glorification, in the following order, viz.: 'Whom God did foreknow (as heirs of salvation), he also did predestinate to be conformed to the image of his Son. Whom he did predestinate, them he also called: and whom he called, them he also justified: and whom he justified, them he also glorified [Rom. 8:29-30].'

5th. That our Lord Jesus Christ will come again, raise the dead—judge the quick and dead, both just and unjust—will punish with everlasting destruction from the glory of his presence all the finally impenitent, and introduce the righteous into the kingdom of glory prepared for them from the foundation of the world.

6th. That baptism and the Lord's Supper are ordinances of Christ to be observed by his people until his second coming, and that the former is requisite to the latter, that is to say, that those only are to be admitted into the church and partake of its ordinances who, on profession of faith in Jesus Christ and obedience to him, have been baptized in water in the name of the Father, the Son, and the Holy Ghost.[79]

In addition to this, a formal statement was issued regarding the time for meeting (the fourth Wednesday in September), and a moderator and clerk were to be voted upon annually by raised hand. Joshua Millet has suggested that in forming the Association, "these central points of gospel light"—the three churches at Bowdoinham, Harpswell and Thomaston,—"encouraged the belief that the prospect was brightening, that other churches would soon arise to co-operate in the general work" of evangelizing Maine.[80]

It was also in this same year (1787) that Potter was beset by a serious physical ailment. He relates that he was troubled by what

---

[79] *Ibid.*, 88-89, citing the 1857 *Minutes of the Bowdoinham Baptist Association*, 17-18. The charts in Burrage, *History of the Baptists in Maine*, 105 and 141, are very important for further study.

[80] Millet, *A History of the Baptists in Maine*, 101.

he termed "a cancerhumour in my blood," which at times gave "symptoms of breaking out in different places." He writes:

> I consulted physicians but their prescriptions did not remove the cause. Soon after this I observed an unusual feeling in my tongue, while travelling, which was exceeding painful, and a tumor soon made its appearance as large as a pepper-corn of a burning red colour, and the flesh raw. I went to a physician who pronounced it to be cancer of the worst kind. I went under a course of physic [i.e. medicine], during the operation of which I had a conviction upon my mind that I was trusting to means instead of trusting in God; by means of this exercise of mind I believe I was led to trust in the Lord Jesus Christ to be my physician for soul and body.[81]

Potter went to his church at Harpswell and there, "gathered at the conclusion of the meeting, I told them my trials and what impressions I had upon my mind." After affirming when he asked them if they believed that God could heal him, Potter later wrote, "I then asked them if they were agreed to ask with me of God that he would heal the dangerous complaint with which I was exercised, to which they all hardily agreed." After praying with them and requesting their further prayers for him, he departed.[82]

Potter returned to his home in Bowdoin for a few days. On the third day at home, he left for the Lewiston church. There he petitioned their prayers as well, recalling, "After we had concluded our prayers, I shewed my tongue to the brethren, which then presented to their view a sore as large as a bean." That night at about ten o'clock, "I went to bed much exercised with pain. . .I awoke about the dawning of the day, found my pain entirely gone and no sore or scar to be seen either by myself or by the family." Potter rejoiced in "this signal interposition" of God's kind providence towards him.[83]

Unshackled from this one thorn in the flesh, Potter continued to visit churches. In 1788, he reported having preached at Buck-

---

[81] Potter, *Narration*, 31.

[82] *Ibid.*

[83] *Ibid.*, 32.

field, Hebron and was also officially "dismissed"[84] from the church at Harpswell to join the Bowdoin church that he had planted some time earlier.[85] With the Bowdoin congregation he would enjoy a settled pastorate, continue some itinerant work, and encourage the establishment of the Bowdoinham Baptist Association. He maintained each of these roles for the remaining twenty-three years of his fruitful ministry.

Potter's post-itinerant ministry

In the United States Federal Population census for 1790, Potter is listed at Bowdoin, with a total of eight family members enumerated (four males and four females). That September, at the annual meeting of the Bowdoinham Association at Harpswell, he preached the opening sermon from the text of Jude 1 and was also honored by being chosen moderator of the sessions.[86]

In 1791, Potter rejoiced in the revival at Turner, Maine,[87] organized a church at Hebron, Maine (August 23rd) and aided in constituting a church at Paris Hill, Maine (November 18th). The latter church was founded by Potter and Elisha Snow.[88] All while, Potter recalls, "traveling in plain clothes; I desired no other badge of distinction but the ornament of my Lord and Master."[89] That same year he settled all temporal concerns by disclosing his living will.[90]

---

[84] An early expression of leaving a church under good favor.

[85] As Burrage writes: "The church in Bowdoin was organized Aug. 1, 1788, with eighteen members and the prominence of its Calvinism is indicated in its designation as 'A Regular, Particular Baptist Church.' " *History of the Baptists in Maine*, 90. See also Millet, *A History of the Baptists in Maine*, 106. The meetinghouse was rebuilt in 1836, after a fire consumed the original building, which had a balcony over the door.

[86] Burrage, *History of the Baptists in Maine*, 91.

[87] Potter, *Narration*, 28.

[88] Millet, *A History of the Baptists in Maine*, 119, 123.

[89] *Ibid.*, 29.

[90] *Ibid.*

In 1795, Potter had a part in a revival at Leeds, Maine, where there were a large number of conversions. Burrage relates a wonderful anecdote about Potter respecting a plan to disciple these new converts:

> By the efforts of some Methodist preachers a class was formed and Mr. [Thomas] Francis [a Baptist minister ordained at Wayne on June 29th of that year,] was appointed class leader, but Mr. Francis and some others were not satisfied with the doctrinal views of the Methodists. Elder Potter visited the place, and the Methodists left the field. When one asked the presiding elder what had become of his class at Leeds, the latter wittingly replied, 'They were marred in the hands of the Potter.'[91]

In the winter of 1797-1798, Potter also participated in a great revival season at Bowdoinham. In a letter dated April 26, 1799, from the town, a minister wrote:

> Since our last association, elder William Stinson, who is ordained over the first church in Litchfield, has baptized 118. The greatest part of them belong to that town.
>
> The winter before last there was the most powerful work in Bowdoinham that I ever saw since I came into these parts. It prevailed through the town. Elder Potter baptized 22 in one day. And it was as powerful in Litchfield last winter; Elder Stinson baptized 13 there in one day. These were two as cold winters as were ever known here. The work has now begun in this town. Six persons have lately manifested a change of heart; two of them are my children. The work still prevails.[92]

---

[91] Burrage, *History of the Baptists in Maine*, 105.

[92] William W. Woodward, compiler, *Increase of Piety, or the Revival of Religion in the United States of America. Containing Several Interesting Letters Not Before Published* (Philadelphia: W. W. Woodward, 1802), "Extract 10," 20.

The Bowdoin church was able to report 58 new additions when the Bowdoinham Association met on August 12-13, 1798, at Brunswick (East Brunswick).[93]

In 1799, on the occasion of a visit by Potter to Topsham, Maine, "occurred what is known as the first revival ever enjoyed in the town," stated Moses Woodman. And thus the way was prepared for the organization of a church.[94] The year also brought sadness to the Potter home, when their son Matthew Potter died.

To be absent from the body

Burrage writes that by 1800, the Bowdoinham Association "had now had an existence of thirteen years." A review of its history to the close of the eighteenth century, he went on to say,

> shows how much of its growth and prosperity was due, under God, to the untiring labors of Elders Case and Potter. They went everywhere preaching the word, and their preaching was in demonstration of the Spirit and of power. That the churches in this time increased from three to twenty-one, and the members from 183 to 1,568, was very largely due to their heroic and self-denying labors divinely blessed.[95]

Elder Potter continued on as pastor at Bowdoin until 1811, "when age and infirmity led him to resign his charge of the church."[96] In summarizing his life in ministry, Potter wrote the following year:

> I found the best means to prepare me for preaching were prayer to God, reading the scripture, and conversing with the people upon things of divine nature. My wife manifested a change of heart several years before me. In the first

---

93 Burrage, *History of the Baptists in Maine*, 103.

94 Moses E. Woodman, "History of Topsham" scrapbook. Continued and compiled by Mary Pelham Hill, ca. 1924.

95 Burrage, *History of the Baptists in Maine*, 105. Burrage includes a chart at the bottom of the page illustrating the growth year by year.

96 Millet, *A History of the Baptists in Maine*, 106.

> reformation, one of my daughters and two of my sons, professed a change, and one daughter since: two of my children have been removed by death.[97]

The early historian of the Maine Baptists, Joshua Millet (1803-1848), gave Potter due credit as "a pioneer to the Baptists in all the interior parts of the State," and for being "instrumental in laying the foundation for many of the now flourishing churches."[98]

Across the undulating hills and down a quiet southeastern Maine road is a small cemetery where neighbors, parishioners and a now silent preacher lie. James Potter died on March 22, 1815, and was buried in South Cemetery across from the South Bowdoin Baptist Church (now Bowdoin Center Baptist Church).[99] The cemetery and church stand on land originally owned by the Potter family. The tombstone marking the gravesite of James and Mary Potter stands nearly three feet high, is broken off and loosely stuck in the ground about ten inches. It is inscribed:

ELD. JAMES POTTER
for 23 years Pastor of
the first Baptist
Church in Bowdoin
DIED March 22 1815
Aged 81 yrs. & 1 month
The memory of the righteous is blessed

(portion now below ground level reads:)
Mary Potter his wife
DIED July 22
1822[100]

---

[97] Potter, *Narration*, 28. As seen earlier, James Potter's narrative was published the following year, in 1813.

[98] *A History of the Baptists in Maine*, 454.

[99] "About 1960, the South Bowdoin Baptist Church was torn down and the materials were used to enlarge the Bowdoin Center Church." Footnote in *Bowdoin Bicentennial: A Pictorial History of Bowdoin, Maine, 1788-1988* (Bowdoin: Falcon Press for the Bowdoin Historical Society, 1988).

[100] As transcribed line by line by the author onsite.

Further Reading

James Potter. *Narration of the Experience, Travels and Labours of Elder James Potter, Minister of the Gospel and Pastor of The Baptized Church in Bowdoin.* Boston, MA: Lincoln and Edmands, 1813.

Henry S. Burrage. *History of the Baptists in Maine.* Portland, ME: Marks Printing House, 1904.

Joshua Millet. *A History of the Baptists in Maine.* Portland, ME: Charles Day and Company, 1845.

George Augustus Wheeler. *History of Brunswick, Topsham, and Harpswell, Maine: including the ancient territory called Pejepscot.* Boston: Alfred McDue and Son, 1872.

Gravemarker for James and Mary Potter.

Samuel Jones (1735-1814)

SAMUEL JONES
1735 - 1814

by Hywel M. Davies

Samuel Jones arrived in Pennsylvania from Wales as a two-year-old in 1737, the son of a Baptist minister. He preserved Wales in his mind while becoming a Baptist of national stature in America. His influence was felt not only in the Middle Colonies but also in New England and in the South and emanated from his leading position in the Philadelphia Baptist Association, the oldest and best organized of the Baptist associations in America.

His ancestry and formative years

Samuel Jones was born in Wales on January 14, 1735, the son of Thomas and Martha Jones. Thomas Jones was born in Newton Nottage in 1703, a village at the western extremity of the Vale of Glamorgan.[1] His family moved up into the hills to a farm called Cefn-y-gelli, in the parish of Betws, very near to Ty'n Ton, the birthplace of the moral philosopher and friend of America, Dr. Richard Price. About 1730, Thomas Jones married Martha Morris from the parish of Monachlogddu, further to the west in north Pembrokeshire. Martha Morris had been baptized a member at Rhydwilym in November 1727, and had submitted to the ordinance of laying on of hands.[2] Martha and Thomas Jones were members of the local church at Pen-y-fai, where Griffith Jones was minister. Thomas Jones soon became one of the ruling elders.

In 1737, Thomas Jones with his family of four—Martha, born in 1730, Thomas, born in 1732 or 1733, Samuel, and Griffith, born in 1736, moved to Pennsylvania. On his arrival, his destination was the "back parts," the frontier with the Native Americans, in what was to become Berks County. In 1738, Thomas Jones became

---

1 Joshua Thomas, *Hanes y Bedyddwyr, ymhlith y Cymru o Amser yr Apostolion, hyd y Flwyddyn hon* (Carmarthen: John Ross, 1778), 308; John Evans, ed., *The Welsh Nonconformists' Memorial; or, Cambro-British Biography; containing sketches of the Founders of the Protestant Dissenting Interest in Wales. By the Late Rev. William Richards, D.D.* (London: Sherwood, Healy and Jones, 1820), 311-313.

2 Rhydwilym Church Register, National Library of Wales, MS 4558D.

the first minister of the Baptist church at Tulpehocken Creek. Tulpehocken joined the Philadelphia Baptist Association in the same year it was constituted. There were nineteen constituent members with Thomas and Martha Jones, all Welsh men and women who were already settled in Pennsylvania, members formerly at either the Great Valley or the Montgomery churches.[3] From their conception as a church and as a settlement in Berks County, the Welsh Baptists struggled to maintain their religious and ethnic identity in the face of the influx of Lutheran Germans and the threat of Native Americans. The peak years of German immigration to Pennsylvania were 1749-1754, but as early as October 1742, writing to his friends in Wales from the significantly named Heidelberg in Berks County, Thomas Jones complained that the advent of Germans into their neighborhood was leading to a crowding out of the Welsh.[4] However, these Welsh Baptists maintained their identity as a distinct religious and ethnic community against the odds and for over thirty years there was a Welsh Baptist church at Tulpehocken Creek.

The diary of Samuel Jones for the years 1757-1758 has survived.[5] It is a remarkable document which sheds light on the survival of Welsh identity in Pennsylvania, the relationship

---

[3] Benjamin Griffith, "A Brief Narrative of the Churches Holding Believers' Baptism in Pennsylvania and the Jerseys," in A. D. Gillette, ed., *Minutes of the Philadelphia Baptist Association from 1707-1807* (Philadelphia: American Baptist Publication Society, 1851), 23-24.

[4] Marianne Wokeck, "The Flow and the Composition of German Immigration to Philadelphia, 1727-1775," *The Pennsylvania Magazine of History and Biography* (Philadelphia: The Historical Society of Pennsylvania), 105 (1981), No. 3 (July): 249-278; Horatio G. Jones, Jr., List of Members for the year 1711 to the year 1787, "Memoranda concerning the History and the Membership of the Great Valley Baptist Church, Chester Co., Pennsylvania," *Collections of the Genealogical Society of Pennsylvania* (Philadelphia: Genealogical Society of Pennsylvania), 23 (1896). Unpaginated.

[5] The diary was first published by Horatio Gates Jones, Vice President of the Historical Society of Pennsylvania, in the *Manayunk Star* in 1859. In 1880, the diary was republished in the *Baptist Family Magazine* (Philadelphia) and the *Manayunk Sentinel*. The work was serialized from January 1880 to December 1881 in the *Baptist Family Magazine* under the title " 'Diary of S. J.' or Extracts from the Journal of a Country Baptist Minister." Extracts quoted here are taken from the *Baptist Family Magazine*.

between father and son, the interaction of family members as well as providing detailed information on the students and school of Isaac Eaton in Hopewell, New Jersey. Samuel paints a colorful picture of life on a backwoods farm in Pennsylvania during the 1750's. The chief characters are his father and mother, his brothers and sister, the Dutch indentured servant, Freddy and the black slaves, Dinah and Cato. The family dog "Carlo" is a firm friend. There is much banter between the servant, the slaves and the young people in the family. It is a very verbal society.

As well as life on the farm and at Isaac Eaton's school in Hopewell, there are descriptions of the trip undertaken by Thomas and Samuel Jones, father and son, to Philadelphia in March 1757, where they met famous figures such as the Baptist scientist Ebenezer Kinnersley, William Logan and Benjamin Franklin. Thomas Jones preached in the Baptist Church in Philadelphia with Franklin present.[6] Thomas Jones was carrying a letter from Conrad Weiser to William Logan on strategy towards the Native Americans. Samuel was surprised that his father was not angry with Logan over the Native Americans; Logan thought they had been "hardly used," while Thomas Jones "mortally hated" them since he had been almost scalped by them in the past. Later that year in July, Samuel and his brothers were sent to Reading with a letter from their father to Weiser expressing concern about their security in Tulpehocken in the face of Native American threat. The news from the Jones brothers that summer was one of a series of reports concerning the new wave of Native American attacks. Weiser told the brothers that the danger was overstated and there was less of a threat since the Easton conference earlier that year. Samuel thought differently—"their horrid cruelties in Berks County have embittered me against the whole race."[7] But, on reflection, he could not deny that the Native Americans had been treated abominably. He recalled "some of the church members talking about the case of two Welshmen who went out one day hunting and deliberately shot two Indians who had done them no harm. When arrested they said they understood it was perfectly proper and lawful to shoot an Indian."[8]

---

[6] *Baptist Family Magazine* (Philadelphia: J. Eugene Reed), 1 (1880), No. 4 (April): 111.

[7] *Ibid.*, 1 (1880), No. 5 (May): 147.

[8] *Ibid.*, 147.

Conversion and baptism

In September 1757, Samuel Jones began studies at Isaac Eaton's school in Hopewell. The uprooting from Berks County to Hopewell had been painful, but by the end of September he was settling in and finding the scholars "of good habits.....from highly respectable families."[9] The school took in boarders as well as day students who lived as members of the Eaton family. They were: James Manning, David Howell, John Stites, David Jones, Isaac Skillman, Stephen Watts and Samuel Jones himself.[10] These names were to become well known in Baptist America.

There were youthful scrapes with the students of the College of New Jersey, which had moved to nearby Princeton in 1756 and in November, Samuel Jones went with another Welsh-Pennsylvanian, David Jones (1736-1820), to visit the Native Americans on the Delaware. David Jones concluded that the Native Americans were descended from the lost tribes of Israel. As evidence, he cited their belief in the "Great Spirit," and their use of lunar months, which were similar customs to the Jews. In December 1757, Isaac Eaton baptized six new converts in a nearby brook. Samuel wrote excitedly in his diary: "There seems to be a great awakening and my own heart prompts me to go forward, but alas! I do not feel the hideous character of my sins."[11] Samuel's continuing search for spiritual reassurance occupied his thoughts and the pages of his diary.

Sunday, January 14, 1758, was a turning point. Isaac Eaton invited John Gano, who had been visiting his parents in the

---

[9] *Ibid.*, 1 (1880), No. 6 (June): 178.

[10] For further information see, for example: Reuben A. Guild, *Life, Times and Correspondence of James Manning, and the Early History of Brown University*. Boston, MA: Gould and Lincoln, 1864; G. Truett Rogers and Terry Wolever, *The Life, Journal and Works of David Jones, 1736-1820. Pastor of Baptist Churches in New Jersey and Pennsylvania and Chaplain in the American Army*. Springfield, MO: Particular Baptist Press, 2007; William G. McLoughlin, *New England Dissent 1630-1820: The Baptists and the Separation of Church and State*. Cambridge, MA: Harvard University Press, 1971, two vols.; and David Spencer, *The Early Baptists of Philadelphia*. Philadelphia: William Syckelmoore, 1877.

[11] *Baptist Family Magazine*, 1 (1880), No. 12 (December): 371.

Hopewell area, to preach.[12] That day Gano preached from John 3:14, "And as Moses lifted up the serpent in the wilderness, even so must the Son of Man be lifted up." Samuel made extensive notes of the sermon, in which Gano compared the condition of the Israelites bitten by the serpents in the wilderness to the condition of the congregation. Samuel Jones and other members of the congregation were deeply affected, as too was Isaac Eaton. Samuel realized that this experience could be the "crisis of my life." He asked himself why he was lingering when he knew "that the river of life is hurrying me rapidly on to the boundless ocean of eternity?" On June 30, he told his brother Griff that he intended to cast his "lot with God's people." Unfortunately, God's people—the Welsh Baptists on Tulpehocken Creek, rejected him—his replies to the deacon on application for membership were not explicit and full enough. He persevered in his faith and Tulpehocken agreed to receive him for baptism. On the afternoon of the last day of the year in 1758, Samuel was baptized in the Creek.[13]

The diary, which concludes there at the end of 1758, gives insight into an ethnic private world and documents the nature and extent of Welsh identity in the lives of Samuel Jones and his family. Welsh was the language of preaching and of biblical exposition, with allowance made for non-Welsh speakers such as the slave, Cato. Welsh was also the language of public worship at the meetinghouse of the Tulpehocken Baptists, but again allowance was made for English-speaking "hearers" and special services were appointed in English. Welsh was most often heard within a religious context, but there were certain customs and events which were regarded as Welsh and celebrated. St David's Day, the festival of the patron saint of Wales, was celebrated as a big day by the Jones's household despite the papist origins of the custom.

While he was at Hopewell, Samuel Jones made a regular habit of reading a chapter from his Welsh Bible. None of the others, with the exception of David Jones, could read Welsh and Samuel often had to help him "both in pronouncing the big words and in rendering them into English."[14] Welsh phrases pepper the diary,

---

[12] For John Gano, see William B. Sprague, ed., *Annals of the American Pulpit* (New York: Robert Carter and Bros., 1865), 6 (Baptist): 62-67.

[13] *Baptist Family Magazine*, 1 (1880), No. 12 (December): 368.

[14] *Ibid.*, 1 (1880), No. 11 (November): 338.

referring in the main to matters domestic. The ties with Wales were rooted in his parents' memory. His father referred to the legends of the *cyhirraeth* (corpse candles and apparitions) and both father and son were proud of the valiant history of the ancient Britons, the ancestors of the Welsh, in fighting the Romans and later the Saxons.[15] However, the Welsh connections were not exclusively related to the past, they also related to the present. Thomas Jones continued to correspond with his former church at Pen-y-fai, and his youngest son, Cradock, born in Heidelberg, Berks County, in 1742, spent some time with his father's sister in Pen-y-fai.[16] He went to Wales around 1756 to try to improve his health, but his "lung trouble" did not improve. Yet he returned home on July 30, 1758, a baptized Christian and was received into the church at Tulpehocken by letter from the church at Pen-y-fai. Welsh identity in the Delaware Valley was constantly being renewed by connections with Wales. Samuel continued to keep in touch with his kinfolk in Wales. Richard Burnell, his father's nephew, who lived at Llansamlet near Swansea, maintained a lively correspondence with his cousin into the late years of the eighteenth century.

Further study at the College of Philadelphia

Thomas Jones had long cherished the ambition that his son Samuel might become a Baptist minister, and in turn, Samuel hoped that his father might live to see his desires gratified.[17] After his baptism, his aspirations turned towards the ministry but at the same time he was anxious to complete his education above grammar school level. Sometime before the end of 1759, Samuel Jones was admitted to the College of Philadelphia.

---

[15] *Ibid.*, 2 (1881), No. 9 (September): 273; No. 10 (October): 307. Corpse candles, harbingers of death, were said to emerge from the body of the doomed person before death and trace the route which the corpse would subsequently take to the place of burial. This belief was not confined to the peasantry, but was widespread throughout all levels of society, particularly in southwest Wales, see Geraint H. Jenkins, "Popular Beliefs in Wales from the Restoration to Methodism," *Bulletin of the Board of Celtic Studies*, 27 (1977): 443-446.

[16] *Baptist Family Magazine*, 2 (1881), No. 10 (October): 307.

[17] *Ibid.*, 2 (1881), No. 6 (June): 177.

The College of Philadelphia catered to the elite of society in Philadelphia and Pennsylvania. It is significant that Thomas Jones had the wealth and the connections to facilitate his son's entry into this elite institution. The elder Jones's friendship with Ebenezer Kinnersley, a fellow Baptist, was important in this respect, but Thomas Jones was a wealthy man in his own right. He owned land in Wales as well as in Berks County and letters received in Wales from Pennsylvania referred to him as a man who was endowed with "worldly wealth."[18]

Samuel Jones kept in touch with his Hopewell friends while he was in the College of Philadelphia. James Manning (1738-1791), on leaving Hopewell Academy, went to the College of New Jersey at Princeton and spoke of their friendship in the warmest of terms. He hoped that their friendship would "not only last during our stay on earth," but would be a "shadow of that everlasting friendship which shall subsist between kindred souls, through all the future periods of our Existence."[19]

Samuel's early studies at Philadelphia were interrupted through illness and it was in April of 1760 before he began his studies in earnest, under the direction and tuition of Rev. Mr. Francis Alison.[20] Unlike Harvard or Princeton where science and secular philosophy vied with a medieval curriculum, Philadelphia committed itself wholly to the Enlightenment. Francis Alison had been taught at Glasgow and the influence of the Scottish Enlightenment was therefore pronounced. Samuel Jones's studies flourished in this atmosphere. Hezekiah Smith (1737-1805), another of his Hopewell friends with whom he was still in touch, was more pleased that godliness was a higher priority for his friend than learning, but he was also gratified that Samuel made

---

[18] Thomas, *Hanes y Bedyddwyr*, 309.

[19] James Manning to Samuel Jones, May 17th, 1760, Nassau Hall, Princeton. Mrs. Irving H. McKesson Collection (Jones section), Historical Society of Pennsylvania (hereafter HSP).

[20] For Francis Alison, a leading Presbyterian Old-Sider, see A. D. Gordon, "The College of Philadelphia, 1749-1779: Impact of an Institution," Ph.D. dissertation, University of Wisconsin, 1975, passim; Charles H. Maxson, *The Great Awakening in the Middle Colonies* (Chicago: University of Chicago Press, 1920), passim.

"so few Blunders to what you used, in writing."[21] On December 5, 1760, Samuel Jones was received into the Philadelphia Baptist Church by letter from Tulpehocken.

Samuel graduated in May 1762, and was now able to fulfill his ambitions of becoming a minister of God. The Philadelphia Baptist church noted that Jones had "of long time been inclined to devote himself to the ministry and with a view to become more capable of the office has gone through a course of college learning."[22] At this time, the Philadelphia Baptist church held its meetings at the College of Philadelphia, and Baptist youths at the college were placed under the supervision of local Baptist ministers. There was therefore, a good relationship between the church and the college. It was at the college that Samuel Jones preached his first sermon, on trial, on June 12, 1762. His text was from Ephesians 3:19: "That ye might be filled with goodness of God." He had prepared the sermon carefully and had written it out in a large, legible hand, on the advice of Morgan Edwards (1722-1795), pastor of the Baptist church at Philadelphia and another Philadelphia Baptist of Welsh origin. Samuel hesitated to make any direct application of his theme—"that would look too assuming in a person of my present circumstances."[23] His trial was successful and he gained his license to preach. Edwards and the deacons signed the certificate on behalf of the church. He did not have long to wait before receiving a call to serve a church with a view to ordination.

His call to the pastorate at Southampton and Pennepek

On July 23, 1762, Joseph Hart, a deacon at Southampton in Bucks County, wrote to Samuel Jones, asking him to "pay us a visit, preach us a sermon, and let us know whether or not you are disposed to settle."[24] He did go there to preach and apparently to their satisfaction, since he was called to the ministry there. Such was his growing reputation as a young preacher of influence

---

[21] Hezekiah Smith to Samuel Jones, November 10th, 1760. McKesson Collection (Jones section), HSP.

[22] "Rev. Dr. Samuel Jones of the Class of 1762." Archives of the University of Pennsylvania, Philadelphia.

[23] *Ibid.*

[24] Joseph Hart to Samuel Jones, July 23, 1762. Society Collection, HSP.

within the Philadelphia Baptist Association, that he was invited to draft the letter from the Association to the churches that year.[25] Not only was he called to Southampton, he also received a call from the church at Pennepek, in Philadelphia County.[26] Pennepek was the oldest surviving Baptist church in Pennsylvania and had powerful and prosperous lay members, notably Alexander Edwards. Southampton and Pennepek agreed, in a spirit of cooperation, to share the ministry of Samuel Jones.

On New Year's Day, 1763, William Marshall and Alexander Edwards for Pennepek and Joseph Hart and David Dungan for Southampton, drew up a "Memorandum of certain Articles, Confession and agreements," which detailed the arrangements agreed upon.[27] Firstly, the agreement was in force for one year only. Secondly, Samuel was to make his home halfway between the churches or spend six months in each. He was to preach alternate Sabbaths in each church until the last day of March, with Communion held once in every two months in each church. When traveling conditions improved he was expected to preach in both places. On condition that these articles were approved "by the said Jones," he would be paid £80 a year, with each church contributing £40.

The day after the legal agreement, Samuel Jones was ordained at College Hall in Philadelphia. Morgan Edwards preached the ordination sermon. In their ordination address, the Baptist Church of Philadelphia stressed his learning, his morality and his "exemplary piety." As the candidate, Samuel Jones signified that he came to the ministry out of free choice, not for any lucrative motives. He indicated that he received the Philadelphia Confes-

---

25 Gillette, *Minutes of the Philadelphia Baptist Association*, 87.

26 Alexander Edwards to Samuel Jones, December 16, 1762. McKesson Collection (Edwards section), HSP.

27 "Memorandum of certain articles, confessions and agreements, made and agreed upon the first day of January Anno. Dom. 1763. By and Between William Marshall and Alexander Edwards Members and Representatives of and for the Church of Christ at Pennepek in the County of Philadelphia, of the one part, and Joseph Hart and David Dungan, members and representatives of the Church of Christ at Southampton....towards the settling the Revd Samuel Jones as their minister Joyntly between the said churches....." McKesson Collection (Edwards section), Miscellaneous Legal papers 1761-1786, HSP.

sion of Faith as the only "human system he approved," but at the same time he was clear that the Confession of Faith did not amount to any form of "human establishment." He was then ordained. Isaac Eaton prayed "that many, by his ministry, may be pricked in the heart with convictions of sin."[28] In private, Samuel felt some misgivings that he was not equal to the greatness of the task and confided these reservations to Evan Pugh and other friends later that year.[29]

Samuel also received solicitations from Hezekiah Smith, his Hopewell friend, to remember the "back parts" and reminded him of the evangelical duties which he might undertake before he settled to a permanent ministry.[30] Smith wrote to him in February from South Carolina and described the spiritual conditions of thousands on the Pee Dee River who had no one "to break with them the Bread of Life—O, my dear Brother! I hope you will be so moved with Pity and with a Probability of a useful Journey, that you will take a Tour this way before you settle."[31] Hezekiah Smith left the Pee Dee early in 1764. Oliver Hart in Charleston complained that the two churches on that river were "entirely destitute.....and the people are vastly numerous."[32] By June 1764, the Pee Dee had the services of Evan Pugh, a Philadelphian again of Welsh descent, who was to continue to inform Samuel of the state of affairs on the Pee Dee River in South Carolina by letter.[33]

We know the main occurrences in Samuel's life during the years 1763-1765, since he compiled a brief summary of these

---

28 "A Narrative of the Ordination of the Rev. Samuel Jones, A. B., January 2, 1763," in William W. Keen, *A Bi-centennial Celebration of the Founding of the First Baptist Church of the City of Philadelphia, 1698-1898* (Philadelphia: American Baptist Publication Society, 1899), 471-475.

29 Evan Pugh to Samuel Jones, January 24, 1763. McKesson Collection (Jones section), HSP.

30 Hezekiah Smith to Samuel Jones, February 23, 1763. McKesson Collection (Jones section), HSP.

31 *Ibid.*

32 Oliver Hart to Samuel Jones, February 7, 1764. McKesson Collection (Jones section), HSP.

33 Evan Pugh to Samuel Jones, Charlestown [i.e. Charleston, SC], June 21, 1764. McKesson Collection (Jones section), HSP.

events in chronological order.[34] His pattern of activity was to repeat itself in other years in a similar fashion. In August and September, Samuel would go to Cape May in New Jersey, the home of his future in-laws. In 1763, he was courting Sylvia Spicer, the daughter of Jacob Spicer of Cape May, whom he had met in the farmhouse of the Eatons in Hopewell when he was at school there. In October, he would frequent the meetings of the Philadelphia Baptist Association. In October 1763, he traveled further afield on the work of the Association. On October 19th he was at New York, on the 23rd at "Seabrook" (i.e. Saybrook, Connecticut), and on the 25th he arrived at Newport, Rhode Island. He stayed there almost a month, returning home on November 17. His business in Rhode Island had to do with preaching the Gospel, but also with drafting the charter of Rhode Island College.

Aid in establishing Rhode Island College (1764)

The "prime mover" in the establishment of Rhode Island College was Morgan Edwards. Edwards, an outstanding if idiosyncratic figure amongst the Baptists in Pennsylvania, had been the minister at the Philadelphia Baptist church since his arrival in May 1761.[35] Edwards took to Jones from the outset. Edwards, a learned man himself who had acquired a thorough knowledge of Greek, Latin and Hebrew at the Baptist Academy in Bristol, England, was struck by Samuel Jones's scholarship. Jones and Edwards were some of the few Baptist ministers in the colonies to have received a college education. Edwards' presence was all pervasive during Samuel Jones's early ministerial career: as seen earlier, it was Edwards who signed Jones's license to preach and delivered his ordination sermon. It was Edwards who was later to officiate at his marriage. Edwards' later career was hounded by

---

[34] Samuel Jones, "Diary 1763-1765 of Main Events." McKesson Collection (Edwards section), Misc. Church Papers, HSP.

[35] For Morgan Edwards, see Sprague, *Annals of the American Pulpit*, 6: 82-85; R. W. Kenny, Typescript article on Morgan Edwards, Archives of John Hay Library, Brown University, Providence, Rhode Island; Thomas R. McKibbens, Jr. and Kenneth L. Smith, *The Life and Works of Morgan Edwards*. New York: Arno Press, 1980; and Howard R. Stewart, *A Dazzling Enigma. The Story of Morgan Edwards*. Lanham, MD: University Press of America, 1995.

controversy, much of it caused by his own doing. Samuel Jones was to be one of the few leading Baptists in the Philadelphia Association to stand by him despite his vicissitudes. Edwards confessed to Samuel Jones in July 1787, that "you have been in my heart for a quarter of a century, how that came to pass I do not know, perhaps a similarity of dispositions, sympathy or *I know not what* was the cause, but so it was that first sight and first talk produced an union or rather unition between me and you."[36]

It was Morgan Edwards who first suggested to the Philadelphia Association in 1762 that a Baptist College should be sited in the "colony of Rhode Island and Providence," because "that legislature is...chiefly in the hands of Baptists and therefore the likeliest place to have a Baptist College established by Law."[37] The Philadelphia Association commissioned James Manning, now a graduate of the College of New Jersey at Princeton, to travel through the Northern Colonies to further this project. A charter for the new college was drafted, but bitter wrangling erupted between the Baptists and the Congregationalists over the composition of the two ruling bodies—the board of trustees and the board of fellows. The Baptists and the Congregationalists each felt betrayed by what they believed to be the other's manipulation of the charter to their advantage. Samuel Jones was able when he came there in the autumn of 1763 soon after his ordination, to intervene. His intervention, together with that of Robert Strettle Jones, resulted in the provision that the majority of the board of trustees and fellows would be Baptists and also that the president would be a Baptist. Nevertheless, the Baptists were disappointed with the final version of the charter. Morgan Edwards believed that the quorum of Baptists had "not been guarded with all diligence." Even so, the Baptists had considerable influence in both branches of the corporation and as stated, the president was to be a Baptist. The college opened in 1765, under the presidency of James Manning, with one fourteen-year-old student, William Rogers (1751-1824), from Newport, Rhode Island.

---

[36] Morgan Edwards to Samuel Jones, Pencader, July 25, 1787. McKesson Collection (Jones section), HSP.

[37] Morgan Edwards, "Materials Towards a History of the Baptists in Rhode Island," in *Collections of the Rhode Island Historical Society* (Providence: Hammond, Angell and Co.), 6 (1867), 348.

His marriage and decision to remain at Pennepek

In his diary of "main events," Jones made the entry for November 10, 1764, simply read: "Was married."[38] Sylvia Spicer was the daughter of Jacob Spicer, a considerable landowner in South Jersey and at one time lieutenant governor of New Jersey.[39] Jones was very impressed with her and noted in his diary, "when she laughed her eyes seemed to laugh also, which made her wonderfully attractive."[40] At the outset, Samuel's relationship with his future father-in-law was quite prickly. Before the marriage in September 1764, Jacob Spicer wrote to him and put it bluntly that the young couple would not get any financial assistance from him; however, he went on to say, if "you happen here on the 20th of October next, in the Interim perhaps a Trifle of Cash may come to hand, and if it does, I shall not object against dispensing with what any want can spare...." He added that he probably would not attend the wedding, but that need be "no obstruction."[41]

Jacob Spicer's anxiety was not due to the fact that his daughter was marrying a Baptist, for he too was a Baptist. Sylvia added considerably to Samuel Jones's personal happiness, was dutiful as a minister's wife and in 1765, added to his wealth through inheritance from her father. As a result of the Spicer inheritance, Samuel Jones came to own land in Cape May, New Jersey. However, Sylvia Jones was English and it would be safe to

---

[38] Samuel Jones, "Diary 1763-1765 of Main Events," McKesson Collection (Edwards section), Misc. Church papers, HSP. [The official marriage register shows they had applied for a license just the day before, on November 9th. See John B. Linn and William H. Egle, compilers, "Names of Persons for whom Marriage Licenses were issued in the Province of Pennsylvania, Previous to 1790." *Pennsylvania Archives.* Second Series (Harrisburg: E. K. Meyers), 2 (1890): 136 —*Ed.*]

[39] For the important Spicer family, see Mary D. Ogden, ed., *Memorial Cyclopedia of New Jersey* (Newark, NJ: Memorial History Co.), 1 (1915): 106-107.

[40] *Baptist Family Magazine*, 1 (1880), No. 12 (December): 370.

[41] Jacob Spicer to Samuel Jones, Cape May, September 8, 1764, Society Collection, HSP.

conclude that his marriage marked the end of Welsh as one of the languages of the hearth in the Pennepek household.

During the early years of his marriage, Samuel was beset by spiritual uncertainties. His confidante in these matters was Oliver Hart (1723-1795), a man of evangelical persuasion influenced by the preaching of Whitefield and the Tennents.[42] A member at Southampton, he was licensed to preach and was ordained there in 1749. He became minister to the Baptist church in Charleston, South Carolina in 1750. He acted to several "as their father in the gospel" and was a source of comfort and reassurance to Samuel Jones. Possibly as a result of Hart's firm reassurance (the Scripture, Hart stressed, "comes handed down to us, with the greatest certainty, and upon the clearest evidence"), Jones's anxieties were gradually allayed.[43] His busy life also possibly did not allow him the time to dwell on such matters.

He had decided to supplement his ministerial stipend and his other earnings from his farm and lands in Cape May by keeping school. Throughout his life, Samuel Jones was an astute man of business and a farmer. In April 1765, he bought the plantation of the Eaton family in Pennepek and moved there with his wife, who was expecting their first child. In August of that year, Thomas Spicer Jones, their first son, was born.[44] That same month he received an invitation to visit from the Baptist church at Boston.

The Boston church had been traumatized by the Great Awakening. An "Old Light" church, it only began to recover during the mid 1760's.[45] The quest for a new minister of sound Calvinistic principles to succeed the urbane, liberal and Arminian Jeremiah Condy, who had turned to bookselling from the ministry, was an integral part of this process. Samuel Jones, college-educated, respectable and scholarly, seemed a very appropriate choice. The invitation was issued by the deacons in August 1765, who presented Boston in its best possible light: "We think Boston a

---

42 For Oliver Hart, see Sprague, *Annals of the American Pulpit*, 6: 47-50.

43 Oliver Hart to Samuel Jones, November 1st, 1764. McKesson Collection (Jones section), HSP.

44 Samuel Jones, "Diary 1763-1765 of Main Events." McKesson Collection (Edwards section), Misc. Church Papers, HSP.

45 Carla G. Pestana, *Quakers and Baptists in Colonial Massachusetts* (Cambridge: Cambridge University Press, 1991), 167-172.

place where many godly people are—a metropolis where a good faithful Baptist minister might do much service, and to that cause in particular."[46] They reminded him that his Hopewell friend, Hezekiah Smith, ministered at nearby Haverhill. Together they would strengthen the Baptist cause in Massachusetts. The prospect of a Baptist college was dangled in front of him. Even though it was likely that a Baptist college would be founded in Newport, Rhode Island; it was not too late for Boston to put in a claim, a claim which would carry more weight if they had an "able head." The Boston deacons lamented the lack of assistance from the direction of Cambridge and wished that there were "as many of our persuasion here as at Philadelphia and neighbourhood." Samuel Jones accepted the invitation to visit, went there in November and stayed there for three weeks. He was attracted by the prospect and went so far as to tell the Baptists there that he would accept the invitation to become their minister. However, Samuel did not reckon upon the attitude of Southampton and Pennepek, or upon the reaction of his wife. Sylvia Jones was not disposed to leave Philadelphia with a young child, but it was the opposition of Pennepek which was crucial and decisive. The Pennepek deacons told him in no uncertain terms that if he could find somebody to replace him at Pennepek, then that somebody could go to Boston. On February 26, 1766, Jones wrote to decline the invitation. Boston felt that they had been let down: why did he think that his church would be willing to part with him and why did he give them encouragement that they might be supplied? "The matter is settled," their bitter reply read, "they will not part with you."[47]

This episode had a lasting effect on Samuel Jones. He traveled widely and received calls from other churches but never again would he be tempted to leave Pennepek—even if Pennepek would have been content to release him. He stayed at Pennepek, declined invitations to succeed Isaac Eaton at Hopewell and Benjamin Miller at Scotch Plains and made his loyalty into a virtue by

---

[46] Thomas Bouches, Joseph Collins and John Bound to Samuel Jones, August 26, 1765. McKesson Collection (Edwards section), HSP.

[47] John Proctor to Samuel Jones, April 21st 1766. Society Misc. Collection, HSP.

Above is the Pennepek Baptist Church as rebuilt in 1805 during Samuel Jones's ministry. Below is the gravemarker for Jones in the church's cemetery. The congregation recently began meeting again in this building.

interpreting longevity of tenure by the minister as a distinct advantage to that church.[48] However, the key point revealed by this episode was the powerlessness of the minister in the face of unanimous opposition from the deacons and the laity (including his wife).

The associational stalwart

Philadelphia at this time exerted a greater influence than Boston in disseminating Baptist ideas and principles. The regular supply of Baptist ministers in Philadelphia was crucial. As late as 1782, James Manning could write to Jones and ask, "Is there no way to break up that Nest of Baptist ministers in Philadelphia and render them useful somewhere amongst the destitute churches? I feel ashamed when I think on that circumstance."[49] Before the Revolution, the Middle Colonies as a whole held sway over the other colonies in Baptist America. The Baptist ministers who dominated Rhode Island College in the eighteenth century were not New Englanders, but men who were born (or had moved to) and had been educated in the Middle Colonies: Manning, Morgan Edwards, Samuel Jones, David Howell, Hezekiah Smith, Samuel Stillman, John Davis—ministers who Manning called "my western friends."[50] One of the reasons for this influence, apart from the sheer number of Baptist ministers there, stemmed from their organizational unity. The Presbyterians in the Middle Colonies divided acrimoniously into New Siders and Old Siders in response to the Great Awakening. Baptists in Virginia and New England divided into Regulars and Separates. Individual Baptists were deeply influenced by the Great Awakening—John Gano, Benjamin Miller, Abel Morgan of Middletown, for example. However, the Baptist evangelicals in the Middle Colonies were

---

48 Samuel Jones to Joshua Thomas, March 10, 1786. McKesson Collection (Jones section), HSP.

49 James Manning to Samuel Jones, Providence, June 17th, 1782. Jones Collection, Archives of John Hay Library, Brown University, Providence, RI.

50 McLoughlin, *New England Dissent*, 1: 500. [The Middle Colonies all lay geographically to the west of New England, therefore the Philadelphia Association was sometimes referred to by New Englanders as "the Western Association" —*Ed.*]

contained within and accommodated by the powerful Philadelphia Baptist Association. Samuel Jones was not a revivalist, nor did he espouse evangelical methods of preaching. Like Morgan Edwards, he opposed extempore preaching. His sermons were carefully structured and prepared beforehand.[51] Samuel Jones was, above all, a Calvinist, and a great admirer of the English divine, John Gill (1697-1771).[52] Jones's favorite theme was the sovereignty of grace. He encouraged denominational growth and supported the evangelical missions of the Philadelphia Association. However, his main energies were directed towards educating the young for the ministry and he was not particularly remembered as a preacher.

Since his purchase of the Eaton plantation at Pennepek in 1765, the arrangement with Southampton had come under strain. Samuel was away a great deal on Association business and Southampton was aware that the link with Pennepek, not least because this is where he lived, made his connection with them weaker than his connection to Pennepek. The yearly memorandum of agreement between the churches continued to be renewed, but matters came to a head in May of 1768. At a special meeting of business, Southampton resolved to force the issue of divided loyalties and call Samuel Jones as their *sole* minister at £40 per annum and the use of the parsonage. If he did not accept "they would seek for another as soon as may be..."[53] Samuel Jones replied that he would not settle with either church, but as he lived at Pennepek, that church would naturally get the major part of his time. Southampton did not get their way and in April 1770, Samuel Jones resigned the care of Southampton.

This did not impede the progress and reputation he was making within the Baptist denomination. When Isaac Eaton died in 1772, Samuel Jones preached at the funeral and the sermon

---

[51] Small volumes; Sermons. McKesson Collection (Edwards section), HSP.

[52] [It could be said that in the cast of his mind, Samuel Jones was a more doctrinally-oriented Calvinist, seeking to establish the saints in truth; as contrasted to those Calvinistic ministers who would be more decidedly evangelistically-oriented and outwardly focused. We certainly wouldn't fault Jones for this. Both kinds of ministers are needed. Rarely, though best, is when each of these qualities is found in good measure united, as with the Apostle Paul, in the same person —*Ed.*]

[53] May 19, 1768, Memorandum of proceedings....at Southampton. Misc. Church papers, McKesson Collection (Edwards section), HSP.

was published.[54] Eaton was mourned by his former students in particular; Oliver Hart told Samuel Jones that "his death is an unspeakable loss to the Baptist Interest in general and to his own church in particular."[55] Samuel Jones was running his own school along the same lines as Eaton's Academy at Hopewell. His school was financed in part by the Philadelphia Association. Students were bound to a trust which included Samuel Jones as trustee, for a sum of money. The obligation to pay back the money would be void as long as the student "justly and properly" sustained the character of minister of the gospel within seven years after the initial agreement. This agreement enabled several students to enter the Baptist ministry: Peter Smith, for instance, and Burgiss Allison.[56]

Samuel Jones exercised his ministerial authority with responsibility. He could, however, be a hard man of business in a slave-owning society and economy and decisive when crossed. In 1768, he complained at a Southampton meeting of business that Joseph Richardson had sold him a "wench as very good when she was one of the worst in the world."[57] Richardson promised to pay him compensation in front of a witness, but he later reneged. The proceedings of the Southampton meeting noted that Richardson had "represented the whole affair and some other things falsely," much to the injury of Jones's character. Richardson was suspended and in December 1769, excommunicated from membership.[58]

Samuel Jones's local influence and standing were enhanced through a growing network of contacts throughout the colonies. This network resulted from the principle of "association" and the

---

[54] Samuel Jones, *Resignation, A Funeral Sermon, occasioned by the death of the Rev Isaac Eaton, A.M. Late Minister of the Baptist Church, at Hopewell, in New Jersey, who departed this life, July 4, 1772. Preached at Hopewell, the 26th of the same month*. Philadelphia: James Humphreys, Jr., 1772.

[55] Oliver Hart to Samuel Jones, April 21, 1773. McKesson Collection (Jones section), HSP.

[56] Spencer, *The Early Baptists of Philadelphia*, 107.

[57] September 3, 1768, Memorandum of proceedings....at Southampton. Misc. Church papers, McKesson Collection (Edwards section), HSP.

[58] December 30, 1769, *Ibid*. [Pennsylvania, as with other colonies, did not pass laws against slavery until after Independence and statehood —*Ed*.]

missionary work of the Philadelphia Association. In 1766, the Philadelphia Association agreed to "yearly intercourse" by letters and messengers between associations to the "east and west of us."[59] John Gano, Abel Griffith and Noah Hammond were sent by the Association, at the request of James Manning, to Rhode Island, where they convinced the embryonic Warren Association of the desirability of "association." Samuel Jones wrote to them on behalf of the Philadelphia Association and stressed the fellowship, mutuality and greater familiarity which emanated from such an association. It is a letter which has been widely and frequently cited by American Baptist historians:

> A long course of experience and observation has taught us to have the highest sense of the advantages which come from association; nor indeed does the nature or thing speak any other language. For, as particular members are collected together and united in one body, which we call a particular church, to answer these ends and purposes which could not be accomplished by any single member, so a collection and union of churches into one associational body may easily be conceived capable of answering those still greater purposes which any particular church would not be equal to. And by the same reason, a union of associations will still increase the body in weight and strength and make it good that a threefold cord is not easily broken."[60]

Through "public service in the Baptist cause," Samuel Jones had, by the eve of the Revolution, become a major figure in Baptist life in Pennsylvania and beyond. He was an important fulcrum in an American network of Baptist communication. He corresponded with James Manning in Providence, Richard Furman in Charleston, Isaac Backus in Middleboro and several others. This network of communication extended across the Atlantic. In Samuel Jones's career, in his public and private lives, local and transatlantic influences were intertwined and interdependent. Before the Revolution, Baptists in America looked to their brethren in London and the Dissenting Deputies for means of redressing legal grievances. The New England Baptists used their

---

[59] Spencer, *The Early Baptists of Philadelphia*, 94.

[60] For example *Ibid*, 95; and H. Leon McBeth, *The Baptist Heritage: Four Centuries of Baptist Witness* (Nashville, TN: Broadman Press, 1987), 240.

transatlantic denominational connections to fight religious oppression in New England. At a time when religious groups were distancing themselves politically from the mother country, the New England Baptists in the 1770's, with the support of their brethren in Philadelphia (Samuel Jones included), were still pursuing traditional means of redressing their grievances.

Through his extensive contacts in New England, Samuel Jones became aware of their campaign against religious taxation, whereby Baptists and Quakers had to pay taxes to support a Congregational or Presbyterian ministry. Samuel Jones supported the leader of the New England Baptists' campaign for religious liberty, Isaac Backus. Jones sympathized with Backus, and in the centenary address of the Philadelphia Association which he gave in 1807, looking back over twenty-five years, he summed up the general Baptist feeling to the Revolution: "It seemed unreasonable to us, that we should be called upon to stand up with them in defense of liberty if, after all, it was to be liberty for one party to oppress another."[61] The Philadelphia Association, which was more deferential in its tone than the Warren Association in New England, agreed to help them defray the expenses of sending an agent to England so that "their cause be laid at the feet of our gracious sovereign."[62] Sums of money were collected in churches throughout Pennsylvania and the proceeds dispatched to agents in Philadelphia and New York and then sent to England. A committee was appointed by the Philadelphia Association to draw a memorandum addressed to Dr. Samuel Stennett, a London Baptist minister "in favour of our New England brethren's design."[63] Stennett's appeal to the Commissions of Trade and Plantations was successful and the Ashfield Law (named after the *cause celebre* of religious taxation in Ashfield, Hampshire County, Massachusetts) was rejected. To achieve complete religious liberty, Backus argued that the Baptists had to reject the system of religious taxation in its entirety and used the treatment of the Baptists by the Congregationalists as analogous to the treatment

---

[61] Samuel Jones, *A Century Sermon. Delivered in Philadelphia, at the Opening of the Philadelphia Baptist Association, October 6th, 1807* (Philadelphia: Bartram and Reynolds, 1807), as republished in Gillette, *Minutes of the Philadelphia Baptist Association*, 459-460.

[62] Spencer, *The Early Baptists of Philadelphia*, 99.

[63] *Ibid.*

of the colonists by Parliament. By the autumn of 1773, Backus hoped to win religious liberty without recourse to the king and wrote to his friend Samuel Jones in Pennepek to this effect in December 1773. He thanked Jones for procuring subscriptions to his *Appeal to the Public for Religious Liberty* (a sixty-two page tract McLoughlin has called "pietistic America's declaration of spiritual independence"), which "added to former kindnesses," wrote Backus, "demand my particular acknowledgements."[64] The New England Baptists took their case to Congress, to a conference with the Massachusetts delegates believed to be friends to religious liberty.[65] This conference was held in Carpenter's Hall on October 14, 1774, and among the Baptists present were Morgan Edwards, James Manning, Isaac Backus and Samuel Jones. To their disappointment, John and Samuel Adams claimed that if there was an establishment then it was a "slender one" and that the General Court of Massachusetts had treated the Baptists fairly "whatever might have been done by executive officers."

The difficult years of the Revolutionary War

When the war with the British broke out in April 1775, there was a great deal of suspicion concerning the loyalty of the Baptists both in New England and the Middle Colonies. The majority of the Baptists sprang to the patriotic ranks. The Delaware Valley was a military arena and Samuel Jones suffered directly from the activities of the enemy: "They took from me 2 horses, one wagon and part of the gears. The horses were worth about 10 pounds a piece and the wagon with what gears they took about 12. They also did damage in grazing their horses in the meadow and wheat field to the value of about 3 pounds."[66] The war disrupted the services of the local churches and also the meetings of the Association. In July 1778, Pennepek resolved to recommence

---

[64] William G. McLoughlin, *Isaac Backus and the American Pietistic Tradition* (Boston: Little, Brown and Co., 1967), 127; Isaac Backus to Samuel Jones, December 13, 1773. McKesson Collection (Jones section), HSP.

[65] See McLoughlin, *New England Dissent*, 1, part 7, chapter 30.

[66] Note on the reverse of a letter from Enoch Edwards to Samuel Jones, 1778, in Samuel Jones's hand. McKesson Collection (Edwards section), HSP.

communion after a disruption caused by the English army "being in our midst."[67] A woman was suspended from the membership of Pennepek on suspicion of collaboration with the enemy.[68] The Philadelphia Association record for 1777 contained one brief entry: "In consequence of the ravages of war, and Philadelphia being occupied by the British Army, the Association held no meeting this year."[69] The war also affected church discipline in an indirect way. Southampton attributed its undisciplined condition to "the coldness arising from sentiment respecting Whig and Tory principals [sic] which too much prevails almost amongst all classes of people."[70]

In the midst of the depravations of war, Samuel Jones and his family experienced a searing tragedy. In August of 1778, the Jones family lost two sons and a daughter from yellow fever. The boys, Thomas aged thirteen and Samuel aged ten, were buried together. Manning wrote to Jones: "I have heard of the trying Dispensations of divine Providence towards you in the loss of three of your children and amongst them your dear Tommy, that most promising boy...."[71]

After the Revolution, Backus addressed the argument that the Baptist cause of religious liberty might have been better served by standing back from involvement in the Revolution. He concluded that the cause of religious liberty had actually benefited from Revolution. A concurrence with the arbitrary claims of the English Parliament would have brought guilt upon their consciences; the cause of Revolution had become the cause of God.[72] Samuel Jones

---

67 July 30, 1778, Memorandum of meetings of preparations....Pennepek. McKesson Collection (Edwards section), HSP.

68 *Ibid*. Also quoted in Spencer, *The Early Baptists of Philadelphia*, 120.

69 Robert G. Torbet, *A Social History of the Philadelphia Baptist Association, 1701-1940* (Philadelphia: Westbrook Publishing Co., 1944), 50.

70 *Ibid*., 51.

71 James Manning to Samuel Jones, Providence, November 24, 1778. McKesson Collection (Jones section), HSP.

72 Isaac Backus, *A History of New England, with Particular Reference to the Denomination of Christians Called Baptists*, 2 (Providence, RI: John Carter, 1784): 299-300.

had joyful news to pass on to the Baptists of the North in this spirit in 1780. In April, he sent Backus the text, copied in his own hand, of a *Bill for Establishing Religious Freedom.*[73] The author of the bill was Thomas Jefferson. The bill had been put before the General Assembly of Virginia in November 1779, but was not enacted until 1785, when it effectively removed sectarian religion from politics in Virginia. Jones played a pivotal role in a Baptist network of communication which was sustained by associational contact. He fully realized the importance of the text he was conveying and its relevance to Isaac Backus. The sentiments, he told Backus, "are excellent not only in themselves, but also on account of the language in which they are conceived. You see I am not for eating my morsel alone, but want you should partake with me of the feast. I am persuaded they would be acceptable at any time to a man of your turn, and who has been so long and so usefully engaged in the same cause, but specially at such a time as this."[74] James Manning copied Samuel Jones's copy of the text in the *Providence Gazette* of May 13, 1780, and afterwards in the Worcester papers.

The transatlantic fellowship

After the Revolution, relationships amongst Baptists in England, Wales and America continued and intensified. Political considerations were more often than not thrust into the background. The main protagonist of transatlantic connection amongst the English Baptists was John Rippon (1751-1836).[75] In writing to James Manning in 1786, he asked for a few hymns from Manning and his American brethren to be included in the "Selection" of hymns which he was compiling, not "that we want hymns" he explained, "but a few American hymns in our English book would show we are yet brethren."[76] Rippon's *Baptist Annual*

---

73 Samuel Jones to Isaac Backus, April 17, 1780. Simon Gratz Collection, HSP.

74 *Ibid.*

75 For John Rippon, see Kenneth R. Manley, "John Rippon D.D., 1751-1836 and the Particular Baptists," D. Phil. thesis, Oxford University, 1967.

76 John Rippon to James Manning, no specific date, 1786. Rippon section, Archives of John Hay Library, Brown University.

Register was a conscious attempt to restore and continue the correspondence which the late "unhappy war" had interrupted. "When peace was restored, it was thought by several persons an object of considerable importance to open a new correspondence with the western world."[77] This "new correspondence" continued the themes which had interested Baptists before the war. Correspondence continued to be of mutual benefit, and lessons were drawn from the similar problems and issues which were experienced.

The leading Baptists on both sides of the Atlantic became active supporters and promoters of associations. Circular letters began to be exchanged between associations in England, Wales and America. John Rippon, as with so many other aspects of transatlantic connection, was instrumental in this exchange. Samuel Jones also regularly received the letters of the Welsh association from his new post-revolutionary contact, the Welsh Baptist historian Joshua Thomas (1719-1797).[78] This transatlantic exchange of associational circular letters was an extension into the transatlantic sphere of the fellowship which Baptists experienced within their own associations and with other associations. Transatlantic exchange gave Baptists the opportunity to enlarge on this fellowship.

Transatlantic correspondence was eagerly sought by the Baptist ministers. Isaac Backus noted in his diary for July 7, 1784: "Received a letter from Pennsylvania which mentions Mr. Timothy Thomas in London who would be glad of a correspondence with me, therefore on the 8th I wrote to him."[79] This "letter from Pennsylvania" had come from Samuel Jones, who was an avid disseminator of transatlantic correspondence. In this way Amer-

---

[77] John Rippon, *The Baptist Annual Register for 1790, 1791, 1792, and Part of 1793* (London: Dilly, Button, and Thomas, et al., 1793), 4.

[78] For Joshua Thomas, see "Memoirs of the Late Rev. Joshua Thomas, of Leominster," *The Evangelical Magazine*, 6 (1798), No. 3 (March): 89-99; *Dictionary of Welsh Biography*; Eric W. Hayden, "Joshua Thomas, Welsh Baptist Historian," *The Baptist Quarterly*, 23 (1969), No. 3 (July): 126-137; Hywel M. Davies, *Transatlantic Brethren. Rev. Samuel Jones (1735-1814) and His Friends: Baptists in Wales, Pennsylvania, and Beyond* (Cranbury, NJ: Associated University Presses, 1995), passim.

[79] William G. McLoughlin, ed., *The Diary of Isaac Backus* (Providence, RI: Brown University Press, 1979), 2: 1143.

ican Baptists came to know and share each others' transatlantic contacts. As a result of the growth in the transatlantic network, Baptists in England and Wales became more familiar with the advance of the Baptist denomination in America. The connections with James Manning and Rhode Island College also continued after the Revolution.

Samuel Jones felt a great affinity with Baptists in England and Wales, particularly "our brethren in [my] native country,"[80] but he was not as active as his friend Manning in Rhode Island and Joshua Thomas in Wales in participating in the Baptist Atlantic. One of the reasons for this reluctance lay in the fact that Samuel Jones was a direct competitor with John Rippon for the Baptist market in hymnbooks in the United States.

In 1790, Samuel Jones together with his former pupil Burgiss Allison (1753-1827), published a hymnbook for the use of Baptist churches on behalf of the Philadelphia Association.[81] They had three objectives in mind in publishing their hymnbook.[82] Firstly, their hymnbook would be considerably cheaper than Watts' *Psalms and Hymns.* Secondly, their hymnbook would be more convenient in that it would contain under one cover the "quintessence" of Watts' *Psalms and Hymns*, together with hymns taken from other authors. Lastly their hymnbook would be easier to use in public worship—the pages would be numbered and the hymns would be identified by the page number, thereby avoiding the minister having to say "the 43rd hymn of the 2nd book, omitting the 3rd and 4th verses long metre." Samuel Jones used his extensive connections to circulate the hymnbooks for purchase. He came face to face with opposition from the churches to a publication which they dismissed as shoddy, and at the same time he faced direct competition from a transatlantic rival, John Rippon. Rippon was both flattered and dismayed to find that two

---

80 Samuel Jones to Joshua Thomas, no date. McKesson Collection (Jones section), HSP.

81 Samuel Jones and Burgiss Allison, *A Selection of Psalms and Hymns, Done under the Appointment of the Philadelphia Association.* Philadelphia: Robert Aitkin and Sons, 1790. [A second (1801), third (1807) and fourth edition (1819) of the work were also printed —*Ed.*]

82 Samuel Jones to unnamed minister, no date. McKesson Collection (Jones section). HSP.

unauthorized editions of his *Selection of Hymns* (1787) were printed in America.[83]

The Allison/Jones *Selection of Psalms and Hymns* used many of the hymns from Rippon's *Selection*. As well as being derivative, their work was also poorly produced. The Baptist church at Baltimore wrote to Samuel Jones and asked him whether the hymnbooks they had received from him could be replaced by a "more perfect Impression."[84] The Baltimore Baptists believed the hymnbooks to be useless for their purpose. Samuel Jones, a man of short temper and often very stubborn, was incensed. He wrote to the minister at Baltimore, Lewis Richards, and accused his members of being both unjust and dishonest. Richards defended his flock. They would take the hymnbooks provided they were as accurate as could be reasonably expected. Richards added that the Philadelphia Association itself would be stigmatized if it was "to suffer so incorrect an Impression to go into the world.[85]

As well as considerable problems caused by inferior printing, Samuel Jones also suffered the aforementioned direct competition from John Rippon. Jones tried to sell his hymnbooks to Richard Furman in Charleston. Furman was grateful for the collection, which he would recommend to his "connections" but, he wrote Jones, "most of our Friends in Charleston have been obtaining Rippon's selection lately, which may be some obstacle to their purchasing this directly."[86]

For his part, John Rippon thought very little of Samuel Jones's hymnbook. He was astonished by its numerous typographical errors and envied the liberty which Jones had to take what he pleased from Isaac Watts. "I'll confess that the pirating of two editions of my book in America while it gives me pain affords me

---

[83] Manley, "John Rippon and the Particular Baptists," 190.

[84] Alex McKim to Samuel Jones, Baltimore, May 16, 1791. McKesson Collection (Jones section), HSP.

[85] Lewis Richards to Samuel Jones, November 10, 1792. McKesson Collection (Jones section), HSP. [The poor quality of the hymnbook is unaccountable since Robert Aitkin was an otherwise reputable printer in Philadelphia —*Ed.*]

[86] Richard Furman to Samuel Jones, February 19, 1791. McKesson Collection (Jones section), HSP.

pleasure. May yours and mine do much good!"[87] Rippon tried to be as diplomatic as possible and endeavored to mollify the influential leader of the Philadelphia Baptist Association.

Rippon's remarks concerning his hymnbooks offended the sensitive Samuel Jones and Rippon was swift to apologize. "I ASK YOUR PARDON A THOUSAND TIMES," he printed.[88]

The general question of American dependence upon English publications was a matter of principle as well as a matter of financial consideration for Samuel Jones. Dependence upon English books and scholarship was a continuation of a prerevolutionary tendency which seemed to militate against their independence as Americans. Samuel Jones and James Manning were proud Americans as well as Baptists, and Jones believed that American Baptists were too dependent upon English scholarship. Dependence upon Britain in the field of learning was again experienced when Manning died in 1791. Samuel Jones, who received an honorary M.A. from Rhode Island College in 1769 and an Honorary Doctor of Divinity from the College of Pennsylvania in 1788, was offered the presidency of Rhode Island College by his former Hopewell schoolmate David Howell, but declined it on account of his age.[89] There were few American Baptists deemed to be of adequate academic standing for the position of president, so again American Baptists looked across the Atlantic. There was astonishment expressed in England that there was no one amongst the American Baptists to fill Manning's place.[90] Samuel Jones answered frankly, "we have but few learned men among the Baptists in America and then every learned man is not qualified for the station."[91]

---

[87] John Rippon to Samuel Jones, February 7, 1793. McKesson Collection (Jones section), HSP.

[88] John Rippon to Samuel Jones, August 24, 1793. McKesson Collection (Jones section), HSP.

[89] David Howell to Samuel Jones, August 3, 1791. McKesson Collection (Jones section), HSP.

[90] Morgan Jones to Samuel Jones, March 1, 1792. McKesson Collection (Jones section), HSP.

[91] Samuel Jones to Morgan Jones, July 16, 1792. McKesson Collection (Jones section), HSP.

An ambivalent attitude towards dependence upon Britain did not interrupt Samuel Jones's own personal transatlantic correspondence with the Welsh Baptist, Joshua Thomas. This correspondence was concerned initially with the history of the Welsh Baptists on the Delaware and was therefore relevant to Jones's own family background and history. It was later broadened to include themes such as the advance of the gospel in their respective countries, news of Rhode Island College, and news of their associations. Joshua Thomas was instrumental in introducing Samuel Jones to other correspondents in England and Wales. Through this correspondence, he strengthened and revealed his own self-identity as a Welshman.

The controversy over laying on of hands

As well as a mutually useful exchange of historical information about common ancestors, Joshua Thomas's correspondence also influenced Samuel Jones in a direct and personal way. Samuel Jones persuaded himself from information provided by Joshua Thomas that the doctrine of laying on of hands practiced by the churches of the Philadelphia Baptist Association, stemmed from Welsh custom and not from scriptural authority.[92] The issue of the laying on of hands first arose in their correspondence as a result of Thomas's claim in his Welsh History of 1778 that the Pennepek church was guilty of irregularity in its founding years.[93] Jones was intensely loyal to his church and to its history, and was hurt by his friend's accusation, which Thomas had based on a Welsh Tract source.

Thomas described the historical development of imposition of hands in Wales in a collection of materials, entitled a "Historical Sketch of the Debate upon the Laying on of Hands."[94] This "Sketch" was completed by 1782. Thomas wrote from a typically neutral stand-point, neither decrying nor supporting the laying on

---

92 [In their view, not only were church officers such as pastors and deacons to undergo imposition of hands (as generally practiced today), but every baptized believer, as a New Testament ordinance in order for membership. The debate was over this latter practice of making it a mandatory rite for every baptized believer —*Ed.*]

93 Thomas, *Hanes y Bedyddwyr*, 346.

94 National Library of Wales, MS21, 161C.

of hands. His aim was "not to stir up contention but to promote peace, free inquiry and free practising according to what is seen."[95] According to Thomas's historical account, the first reference to imposition occurred at the "Association" at Llantrisant in June 1654. Support for laying on of hands as a "foundation principle" grew after 1655, mainly, Thomas surmised, as a result of lay pressure. In 1668, the large and influential church at Rhydwilym in Pembrokeshire was persuaded that imposition of hands on the baptized was right—a conviction brought by Welsh emigrants to America. Joshua Thomas then brought his account up to the present day. He informed Samuel Jones in 1784: " 'Tis remarkable, I had two brothers, both in the ministry, one very zealous for and the other as steady against the practice."[96]

By shedding light on the origins of the practice in Wales, the exchange of information with Thomas confirmed Jones's doubts and enabled him to consign the practice to Welsh custom and not to scriptural authority. Jones was more than prepared to use matters pertaining to Wales to suit his own purposes as a Baptist writing with the needs of the Philadelphia Association in mind. He was a firm opponent of imposition as a fundamental ordinance of the Gospel. His position in this respect was clarified and reinforced by the historical and ethnic perspective which he derived from his correspondence with Joshua Thomas.

The Philadelphia Association had long endorsed the laying on of hands. In 1729, the church at Philadelphia had queried the status of a minister who was opposed to the doctrine. The Association stated categorically that such a minister should not be allowed to administer the ordinances of baptism or the Lord's Supper.[97] By 1783, the Association's position had moderated and it was resolved to admit any person who had scruples concerning imposition into the fellowship of the church.[98] Samuel Jones played a leading part in achieving this resolution.

Among Samuel Jones's papers is a printed, one-sheet handbill entitled *A brief History of the Imposition of Hands on baptised*

---

[95] *Ibid.*

[96] Joshua Thomas to Samuel Jones, September 18, 1784. McKesson Collection (Jones section), HSP.

[97] Gillette, *Minutes of the Philadelphia Baptist Association*, 30.

[98] *Ibid.*, 193.

Persons, in which he delineated the development of his thinking on the subject. The *brief History* was probably written in the late 1780's. According to this account, Jones had not questioned the doctrine until he was ordained, when he had to implement the laying on of hands for the first time. He investigated the Scriptures more closely and found to his dismay that in the Gospel it "was practiced for the purpose of conveying miraculous gifts, and only by Apostles who had that power." He confessed that he continued to lay his hands on the baptized despite his reservations because he "had not resolution sufficient to stem the torrent of custom." Jones attributed the laying on of hands to "custom" and not to the authority of Scripture, and this custom he realized through his dialogue with Joshua Thomas, had originated in Wales. Jones concluded that the laying on of hands "was imported here from Wales, where it took its rise on the authority of a few members in one church only." This church was Rhydwilym, the "mother church" of the Welsh Tract Baptist Church in Delaware, a church which had included an article on the laying on of hands in its own Confession of Faith.[99] Therefore the imposition of hands in Pennsylvania had arisen as a result of a historical legacy from Wales, writes Jones, for "in England they knew nothing of it." Since so many of the early churches of the Philadelphia Association had ministers from Wales "and the power of the Association resting in their hands, the practise became general through the whole Association." The churches without a Welsh background or influence knew nothing about it.

Samuel Jones's opposition to the laying on of hands did not go unchallenged. David Jones, his former schoolmate, was deeply shocked by the Association's resolution of 1783 and, defending imposition as a fundamental ordinance, redirected his anger against the leaders of the Association, Samuel Jones in particular, in his 1786 pamphlet, *The Doctrine of "Laying on of Hands" Examined and Vindicated*. This defense was aimed at the decision of the Philadelphia Association in 1783 to downgrade the historical importance of the laying on of hands by not making it a bar to communion. This resolution on the part of the Association reversed an article of faith contained in its Confession and was a disturbing precedent: "By this example, a future Association might resolve another article away as no bar of communion, till, at last,

---

99 The Rhydwilym Confession of Faith is printed in full in *Trafodion Cymdeithas Hanes Bedyddwyr Cymru.* Caerfyrddin: Cymdeithas Hanes Bedyddwyr Cymru, 1979.

it would be impossible to know what is the faith and practice of a regular Baptist church."[100] He predicted there would be "confusion in our churches" and even worse—schism.

Samuel Jones's handbill revived the quarrel and drew a direct reply from David Jones in the form of a seventy-two page tract entitled *A True History of Laying on of Hands upon Baptized Believers as Such: in Answer to a Hand-Bill*. The *True History* was published in 1805 at Burlington, New Jersey. The emotional pitch of the *True History* is high and the emotion did partly spring from a defense of tradition. David Jones was a son of the Welsh Tract. He recalled Samuel visiting the Welsh Tract and baptizing a believer but refusing the laying on of hands. David Jones was informed by many of the Welsh Tract members that this was a matter of great grief to them, that they had submitted for "peace sake," but that "none have been admitted after that disorderly manner to this day."[101] David Jones had little difficulty in dismissing the historical evidence of Samuel's handbill as inappropriate and unnecessary. He should have consulted Scripture, "but instead of that, we have been amused with some trifling details of his correspondence with one Joshua Thomas, who by his name I suppose to be a Welshman."[102] David Jones argued that Samuel should have applied to God for relief of his "perplexity," "instead of sending more than three thousand miles for advice, to a Welshman too."[103] His stance on the Welsh and the Welsh in America was ambivalent, sarcastic and dismissive, but also a shared sense of heritage, a sense of knowing which target to hit that would hurt the most. The language of David Jones's attack was intemperate and even bitter; when he saw Samuel Jones's handbill with the minutes of the Association, he was sorry that Samuel "could not die in peace and not again trouble the

---

100 David Jones, *The Doctrine of "Laying on of Hands" Examined and Vindicated* (Philadelphia: Francis Bailey, 1786), 3.

101 David Jones, *A True History of Laying on of Hands upon Baptized Believers as Such: in Answer to a Hand-Bill, Intitled, A Brief History of the Imposition of Hands on Baptized Persons; Published by Samuel Jones, D.D. Wherein His Mistakes are Attempted to be Corrected* (Burlington, NJ: S. C. Ustick, 1805), 14.

102 *Ibid.*, 4-5.

103 *Ibid.*, 15-16.

church on the subject of laying on of hands upon baptized believers..."[104] The intensity of invective is remarkable when the debate was not a point, as David Jones himself admitted, "on which salvation depends."[105]

In 1783, Samuel Jones had his first work published, his sermon on the doctrine of "God's Covenant," by the Philadelphia Association. It had been originally printed as their Circular Letter two years before.[106] This sermon made Samuel Jones's name as a theologian of some weight. It was of functional importance, since it had been published to refute the Universalist heresy promulgated by Elhanan Winchester (1757-1797), then minister at the First Baptist Church in Philadelphia.[107] The orthodox majority in the church had requested the intervention of a counsel of ministers from the Association in their behalf. The opposition of the Association was decisive in getting Winchester excluded from the church, because there was a sizeable (and determined) minority there who had become loyal to Winchester. In his Circular Letter on "God's Covenant," Jones showed the manner in which God works to redeem lost men through Jesus Christ. The letter took up Winchester's heresy by referring to the same Scripture in Genesis which Winchester had used in his sermon, *The Seed of the Woman Bruising the Serpent's Head* (Philadelphia, 1781), to justify universal restoration on the grounds of God's covenant with Adam. Jones argued that this passage did not refer to a covenant between

---

[104] *Ibid.*, 66.

[105] *Ibid.* [Both the handbill by Samuel Jones and David Jones's lengthy reply in 1805 have been reprinted in full in Rogers and Wolever, *The Life, Journal and Works of David Jones*, Part IV, "Controversial Works concerning the origin and practice of Laying on of Hands," 527-578 —*Ed.*]

[106] Samuel Jones, *The Doctrine of the Covenants. A Sermon Preached at Pennepeck in Pennsylvania, September 14, 1783. Wherein is Shewn, That there never was a Covenant of Works made with Adam; nor any other Covenant ever made with Man, respecting Things purely of a Spiritual Nature*. Philadelphia: F. Bailey, 1783. [Jones's letter on "God's Covenant" was originally presented before the Association on Thursday morning, October 25, 1781. See Gillette, *Minutes of the Philadelphia Baptist Association*, 174-178 —*Ed.*]

[107] For Elhanan Winchester, see Joseph R. Sweeney, "Elhanan Winchester and the Universal Baptists," Ph.D. thesis, University of Pennsylvania, 1969.

God and Man, but referred rather to the discovery, revelation and manifestation of God's Will and purposes for the eternal life of Man. The term "covenant" did not mean a compact between God and Man; on the contrary, it implied a statute, an ordinance or a decree. Through his careful definition of "covenant," Jones reaffirmed the justice of God and the doctrine of particular election against the general salvation proposed by Winchester.[108] This sermon established Jones's role as a theological trouble-shooter and a definer of "orthodox" on behalf of the Association, a reputation further confirmed in 1783 as the author of the Association's Circular letter of that year on "the freedom of man's will." In this letter Samuel argued that a distinction should be drawn between that which is natural and that which is sinful, the former being from God, the latter from us. Thus the power of speech was God given, but blasphemy came from the corruption of the human heart.[109] The next year the Philadelphia Association met at New York, but Jones was for once absent. Yet even in his absence, he was recommended to write on their behalf to those churches in the "western parts of this Association," in order to "press them to a due regard" as to the responsibilities of their associational connection and correspondence, since there had been "much inattention" on the part of some of these churches.[110]

It was partly on behalf of the Association that Jones undertook to visit Kentucky in the spring of 1786. He had been invited by Elijah Craig, one of the few Baptist ministers in the territory, to establish a college there along the same lines as his boarding school at Pennepek. Jones had been strongly recommended to Craig by Thomas Ustick, and as the fellow Philadelphia Baptist minister wrote him: "When Mr. Jones comes to realise the prospect of that luxuriant soil and the simplicity of their manners by whom it is inhabited together with all the great and growing prospects of that new discovered Canaan, I think it will be hardly possible for him ever after to be contented upon his old and I suppose worn out plantation at Pennepek."[111] Samuel visited

---

108 Jones, *The Doctrine of the Covenants,* 44. See also *Transatlantic Brethren,* 161-163.

109 Gillette, *Minutes of the Philadelphia Baptist Association*, 196-197.

110 *Ibid.*, 201.

111 Thomas Ustick to Elijah Craig, March 1786. Ustick Collection, American Baptist Historical Society, Atlanta, Georgia.

Kentucky knowing that his position at Pennepek was unassailable. In March 1786, Pennepek took the unusual step of establishing itself as a chartered body with the minister as trustee and president of the Board.[112] He returned from Kentucky by the end of the year—it had been a successful visit. He had established a school which he promised to supply with instructors from his own boarding school at Pennepek. He had purchased some land there and also preached the gospel. He used his experience of gospel success in Kentucky as a theme in his correspondence with Joshua Thomas. Their transatlantic correspondence dwelt on the spread of the gospel with particular reference to the increase of the Baptist denomination in their respective countries. Samuel Jones was active on behalf of the Philadelphia Association in Kentucky, while Joshua Thomas supported and encouraged the Welsh Association's mission to North Wales.[113]

In November 1785, Samuel Jones had mentioned to Joshua Thomas his regret "that emigration from my native country to America has in a manner ceased for these 30 or 40 years past."[114] As a beneficiary of emigration himself, Jones was sure that it would be in their "interest to come over." Emigration from Wales to America increased for a number of reasons during the early years of the French Revolution. Joshua Thomas advised Samuel to be wary and avoid the indiscriminate accommodation of emigrants, for there were, he admitted "very different springs of uneasiness."[115] Jones was aware of the varying character of the Baptist emigrants through his own direct experience, but at the same time he was sensitive to the bias and prejudices which were held by ministers in England and Wales in attributing a certain "character" to ministers who had left their midst to preach and settle in America. He was prepared to stand by John Stanford of New York, whom he thought had been traduced by his brethren in England. Jones preferred to trust his own judgment of men based on his experience of them in America and forgive any misde-

---

112 Spencer, *The Early Baptists of Philadelphia*, 41.

113 Davies, *Transatlantic Brethren*, Chapter 5.

114 Samuel Jones to Joshua Thomas, November 29, 1785. McKesson Collection (Jones section), HSP.

115 Joshua Thomas to Samuel Jones, November 4, 1796. McKesson Collection (Jones section), HSP.

meanors of a foreign past as essentially irrelevant to their present situations.

Samuel Jones used his transatlantic connections to tap the pro-American sentiment of his Welsh brethren. He was an active encourager of emigration and tried to sell his own land in Kentucky to prospective emigrants. His motivation was only partly mercenary. His main motive was to share the benefits, both spiritual and material, of America with his fellow brethren in Wales. His American patriotism was conceived in religious terms —America had a providential role in the Divine scheme. By the same token, Samuel was an inveterate enemy of England and the impiety which he associated with it. England had never forgiven America for its "humiliation" in the War of Independence "after spending so many millions to save it."[116] Samuel was also convinced that England realized the benefits which emigration would bring to those who emigrated and that this added to their "humiliation." Jones presented emigration to America to his brethren elsewhere as being "always in their interest."[117] Jones confirmed from the American perspective what radical, disaffected Baptists in Wales and England held to be the case: namely that Britain was in absolute decline. Consequently, at a time of decline, predicted by the Scriptures, emigration was a necessary option for them to take. Jones was a staunch advocate of America and of American republicanism. His particular identification with the land of his birth made him particularly anxious that his Welsh countrymen and fellow believers should share in its benefits. An undated draft letter begins: "What would you think of encouraging some of our brethren in Wales to come over?"[118] His extensive transatlantic contacts, combined with this denominational and ethnic identification, made Samuel a well-known figure, albeit by reputation, among the transatlantic brethren. A group of Welsh artisans in New York collectively petitioned Samuel Jones for aid and claimed: "We heard much of you in our native land that you

---

116 Samuel Jones to Morgan Jones, July 16, 1792. McKesson Collection (Jones section), HSP.

117 *Ibid.*

118 Samuel Jones to Joshua Thomas, no date, but probably some time in 1789. The letter refers to recent funeral of Thomas Jones, who died that year. McKesson Collection (Jones section), HSP.

was a well wisher to your countrymen."[119] Another Welsh Baptist wrote, "your name is known in our country among the Brethren of every denomination."[120] Even allowing for some flattering overstatement, there is an element of truth in these remarks. Samuel Jones's correspondence from Wales is immense, and there are extant over seventy letters from twenty Welsh-born correspondents (excluding Morgan Edwards). Jones described the material benefits of moving to America and also tried to facilitate their passage and settlement. He would make the land he owned in Kentucky available to settlers on easy terms, but he realized that even such attractive propositions would not counter the "hiraeth" of the Welsh who "would for the first few years be longing for the onions and leeks of Egypt."[121] His belief in the benefits of emigration was sincere and was based on the conviction that "we live in a land of liberty in every sense of the word."[122] Welsh Baptists were welcomed in Pennepek, both in the church and in the Jones's household. It was also two-way traffic across the Atlantic. Enoch Edwards, the son of Alexander Edwards and former student of Samuel Jones, traveled in England and Wales, using his minister's connections, as a land agent for John Nicholson. Baptists traveled long distances to visit him, including some who were already in correspondence with Samuel Jones.[123]

In 1793, a letter appeared in Morgan John Rhys's Welsh magazine which referred to Samuel Jones in Welsh as "Samuel Jones, Cymro"—"Samuel Jones, a Welshman."[124] To newly-arrived immigrants from Wales, Samuel Jones's identity as a Welshman

---

119 "Welsh artisans" to Samuel Jones, April 10, 1795. McKesson Collection (Jones section), HSP.

120 John Williams to Samuel Jones, May 6, 1795. McKesson Collection (Jones section), HSP.

121 Samuel Jones to Joshua Thomas, no date, probably 1788. McKesson Collection (Jones section), HSP.

122 Samuel Jones to Morgan Jones, October 31, 1791. McKesson Collection (Jones section), HSP.

123 For Enoch Edwards' trip to England and Wales, see Davies, *Transatlantic Brethren*, 208-211.

124 "Taith at y Madogion. Copi o lythyr oddiwrth John Evans o'r Waunfawr, yn Arfon, at ei frawd," *Cylchgrawn Cymraeg*, 2 (May, 1793): 115.

was not in doubt. In the oration he preached at Jones's funeral, William Staughton (1770-1829), a Baptist minister and immigrant from England, said of him: "If he cherished a peculiar regard for the Welsh as his country-men, it never prevented the flow of Christian affection to any of the followers of God."[125] His peculiar regard for the Welsh was a particular manifestation of his general fellowship to "any of the followers of God."

His established reputation and closing days

Samuel Jones's reputation was made by and large through his work on behalf of the Philadelphia Association. His long-standing ministry, his scholarship, his Calvinism and his business acumen made him a leading light within the Association. Samuel Jones was in great demand to counter heretical teaching or unorthodoxy. For example, John Stancliff beseeched him to go to Cape May in the summer of 1790, to counter the universalist teachings there.[126] It was Jones who, on behalf of the Association, revised Morgan Edwards's *Materials for a History of the Baptist Churches in the State of New Jersey* (1792). Jones also amended and revised the Association's System of Discipline, which was then published in 1798.[127] It was with intentional irony that one Baptist referred to the Jones's farmhouse as the "Bishop's Palace" and to Jones as "his Lordship" in a letter of 1805, but these remarks revealed Samuel Jones's high status amongst the Baptists, not only within the Philadelphia Association, but beyond as well.[128] Jones was one

---

[125] William Staughton, *The Servant of God Concluding His Labours. A Sermon on the Death of The Rev. Samuel Jones, D. D. Delivered before the Baptist Church and Congregation at Pennepek, of which he had been the beloved and affectionate Pastor, upwards of 51 years* (Philadelphia: R. P. and W. Anderson, 1814), 28.

[126] John Stancliff to Samuel Jones, August 4, 1790. McKesson Collection (Jones section), HSP.

[127] Samuel Jones, *A Treatise of Church Discipline, and a Directory. Done by Appointment of the Philadelphia Association*. Philadelphia: S. C. Ustick, 1798.

[128] John Stanford to Samuel Jones, July 28, 1805. McKesson Collection (Jones section), HSP.

of the three asked by the New York and Warwick Associations in New York City in 1803 to help to reconcile their differences.

Samuel Jones was not a sentimental man, he brooked no opposition in business, but he was held in high esteem locally in Pennepek as a man of business, farmer and landowner. His former students also remembered him and Mrs. Jones with affection. Samuel Jones was a devoted family man. Since their loss in 1778, Samuel and Sylvia Jones had concentrated their affections upon their only surviving daughter, Sarah or Sally Jones. On July 23, 1802, Samuel's wife Sylvia died. Jones came to rely increasingly on his son-in-law, Theophilus Harris, an immigrant from Wales,[129] who had married Sarah (her second husband, she was the widow of the Philadelphia merchant, Robert Henderson). Theophilus Harris was admitted to the church at Pennepek in 1808.[130] In 1810, Samuel Jones sold his 100-acre farm at Pennepek to Harris for $8,000. Harris was to pay him $2,000 in four installments.[131]

In his advancing years, Samuel Jones was widely regarded in high esteem as the *eminence grise* of the Philadelphia Association. His advice was more eagerly sought than ever. The younger Baptist ministers consulted him about any innovations and encouraged his support.[132] It was a compliment to his influence and standing that he was invited to give the sermon to commemorate the centenary of the Association in 1807.[133] The

---

[129] For Theophilus Harris see John H. Moore, "Theophilus Harris's Thoughts on Emigrating to America in 1793," *William and Mary Quarterly.* Third Series (Williamsburg, VA: Institute of Early American History and Culture), 36 (1979), No. 4 (October): 602-614.

[130] Meetings of Preparation and Business, Pennepek, (Edwards section), HSP.

[131] "On the third day of May 1810 it was agreed between Samuel Jones of Lower Dublin and Theophilus Harris of Philadelphia..." McKesson Collection (Henderson section), HSP.

[132] For example, William Rogers, William White, Thomas Shields, I. Healy, B. Allison, W. Staughton to Samuel Jones, January 14, 1813. McKesson Collection (Jones section), HSP.

[133] Samuel Jones, *A Century Sermon. Delivered in Philadelphia, at the Opening of the Philadelphia Baptist Association, October 6th, 1807* (Philadelphia: Bartram and Reynolds, 1807), which may be seen in Gillette, *Minutes of the Philadelphia Baptist Association*, 453-468.

sermon was a *tour de force*, the work of an accomplished historian, and was a reverential and balanced historical analysis of the Philadelphia Association. As Samuel Jones concluded, it was well worthwhile "to devote one hour, once in a hundred years at least, to review the ways and doings of God with his church and people, in accomplishing the purposes and decrees of his grace and goodness."[134] It is also the sermon of an *American* Baptist. No specific claims were attributed to contributions made by non-American elements such as the Welsh, to the development of the Philadelphia Association.

Jones pursued his life to its full measure. He was deeply beloved by his family, his church and his neighbors. He was materially comfortable, to say the least, and when he died on February 7, 1814, untypically leaving no will, his estate was valued at $40,000.[135] He was buried at the back of the Pennepek meetinghouse at the side of his wife and the row of little gravestones for his children, who had died in their youth.

---

[134] *Ibid.*, 468.

[135] Letter of Administration granted to Theophilus Harris on the 14th day of February, 1814, to the estate of Samuel Jones deceased. Archives, Philadelphia City Hall.

Further Reading

Hywel M. Davies. *Transatlantic Brethren. Rev. Samuel Jones (1735-1814) and His Friends: Baptists in Wales, Pennsylvania, and Beyond*. Cranbury, NJ: Associated University Presses, 1995.

Abram D. Gillette, ed. *Minutes of the Philadelphia Baptist Association, 1707-1807*. Philadelphia: American Baptist Publication Society, 1851; reprinted Tricentennial Edition with new comprehensive indexes, maps and illustrations, Springfield, MO: Particular Baptist Press, 2002.

Horatio G. Jones, Jr. *Historical Sketch of the Lower Dublin (or Pennepek) Baptist Church. With Notices of the Pastors*. Morrisania, NY, 1869; facsimile reprint in James L. Clark, *To Set Them in Order; Some Influences of the Philadelphia Baptist Association Upon Baptists of America to 1814*. Springfield, MO: Particular Baptist Press, 2001, 367-411.

David Jones (1736-1820)

DAVID JONES
1736 - 1820

by George Truett Rogers

Do the times make the man or the man make the times? David Jones, 1736-1820, could hardly be credited with "making" the time of the American Revolution, though he did play a small, yet significant, role in that period. However, the times most certainly helped make the man in his case. Combining the national conflict with the energy and enthusiasm of his physical, spiritual, familial and energetic personality, David Jones and his times seem to have been a perfect match. The combination of national and international revolution, warfare and nation building and an energetic natural leader, met. Baptist work was growing in the new world, and Jones became an integral part of that growth in both pastoral ministry and military chaplaincy for all his adult life.

These were years of the ending of the long English-French struggle for control of North America, the fight for independence, the formation of a new government, the enlargement of our western frontiers, and a second war with Great Britain. This minister, soldier, farmer, missionary, doctor, and writer threw himself into every phase of his religion and his country's activities. He was a leader among his Baptist contemporaries as a vital part of the Philadelphia Baptist Association. He was an early and well known soldier-chaplain in three wars and a militiaman in another. He was a pastor of several important Baptist churches. He traveled in the West, attempting to evangelize the Native Americans. He was pressed into service as a doctor during the Revolution, and in the midst of all the above, he maintained and enlarged his land holdings.

Brief biography of David Jones

An understanding of the early Welsh settlers in Delaware is necessary to appreciate David Jones, and many other Welsh Baptists, and their unique influence on later American history. An unknown writer noted that need for understanding when the following words were penned concerning descendants of early Welsh Tract families. Those descendants were primarily of the Morgan and Griffith families, the heritage of David Jones, born May 12, 1736:

> If we would understand our present drift and the lines upon which we, as a people, are moving socially, politically, and religiously, we must study that portion of our history which preceded the immense foreign emigration of the last forty years. It was during that period that the ideals we as a people are endeavoring, consciously or unconsciously, to realize, and which the necessity is imposed upon us of realizing, were wrought into the very inner nature of our people.[1]

A large immigration of settlers from South Wales came to America in 1701. Settling temporarily in Philadelphia, they negotiated with William Penn for a tract of land to the south where they might maintain their religious, linguistic, and other social customs. "Penn granted to David Evans and William Davis thirty thousand acres of land to be divided and deeded to settlers from South Wales." In 1703, they "set [their church] meetings in order" at Pencader Hundred, "placing their Meeting House on the banks of Christiana Creek, at the foot of Iron Hill."[2] That land is now part of the state of Delaware.

David Jones's family joined the American Welsh immigrants in 1710. His great grandparents were John Griffith and Jane Rhydderch, widow of Morgan ap Rhydderch of Wales. The tradition of the Welsh Tract holds that a brother of Morgan ap Rhydderch, Rhees, "was a soldier in Cromwell's Army. William A. Johnson, in his history of Cecil County, Maryland, embodying this general tradition says: he was 'an officer and served in Cromwell's Army in the troublesome times that preceded the trial and execution of Charles I.' "[3] John and Jane Rhydderch Griffith came to America in 1710 with at least two children, Benjamin and Sarah, joining the Welsh Tract Baptist Church on their arrival from Wales.

---

[1] "Descendants of Early Welsh Tract Families, Newark, Delaware: The Morgans and Griffiths," typescript in the Historical Society of Delaware, Wilmington, Delaware, n.d., n.a., 1.

[2] *Records of the Welsh Tract Baptist Meeting, Pencader Hundred, New Castle County, Delaware, 1701 to 1828* (Wilmington: The Historical Society of Delaware, 1904), 3, 8; "Descendants of Early Welsh Tract Families," 1. The church had been constituted in Wales in 1701.

[3] *Ibid.*, ix.

These Welsh Baptists tended to be exclusive in their religious associations, preferring not to unite with American Baptist churches of similar faith and order. Two reasons were given for their desire to remain separate: retention of the Welsh language in public worship and the practice of certain unique doctrinal matters, especially the practice of the laying on of hands on baptized believers. They obviously continued their use of Welsh since it was stated that "The gospel was preached in the Welsh language in this meeting [Welsh Tract Baptist meetinghouse] until about the year 1800."[4]

David Jones was described as "about five feet ten inches in height, of a spare habit of body."[5] He gave poor health as one of the reasons for his later traveling to preach to Indians, military campaigns and looking for land—seemingly strenuous activities for one in poor health. Perhaps a more understandable reason for his many travels was given in a personal note to a friend: "you know me to be a great Rambler."[6] And ramble he did, through preaching, travels to Ohio Indian country, military campaigns in three wars, and numerous trips up and down the eastern seaboard, well into his late 70's.

One item began to recur in his diary during the years following the Revolutionary War: frequent and lengthy visits away from his home and church. His grandson attributed those visits to a previously established pattern of travel during the Revolutionary War. "His previous active life made him useless as a settled pastor and hence he frequently visited Delaware and the Jerseys, preaching as he went."[7] One should question the choice of the word "useless" as a settled pastor, since each of Jones's churches experienced physical growth during his pastorates. Also, his visits did, indeed, include "Delaware and the Jerseys," but of far more frequency and duration were his treks to the Ohio River Valley on

---

[4] *Records of the Welsh Tract Baptist Meeting*, 4.

[5] David Jones, *A Journal of Two Visits Made to Some Nations of Indians on the West Side of the River Ohio, in the Years 1772, 1773* (Burlington, VT: Isaac Collins, 1774), 38-39.

[6] MS letter of David Jones to Nancy Botts, dated August 16, 1775. American Baptist Historical Society, Atlanta, Georgia.

[7] Horatio G. Jones, Jr., "A Memoir of the Rev. David Jones A. M. by his Grandson Horatio Gates Jones of Leverington, Near Philadelphia," 21. MS in the collections of the American Baptist Historical Society, Atlanta. Hereafter cited as Jones, "Memoir."

visitations to his personal land holdings. His own estimation of being a rambler seems justified.

His temperament was sometimes rather brittle. Given his appointment to numerous positions within Baptist organizations such as the Philadelphia Baptist Association, his three military service appointments until he was almost 80 years of age, and his reception as a writer for several publications, it is obvious that he had the ability to work harmoniously with his contemporaries. However, when provoked or challenged, he also demonstrated a censorious side of his personality. Several instances of such behavior are recorded by churches he served, close companions and Jones himself.

As a young man seeking ordination at the Middletown Baptist Church in 1764, he claimed it was his "right" and reproached the church for their delay in ordaining him. He was however, denied the ordination. Later in the year, he appealed to the church for a second time and was rejected once again with the statement of "his Unreasonable Demand: And ill treating of his Brethern."[8] Two years later, and perhaps with more maturity and a bit more humility, he was ordained as pastor of the newly-constituted Baptist church at Crosswicks (Upper Freehold), New Jersey, on November 12, 1766.[9] The congregation had formerly been a branch of the Morristown church.

A second view of Jones's strong disposition occurred during his early Revolutionary War experience. In a 1776 message from Jones's commander at Ticonderoga, General Anthony Wayne, to Benjamin Franklin, the General wrote: "Through the medium of my Chaplain, I hope this will reach you as he has promised to blow out any man's brains who will attempt to take it from him."[10] The chaplain was evidently not a pacifistic man of the cloth.

That willful nature asserted itself once again in a confrontation in a stagecoach on his way to the front lines to assume his duties

---

[8] Minutes of the Baptist Church, Middletown, New Jersey, MS in the Middletown Public Library.

[9] Helen Polhemus, ed., *The Church Book of the Upper Freehold Baptist Church. A Copy of the Introduction of the Original Church Records Begun in 1766* (Imlaystown, NJ: The Upper Freehold Baptist Church, 1972), 6-7.

[10] Charles J. Stille, *Major-General Anthony Wayne and the Pennsylvania Line in the Continental Army* (Port Washington, NY: Kennikat Press, Inc., 1968), 37.

as a chaplain in the War of 1812. He was seventy-six years old and in company with a number of gentlemen,

> all of whom seemed to take a lively interest in the political affairs of the day. Among them was a young lawyer, who was criticising, in no measured terms, the policy and spirit of President Madison. 'A weak administration—a miserably weak administration,' was the epithet which he applied to the powers that then were. Mr. Jones had sat quietly, taking but little part in the animated discussion. But now he woke up—'Yes Sir,' said he, 'it is a weak administration,—a miserably weak administration—if President Madison were half the man he ought to be,' looking full in the eye of the young lawyer,—'he would have hung, long ago, scores of such confounded Tories as you!' 'Sir,' said the lawyer, with a great deal of warmth,—'if you were not an old man, you would not say that to me.' 'Yes, yes Sir'— replied Mr. Jones, shaking his head energetically toward the angry youth—'and if I were not an old man, you would not dare to say that to me.'[11]

Energetic, strong willed, loving, combative, spiritual, opinionated and caring, David Jones made a lasting impression on all who knew him.

The theology of David Jones as pastor/preacher

There were two major influences in Jones's ministerial training. One of those influences in his life was his early education at Hopewell Baptist Academy and the formation of many friendships with young men there who later became important Baptist leaders. One of those, Samuel Jones (1735-1814), an English-speaking Welshman, aided him each evening in vocabulary, translations, and pronunciation of English words, since Welsh-speaking David had limited abilities in written and spoken English. No further mention is made of any difficulty with his language or formal studies, and Jones evidently succeeded comparatively well with his study at Hopewell Academy. Among his fellow students at the school were James Manning, first president of Rhode Island College (now Brown University),

---

[11] William B. Sprague, ed., *Annals of the American Pulpit* (New York: Robert Carter and Brothers, 1865), 6 (Baptist): 88.

Hezekiah Smith, who became a leading itinerant preacher in Massachusetts, and the aforementioned Samuel Jones, later an outstanding Baptist pastor in Pennsylvania. Of the students at the Academy,

> about 20 men became preachers, about half of the total. Five others became lawyers, two holding judgeships, and several were in the Revolutionary War. Five later enrolled in Princeton, two in the College of Philadelphia, and several in the College of Rhode Island.[12]

Hopewell Baptist Academy, or "Isaac Eaton's Latin Grammar School" as it was sometimes called, was an outgrowth of the Baptist church in the same town. The church had a rich heritage of outstanding pastors and members such as John Gano, pastor and associational missionary, Isaac Eaton, pastor and founder of this first Baptist school in America, and Oliver Hart, pastor and denominational leader. Eaton, particularly, was instrumental in the formation and teaching at Hopewell Academy. Having studied medicine at Montgomery, Pennsylvania, and taught school in Southampton, Pennsylvania, he became pastor of the Hopewell Baptist Church in 1748. Eaton joined with other Baptist pastors in a concerted effort to establish a Baptist school because of the fear of a negative influence of other denominational training centers.

> They distrusted Harvard because of its liberalism, Yale because of too many New Englanders, and the College of Pennsylvania, it was said, would lead to a taste of high life, and people there became Episcopalians because they could sin and not be held accountable.[13]

The second major theological training of Jones concerned his relationship with Abel Morgan (1713-1785), his tutor. Morgan was pastor of the Middletown, New Jersey, Baptist church for forty-seven years. Sometime during the fall of 1761, Jones arrived in Middletown to live. It appears that he came for at least two reasons. First, he moved to that place "to improve himself in Divinity under the care of his relative, the Reverend Abel Morgan." The recipient of an honorary A.M. degree from Rhode

---

[12] Dean Henderson Ashton, "Hopewell Academy," n. d., typescript in Hopewell Museum, Hopewell, New Jersey.

[13] *Ibid.*, 78-79.

Island College in 1769, Morgan was known as an outstanding Greek scholar. His young protégé, Jones, used his study of that original New Testament language to good advantage as his later writings indicate. The second reason undoubtedly pertained to a young lady named Ann Stillwell, a member of the Middletown Baptist congregation, who became his wife within six months after his arrival.[14]

David Jones was the pastor of three churches: a charter member and first pastor of the Crosswicks (or Upper Freehold) Baptist Church, New Jersey—1766-1775; Baptist Church in the Great Valley, Pennsylvania—1775-1786; and Southampton Baptist Church—1786-1792. He returned to the Great Valley church in 1792 and remained there as pastor until his death on February 5, 1820; he is buried in the church's cemetery. In addition to preaching as a pastor, he preached to many military men during his sixteen-year Army service. A minister's doctrinal subjects, the topics he chooses, and the frequent repetition of certain texts explain, to some degree, what the man believed. If he preached extensively from the prophetic sections of the Bible, for example, his emphasis would be quite different from the pastor who preached from the ethical portions of scripture. Thus, a close reading of his textual choices can reveal what he thought to be most important.

From May 30, 1786, to October 30, 1814, Jones kept a diary of his sermon texts. Each time he preached he noted the date, the scripture, and usually a portion of that text was written in his own hand. Sometimes he also wrote his sermon outline, and twice he set down the entire sermon in abbreviated form. A few other items were also noted in the diary such as medicinal remedies and horticultural notes, but the major space was given to the listing of sermon texts.

Unfortunately, he did not keep a diary of his varied activities during the Revolutionary War, but Jones began his first diary on the occasion of his first sermon as pastor of the Southampton Baptist Church of Bucks County, Pennsylvania in 1786. When he returned to his former pastorate, The Baptist Church in the Great Valley, in 1792, he continued to note his sermon texts until 1814. There are two duplications of his recorded sermon texts. The first occurred when he entered the U.S. Army as chaplain in 1794, and

---

[14] [The couple's youngest son, Horatio Gates Jones (1777-1853) and grandson, Horatio Gates Jones, Jr. (1822-1893), would each become significant members of the Philadelphia Association as pastor and historian, respectively —*Ed.*]

the second when he re-entered the Army in 1813. On each of these occasions he kept a field or memorandum book, but continued to enter his sermon references in the diary begun in 1786, oftentimes entering the texts in both his personal diary and field book.

There are a total of 678 sermon texts listed in the diary, including the few overlapping texts used while preaching as chaplain. These biblical verses can be categorized as follows:

The entire Old Testament ....79 texts or 11.7%
The Gospels (Matthew, Mark, Luke,
and John) ....192 texts or 28.3%
The Book of Acts.................................61 texts or 8.9%
The Book of Romans...........................70 texts or 10.3%
The Books of Corinthians, Galatians, Ephesians,
Philippians, Colossians, Thessalonians,
Timothy..................................174 texts or 25.7%
The General Epistles – Hebrews, James,
Peter, John, Jude ....77 texts or 11.4%
The Book of Revelation.........................25 texts or 3.7%[15]

Several observations can be made from these statistics revealing Jones's attitude in the selection of preaching topics. The major themes contained in the books of the previous list indicates that Jones was most concerned with the life, death, and resurrection of Christ. His frequent use of Paul's letters with their strong doctrinal and practical sections emphasized a utilitarian character of the Christian life, while the doctrinal passages of the General Epistles and Romans appeared less often. Acts, the book of the beginnings, growth, and difficulties of the early church, was sparingly used as was the prophetic book of Revelation.

David Jones was not primarily a theologian. Rather, his strengths as a minister were in preaching, performing pastoral duties, and rendering service to God and country through his military role as a chaplain. He did preach and write concerning specific theological subjects in his profession, of course, as ministers must. However, proclaiming God's Word rather than explaining theological nuances was his main concern.

He was Calvinistic in doctrine as was essentially the entire Philadelphia Baptist Association. Sermons and other written

---

[15] George Truett Rogers and Terry Wolever, *The Life, Journal and Works of David Jones, 1736-1820* (Springfield, MO: Particular Baptist Press, 2007), 30.

material of ministers such as Abel Morgan of New Jersey and Isaac Backus of Massachusetts concerning subjects such as God's grace, the atoning work of Christ, the kingdom of God, and baptism are in line with Jones's basic positions on those subjects. In addition, most American Baptists of his day in the Middle Colonies certainly agreed with all of the five points of Calvinism adopted by the Council of Dort in 1619: the total depravity of man, God's unconditional election, the limited atonement of Christ, the irresistible grace of God, and the perseverance of the saints. And David Jones was known to have welcomed Baptist ministers from England and Wales on the condition that "they must not be of the class of velvet mouths, you may tell many of your acquaintances in the ministry that there is a great call for servants of Jesus in America; but they must be true Calvinists and men of Christian experience."[16]

Of special interest to Jones, as to most of the Welsh Baptists, was the issue of laying on of hands on baptized believers as an ordinance. Using the practice of laying on of hands of the early church in the book of Acts, and citing Hebrews 6:1-2, Jones advocated for the practice as an ordinance and continued observance for post-biblical usage. In 1795, he engaged in a handbill/pamphlet debate with another Welsh Baptist and friend, Samuel Jones, who decried this practice as an ordinance in the Baptist churches of the Philadelphia Baptist Association.[17] However, the issue had been somewhat laid to rest many years earlier.

In 1706, Welsh Tract Baptist Meeting members met with several members of local American Baptist churches at the home of Richard Miles in Radnor, Chester County, Pennsylvania in July to discuss the question of fellowship. Since the practice of "hands" was a critical issue, the following agreement, was made:

---

[16] Letter from David Jones to John Rippon, The British Library, London, as cited in Hywel M. Davies, *Transatlantic Brethren: Rev. Samuel Jones (1735-1814) and His Friends, Baptists in Wales, Pennsylvania, and Beyond* (Cranbury, NJ: Associated University Presses, 1995), 196.

[17] David Jones, *A True History of Laying on of Hands Upon Baptized Believers as Such: In Answer to a Hand-Bill, Intitled, A Brief History of the Imposition of Hands on Baptized Persons: Published by Samuel Jones, D.D. Wherein His Mistakes are Attempted to Be Corrected* (Burlington, NJ: S. C. Ustick, 1805), 1-5. See Rogers and Wolever, *The Life, Journal and Works of David Jones,* 533-578, for the complete text.

> 1) With regard to them who believe in the ordinance of laying-on-of-hands on every believer. That they are to enjoy all liberty, within the bounds of brotherly love, to preach on the subject, and to practice according to their belief.
>
> 2) And with regard to them who do not think it duty to practice the ordinance, that they be left to their liberty.
>
> 3) And further it was agreed, that neither of the parties were to make opposition in any mixed assembly, but that the members of either church might enjoy occasional communion with the other.[18]

Because of such agreements, early union with other American Baptists was attained, so that Welsh Baptists were an integral part of the foundation of the first formal Baptist associational organization in America, the Philadelphia Baptist Association, in September of 1707.

David Jones also published several works on other doctrinal and ecclesiological issues. Beginning in 1773, ministers within the Philadelphia Baptist Association were commissioned to write circular letters on various aspects of the Association's doctrinal positions. Jones wrote two: *The Doctrine of Saving Faith and Religious Worship* and the *Sabbath Day* were published in 1788 and 1798 respectively as expositions of chapters XIV and XXII of the Philadelphia Confession of Faith. On his own initiative he published *A Treatise of the Work of the Holy Ghost under the Gospel Dispensation* in 1804.

A summary of Jones's theological views should indicate, first, as noted earlier, that in his ministry he was not primarily a theologian. Unlike many of his contemporaries, however, some of his theological views on certain subjects were published, either as books, sermons, or circular letters. From these works and some existing correspondence we may glean a portion of his beliefs.

Jones added little new theological insights to the body of doctrinal literature. He was strict in his interpretation of the Bible, and went so far as to forbid the celebration of Christmas because that holiday could not be scripturally proven to be in late December. Thus this strict minister-chaplain with minimal formal education was a traditional American Baptist with a distinctive Welsh and Calvinistic background.

---

[18] *Records of the Welsh Tract Baptist Meeting,* 10.

David Jones as an early American Army chaplain

Tradition has taught that most people wish to be remembered for their greatest accomplishment in life. If one built a great company, engaged in a great victory, invented a new process, or created a masterpiece, the thought runs that, all other achievements pale beside his one great *éclat*. It might be argued that David Jones shared that feeling when, in spite of varying degrees of success as a minister, a missionary, a writer and a denominational activist, he desired to be known in his later years as "The Old Soldier." That self-denoted appellation is probably indicative of an unusual pride in being a part of the Delaware Colonial militia, the Continental Army, and the United States Army in four separate wars: the French and Indian War as an eighteen-year-old non-combat militiaman (1754-1763), the Revolutionary War (1775-1783), the Indian War in the Northwest Territory of 1794-1796 and the War of 1812. As a result of this activity, he addressed himself as the "Old Soldier" to the readers of the *Philadelphia Aurora*, December 20, 1811, through January 24, 1816, and in personal letters.

Several aspects of Jones's almost sixteen years as a military chaplain bear analysis, since his duty was varied and involved him in some extremely important Army events of early America. The various facets of the chaplain's activities reveal an interesting, exciting and productive military career.

Motivations to service.—Early in his ministry, Jones turned his attention to the spread of the gospel to the American Indians. This religious motivation led him, at last, to a brief ministry with the Shawnee and Delaware tribes of Ohio in 1772 and 1773. While traveling through the West in this missionary activity, he noted the need for chaplains at Ft. Pitt, where there was neither a military chaplain nor a civilian minister. His notation of the absence of chaplains in the West at so early a date, 1772, indicated his deep-seated interest in such a ministry. Undoubtedly, his previous experience as a militiaman with a Delaware unit during the French and Indian War increased his sensitivity to the religious needs of military men as he traveled through the West.[19]

There is even more evidence, however, to indicate another motivation toward the chaplaincy on Jones's part: a strong and never-flagging patriotism. He was forced to resign his first pastorate in New Jersey because of his strong stand against

[19] David Jones, *Journal of Two Visits,* 12.

British policies toward the American Colonies. His grandson believed that the cause for that removal was a "bold courage [which] rendered him obnoxious to the Tories who abounded there."[20] Since his enlistment as a chaplain in the 3rd Pennsylvania Regiment followed within one year, it is clear that Jones stood early, and solidly, with the Patriot cause. In 1794, he wrote to a Baptist leader in England, Dr. John Rippon, that his religious and patriotic inducements to rejoin the army were reinforced by his pride in being the only Baptist then serving as a chaplain. That statement, perhaps more than any other, expressed the combination of patriotic, religious and personal motivations for serving as a chaplain:

> I am now appointed chaplain to the army, and am the only one in America: by this you may learn that our Society [the Baptists] appears in a different point of view to your's in England where you are abused with the odious character of a DISSENTER. I am to set out in a few days for head quarters, which is near 900 miles in the rout[e] I am to go. Several reasons prevailed on me once more to enter into the service of my country 1. My health is impaired, and travelling in times past has had a good effect on it. 2. The army lies opposite to Kentucke where I have business to transact. 3. I am a neighbour to the commander in chief, General Wayne, whose chaplain I was during the last war, and to whom I am much attached; and lastly, I am in hopes once more of having an opportunity to speak to the Indians, should I live to the end of the war.[21]

Variety of services rendered

The war moved to the Philadelphia area in 1777, and as it grew in intensity, many citizens were called on to perform extra duties, especially those who lived in the immediate area of the hostilities. Because Jones knew the geography of the Philadelphia-Wilmington area quite well, he was detached from his chaplain-surgeon's duty to act as a scout. The need to locate the British

---

[20] Jones, "Memoir," 7.

[21] John Rippon, ed., *The Baptist Annual Register for 1794, 1795, 1796-1797* (London: Dilly, Button and Thomas, 1797), 132-133.

movement northward from the Chesapeake Bay forced the chaplain to command a patrol in search of the redcoats.

Chaplain Jones was also close to the front lines at the Battle of Brandywine, so close in fact, that the horse he was riding was wounded in the leg. After that battle, Jones accompanied General Anthony Wayne and a small contingent of troops on a secretive mission behind the British lines. A nearby Tory informed the British commander, General William Howe, of the presence of the Americans, and a force twice the size of Wayne's encircled the Americans on the night of September 21, 1777. Later called the "Paoli Massacre," the British, led by a force of hired German mercenaries (Hessians), attacked quietly with bayonets and unloaded muskets. Jones barely escaped as 300 Americans were killed.

> He seemed to be impressed with a sense of forboding and so had his servant prepare his horse and he slept in his clothes. He said he heard the first alarm and mounted his horse and when the dark cloud came over the moon—which happened as if by direction of Providence—he succeeded in escaping, many of the soldiers following his lead.[22]

Forty years later, Jones was the featured speaker at the dedication of a monument, still standing, at that spot.

During the Philadelphia campaign, Jones was never far from his Chester County home and church. When the fighting subsided following the Battle of Germantown, the Continental Army retired to Valley Forge, within sight of The Baptist church in the Great Valley. Because of the proximity of his family to the army camp, he often left his duties as chaplain-surgeon to gather supplies, preach at his church and visit his family.

During such travels between his home and the camp, an interesting event transpired as the chaplain once more stepped out of his role as a spiritual leader and acted the part of a fighting patriot. He stopped at a nearby inn to feed himself and his horse.

> While eating, he heard a rider dismount and inquire about the location of the British camp, saying that he had lost his way. David Jones quietly stole out, got his pistol and returned to the stranger, evidently concealing his weapon. 'So you have lost your way?' 'Yes sir,' was the reply. 'Well,

---

[22] Jones, "Memoir," 9.

then,' replied the chaplain, 'I am one of those whom you call rebels,' and cocking his pistol and presenting it he said, 'You are my prisoner and I'll lead you to Headquarters.' He made the British dragoon ride ahead of him and entered the American lines. As news of this passed along, the lines of American soldiers 'were on the qui vive' [or, on the alert] and many gathered to watch the men ride in. General Wayne laughed 'immoderately' at the entire proceeding. Later at Staunton, Virginia, Jones saw a group of English prisoners and in their midst one took off his hat and bowed to him as Jones rode by. It was this prisoner.[23]

A local minister-chaplain serving in the American Army, gathering supplies at his home, preaching and reporting on Washington's Army at local churches and capturing a British dragoon captain could hardly remain unknown to the English authorities for long. Consequently, the British commander, Howe, ordered Jones arrested. A cavalry patrol was sent to wait for the chaplain to return home by way of Valley Forge, but instead of capturing a Baptist chaplain, they unwittingly arrested the local Methodist minister, thus alerting Jones to discontinue his frequent journeys. One can imagine the consternation of the Methodist, the Reverend Miller, "whose hair was black and curled behind like Jones," and the relief of the Baptist Jones, who remained with his troops, over the mistaken identity.

Two sermons best illustrate Jones's style of preaching to soldiers. The first message was delivered on July 20, 1775 at the Log House before Colonel Joseph Owen Dewees's Regiment. Though Jones was not yet an official Army chaplain, he was preaching to Army troops—perhaps his first such experience. The occasion was a Continental Congress-proclaimed Fast Day for prayer and supplication to God for His help in the struggle, already begun in the Boston area. The sermon was titled "Defensive War in a Just Cause Sinless," with Nehemiah 4:14 as the text:

> And I looked, and rose up, and said unto the nobles, and to the rulers, and to the rest of the people, Be ye not afraid of them: remember the Lord, which is great and terrible, and fight for your brethren, your sons, and your daughters, your wives, and your houses.

---

[23] *Ibid.*, 16-17.

After tracing the historical background of the text, Jones listed three purposes of his sermon:

1. A caution against cowardice, or fear of an enemy unjustly engaged. Be not ye afraid of them. It is of great importance in war to be delivered from fear of the enemy; for soldiers in a panic generally fall a victim in the dispute.
2. We have an argument to excite fortitude and firmness of mind in martial engagements. Remember the Lord, which is great and terrible.
3. A fervent call to present duty in times of distress. And fight for your brethren, your sons, your daughters, your wives and your houses.[24]

He then sought to prove that when people have no other redress for legitimate grievances, it is their right and duty to fight for liberty and property. *Defensive War in A Just Cause Sinless*, received wide acclaim when published in 1775. Its delivery and publication were timely, of course, but beyond the emotion of the day, the sermon is a favorite example for many of patriotism founded on biblical and spiritual principles.

A second sermon, also published, served as a good example of preaching to troops immediately prior to their entry into combat. As American troops attempted to halt the advance of General Sir Guy Carleton's British army southward from Canada, a stand was made by the Americans at Ft. Ticonderoga. The Americans had invaded Canada earlier, in 1775, but costly defeats followed early victories and by October, 1776, the danger of the Canadian force pushing all the way to New York City, uniting the main British Army, caused a desperate defense at Ft. "Ti," as the soldiers called Ticonderoga. Jones preached a sermon as "the enemy was expected hourly from Crown Point." Thus, the message is illustrative of the kind of sermon chaplains preached to troops readied for imminent combat.

This second sermon began with many references to our common faith, and that we are fighting for all that is "near and dear to us, while our enemies are engaged in the worst of causes..." Then followed some interesting blessings and "accursings" in his emotional conclusion. A few examples are listed:

---

[24] David Jones, *Defensive War in a Just Cause Sinless* (Philadelphia: Printed by Henry Miller, 1775), 5-6.

Defensive WAR in a just Cause
SINLESS.

A SERMON,

PREACHED

On the Day of the CONTINENTAL FAST,

AT

TREDYFFRYN, in CHESTER COUNTY,

BY

The Revd DAVID JONES, *A. M.*

PUBLISHED BY REQUEST.

Our GOD whom we serve, is able to deliver us.
DAN. iii. 17.

PHILADELPHIA:
Printed by HENRY MILLER. 1775.

Facsimile of the original title page to David Jones's *Defensive War in a Just Cause Sinless* (1775).

1. Blessed be the man who is possessed of true love of liberty; and let all the people say, Amen.
2. Blessed be the man who is a friend to the common rights of mankind; and let all the people say, Amen.
3. Blessed be the man who is a friend to the United States of America; and let all the people say, Amen.

Now, on the other hand, as far as is consistent with the Holy Scriptures, let all these blessings be turned to curses to him who deserts the noble cause in which we are engaged, and turns his back to the enemy before he receives proper orders to retreat; and let all the people say, Amen.

Let him be abhorred by all the United States of America.

Let faintness of heart and fear never forsake him on earth.

Let him be a magor missabile, a terror to himself and all around him.

Let him be accursed in his outgoing, and cursed in his incoming; cursed in lying down, and cursed in uprising; cursed in basket, and cursed in store.

Let him be cursed in all his connections, till his wretched head with dishonor is laid low in the dust; and let all the soldiers say, Amen.

And may the God of all grace, in whom we live, enable us, in defense of our country, to acquit ourselves like men, to his honor and praise. Amen and Amen.[25]

The sermon was published both during and following the war. A Colonel Johnson told Jones's grandson that he had had copies made even after the war to demonstrate this as an example of Jones's preaching. It was this Colonel Johnson who had appended the note to the sermon seen earlier about the "powerful effect" it had "in animating the men."[26]

An interesting point concerning his preaching to troops is the location of his biblical texts. Of the thirty-five total references, eighteen, slightly over 50%, are from the Old Testament. His sermons to civilians during the war contained far fewer Old

---

[25] Benson J. Lossing, *The Pictorial Field Book of the Revolution* (New York: Harper and Brothers, 1855), 165-166.

[26] Rogers and Wolever, *The Life, Journal and Works of David Jones*, 134.

Testament references; not more than 10%. Since the Old Covenant writers recorded numerous acts of war on the part of God's people, it is not surprising that a chaplain would turn to that section of the Bible for authority in speaking to fighting men in wartime.

The context of his sermons, then, was directed at the immediate needs of the troops: remaining under authority, the right to bear arms, personal morality, inspiration in the face of enemy fire and the promise of a future life for faithful Christian soldiers. Evidently the chaplain's sermons were well received as evidenced by the publication of two of the messages and the invitation to preach at important gatherings. Following the significant victory at Saratoga in October of 1777, and the subsequent entry of the French into the American cause, Washington's Army at Valley Forge was assembled to give thanks to God. Chaplain Jones was the featured speaker at the service of worship.[27]

Jones most certainly enjoyed his role as a preaching chaplain. The desire to preach the Word of God fit well with an innate patriotic verve. Several innovations in the art of preaching to military personnel inevitably followed from such dedication to the task. One was having drummers arranged in front of him as he spoke to troops in the Ohio Indian campaign. These drummers were ordered by the chaplain to beat a slow roll as he began preaching. Also, when asked to preach at First Baptist Church, Philadelphia, during peace times, he sent to the Navy Yard for Marines to sit in front of the church, for he fancied he could preach better if there were soldiers around him.[28]

Other duties of this chaplain-soldier included marriages and funerals for both military and civilians, and ministering at the execution of deserters, a particularly difficult assignment. He also served as a clerk/recorder at the Treaty of Greenville (1795) which concluded the Indian wars of 1794. His duties as an Army chaplain were far broader than preaching and giving spiritual aid to the troops. Serving as a scout for his commander, serving as a doctor when needed, gathering supplies and acting as a messenger demonstrate a total commitment to his commission as well as a confident trust on the part of his commanders.

---

[27] Mildred Goshow, Unpublished Genealogy, April 1973, typescript in possession of Mildred Goshow of Roxborough, Pennsylvania and Daniel Cornog of Wayne, Pennsylvania, 45.

[28] Jones, "Memoir," 70-71.

Jones's thought on Indian-white relationships

Two other events in Jones's life were of such concern to him that he kept journals and published his actions, thoughts, and interviews in his later years. One of those endeavors was directly related to his Christian ministry. That was an early effort to evangelize the Indians of the Ohio River Valley. On May 4, 1772, Jones left his home for a preaching and surveying tour of the people and land of Ohio. He returned home in September of 1772 for a brief visit, but left for a second tour on October 26th, returning, at last, on April 30, 1773.

Jones stated that his first concern was to visit the Shawnee Indian towns west of the Scioto River "with efforts to civilize the Heathens." In addition to that spiritual motivation, Jones also had a personal and physical reason for his trip. He wished to invest in land on the east side of the Ohio River "in a province then expected to take place under the propriety of messrs: Franklin, Wharton, Baynton, Morgan and others."[29] He also wished to travel for his health, as he believed that exposure to the pure air of the West would he salubrious to a condition possibly indicating asthma.

He noted that he departed from Fort Pitt "in company with Mr. George Rogers Clark, and several others," in canoes moving down river past several Indian towns. Messages previously sent to the Shawnee villages requesting permission to preach were received, but with something less than enthusiasm on the part of the Indians. He began a journey home on July 28th, due to ill health, but his stay in New Jersey was short-lived, since he still anticipated a breakthrough in his ministry to the Indians, a breakthrough that never occurred.

Still, Jones learned a great deal about the Indians on these two trips in 1772-1773, as well as subsequent visits. His success was minimal, for even he admitted to his grandson in later years that his efforts at preaching were "not very successful." Though he was not among the Indians of the Ohio region for long periods of time until 1795, when he served as chaplain in the Indian War, he visited their area numerous times in the interim. He did, however, observe first-hand two native tribes (Shawnee and Delaware), their geography, their habits, their speech and something of their attitudes and opinions. Those observations were kept in a diary

---

[29] Jones, *A Journal of Two Visits*, 3-4.

which was later used as a basis for publication in a series of articles in the *Philadelphia Aurora* beginning in 1811.

Those articles focused on three major points. His first, and major, consideration in relating his views on the Indian problem was to discuss ownership of western lands. His first mention of Indian rights to specific parcels of land was in 1773, during his second missionary journey. Establishing a theory to be developed more fully in his later writings, he said, "Nor could I understand that they [the Indians] have any fixed bounds to a nation, esteeming it chiefly useful for hunting."[30] He noted in his diary that the speech by a Chippewa Chief claiming certain lands in Ohio "very much displeased the waindots [Wyandots] and Delawares." It was made manifestly clear to Jones by such disputes among the Indians that no one could agree on title to land, including the Indians, and no one held rights to land except by "civil compact." To Jones's thinking, specific property rights, then, are civil and not natural rights.

Conquest was the alternative to civil treaties, Jones believed, and any agreement made with a vanquished enemy should be at the initiative of the victor, on the winner's terms alone. The conquest theory came late to him after observing many failures of attempts of conciliation over many years. As he wrote, "we must humble the Savages, they must be conquered. People ask for Peace, that we must grant only on condition of their engaging to cultivate the Land, and abandon the former way of life."[31] A full-scale war against the natives was thus suggested by Jones, a war lasting as long as required for the Indians to accept the complete terms of the white men.

The second attitude of Jones toward Indians is his concept of the Indian personality. Whatever "noble savage" concepts he had earlier of the Indians dissolved through the years as he noted their thievery, cowardice and constant deception. A white captive, Mrs. Henry, related to him that during her captivity, it was not uncommon for [Shawnee] women to hang or drown their children, when they did not like them, and never concern themselves so much as to bury them. Nor were they guilty of this cruelty

---

[30] David Jones, "Indian Affairs," *Philadelphia Aurora,* December 20, 1811.

[31] MS letter of David Jones to James Madison, dated November 26, 1812. American Baptist Historical Society, Atlanta, Georgia.

secretly, for nothing would be said on the occasion more than if a puppy had been drowned.[32]

The severe cruelty dealt out by the Indians was a custom especially revolting to Jones. Writing of the savage treatment of captives, the missionary related how holes were punched in the foreigner's wrists, and as a rope was threaded in the hole, the subjects were tied around a stake. Amid howls of laughter, the noses of the victims were cut off, and, at last, they were tomahawked, their bodies left for the birds and wild animals. Such behavior combined with their refusal to be attentive to the Christian gospel, being personally attacked on occasion, and having his horse taken from him, drove Jones to view Indian nature very negatively.

Following future and inevitable conquest of the Indians, Jones wrote that the best solution to the Indian-white problem was the transformation of the natives from a nomadic to a settled, sedentary life, a theory promulgated by the federal government for many years. The writer's personal values of a life rooted in the soil are easily understood, of course, since he was born to a land-cultivating, God-fearing farm family, and worked as a farmer-minister-chaplain throughout his lifetime. He also offered another suggestion as a long-range solution to the continuous Indian-white conflict—the amalgamation of the two races. He felt that at the root of the conflict was a basic racial, ethnic difference that could be solved only by the extinction of inherent phyletic variations.

The judgment of one who changed his Indian views from exclusively preaching the gospel to them to actively promoting their subjugation in order to further their civilization, appears extremely harsh, though many others, of course, shared his opinions. When Jones is presented, however, as a first-hand observer of an unwillingness on the part of Indians even to hear the gospel, while at the same time he noted their extreme forms of physical cruelty, attacks on his person, union with a longtime enemy (Britain), murders of his settler friends and their failure to cultivate good land, then his attitude changes appear more understandable, if not entirely acceptable by modern thought. Knowing his intimate relations with Indians as both friend and foe may not justify his strong Indian philosophy of 1816, but it does make his later views (make no treaties, conquest, cultivation of the soil and amalgamation) at least understandable.

---

[32] Jones, *A Journal of Two Visits*, 55.

Second Bank of the United States

A second series of publications published late in Jones's life were purely political in nature. One's tendency toward conservatism or progressivism probably invades most areas of one's thought with consistency. David Jones, for example, was certainly a religious conservative and that position carried over into the realm of politics and finances as well. He wrote very little concerning economics until 1816, when a series of articles appeared in the *Philadelphia Aurora* on that subject under his pen name, "The Old Soldier."[33] The impetus for his taking up the pen was the issue of the proposed chartering of the Second Bank of the United States. Generally, Jones was against the proposal, but if the Bank was to be an inevitable reality, then he proposed several qualifications for it.

Of the seven basic arguments against the Second Bank (i.e., constitutionality, concentration of financial power, state bank advocacy, foreign stock holders, enemies of the administration, war politics and centralized federal government), Jones joined the enemies of the bank on most of the objections. His reasons for doing so were founded not so much in party politics, however, as in his conservative economic philosophy. His desire for a sound national economy was expressed in terms of government land and equitable taxes based on that land ownership. His objection to inflated paper money was due to his past experience of holding securities in land or specie. Any other forms of fiscal policy depending on unsecured credit, he reasoned, were extremely tenuous.

His economic philosophy was rooted in agriculture, involvement of the common man in the fiscal affairs of his country and hard money backed by land and taxation. He was a die-hard, old line Jeffersonian Republican who stood by the strict interpretation of the Constitution, and he desired that Congress, alone, manage the country's economy. His was not a major voice of educated economic theory or the respected political leadership of a founding father, but it did represent a significant segment of solid middle class, Jeffersonian Republicans. Undoubtedly, many of his neighbor-farmer-fellow-churchmen-Republicans echoed a hearty "amen" to his printed words on the nation's economy.

---

[33] David Jones, "To the Senate and House of Representatives of the United States." *Philadelphia Aurora*, January 5, 1816 - January 24, 1816. Five articles on national economy.

Summary of his contributions

David Jones was not a major figure in American history in any of the specific political, intellectual, or religious fields of his interests. Men of his acquaintance and friendship such as George Washington, James Madison, James Monroe, Anthony Wayne, James Wilkinson, Isaac Backus and John Gano all served their individual causes with more relevance to important world and national events than did Jones. Yet, he was involved with many major personalities and events of American history, and as a thinker, writer, activist and patriot, his contributions, if less than the Founding Fathers, add to the knowledge of his era.

There were certain innate handicaps inhibiting Jones's larger influence. He was, for example, a part of a small provincial foreign language group. Welsh-American Baptists of upper Delaware in the mid-eighteenth century did not have the wide political, social and religious prestige as did New England's English-speaking Congregationalists or Virginia's Anglicans. In addition, formal educational opportunities were limited for one desiring to study with Baptist tutors. Since there was no Baptist-supported college in America in Jones's youth, he was forced to be content with a brief academy training. Perhaps it was because of his short rural education with Welsh teachers and friends that he was criticized for having an unpolished style of speaking. Lack of participation in cultural activities afforded in the larger cities and universities may also account for a blunt, censorious style of writing as noted earlier in his books and letters. Yet David Jones was considered an influential man by his contemporaries.

1) Jones was a leader among Baptists in the Middle Colonies of America. As a life-long member of the earliest and most influential Baptist association, the Philadelphia Association, he was active in pastoring, organizing and administering the affairs of several church and associational organizations. He served as the moderator and clerk of the same Association, and was a charter member and first pastor of the Crosswicks (or Upper Freehold) Baptist Church in 1766. Serving a total of three Baptist churches in New Jersey and Pennsylvania, he was a full and part-time pastor for fifty-four years.

2) Jones represents the thought and social background of the early Welsh-American tradition of the Middle Colonies. He was born to the Welsh language and customs in the Welsh Tract of Delaware, retaining these ties throughout his life.

3) He was an early and faithful patriot in the struggle for American independence. His advocacy for American protestations against British rule led him to unresolved differences with his neighbors in New Jersey in 1775, causing him to move from that area. His best known sermon, "Defensive War in a Just Cause Sinless," was published shortly after his removal. Throughout the war, he served as an active, preaching, chaplain-surgeon. Though his house and farm were ransacked by the invaders, and though he suffered through personal privations and illness, he persevered to the end of the war. He never received his full promised pay for services performed during the Revolutionary War, as was often the case, though he did receive donation lands in lieu of cash. Yet, the patriotism he exhibited throughout the war remained constant during his lifetime.

4) Jones was a part of the first Baptist school in America. As a student of that school, the Hopewell Academy, Hopewell, New Jersey, he not only received his only formal education, but he also made many valuable contacts with future Baptist leaders.

5) He brought Baptist influence to a national endeavor. During the Indian Wars of 1790-1795, Jones served as the only chaplain in the United States Army. His recognition of the significance of that unique service is evident in his correspondence, as he spoke of how Baptists were given increasingly important roles in America's affairs.

6) An examination of his sermons reveals a considerable homiletic gift. Soldiers recognized him as a chaplain who could "rouse their spirits with harangues [or passionate speech]," and civilians and soldiers alike responded to his preaching in personal exhortations as well as published messages. Two of his sermons received wide distribution during the Revolutionary War.

7) He was an early Baptist leader to recognize the necessity and opportunity for missionary work among the Indians. Many mission societies and individual Christian missionaries had served among the natives before Jones's trips of 1772-1773, of course, but Baptists were lacking in financial resources in the late Colonial period to sustain a cooperative missionary effort.

8) David Jones was an important and early United States Army chaplain. He served sixteen years as a chaplain in three different wars. At one time he was the only American Army chaplain, and the fact that the government would later appoint him as a seventy-six-year-old chaplain indicated others' respect for the quality of his service. Two diaries kept during wartime provide helpful insights to the life and duties of early Army chaplains as

well as serving to supplement other accounts of military campaigns.

Jones's influence, in the final analysis, cannot be traced to intellectual, theological, or political distinction. It may be seen most clearly in the growth of the American Baptist witness during his lifetime and after. He was an important, if not leading, character in the religious life of the United States. As a minister, denominational worker, short-term missionary and effective Army chaplain, Jones contributed his personality, thoughts and writings to a struggling new nation.

Further Reading

The Life, Journal and Works of David Jones, 1736-1820. Pastor of Baptist churches in New Jersey and Pennsylvania and Chaplain in the American Army. With the biography of his life by George Truett Rogers and the published Journal and other works of David Jones edited by Terry Wolever. Springfield, MO: Particular Baptist Press, 2007.

Abram D. Gillette, ed. *Minutes of the Philadelphia Baptist Association, 1707-1807*. Philadelphia: American Baptist Publication Society, 1851; reprinted Tricentennial Edition with new comprehensive indexes, maps and illustrations, Springfield, MO: Particular Baptist Press, 2002.

Horatio Gates Jones, Jr. *History of the Baptist Church in the Great Valley. Treadyffrin Township, Chester County, Pennsylvania*. Philadelphia: William Syckelmoore, 1883; reprinted in James L. Clark. *"To Set Them in Order;" Some Influences of the Philadelphia Baptist Association Upon Baptists of America to 1814*. Springfield, MO: Particular Baptist Press, 2001, 413-434.

Samuel Stillman (1737-1807)

SAMUEL STILLMAN
1737 - 1807

by Peter Beck

American history begs to be read. Thrilling stories of heroes raise pulses. Amazing accounts of revival and spiritual successes enervate the soul. Yet, rarely do these two sides of America's legacy meet on the same page. Historical malpractice and urban legend have conspired to build a wall of separation between the secular and the sacred. In the minds of many, declarations and constitutions were the province of the former while theological debate and sectarian division belong to the latter. The dichotomy between the history of religion and the republic in America reveals modern biases and historical ignorance.

In truth, the pages of American history run red with the blood of men and women who were passionate about their God and their country. Their religion informed their nationalism. Their faith fed souls and fueled desires for freedom. Such a man was Samuel Stillman.

Serving First Baptist Church, Boston, during America's belabored deliverance from English domination, Stillman was both a patriot and a pastor, a man of political and prophetic conviction. As one contributing writer to the *Baptist Encyclopedia* reported, "Among the honored names that have been handed down to us in the annals of the eighteenth century, that of Samuel Stillman is not the least worthy of mention."[1]

"O that I could live much in a little time"[2]

The middle half of the eighteenth century flowed with the tides of change. The Great Awakening and the war between England and France raged on both sides of the Atlantic Ocean. The American colonists would eventually struggle with their religious and British identities. Into this world Samuel Stillman was born

---

[1] William Cathcart, ed., *The Baptist Encyclopedia* (Philadelphia: Louis H. Everts, 1881), 1107.

[2] Thomas Baldwin, "Biographical Sketch of the Author's Life," in *Select Sermons on Doctrinal and Practical Subjects by the Late Samuel Stillman* (Boston: Manning and Loring, 1808), xx.

on February 27, 1737. And, on both accounts, Stillman would leave his mark.

History reveals little about Stillman's birth and upbringing. What is known is that he was born in Philadelphia to "respectable parents." Of his mother, Stillman in her funeral sermon eulogized,

> She maintained a close communion with God; was often engaged in her closet, and constant in her attendance on the word and ordinances of the gospel. Out of the abundance of her heart, her mouth frequently spake of divine things; and which she did in a way suitable to the cases of those with whom she conversed.[3]

Otherwise, contemporary accounts provide scant information about Stillman's family or early childhood.

History does reveal the fact that the first eleven years of his life were lived amongst the people of the city of brotherly love before the Stillman family moved to the Holy City of the South, Charleston, South Carolina, in 1748, for reasons lost to time. There, it has been argued, "was laid the foundation upon which he afterwards built the magnificent superstructure of his life."[4]

The move to Charleston would prove to be fortuitous for Stillman, American Baptists, and quite likely the nation itself. There he entered into the highly regarded academy of a Mr. Rind where he received a thorough, classic education while displaying great intellectual potential. Of his native intelligence, Stillman's peer Thomas Baldwin would remark, "By nature he was endowed with a sprightly genius, a good capacity, and uncommon vivacity and quickness of apprehension."[5] Such an education and intellectual gifts would serve Stillman and later generations well as he would eventually be awarded degrees from the College of Philadelphia and Harvard as well as play an influential role in the formation and sustenance of what would become Brown University in Rhode Island. The value of a quality education never escaped Stillman and was a regular component of his hopes for America.

---

[3] Samuel Stillman, *A Sermon Occasioned by the Decease of Mrs. Mary Stillman* (Boston: Philip Freeman, 1768), 30.

[4] Cathcart, *The Baptist Encyclopedia*, 1107.

[5] Baldwin, "Biographical Sketch of the Author's Life," vii.

Of eternal consequence, the move to Charleston placed the young Stillman in the midst of a stream of growing Baptist sentiment. Having experienced religious impressions earlier in his childhood, Stillman had not as yet come to a conclusion concerning matters of his soul. In Charleston, however, he and his family would find themselves under the preaching ministry of the eminent Oliver Hart, pastor of First Baptist Church. Remarking later on the nature of his conversion, Stillman noted,

> My mind was again solemnly impressed with a sense of my awful condition as a sinner. This conviction grew stronger and stronger. My condition alarmed me. I saw myself without Christ and without hope. I found that I deserved the wrath to come, and that God would be just to send me to hell. I was now frequently on my knees, pleading for mercy. As a beggar I went, having nothing but guilt, and no plea but mercy.[6]

Thus convinced and convicted of his fallen nature, Stillman found no peace until he heard Hart preach from Matthew 1:21, "And she shall bring forth a son, and thou shalt call his name Jesus; for he shall save his people from their sins." Impacted by the power of these words, Stillman commented,

> Christ then became precious to me, yea, all in all. Then I could say of wisdom, "Her ways are the ways of pleasantness, and all her paths are peace." That I shall think was the day of my espousal. Glory be to God, for the riches of his grace to me.[7]

He was admitted shortly thereafter into the membership of First Baptist Church by baptism.[8] By all accounts, these events seem to have occurred before Stillman's twentieth birthday.

Having settled the matter of his eternal destiny, Stillman turned to the question of his eternal purpose. According to one writer,

---

[6] *Ibid.*, vi.

[7] *Ibid.*

[8] *Ibid.*

> At this time his mind was directed towards the work of the ministry, and he determined to enter at once upon the preparation necessary for that service, which seemed to him of all others most imperatively to demand his attention.

To that end, Stillman placed himself under the spiritual tutelage of Hart for the study of theology, a theology that was decidedly Calvinistic, thus forever securing Stillman's place among the Particular Baptists in America.[9]

Upon completion of his one year mentorship under Hart, the church acknowledged Stillman's call to the ministry. A short time later, he preached his first sermon just days short of his twenty-first birthday on February 17, 1758. The Charleston Association of Baptists would officially recognize the hand of God on Stillman in November of the same year, calling him "an orderly and worthy minister of the gospel." Finally, one day before his twenty-second birthday, Stillman was ordained to the Gospel ministry as an evangelist by that same association on February 26, 1759.[10]

Following his ordination, Stillman assumed his first pastorate on neighboring James Island, just to the southwest of Charleston. While serving there, Stillman journeyed north to Philadelphia where on May 23, 1759, he "formed a matrimonial connection" with Hannah Morgan, the daughter of a prominent merchant and sister of John Morgan who would later distinguish himself in the service of the fledgling nation during the Revolution. Hannah would remain by her husband's side until his death nearly fifty years later. Together the Stillmans would have fourteen children, of whom only two would survive their father.[11]

After returning to James Island with the new Mrs. Stillman, Samuel would serve faithfully for another eighteen months before physical ailments would necessitate a move north to friendlier climes. For two years the family remained in Bordentown, New Jersey, where Stillman continued to exercise his spiritual gifts in the service of two congregations, filling their pulpits as needed.

---

[9] Cathcart, *The Baptist Encyclopedia*, 1107.

[10] Wood Furman, *A History of the Charleston Association of Baptist Chuches in the State of South Carolina* (Charleston, SC: J. Hoff, 1811), 12.

[11] Baldwin, "Biographical Sketch of the Author's Life," vii; William B. Sprague, ed., *Annals of the American Pulpit* (New York: Robert Carter and Bros., 1865), 6 (Baptist): 71.

From there, he would venture even further north into New England where, according to the account in Sprague's *Annals of the American Pulpit*, "His services in the pulpit were everywhere eminently acceptable and useful."[12]

Such were Stillman's preaching skills that the Second Baptist Church of Boston secured his services as assistant to their pastor in 1763. The arrangement quickly proved difficult as some in the congregation allied themselves with the aged pastor, Ephraim Bownd, while others cast their lot with the talented, young Stillman. Handicapped by the difficult situation wherein his gifts were improperly exercised and desirous of not becoming the source of division, Stillman accepted the invitation of First Baptist Church to fill their vacant pulpit and began his forty-two year pastorate on January 9, 1765.

Contrary to custom, First Baptist asked Stillman to preach his own installation sermon because "of the enviable position which he had already won as an eloquent preacher."[13] A large crowd gathered for this occasion in spite of the fact that the church was out of fellowship with other Baptist churches in the area because of the questionable theological positions of earlier pastors. Giving even further testimony to his eloquence, many members of Second Baptist joined those who thronged to hear Stillman preach.

Stillman's reputation grew as did his congregation. The greatness of both seemed predestined. His sermons were clear and powerful. Presidents and generals listened raptly. More importantly, however, Stillman proved to be a great pastor.

> As a pastor, he was untiring in his devotion to his work, declining to enter upon any festivity or social pleasure which in the least interfered with his duties to his church. His own private interests were ever secondary to those of his flock, and even for persons in no way connected with his ministry he had at all times a ready hearing and an open hand.[14]

---

[12] *Ibid.*, 72.

[13] Nathan E. Wood, *The History of First Baptist Church of Boston, 1665-1899* (Philadelphia: American Baptist Publication Society, 1899), 249.

[14] *Ibid.*

As Baldwin later recounted, "In the chamber of sickness and affliction he was always a welcome visitor. . . .The sick would almost forget their pains, and the mourner cease to sigh."[15] Continuing, he praised the charity of Stillman's pastoral ministry,

> How many wounded hearts he has bound up, and from how many weeping eyes he has wiped the tears away—how many thoughtless sinners he was the means of awakening, and how many saints he has edified and built up unto eternal life—how many wavering minds he has settled, and to how many repenting sinners his words have administered peace, can be fully known only at the great day![16]

This pastoral care frequently extended to non-Baptists as well. Of these opportunities, Stillman noted, "In Boston I have also enjoyed a pleasing intimacy with Christians of different denominations."[17] As a result of God's grace and Stillman's faithfulness, "Baptisms were numerous, congregations were large, and the church prospered."[18] In total, 519 people joined the church during his long tenure.[19]

Ever the pastor, Stillman led First Baptist through dark hours and great victories. He led the church in the adoption of the singing of metrical hymns in 1771. Stillman stayed with the church through the evacuation of Boston during the Revolution for all but a brief time and was the only pastor to reclaim his church and guide them through the tumultuous years of the war. He orchestrated the building of a new sanctuary and two subsequent renovations to accommodate the continued growth. Following their pastor's lead, First Baptist broke tradition and began to hold weekly prayer meetings in 1793. God blessed the church with repeated visitations of revival, most notably in 1804 and 1805 when most of the dramatic effects of the Second Great Awakening

---

[15] Baldwin, "Biographical Sketch of the Author's Life," xiii.

[16] *Ibid.*

[17] *Ibid.*, xix.

[18] Wood, *The History of First Baptist Church of Boston*, 266.

[19] *Ibid.*, 302.

were typically limited to upstate New York and the frontier territories of the expanding West.

Christians in Boston and New England also enjoyed the touch of Stillman's ministry. Convinced of the need for educated Baptist pastors, he was among the founding supporters of Rhode Island College, now Brown University, in 1764. Displaying his continued commitment to that institution, he would preach the opening convocation sermon every other year and eventually be awarded an honorary doctorate. He was instrumental in reconciling First Baptist with other likeminded congregations and spearheaded the effort to form the first Baptist association in New England in 1767. Stillman's efforts and popularity proved vital in many benevolent endeavors including the Humane Society of Massachusetts, the Massachusetts Charitable Fire Society, and the Boston Female Asylum, a ministry dedicated to female orphans. Even in his twilight, following the lead of British Particular Baptists, Stillman continued serving the needs of others with his instrumental role in the formation of the Massachusetts Baptist Missionary Society in 1802.

Stillman's service to God and man did not end with Christian ministries and charities. He was deeply involved in the struggle for independence and the foundation of his new country in the 1760's and 70's. As a British citizen, he rejoiced at the repeal of the Stamp Act in 1766. He led his church through the dark years of the Revolution when British troops occupied Boston. At times, First Baptist under Stillman's leadership was the only house of worship open. In 1779, he was selected to preach the all-important, and very public, election day sermon by the legislature in Massachusetts, the first Baptist to enjoy this honor. Eight years later, Stillman was recognized again for his patriotism as he was one of twelve men elected to serve the people of Boston at the Federal Convention of Massachusetts, where he argued powerfully for the ratification of the new national constitution. Two years later, it was Stillman who was again asked to speak for God before the citizenry to commemorate the nation's independence.

For all of his influence, his usefulness to those within the church and those without, Samuel Stillman longed to be more useful. On one anniversary of his ministry, Stillman prayed,

> How long have I lived, and to how little purpose! Yet I trust I can say, through grace, that my poor labours have not been in vain in the Lord. When I shall sleep in the tomb, may the Lord Jesus bless the people of my charge with a plain, able,

> faithful preacher of his gospel. O that they may not be as sheep without a shepherd. Lord Jesus, send them a pastor after thine own heart; and may those truths which thou hast enabled thine unworthy servant repeatedly to deliver to them, be attended with a divine blessing, when I am no more on earth; and thine shall be the glory forever. The short time that yet remains to me, help me to devote to them. O that I could live much in a little time, and stand waiting to be gone whenever thou shalt call me hence. Glorify thyself of me, whether it be by life or by death.[20]

Just a year before his death, he added this entry in his diary,

> One year more of my life and ministry is gone. How wonderfully hath the Lord preserved such an unworthy creature as I am! O how little have I done for God! The Lord forgive me, and help me, the few days that may remain, to live for him alone. Help, Lord; help me to finish my course with joy, and the ministry which I have received of thee, so that thou mayest be glorified. I wait till thou call me hence.[21]

Twelve months later, on his death bed and aware of his impending demise, Stillman's last words reveal that his concern was not for himself but for the God who had led him so faithfully. "I desire to have no will of my own: God's government is infinitely perfect."[22] Samuel Stillman went to be with his Lord less than twelve hours later on March 12, 1807, faithful to the last.

"one of the foremost of the patriot orators"[23]

From his birth in Philadelphia, the birthplace of freedom, to his fortuitous arrival in Boston amidst the uprising of American sentiment, the life and ministry of Samuel Stillman were inextricably linked to the momentous times in which they took

---

[20] Baldwin, "Biographical Sketch of the Author's Life," xx.

[21] *Ibid.*, xix-xx.

[22] Wood, *The History of First Baptist Church of Boston*, 299.

[23] *Ibid.*, 268.

place. Yet, just as one cannot separate the man from the times of his life, one cannot divorce his politics from his theology. As one writer observed a generation later,

> As a public citizen, he had at heart the good of his country, and he was never deaf to the calls that were made upon him to take part in her affairs. Without being a partisan in his politics, he was firm in his convictions.[24]

From his initial loyalty to Britain, to his insistent defense of the liberties gained in revolution, Stillman was first and foremost a Christian who also happened to be a patriot.

A number of extant sermons display the extent to which Christianity and citizenship were intertwined in the heart and mind of Stillman. A brief survey of several that parallel key turning points in American history illustrates the manner in which he brought faith and civic duty together. Each is pertinent to the occasion which precipitated its proclamation. Yet, Stillman's observations are based on the timeless truths of Scripture, his view of God's sovereignty and man's depravity, and the God-given grace of human governance.

When the British Parliament enacted the Stamp Act in 1765, Stillman was yet a committed Englishman. "We aim not at INDEPENDENCY," he announced. Enacted to raise funds necessary to support British troops stationed in the colonies, the Stamp Act angered those subjects affected—the colonists. After much protest about the issue of taxation without representation, Parliament repealed the measure on March 18, 1766. Stillman commented on the change in circumstances on the 17th of May that same year.[25]

As Stillman proclaimed, the end of the Stamp Act was welcomed as "good news from a far country." Such news brought great joy throughout the land as the colonists believed that their fellow countrymen had dealt justly with them. "Look upon [this news] as a royal confirmation of your civil and religious liberties," he celebrated.[26] Yet, warning his auditors against over-zealous

---

[24] Cathcart, *The Baptist Encyclopedia*, 1108.

[25] Samuel Stillman, *Good News from a far Country. A Sermon Preached at Boston, May 17. 1766. Upon the Arrival of the important News of the Repeal of the Stamp-Act* (Boston: Kneeland and Adams, 1766), 33.

[26] *Ibid.*, 31.

celebration, Stillman took the opportunity to turn the church's eyes from the government of man to that of God.

> Are we tenacious of our rights and liberties? And do we fear every thing that looks like an infringement? What think we then of our conduct towards Him, who is the only Potentate? How often have we been for wresting the government from Him, and have practically said, *'We will not have the Lord to reign over us?'*[27]

Instead, he chided, there is indeed "good news from a far country," the Gospel itself, "a method of salvation. . .that effectually secures the honours of the divine government, and the harmony of Jehovah's attributes; while the chief of sinners are made heirs of God, and joint-heirs with Jesus Christ!"[28]

The good news of the Gospel, Stillman believed, began in the "counsel of peace" with the covenant of grace as Father and Son conspired to save a fallen humanity while exercising His sovereignty and magnifying His glory.

> This great truth, which appears to me to shine with distinguished brightness, in the holy Bible, is full of solid comfort to the pious soul; an article of high importance in the church of Christ; and when rightly understood, has a most powerful influence on the believer's practice. . . .That a deviation from this and the other glorious doctrines, that are connected with it, has generally been attended with a decay of vital religion.

That sinful man would reject the notion of such a benevolent yet sovereign plan should come as no surprise, he added. It is "a doctrine from heaven."[29]

Orthodox in his faith, Reformed in his soteriology, Stillman introduced nothing new in his sermon that day. Instead, he chose to remind them that the true Gospel must influence the heart. "It begins with the heart," he added, "laying the ax to the root of the tree. . . .Hence the man becomes a new creature, old things pass

---

[27] *Ibid.*, 7-8.

[28] *Ibid.*, 8.

[29] *Ibid.*, 10-11.

away, and all things become new," he said. With the new heart comes "new apprehensions of divine things, new feelings, 'Joy and peace in believing' " and "different conduct." The changes don't end there, however. Regeneration has a "special influence also on the believer's mind." He discovers himself to be newly "spiritually minded." He sees the "intrinsic beauty of holiness." So comprehensive is the change, Stillman reminded his church, "Nothing will satisfy him short of perfect holiness." At conversion, the citizenship of the soul passes from earth to heaven where a sovereign yet benevolent God reigns. To that government he called his people to submit.[30]

In short order, Stillman's English sympathies would change. As pressure mounted on the colonies to submit or surrender, Stillman commended the officers and men of the Massachusetts militia for their service and their skills. A few years later when British troops took Boston by force in 1775, Stillman and family would remove to Philadelphia. There his reputation as a preacher would precede him and in short order he was invited to preach before the Continental Congress meeting to consider the future of the nation. Stillman returned to Boston in 1776 and remained active in his pulpit for remainder of the hostilities.

With the war for independence won and British domination behind, America set her sights on a new future, one bright with possibilities and heavy with responsibility. To move forward, a new government had to be established, but to prevent moving backward, this new government had to be governed itself. To that end, the representatives of the people put forth a proposed Constitution. Stillman found himself in favor of the document and spoke publicly of his support.

In 1779, Stillman was called upon again by the legislature to preach on a day of great civic import. The first Baptist to enjoy this honor, Stillman's invitation was initially revoked. A second vote, however, proved that his popularity was greater than the opposition realized and the invitation was quickly extended once more. On May 26, 1779, he preached before the Massachusetts House of Representatives. His topic? The rights and responsibilities of a Christian people in this newfound democracy.

The text Stillman chose for his sermon was the twenty-first verse of Matthew 22: "Then faith be unto them, Render therefore unto Caesar, the things that are Caesar's: and unto God, the things that are God's." After explaining the biblical context of the

[30] *Ibid.*, 15-16.

passage, Stillman moved to address the context of their gathering that day.

> The time has been when the divine right of kings sounded from the pulpit and the press; and when the sacred name of religion was brought in, to sanctify the most horrid systems of despotism and cruelty.—But blessed be God, we live in a more happy era, in which the great principles of liberty are better understood. With us it is a *first* and *fundamental* principle, *that God made all men equal*.[31]

This new state of "entire freedom" in which Stillman and his contemporaries found themselves required great care, he counseled. Operating with the consent of the people, the new government must be "the best calculated to promote the happiness of themselves and of their posterity."[32]

While he gave attention to a wide variety of civic matters in his sermon, Stillman gave the greatest amount to the role of the state and religion. Of particular concern was the freedom of conscience.

> From hence arises, in my view, the indispensable necessity of a Bill of Rights, drawn up in the most explicit language, previously to the ratification of a constitution of government; which should contain its fundamental principles, and which no person in the state, however dignified, should dare to violate but at his peril.[33]

This Bill of Rights, he contended must protect the citizen from governmental interference in matters wherein the Deity alone is sovereign.

While acknowledging that the magistrate exercises a God-given authority, Stillman reasoned that same authority is God-limited as well. Arguing from the sermon's text, he added, that "there are some things which Caesar, or the magistrate, cannot of right

---

[31] Samuel Stillman, *A Sermon Preached before the Honorable Council and the Honorable House of Representatives of the State of Massachusetts-Bay, in New-England, at Boston, May 26, 1779. Being the Anniversary for the Election of the Honorable Council* (Boston: T. and J. Fleet, 1779), 8.

[32] *Ibid.*, 9.

[33] *Ibid.*, 10.

demand, nor the people yield." Continuing, he reminded the Representatives,

> We are engaged in a most important contest; not for POWER, but FREEDOM. We mean not to change our masters, but to secure to ourselves, and to generations yet unborn, the perpetual enjoyment of civil and religious liberty, in their fullest extent.[34]

Thus, the power of the state must of necessity be limited to the things of this world. For, as he would add later, man is bound to the precepts of the Bible before the principles of man.

> The doctrines that we are to believe, the duties that we are to perform, the officers who are to serve in [the church], and the laws by which all its subjects are to be governed, we become acquainted with by the oracles of God, which are the Christian's infallible directory: To which he is bound to yield obedience, at the risque [risk] of his reputation and life.[35]

Matters of faith belong to the kingdom of God over which man holds no sway. "The subjects of this kingdom are bound by no laws in matters of religion, but as such as they receive from Christ, who is the only lawgiver and head of his church."[36] Such the Bible teaches, Stillman told his audience that day, and such they must remember in the exercise of their appointed duties.

The Christian citizen, Stillman added, also bears responsibility in the outworking of the new democracy.

> For though Christians may contend amongst themselves about their religious differences, they will all unite to promote the good of the community, because it is their interest, so long as they all enjoy the blessings of a free, and equal administration of government.[37]

---

[34] *Ibid.*, 21-22.

[35] *Ibid.*, 26.

[36] *Ibid.*, 27-28.

[37] *Ibid.*, 30.

Working together, the church and the state provide an atmosphere in which the freedom of all citizens might flourish.

Likewise, the establishment of one system of belief, of one sect, or denomination over against all others, also merited Stillman's words of caution.

> Happy are the inhabitants of that common wealth, in which every man sits under his vine and fig-tree, having none to make him afraid [Micah 4:4].—In which all are *protected*, but none *established*![38]

For the independence declared in Philadelphia and defined in the Constitution to be truly free, the citizens of America must be free to choose their form of government and their form of religion.

In the end, Stillman called on his fellow Christians to see their civic duty in light of eternity.

> They should study to imbibe more of the spirit of their divine Master, to love as brethren, and to preserve the unity of the spirit in the bonds of peace. In the present state of ignorance and prejudice they cannot expect to see eye to eye. There will be a variety of opinions and modes of worship among the disciples of the same Lord; men equally honest, pious, and sensible, while they remain in this world of imperfection. Let them therefore be faithful to their respective principles, and kind, and forbearing towards one another. Their chief study should be to advance the cause of morality and religion in the world; and by their good works to glorify their Father who is in heaven.[39]

While the results of the Fall are too far reaching to permit the illusion of a present perfection in the form of government, Christians should strive as pious members of society to promote the good of all mankind. Such is their secular and sacred duty.

Sermons dealing with civic and Christian sensibilities dot the landscape of Stillman's work. On July 4, 1789, he was called upon by the leaders of Boston to deliver a sermon "in celebration of the anniversary of American independence." With this oration Still-

---

[38] *Ibid.*

[39] *Ibid.*, 37-38.

man reminded his hearers of God's grace in the establishment of the American nation and the disestablishment of the state church.

> The American Revolution, my Fellow-Citizens, is a great event in the moral government of God: new and astonishing to us and to surrounding nations, but not so to that Omniscient Being, who is said in the language of inspiration, to see the end from the beginning. That it was the purpose of God it should be, is evident in his almost miraculous interpositions in favor of it.[40]

Stillman went on to recount the key principles of liberty adopted by the nation so recently in the Constitution, notably freedom of the press and freedom of religion. He also took the opportunity to call upon elected officials to engage their Christian beliefs in the service of and for the benefit of the people.

> Civil rulers ought to go before the people as examples of everything amiable and praiseworthy; be the constant patrons of religion and learning, and do everything in their power to promote that righteousness which exalteth a nation.[41]

In fact, he said, the want of such true virtue ought to disqualify a politician from public service.

Five years later in 1794, Stillman again displayed the harmonious union of the Christian faith and the civic reality as he preached on the day "of thanksgiving to God, who guides the affairs of empire."[42] His thanksgiving extended to his own providential birth during such a time as his, "at a period, which gave me an opportunity of observing the origin, progress and glorious issue of my country's contest with her oppressors."[43]

---

[40] Samuel Stillman, *An Oration, Delivered July 4th, 1789, at the Request of the Inhabitants of the Town of Boston in Celebration of the Anniversary of American Independence* (Boston: B. Edes & Sons, 1789), 5.

[41] *Ibid.*, 28.

[42] Samuel Stillman, *Thoughts on the French Revolution. A Sermon, Delivered November 20, 1794: Being the Day of Annual Thanksgiving* (Boston: Manning and Loring, 1795), 5.

[43] *Ibid.*, 11.

Comparing the Revolution in America with that taking place in France, Stillman acknowledged that human depravity necessitates the grace of God in that he preserved true religion in the former even while man rejected it in the latter. Through it all, Stillman believed, God ordained and preserved the United States in the face of human ambition and the tendency toward sinful self-destruction. "Let us unite in giving glory to God for our Federal Government," he said, "which hath already raised the United States to wealth and eminence."[44]

Not long before the turn of the century, on April 25, 1799, Stillman again revealed his commitment to federal form of representation because of his Christian beliefs. When the President called for a national day of fasting, Stillman responded with a sermon drawn from Joel 2:15-17. In this message, he issued a clarion call to faithfulness in light of the degradation of the situation in France toward civil war. Warning his American audience that day, Stillman told them that the human proclivity to sin placed them in a situation not far removed from that of France. To forestall such dire events in the United States, he urged them to admit their dependence on God in all matters. "We pray God, that sad necessity may not drive us into this awful condition as a nation."[45] To prevent such a tragedy, Stillman called on the people to reject the atheism that marked the French Revolution and the deism that presented little more than a "political religion," a religion devoid of Christ yet posing as Christian.[46] "The state must," he contended, "have some kind of religion, in order to preserve the peace of society, and the obligation of an oath."[47]

To preserve the Christian religion in America, Stillman presented a two-fold plan. First, Christians must pray. "Let us then beseech the Father of mercies, to spare us as a nation, and to revive his own work among us, that there may be a universal reformation in our country."[48] Second, ministers of the Gospel

---

[44] *Ibid.*, 25.

[45] Samuel Stillman, *A Sermon, Preached at Boston, April 25, 1799; the Day Recommended by the President of the United States for a National Fast* (Boston: Manning and Loring), 9.

[46] *Ibid.*, 10-11.

[47] *Ibid.*, 11.

[48] *Ibid.*, 14.

must rise up and take on the role of leadership in the church and the nation. They must lament the sinful condition of the people[49] and they must sound the alarm for those same people so in love with their own sinfulness.[50] Recognizing the tendency of the people and their government to silence their critics, Stillman responded to the unspoken criticism of his opponents:

> Shall the ministers of religion be censured, for endeavouring, like Paul, to support government?—the government of their own choice? Is it not their duty to use their influence to promote the peace, the order, and safety of society? Most certainly it is.[51]

The problem he realized was not that his peers denied a role for religion in politics. As he said, "The objection does not lie so much against their '*preaching* politics,' as against the '*politics* they preach.' "[52]

Finally, Stillman called on his people to humble themselves and pray that God would preserve the nation from the evils that she so justly deserves for her sins against him.[53] As he closed that sermon, Stillman reminded them of their duty to pray for the President:

> Brethren, pray for him, that God will graciously sustain him, and inspire him with that wisdom that is profitable to direct: also, that the councils of our nation may be under the divine direction; and that the happy period may soon arrive, when that kingdom which is righteousness, peace, and joy in the Holy Ghost [Rom. 14:17], shall be universally established, and all men dwell together in friendship and in love. And let all the people say, 'AMEN.'[54]

---

[49] *Ibid.*, 17.

[50] *Ibid.*, 19.

[51] *Ibid.*, 21.

[52] *Ibid.*

[53] *Ibid.*, 22.

[54] *Ibid.*, 23.

In Stillman's mind, God's providence and human institutions were conjoined. The latter could not succeed without the success of the former. The Christian citizen, he believed, would do well to seek them both.

In the death of George Washington, Stillman recognized the sweet hand of God's providence as well. Washington died on December 14, 1799. Stillman spoke of it two weeks later in a sermon that compared the death of the great general and president to that of King Hezekiah in 2 Chronicles 32. So powerful was that sermon that his fellow Baptists sought and received his permission to reprint the message in its entirety for the benefit of all the people of Boston.

When originally preached, the sermon sought to soothe the broken heart of a mourning people. While acknowledging that all men must die, God remained sovereign, even in the case of "our beloved WASHINGTON."[55] Rather than dwell on the sorrow of the moment, Stillman chose to remind his audience that "though dead. . . .he speaketh to us by his *private*, and his *public* life."[56] Washington's life, he said, should serve as a model for the Christian and the citizen.

While later historians may doubt the depth and orthodoxy of Washington's faith, Stillman entertained no such reservations. "His *religious* character will be established in the view of every candid mind by the tenor of his life," he announced. "In his public acts we have repeated evidence of his reverence for Deity, and dependence on his Providence."[57] Clearly rebutting any accusations of deism, Washington told Congress upon his resignation from service,

> The successful termination of the war has verified the most sanguine expectations, and my gratitude for the interposition of Providence, and the assistance I have received from my countrymen, increases with every review of the momentous subject. I consider it as an indispensable duty to close this last solemn act of my official life, by commending

---

[55] Samuel Stillman, *A Sermon, Occasioned by the Death of George Washington, Late Commander in Chief of the Armies of the United States of America* (Boston: Manning and Loring, 1800), 9.

[56] *Ibid.*, 10.

[57] *Ibid*, 12-13.

> the interests of my dearest country to the protection of Almighty God, and those who have the superintendence of them to his holy keeping.[58]

Shortly after leaving the public eye, Washington was called back to the service of his country when elected its first president. To that task, Stillman pointed out, Washington brought his faith as well. In his acceptance address before a joint session of Congress, the president announced,

> Such being the impressions under which I have, in obedience to the public summons, repaired to the present station; it would be peculiarly improper to omit, in this first official act, my fervent supplications to that Almighty Being, who rules over the universe—who presides in the councils of nations—and whose providential aids can supply every human defect—that his benediction may consecrate to the liberties and happiness of the United States, a government instituted by themselves for these essential purposes;. . . .[59]

Washington's public proclamation of his faith, Stillman wanted his congregation to see, was sincere and intimately related to his service of a people with whom he shared a common vision and belief. For, as Washington added in another address,

> Whatever may be conceded of the influence of refined education on minds of peculiar structure; reason and experience both forbid us to expect, that national morality can prevail in exclusion of religious principle.[60]

This faith, Stillman concluded, accompanied the president to his grave.

Stillman brought these observations to his congregation not to simply add his praises to the chorus of many that followed Washington's death. Instead, he used this event of national import to call them to action. People should do more than pay mere verbal homage to the man, he said. The greatest compliment that could

---

[58] *Ibid.*, 13.

[59] *Ibid.*, 14.

[60] *Ibid.*, 15.

be paid to Washington would be to "*imitate* his virtues."[61] Even more importantly, his life and example ought to inspire thoughts of greater import.

> If the personal excellencies of a man can attract the admiration of a nation, how ought we to be swallowed up in love and adoration of that God, in whom dwells essentially every possible perfection![62]

The perfections of the infinitely great God, Stillman said, merit man's worship.

Washington's demise was also used by Stillman to point his audience to the reality of their own coming death. "The solemn instance of death which now arrests our attention," he said, "is a loud call to all. . . .to be always ready, because they know not the day nor the hour when the Son of Man will come." When death comes, he continued, it ignores all social distinctions, from the greatest to the least all must die and face the eternal consequences of their life. Thus, he deduced, "It becomes us all to entertain a lively sense of that awful period, when God will judge the secrets of men by Jesus Christ; and to be prepared for it, that we may give up our account with joy, and not with grief."[63] Even in the instance of the death of America's first citizen, Stillman was compelled to point his auditor's to God as the source and the hope of the nation. "We are under every obligation to mingle thanksgivings to God," he preached, "with the sorrows of the occasion, because a life so important to our country hath been spared so long. A kind Providence lent us a WASHINGTON."[64] Rather than be lost in sorrow, he concluded, "we leave for a moment the tomb of our much loved friend, to offer praise to Almighty God, for the many promising and useful characters that rise before us."[65] After all, as the people go to God, so goes the country, for its future is only as great as its faith.

---

[61] *Ibid.*, 22.

[62] *Ibid.*, 23.

[63] *Ibid.*, 24.

[64] *Ibid.*, 24-25.

[65] *Ibid.*, 25-26.

Concluding observations

Samuel Stillman was truly a man of two countries—one heavenly, the other earthly—a citizen of two worlds. He was a man of God and a man of and for his times. He proved that one can and should separate the state from the church but that you cannot and should not separate the church from the state.

Stillman's life and thought impacted the spiritual life of Baptists, Boston, New England and the new country. His friend and fellow pastor, Thomas Baldwin remarked,

> He was always the polite and attentive Christian gentleman. He was a diligent pastor and student. He was an ardent patriot. No pulpit orator was heard with greater delight in the stormy times preceding the Revolution. He deemed it his duty to preach upon political questions which agitated the people, and spoke with no compromising voice. He was a born leader of men.[66]

Baldwin's account was not alone in its commendation of Samuel Stillman. His approval was near universal among his contemporaries, both congregants and ordinary citizens. Friend and frequent publisher James Loring commented forty years after Stillman's death, "In death, as well as in life, he evinced the living power, the sublimity, and greatness, of Christian faith."[67] Samuel Stillman had, just as he had asked of God, lived a life of consequence. He lived much in a little time.

---

[66] Wood, *The History of First Baptist Church of Boston*, 300.

[67] Sprague, *Annals of the American Pulpit*, 77.

Further Reading

Thomas Baldwin, "Biographical Sketch of the Author's Life." *Select Sermons on Doctrinal and Practical Subjects by the Late Samuel Stillman.* Boston: Manning and Loring, 1808, v–xviii.

Thomas Baldwin, David Benedict, James M. Winchell, John Pierce, James Loring and William Jenks, "Samuel Stillman, D.D." William B. Sprague, ed. *Annals of the American Pulpit.* New York: Robert Carter and Brothers, 1865, Volume 6 (Baptist), 71-79

Baron Stow. *A Discourse, delivered at the One Hundredth Anniversary of the Organization of The Baldwin Place [formerly Second] Baptist Church, July 27, 1743.* Boston: Gould, Kendall and Lincoln, 1843.

Nathan E. Wood. *The History of the First Baptist Church of Boston, 1665-1899.* Philadelphia: American Baptist Publication Society, 1899.

HEZEKIAH SMITH
1737 - 1805

by John David Broome

On May 9, 2010, the First Baptist Church of Haverhill, Massachusetts, observed its two hundredth and forty-fifth anniversary. This large and affluent church owes much of its heritage to one man—Hezekiah Smith, its founder and first pastor. Baptists of America also have cause to be interested in this man. In New England, he forged the spearhead of Baptist advance into the region north of Boston. His religious heritage and education were received among the Baptists of the Middle Colonies. He was ordained to the ministry in the South. In this brief essay we will revisit his wide-ranging life and influence.

Early years

Hezekiah Smith was born on April 21, 1737, at Hempstead, Long Island, to well-to-do Anglican parents. When Smith was but a child, the family moved to Hanover, New Jersey. Several years later, he was providentially led to hear John Gano, the intrepid Baptist pastor at nearby Morristown; young Smith became a Baptist. Eager for an education, he was among the first students of the Baptist Academy at Hopewell. He later graduated from the College of New Jersey (now Princeton University) in 1762. Meanwhile, the Hopewell Baptist Church had licensed the aspiring young preacher.

A visit to the South followed graduation from college. The historic First Baptist Church of Charleston, South Carolina, ordained Hezekiah Smith on September 20, 1763. The Cashaway Church in the Pee Dee region called him to be their pastor. He served the church for several months. In addition to the valuable pulpit experience which he gained in the South, Smith established friendships which were to influence his subsequent life. He was introduced to the actual work of the great evangelist George Whitefield in Savannah. He saw the success of Oliver Hart among the aristocratic society of Charleston. Friendships with wealthy South Carolina and Georgia planters were later to be valuable assets. Perhaps the most important experience of all to the later ministry of Smith was the introduction which he received to the Baptists of the Separate tradition—Shubal Stearns, Daniel Marshall, Samuel Harriss, and the like.

Soon after his return to New Jersey in early 1764, Hezekiah Smith went with his friend James Manning to Rhode Island, to the site of a proposed Baptist college which Manning hoped to establish. After a short stay there, Smith embarked on a preaching tour which carried him as far north as Maine. Large crowds attended his services at most places. Haverhill, Massachusetts, was the scene of an enthusiastic reception for the itinerating evangelist. Smith wrote in his journal, "Oh that the Time might now come that Haverhill Town might be as one Man in God's service."[1] Smith was solicited to remain in Haverhill by many of the town's inhabitants. After a careful examination of the situation, Hezekiah Smith decided that Haverhill was the locale where he wanted to invest his ministry; it was to last forty years and was to extend far beyond the environs of the little town by the Merrimack River.

Pastor at Haverhill

The decision of Hezekiah Smith to remain in Haverhill elicited both adverse and favorable reactions. The pastors of the established Congregational churches vigorously opposed his efforts to begin a Baptist congregation—there was but one Baptist church north of Boston at the time. On the other hand, there were people in Haverhill who welcomed the opportunity to sit under the preaching of a man who bore the marks of "a second Whitefield."[2]

On January 1, 1765, a religious society was organized for the support of the ministry of Smith. The Haverhill Baptist Society was necessitated because a Baptist church had no property rights in Massachusetts. A large majority of those in the society were not Baptists. However, it was but a short time until many society members accepted the Baptist tenet of believer's baptism. On April 13, 1765, Smith baptized eight persons in the Merrimack.

---

[1] John David Broome, *The Life, Ministry and Journals of Hezekiah Smith, 1737-1805. Pastor of the First Baptist Church of Haverhill, Massachusetts and Chaplain in the Revolution* (Springfield, MO: Particular Baptist Press 2004), 272.

[2] William W. Everts and John H. Davis, *Historical Discourse delivered on the One Hundred and Twenty-Fifth Anniversary of the First Baptist Church of Haverhill, Massachusetts, May 9, 1890, and the Historical Sketch of the Sunday School* (Haverhill, MA: Chase Brothers, Printers, 1890), 12.

Five days later, he preached in the open to about two thousand persons, most of whom had come to view the baptism of eight more candidates.[3]

An early Haverhill historian noted that Smith's "ardent manner, and his calvinistic sentiments. . .drew together considerable numbers" in Haverhill.[4] On May 9, 1765, twenty-three persons joined in the formal organization of a Baptist church.[5] Less than a month later, these and other worshipers held services in their own building, an imposing edifice which seated five hundred persons. Hezekiah Smith was formally installed as the pastor of the church on November 12, 1766. His close friends, John Gano, James Manning, and Samuel Stillman, participated in the service.

The infant church grew rapidly under the leadership of its first pastor. By the fall of 1767, the church had 107 members.[6] The pastoral concern of Smith extended into the nearby towns and villages in Massachusetts, New Hampshire, and Maine. Soon, the membership of the Haverhill Church included persons who lived far removed from Haverhill. By 1783, the church had grown in membership until it was the fifth largest Baptist congregation in New England, having 190 members.[7] A larger membership was prevented by the steady dismissal of members over the years to form new Baptist churches, as well as by the rigid discipline enforced by the church.

The journal of Smith reveals that he had unusual concern as a pastor for his people. For those who could not attend services because of sickness, he would hold services in their homes. For the members of the church who lived at locales distant from Haverhill,

---

[3] Broome, *Life, Ministry, and Journals of Hezekiah Smith*, 283.

[4] Leverett Saltonstall, *An Historical Sketch of Haverhill, in the County of Essex, and the Commonwealth of Massachusetts; with Biographical Notices* (Boston: John Eliot, 1816), 31.

[5] "In Haverhill. The Baptist Church-Book. 1765," 21. (This unpublished records book of the early days of the Haverhill Church is in the Haverhill Public Library.)

[6] *Ibid.*, 28.

[7] Isaac Backus, *A History of New England, with Particular Reference to the Denomination of Christians Called Baptists*. Second Edition, with Notes by David Weston (Newton, MA: Backus Historical Society, 1871), 2: 306-310.

he was a constant visitor. Respect for Smith increased over the years among his Congregational neighbors. A tribute of note is the fact that he actually preached the funeral sermons of two neighboring Congregational ministers late in his ministry.[8] Such was in keeping with the established practice of the Haverhill pastor to accept any and all preaching opportunities.

Preacher

Hezekiah Smith took his calling quite literally. Scarcely a week went by that he did not preach or "exhort" five or six times. Scenes for his preaching included such places as taverns, orchards, barns, log cabins, wharves, gallows, army camps—anywhere he could secure a hearing. During the course of his ministry, he preached in each of the original thirteen states, as well as in Maine, which was a part of Massachusetts until 1820. Everywhere he went, crowds attended his services—a mark of an outstanding pulpiteer.

The messages of Smith were usually textual in style. Each sermon always concluded with an "application," which presented the challenge of the message to the audience. In a day when sermons of marathon length were not unusual, Smith seldom let his services exceed an hour.[9] He was a master in the choice of appropriate texts to suit the occasion. A funeral sermon for two young boys occasioned the use of Job 1:19: "and it fell upon the young men, and they are dead."[10] Just prior to the crucial battle to save Albany, New York, in 1777, Smith preached to the American troops from Psalm 60:11: "Give us help from trouble: for vain is the help of man."[11]

Samuel Davies (1723-1761), the noted colonial preacher and orator, taught Hezekiah Smith at the College of New Jersey. Smith oft waxed eloquent in the style of his teacher, as in a description of the "Church of God":

---

[8] Broome, *Life, Ministry, and Journals of Hezekiah Smith,* 567, 579.

[9] Samuel F. Smith and Laban Clark, "Hezekiah Smith, D.D.," in William B. Sprague, ed., *Annals of the American Pulpit* (New York: Robert Carter and Bros., 1865), 6 (Baptist): 103.

[10] Broome, *Life, Ministry, and Journals of Hezekiah Smith*, 348.

[11] *Ibid.*, 452.

> It is fitly framed together, by the materials being taken out from the quarry of fallen nature, broken by the law, hewn and squared by God's Word in the hands of the divine Spirit, and polished with grace, and each material placed in the building in proper order by the great Architect.[12]

Such eloquence, however, did not alienate Smith from the rank and file hearers. His preaching met with marked success among the rough backwoodsmen of South Carolina and New Hampshire, as well as among the elite of Charleston and Boston. James Manning called Smith a "son of thunder."[13] Laban Clark commented that the Haverhill pastor "fed, not glutted, his flock with the sincere milk of the Word."[14]

Theologically, Hezekiah Smith stood in the camp of evangelical Calvinism. In his early years in New England, he was often embroiled in theological debates with neighboring Arminian Congregational pastors. His position relative to believer's baptism involved him in conflicts with *all* of the clergy of the established church. Several works which condemned Smith and his views were published. He int turn capably defended himself and the Baptist viewpoint in two printed replies to his attackers. He also employed other means to solidify the Baptist position in Haverhill and New England.

Citizen and patriot

A man often dissuades potent opposition on the one hand by an appreciable exhibition at other points. Hezekiah Smith alleviated the bitter religious opposition which he experienced in Haverhill by an obvious and successful attempt to be a good citizen of his town and country. Leverett Saltonstall wrote of Smith, "As a

---

[12] *Ibid.,* "God's Church or Building described," (n.p.). (This is a sermon outline found in the Backus Historical Collection at Andover Newton Theological School, Newton Centre, Massachusetts.)

[13] Reuben A. Guild, *Life, Times, and Correspondence of James Manning, and the Early History of Brown University* (Boston: Gould and Lincoln, 1864), 181.

[14] Smith and Clark, "Hezekiah Smith, D.D.," in Sprague, *Annals of the American Pulpit,* 6: 103.

husband, parent, friend, and neighbor, he was highly exemplary."[15]

When he was thirty-four years of age, Smith married Miss Hephzibah Kimball of Boxford, Massachusetts. They had six children, two of whom died in infancy. In addition to the income which was brought into the family by the sale of considerable property owned by his wife, Hezekiah Smith taught school, wrote legal papers, and took in boarders in order to provide income for his growing family. He was a member of the town school board, participated in various literary and civic organizations, and played an active role in the civic affairs of Haverhill.

Hezekiah Smith also proved to be a good citizen of his country. In the 1774 Warren Association circular letter, he wrote, "It is a day of great affliction, when our civil rights are invaded."[16] Soon after the shots were fired on Lexington green, he became a chaplain in the Massachusetts regiment of Colonel John Nixon. Smith was present at the battle of Bunker Hill in June of 1775. Officially commissioned by the Continental Congress on January 1, 1777, Smith served the American cause with valor in the New York area. He became acquainted with George Washington, who attended the services he conducted on several occasions.[17] Smith served until late 1780, when he was "discharged by permission of General Washington."[18] Upon arriving home in Haverhill, he preached to his people from Isaiah 54:7: "For a small moment have I forsaken thee; but with great mercies will I gather thee."[19] The Baptists of New England, as well as those of Haverhill, felt the impact of the "gathering" by Hezekiah Smith.

---

[15] Saltonstall, *An Historical Sketch of Haverhill,* 31.

[16] *Minutes of the Proceedings of the Warren-Association, in their Meeting at Medfield, September 13th and 14th, 1774* (Boston: John Kneeland, 1774), 7.

[17] Broome, *Life, Ministry, and Journals of Hezekiah Smith*, 462.

[18] *Massachusetts Soldiers and Sailors of the Revolutionary War* (Boston: Wright and Potter Printing Co., 1906), 14: 412.

[19] Reuben A. Guild, *Chaplain Smith and the Baptists; or Life, Journals, Letters, and Addresses of the Rev. Hezekiah Smith, D.D., of Haverhill, Massachusetts, 1737-1805* (Philadelphia: American Baptist Publication Society, 1885), 282.

Denominational leader

Aside from Isaac Backus, there was a lack of strong leadership among New England Baptists in 1764. Hezekiah Smith soon gained a reputation as a leader among the Baptists of New England. In his later years, he was known among the Baptists as the "great man of Haverhill."[20] His denominational work centered around educational and associational projects.

Rhode Island College opened its doors in 1765. Hezekiah Smith was elected as one of the college's twelve fellows, its governing body.[21] Much of the remainder of his life was devoted to the benefit of the college; in fact, he missed but three meetings of the college board in forty years. Lack of funds and students plagued the college in its early years. Smith went to the South in late 1769 "to beg for the college."[22] His friends in the region responded to his appeals, for he obtained subscriptions in the amount of £3,710 for the college. Smith also "recruited" students for the school. One of these, Asa Messer (1769-1836), was later to be president of the college, renamed Brown University, from 1802-1826. In 1797, the college recognized Smith's achievements by conferring an honorary Doctor of Divinity degree upon him.

Begun in 1767, the Warren Association was the first such organization among the Regular Baptists of New England. The Haverhill Church was one of the four churches which formed the association. Hezekiah Smith was an active participant in the affairs of the association. He was a member of its religious liberty committee from its inception in 1769 until his death in 1805. This committee led in the Baptist quest for the separation of church and state in Massachusetts. Moderator of the association on twelve occasions, Smith was a trustee of its education fund for young ministers, was its representative to other such bodies on numerous occasions, and wrote the associational circular letter on three occasions. However, Hezekiah Smith did not depend solely on organized effects to advance the Baptist cause; he went himself.

---

[20] William H. Allison, "Smith, Hezekiah," *Dictionary of American Biography* (New York: Charles Scribner's Sons), 17 (1935): 280.

[21] *Ibid.*, 106-107, 296; Harry L. Koopman, ed., *Historical Catalogue of Brown University, Providence, Rhode Island, 1764-1894* (Providence: P. S. Remington and Co., 1895), 2.

[22] Broome, *Life, Ministry, and Journals of Hezekiah Smith*, 355.

Missionary

Apart from a feeble congregation at Newton, New Hampshire, there were no Baptist churches northeast of Boston in 1764. Not content to be localized to the immediate environs of Haverhill, Hezekiah Smith "lived chiefly in the saddle."[23] His preaching tours carried him to many locales in Massachusetts, New Hampshire, Vermont, and Maine. Though not always welcomed, he usually had little trouble securing an audience; many of the remote towns and hamlets were devoid of regular preaching of any kind. In 1767, the tireless itinerant preached at least 127 sermons in some thirty-nine places other than Haverhill.[24] At one town in Maine, he spoke in a barn because the meetinghouse could not hold the crowd, and "likewise because the barn was handier to the river...."[25]

There were many other places where Smith baptized converts to the Baptist faith. These converts, along with many Separate Baptists, became the foundations of numerous Baptist churches which Smith helped to establish. Among these were churches in the New Hampshire towns of Weare, Deerfield, Stratham, Brentwood, Nottingham, Hopkinton, and Exeter. Baptist work in Maine had lain dormant since the expulsion of William Screven in the late seventeenth century. In June 1768, Smith "assisted in constituting" Baptist churches in Gorham and Berwick, Maine.[26] Immediate success was not always gained by Smith. A historian of Concord, New Hampshire, wrote:

> It does not appear that his [Smith's] preaching had immediate effect; but some of the early Baptists of Concord seemed to regard the seed then sown as ripening afterward in the formation of the First Baptist Society of this city.[27]

---

[23] Everts and Davis, *Historical Discourse,* 13.

[24] Broome, *Life, Ministry, and Journals of Hezekiah Smith*, 320-334, where Journal entries reveal this information.

[25] *Ibid.*, 326-327.

[26] *Ibid.*, 339-340.

[27] James O. Lyford, ed., *History of Concord, New Hampshire, from the original Grant in seventeen hundred and twenty-five to the Opening of the*

A number of Smith's converts became Baptist preachers, including several from among the Congregational clergy.

The missionary vision of Hezekiah Smith extended beyond the bounds of northern New England. On May 26, 1802, he "met with a number of ministers and other Christians, to form and establish a missionary Society."[28] He was the moderator of the meeting and opened it with prayer.[29] Smith was also elected a trustee of the new society, which was designated The Massachusetts Baptist Missionary Society, the first such organization among American Baptists. At the encouragement of their pastor, several members of the Haverhill Church joined the newly-organized group; these Haverhill Baptists were among the first to rally around Luther Rice and the Judsons less than a decade later.[30]

Measure of his ministry

Hezekiah Smith preached his last sermon on January 13, 1805. Almost prophetically, he drew his text from John 12:24: "Except a corn of wheat fall into the ground and die, it abideth alone: But if it die, it bringeth forth much fruit."[31] Four days later, he was seized with a paralytic stroke. He died on January 24, 1805.

The most immediate effect of his death was a revival which swept Haverhill and the nearby towns. Almost a hundred new members were received by baptism into the Haverhill Church in a little over a year.[32] Ann Hasseltine, the future wife of Adoniram Judson, lived across the river from Haverhill in Bradford. She

---

Twentieth Century (Concord, New Hampshire: The Rumford Press, 1877), 1: 727.

[28] Broome, *Life, Ministry, and Journals of Hezekiah Smith,* 608.

[29] W. H. Eaton, *Historical Sketch of the Massachusetts Baptist Missionary Society and Convention* (Boston: Massachusetts Baptist Convention, 1903), 12.

[30] James B. Taylor, *Memoir of the Rev. Luther Rice, One of the First American Missionaries to the East* (Baltimore: Armstrong and Berry, 1840), 137.

[31] Broome, *Life, Ministry, and Journals of Hezekiah Smith*, 625.

[32] Everts and Davis, *Historical Discourse,* 27-28.

became a Christian in the revival, although she did not join the Baptist church at the time.[33]

The fruits of the life of Hezekiah Smith were manifold. Fifty years after his arrival in a region which had only one Baptist church, there were 277 "regular Baptist churches" with a total of 17,878 members in the area east of the Merrimack River in New Hampshire, Vermont, and Maine.[34] Many factors contributed to this rapid growth, but one must agree with a later historian who wrote of Smith, "It is safe to say that no man did more than he to give character to the denomination."[35]

As a pastor, the progress of the Haverhill Church under his ministry is evidence enough of his capacity to lead a congregation in the paths of Christian service. According to John Greenleaf Whittier, "but few excelled him [Smith] as a preacher."[36] Smith served his country well as a chaplain, in addition to being a good citizen of his town. He was an acknowledged leader among the Baptists of his day. Evidence of his widespread influence can be seen in the fact that he served as moderator of the New Hampshire Association in 1800,[37] of the Warren Association in 1801,[38] and of the Philadelphia Association in 1802.[39]

---

[33] *Ibid.*, 28.

[34] William Batchelder, *A Discourse delivered in Haverhill, July 1816, on a Baptismal Occasion*. Second edition (Exeter, NH: Samuel T. Moses, 1823), 18.

[35] Anon., "Smith, Hezekiah, D.D.," William Cathcart, ed., *The Baptist Encyclopedia* (Philadelphia: Louis H. Everts, 1881), 1066.

[36] B. L. Mirick, *The History of Haverhill, Massachusetts* (Haverhill, MA: A. W. Thayer, 1832), 191. (John Greenleaf Whittier compiled the material for this work, but the great poet left Haverhill before he had opportunity to publish the work. Mirick then published it as his work.)

[37] Broome, *Life, Ministry, and Journals of Hezekiah Smith*, 597.

[38] *Minutes of the Warren Association, held at the Meeting-House belonging to the First Baptist Church in Sutton, September 8 & 9, 1801* (Boston: Manning and Loring, 1801), 3.

[39] A. D. Gillette, ed., *Minutes of the Philadelphia Baptist Association, 1707-1807* (Philadelphia: American Baptist Publication Society, 1851), 369.

The efforts of Smith as a missionary of the Baptist cause were boundless. Henry C. Vedder wrote that Smith "was a whole State mission society in himself."[40] Perhaps a summation of the impact of Hezekiah Smith upon men can be seen in the experience of a New Hampshire backwoodsman when he confronted the Haverhill pastor for the first time. Andrew Sherburne later wrote as follows:

> I was surprised to see how perfectly at home he seemed to be in the humble cottage (log cabin); but I was astonished when I heard him preach. . . .His preaching caused my very soul to tremble. . . .At the close of the last exercise, I retired to the deep forest. . . .I resolved to unfold my soul to God, and plead for mercy; concluding that I could not make too great a sacrifice for the salvation of my soul.[41]

Such was the impact of Hezekiah Smith of Haverhill.

Further Reading

John David Broome. *The Life, Ministry, and Journals of Hezekiah Smith, 1737-1805. Pastor of the First Baptist Church of Haverhill, Massachusetts and Chaplain in the Revolution.* Springfield, MO: Particular Baptist Press, 2004.

Henry C. Graves. *Historical Sketch of the Baptist Religious Society of Haverhill, Massachusetts, and of the Church Edifices Built under its Direction.* Haverhill: James A. Hale, 1886.

Reuben A. Guild. *Chaplain Smith and the Baptists; or, Life, Journals, Letters, and Addresses of the Rev. Hezekiah Smith, D.D., of Haverhill, Massachusetts, 1737-1805.* Philadelphia: American Baptist Publication Society, 1885.

---

[40] Henry C. Vedder, *A Short History of the Baptists.* New and illustrated edition (Philadelphia: American Baptist Publication Society, 1907), 311.

[41] Andrew Sherburne, *Memoirs of Andrew Sherburne: A Pensioner of the Navy of the Revolution* (Utica, NY: William Williams, 1828), 146-147.

Andrew Bryan (1737-1812)

ANDREW BRYAN
1737 - 1812

by Walter E. Johnson

Andrew Bryan's contribution to Baptist life in America is interwoven with the establishment of what arguably is the oldest African-American church in continued existence. Baptist historian Leon McBeth noted that extant records do not allow for scholarly consensus concerning the identity of the first African-American Baptist church in America.[1] While it is certain that some African-American churches existed before Bryan's church, substantial evidence can be marshaled that this is the oldest such church *in continuous existence*. That Bryan's church was the first African-American church in Georgia, founded even prior to the white First Baptist Church of Savannah in 1800, is beyond question.

Background of the First African Baptist Church

Bryan is considered the first African-American to be ordained in America. This event, however, is also in question in that while other blacks were licensed to preach or were appointed to carry out evangelistic work on the Southern plantations, it not clear that prior to Bryan anyone had received ordination to the gospel ministry in association with a local church. If not the first, he had to be among the first so ordained.

Prior to the Revolutionary War, blacks often attended services in white churches. Winds of change however, were blowing in the 1770's:

> Only a few slaves in these two British Colonies [Virginia and Georgia] or anywhere else in the New World freely joined churches before the 1770s. But the preaching of the new wave of revivalists who emerged during the political revolutionary mood of the 1770s emboldened them to believe that maybe a few white people would assist them in establishing their own congregations. This required developing their own indigenous leadership, or at least relying on

[1] H. Leon McBeth, *The Baptist Heritage: Four Centuries of Baptist Witness* (Nashville: Broadman & Holman, 1987), 778.

bold white Christians willing to offer political protection in addition to spiritual nurture.[2]

The movement toward establishing independent black churches in America received a boost with the conversion of George Liele (sometimes spelled Lisle), a slave born in Virginia around 1750. Sometime before 1773, Liele's master, Henry Sharpe, brought Liele to Georgia where Liele was converted and received into the Buckhead Baptist Church under pastor Matthew Moore in 1772. Liele's gifts soon became evident and he was licensed to preach in 1775. Later that year, he was ordained by the Baptist Association of Burke County with the charge to preach to the slaves on the plantations along the Savannah River. At some point, Sharpe freed Liele to enhance the effectiveness of his ministry.[3] Liele preached successfully in the area of Savannah for three years.

In December 1777, without notice or approval, Liele constituted a church in Savannah and served as pastor. By 1780, the church had about thirty-eight members with the aid of several members who joined upon leaving the black church at Silver Bluff, South Carolina, which had been led by David George, a convert of Liele's. The Silver Bluff church disbanded due to problems associated with the Revolutionary War.[4] After Sharpe's death, efforts were made to re-enslave Liele, an attempt thwarted by a British officer who was part of the British occupation of Savannah. Realizing that re-enslavement after the war was a possibility, Liele decided to leave for Jamaica in 1783. Before the ship departed, Liele returned to Savannah and baptized Andrew Bryan and his wife Hannah, Kate Hogue, Hagar Simpson, and Samson Brown.[5] All were black

---

[2] James M. Washington, *Frustrated Fellowship: The Black Baptist Quest for Social Power* (Macon, GA: Mercer University Press, 1986), 8.

[3] Thomas Ray, *Daniel and Abraham Marshall—Pioneer Baptist Evangelists to the South*, including the *Memoirs of Abraham Marshall*, eds. Jabez P. Marshall and Thomas Ray (Springfield, MO: Particular Baptist Press, 2006), 59.

[4] Robert G. Gardner, et al., *A History of the Georgia Baptist Association 1784-1984* (Atlanta: Georgia Baptist Historical Society, 1996), 17.

[5] Edgar G. Thomas, *The First African Baptist Church of North America* (Savannah: copyrighted by the author, 1925), 25.

slaves.[6] Ultimately, Bryan succeeded Liele as pastor.[7] According to Edgar G. Thomas,

> Nine months after the departure of Rev. Liele, Andrew Bryan, who, through prayer meetings and fatherly advice, had held the little flock together, felt the divine call to preach the gospel and lead this yearning band. Without an available authorizing council, or even an instructor save the Holy Spirit to point the way on this untrodden path, Andrew meekly assumed the arduous task.[8]

Bryan's early life and trials

Andrew Bryan was born into slavery in 1737 at Goose Creek, South Carolina, near Charleston. Bryan's owner, Jonathan Bryan, a planter and politician, was a "New Light" Presbyterian. In 1738, Jonathan Bryan met George Whitefield, who believed that conversion to Christianity made slaves better workers and easier to handle. Influenced by Whitefield, Jonathan Bryan greatly encouraged Andrew in his preaching ministry among the slaves.[9] Bryan had been converted under Liele's preaching from John 3:7, "Ye must be born again."[10]

---

[6] Charles J. Elmore, *First Bryan—1788-2001: The Oldest Continuous Black Baptist Church in America* (Savannah: First Bryan Baptist Church, 2002), 3.

[7] Gardner, et al., *A History of the Georgia Baptist Association*, 17.

[8] Thomas, *The First African Baptist Church of North America*, 33.

[9] Uche Egemonye, "A History of First African Baptist Church, The Oldest Continuous Black Baptist Church in North America 1788-1939" (Ph.D. diss., Emory University, 2003), 53. [Without knowing the context of this sentiment attributed to Whitefield, which I have not met with before, the reader should not be left with the impression that Whitefield approved of the institution of slavery, for we know he did not. See in this regard Arnold A. Dallimore, "Whitefield and the American Negro," in Chapter 30 of his *George Whitefield, The Life and Times of the Great Evangelist of the Eighteenth-Century Revival* (London: The Banner of Truth Trust, 1989), 1: 495-509 —*Ed.*]

[10] From a letter by Abraham Marshall printed in Ray, *Daniel and Abraham Marshall*, 231.

After the American Revolution, Bryan continued to preach to blacks, as well as a few whites, but social and political circumstances weighed against Bryan's efforts. Bryan's early work was taking place soon after many blacks had fled from their owners to Savannah, which had been occupied by the British from 1778-1782. Apparently, many whites associated the rise of independent black churches with this loss of slaves and British occupation. Many whites in Savannah may have concluded that these black Baptists were Loyalists, following the lead of George Liele and his owner, Henry Sharpe.[11]

Such resentment toward the blacks led to various persecutions. According to a letter by Abraham Marshall, about eight or nine months after Liele's departure, Edward Davis allowed Bryan's congregation to construct a building on his land at Yamacraw, a suburb of Savannah. Marshall further stated that it was a building "of which they have been artfully dispossessed."[12] In 1787, as a part of this systemic persecution, Bryan, along with his brother Samson, a convert of Bryan's, and about fifty of Bryan's followers were attacked in public and severely beaten and whipped. Bryan was warned to cease preaching. He replied, "If you would stop me from preaching, cut off my head! For I am willing not only to be whipped, but would freely suffer death for the cause of the Lord Jesus."[13]

Many of these black Baptists were confined to prison. Jonathan Bryan interceded for them and secured their release, although opinions vary concerning Bryan's motive. Thomas wrote that Bryan considered them to be martyrs.[14] Egemonye claimed that the motivation was "paternalism and financial considerations, not racial egalitarianism."[15] E. K. Love was even critical in his evaluation. Concerning Jonathan Bryan's intervention, Love wrote, "We are disposed to believe that the sympathy of the community excited in favor of the persecuted disciples moved him rather than the magnanimity of his own heart. Where was he

---

[11] Egemonye, "A History of First African Baptist Church," 49.

[12] Quoted in Ray, *Daniel and Abraham Marshall*, 231.

[13] Thomas, *The First African Baptist Church of North America*, 34.

[14] *Ibid.*

[15] Egemonye, "A History of First African Baptist Church," 52.

while all this persecution was going on?"[16] Regardless of the motivation, Jonathan Bryan came to their rescue and offered the use of his barn at Brampton for Bryan's congregation to conduct worship in, which they did for about two years.[17]

George Walton, an attorney and two-time governor of Georgia, took up the blacks' case from a legal standpoint. Walton believed that the slaves had a right to congregate and practice their religion publicly. He petitioned the court to allow blacks to worship on Sundays; the court ruled in their favor—determining that they could worship between sunrise and sunset.[18] Thus, worship in Jonathan Bryan's barn was protected by law. Such protection facilitated the church's significant growth in subsequent years.

His church is formally constituted

Another giant step forward for the congregation came in 1788, when Bryan was ordained and the church constituted as a Baptist church.[19] Jesse Galphin, also known as Jesse Peter, another convert of Liele's and later a pastor at Silver Bluff, concluded that the persecution could be ameliorated if the church was duly constituted as a Baptist church. Knowing that Abraham Marshall (1748-1819) of Kiokee, Georgia, was a highly esteemed Baptist minister, Galphin secured Marshall's services to ordain Bryan and formally constitute the church. Marshall himself ordained Bryan, contrary to traditional Baptist polity, which called for the participation of one or more churches to form a new congregation.

Marshall left the congregation with two certificates. The first certificate verified they had formally constituted the church:

---

[16] E. K. Love, *History of the First African Baptist Church, from its Organization, January 20th, 1788, to July 1st, 1888. Including the Centennial Celebration, Addresses, Sermons, Etc.* (Savannah: The Morning News Press, 1888), 39.

[17] Egemonye, "A History of First African Baptist Church," 55.

[18] *Ibid.*

[19] Thomas claimed that this "was not the constitution of the church," but that the church was merely "organized anew." See Thomas, *The First African Baptist Church of North America*, 18-19.

> This is to *certify* that upon examination into the experiences and characters of a number of *Ethiopians*, at and adjacent to Savannah, it appears that God has brought them out of darkness into the light of the Gospel, and given them fellowship one with the other: believing it is the will of Christ, we have constituted them a church of Jesus Christ, to keep his worship and ordinances.
> January 19, 1788. A. Marshall, V.D.M.[20]

The second document certified Bryan's ordination, authorizing him to preach the gospel and administer the ordinances in a Baptist church:

> This is to certify that the Ethiopian church of Jesus Christ at Savannah, have called their beloved brother *Andrew* [Bryan] to the work of the ministry. We have examined into his qualifications, and believing it to be the will of the great Head of the church, we have appointed him to preach the Gospel, and administer the ordinances as God in his providence may call.
> January 20, 1788. A. Marshall, V.D.M.[21]

On January 20, 1788, Jesse Galphin baptized forty-five of Bryan's followers into the church.[22] These, along with twenty-four others, probably some from Liele's disbanded church, constituted the original members of the First African Baptist Church.[23]

Soon afterward, Bryan became aware that the method of his ordination and the church's constitution was highly irregular, seeing that no council of ministers had been called. In 1790, fearing for the denominational legitimacy of his church and the validity of his ordination, Bryan asked for an opinion from the Georgia Baptist Association. This evidently was very embar-

---

[20] John Rippon, *The Baptist Annual Register, for 1790, 1791, 1792, and Part of 1793* (London: Dilly, Button and Thomas, 1793), 341; as cited in Ray, *Daniel and Abraham Marshall*, 233-234.

[21] *Ibid.*, 234. [V.D.M. is an abbreviation for the Latin, Verbei Dei Minister: "Preacher of the Word of God" —*Ed.*]

[22] Elmore, *First Bryan*, 3.

[23] Egemonye, "A History of First African Baptist Church," 55.

rassing to Marshall, who was serving as the association's moderator that year. Ruling that Marshall's actions occurred in extraordinary circumstances, the Association affirmed his actions and admitted the First African Church into its fellowship, where it remained until 1802, when it joined the newly-formed Savannah River Association.[24]

Persecution subsided, but did not cease. Later in 1788, a Chatham County grand jury charged William Bryan, who received ownership of Andrew upon the death of his father Jonathan, with "permitting negroes to assemble, in large bodies," in violation of the law.[25] Andrew Bryan secured the services of a white attorney to draw up a petition on behalf of the church and presented it to the court with endorsements of fifty-three white slave owners. The court was unimpressed and refused the church the right to congregate.[26] The church prospered even in these adverse circumstances, growing from approximately sixty-seven members in 1788, to over 250 by 1790.[27]

The year 1790 brought other blessings as well to Bryan. According to Chatham County records, William Bryan sold Rev. Andrew Bryan his freedom for ,50 sterling, "acknowledging also the faithful services of my Negro fellow Andrew," and serving notice to "give and grant the said Negro fellow Andrew his full and absolute manumission."[28] The same year, Thomas Gibbons, three-time mayor of Savannah, donated a lot to the congregation to erect a church building, which they did with little or no outside financial help. In 1792, when the church decided to build again, Jonathan Clarke, an attorney and Baptist layman, wrote a fund-raising letter to Richard Furman, who was serving as pastor of the First Baptist Church of Charleston, South Carolina.[29] No information is available concerning Furman's response. Bryan did purchase a lot for what was equal to $150, and the congregation constructed a

---

[24] Washington, *Frustrated Fellowship*, 11.

[25] Egemonye, "A History of First African Baptist Church," 56.

[26] *Ibid.*, 58, 60.

[27] *Ibid.*, 61.

[28] From Chatham County Record, Book G, 1789-90, quoted in Thomas, *The First African Baptist Church of North America*, 37.

[29] Egemonye, "A History of First African Baptist Church," 61-62.

larger building, which was described as being "very plain, without any attempt at architectural beauty."[30]

By 1794, Bryan's church was confronted with further opposition from Savannah's white citizenry. The Chatham County Grand Jury noted that between five and six hundred Baptist slaves in Savannah were congregating regularly, in violation of the 1792 ordinance prohibiting their assembly. The jury ruled that blacks could not hold services separate from whites. The courts moved to close the church, but by using white ministers to preach in the services, the church remained open.[31]

This need of having white ministers to preach in his church likely was the occasion for which Bryan wrote this letter to Isaac Backus (1724-1806), an illustrious Baptist minister in Massachusetts:

> We request you and Gods people will pray for us; we are distressed and persicuted, but hope to trust in the Lord; we have built a place of worship, but have not had the opportunity of enjoying it much; since it was built, we have been prohibited from preaching in it for four months at one time and two months at another. Brother, pray for us; that the Lord would grant us Grace to walk in his fear and give us favour in the eyes of those that rule over us. We shall be happy to hear from you and our Brethern at the Northword, we are distitute of the Gospel here in a great measure; there are a few of our white Brethern visit from above [the North], but very few. . .should be glad if some of the ministering B[rethren] would visit us.[32]

Egemonye believes that Bryan was cognizant that Backus would have little influence in curbing the persecution and that the purpose of the correspondence was to request that Backus use his influence to encourage white ministers to preach in Bryan's church, insuring that the doors would remain open.[33]

---

30 *Ibid.*, 63.

31 *Ibid.*, 64.

32 Quoted as printed in William H. Brackney, ed., *Baptist Life and Thought: 1600-1980* (Valley Forge: Judson Press, 1983), 107.

33 Egemonye, "A History of First African Baptist Church," 67.

By 1796, events were such that Bryan perceived that the fears and concerns of the white citizens were abating. With that thought in mind, he re-submitted his 1790 petition, this time receiving a favorable ruling allowing them to worship.[34] In a very informative letter written to Dr. John Rippon in late December 1800, Bryan noted the significant attitude change toward the black Baptists:

Savannah-Georgia, U.S.A. Dec. 23, 1800.

My Dear and Rev. Brother,

After a long silence, occasioned by various hindrances, I sit down to answer your inestimable favour by the late dear Mr. White, who I hope is rejoicing, far above the troubles and trials of this frail sinful state. All the books, mentioned in your truly condescending and affectionate letter, came safe, and were distributed according to your humane directions. You can scarcely conceive, much less can I describe, the gratitude excited by so seasonable and precious a supply of the means of knowledge and grace, accompanied with benevolent proposals of further assistance. Deign, dear sir, to accept our united, and sincere thanks for your great kindness to us, who have been so little accustomed to such attentions. Be assured our prayers have ascended, and I trust will continue to ascend to God, for your health and happiness. And that you may be rendered a lasting ornament to our holy Religion, and a successful Minister of the Gospel.

With much pleasure, I inform you, dear sir, that I enjoy good health, and am strong in body, tho' 63 years old,[35] and am blessed with a pious wife, whose freedom I have obtained, and an only daughter and child, who is married to a free man, tho' she, and consequently, under our laws, her seven children, five sons and two daughters, are slaves. By a kind Providence I am well provided for, as to worldly comforts, (tho' I have had very little given me as a minister,) having a house and lot in this city, besides the land on which several buildings stand, for which I receive a small rent, and a fifty-six acre-tract of land, with all necessary

---

[34] *Ibid.*, 70.

[35] [It is from this statement that we determine Bryan was born in 1737 — *Ed.*]

buildings, four miles in the country, and eight slaves; for whose education and happiness, I am enabled, thro' mercy to provide.

But what will be infinitely more interesting to my friend, and is so much more prized by myself, we enjoy the rights of conscience to a valuable extent, worshiping in our families, and preaching three times every Lord's-day, baptizing frequently from 10 to 30 at a time in the Savannah [River], and administering the sacred supper, not only without molestation, but in the presence, and with the approbation and encouragement of many of the white people. We are now about 700 in number, and the work of the Lord goes on prosperously.

An event which has had a happy influence on our affairs was the coming of Mr. Holcombe, late pastor of the Euhaw Church, to this place, at the call of the heads of the city, of all denominations, who have remained for the 13 months he has been here, among his constant hearers, and liberal supporters. His salary is 2000* a year. He has just had a baptistery, with convenient appendages, built in his place of worship, and has commenced baptizing.

Another dispensation of Providence has much strengthened our hands, and increased our means of information: Henry Francis, lately a slave to the widow of the late Col. Leroy Hammond, of Augusta, has been purchased, by a few humane gentlemen of this place, and liberated to exercise the handsome ministerial gifts he possesses amongst us, and teach our youth to read and write. He is a strong man, about 49 years of age, whose mother was white, and whose father was an Indian. His wife and only son are slaves.

Brother Francis has been in the ministry 15 years, and will soon receive ordination, and will probably become the pastor of a branch of my large church, which is getting too unwieldly for one body. Should this event take place, and his charge receive constitution, it will take the rank and title of *the 3d Baptist Church in Savannah.*

With the most sincere and ardent prayers to God for your temporal and eternal welfare, and with the most unfeigned gratitude, I remain, reverend and dear sir, your obliged servant in the gospel.

Andrew Bryan

* Probably dollars. Editor [John Rippon].

> P.S. I should be glad that my African friends could hear the above account of our affairs.[36]

In 1795, in the midst of an effort to construct another building, Bryan appealed to the Philadelphia Baptist Association for financial aid. This appeal is significant, among other things, in that it indicates Bryan's affinity with this Calvinistic Baptist Association. The minutes of the association's session that October 8th recorded the request as follows:

> On application for assistance to build a meeting-house in Savannah, Georgia, large enough to admit some hundreds of blacks in the galleries, we recommend to the churches to make subscriptions or collections for the above purpose, and to forward the amount to Mr. Ustick[37] by the 20th of November next; which Mr. Ustick is requested to convey by the first opportunity; together with a letter of condolence to the above-mentioned blacks, and our ardent wishes that Providence may interfere in their favor, at least so far, that their masters may be moved to allow them the free enjoyment of public and private worship.[38]

The resulting amount collected is not known.

A division in Israel

By 1802, the First African Baptist Church had experienced substantial growth, to the point that some of the members left and

---

[36] John Rippon, ed., *The Baptist Annual Register, for 1798, 1799, 1800, and Part of 1801* (London: Button and Conder, et al., 1801), 366-367. Rippon suggested in a footnote that this letter was written for Bryan, "perhaps by the Rev. Mr. [Henry] Holcombe."

[37] Thomas Ustick (1753-1803), pastor of the First Baptist Church, Philadelphia and moderator of the Association's meetings that year.

[38] A. D. Gillette, *Minutes of the Philadelphia Baptist Association, 1707-1807* (Philadelphia: American Baptist Publication Society, 1851), 307; Egemonye, "A History of First African Baptist Church," 68. [Bryan's connections and correspondents all strongly suggest that he was Calvinistic, as does the subsequent history of his church —*Ed.*]

formed the Second African Baptist Church.[39] Charles J. Elmore offered an account of the events leading to the establishment of this second church, and the third one as well—the Ogeechee Baptist Church, constituted on January 1, 1803.[40]

Henry Cunningham and Henry Francis, both members of Bryan's church, were well-qualified to be Baptist pastors. In order to give the advantage to Francis, who was Bryan's choice to become the pastor of Second African, Bryan's church called an ordaining council for Francis. Cunningham, ascertaining that he would not become the pastor, left Bryan's church, along with a significant number of others, to join the white Savannah Baptist Church, which had been organized in 1800 and led by pastor Henry Holcombe.

Joining Savannah Baptist Church, Cunningham became Holcombe's favored candidate to pastor Second African. According to Elmore, Bryan, a former slave, was no match for the power and influence of Holcombe; Cunningham became the pastor. Elmore also noted that Cunningham likely was favored over Francis because Second Baptist was located in an area of town comprised of the "upper level" blacks of Savannah. Elmore did not indicate why this social milieu would favor Cunningham over Francis. Nevertheless, Francis was not totally overlooked. He was given the pastorate of the Ogeechee church fourteen miles from Savannah, a church for slaves along the Ogeechee River. Thus, the success of Bryan's ministry led directly to the founding of the second and third black Baptist churches in the Savannah area.

By 1803, there were five Baptist churches in the Savannah River Baptist Association: First African with pastor Andrew Bryan; Newington, with pastor John Goldwire; Savannah, with pastor Henry Holcombe; Second African Baptist of Savannah, with pastor Henry Cunningham; and Ogeechee, with pastor Henry Francis.

---

[39] The First African Baptist Church had 69 members in 1788, 250 members in 1790, 400 in about 1794, and about 700 in 1800. Gardner et al., *A History of the Georgia Baptist Association*, 17.

[40] Elmore, *First Bryan*. The following discussion is from pages 4-6.

His last days

By the end of his life, Bryan had accumulated a sizeable fortune of over five-thousand dollars.[41] Records indicate that Bryan also was a slave-owner. Egemonye cogently argues that this ownership was "benevolent ownership":

> A close examination of the extant deeds of slave purchase involving Bryan reveals that two of the slaves that he purchased were his relatives. In 1803, he bought Hannah, his daughter, and Carolina, his grandson, for four hundred fifty dollars. On August 13, 1804, Bryan sold Hannah and her son to Adam Whitfield, his free son-in-law and Hannah's husband, for ten dollars. The deed stipulated that Whitfield would exercise no control over his wife and son, except to receive an annual fee of twenty-five cents from them.[42]

From the widow of the former mayor of Savannah, Bryan purchased Rachel, a slave that was not a relative. It may be that Bryan purchased Rachel because she was married to or engaged to Bryan's nephew, Andrew Marshall. The deed stipulated that Bryan would exercise essentially no control over Rachel. From all appearances, Bryan would have freed his slaves had an 1801 statute not been passed, which required a special act of the Georgia legislature to free a slave.[43]

Bryan's eventful life came to an end on October 6, 1812, after twenty-four years of faithful service to his congregation. Such faithful service to Christ and His church eventually won the admiration of many. Several distinguished white men delivered eulogies at his funeral, including Henry Holcombe. In its first session following Bryan's death, the Savannah River Association adopted the following resolution:

> Resolved, That this Association is sensibly affected by the death of Rev. Andrew Bryan, a man of color, a pastor of the First Colored Church in Savannah. This son of Africa, after

---

[41] Love, *History of the First African Baptist Church,* 40.

[42] Egemonye, "A History of First African Baptist Church," 81.

[43] *Ibid.*, 83. The law was passed to stem the tide of slaves being freed for various reasons after the Revolutionary War.

suffering inexpressible persecution in the cause of his divine Master, was at length permitted to discharge the duties of ministry among his colored friends in peace and quiet, hundreds of whom through his instrumentality, were brought to the knowledge of the truth as it is in Jesus. He closed his extensively useful and amazingly luminous course in the lively exercise of faith, and the joyful hope of a happy immortality.[44]

Further Reading

Uche Egemonye. "A History of First African Baptist Church, the Oldest Continuous Baptist Church in North America 1788-1939." Ph.D. dissertation, Emory University, 2003.

Charles J. Elmore. *First Bryan—1788-2001: The Oldest Continuous Black Baptist Church in America.* Savannah, GA: First Bryan Baptist Church, 2002.

Emanuel K. Love. *History of the First African Baptist Church, from its Organization, January 20th, 1788, to July 1st, 1888. Including the Centennial Celebration, Addresses, Sermons, etc.* Savannah: the Morning News Press, 1888.

Thomas G. Ray. *Daniel and Abraham Marshall—Pioneer Baptist Evangelists to the South.* Springfield, MO: Particular Baptist Press, 2006.

Edgar G. Thomas. *The First African Baptist Church of North America.* Savannah: printed for the Author, 1925.

---

[44] Thomas, *The First African Baptist Church of North America*, 40-41.

JOHN DAVIS
1737 - 1772

by Thomas Ray

John Davis rightly deserves to be listed among the champions of religious liberty. Born in 1737 at Welsh Tract, Pencader Hundred, New Castle County, Delaware, his father was David Davis,[1] pastor of the Welsh Tract Baptist Church. His mother was Mary Davis,[2] who died on July 24, 1743, when John was only six years old.[3] Upon the death of his beloved wife, Elder Davis was left with six motherless children ranging in age from 11 years to 1 month. David Davis's second wife was Rachel Thomas Jones,[4] the daugh-

---

1 David Davis was born at Whitchurch, Pembrokeshire, Wales, in 1708 and brought to America as an infant in 1710. He was ordained in 1734 as the Teaching Elder of the Welsh Tract Baptist Church and installed as pastor on May 27, 1748, upon the resignation of Elder Owen Thomas. Davis died at the Welsh Tract on August 19, 1769, at the age of 61.

2 The records of the Welsh Tract church state that "Mary Davis, the wife of David Davis teaching elder, was buried July 24, 1743." *Records of the Welsh Tract Baptist Meeting, Pencader Hundred, New Castle County, Delaware, 1701-1828* (Wilmington: The Historical Society of Delaware, 1904), 69 (original records, Book 3, page 2).

3 John Davis had two brothers: Rees, born in 1731 or 1732, who died November 7, 1756, age 24 (*Records of the Welsh Tract Baptist Meeting*, 127); and Jonathan, who was born at nearby Newark, Delaware, on July 7, 1734, and ordained at Shiloh (near Cohansey), New Jersey, November 12, 1768. He was pastor of the Seventh Day Baptist Church, Shiloh, from 1768 until his death on July 23, 1785, age 51. John Davis also had three sisters: Susanna, Mary, and Margaret. No information came to hand on Susanna and Mary, but Margaret Davis was born June 28, 1743 and married Major Thomas Booth. She died on December 2, 1820, age 77. *Records of the Welsh Tract Baptist Meeting*, 127.

4 Morgan Edwards informs us that Rachel Thomas had married a member of the Jones family by whom she had one daughter. The time of this husband's death is unknown, but it would have occurred before 1743. David Davis was her second husband. She lived several years after the death of Elder Davis, but the exact date of her death is unknown. Eve B. Weeks and Mary B. Warren, eds., *Materials Towards a History of the Baptists. By Morgan Edwards, A.M.* (Danielsville, GA: Heritage Papers, 1984), 1: 11.

ter of Elisha Thomas, the second pastor of the Welsh Tract church. Rachel Davis was not only a loving and faithful wife, she was also responsible for the care and the instilling of Christian principles into the hearts and minds of these six minor children.

His early education and call to the ministry

Information about John Davis's childhood is almost nonexistent, but we are informed that at an early age he exhibited a taste for literature and mathematics.[5] His parents, desiring to nurture his talents, enrolled him in Isaac Eaton's Hopewell Academy in Hopewell, New Jersey. Eaton, in addition to being the founder of the school, was also the pastor of the Hopewell Baptist Church. He not only trained some of America's most famous Baptist ministers, he was also responsible for educating several outstanding attorneys and physicians. Davis completed his academic training at Hopewell in 1759 and, desiring to continue his education, enrolled at the College of Philadelphia (later University of Pennsylvania) in 1760. It was while a student at the College of Philadelphia that Davis came under the influence of another Baptist minister, the eccentric but brilliant (and extremely popular) Ebenezer Kinnersley (1711-1778), professor of English and Oratory. Kinnersley had achieved fame due to his experiments and collaboration with Benjamin Franklin in the study of electricity (then known as "electric fire"). Among his many achievements was the invention of an electrical thermometer, by which he successfully demonstrated that electricity produced heat. It was through his extraordinary efforts that the public was eventually convinced that lightning rods could protect their homes and barns from electric lightning strikes. Kinnersley was so impressed by John Davis's intellectual abilities and academic achievements that he made him his assistant in November 1761. And Davis performed this task so well that the trustees of the college voted him a salary of £25 a year. Shortly before his graduation in May 1763, the trustees, recognizing Davis's ability not only as a scholar but as an instructor, appointed him usser (i.e. assistant teacher) in the English school. Two months later, they appointed him to a more prestigious position as tutor in the Latin

---

[5] Horatio G. Jones, "John Davis," in William B. Sprague, ed., *Annals of the American Pulpit* (New York: Robert Carter and Bros., 1865), 6 (Baptist): 117.

School, at a salary of £100 per year.[6] It is almost certain that during his years as a student he attended the First Baptist Church of Philadelphia, where he developed a friendship with the pastor, Morgan Edwards (1722-1795). It is worth noting that Ebenezer Kinnersley was also a member of First Baptist. For some unknown reason, and to the disappointment of the trustees of the College of Philadelphia, Davis resigned his position in May 1764, and accepted a teaching position at the Newark Academy[7] (later University of Delaware), where he would remain two or three years. In 1765, the trustees of the College of Philadelphia, in recognition of Davis's achievements, awarded him an honorary Masters Degree. Three years later, on August 16, 1768, the prestigious and exclusive American Philosophical Society[8] elected him as a member, in recognition of his academic achievements in mathematics. According to one of Davis's associates and friends, mathematics was "his favourite pursuit" and "he relished, with more than common satisfaction, the writings of antiquity, and the most ingenious [authors] of the present age."[9]

John Davis had been converted and baptized at the age of twenty-one on May 6, 1758.[10] Unfortunately, we do not know the exact time John Davis yielded his life to preach the Gospel, but it

---

[6] Tutors then and now are private instructors who give additional, special, or remedial instruction.

[7] Newark Academy had been moved from New London, Pennsylvania to Delaware in 1765. The school was founded by Dr. Francis Alison (1705-1779), a Presbyterian minister, who was also an instructor at the College at Philadelphia from 1752 to 1779, where he taught among other subjects, Latin. John Davis was a tutor in the Latin School. It was probably through the influence of Dr. Alison that Davis accepted the teaching position at Newark Academy.

[8] The American Philosophical Society was founded in 1743 by Benjamin Franklin and other likeminded men, to promote useful knowledge in the sciences and humanities through excellence and scholarly research.

[9] David Jones, *A Journal of Two Visits made to Some Nations of Indians on the West Side of the River Ohio, in the years 1772, 1773* (Burlington, NJ: Isaac Collins, 1774; reprinted from the second edition of 1865, in G. Truett Rogers and Terry Wolever, *The Life, Journal and Works of David Jones, 1736-1820*, Springfield, MO: Particular Baptist Press, 2007), 215-216.

[10] *Records of the Welsh Tract Baptist Meeting*, 48.

is almost certain that it was after he had completed his college education, which was sometime between 1763 and 1768. The records of the American Philosophical Society recorded that he attended the meetings of October 18, 1768 and July 20, 1769. On the latter date the secretary recorded him as "Revd. J. Davis." This is the first time we find Davis referred to as 'Reverend.'[11] We cannot find any record of the Welsh Tract Baptist Church having licensed Davis to exercise his gifts. However, there can be no doubt the Welsh Tract church had officially recognized the work of God in John Davis's life and had encouraged him to preach the Gospel.

Fellow of Rhode Island College

Rhode Island College (later Brown University) was born in the hearts of the ministers of the Philadelphia Baptist Association. It was their desire to provide a college that would unite higher learning with preaching the Gospel. The Philadelphia Baptist Association sent James Manning to Rhode Island in 1762 in an attempt to establish a Baptist college. Through the efforts of Manning and other interested citizens, they were able to achieve their goal. The general assembly granted the college a charter in 1764, and Manning was elected president of the college the following year. The college was officially opened in Warren, Rhode Island, in 1766, with the first commencement taking place three years later on September 10, 1769. The college was moved in February 1770, to its present home in Providence, Rhode Island. Davis's involvement in the early years of the college was extensive. Reuben Guild, author of the *Early History of Brown University*, provides a list of the originators and founders of the college, among whom was John Davis.[12] While Davis is also named in this source as a Fellow (or member of the governing body) of the College in 1770, a biographical notice of Davis by the American Philosophical Society says he was elected a Fellow in 1768,[13] per-

---

[11] American Philosophical Society, unpublished biographical sketch by Dr. Whitfield Bell.

[12] Reuben A. Guild, *Early History of Brown University, including the Life, Times, and Correspondence of President Manning,* (Providence, RI: Snow and Farnham, 1897), 520.

[13] American Philosophical Society, unpublished biographical sketch by Dr. Whitefield Bell.

haps following Backus, who also stated that Davis was made a Fellow in 1768.[14] In 1769, the college in recognition of John Davis's literary skills, awarded him an honorary Master of Arts degree.[15]

Davis probably began his trip to Rhode Island to attend the meeting of the corporation the latter part of July, or the first of August, 1769. It is unfortunate that Davis did not keep a record of the journey. Although we do not have a complete record of his activities, we learn from the diary of Congregational minister Ezra Stiles (1727-1795), that John Davis was in Newport, Rhode Island on August 9, 1769, where he delivered a lecture that Saturday night, which Stiles attended.[16] Stiles provides no information about the location, the subject matter, or the lecture's value, but there is no doubt he thought well of Davis, whom he referred to as a "sensible man."[17] The college records reveal that the corporation met on September 6, 1769, and among the items approved was the appointment of a committee to prepare a curriculum and design the college's first building. It was "Resolved, that Hon. Stephen Hopkins, Esq., Mr. Joseph Brown, and Rev. John Davis to be a committee to draft instructions and prepare a model of the house proposed to be erected, to be directions, approbation of the corporation for the committee to carry the same into execution."[18] The committee submitted their recommendations and they were taken under consideration and acted upon by the corporation. The following year Davis returned to participate in the college's commencement exercises. The graduation was held on Wednesday morning, September 5, 1770, in Joseph Snow's meetinghouse.[19]

---

[14] William G. McLoughlin, ed., *The Diary of Isaac Backus* (Providence, RI: Brown University Press, 1979), 2: 732.

[15] Guild, *Early History of Brown University*, 84.

[16] John Davis was introduced by Dr. Francis Allison. Franklin H. Dexter, ed., *The Literary Diary of Ezra Stiles* (New York: Charles Scribner's Sons, 1901), 1: 19.

[17] *Ibid.*, 1: 241.

[18] Guild, *Early History of Brown University*, 110-111.

[19] Joseph Snow, Jr. (1715-1803), Separate Congregationalist, was pastor of the Beneficent Congregational Church, Providence, Rhode Island from 1745-1803. The college commencement exercises were held at Mr. Snow's meetinghouse from 1770 to 1774. The college graduated four in 1770. Guild, *Early History of Brown University*, 164.

Davis was chosen to deliver the sermon that evening. Taking as his text 1 Corinthians 2:4, "And my speech and my preaching was not with enticing words of man's wisdom, but in demonstration of the Spirit and of power," Davis preached "a good sermon," in the estimation of Isaac Backus.[20]

Work with the Warren Association

After the commencement at Rhode Island College, Davis, Morgan Edwards and Samuel Jones attended the meeting of the Warren Association, which was held Tuesday through Thursday, September 12-14, 1769. Backus in his Diary tells us that Davis preached on Tuesday evening and Jones preached the following evening. At this meeting, the pastors discussed the persecution that certain Baptists in Massachusetts had been subjected to as a result of their refusal to pay the established Church's ministerial tax. The pastors decided that these unjust actions must be exposed and confronted. They agreed to establish a Grievance Committee and elected John Davis, Henry Williams, Isaac Backus, Richard Montague, John Fulsham, and Ebenezer Davis to prepare petitions to the General Court of Massachusetts and Connecticut for redress.[21] The Committee in turn selected John Davis to act as chairman.[22] The Committee drew up the petitions which were read to the Association and approved. The petitions were presented to Samuel Stillman, Philip Freeman, Jr., John Proctor, and Nathan S. Spear, who were directed by the Association to present them to the General Court.[23]

At the next annual meeting of the Association in 1770, held at Bellingham, Massachusetts, John Davis was again appointed to the Grievance Committee, along with Samuel Stillman, Hezekiah Smith, Isaac Backus, Philip Freeman, Nathan Plimpton, Philip Freeman, Jr., Richard Gridley and Noah Alden.[24] Hezekiah Smith

---

[20] McLoughlin, *The Diary of Isaac Backus*, 2: 773.

[21] *Ibid.*, 2: 731-732.

[22] Guild, *Early History of Brown University*, 78.

[23] McLoughlin, *The Diary of Isaac Backus*, 2: 732.

[24] *Hezekiah Smith* (1737-1805), A.B., A.M., Princeton, 1762; A.M., Rhode Island College, 1769; A.M., Yale College, 1772; D.D., Rhode Island College, 1797; was founding pastor of the First Baptist Church, Haverhill,

was appointed agent to the court of Great Britain to act in conjunction with English Particular Baptists Samuel Stennett and Thomas Llewellyn.[25] It is worth noting that John Davis and Isaac Backus became close personal friends as a result of their work on the Grievance Committee. Their attitude and ideas about how to deal with the outrages inflicted upon their Baptist brethren were in complete harmony, though their views were at odds with their more conservative brethren.

Travels to Newport and Boston

At the conclusion of the Warren Association's meeting in 1769, John Davis and Morgan Edwards, having received an invitation from Ezra Stiles, traveled to Newport, Rhode Island, where they both delivered sermons at the First Congregational Church on September 17th. Edwards spoke in the morning service from John

---

Massachusetts, 1765-1805; *Philip Freeman* (1712-1789), was born in England and came to Boston some time before 1746; he was a deacon in the Second Baptist Church; on October 7, 1764, Deacon Philip Freeman and six other members followed Samuel Stillman to First Baptist Church; was made a deacon at First Baptist on October 29, 1779; *Nathan Plimpton* (1711-1781) was a weaver and dyer in Medford, Massachusetts; he served as the town clerk for four years; in 1742, Plimpton and several other 'New Lights' were excommunicated from the Medford Congregational Church; in 1752, he united with the Second Baptist Church, Boston; he and six other men obtained permission from the town of Medford to hold meetings as a branch of the Second Baptist Church; *Philip Freeman, Jr.* was the son of Philip Freeman, and also member of Second Baptist Church, Boston; when Freeman Sr. followed Stillman to First Baptist Church, Freeman Jr. chose to remain at Second Baptist; at the founding of the Warren Association in 1767, Philip Freeman, Jr. represented the Second Baptist Church; in 1771, though Philip Freeman, Sr. chose to follow his pastor Samuel Stillman in not supporting the Grievance Committee petition to the General Court, Philip Freeman, Jr. chose to support the petition; *Richard Gridley* (1728-1798), in 1771, he chose to support the Grievance Committee petition to the general court in spite of pastor Stillman's objections; he was a deacon at First Baptist Church, Boston from 1779 to 1798; *Noah Alden* (1725-1797), was converted in 1741 and joined the Congregational Church in Middleboro, Massachusetts; he adopted Baptist principles and was immersed by Shubal Stearns in July 1754; he was pastor at First Baptist, Bellingham, Massachusetts; he faithfully worked for religious liberty.

[25] McLoughlin, *The Diary of Isaac Backus*, 2: 775.

3:7 and Davis preached that evening from Matthew 5:26.[26] From Newport, Davis traveled to Boston, where Backus informs us that he paid the pastor-less Second Baptist Church "a visit" that fall.[27] We have no record of how long Davis remained in Boston, but he probably had returned to Delaware when the news finally reached him that his father had died on August 19th. Davis did not return to Boston until the next spring on May 16, 1770, after the Second Church extended him a call.[28] Little is known of Davis's activities during this interim. However, it is highly likely that he spent most of this time settling his late father's estate. He also filled the vacant pulpit at the Welsh Tract Baptist Church until a new pastor was settled. The last mention of John Davis in The Welsh Tract records reveal that he attended their business meeting on March 31, 1770.[29] It is pure speculation, but it would seem reasonable to think that the Welsh Tract Church would have called John Davis as their pastor if he had not already committed to Second Baptist Church, Boston.

Ministry at Second Baptist, Boston

John Davis had been represented to the Second Baptist Church of Boston as "a man of fine talents, and of a finished education," as well as "a truly pious man, and an excellent preacher."[30] He began

---

[26] Dexter, *The Literary Diary of Ezra Stiles*, 1: 24.

[27] Backus, *A History of New England*, 2: 423. Stiles, in his Diary entry of September 17, 1769, referred to Davis as a candidate. Dexter, *The Literary Diary of Ezra Stiles*, 1: 24.

[28] Backus, *A History of New England*, 2: 423; Dexter, *The Literary Diary of Ezra Stiles*, 1: 763.

[29] *Records of the Welsh Tract Baptist Meeting*, 13.

[30] Baron Stow, *A Discourse Delivered at the One Hundredth Anniversary of the Organization of the Baldwin Place Baptist Church, July 27, 1843* (Boston: Gould, Kendall and Lincoln, 1843), 24. An example of the esteem in which John Davis was held was demonstrated upon the resignation of Morgan Edwards as pastor of the First Baptist Church, Philadelphia. In a specially called business meeting, the congregation was asked to present nominees to fill the vacant pastorate. The second person nominated was John Davis. David Spencer, *The Early Baptists of Philadelphia* (Philadelphia: William Syckelmoore, 1872), 103.

his ministerial labors there on a probationary basis in May of 1770. His ministry must have met with approval, for that September 9th he was formally ordained as pastor. His friends and fellow pastors, Morgan Edwards and James Manning, officiated.[31] You will notice that Samuel Stillman, the pastor of the First Baptist Church, Boston, did not participate. We will shortly explain the reason for his absence.

Davis was not stepping into an ideal situation. The church had been without a pastor for five years and internal dissention and transfers had left the church greatly diminished from former years. Second Baptist had come into existence through a doctrinal dispute that occurred within the First Baptist Church. The church upon the death of their beloved pastor, Elisha Callender in 1738, sent to England and soon called Jeremiah Condy (1708-1768) to fill the vacant pastorate. He was installed into office on February 14, 1739. Shortly after his arrival, some of the members began to feel there was a lack of spirituality on the part of Pastor Condy, as he was opposed to the revival going on in New England under the ministry of George Whitefield and others. They were also disturbed about the doctrinal views he taught in the pulpit. They spoke to him about their concerns, but to little effect. The concerned members withdrew from the church and began meeting in private homes. They wrote a letter to the church on September 29, 1742, expressing their belief that Condy was an Arminian, a "Free-willer," holding to a falling from grace and denying original sin. They declared their belief that he had denied the doctrines of election and predestination. They reminded the congregation that the church was founded by strict Calvinists on the principle of free grace. The dissenting members stated they would happily return to their places in the church if the church would return to the principles upon which it was founded. The church ignored the letter, consequently, the dissenting members continued to hold separate meetings. These continued until July 27, 1743, when they were organized as a Baptist church with seven members. The new church chose as their first minister Ephraim Bownd (or Bound), who was one of the original founders. Bownd's ministry was blessed of God. Baptisms were frequent and there were numerous additions to the church. Bownd served the church for twenty-two years until his death in 1765. During the last years of his life he

---

[31] Backus, *A History of New England*, 2: 423; Stow, *A Discourse Delivered at the One Hundredth Anniversary of the Organization of the Baldwin Place Baptist Church*, 24.

was subjected to great physical suffering, which left him incapable of fulfilling his ministry for several months at a time. In 1763, the church invited Samuel Stillman to become Bownd's assistant. Stillman accepted the church's invitation, but he limited his term of service to one year. Stillman won the hearts of the people by his eloquence and piety. The membership at Second Baptist took it for granted that he would succeed Bownd as pastor, but to their shock and dismay, Stillman at the conclusion of his agreed-upon one-year service, was called to the pastorate of the First Baptist Church, which had been made vacant by the resignation of Condy. This decision by Stillman created a great deal of resentment among some of the members of Second Baptist. Adding to their resentment was the fact that other members who had become attached to him moved their membership to First Baptist. This event created a complete break in fellowship between the two Baptist bodies. In fact, Dr. Stillman was not allowed to speak in the pulpit of Second Baptist until 1772, a period of seven years.[32]

Davis's ministry brought new hope and life to this afflicted and suffering church. For a season, it seemed as if the old days of prosperity were returning. New faces appeared in the house of worship, and sinners were being converted to God. The congregation not only increased in numbers, but in respectability.[33]

Davis and the fight for religious liberty

In writing to Samuel Stennett, Backus informed his London friend that John Davis had been educated "in the genuine principles of liberty," and having been "born under one of the happiest of civil constitutions, he felt with the keenest sensibility for the oppressed, and when his duty called him, with a manly and vertuous [sic] boldness defended them."[34] Indeed, Davis was ap-

---

32 [In Stillman's defense, the situation for him at the Second Baptist Church had become strained. See Nathan E. Wood, *The History of the First Baptist Church of Boston, 1665-1899* (Philadelphia: American Baptist Publication Society, 1899), 245-250 –*Ed.*]

33 Stow, *A Discourse Delivered at the One Hundredth Anniversary of the Organization of the Baldwin Place Baptist Church*, 24-25.

34 MS copy of a letter from Isaac Backus to Samuel Stennett, dated Middleborough, October 9, 1773. Andover Newton Theological School, Newton Centre, Massachusetts.

palled when he first heard of the injustice inflicted upon the Baptists of New England. When he arrived at Boston in 1770, he was determined not only to revive the ministry of the Second Baptist Church, but to do everything in his power to assist his Baptist brethren in obtaining complete religious liberty.

As related earlier, Davis began his work in this regard through his appointments on the Warren Association's Grievance Committee in 1769-1770. Following the resignation of Hezekiah Smith, the Association at their next meeting on September 10, 1771, appointed Davis their new agent, instructing him "to use his best endeavors, by the advice of their committee, in concert with their agents in London, to obtain the establishment of equal religious liberty in this land"[35]—even if it meant appealing directly to the king. Davis did not have to accept the responsibility and perils of being the Warren Association's agent. As the pastor of a Boston Baptist church, he and his members were exempted from the ministerial tax. By becoming the Baptist agent, and aggressively seeking justice for his oppressed brethren, he soon found himself subjected to personal attacks and vilification by the establishment. Still worse, he would have to endure the desertion of some of his fellow Baptist ministers from the cause. But in the end, what strengthened his resolve was the fact that he strongly believed the Baptist quest for religious liberty was also the Lord's cause. In a letter to Backus, Davis revealed the depth of his feelings in undertaking this great work when he wrote,

> For [being] young and unexperienced, I walk with Diffidence, and wishing to do all things right am anxious for the best—Brother, pray for me, that I may be directed and enabled to glorify my God, and Saviour; which to do is the hearty Desire of your friend and Brother in the work of the Lord Jesus."[36]

---

[35] Isaac Backus, *A History of New England with Particular Reference to the Denomination of Christians Called Baptists.* Second Edition, with Notes by David Weston (Newton, MA: The Backus Historical Society, 1871; reprinted, New York: Arno Press, 1969), 2: 176. The Association also elected Davis that year to serve as their clerk. McLoughlin, *The Diary of Isaac Backus*, 2: 732.

[36] MS Letter of John Davis to Isaac Backus, dated Boston, February 18, 1771. Andover Newton Theological School.

The mandate was no easy task. He would be forced to contend with a government where the state and church were united. It was obvious that the Congregationalists would not easily surrender their advantages. Still another obstacle Davis faced was his more timid Baptist brethren, who seemed willing to compromise their principles for a few crumbs from their oppressors' table.

One of the first steps that Davis took in his battle to gain religious liberty for the Baptists was to carefully study the king's charter, which determined the rules and laws under which the Massachusetts Bay Colony was to be governed. His study revealed that the charter guaranteed to the "Loving Subjects of His Majesty" exemption from "fines, forfeitures, or other incapacities," even to those who "do not agree in the congregational way."[37] This meant the laws and rulings by the courts that forced dissenters to pay ministerial taxes to support Congregational ministries were in violation of the king's charter. Davis believed the Baptists had neglected to strike more directly at the root of their oppressions and he was determined to expose the established Church's illegal measures in pursuing its religious intolerance.[38]

Some background as to the making of this conflict of interests between the established Church or Congregationalists and the Baptists might be helpful at this point.

The Puritans or Congregationalists

The Puritans were a movement within the Church of England who in seeking to 'purify' their church, found themselves in constant conflict with the church's establishment, criticizing and opposing what they considered their worldly and unscriptural practices. The Puritans left England to escape religious persecution and to establish what they hoped would be an ideal religious community, based upon their interpretation of the Bible. They began arriving in New England in the summer of 1630, and soon established what became known as the Massachusetts Bay Colony, a theocracy ruled by ministers, who aggressively attempted to keep their community free from all 'radical' dissenters.

---

[37] David B. Ford, *New England's Struggles for Religious Liberty* (Philadelphia: American Baptist Publication Society, 1896), 184.

[38] Alvah Hovey, *A Memoir of the Life and Times of the Rev. Isaac Backus* (Boston: Gould and Lincoln, 1858; facsimile reprint, Harrisonburg, VA: Gano Books, 1991), 191.

It is ironic that these Puritans (or Congregationalists) who had fled England to escape religious persecution would now in turn become the persecutors of fellow Christians. They utilized fines, imprisonments, banishments, public whippings and even hangings[39] in an effort to achieve their purposes. Thankfully by the 1770's, the established Congregational churches (or Standing Order) had abandoned their more barbaric practices of public beatings and executions of religious dissenters, but they did not cease to oppress and persecute the Baptists by fines, imprisonments, and seizure of their property, which was sold for a fraction of its actual value to pay the ministerial rates. The Congregationalists had, from the beginning, imposed a ministerial tax upon all the inhabitants of the colony. The tax was used to build, enlarge, and repair their own meetinghouses and to pay the salaries of their ministers. The Baptists resisted and in many cases refused to pay what they considered an unjust tax. They claimed they should not be taxed to build meetinghouses they did not attend, or support ministers whom they never heard. They also claimed they had their own meetinghouses to build and ministers to support and it was unfair to take money from their community and give it to another religious body with whom they so strongly disagreed. The Baptists had for years consistently gone to the court in an attempt to gain exemption from the ministerial rates. The courts and the legislature had made some concessions to the Baptists. They had ruled that once the local established church's meetinghouse had been constructed and their ministers settled, the Baptists could get a certificate of exemption which must be signed by three fellow Baptists and the Baptist minister. The certificate was then to be submitted to the assessor of taxes in their particular parish or town, who would proceed to grant them the exemption. A new certificate of exemption had to be filed every year for their tax exemption to remain valid. The law also allowed the Congregationalists to vote to issue a permanent exemption to their Baptist neighbors. However, this privilege was rarely granted, due to the fact that if the Baptists were exempted from the ministerial tax, revenues would decrease. This decrease would in turn increase the tax burden to be borne by the Congregationalists themselves in order to meet the expenses.

---

[39] [Four Quakers, three men and one woman, were hung on Boston Common by the Puritans between 1659 and 1661 –*Ed.*]

Baptist growth, 1740-1770

The Puritans considered the Baptists to be a group of fanatical, ignorant enthusiasts,[40] who would only become a threat to the establishment if their meetings were allowed to multiply. Initially, the establishment had largely ignored the obscure, small sect of "Anabaptists" among them, but between 1740 and 1770, the Baptists of New England were transformed into a dissenting body of sufficient strength to constitute a serious threat to the stability of the Standing Order. The Baptist churches in Connecticut during this period increased from three to twenty-three and in Massachusetts from eight to thirty-two. Although the Congregationalists also increased, the Baptists rate of growth was considerably higher.[41] This Baptist growth can be directly attributed to what is known as the Great Awakening, which began in Massachusetts about the year 1740, when the before-mentioned George Whitefield began preaching in New England. His preaching generated vast crowds. It was estimated that 25,000 persons had gathered on the Boston Common to hear him preach. This is remarkable when considering the population of Boston in 1740 was only 16,400. Whitefield's preaching produced hundreds of new converts, most of whom were initially Congregationalists.[42] These "New Lights," as they were called, returned to their Congregational churches, where they soon discovered not only a coolness, but an open hostility toward them and their new-found faith. Realizing they could not grow spiritually in this atmosphere, the New Lights chose to withdraw from what they considered dead churches and organize what became known as Separate churches. It is estimated that 50% of all of the Separate churches eventually adopted Baptist principles and became Separate Baptists. These new Baptists were very aggressive in demanding religious freedom and often found themselves in conflict with the old Baptists, who tended to be more conservative. The new Baptists were much more

---

[40] [Mainly due to their insistence on the baptism of believers only by immersion only, as being the sole scriptural subjects and mode –*Ed.*]

[41] William G. McLoughlin, *New England Dissent, 1630-1833: The Baptists and the Separation of Church and State* (Cambridge, MA: Harvard University Press, 1971), 1: 438.

[42] In the Boston area, not less than twenty ministers confessed they had never been converted until they heard Whitefield preach in 1740.

forceful in stating their grievances, while the more conservative pastors had, according to one historian, sought to appease the Standing Order and gain concessions by using flattery, showing deference, and adopting several of their standards.[43] This philosophy was unacceptable to the majority of the new Baptists. Samuel Stillman, Ebenezer Hinds, and Hezekiah Smith constituted the leadership of the more conservative wing of the denomination. The conservatives attempted to subdue and restrain the demands of their more aggressive brethren, and stood against the Separate Baptists' petitions when they felt they were too radical.[44]

The Grievance Committee collects documentation

The Grievance Committee placed an advertisement in the *Boston Evening Post* on August 20, 1770, requesting that all the Baptists in the Province of Massachusetts Bay who had been oppressed for religious reasons attend the Warren Association meeting that September. They encouraged the churches "to collect your cases of suffering, and have them well attested; such as, the taxes you have paid to build meeting-houses, to settle ministers and support them, with all the time, money, and labor you have lost in waiting on courts, seeing lawyers, &c.; and bring or send such cases to the Baptist Association to be held at Bellingham."[45] The response was overwhelming. There were dozens of affidavits and letters from all over the province, clearly demonstrating that the exemptions act "was being unjustly administered to the injury of the Baptists."[46] The Grievance Committee was shocked by the amount of documentation detailing religious intolerance and the unjust taxation which the Standing Order had been imposing upon individual Baptists and Baptist churches. The sheer volume made it impossible to appeal all the cases, therefore the Committee chose to focus on the Ashfield Case as an example. Davis however, as the agent for the Association, did not neglect the numerous other churches that had experienced discrimination

---

[43] McLoughlin, *New England Dissent*, 1: 439.

[44] McLoughlin, *The Diary of Isaac Backus*, 2: 812*n*.

[45] Backus, *A History of New England*, 2: 155*n*.

[46] William G. McLoughlin, *Isaac Backus and the American Pietistic Tradition* (Boston: Little, Brown and Co., 1967), 119.

and illegal taxation at the hands of the establishment. He often visited these churches, providing them with information and assistance in filing the correct certificates with the taxing authorities. Unfortunately, each Baptist church and individual had to design their own certificates of exemption, petitions and enactments. At the Warren Association's meeting on November 9, 1770, Davis recommended that the Association adopt uniformity in its wording "for enactments, certificates, and petitions" and even supplied his own suggestions.[47] These recommendations proved to be a great benefit to the Baptists.

Their petition is presented before the General Court

John Davis was well aware of the perils of filing a petition with the General Court stating the Baptists' grievances. It is important to know that this is the first time the Baptists as a body had filed a petition of grievance with the General Court. John Davis sought and obtained the aid of Hezekiah Smith in drawing up a petition to be presented before the Committee. As McLoughlin observed, Davis and Smith in their petition took the then current phrase, "No taxation without representation" and turned it into a plea for "no religious taxation against liberty of conscience."[48] The Baptists, he wrote, "sincerely believed that they were being treated unjustly and they sensed a kind of hypocrisy in their neighbors who shouted so loudly for their rights against England, but would grant none of the rights which the dissenters in their midst felt was equally valid."[49] Davis and Smith met with the Committee on October 18 and 19, 1770, to discuss the Baptists' complaints and officially file their petition. The petition asked the authorities to restore property taken from the Baptists in order to satisfy parish religious taxes, to allow Baptists "to recover damages for the losses they have been made to sustain on a religious account," and "to grant perpetual exemption to all Baptists and their congregations

---

[47] MS by John Davis, recommending wording "for enactments, certificates, and petitions," presented to the Warren Baptist Association, November 9, 1770. Andover Newton Theological School.

[48] McLoughlin, *New England Dissent,* 1: 538.

[49] *Ibid.*, 542. [A similar deduction would later be drawn by some members of the Warren Association respecting the rights of black persons –*Ed.*]

from all ministerial rates."[50] The petition was signed by Samuel Stillman, Hezekiah Smith, and John Davis.[51]

The Baptists had not only suffered from the unjust laws the legislature had passed, but by the courts manipulation of these laws. The legislature in response to Baptist complaints had amended and updated the exemption laws on several occasions. But, the benefits the Baptists received were miniscule. The new laws were just old laws dressed up in new clothing and Davis had no expectation that the current petition would produce the results the Baptists desired. The General Court had appointed its own committee to hear and evaluate the grievances of the Baptists. Davis had another major concern which related to his conservative Baptist brethren. He was fearful that when the criticism and public indignation over the Baptist petition became aroused, the conservatives would abandon the petition. He was especially concerned about Samuel Stillman's continued support, even though he was one of the signers of the petition. In a letter to Morgan Edwards, Davis states, "What he [Stillman] will be, whether for us or against us I cannot certainly tell—He seems to be more directed by petticoats than by a love of the good old cause [i.e. religious liberty]." The 'petticoat' reference is to Mrs. Stillman, who had not been silent about her opposition to the Committee's petition.[52] Unfortunately, Davis's concern about Stillman became a reality. In a letter to Backus in February 1771, Davis explains to his friend the events that led to Stillman's withdrawal of his support from the Grievance Committee's petition:

> There Never has been such an attempt made by the Baptists against the powers That be as we have Made of late—if we are beat[en] off, the Conquest, on the Other Side, will be important to them, and will avail much against Us; more especially as they have removed some, pretended Baptists, from our Interest, and, like Satan when changed into an Angel of Light, fought us with our own weapons—This therefor[e] must be a spur to those that remain; who prize

---

[50] John D. Broome, *The Life, Ministry, and Journals of Hezekiah Smith, 1737-1805* (Springfield, MO: Particular Baptist Press, 2004), 372*n*.; Hovey, *Memoir of the Rev. Isaac Backus*, 179-180.

[51] Hovey, *Memoir of the Rev. Isaac Backus*, 177-180.

[52] MS Letter of John Davis to Morgan Edwards, dated September 26, 1770. Andover Newton Theological School.

> the Truth more than their present gain; and who love the Lord Jesus more than Wife, or Children, friends or Neighbours; Nay more than this world—For my own part I am ready to forego all things else that I may hold fast the Truth—Let me then inform you, that Messrs. Smith and Stillman, and myself, being chosen a standing Committee did, as you know, address the general Court; and we were order'd by the Court to summon the proprietors of Ashfield to appear, to defend themselves against our Complaint. Now, Mr. Stillman says he will Never More sit in the Committee nor wait on the Court to support the prayer [i.e. entreaty] of the Committee in their petition and [if] by his thus refusing the Court should not repeal that Law, the blame will not fall on the Court but on Us; and they will say we have complain'd without a cause; as they say of the people of Ashfield have done before, and when the Matter came to the point, the Complain[t]ants fell off; and if they have suffer'd it was by their own default.[53]

Davis is obviously angered by Stillman's desertion and he believes that it has given the court leverage not to repeal the Ashfield Law, nor grant the Baptists permanent exemption from all ministerial taxes. He feels Stillman by his action "will betray the Cause of his Constituents," and thereby forfeit "the Confidence his Brethren have reposed in Him; and ought Never More to be trusted."[54] Davis does not make any similar negative comments about Hezekiah Smith, but it is obvious that Smith, even though he was the co-author of the petition, also forsook the Grievance Committee and its petition. The records reveal that Smith did not attend any of the court hearings nor offer any more support for the petition.[55] Davis was disappointed by these important desertions, but the majority of the Committee continued to support the

---

53 MS Letter of John Davis to Isaac Backus, dated February 18, 1771. Andover Newton Theological School.

54 *Ibid.*

55 [It is difficult to understand today exactly what factors might have prompted Stillman and Smith to abandon such an important cause just when the weight of their support was greatly needed. Was it a matter of personality conflicts with other members of the Grievance Committee, or possibly a strong disagreement over how best to achieve the same end? We may never know –*Ed.*]

petition. The following six men signed a petition demonstrating their continued support: Isaac Backus, Noah Alden, Richard Gridley, Nathan Plimpton, Philip Freeman, Jr., and John Davis. The only three committee members whose signatures were missing are Samuel Stillman, Hezekiah Smith, and Philip Freeman, Sr., a member of First Baptist Church.

Critics attack the Baptist petition

McLoughlin's research reveals that an anonymous letter from Cambridge, Massachusetts, appeared in the *Boston Newsletter* of October 25, the *Boston Evening Post* of October 29, and the *Boston Gazette* of November 12, 1770, expressing "great surprise" that the Baptists had petitioned the General Court for redress of persecutions and claiming the Baptists had always been treated with great charity and consideration: "there is no greater place in the whole Christian world, where there was more candor, charity, and lenity expressed toward the Baptists in particular." It was further stated that, in regards to the Ashfield Case, few persons were actually acquainted with it, and a true account of all its details was needed. It was suggested that if the Baptists have suffered in any way due to their religious principles, it was "not owing to the want, either of all reasonable legal protection, or a real hearty desire, both in rulers and ruled, that they might enjoy as perfect freedom in the exercise of religion, in their own way, as any denomination of Christians in the land."[56]

The Grievance Committee requested that Davis answer the Cambridge letter and demonstrate the legitimacy of their claims. Davis prepared a reply, with an article explaining why they had filed a petition in supporting the Baptists in Ashfield. Signing himself "A Baptist," Davis's article appeared as a letter to the editor in a Boston newspaper in December of 1770, as follows:

> Mr. Draper,
>
> When general Charges are brought against Individuals, or Societies, or Governments, if they involve no Absurdity, 'tis presumed that they are true, until contradicted: And when contradicted, 'tis presumed that one Alegation is as good as another; and the *Charger* is put to the Proof. I, feeling no other will appear, hold myself bound to support, what have been called *just & grievous* Complaints, on the

---

[56] McLoughlin, *The Diary of Isaac Backus*, 2: 787.

one hand; on the other, 'News-Paper Complaints.' The Gentleman who has appeared to act the Defendant in the Case, and I think with no small stock of Effrontery, after saying many things, respecting the Baptists, which serve only to show his ignorance of 'the whole Christian world'; by which I must suppose he intends the Province of Massachusets-Bay, asks, 'Can any thing more be done than hath been enacted in their (the Baptists) Favour?'—Every man that knows what the rights of Conscience are, taking the Matter to be just as he represents it, or to use, a popular Phrase, Misrepresents it, will answer, That much more can be done than has been enacted in their Favour.—But, to take off a little of their Surprise, and to enable 'the many' to *guess* at the reasons of the Complaints, I shall gratify this Gentleman, and the many who are like himself ignorant of a grand Cause, and I will venture to say the *sole* Cause, of our Complaining publickly at *this* Time, by laying before them a sketch of the state of Ashfield.

The Baptists of Ashfield paid their Money to build a Congregational Meeting-House; the good People for whom they built it, did not, as it seems like the situation of the House; they moved it to a considerable Distance, and taxed the Baptists to pay for removing it, and repairing it, when removed: Some were so heterodox as shrewdly to suspect that the true Cause of the Removal was to increase the Town Charges, as almost all the Inhabitants were Baptists; and they support their Suspicion by saying that the House is built, at least, one third larger than necessary.—The Baptists also paid their Money to support the Congregational Ministry in the Town until they settled the present able, learned, orthodox, Protestant Minister, of whom the first Cost was One Hundred Pounds lawful Money; of which the Baptists paid their Proportionable Part—After which they expected to get clear; but were told, that the Town not being incorporated the Act of Court made to exempt the People commonly called Anabaptists did not take place there. In Consequence of this a Number of the Inhabitants of the Town petitioned the General Court for an Incorporation; but did not obtain it. Shortly after a very small Number of the Inhabitants, joined by non-resident Proprietors petitioned for an Incorporation, and they obtained it; but were not fortunate enough to frame the Incorporating Law in such Manner as to enable them to execute all their Pleasure upon the Baptists.—During the Time of this Law the Baptist[s] Petitioned the General Court, praying Relief from Ministerial Rates.—the Court read their Petition and ordered upon it, That the Proprietors of the Town of Ashfield should be summoned to appear, to shew Cause, if they had any, why the Baptists Petition should not be granted—and that the further levying of Taxes, so far as it respected the Petitioners, should be suspended, in the mean Time.—This Act did no good service. They petitioned again—and obtained a like Act of Court with this Difference, that instead of, 'in the mean time, it was said, That the further levying of Taxes so far as it respected the Petitioners, should be suspended *till further Orders* from this Court.—So far all Things seem to have gone on well, and the Baptists were pleased, tho' they had an Hundred and ten Miles nearly, to come every Time down to attend the Court; the Expences, Fatigue, and Trouble of which they bore with a Degree of Patience; having Hope that finally the Court would order that they should have the Benefit of the Act aforementioned, respecting Baptists; for this seems to have been their whole Aim.—But tell it not in a Land of Liberty! In this same Session of the Court, and therefore by the same House, a Law passed *inperpetuum*,[57] by which every Proprietor in the Town of Ashfield, Baptists with the rest, must SUPPORT the orthodox [i.e. Congregational] Minister; and upon refusal, his Houses, Lands, &c. shall be sold, according to the Discretion of those whose Interest it is to sell the same.—This law is now in being, together with two Acts of Court, passed upon Petitions, and one Act that is said *to exempt Baptists in this Government from all Ministerial Rates*, &c.—Which Law and Acts do directly and positively contradict each other.

If this short Account of this Matter should not please the Gentleman of Cambridge when I have Leisure shall give a more circumstantial Account of Ashfield, together with many other Things that may tend to ascertain the Ideas the Gentleman affixes to the Words '*Charity, Candor, and Lenity.*'

A BAPTIST[58]

---

57 Inperpetuum: Latin, meaning *forever*.

58 *The Massachusetts and Boston Weekly Gazette: The News-Letter*, Number 3508, Thursday, December 27, 1770, 1. Courtesy Massachusetts

The critics of the Baptist position, instead of attempting to refute Davis's claims, chose to attack him personally in the newspaper. Their response appeared in the *Boston Evening Post* of January 7, 1771, which in part stated:

> There is a little upstart gentleman, lately settled in [this] town, who calls himself A BAPTIST; and the youth discovers a most insufferable arrogance and self-sufficiency. . .I very much suspect, that he is one of those deluded young men, who are employed [by the enemies of America] to defame and blacken the colonies, and this town and province in particular. . .I am of the same persuasion in religion with this young hero. . .and I cannot say what the General Assembly could do for the Baptists in general, or the Ashfield Brethren in particular, that they have not done, . . .and I believe this is the opinion of the Baptists in general, and of all others but enthusiastical bigots. [59]

The author of this article had the audacity to sign this article, "A Catholic Baptist," though it is obvious this article was not written by anyone affiliated with the Baptists. It was suspected that this was the work of one of the ministers of the established church who was involved in the Ashfield Case.

Davis read the attack on his character, but, says Backus, he refused to engage in a debate with a man who would write such "mean and dirty stuff." In the *Gazette* of February 7th, came another piece from a minister near Ashfield, stating, "It is a very common observation among us, that the people called Separate Baptists in these parts will not stick at any false representation to serve their purpose," which he then attempted to prove by facts. But Ebenezer Smith (1734-1824), pastor of the Baptist church at Ashfield since 1761, came down and answered him in the same paper on March 21, 1771. Utilizing the public records, Smith was able to prove the injustice the Baptists of Ashfield had been subjected to and in the words of Backus, "fairly turned that charge back upon the minister who advanced it."[60]

Historical Society, Boston. McLoughlin notes that a longer letter in answer to their critics was written by Ebenezer Smith and published in the *Boston Gazette* of March 21, 1771. *The Diary of Isaac Backus*, 2: 787.

[59] Backus, *A History of New England*, 2: 157.

[60] *Ibid.*

The tone of the letter by the so-called "Catholic Baptist" succeeded in adding more fuel to an already dangerous and volatile situation in Boston. By this time the political atmosphere in town had already reached a boiling point. Resentment towards the British Parliament and monarchy had been increasing since 1766, when Parliament passed a series of bills increasing taxes. This legislation, collectively known as the Townsend Acts, raised taxes on glass, paint, oil, lead, paper, and tea. The colonists resisted what they believed to be an unlawful taxation. The British government, in an attempt to demonstrate their authority and right to raise taxes, sent British troops to occupy the city of Boston. This action did not subdue the Bostonians, but only infuriated them, resulting in what was known as the "Boston Massacre," which occurred on March 5, 1770, when British soldiers, believing their lives were in danger, fired upon an angry crowd, killing five unarmed civilians.

Public anger now also became directed towards Davis, who was accused of being an agent of the English government and an enemy of the Commonwealth. Davis's friends feared for his life. The animosity grew to be so intense that it was unsafe for Davis to walk the streets.[61] Davis, however, was not surprised by the reaction his article produced and the threats to his own safety did not alter his determination or cause him to abandon what he felt was his duty; he continued to pressure the courts and the legislature in an attempt to obtain justice and religious liberty.

The Ashfield Case

Chileab Smith, a key figure in the unfolding of the Ashfield Case, was converted during the Great Awakening and joined the local Congregational Church in Hadley. A doctrinal dispute with the church soon led him to withdraw from it with his family. In 1739 or 1740, he removed his family to Huntstown, Massachusetts, which at that time was in a wilderness area. Since there was no church there, he began exercising his spiritual gifts as a New Light exhorter to his family and neighbors. Eventually, he and his family and neighbors adopted Baptist principles and were immersed on June 27, 1761. About a month later, on August 20, 1761, a Baptist church was organized and Chileab Smith's eldest son, Ebenezer was ordained as pastor. In 1762, a state tax was imposed upon the town; however, the law exempted all settled

[61] McLoughlin, *New England Dissent*, 1: 578.

ministers. The Baptists of Huntstown, being the majority, decided to take advantage of this law and file an exemption, seeking to have the court certify Ebenezer Smith as the settled minister of Huntstown. However, the court refused to recognize Ebenezer Smith's ordination, stating he lacked a college degree or its equivalent, and refused to allow any appeal. The Baptists were disappointed by the court's rejection of their pastor, but were determined to build a Baptist meetinghouse. Thereupon the nonresident proprietors, who owned most of the land in the town, became alarmed, believing that Baptist control would drive down the value of the land and ruin their future prospects. Their thinking was that respectable people would not live in a town where the Baptists were the majority and taxes for the support of the Congregational church would be sky high on the minority.[62]

The Congregationalists proceeded to obtain the services of "an orthodox minister," Yale graduate Jacob Sherwin (1736-1803). They voted to provide Sherwin with a settlement fee of £100 and a yearly salary of £64. Sherwin immediately organized a new church and they proceeded to build a new meetinghouse. The proprietors proceeded to tax the Baptists for the construction of this Congregational meetinghouse as well as Sherwin's settlement fee and salary. The law stated that all the inhabitants of an unincorporated town were required to pay the ministerial tax until the meetinghouse was built, a pastor settled and the town incorporated. The Baptists therefore, were legally obligated to pay for the Congregationalist meetinghouse and the expenses of settling Mr. Sherwin. The Congregationalists, adding insult to injury, decided they did not like the location of their new meetinghouse and proceeded to move it and tax the Baptists for its removal and repair. The Baptists were forced to abandon building their own meetinghouse—they could not afford to pay for both. In 1765, the town was incorporated and the name changed to Ashfield. Technically, at that moment the Baptists ceased to be legally responsible for paying religious taxes according to the exemption act. Nevertheless, the town continued to tax the Baptists on the grounds the meetinghouse was not completed. The Baptists continued to pay taxes for three years, but under protest. Upon completion of the Congregational meetinghouse, the Baptists applied for relief from the ministerial rates. The court took up their petition and ordered the proprietors to show just

---

[62] McLoughlin, *Isaac Backus and the American Pietistic Tradition*, 115-116.

cause why the Baptists should not be exempted from all ministerial taxes. The court also ruled to suspend the taxes imposed upon the Baptists. The Baptists were given the impression the court would rule in their favor. But Israel Williams, one of the chief proprietors of Ashfield and the most important political figure in Western Massachusetts, pointed out that Smith and his group were really Separates, or 'New Light fanatics,' and not entitled to exemption as Baptists. At his urging, the legislature passed in June 1768, the "Ashfield Law," which required all the inhabitants of Ashfield to support Sherwin and the Standing Order church, despite the general exemption statues. The Baptists filed a petition for relief in 1768, which was dismissed.[63] The town proceeded to levy taxes upon the Baptists, which they refused to pay.[64] The Ashfield assessor, in a move that was strictly vindictive and would eventually prove to be illegal, proceeded to seize 398 acres of the Baptists' property for non-payment of the ministerial tax and sold it for only a fraction of its true value. The land, which was valued at £363 and 13 shillings, was sold at auction on April 4, 1770, for £19 and 3 shillings.[65] The Ashfield Baptists suffered a loss of £344. The perpetrators of these crimes even sold the Baptist burial grounds![66] John Davis traveled to Ashfield in June 1770, where he assisted Ebenezer Smith in writing a new petition seeking relief and restoration of the property that the tax assessor had seized.[67]

The court rejects the Ashfield petition

In October 1770, Davis, Stillman and Smith of the Grievance Committee had appeared before the General Court. According to Davis,

> The members of the Court say, they will repeal the Ashfield Law; but say they cannot restore the Lands, because [they

---

[63] For this petition, see Hovey, *Memoir of the Rev. Isaac Backus*, 346-348.

[64] McLoughlin, *Isaac Backus and the American Pietistic Tradition*, 115-116.

[65] McLoughlin, *New England Dissent*, 1: 538.

[66] Backus, *A History of New England*, 2: 149-155.

[67] McLoughlin, *Isaac Backus and the American Pietistic Tradition*, 117.

> were] taken according to, or by Law—But, says the Speaker to Mr. Stillman, some illegality in the Conduct of the Town, would or may enable the Baptists to recover their Lands—[68]

But, as Davis argues, this decision not only compelled the Baptists to have to pay the cost of recovering their own lands, which were "taken from them unrighteously," but in essence covered up the illegality of the whole proceedings against them, for as the members insisted, "the Conduct of the Court must not be censured."[69]

In March, the proprietors of Ashfield presented a lengthy (and it must be said, abusive) reply to the General Court regarding the Baptist petition. William McLoughlin believed the reply to be significant due to the fact that "it reveals the kind of prejudice that operated so strongly among many of the Congregationalists against the Baptists," while adding that it "probably presents as well the common man's view of church-state relations at that time."[70]

On April 24, 1771, the council hearing the Ashfield petition voted to reject it. The committee ruled that the taxes imposed upon them were just and the authorities had no choice but to sell their lands. "Your committee find, that in the sale of those lands there was no unfairness, but everything was quite fair, quite neighborly, and quite legal. . .It is our opinion that said petition is dismissed. W. Brattle, by order."[71] Several members of the house were shocked by the committee's ruling. They presented a bill to have the Ashfield Law repealed, however, the bill was rejected and the petition along with it. The Baptists were both appalled and dejected by the injustice of the committee's ruling, while their oppressors rejoiced in their victory. But that joy was soon turned, as we shortly shall see, to their dismay and confusion.

---

[68] MS remarks on the Ashfield Case, by John Davis, dated January 23, 1771. Andover Newton Theological School.

[69] *Ibid.*

[70] McLoughlin, *New England Dissent*, 1: 539.

[71] Backus, *A History of New England*, 2: 159. [This "W. Brattle," as will be seen, was Col. William Brattle (1706-1776), head of the five-member General Court hearing their case —*Ed.*]

The court rejects the Grievance Committee's petition

In order to fully understand the Ashfield Petition and the Grievance Committee's petition we need to know that at the same time the court was hearing the Ashfield Case, they were also taking testimony concerning the Grievance Committee's petition. Col. William Brattle was chosen the chairman of the committee appointed to hear and rule on the Baptist petition. Davis states that during the ensuing proceedings, the Baptists were "treated very roughly." Chairman Brattle personally attacked Davis and the Grievance Committee. When Brattle had finished, Backus tells us that "Davis arose, and distinctly answered his arguments without taking any notice of the personal abuse that was heaped upon him. A gentleman present said, the worth of the man never appeared so great before."[72] The court indicated that it might be willing to do something for the Baptists of Ashfield, writes McLoughlin, "but it would not be abused and bullied by a Baptist committee."[73] They also stated, "That if said Reverend Gentleman had in their Petition treated the General Court with more good manners and truth, they would have cast no blemish upon their sacred Character by so doing." The abuse the committee subjected Davis to and the attacks made upon the Grievance Committee are explained by Davis in two letters he wrote to Backus in May 1771. In the first letter, dated May 1, 1771, Davis writes:

> The court met; Mr. Stillman would not support the petition; I went, Mr. Gridley, with me. The Committee of both Houses sat upon the Baptist petition—I appear'd [or came forward] to support it; They abused me and the petition much; and finally did not repeal the Ashfield Law; for, as they ([the] Council) told Smith, they would have respected it if the Baptists of Ashfield had petition'd; but they would not for a Committee of Grievances—and called the Committee of the Baptists all the Bad things imaginable—The presbyterian [i.e. Congregational] petition against the Baptists...contained seven pages [of] charges and a half; fill'd mostly with slanders against the Baptists. I intend to get a copy of it.[74]

---

[72] *Ibid.*, 176.

[73] McLoughlin, *New England Dissent*, 1: 541.

[74] MS letter of John Davis to Isaac Backus, dated May 1, 1771. Andover Newton Theological School.

The second letter is dated May 3, 1771. Davis reports,

> The general Court has not repealed the Ashfield Law—The people of Ashfield sent down a Committee and Counter petition, in which they deny every thing we have said—I intend to set out for Ashfield next tuesday—I expect a Committee will [be] called to Meet the 25th day of this next May—I went alone to the Court to support the petition; and was treated very roughly by the Committee of Both Houses —"[75]

Even so, he also was able to say that the king was already expecting their petition. These letters demonstrate that the court had no interest in investigating the truth of the Baptists' claims. The committee submitted a report to the general court on April 25, 1771, to dismiss the Grievance Committee's petition. The lack of impartiality inherent in the court can be observed by the fact that the chairman of the committee hearing the Grievance Committee's petition, Col. William Brattle, was the same man who heard and dismissed the Ashfield petition a day earlier on April 24, 1771. The General Court had no intention of assisting the Baptists. Their plan from the beginning was to portray them as a group of malcontents.

Davis was disappointed, but not surprised by the committee's ruling. Seeing he could obtain no help from the courts, he turned his attention to the legislature in an attempt to have the court's miscarriage of justice overturned. All during that summer he pressured the legislature until they looked upon him as a nuisance. One of the members of the assembly told him plainly, in the presence of several witnesses, it was not worthwhile to wait on the court any longer, "for they would keep them [the Ashfield Baptists] under the law...as long as they saw fit."[76] Davis, realizing he could not receive any help from the legislature, called a meeting of the Grievance Committee, and they decided it was time to petition the king. The Grievance Committee presented their recommendation that they appeal to the king for relief. The Warren Association ratified the decision of the Grievance Com-

---

[75] MS letter of John Davis to Isaac Backus, dated May 3, 1771. Andover Newton Theological School.

[76] McLoughlin, *New England Dissent*, 1: 537.

mittee, although several prominent members objected.[77] Davis was disgusted with the willingness of the conservatives to compromise with the establishment at the expense of their suffering Baptist brethren.

The Baptists appeal to the king

John Davis and the Grievance Committee were well aware that an appeal to the king would result in resentment and outright hostility from their neighbors. Yet Davis was correct when he told Backus, that through the Massachusetts legal system "we seldom, hardly ever, can get a judgment in our favor."[78] The Grievance Committee's love of religious liberty was greater than their fear of public hostility, and acting upon principle, they agreed to send their petition to Samuel Stennett in London and seek his assistance in convincing the king to repeal the Ashfield Law. John Davis had known from the beginning that the best chance the Baptists had of seeing the Ashfield Law set aside was to appeal to the king. Consequently, even before the courts rejected the Grievance Committee's petition, Davis had corresponded with Stennett, who was a personal friend of the family of King George III. Davis had already informed Stennett that if their petitions were rejected, the Grievance Committee would desire that he would present the facts of the Ashfield Case and petition the king on their behalf.

In early May 1771, when the Grievance Committee realized its petition had failed, it forwarded letters and evidence to Stennett. On May 22nd, Stennett presented a petition to the Lords Commissioners of Trades and Plantations, stating that the

---

[77] The prominent members were led by Samuel Stillman. In light of what Davis tells us of Stillman's lack of support for their petition, it is ironic that Stillman in a letter to Henry Van Schaack, dated January 2, 1792, takes credit for helping repeal the Ashfield Law. He states that he wrote a letter to Samuel Stennett at the request of Governor Thomas Hutchinson, who had told him in confidence that he believed the Ashfield Law was unjust. Stennett made no mention of ever receiving this letter, nor do Backus or Davis ever mention it in connection with the Ashfield Case. See McLoughlin, *New England Dissent*, 1: 733*n*., citing H. C. Van Schaack, ed., *Memoirs of Henry Van Schaack* (Chicago, 1892), 180-181.

[78] Letter of John Davis to Isaac Backus, dated Boston, September 26, 1770. Andover Newton Theological School.

incorporation act of 1765, "Requiring the Baptists to support their minister," was perhaps "agreeable to the terms of the grant [of 1735] but contrary to the general law freeing Baptists and Quakers from taxation toward the support of other churches" in incorporated towns and parishes. The Ashfield Act of 1768, "which confirmed the grievance" of the Baptists after 1765, should therefore be disallowed. Governor Hutchinson,[79] Stennett noted, had expressed his complete agreement with this. The board of trade reacted favorably to Stennett's argument, recommending to the king "that the clause whereby all persons of whatever sect or persuasion in religion, occupying lands in this township are equally and indiscriminately taxed for the support of the Independent [Congregational] Church therein established, is in our opinion equally unusual and unreasonable particularly in the case of the Sect commonly called Antipedobaptists." On July 31, 1771, King George III in council accepted this recommendation and declared his disallowance of the Act.[80] The king's decision was published in a Boston paper on October 21, 1771, giving official notice that the king had indeed disannulled the Ashfield Law. The establishment could not believe the news. How could so despised a people get access to the throne, and obtain such an act, especially in so short a time! This is a great victory for John Davis and the Baptists of Massachusetts—especially those in Ashfield. In this bold move to petition the king, resulting in the disallowance of an oppressive law, McLoughlin believed Davis had been "particularly effective."[81] But though the Baptists of Ashfield recovered their lost property, they never felt they had received full justice, based upon the fact that the money they were forced to invest in the lawsuit was never fully recovered and quarrels over these lands continued to vex the town for many years.[82] Nonetheless, Davis's three-year pursuit, as McLoughlin points out, "gave impressive

---

[79] Lt. Governor Thomas Hutchinson (1711-1786), was a businessman, historian, and prominent loyalist politician. As governor of Massachusetts from 1758 to 1774, Hutchinson was no friend to the Baptists nor of their desire for religious liberty. His support of their petition was a political move calculated to drive a wedge between the Baptists and the Establishment. See McLoughlin, *New England Dissent*, 1: 543.

[80] *Ibid.*, 1: 545.

[81] McLoughlin, *The Diary of Isaac Backus*, 2: 732.

[82] McLoughlin, *New England Dissent*, 1: 544.

impetus to the movement for disestablishment."[83] Although the Ashfield Baptists were never fully reimbursed for their losses, they were finally exempt from religious taxes and for that they could thank John Davis and the Grievance Committee.

Backus and Davis's last parting

Backus and Davis had become close personal friends and when Backus came to Boston, which he often did, he always preached for Davis and stayed in his home. Backus arrived in Boston in July 1772, where on the 12th he recorded that he preached twice "to Elder Davis' people, with some freedom."[84] Davis had previously agreed to assist Backus in writing a history of the New England Baptists. Believing his time was short, the next day he delivered to Backus all the papers he had collected towards the history.[85] He informed Backus he was waiting for his sister to arrive from Philadelphia and assist him in returning to Pennsylvania. Davis also stated to his friend it was "doubtful whether he shall live ever to return here again." He told me, writes Backus, "it grieved him to think he had had so many advantages, and yet now seemed to be a useless creature; he longed to do something for God, but seemed to be denyed. Rarely have I had such a parting from any friend in my life."[86] This was the last visit Backus had with John Davis. Davis and his sister sailed from Boston to Philadelphia in August 1772. His death occurred only four months later, at the age of thirty-five. Backus would subsequently take over the position as agent and would faithfully carry on the battle for religious freedom until his death in 1806. Surprisingly, even though Davis

---

[83] McLoughlin, *Isaac Backus and the American Pietistic Tradition*, 112.

[84] McLoughlin, *The Diary of Isaac Backus*, 2: 848.

[85] McLoughlin, *New England Dissent*, 14*n*. John Davis had tried to discover who was the first Baptist in Massachusetts. He claimed that Seth Sweetser of Charlestown, deserved that title. According to Davis, Sweetser and his family came from Tring, in Hartford, England, in 1638. Because of his Baptist views, Sweetser was denied the right of a citizen and could not share in the town common land; yet he was required to pay taxes for the support of the Congregational ministers in Charlestown. His son, Benjamin Sweetser, became an early member of Thomas Goold's Baptist Church in Boston.

[86] McLoughlin, *The Diary of Isaac Backus*, 2: 848.

and Backus fought valiantly for religious freedom for the Baptists of Massachusetts, it did not stop the Standing Order from enforcing the unjust ministerial taxes upon the Baptists. But Davis's aggressive and persistent battle for religious liberty which was continued by Isaac Backus, eventually began to produce positive results. Town after town began to vote to exempt the Baptists from all ministerial taxes. Consequently, the Grievance Committee could boast that by 1785, the number of complaints concerning unjust taxation had almost ceased.[87] Complete religious freedom did not come to Massachusetts until 1833, when the legislature abolished all relationships between the government and the established church, placing all churches on equal footing. This was sixty years after the death of John Davis and twenty-seven years after the death of Isaac Backus.[88]

Davis's mission trip to the West and his death

In early 1772, David Jones (1736-1820), then pastor of the Crosswicks (or Upper Freehold) Baptist Church in Monmouth County, New Jersey, made a missionary journey to the American Indians residing in what is now Ohio. In October of that same year, Jones began making plans to revisit the Indians. He traveled from New Jersey into Pennsylvania, where he crossed the Alleghany Mountains and arrived at Redstone, in the south-western part of the colony, on November 17th. Unknown to Jones, John Davis had arrived a few days earlier and was planning to accompany him on his journey. Jones and Davis had been lifelong friends. Both had attended the Welsh Tract Baptist Church, where both were baptized on May 6, 1758.[89] Jones was pleased to see his friend, but he was shocked at the deterioration of Davis's health. When Davis informed him that he intended to accompany him at least as far as the Ohio River, Jones, fearing his friend could not survive the journey, implored him not to attempt such an arduous trip. But Davis was determined to make the trip and Jones, seeing

---

[87] McLoughlin, *Isaac Backus and the American Pietistic Tradition*, 166.

[88] McLoughlin, *The Diary of Isaac Backus*, 2: 848, 869.

[89] Jones, *A Journal of Two Visits made to Some Nations of Indians on the West Side of the River Ohio, in the years 1772, 1773* in Rogers and Wolever, *The Life, Journal and Works of David Jones*, 15, 192; *Records of the Welsh Tract Baptist Meeting*, 48 (Jones's surname appears as John).

he could not prevail, reluctantly consented. Jones and Davis began their journey to the Ohio River, but high waters and stormy weather impeded their progress and they did not reach the river until December 2nd. Shortly after their arrival, they came to the house of Dr. James McMechen (1748-1825), a former neighbor of Davis. Upon seeing his old friend, Davis was overjoyed and seemed to forget his physical problems. Sadly, however, a short time after their arrival, he became critically ill. I think it is best to let Davis's friend, David Jones, describe his final days:

> During the time of his illness, he was very submissive to the will of GOD; and was so far from the fear of death, that he was often heard to say, 'Oh! that the final blow was struck!' He had a complication of disorders, and all the medicines used either by Dr. McMechen or myself seem to have none effect. When he drew near his last, he was very delirious, and could give few rational answers, tho' he still knew me, and would always have me by him, till all senses failed. To compose him a little, [I] gave him a strong anodyne, which had so much effect, that for about fifteen minutes he enjoyed the use of his reason. In this time he told me, that he firmly believed the LOCALITY of heaven—that in a little time he expected to be with CHRIST, *and see and know HIM as he is now known, and as he is not known*. He said his faith in his Saviour was *unshaken*. Then he made as humble addresses to GOD, as ever I heard drop from mortal lips. Soon after his delirium returned, and never remitted more. On the 13th of December 1772, being the Lord's day, about an hour and an half before the sun set, this great man, took his final departure from this world of sorrows.

"No scene of life past at that time more affected me than the death of Mr. Davis," added Jones.[90] In order to make his friend a coffin and give him a decent Christian burial, Jones traveled eight miles to obtain some sawed boards and a spade. And with the assistance of a man who was skilled with tools, they constructed a coffin. His remains, wrote Jones, were "interred near a brook, at the north end of the level land adjacent to Grave Creek," near the present Moundsville, West Virginia. About fifteen feet north of his grave was a large black oak tree, where Jones carved the name of

---

[90] Jones, *A Journal of Two Visits made to Some Nations of Indians on the West Side of the River Ohio, in the years 1772, 1773* in Rogers and Wolever, *The Life, Journal and Works of David Jones*, 213-214, 216.

Davis, the date of the year, and the day of the month with his tomahawk.[91] He then penned in his journal this brief evaluation of his friend:

> Mr. Davis, it is well known, was a great scholar, possessed of a good judgment, and a very retentive memory. He had truly a great soul, and despised any thing that was little or mercenary. In our journey he told me one reason why he left Boston was, because he abhorred a dependent life and popularity:[92] that if GOD continued him, he intended to settle in this new country, where he could preach the gospel of his Saviour freely. His address, in all his religious performances was easy, sweet and pleasing: his private conversation both informing and engaging; though at times he was a little reserved, yet it was only when not suited. And what exceeded all, I believe he was a humble disciple of our blessed Saviour. In this point, [I] was more confirmed by conversing with him in our journey, than what I had been in any part of former acquaintance.[93]

Jones also composed the following verses as an expression of Davis's faith:

> How learn'd, how fam'd, now avails me not!
> By whom admir'd, or by whom begot!
> Ohio's bank my body now confines
> In safe repose, till CHRIST in triumph shines;
> But when the last trump's alarming sound
> Shall shake the foundations of the ground:
> And CHRIST in full glory shall descend,
> The rights of pure justice to defend:
> Then in bright honour shall this body rise,
> To meet my dearest LORD up in the skies.[94]

---

[91] *Ibid.*, 215.

[92] Dependent life and popularity: contingent on the support and approval of others.

[93] Jones, *A Journal of Two Visits made to Some Nations of Indians on the West Side of the River Ohio, in the years 1772, 1773* in Rogers and Wolever, *The Life, Journal and Works of David Jones*, 214.

[94] *Ibid.*, 214-215.

Further Reading

Horatio G. Jones, "John Davis," in William B. Sprague, ed. *Annals of the American Pulpit*. New York: Robert Carter and Brothers, 1865, 6 (Baptist), 117-120.

David B. Ford. *New England's Struggles for Religious Liberty*. Philadelphia: American Baptist Publication Society, 1896.

David Jones, *A Journal of Two Visits made to Some Nations of Indians on the West Side of the River Ohio, in the years 1772, 1773* (Burlington, NJ: Isaac Collins, 1774; reprinted from the second edition of 1865, in G. Truett Rogers and Terry Wolever, *The Life, Journal and Works of David Jones, 1736-1820*, Springfield, MO: Particular Baptist Press, 2007), 190-266.

William G. McLoughlin. *New England Dissent, 1630-1833: The Baptists and the Separation of Church and State*. Cambridge, MA: Harvard University Press, 1971. Two volumes.

Baron Stow. *A Discourse Delivered at the One Hundredth Anniversary of the Organization of the Baldwin Place Baptist Church, July 27, 1843*. Boston: Gould, Kendall and Lincoln, 1843.

Portrait of James Manning (1738-1791) at the age of 32, painted in 1770 by Cosmo Alexander (1724-1772). Courtesy Brown University portrait collection.

JAMES MANNING
1738 - 1791

by William H. Brackney

James Manning was born October 22, 1738,[1] at Piscataway, New Jersey, and he died July 29, 1791, at Providence, Rhode Island. He was one of the most eminent Baptist clergy of the later colonial and early national periods of American history, a pioneering American educator, and a Baptist pastoral luminary.[2] James was the son of James Manning, Sr. and Grace (Fitz-Randolph), both from among the earliest families in the colony of West Jersey. James, Sr. was a farmer who aspired to great accomplishments for his son.[3] The immediate family is identified with a large farm near the villages of Brooklin and Samptown on the Cedar Brook. James's grandfather, Jeffrey, was a pioneer in Piscataway and he left a substantial estate. Grace Fitz-Randolph was likewise descended from a prominent Baptist family in Piscataway. Grace received a portion of her father's significant estate as well.

Young man with a calling

In 1756, upon the opening of a Latin Grammar School in Hopewell, New Jersey, James, Jr. began his educational pilgrimage. The school was conducted by Isaac Eaton,[4] pastor at

---

[1] Isaac Backus's obituary notice for Manning, dated November 11, 1791, dates his birth on October 23. See "Obituary Notice for James Manning" in William G. McLoughlin, *Soul Liberty: The Baptists' Struggle in New England, 1630-1833* (Hanover, NH: University Press of New England, 1991), 271.

[2] For the important biographical sources in Manning, see the author's note at the conclusion of the essay.

[3] Apparently father and son remained close through life, as Isaac Backus noted in his diary for April 10, 1767, that Manning received the "heavy news" that his father had died on March 7th. William G. McLoughlin, ed., *The Diary of Isaac Backus* (Providence, RI: Brown University Press, 1979) 1: 663.

[4] Isaac Eaton (1725?-1772) studied under Oliver Hart in Charleston, South Carolina, and was pastor at Hopewell all of his career.

Hopewell Baptist Church, whose students would qualify for admission to further studies in law, theology, or medicine. The principal goal for Eaton's students was the College of New Jersey at Princeton, opened in 1746. This school, previously inspired by the "Log College," was started by William and Gilbert Tennent to provide learning in spiritual matters for those who had been converted in the Great Awakening.[5] Having matriculated in the college in September 1758, the athletic James Manning became an outstanding student. He was accompanied by his cousin, Nathaniel Manning, in the undergraduate course. James and Nathaniel graduated from the College of New Jersey in December, 1762, both with bachelor of arts degrees. James took second place standing in a class of twenty-one men. Only Isaac Allen stood higher in rank.[6] At the commencement exercises, James, as salutatorian, gave a Latin oration described as "a delight to all."[7]

As a young man, James Manning was remembered as having remarkable dexterity in athletics. He devoted many hours to recreation and was a leading player in team sports among the students at the College of New Jersey and later in his own Latin Grammar School. At six feet tall, people described him as having a symmetrical form and moving with grace.[8] One observer remarked that young Manning had no difficulty finding favor with the cultured Newport, Rhode Island constituency, and had no rival for the presidency of the proposed college—in other words, he was a well-rounded person. One early critic, in contrast, thought that as

---

[5] William (1673-1746) and Gilbert (1703-1764) were a father/son embodiment of the Great Awakening. William founded a New Side Presbyterian theological school at Neshaminy, Pennsylvania, that inculcated the ideals of the revival. The Log College, as it was derisively called, was a precursor to what became in 1746 the College of New Jersey. Gilbert itinerated widely in the Middle Colonies during the awakenings.

[6] Isaac Allen (1741-1806) became a lawyer and public official in the Revolutionary era. A Loyalist, Allen gave up his home in New Jersey and moved to a 2,000-acre grant near Fredericton, New Brunswick, where he became a judge of the provincial Supreme Court.

[7] Newspaper account of the exercises reprinted in *New Jersey Colonial Documents*, 87-88.

[8] Reuben A. Guild, *Early History of Brown University, Including the Life, Times, and Correspondence of President Manning, 1756-1791* (Providence, RI: Snow and Farnham, 1897), 31*n*.

a young man, James was "ambitious and haughty, intriguing and avaricious."[9] Indeed, young Manning was aware that small details were important in making impressions, even at the risk of being brash: in 1769, at the new Rhode Island College's first commencement, he led his graduating class in wearing American manufactured clothing as a political statement of colonial solidarity.[10]

Of significant spiritual and intellectual influence upon the theological student, James Manning, was Samuel Davies (1723-1761), a New Side Presbyterian divine who carried forth the spiritual energies of the Great Awakening. Davies had been ordained as an evangelist to travel in Virginia at a time when few dissenting congregations existed in that colony. His preaching skills and evangelical zeal won many converts and he firmly established Presbyterianism in Virginia. Davies made use of rhetorical devices in his preaching of familiar Calvinistic doctrines, and he is said to have had a unique style of diction and delivery. From 1753-1755, he intinerated on behalf of the College of New Jersey, raising funds tirelessly in the colonies and beyond. In a tour of Britain with Gilbert Tennent, he identified with prominent evangelicals like George Whitefield and the Wesleys. As president of the College of New Jersey 1758-1761, he created a curriculum that stressed oratory and English composition, and he built a fine library of both classics and contemporary theology. He was also one of the earliest antislavery activists in the American Colonies.[11] Davies' many assets came forth in his chief understudy, James Manning.

Manning's experience as a student in the College of New Jersey laid a foundation for his educational philosophy. Later, he would borrow heavily from the school in setting up Rhode Island College. College of New Jersey students matriculated in the baccalaureate program and after four years, graduated with a Bachelor of Arts degree. B.A. Students were admitted on Latin capability, as well

---

[9] Ezra Stiles, quoted in James McLachlan, *Princetonians 1748-1768* (Princeton, NJ: Princeton University Press, 1976), 393.

[10] Newspaper account, *Newport Mercury*, September 11, 1769, quoted in Guild, *Early History of Brown University*, 42.

[11] Davies was himself a slaveholder, but baptized 100 slaves and preached to hundreds more. He taught slaves to read, encouraged them to join congregations, and he understood them to be fully human. In 1754, Davies wrote *The Duty of Christians to Propagate Their Religion among the heathens, Earnestly Recommended to the Masters of Negro Slaves in Virginia*.

as being able to translate from Greek the Four Gospels. Strict examinations were given from start to finish. Attendance at religious services in the college were required as well as on the Lord's Day. Forbidden past-times were frequenting taverns, public entertainment, scandalous friendships, cards, and dice, upon pain of a fine. Fines were likewise levied for chewing tobacco and smoking. Tutors visited rooms to insure study habits and that there were no snacks or meals or entertainment in the rooms. The College of New Jersey maintained a deferential student code toward professors, taking off hats at the space of ten rods, making obeisance upon the president's entering or leaving a room, the use of the term "Sir" in address, and never being seen in indecent or slovenly attire. Shoes, stockings, and shirts were required in the college dining room at all times. "No jumping or hallooing or boisterous noise" was permitted at any time on the college premises. Students paid tuition charges of fifteen shillings per quarter.[12] Three formative themes were impressed upon young James at Princeton: a serious Christian worldview, proper decorum befitting a gentleman, and rigorous scholarship. During his student days in Princeton, his closest friend was Hezekiah Smith, who would also become a significant Baptist pastor in New England.[13]

Manning clearly prepared for the Gospel ministry and he took the first step on February 6, 1763, when the Scotch Plains (NJ) Baptist Church licensed him to preach, a prerequisite among associational Baptists. Manning understood that ministry "is emphatically a *work*, a very *extensive work*, for which natural and acquired gifts are necessary; as also *saving grace*, without which all the cupidity of this world could [not] qualify a man for the gospel ministry."[14] His home church, founded in 1747, was served

---

[12] "Laws and Customs of the College of New Jersey," as quoted in Guild, *Early History of Brown University*, 29-31.

[13] Hezekiah Smith (1737-1805) was ordained at Charleston, SC, in 1763 and moved to New England shortly thereafter. He organized the Baptist congregation at Haverhill in 1765, which he served till his death. During the American Revolution he was a chaplain in the Continental Army. See Reuben A. Guild, *Chaplain Smith and the Baptists*. Philadelphia American Baptist Publication Society, 1885; and John D. Broome, *The Life, Ministry, and Journals of Hezekiah Smith*. Springfield, MO: Particular Baptist Press, 2004.

[14] Per comment of Isaac Backus on Manning's philosophy of ministry: McLoughlin, *Diary of Isaac Backus*, 3: 1211, entry for December 5, 1787.

by Benjamin Miller (1715?-1781), who had been converted under the preaching of the Great Awakener, Gilbert Tennent. At Scotch Plains, Miller enjoyed a solid reputation from 1748 to 1780 as an evangelical pastor among the Baptists, whose funeral sermon was delivered by the eminent John Gano (1727-1804) of New York.

On April 19, 1763, James Manning was ordained by the Scotch Plains Baptist Church. He had both the funds and the opportunity as a young, unsettled ordinand to travel through the colonies in order to gain a perspective on Baptist and evangelical work in North America. The Scotch Plains Church was a member of the Philadelphia Baptist Association, the oldest Regular Baptist association in the United States, which stretched from Virginia to Nova Scotia at one time. Shortly after his ordination, Manning married Margaret Stites of Elizabethtown,[15] New Jersey, sister to Sarah Stites, who had married John Gano. Described as an attractive and lovely person, Margaret was not a professor of religion at the time of their marriage. James had written what could only be described as an evangelistic letter to his "Affectionate Friend" Margaret in 1759, but to no avail. Her conversion may be dated from 1775, when under the influence of her husband's preaching, she was converted and baptized at Providence.[16] The couple had no children.

Church planter and bi-vocational pastor

Manning's reputation as an outstanding candidate for a settled pastoral appointment extended throughout the colonial Baptist community. He received an offer to be the associate pastor at historic First Baptist Charleston, South Carolina, under the distinguished Oliver Hart (1723-1795), but refused the opportunity. On a journey of personal discovery in 1763, Manning was traveling through New England to Halifax, Nova Scotia,[17] when he met several Baptist leaders in southern Massachusetts and Rhode Island at Newport. Pastoral leaders from the Philadelphia Association, led by the eminent Morgan Edwards of the First Baptist Church in that city, had recently been in correspondence

---

[15] Margaret was the daughter of John and Margaret Stites of Elizabethtown, New Jersey. She died on November 9, 1815.

[16] The date of her baptism was January 1775.

[17] On this trip, Manning visited western Nova Scotia, in the vicinity of Falmouth on the Avon River, where he witnessed several baptisms.

about commencing a college in New England to be under the direction and with the support of the Baptists. This strategic meeting in July 1763 included Samuel Ward, the governor of Rhode Island, Col. John Gardiner, the deputy governor, Josias Lyndon, and twelve others from the Baptist community.[18] Manning also favorably impressed Ezra Stiles (1727-1795), pastor at the Second Congregational Church in Newport (later to become president of Yale College), and he hastily laid a plan before Stiles and principally the Rhode Island Baptists for an educational institution. In the next few months, the local clergy engaged in a sometimes-heated debate over a charter for the school that could be presented to the Rhode Island legislature. Plenty of intrigue characterized the process, with charges of deception and roguish tactics thrown at Stiles who seemed reluctant to have the Baptists actually control the project.[19] In March 1764, the Rhode Island Assembly approved the charter and the governor issued the charter over his signature on October 24, 1764.

During the summer of 1764, Manning relocated to Warren, Rhode Island, where he opened a Latin Grammar School of his own on the model of Isaac Eaton, at the same time planting a Baptist congregation there in November 1764. It is likely that in addition to his own resources, he received support from the Scotch Plains church.[20] When the educational charter for the college came down through the colonial governor's office, James Manning was

---

[18] The majority of the Baptist inhabitants in Warren were members of the Swansea Church, located about three miles distant across the Warren River.

[19] Unfortunately, Manning departed from these discussions prematurely to continue his travel plans to Halifax. His absence led to changes in the Baptist character of the charter as Manning had originally intended. Ezra Stiles in particular attempted to open up the governance to the Standing Order.

[20] Manning returned to the College of New Jersey in 1765 to receive his M.A. degree. During the presidency of Samuel Davies, requirements in the College of New Jersey for the second degree were tightened to three years, preferably in residence. It is not known whether Manning was actually in residence for that period, but he must have presented an additional thesis and paid the fees. Master's degree candidates were required to demonstrate advanced competency in the languages by disputes and exercises. See Willard Thorp, Minor Myers, Jr., Jeremiah Stanton Finch, *The Princeton Graduate School: A History* (Princeton, NJ: Association of Princeton Graduate Alumni, 2000), 4.

elected president and professor of languages, "and other Branches of learning, with full power to act immediately in these capacities, at Warren or elsewhere" of the newly-designated Rhode Island College.[21] He was only twenty-five years old. Through the years of his leadership, the fledgling college would take shape and develop a national reputation and Manning himself would become a leading pastor in New England amidst the great era of the American Revolution.

By autumn of 1764, a coalition of members from the Baptist Church in nearby Swansea, Massachusetts, formally organized themselves a church in Warren on the basis of the doctrines of regeneration and perseverance in grace. They issued a call to the Rev. James Manning, "late of Nassau Hall in New Jersey" to take up the work of a pastor "over and amongst them."[22] The organization of the new church came about as a response to Manning's effective preaching in the vicinity. Warren was a small Narragansett Bay seaport in the making as the decade of the 1760's commenced. It was situated about ten miles from Providence, the colonial capital. Manning saw possibilities in Warren and was encouraged by the Swansea folk who included Sylvester Child, Ebenezer Cole, and John Wheaton. Swansea, the oldest Baptist church in the Bay Colony, was only three miles from Warren, but at this point in time it was declining under the eldership of Jabez Wood, who had been its pastor for about five years. Many of the prominent families of the Swansea Church lived in Rehoboth or Warren and were anxious to make a new beginning.

When the Warren Church was thus constituted in 1764, the Swansea Church dismissed twenty-five members to the new venture. Mr. Manning was called formally on November 15, 1764, to become Warren's first resident Baptist pastor, with a beginning membership of fifty-eight souls. Three distinguished Baptist elders participated in the installation service that day for Manning: John Gano of New York (his wife's brother-in-law), Gardner Thurston of Newport, and Ebenezer Hinds of Middleborough, Massachusetts. Following the usual Baptist practice of fasting and prayer, Mr. Thurston gave the sermon. A meetinghouse, planned as early as

---

[21] Guild, *Early History of Brown University,* 53, 59.

[22] The call letter is reproduced in Josiah P. Tustin, *A Discourse Delivered at the Dedication of the New Church Edifice of the Baptist Church and Society in Warren, R.I. May 8, 1845* (Providence, RI: H.N. Brown, 1845), 171-173.

1763, was erected, as well as a parsonage for the pastor and his bride. In their call to Manning, the church leaders declared their intention to render his life as happy as possible. . ."communicating our temporal things to your necessities so long as God in his Providence shall continue us together."[23] Manning, the college, and the church remained in Warren, Rhode Island, for five years.

Manning's theological acuity was quickly put to the test in the Warren pastorate. His six-paragraph covenant covered all of the major tenets of five principle, first-day colonial Baptist character. He wrote of human sinfulness, free grace, a visible church and growth in grace and knowledge of the Lord God. He also echoed the theology of English General Baptist John Smyth a century and a half earlier, by speaking of performing duties toward God and each other and by walking according to God's revealed word and to "what is and shall be made known to us," indicating a progressive rather than a fixed system.[24] He defined a believer's church, as having evidence of a "living faith," preceding baptism by immersion in the name of the Holy Trinity. On the thorny issue dividing many Baptists in New England, the laying on of hands to signify the presence of the Holy Spirit in the believer (the "sixth principle"), Manning took the middle ground that it was a non-essential issue, and that persons of both positions who walked in an orderly way, were welcome in Warren.[25] In many respects, the

---

[23] Guild, *Early History of Brown University*, 51, quoting the letter of call dated November 15, 1764.

[24] [The covenant statement reads: "And we do humbly engage, that, through his strength [i.e. Christ], we will endeavor to perform all our respective duties toward God and each other, and to practice all the ordinances of Christ, according to what is and shall be made known to us in our respective places; to exercise, practise, and submit to the government of Christ in his church." Guild, *Early History of Brown University*, 49. Which is to say, that having determined, "through Jesus Christ, to walk together according to his revealed Word," the members at Warren should expect that as they grew in the grace and knowledge of the Lord (2 Peter 3:18) through the faithful teaching and preaching of that unchanging Word (Ps. 119:89), so too would their understanding of what they presently know and shall yet learn of the duties of their respective places in the church towards God and one another and of the ordinances (or authoritative commands) of Christ —*Ed.*]

[25] The Warren Covenant is found in Tustin, *A Discourse*, 169-171. In 1845, Tustin, pastor at Warren 1842-1849, claimed to have had the original copy of the covenant in Manning's own hand.

Warren Church covenant resembled that of nearby Swansea, which had been composed in 1663 by the venerable John Myles, plus additional influences of the Great Awakening.[26] In the ensuing years, the key theological principles at work were regeneration, perseverance in grace, and a personal profession of faith. Overall, Manning was a consistent Calvinist in the tradition of his contemporary, the English Baptist divine, Dr. John Gill, yet slightly more experimental.[27] According to one of his students, the works of Philip Doddridge, Isaac Watts, Richard Baxter, Jacques Saurin, and Archbishop John Tillotson were in his near reach, along with Gill's commentaries.[28]

James Manning was pre-eminently an organizational genius. In an age where opportunities abounded for church planting, religious education, and ecclesiastical cooperation, Manning seemed to be in the right places at the right times. Once the foundation of Warren Baptist Church had been laid, he turned to organizing the other Baptists of New England. Manning had good reason to try to unite the churches, namely to form a support base for the college. He traveled extensively in the spring and summer of 1766, advancing the idea of an association. In September, a regional association took definite shape. At an informational

---

[26] For the Swansea Covenant, see Henry M. King, *Rev. John Myles and the Founding of The First Baptist Church in Massachusetts* (Providence, RI: Preston and Rounds Co., 1905), 52-55.

[27] This may be legitimately inferred from a listing of subscribers to the publication the first edition of Dr. Gill's *Body of Divinity* in 1769. Manning purchased six copies and was listed as "President of Rhode Island College." One may speculate that one set was for his personal library, another for the College, and the remainder for theology students. See John Gill, *A Body of Doctrinal Divinity; or A System of Evangelical Truths, Deduced from the Sacred Scriptures.* In Two Volumes, Vol. I. (London: George Keith, 1769), list of subscriber names.

[28] "William Hunter Statement," included in William B. Sprague, ed., *Annals of the American Pulpit* (New York: Robert Carter and Bros., 1865), 6 (Baptist): 97. Doddridge was a dissenting minister who was among the early leading evangelicals in the 18th century awakenings and author of *The Rise and Progress of Religion in the Soul* (1745). Tillotson was a nonconformist-leaning Anglican divine and Archbishop of Canterbury, known for his Zwinglian positions and apologetics. Saurin was a French pastor in The Hague and later in London, whose published *Sermons* (1708-1725), were highly regarded. Baxter was the last of the English Puritans, whose work on the role of the pastor, *The Reformed Pastor* (1656), was widely quoted.

meeting on September 8th at Warren, the elders and delegates of eleven churches met: Warren, Rehoboth, Haverhill, Norton, First, Middleborough, Second Middleborough, Cumberland, First Boston, Second Boston, and Attleborough. Delegates from the Philadelphia Association included John Gano of New York, and Abel Griffith and Noah Hammond from Pennsylvania. Manning invited churches to unite their witness on the model of the Philadelphia plan.

Following carefully Benjamin Griffith's advice on the purpose of associations, the blueprint for the Warren Association suggested it would serve as an advisory council, disclaiming superiority, jurisdiction, coercive right and infallibility over the churches.[29] Leaders were to be men trained in the knowledge of the Scriptures, especially since the Scriptures were the only rule of faith and practice in religious matters. The independency and power of local churches were paramount. The Second London Confession of Faith, as amended by Philadelphia, was the doctrinal standard.[30] Especially noteworthy were doctrines of original and imputed sin; inability of humans to recover themselves; effectual calling by sovereign grace; justification by imputed righteousness; baptism by immersion upon a profession of faith; congregational church independency; and reception into membership upon a sound conversion.[31]

Manning continued to be concerned for the wider interests of the church. In September 1782, Manning joined Isaac Backus (a late-comer to the association) and others in the Warren Association in their concern for the propagation of infant baptism being subtly taught in the public schools through a catechism and accompanying English grammar book; the result of their efforts was the production of a Baptist spelling book.[32] In the mid-1780's, he was praiseworthy of revivals in New York, New Jersey, and Vermont, especially news of the spiritual awakenings associated

---

[29] Benjamin Griffith, "An essay on the power and duty of an Association of churches," in A. D. Gillette, ed., *Minutes of the Philadelphia Baptist Association, 1707-1807* (Philadelphia: American Baptist Publication Society, 1851), 60-62.

[30] See "Second London Confession" in William L. Lumpkin, ed., *Baptist Confessions of Faith* (Valley Forge, PA: Judson Press, 1963), 240.

[31] Guild, *Early History of Brown University*, 76-77.

[32] McLoughlin, *Diary of Isaac Backus*, 2: 1118.

with his friend and relative, John Gano, in New York City. Manning had a special burden for evangelical work in Kentucky and the Ohio River Valley, and he even considered leaving Rhode Island to devote himself to western evangelization. In 1785, he took on the project of providing a library to train new ministers in the West. Through the Elkhorn Baptist Association in Kentucky, he laid plans to help qualify ministers with useful knowledge. He used the good offices of Thomas Ustick in the Philadelphia Baptist Association to coordinate this timely project.

Forces much larger in political realities and the providence of God as Manning understood it, created a significant opportunity to move Rhode Island College to Providence in 1770. The first issue was lack of funding: Manning had been without sufficient funds for five years, except the income from his pastorate and the Latin Grammar School. Leading men of Providence had laid a plan on the table for provision for a building and operating expenses for a college. Second was the troubling proposal before the Legislature to establish another college at Providence. Some thought the Baptists incapable of managing an institution and wanted the school in the hands of Congregationalists.[33]

Several Rhode Island towns were interested in hosting the college and made viable proposals in what amounted to an inter-village contest among Newport, Bristol, Kent, East Greenwich, and Providence. Newport was actually the most viable possibility, but its disadvantages included a heavy Congregationalist contingency and the presence of strong Church of England influence. Manning weighed in personally by writing an "anonymous letter" to Nicholas Brown (1729-1791) in Providence, whom he had met and favorably impressed. Manning suggested a strategy to enhance the Providence subscriptions by having Brown underwrite the construction of a building for the college. In a crucial meeting on February 7, 1770, the trustees of the college corporation voted 21-14 to build the college edifice in Providence, where "it shall continue forever."[34] Charges of hypocrisy were hurled at the trustees (and Manning!), the Newport representatives expressed unreasonable enmity toward the chancellor,

---

[33] Ezra Stiles, then in Newport, watched the young Manning closely and became a vocal antagonist for years to come over the relocation plans. Yale College, where Stiles became president in 1778, was in direct competition with Rhode Island College.

[34] Minute taken from Corporation, quoted in Guild, *Early History of Brown University*, 121.

and the Baptist people in Warren were devastated. They had pledged themselves to Mr. Manning's support, had built a meetinghouse and parsonage for him to live in and conduct his Latin Grammar School, and they highly esteemed Manning as their pastor. To offset the travail of his decision to go to Providence, Manning sought the advice of seven of his Baptist minister colleagues in the Warren Association. Messrs. Edward Upham (1710-1797), Isaac Backus (1724-1806), Samuel Stillman (1737-1807), Gardner Thurston (1721-1802), John Maxson (1701-1778), Samuel Mason (1714-1786), and Samuel Winsor (1721-c.1803; also spelled Windsor)[35] gave Manning hearty approbation of his conduct, care, and government of the college, and told him to go with the college to Providence.

President Manning did in fact relocate to Providence, and commenced attending the First Baptist Church, a much-divided congregation, socially and theologically, laboring under an elderly pastor. An opportunity to preach led to a growing affection for the young educator. Manning easily became the choice of the emerging urban elite that wanted to set aside the existing rigid nature of Six Principle,[36] closed communion ministry in what a recent historian of the congregation has called the "iron law of creeping respectability."[37] Manning was originally considered in a support role to Elder Samuel Winsor, Jr., who was in his fortieth year with the congregation, but Manning's Calvinistic theology, winsome preaching, and openness to new worship styles that involved singing,[38] led him to be admitted to the old congregation and he

---

[35] This roster was a virtual "Who's Who" list of New England Baptist luminaries.

[36] The Six Principle orientation of the Providence Church at the time of Manning's arrival is narrated in Richard Knight, *History of the General or Six Principle Baptists, In Europe and America: In Two Parts* (Providence, RI: Smith and Parmenter, 1827), 255-259.

[37] J. Stanley Lemons, *First: The First Baptist Church in America* (Providence, RI: The Charitable Baptist Society, 2001), 14-18.

[38] W. G. McLoughlin speculated that the real issue was singing, but the contemporary accounts suggest it was a disagreement over the sixth principle and Manning's being barred from the Lord's Supper. See McLoughlin's note, *Diary of Isaac Backus*, 2: 730-731.

became the leading pastoral presence.[39] In the crucial vote to admit Manning that offended Elder Winsor and which was heavily supported by the women of the congregation, the door opened wide for the 33-year-old. In May 1771, James Manning was invited to become pastor at First Baptist Church, arguably the oldest congregation belonging to Baptists in North America.[40] His salary as pastor was £50, and from the college he received £100, plus his house.[41]

As Manning moved to the colonial capital, a modest revival of religion was being felt in the city.[42] Providence was quite a contrast to Warren, with its wagon and carriage noises, huckstering, shops, and slave marketing. The president's first two challenges were an inadequate meetinghouse and the church's relation to other Baptists in New England. President Manning found the existing meetinghouse unsuitable for commencements. He spearheaded the campaign to build a new, commodious house of worship at a cost of nearly $21,000 (£7,000). It was a striking

---

[39] Manning was best known for practical sermons rather than heavily emphasizing doctrine. His extemporaneous style was directed at the affections more than the intellect, a characteristic of New Light preachers.

[40] Lemons, *First: The First Baptist Church*, 8, 13. This congregation was founded by Roger Williams and Ezekiel Holliman in 1638/39. Though its records are not surviving from this era, other sources indicate that the church was then founded. A decade later, the Newport Baptist congregation was founded by John Clarke and because their records are clearer to some extent, they make a claim as the oldest church of the denomination in America.

[41] Guild, *Early History of Brown University,* 191. At first, the Mannings lived in the older house formerly belonging to Benjamin Bowen on Bowen Street. Manning's new residence, finished by the autumn of 1770, was described as "a plain two and a half storey house" located to the northwest of the College Edifice. Funds to construct the parsonage were raised through a public lottery. In addition, for many years up to the Revolution, Manning received funds from tuition at the Latin Grammar School he conducted. In 1772, this was moved to the College Edifice and essentially combined with the College. Walter C. Bronson, *History of Brown University, 1764-1914* (Providence, RI: D. B. Updike, 1914), 57-58.

[42] See Iain H. Murray, *Revival and Revivalism: The Making and Marring of American Evangelicalism 1750-1858* (Edinburgh: The Banner of Truth Trust, 2009), 306. Murray offers no primary sources for his claim.

structure at 80′ square with seating for 1,200 in a city that had slightly over 4,000 inhabitants.[43] Supporters of several kinds and stations were solicited by the pastor, some giving cash, others materials in kind. It was described as a noble example of colonial church architecture and the principal landmark in the city of Providence of the eighteenth century. Compared to existing Baptist meetinghouses which were simple, square floor plans, lacking steeples that were associated with "formalism, bigotry, and intolerance," the first Baptist steeple in North America, inspired by James Gibbs' design for St. Martin-in-the-Fields in London, at 200 feet high, immediately dominated the city landscape.[44] The eminent American Baptist historian and pastor at Pawtucket, Rhode Island, David Benedict, when he first saw the church, remarked,

> I myself was not a little surprised, when I first saw this stately temple, at being informed that it was the place of meeting for our plain, old-fashioned sort of people, as I had resided mostly in a region of country where our people would not suppose there could be found any Holy Ghost in such a house as that. . .[45]

Once in the elaborate new meetinghouse, Pastor Manning continued to preach extemporaneously twice every Lord's Day (sometimes more frequently), excepting when he was traveling for the College. Important hearers of the pastor described his popular preaching as earnest, excellent, and with passion.[46] His pastoral

---

[43] See the details in Lemons, *First: The First Baptist Church,* 22-27; also Henry M. King, compiler and editor, *Historical Catalogue of the Members of the First Baptist Church in Providence, Rhode Island* (Providence, RI: F. H. Townsend, 1908), 3. The architect, James Gibbs, was a student of Christopher Wren. The construction project took slightly under a year and the meetinghouse was dedicated midway between the Revolutionary War Battles of Lexington and Bunker Hill.

[44] Lemons, *First: The First Baptist Church*, 25-26.

[45] David Benedict, *Fifty Years Among the Baptists* (New York: Sheldon and Co.; Boston, MA: Gould and Lincoln, 1860), 71.

[46] His successor, Jonathan Maxcy, used terms like "eloquence," "forcible," "spontaneous," "fluent" and "powerful." He thought Manning's intellect was exceedingly great. See quotations in Bronson, *History of Brown University*, 93.

duties were not neglected, as he candidly assessed his own ministry:

> I attended, by solicitation, the funeral of every baby that died in Providence; visited the sick of my own Society, and, not unfrequently, the sick of other Societies; made numerous parochial visits, the poorest people exacting the longest, and, in case of any seeming neglect, finding fault the most.[47]

Church records indicate that 283 members were received into the congregation during Manning's two-decade ministry. A considerable revival occurred in late 1774, when upwards of a hundred members were added to the congregation in ten months.[48] According to Isaac Backus, in 1775, Manning baptized a hundred and ten persons, and several more who joined the New Light Congregational Church under Joseph Snow's ministry.[49] At his death in 1791, the church reported a total enrollment of 159.[50]

Manning developed long term and close friendships with Baptists. His close association with Hezekiah Smith was likely his fondest friendship, the two having met in New Jersey college days. Manning's next closest confidante was doubtless Isaac Backus, whom he first met in November, 1764. Backus noted in his diary his personal esteem for Manning's Christian temper and gift in understanding the scriptures.[51] Backus stayed at the Manning home frequently and exchanged scores of letters with the president. In return, Manning was a conduit of details for Backus's history and he helped to distribute Backus's tracts. The two colleagues frequently served on association boards and participated in ordinations. Beyond his inner Baptist circle,

---

[47] Recollection of Dr. Waterhouse from Manning, quoted in Bronson, *History of Brown University*, 96.

[48] So reported Isaac Backus in his "Obituary Notice for James Manning," McLoughlin, *Soul Liberty*, 272. This is likely the revival that Murray, above, note 42, conflates into 1771.

[49] Backus, *History of New England*, 2: 493. Joseph Snow was pastor of the Beneficent Congregational Church in Providence.

[50] King, *Historical Catalogue*, 3.

[51] McLoughlin, *Diary of Isaac Backus*, 1: 582, entry for November 7th.

Manning's political acquaintances reached to the heights of Rhode Island luminaries, including Governor Joseph Wanton, and the two signers of the Declaration of Independence, Stephen Hopkins and William Ellery. In the Providence environs, Manning successfully courted prominent families and even allowed them to be adherents, or "hearers," rather than requiring them to be baptized as full members of the church.[52] His mildly latitudinarian tendencies extended to the organization of First Baptist, which, following the example of several leading Baptist and Congregationalist churches in New England and the Middle Colonies, conducted business through a parallel "society," in this case the "Charitable Baptist Society."[53] Leading the life of Manning's "extended" congregation were the Brown brothers, John (1736-1803) and Nicholas (1729-1791), wealthy and powerful Providence merchants, and Nicholas, Jr. (son of Nicholas), and his sister, Hope. Manning became their pastor and spiritual advisor. In 1792, in part in grateful memory of the sainted Manning, Nicholas, Jr. gave $2,000 to purchase a lot and construct a parsonage, and in 1834 he donated a pipe organ to the church. Hope gave the funds for the magnificent chandelier in the center of the meetinghouse in 1792. The generosity of Nicholas Brown extended as well to the College, and in recognition of his munificence, in 1804, the college was renamed Brown University.[54]

Ironically, James Manning was characterized unfairly by a contemporary as religiously bigoted because of his ecclesiological stance on believer's baptism. Some considered him rigid and overly attached to externals.[55] This was unfair personally because President Manning could not afford to be limited in his religious associations only to the Baptists. As he responded to one non-Baptist correspondent, "I think I love the followers of the Lamb, under whatever Denomination they pass amongst Men. I esteem them my Brethren; and feel disposed to make all proper Allow-

---

[52] This amounted to a de facto form of open membership.

[53] The model of separating the spiritual life of a congregation from its trustee and property management was used widely among New England Congregationalist churches and more urbane Baptists. Manning was thus able to integrate a broader spectrum of people in the life of First Baptist.

[54] It is said that Mr. Brown's total gifts exceeded $160,000.

[55] Quoted in Bronson, *History of Brown University*, 92.

ances for the Prejudices of Institution, and ye Weaknesses of human Nature, knowing that I myself also am in the Body; and peculiarly need the Candour of my Xtn. [Christian] friends."[56]

A humble and self-effacing man, Manning attempted to raise the prospects of Rhode Island College by preaching in Presbyterian, Congregationalist, Quaker, and likely Jewish and Sabbatarian assemblies and services. To his friend, Hezekiah Smith, he quipped, "See what it is to be catholic like me."[57] In local associations, he was active in promoting free schools in Providence, the first in the colony of Rhode Island. The breadth of his interests and attitudes led the College of Philadelphia (later the University of Pennsylvania) to confer upon him the degree of doctor of divinity in 1785. By the mid-1780's, James Manning was acclaimed as the acknowledged head of the Baptist clergy of his time, both in America and England.[58]

Builder, teacher, and administrator

President Manning was specifically involved in every phase of the college's life. He designed the curriculum at Rhode Island College and personally delivered much of the lectures in the first years in what came to be called the "old system." He underscored the need for languages, the liberal arts and sciences—all to be examined publicly each quarter.[59] A colleague in ministry, Benjamin Waterhouse, recalled that the president taught two classes every day, held office hours during which he received complaints from students and their parents, responded to voluminous correspondence, and entertained visitors to the college. This was supplemented by the daily routine of his pastoral

---

[56] Bronson, *History of Brown University*, 92.

[57] Manning to Hezekiah Smith, May 5, 1773, quoted in Bronson, *History of Brown University*, 91.

[58] So wrote Ashur Robbins, a 1782 Yale alumnus and Manning's first faculty appointment after the War of Independence. Quoted in Bronson, *History of Brown University*, 92.

[59] The authors read as texts included Virgil, Xenophon, Homer, Cicero, Duncan (Logic), Watts (Logic), Hutchinson (Moral Philosophy), Doddridge (Philosophy), Hammond (Algebra), Wilson (navigation), Ferguson (astronomy), Bolingbroke (history), and Locke (political philosophy). Guild, *Early History of Brown University*, 356.

ministry.[60] In 1766, there were five students in the college, which grew to eleven in 1769. The highest enrollment prior to the Revolution was forty-one.

Upon removal to Providence, the college obtained a hilltop site overlooking the port and lower town, just above where the new 1774 meetinghouse would be erected. Manning's hope was that enrollment in the college would grow dramatically in its new environment. Activities, including religious exercises, meals, and lodgings for Manning's extended family were eventually centered in "the College Edifice," the original building erected in 1770-1771. It was constructed under his watchful eyes on the design of Nassau Hall in Princeton. It still stands as a solid four-story structure constructed of brick, 150 x 46 feet with side projections.[61] Morgan Edwards (1722-1795), a Philadelphia mentor of Manning, noted in 1771 that the college had a commanding view of the town, Narragansett Bay, the islands, and the variegated hills and countryside, "a spot made for the seat of the Muses."[62]

As Manning's administrative and development responsibilities increased, he enlisted an underclassman friend from the College of New Jersey, David Howell, as lecturer.[63] In the early years, Manning and Howell constituted the admissions committee of the college and carefully selected the incoming classes. Howell also became indispensable to instruction, covering the sciences and classics, but was often a difficult colleague. In 1787, Manning

---

[60] Correspondence quoted in Bronson, *History of Brown University*, 96.

[61] The foundation stone was laid on May 14, 1770; only the first two stories were finished before the Revolution. The cost was about $9,400, including the erection of the president's home. Since 1823, the building has been known as University Hall. During the War and French occupation, the building was substantially gutted of its wooden appointments, including the closets and windows, plus walls and part of the roof were removed to accommodate a stable and access for invalids. The circumstances grieved Manning greatly. See Bronson's citation of a note from Manning to Joseph and Nicholas Brown, July 17, 1782, *History of Brown University*, 72-73.

[62] Quoted in Bronson, *History of Brown University*, 55.

[63] Howell (1747-1824; Princeton Class of 1766; A.M. Rhode Island College, 1769) delivered most of the curriculum in the early years, ultimately becoming a professor of Law, a distinguished jurist and political leader. In the early years, Howell was single and boarded near the college rooms.

dismissed a student from the college for breaking the rules, only to have Professor Howell advise the student and his family to appeal the judgment. Manning came to distrust Howell, whom he called an "assiduous Antagonist." Friends advised the president that Howell wanted to displace him from office.[64] Ironically, the Corporation invited Howell to assume interim presidential duties in 1791-1792 as Manning retired.

At Rhode Island College, student behavior toward faculty, ministers, magistrates, and parents was highly regulated and deferential, as it had been in Princeton, "in no case using reproachful, disrespectful, or contumacious language."[65] In fact, Latin only was to be spoken in the college or college yard. Tutors regularly visited the student rooms to see if they were at study, punishing those who were frivolously employed. The religious character of the institution was evident in morning and evening prayers, required attendance at public worship on the first day of the week, the exceptions being Seventh Day Baptists and Jewish students. Senior students read passages from the Greek New Testament into English before morning prayers. President Manning loved academic decorum and built a tradition in the College of pomp and splendor, English orations, and democratic entertainments to the commencements.[66]

President Manning was also a surrogate parent to his students. Of note was the great favor he provided for his friend, Robert 'Councillor' Carter, III of Nomini Hall in Virginia, one of the wealthiest men in colonial America, whose two sons, George and John Tasker, Manning adopted as a "foster father" during their stay in Providence.[67] The two brothers boarded in the president's

---

[64] The 1787 incident and Manning's assessment of Howell are reproduced from the Manning Correspondence in Bronson, *History of Brown University*, 84.

[65] Guild, *Early History of Brown University*, 357

[66] Observation of Ezra Stiles, noted in Bronson, *History of Brown University*, 96.

[67] Carter (1727/28-1804) was an antislavery advocate in Virginia and may have had an influence upon Manning's thinking. He wrote to the president expressing his abhorrence over the institution of slavery. In 1791, the year of Manning's death, Carter manumitted the slaves on his plantations, the largest release of slaves in the United States before the Civil War.

home. In contrast, the president was doubtless grieved and embarrassed in 1770 at having to make amends for a student who vandalized a Quaker meetinghouse in Smithfield, giving him the severest possible punishment short of expulsion. Four years later, he publicly rebuked five students for breaches of curfews and study habits, the sons of close and important friends, John Gano, Morgan Edwards, and Oliver Hart. After withholding their diplomas for a year, 'Father' Manning later declared them "well-behaved boys" and received the thanks of grateful parents.[68]

As an academic, Manning concentrated his efforts in his strength, the classics, lecturing on the works of Horace, Cicero, and Longinus. According to William Hunter, a member of Manning's last class and later a United States Senator, the president taught sophomores from Isaac Watts' *Logic or the Right Use of Reason in the Enquiry After Truth* (1724), and with the seniors he discoursed from John Locke's *Essay on Human Understanding* (1690), both important in his own formation.[69] He also used state-of-the-discipline works in metaphysics and moral philosophy, notably William Paley's *Principles of Moral and Political Philosophy* (1785). Manning's friends did not think of him as a writing scholar, in part because of his attention to administrative details and traveling in the interests of the College.[70] In response to the ever-present critique of Ezra Stiles, who characterized Manning as having a superficial general knowledge of languages and sciences, and studying "too little to make any Thing very great,"[71] Isaac Backus attributed lack of

---

[68] The incident is recounted in Bronson, *History of Brown University*, 113-115.

[69] Isaac Watts (1674-1749) was an English logician, theologian, and hymnist who was much influenced by the British Empiricist school. He was a nonconformist in religious matters. His *Logic* went through 20 editions.

[70] His literary output amounts to a single published item, and that printed posthumously: *A Charge from the President to the Graduates at the Commencement at Providence, September 2, 1789*. Boston, MA: Manning and Loring, 1806. John Hay Library, Brown University, has the only available copies.

[71] Franklin H. Dexter, ed., *The Literary Diary of Ezra Stiles* (New York: Charles Scribner's Sons, 1901), 2: 339. Stiles did later note, however, "He was a pretty good Linguist." *Ibid.*, 3: 425.

published scholarship to Manning's unfeigned humility that prevented him from publishing any discourses.[72] Manning's own library amounted to about $50 in value at his death.

A man of old friendships and new loyalties

James Manning was born a British colonist and thought of himself as a Christian man with Old Country connections. Prior to the Revolution, Manning was anxious to connect with Baptists in Great Britain. He had correspondence with John Collett Ryland (1723-1792) at Northampton and Benjamin Wallin (1711-1782) of London.[73] These letters reveal Manning's assessment of theological treatises by prominent English clergy whom Manning was considering for honorary degrees at the College. One of those in the exchange was Augustus Toplady (1740-1778) of the Church of England, author of the hymn "Rock of Ages," who received a degree in 1773, and Isaac Woodman, who was likewise honored in 1770. Manning's papers contain a list of twenty-one Calvinistic Baptist ministers in England who could read the Greek Testament, a choice selection of Baptist pastor-scholars fit for recognition. His wide-ranging friendships in Britain probably placed him among the lukewarm supporters of the Revolution. Certainly his personal advocacy accompanied by Isaac Backus before the Continental Congress in 1774 of a church exemption from taxation, led some to question his patriotism.

This latter issue demonstrated that Manning was a significant player in the political realities of his day. As part of the Warren Association delegation that went to the First Continental Congress that year to redress Baptist grievances at having to pay church taxes in Massachusetts, Manning had the honor of reading the memorial to the Massachusetts delegation composed of Samuel Adams, John Adams, Robert Treat Paine, and Thomas Cushing. Two years later, it was from the steps of his church, First Baptist, Providence, that the Declaration of Independence was read on July 25, 1776. Yet, the effects of the war in Providence and upon the college were devastating. The school was closed twice and was

---

[72] "Obituary Notice," 273.

[73] The war did not alienate the English Baptists. Wallin remained a correspondent as did John Rippon and Thomas Llewellyn.

eventually commandeered as a hospital for French soldiers.[74] Only five students who had studied privately with Mr. Manning remained at the close of military hostilities, and the building was left in shambles. Manning wrote to his friend, Samuel Stennett (1727-1795), in England,

> I cannot say in what light you view the American Revolution, but to serious people here it appears to be of God; and if the counsels of Great Britain are conducted with wisdom and moderation, it will in the issue be of no disadvantage to her in a national view. In a religious view I am certain it should not operate to produce any discord among the subjects of that Prince whose kingdom is not of this world. As far as my acquaintance extends, I am convinced that, on our part, the former attachment still continues; and I am sure I have as little reason to doubt it on yours.[75]

One close observer of Manning noted that during the years of the Revolution, Mr. Manning did not pray for the Continental Congress or the Army until George Washington visited the church in the 1780's.[76] Doubtless his own personal deprivation during the war years and the early Confederation played a role in his thinking about military conflicts:

> At the last session [of the Continental Congress] I petitioned them to pay my advances, and the remainder of my salary as delegate, amounting to upwards of four hundred dollars. This they offered to do in their paper, but in no other way.... A more infamous set of men under the character of a legislature, never, I believe, disgraced the annals of the world. And there is no prospect of a change for the better. Of

---

[74] Backus reported that the school building was used from December 1776 to April 1780 to house Continental Army troops and again on June 25, 1780, it was violently commandeered by order of the Council of War to become a French soldiers hospital until June 1782. Manning's use of his beloved edifice came to a halt one Sunday evening. See McLoughlin, *Diary of Isaac Backus*, 2: 1053, entry for June 30, 1780.

[75] Manning to Stennett, November 8, 1783. Guild, *Early History of Brown University*, 367.

[76] The observer was none other than Manning's constant critic, Ezra Stiles. See Dexter, *Literary Diary of Ezra Stiles*, post 2: 23; post 3: 425.

> all the arrearages of tuition for the last year, and the quarter advanced in this, I have not received ten pounds. I was taken sick the day after the second great snow, with no provisions in the cellar except one hundred-weight of cheese, two barrels of cider, and some potatoes; with not a load of wood at my door; nor could I command a single dollar to supply these wants. The kindness of my neighbors, however, kept me from suffering. But when a man has hardly earned money, to be reduced to this abject state of dependence requires the exercise of more grace than I can boast of....I have serious thought of removing to the farm at the Jerseys, and undertake *digging* for my support. Should things wear the same unfavorable aspect next year, I believe I shall make the experiment, if my life is spared.[77]

Like most reluctant Revolutionary Americans in the 1780's, Manning rebuilt and recovered his position in the community. In 1786, the Rhode Island Assembly unanimously elected Manning to the Congress under the Articles of Confederation. He reluctantly accepted and said his motivation was entirely to recover the college damages from the War. In Philadelphia, the Rhode Island member advocated a federalist stance and he helped to sway the vote in favor of ratification of the U.S. constitution in 1788. At first, one of the few clergy in favor of the proposed constitution, Manning labored hard to persuade others to join ratification. He was particularly keen that Massachusetts should support the cause, noting that state was "the hinge on which the whole must turn."[78] The following year, Manning became one of the earliest anti-slavery advocates in New England when he became a member of Moses Brown's abolitionist society in Providence. He joined several of his ministerial colleagues, including Stephen Hopkins, the signer of the Declaration of Independence.[79] Manning's involvement in the slavery issue alienated him from some of the

---

77 Quoted in Martha Mitchell, "James Manning" in *Encyclopedia Brunonia* (Providence, RI: Brown University Library, 1993), online edition.

78 Manning to Hezekiah Smith, February 11, 1788, quoted in Guild, *Early History of Brown University*, 94.

79 Hopkins, Brown, and Manning had led Rhode Island in passing an emancipation law in 1784, and a second act restricting the slave trade in 1787. See Lemons, *First: The First Baptist Church,* 27.

leading Baptist merchants in Rhode Island, including his friend John Brown, who resigned from the Charitable Baptist Society.[80] Capping Manning's social and political experiences was the College's commencement of 1790 (Manning's last), when President George Washington, accompanied by Secretary of State Thomas Jefferson, visited Providence and was hosted by President Manning. Later in that visit, Manning conferred upon the first president the degree of L.L.D.

Neighbor and citizen in Providence

On a personal and social level, Manning was one of the most beloved citizens of Providence. Neighbors often saw him building stone walls about his residence and energetically cutting grass with a scythe in his meadow.[81] He could be seen at the market every day where he joined in friendly discourse. One French visitor to the College noted Mr. Manning's fondness for anecdotes and his pleasant, happy disposition. A portrait of the president that hung in Sayles Hall for many years and once belonged to Mrs. Manning, shows James at about 32 years old with his own hair (as opposed to wearing a wig) and of a robust profile.[82] His energy both before and following the Revolution seemed inexhaustible: he wrote to his close friend of college days, Hezekiah Smith of Haverhill, Massachusetts, that he had preached fifteen times in fourteen days in one stint during the spring of 1773.[83] And as late as the summer of 1790, James Manning was at the center of evangelical activity in his city, preaching twice on a Sunday and baptizing three persons in the afternoon.[84]

Manning's life was not without its trials and stresses. His critics defamed him as conniving and religiously unyielding, which must have penetrated his affable personality. His 1770 departure

---

[80] Manning had two slaves, Zip and Cato, the latter whom he inherited from his father, James, Sr., in 1767. James, Jr. freed them in 1770.

[81] In 1771, Manning purchased seven acres adjacent to the college grounds, which he successfully cultivated. In 1777, he constructed a stone wall 32 rods long on College property, for which he billed the college.

[82] [This portrait appears at the beginning of this essay —*Ed.*]

[83] Guild, *Early History of Brown University*, 237.

[84] McLoughlin, *Diary of Isaac Backus*, 3: 1292, entry for June 21st.

from Warren left a permanent disappointment in the town toward him. Their high hopes of Warren's being a commercial center and the seat of a university faded with Manning's individual decision.[85] As Manning moved to Providence and became the popular choice to be the lead Baptist minister of that town, Elder Winsor's "Six Principle Schism" continued to be an irritation in the Providence environment, raising questions over the legitimacy of the new ministry and theology at First Baptist.[86] In 1769, one of the leading Particular Baptist ministers in London, Benjamin Wallin, had serious questions about Manning not being sound in the faith, charges that Isaac Backus dismissed by affirming Manning's consistency in the "doctrines of grace," eighteenth century theological code language for evangelical five-point Calvinism. Wallin's criticism stung because Manning hoped to garner financial support for the fledgling college from English pastors.[87]

From time to time, Dr. Manning even had his detractors in the congregation at First Baptist. In early 1776, it was apparent that Universalism was creating dissent in the church on a fairly widespread basis. John Murray (1741-1815), the English Methodist-become-Universalist, had toured New England and won many converts. Murray had preached to large crowds at nearby Elder Snow's meetinghouse. Manning and other evangelical Calvinists were abhorred at the doctrinal deviation and Manning requested an explicit response to criticisms of his preaching by the pro-Universalist faction. Included in the critics was William Seamans, a relative of Baptist Elder Job Seamans, who had gone over to Universalism. The church affirmed its pastor and the Universalists were ultimately rooted out.[88] Sometimes, as in 1780, the pastor was unable to attend directly to his church responsibilities

---

[85] Tustin, *Historical Discourse*, 129.

[86] Lemons, *First: The First Baptist Church*, 19.

[87] McLoughlin, *Diary of Isaac Backus*, 2: 744.

[88] Stanley J. Lemons, *First Baptist, Providence, Rhode Island: Records of First Baptist, Providence*, Baptists in Early North America Series, Vol. II, edited by William H. Brackney (Macon. GA: Mercer University Press, 2013), Vol. I, (1775-1784), entries for December 12, 1775-February 29, 1776. Hereinafter cited as *First Baptist, Providence, Rhode Island: Records.*

and he had to rely on deacons to visit and resolve conflicts.[89] Nevertheless, his wisdom in theological matters remained valued, as he was requested six years later to prepare a "suitable form of admonition" for all those who were overtaken by the Universalist tendency. Six persons were dismissed from the congregation over Universalism between April 9, 1775 and May 1782.[90]

As the decade of the nineties emerged, Mr. Manning's circumstances remained frustrating. Inside the college family, David Howell's erratic support of his president often manifested itself in criticism of policies and the making of a college image. In the later 1780's, Manning had his critics in building and rebuilding the College; Isaac Backus thought that there were those in both the colony and the college that envied Manning's position and who even sought to obstruct his designs.[91] Great was the president's chagrin at his own inability to recover costs and damages from the closure of the college from June 1780 to May 1782. Manning, an elected delegate from Rhode Island, and a group of New Englanders, had implored the Continental Congress to make a grant to cover the incurred wartime debts of the college. The effort had failed, and to make matters worse for President Manning personally, the part of his salary that he did receive was in Rhode Island currency that was substantially devalued. At length, one can detect that Manning's bi-vocational career finally took its toll, as the restored college's responsibilities exacted greater amounts of the president's time by 1788. Part of a short-term solution came that year when the congregation hired John Stanford to assist Mr. Manning in the ministry. After only twenty months, however, Stanford was forced to leave under slanderous charges about his character.[92] In early 1791, Manning reluctantly requested the

---

[89] Lemons, *First Baptist, Providence, Rhode Island: Records,* entry for September 28, 1780. Manning actually served as interim church clerk in this period.

[90] *Ibid.*, entry for May 2, 1782.

[91] Backus, "Obituary Notice," in McLoughlin, *Soul Liberty,* 275.

[92] John Stanford (1754-1834) was originally an English Baptist minister, ordained at London's famous Maze Pond Church, having previously served at Hammersmith before emigrating to Norfolk, Virginia. For a time he supplied the pulpit of the First Baptist Church in New York after John Gano's departure and ran an academy. Though he was well-received in Providence, a letter from English sources laid charges of sodomy against him which forced his resignation. He later cleared himself of the

board to secure a successor in the college and he preached his farewell sermon to the church in April.[93]

Twilight of life

Close friends felt that President Manning was waning in strength after the Commencement of 1790, and at 52 years old, he confided that he felt his work was almost done. In the later years of his work at the College and church, he had gained a good deal of weight, weighing upwards of three hundred pounds.[94] Benjamin Rush, the respected Philadelphia physician who knew Manning personally, opined that Manning "died of his knife and fork." This was attributed more to a sedentary lifestyle than to an intemperate diet, and it doubtless contributed to his demise. David Howell, Manning's oldest faculty colleague and his faculty successor, provided an account of Manning's death and funeral: after being unwell for about five days, the president fainted at family prayers and apparently suffered a stroke.[95] James Manning died at 4 a.m. Friday, the 29th of July, 1791. He had been unable to speak after the 27th. His funeral on July 30th was one of the largest in the history of Providence to that date, lamented by all ranks of people. Manning's successor in the pastorate, Jonathan

---

accusations and enjoyed an effective ministry in New York. See King, *Historical Catalogue*, 4; Lemons, *First: The First Baptist Church,* 28; 109-110; Lemons, *First Baptist, Providence, Rhode Island: Records*, Book II (1782-1793), various entries between August 10 - December 3, 1789.

93 While not preaching regularly at the church due to travel and workload, Dr. Manning was requested to speak on special occasions, like the Thanksgiving Service on November 24, 1789. The next year, the church showed its affection for the senior pastor by resolving unanimously in late 1790 still to have Dr. Manning superintend and administer the ordinances of the gospel. See Lemons, *First Baptist, Providence, Rhode Island: Records*, entry for November 4, 1790.

94 Manning's neighbors and students noted his "immense volume of flesh," but as well, his spontaneous and energetic care of his yard. Noted in Bronson, *History of Brown University*, 91.

95 Backus's obituary, based largely on David Howell's account, claimed that the "apoplexy" occurred five days before. See "Obituary Notice for James Manning," in McLoughlin, *Soul Liberty,* 275.

Maxcy, presided over the service and delivered the sermon.[96] At the college commencement of 1791, a funeral oration was delivered by Simeon Doggett, a graduate and M. A. candidate. President Manning was buried in the North Burial Ground in Providence, next to his friend Nicholas Brown, also recently deceased.

Isaac Backus, not given to "extravagant character drawings of the dead," best honored his friend, President Manning, with the words, "Dr. Manning was a noble witness, both in public and private, in profession and practice. He was a burning and shining light, and his extensive benefits were greatly admired and rejoiced in. . ."[97] Almost a century later, another eminent American Baptist historian, Thomas Armitage, put James Manning in proper context: "He was far in advance of his times, both as a Baptist and an American. Broad, disinterested and self-sacrificing, his memory cannot be too sacredly cherished."[98]

---

[96] Maxcy (1768-1820) was a favorite son of Manning, having given evidence of a clear conversion after an eleven-day period of conviction in a typical Great Awakening morphology. Manning baptized Maxcy and took pleasure in his Christian testimony. McLoughlin, *Diary of Isaac Backus*, 3: 1285, entry for January 10, 1790. Maxcy was president of Rhode Island College, 1792-1802, as well as its professor of divinity. In 1802, he was under scrutiny for Universalist leanings, Isaac Backus being among his critics. He resigned to accept first, the presidency of Union College in Schenectady, New York, and in 1804, South Carolina College, Columbia (later University of South Carolina).

[97] *Ibid.*

[98] Thomas Armitage, *A History of the Baptists; Traced by Their Vital Principles and Practices, from the Time of Our Lord and Saviour Jesus Christ to the year 1886* (New York: Bryan, Taylor, and Co., 1887), 787.

In the research for this essay, I am especially grateful for the assistance of the late Martha Mitchell, former archivist and Gayle Lynch, the current Brown University Archivist, in the John Hay Library, Brown University; Terry Wolever at Particular Baptist Press; and Rosalba Reccia and Christie Petersen at the Seeley G. Mudd Library, Princeton University.

Further Reading

Reuben A. Guild. *Life, Times, and Correspondence of James Manning, and the Early History of Brown University*. Boston: Gould and Lincoln, 1864. Republished as *Early History of Brown University, Including the Life, Times, and Correspondence of President Manning, 1756-1791*. Providence, RI: Snow and Farnham, 1897.[99]

Walter C. Bronson. *The History of Brown University, 1764-1914*. Boston: D. B. Updike, The Merrymount Press, for Brown University, 1914.

[99] Other important biographical sources on Manning include, "James Manning," in William H. Brackney, *Historical Dictionary of the Baptists, Second Edition* (Lanham, MD: Scarecrow Press, 2009), 365; "Biographical Note" in *Guide to the James Manning Papers 1761-1827* (Brown Archival and Manuscript Collections Online, 2005); Timothy P. Weber, "James Manning," in Donald M. Lewis, ed., *Dictionary of Evangelical Biography* (Peabody, MA: Hendrickson Publishers, 2004), 2: 739; "James Manning," in *Dictionary of American National Biography* (New York: Oxford University Press, 1999); "James Manning" in Henry W. Bowden, ed., *Dictionary of American Religious Biography*, Revised Edition (Westport, CT: Greenwood Press, [1977] 1993), 287-288; "James Manning," in Martha L. Mitchell, comp., *Encyclopedia Brunonia* (Providence, RI: Brown University Libraries, 1993); "James Manning," in Daniel G. Reid, ed., *Dictionary of Christianity in America* (Downers Grove, IL: Inter-Varsity Press, 1990), 204; William G. McLoughlin, ed., *The Diary of Isaac Backus,* 3 vols. (Providence, RI: Brown University Press, 1979), 1: 579-580; "James Manning" in *Who Was Who in America: Historical Volume 1607-1896* (Chicago, IL: Marquis Who's Who, 1963), 331; Harris E. Starr, "James Manning," in Dumas Malone, ed., *Dictionary of American Biography* (New York: American Council of Learned Societies, 1930), 12: 249-251; "James Manning," in *National Cyclopedia of American Biography,* 55 vols. (New York: 1892), 8: 20-21; Thomas Armitage, *A History of the Baptists* (New York: Bryan, Taylor & Co., 1887), 782-787; William Cathcart, ed., *The Baptist Encyclopedia* (Philadelphia, PA: Louis H. Everts, 1881), 745-746; David Benedict, William G. Goddard, and William Hunter, "James Manning, D.D.," in William B. Sprague, ed., *Annals of the American Pulpit* (New York: Robert Carter and Bros., 1865), 6 (Baptist): 89-97; W. G. Goddard, "Memoir of the Rev. James Manning," *American Quarterly Register* (May, 1839); and likely the first biographical notice of his career, an entry made by Isaac Backus, August 1-6, 1791, in McLoughlin, *Diary of Isaac Backus*, 3: 1313-1314.

Appendix

Letter of dismissal granted to Peter Peterson VanHorne and to his wife Margaret from the Baptist church at Pennepek to the Baptist church at Cape May, New Jersey, written by Samuel Jones and dated September 13, 1770.[1]

The Baptist Church at Pennepack:
To y^e [the] Church of Christ of ye same faith meeting
in Cape-May West-New Jersey:[2] sendeth Greeting.

Beloved Brethren,

Forasmuch as ye Revd Peter Peter son Vanhorn & Margaret his Wife are settled among you, & have requested a dismission from us y^t [that] they might give themselves Members among you: We think it our duty to comply, & do therefore hereby testify y^t they are both Members of regular standing among us, in full union & Communion, & as such we recommend them to your acceptance and care; & when they shall be received among you they will be fully dismissed from us. So commending them & you to ye Lord & to ye word of his Grace which is able to build you up:[3] and hoping they may be long a blessing to you & you a comfort to them, we subscribe ourselves your Brethren in Gospel Relation.

At Our Meeting of Business	Samuel Jones
September 13th 1770.	Clerk.
Signed Oct. 6th 1770 at our	Alexander Edwards
Meeting of Preparation.	Deacon

---

[1] Transcribed by the editor from the photograph of the original letter reproduced in Susan Armour, *300: 1712-2012. First Baptist Church of Cape May* (Cape May, NJ: First Baptist Church, 2012), 22. Courtesy Susan Armour, First Baptist Church. A nice photograph of the gravestone of Margaret VanHorne appears on page 23 of the book, opposite the letter.

[2] Though the two former provinces of West New Jersey and East New Jersey had been reunited in 1712, their respective names persisted in the minds of the general public long afterwards, as here.

[3] Acts 20:32.

A

B

D

E

F

R

S

X

Y

Z

Biblical Persons

Index of Subjects

A

C

F

G

I

O

T

U

Y

Index of Churches

Baptist churches are listed in regular type with their dates of constitution when known. Those of other faiths are italicized and otherwise indicated.

Connecticut

Delaware

District of Columbia

Georgia

Kentucky

Maine

Maryland

Massachusetts

New Hampshire

New Jersey

New York

North Carolina

Ohio

Pennsylvania

Rhode Island

South Carolina

Vermont

Virginia

England

Ireland

Wales

West Indies

The Life of John Gano, 1727-1804. Pastor-Evangelist of the Philadelphia Association

by *Terry Wolever*

In this new and greatly expanded volume, incorporating a completely revised and corrected edition of the author's 1998 book, *The Life and Ministry of John Gano, 1727-1804,* the story of this leading evangelical figure of the eighteenth century is related in greater depth, utilizing a number of previously untapped sources.

This volume presents in detail Gano's ancestry, early life, conversion experience, ordination and subsequent ministry at Morristown, New Jersey, the Jersey Settlement in North Carolina, Philadelphia, New York, his chaplaincy with the Continental Army during the Revolutionary War and his final years of ministry in Kentucky.

Twelve appendixes cover information on John Gano's children, sermons, land deeds, diary and expense account for his 1773-1774 evangelistic tour of New England, the South and upstate New York and his Last Will and Testament, as well as a 30-page discussion on the strengths and weaknesses of the Gano family evidence on the baptism of General George Washington during the Revolutionary War, as presented by descendants and L. C. Barnes in a controversial 1926 paper.

704 pages, including over 35 illustrations (three in color), four maps and extensive indexes of persons, subjects and churches. $42.50.

The Life, Ministry and Journals of Hezekiah Smith

by *John David Broome*

The manuscript journals of Hezekiah Smith (1737-1805), now published for the first time, along with a new biography, will prove to be an invaluable source-book for any research into colonial Baptist history, and the growth of Baptist principles in New England.

Hezekiah Smith "by the eloquence of his preaching, and the weight of his character, bore down the strong prejudice against the Baptists, and was the means of abundantly extending their cause."—David Benedict, *A General History of the Baptist Denomination in America* (1813)

Bound in dark navy vellum with gold stamping. 717 pages. Extensive indexes. Illustrations and one map. $43.

The Life, Journal and Works of David Jones, 1736-1820

In addition to pastoring churches in New Jersey and Pennsylvania, David Jones also undertook one of the earliest Baptist missionary endeavors among the American Indians in 1772-1773. During the Revolutionary War and again in the Indian Wars of 1794-1796 and the War of 1812, Jones served as a chaplain in the American Army.

This first-time compilation of material on this Philadelphia Association minister includes a full-length biography of his life by Dr. G. Truett Rogers, the Journal of his two missionary visits to the Indians of the old Northwest Territory and his various other published works, which have never been reprinted or made generally available until now.

In this unique volume the controversy over whether Laying on of Hands should be a New Testament church ordinance is examined in detail.

Bound in dark navy vellum with gold stamping. Over 600 pages. Extensive indexes. Illustrated. $31.50.

Volumes Published in the Newport Commentary Series

- ***Exposition of Genesis,* by John Gill.** Complete and unabridged in a new easy to read format. Originally published in 1763. 839 pages.

- ***Exposition of the Psalms,* by Samuel Eyles Pierce.** The first reprinting of this very rare two-volume set, originally published in 1817-1818. Includes some additional related shorter works by Pierce. Volume One 669 pages; Volume Two 703 pages.

- ***Exposition of Matthew 13: The Parable of the Sower,* by Samuel Stennett.** Complete and unabridged in a new easy to read format. Originally published in 1786, our reprint is from the second enlarged edition of 1787. 224 pages.

- ***Exposition of the Gospel of John,* by John Gill.** Complete and unabridged in a new easy to read format. Originally published in 1746-1747. 742 pages.

- ***Exposition of Galatians,* by James Alexander Haldane.** The first reprinting of this excellent work, originally published in 1848. Includes four additional shorter works by this author. 462 pages.

- ***Exposition of Ephesians,* by Robert E. Pattison.** Originally published in 1859. Includes Appendix of a sermon by Hanserd Knollys on Ephesians 1:4. 264 pages.

- ***Exposition of Hebrews,* by James Alexander Haldane.** A first reprinting of this other work by an important Scottish Baptist. Includes four additional published works by the author. Originally published in 1846. 424 pages.

- ***Exposition of First John,* by Samuel Eyles Pierce.** Two volumes in one. Originally published in 1835. 503 pages and 347 pages, respectively.

Each of the volumes in this series are uniformly bound in Grade B black vellum with gold stamping and colored dust jackets.